John Wesley's
SCRIPTURAL
CHRISTIANITY

John Wesley's
SCRIPTURAL CHRISTIANITY

A Plain Exposition of His Teaching on Christian Doctrine

THOMAS C. ODEN

ZondervanPublishingHouse
Grand Rapids, Michigan

A Division of HarperCollinsPublishers

John Wesley's Scriptural Christianity,
Copyright © 1994 by Thomas C. Oden

Requests for information should be addressed to:
Zondervan Publishing House
Academic and Professional Books
Grand Rapids, Michigan 49530

Library of Congress Cataloging-in-Publication Data

Oden, Thomas C.
     John Wesley's scriptural Christianity : a plain exposition of his teaching on Christian doctrine
/ Thomas C. Oden
         p.   cm.
     Includes bibliographical references.
     ISBN 0-310-75321-X (v. 1 : pbk.)
     1. Wesley, John, 1703–1791. 2. Theology, Doctrinal. 3. Methodist Church—Doctrines. 4.
Theology, Doctrinal—History—18th century. 5. Methodist Church—Doctrines—History—18th
century. I. Title.
BX8331.2.035   1994   93-40450
230'.7'092—dc20   CIP

Edited by Robert D. Wood
Cover designed by Tammy Johnson

Printed in the United States of America

94 95 96 97 98 99 / DH / 10 9 8 7 6 5 4 3 2 1

CONTENTS

PREFACE

This series is best understood as a reader's guide to John Wesley's teaching. It introduces his thought on basic tenets of Christian doctrine (volume 1), the practice of pastoral care (volume 2), and issues of ethics and society (volume 3). This first volume seeks to offer a plain exposition of Wesley's systematic theology, with steady reference to his own published texts, noting their distinctive earmarks, singular features, quirks, and oddities.

TO WHOM ADDRESSED

There are three houses of evangelicalism: Reformed, liturgical, and pietistic. The largest house encompasses the classic Protestant (Lutheran, Reformed, Baptist) evangelical traditions, especially as they have been affected by the revivalist tradition. The second includes sincere believers in the gospel who are rooted in liturgically oriented, sacramentally focused traditions: Anglican, Roman, and Eastern Orthodox. The third embraces Wesleyan evangelicals and the holiness traditions of evangelical revivalism, from whom have sprung allied traditions of charismatic and Pentecostal evangelicals.

My purpose is to show that the leading figure of the third house of evangelicalism, John Wesley, deserves wider reading in the other two houses. Non-Wesleyan evangelicals have a right to equal access to his reflection. I hope to set forth an informative account that will usher nonprofessional readers of both Reformed and Catholic traditions into the Wesleyan corpus without eliciting defensiveness. My intent is not to insinuate that Wesley become normative for other traditions, but that Wesley be viewed as a thoughtful partner in dialogue.

This exploration intentionally addresses nonprofessional lay readers of wider religious traditions with the ordered thoughts of a standard writer of the eighteenth century evangelical revival. These are the colleagues with whom I most desire to converse—not just nostalgic Wesleyan sentimentalists, but rather Christian lay persons of diverse traditions who have been offered too few plausible reasons to think that Wesley's work is at all useful or applicable to them. I am inviting not merely those who serve in the Wesleyan connection of spiritual formation to think systematically with me about Wesley, but especially those in these related evangelical traditions—Reformed, charismatic and Pentecostal, as well as those in liturgical and orthodox traditions. Wesley's own instinctive audience was ordinary lay Christians of varied opinions and modes of religious observance who were earnestly seeking a life of complete accountability to God.[1]

Meanwhile, working pastors craving their weekly nourishment of sermon ideas and illustrative materials and homiletic outlines will not go away disappointed, either by the structure or content of these homilies. Though some may view this as a functional collection of classic sermon outlines, this is more a study in how to use the homily as a practical means of systematic Christian teaching.

In the course of the last decade I have had the unique privilege, as a wayward son of the liberal tradition, of entering increasingly into an intriguing series of colloquies with conservative Protestant evangelicals. This led to illuminating outings to Lutheran, Reformed, Baptist, Pentecostal, and nondenominational evangelical theological schools. Serving as a Senior Editor of *Christianity Today* has been a major part of my evangelical education, as well as serving as a consultant of evangelical publishing houses, and of the Pew Trust's study on the future of evangelicalism. All of this has complemented significantly a fruitful conversation with Jewish and Catholic scholars in the American Theological Society and the Dulles Colloquium of the Institute for Religion and Public Policy, and with respected Roman Catholic partners in dialogue in the Gregorian University in Rome, Communio, Opus Dei, and the Fellowship of Catholic Scholars. Through these associations, I have become keenly aware that non-Wesleyan Protestants, Catholics and Orthodox have had pathetically limited access to Wesley, partly due to long-perpetuated mental habits and divisions within competing religious publishing traditions. This study seeks to reach out beyond the usual boundaries of Christian divisions.

TRACKING REFERENCES

Even if this book were nothing but footnotes, my unblushing resolve would be to seek to make the scholarly apparatus, notes, and bibliographies alone worth the price for those who wish to study further. A series of short bibliographies are appended to each section to point the reader toward further reading on that topic.

The preferred text is the Oxford/Abingdon Bicentennial edition (Oxford: 1975–1983, Nashville: 1984–).[2] Where volume references to

---

[1] In the Preface to *Sermons on Several Occasions*, 1741, Wesley wrote: "I now write (as I generally speak) *ad populum* . . . to those who neither relish nor understand the art of speaking, but who notwithstanding are competent judges of those truths which are necessary to present and future happiness. . . . I design plain truth for plain people." Preface 2, 3, B1:103-4; FA 11:254f.

[2] In rare cases where Curnock's edition of the Standard Sermons [SS] is quoted, the reader's attention is directed especially to his annotations.

sermons appear in *Arabic numerals*, they are quoted from Albert C. Outler's edition of the four volumes of sermons, volumes 1–4 of the Bicentennial edition (hence 2:133 = Bicentennial volume 2, page 133). In references to the Bicentennial edition of texts other than the four volumes of sermons, I have used the symbol B for Bicentennial, followed by arabic volume number and page number. The sermon number in the Bicentennial edition is marked with a cross-hatch (thus #109 = Sermon 109 in the Bicentennial edition). When the sermon number differs in the Jackson edition, it will be marked with a J plus a cross-hatch (J#127 = Sermon 127 in Jackson).[3]

References in *lower case Roman numerals* refer to the section of the particular homily or tract under discussion (ii.7 = part two, section 7 of the work being presently considered). References in *upper case Roman numerals* are from the 1829–31 Thomas Jackson edition (III:144 = volume III, page 144, reprinted by Eerdmans, Zondervan, and others). In a format departure that seemed reasonable to me, I have listed the homily number (preceded by a cross-hatch, #), the date, and the page references in the Bicentennial (with Arabic volume number) and Jackson (with Roman volume number) editions on the line immediately following the text next to be discussed.

One of my chief motivations is to render Wesley's teaching in plain modern English, with few archaisms, so as to communicate the meaning as clearly as possible in dynamically equivalent contemporary terms. I will normally use the convention of italicizing the scriptural text that formed the basis of Wesley's homily, using the New International Version throughout unless otherwise noted (excepting the text headings that are customarily cited in the Authorized Version). To those who might imagine that Wesley himself was working out of the King James Version, I would note that Wesley read fluently the Greek New Testament, studied it daily in his early morning and evening meditation, and when he published his own translation of the New Testament, many references in the Authorized Version of 1611 were altered to communicate better with his plain-speaking audience. There is no reason to think that Wesley regarded his own English rendering of the Greek as definitive for future centuries of English readers for whom the language protocols and usages would have shifted as they normally do over decades. Since he worked directly out of both Hebrew and Greek texts, one may safely assume that he was not inordinately fixated upon the Authorized Version, though he expressed abiding gratitude for it.

The only collected edition published during Wesley's lifetime was the 32-volume Bristol edition (Bristol: William Pine, 1771–74). The second edition was edited by Joseph Benson, 17 vol., London: 1809–13 (repub-

---

[3]"The Trouble and Rest of Good Men" appears as Sermon 109 in the Bicentennial edition (#109), and as Sermon 127 in the Jackson edition (J#127). The numbering is often the same, but in some instances different.

lished in New York and Philadelphia in 10 volumes, 1826–27). The third edition, edited by Thomas Jackson, 14 volumes, London, 1829–31, has been frequently reprinted in America.[4] The fashioning of an annotated editorial apparatus to the works of Wesley, with scholarly introductions according to modern standards, had to await the publication of Curnock's edition (JJW) in 1916, Sugden's (SS) in 1921, Telford's (LJW) in 1931, and Outler's (JWO) in 1964, and especially the Oxford/Abingdon Bicentennial edition.[5]

---

[4]That Telford, Sugden, Curnock, and Jackson are hardly mentioned in the Bicentennial edition of the Sermons is a curious study in systematic neglect. The American edition, edited by Emory, was published in New York, in 1831, based on Jackson.

[5]When "Articles of Religion" are indicated, I refer to Wesley's own recension of Twenty-four Articles (to which the 1784 American Methodist Church added a twenty-fifth), derived and edited down from the Anglican Thirty-nine Articles. The text of the Articles will be italicized, since they have played such a central role in the American Wesleyan doctrinal traditions. When Confession (or Confes.) is referenced, it refers to the summary of Wesleyan faith set forth in the 1962 Confession of the Evangelical United Brethren, which by a constitutionally restrictive rule has become a doctrinal standard of the United Methodist Church. The first article of the Confession will be referenced: Confes.1.

ABBREVIATIONS

Art.	Twenty-five Articles of Religion
AM	*Arminian Magazine*
AS	*Asbury Seminarian*
B	Bicentennial Edition of *The Works of John Wesley*, General Editors, Frank Baker, Richard Heitzenrater, Oxford: Clarendon Press; Nashville: Abingdon Press, 1975–
BCP	Book of Common Prayer
Bull.	Bulletin
CH	*A Collection of Hymns for the Use of the People Called Methodists*, vol. 7 of the Bicentennial edition
Chr.	Christian
CL	Christian Library
Confes.	1962 Confession of the Evangelical United Brethren
CWT	R. Burtner and R. Chiles, *A Compend of Wesley's Theology,* Nashville: Abingdon
Diss.	Dissertation
Div.	Divinity
DOS	The Doctrine of Original Sin
DPF	"Dialogue Between a Predestinarian and His Friend"
DSF	"The Doctrine of Salvation, Faith and Good Works" (Extracted from the Edwardian Homilies)
DSWT	Thomas C. Oden, *Doctrinal Standards in the Wesleyan Tradition*, Grand Rapids: Francis Asbury Press, Zondervan, 1988
EA	"An Earnest Appeal to Men of Reason and Religion"
ENNT	*Explanatory Notes Upon the New Testament*
ENOT	*Explanatory Notes Upon the Old Testament*
ETS	Evangelical Theological Society
Ev.	Evangelical
EWT	Paul Mickey, *Essentials of Wesleyan Theology*, Grand Rapids, Francis Asbury Press, Zondervan, 1980
FA	"A Farther Appeal to Men of Reason and Religion"

FAP   Francis Asbury Press, Zondervan Publishing House

FB   Howard Slaate, *Fire in the Brand*, Exposition Press, 1963

FW   Kenneth Collins, *A Faithful Witness: John Wesley's Homiletical Theology*, Wilmore: Wesleyan Heritage Press, 1993

FWAT   Mildred Bangs Wynkoop, *Foundations of Wesleyan-Arminian Theology*, Kansas City: Beacon Hill, 1967

HSP   *Hymns and Sacred Poems*

JBR   *Journal of Bible and Religion*

JWPH   Robert Monk, *John Wesley: His Puritan Heritage*, Nashville: Abingdon, 1966

JWTT   Colin Williams, *John Wesley's Theology Today*, Nashville: Abingdon, 1960

JJW   *The Journal of John Wesley*, ed. N. Curnock, 8 vols. London: Epworth, 1916

Jnl.   Journal

JWO   *John Wesley*, edited by Albert C. Outler, Library of Protestant Theology, New York: Oxford, 1964

LCM   "Letter to the Rev. Dr. Conyers Middleton"

LJW   *Letters of John Wesley*, ed. John Telford, 8 vols. London: Epworth Press, 1931

LLBL   "A Letter to the Right Reverend Lord Bishop of London"

LPC   "Letter on Preaching Christ" [same as "Letter to an Evangelical Layman," Dec. 20, 1751]

LQHR   *London Quarterly and Holborn Review*

LS   *Life in the Spirit*, Thomas C. Oden, San Francisco: HarperSanFrancisco, 1992

Mag.   Magazine

Meth.   Methodist

MH   *Methodist History*

Minutes   "Minutes of Some Late Conversations Between the Rev. Mr. Wesley and Others"

MLS   *Martin Luther: Selections from his Writings*, ed. John Dillenberger, New York: Doubleday, 1961

MM   *Methodist Magazine*

MOB   William M. Arnett, "John Wesley: Man of One Book," Drew University Ph.D. Dissertation, 1954

MPL   *Patrologia Latina*, J. P. Migne, ed., Patrologiae Cursus Completus, Paris, Series Graeca, 1857–66, Series Latina, 1878–90

MQR   *Methodist Quarterly Review*

MR   *Methodist Review*

NDM   Reinhold Niebuhr, *The Nature and Destiny of Man*, 2 vols.,
        New York: Scribner, 1941, 1943

NRSV   New Revised Standard Version

NT   New Testament

OED   Oxford English Dictionary

OT   Old Testament

PACP   *A Plain Account of Christian Perfection*

PCC   "Predestination Calmly Considered"

PM   *Preacher's Magazine*

Pref.   Preface

Publ.   Publishing, Publishers

PW   *Poetical Works of Charles Wesley and John Wesley*, ed.
        George Osborn, 13 vols. London: Wesleyan Methodist
        Conference, 1868–1872

PWHS   *Proceedings of the Wesleyan Historical Society*

Q   Quarterly

QR   *Quarterly Review*

RC   Roman Catholic

RE   Henry D. Rack, *Reasonable Enthusiast*, Philadelphia: Trinity
        Press Intl., 1985

RJW   George Croft Cell, *The Rediscovery of John Wesley*, New
        York: Henry Holt, 1935

RL   *Religion in Life*

SS   *The Standard Sermons of John Wesley*, ed. E. H. Sugden,
        2 vols., London: Epworth, 1921 (third ed. 1951)

SSM   *Sunday Service of the Methodists of the United States of
        America*, 1784, ed. Edward Hobbs, Nashville: MSM, 1956

TCNT   Twentieth Century New Testament

Theo.   Theological

TIRC   "Thoughts on the Imputation of the Righteousness of
        Christ"

TJW   William R. Cannon, *Theology of John Wesley: With Special
        Reference to the Doctrine of Justification*, New York:
        Abingdon, 1946.

TUN   "Thoughts Upon Necessity"

UMC   United Methodist Church

unpubl. unpublished dissertation
diss.

WC   John Deschner, *Wesley's Christology*, Grand Rapids: Francis
        Asbury Press, Zondervan, 1989

WHS Lycargus M. Starkey, *The Work of the Holy Spirit*, Nashville: Abingdon, 1962

WMM *Wesleyan Methodist Magazine*

WQ Donald Thorsen, *The Wesleyan Quadrilateral*, Grand Rapids: Francis Asbury Press, Zondervan, 1990

WQR *Wesleyan Quarterly Review*

WRE John W. Prince, *Wesley on Religious Education*, New York: Methodist Book Concern, 1926

WS Harold G. A. Lindstrom, *Wesley and Sanctification*, Nashville, Abingdon, n.d.

WTH Albert C. Outler, *The Wesleyan Theological Heritage, Essays*, ed. by T. Oden and L. Longden, Grand Rapids: Francis Asbury Press, Zondervan, 1991

WTJ *Wesleyan Theological Journal*

XXV Twenty-five Articles, adapted from the Sunday Service of 1784

INTRODUCTION

WHETHER WESLEY WAS THEOLOGICALLY SYSTEMATIC

By arranging the themes of Wesley's major homilies and essays in systematic sequence, it becomes evident that no major Christian doctrine is neglected and all systematic points are treated with reasonable internal cohesion. My objective is simply to set forth the implicit inner cohesion of these diverse points of Wesley's teaching.

The notion of an established, reliably transmitted Book of Homilies was a familiar pattern of the English church tradition (following Thomas Cranmer, John Jewel, and Matthew Parker), where it referred to a collection of prepared thematic teaching sermons designed to instruct congregations on received Christian doctrine.[1] Wesley followed this two hundred year Anglican tradition by modestly offering his own tutorial homilies to those in his direct connection of spiritual formation.[2]

At first glance, we seem not to have from Wesley's hand, as from Calvin or Suarez or Melanchthon, a definitive systematic theology in the sense of a comprehensive and sequential organization of the topics of theology. With Wesley we have what seem to be occasional instructional homilies. Though not organized as systematic theology, they were designed for standard doctrinal instruction, and clearly intended to inform the entire curriculum of evangelical life concerning the "whole compass of divinity."[3]

Among the charges made against Wesley in his lifetime,[4] which he answered in detail, was the indictment that he remained "absolutely unsettled with regard to every fundamental doctrine of the gospel," and that "no two disputants in the Schools can be more opposite to each other

---

[1] LJW 1:305, 312; 3:382; 4:125f., 379–81; JWO 119–33, 204–6, 417; FA 11:175, cf. 279.

[2] The root word of homily is *homos*, the same, from which our terms homogeneity, homogenize, and homoousian come. A *homilios* is an assembly, and a *homilia* is an intentional, reflective, deliberate, considered instruction to gathered hearers. Since so many have a distasteful aversion to the very word "sermon," tarred by a long history of browbeating, legalistic emotivism, I prefer the more descriptive term "teaching homily," as a contemporary dynamic equivalent. Cf. Collins, FW, 11-14.

[3] LJW 4:181; LJW 5:326.

[4] Among other complaints, he was charged with contradictions, inconsistencies, B9:56, 375, evasions, 374f., and hypocrisy, B9:304.

than he is to himself.''[5] His detailed and amusing responses to critics like Roland Hill, Conyers Middleton, and George Lavington show how ardently he sought to demonstrate the internal consistencies that others had impatiently failed to grasp or hastily misstated.[6]

Neither Wesley nor his successors ever issued an edition or précis of his published works deliberately sequenced in the order of the standard topics of systematic theology.[7] Had this been sooner done, Wesley might have been straightaway acknowledged as a systematic theological thinker. To those who imagine that Wesley lacked a systematic mind,[8] I wish to show that every major point of systematic theology is addressed in his instructional homilies, supplemented by his essays, journals, prefaces, and letters, with minimal lapses and incongruities.[9]

These homilies were intentionally designed by Wesley to cover every pivotal issue of Christian teaching. I challenge those who scold Wesley as unsystematic to propose any major question of Christian doctrine that he grossly disregarded. Though there is nothing in Wesley or most other Anglican sources that has the structural appearance of the ponderous dogmatic style of the seventeenth-century Lutheran or Reformed orthodox dogmatics, still no essential article of faith is left unattended, as we will see.[10]

To track carefully Wesley's own path and language is to offer a veritable course in systematic theology. This study could assist in devising a plan of instruction that would feature Wesley's teaching to constituencies who supposedly stand in his tradition of spiritual formation but who have in this century never been given a fair opportunity to be intellectually formed by him.

---

[5]Some Remarks of Mr. Hill's "Review of All the Doctrines Taught by Mr. John Wesley" X:377, quoting Roland Hill.

[6]Some Remarks of Mr. Hill's "Review of All the Doctrines Taught by Mr. John Wesley" X:381. In response to Hill he patiently refuted a hundred and one specific arguments ranged under twenty-four heads. As an experienced former teacher of logic, he did not lack confidence that he could "unravel truth and falsehood, although artfully twisted together."

[7]With the swollen footage of Wesley studies in history archives, it is surprising that this sort of inquiry has never been attempted.

[8]John Deschner, who has written the definitive work on Wesley's Christology, maintains that "Wesley's theology is not a settled system of doctrine, as Calvin's or Schleiermacher's theologies are. It is rather the effort of an energetic mind to organize for popular use the principal element of a message." WC 14. Cf. Albert C. Outler, "John Wesley: Folk-Theologian," *Theology Today*, 34 (1977) 150–66. The most eminent interpreters of Wesley—G. Cell, A. Outler, T. Langford, J. Deschner, D. Thorsen—all are uncomfortable with the claim that Wesley was a systematic theologian. They think it is a stretch of the imagination to view Wesley under the rubric of dogmatician or systematic theological teacher or exacting catechist. My purpose is to show that this is more plausible than usually thought.

[9]LJW 5:326.

[10]For doctrinal summaries, see JWO 183–85, 386ff.

STANDING IN WESLEY'S EVANGELICAL CONNECTION OF SPIRITUAL FORMATION

To stand "in Wesley's connection" traditionally has meant that one looks to him for spiritual formation. Millions in the eighteenth and nineteenth centuries have stood (with greater or lesser distance) in this connection. The entire early Methodist movement was intensely and personally bound with and configured by this remarkable pastoral guide. He gave himself unreservedly to the pastoral care of thousands in countless English, Irish, Welsh, and Scottish villages, traveling incessantly to serve the interests of their spiritual maturation.

Many today remain obliquely in Wesley's evangelical connection or remnants of it, though more distanced by time and history. Some remain committed to the churches resulting from his ministry who are now asking how they might again be formed by his wisdom, by the truth of his message and the joyful integrity of his outlook. Others not in the Wesleyan family of evangelical churches see in Wesley a godly leader of special spiritual power, and are willing to hear more.

The study of Wesley's doctrine is inevitably an exercise in daily practical spiritual maturation, if one is to credit at all Wesley's own understanding of himself. It is still possible for persons thoroughly immersed in post-modern consciousness to seek and reappropriate Wesley's counsel, not only by means of the text of his writings and sermons, but also by attending to the roots from which he drew strength (especially the patristic, Anglican, holy living, and Puritan traditions), and by personally meeting with those formed today by this spirit.

Even if one were only slightly intrigued conceptually by the cohesion of Wesley's ideas, the study of his theology would remain important for the understanding of the history of religion in our times. The family of churches his ministry spawned is vast and worldwide. It includes not only the eight-million-member United Methodist Church (larger than combined Lutheran and Episcopalian bodies in the United States), but also a conspicuous assortment of worldwide church bodies that have spun off from Methodist and holiness revival preaching, including the Wesleyan Church, the Free Methodist Church, the Church of the Nazarene, the Salvation Army, the African Methodist Episcopal and AME Zion traditions, and, arguably, many forms of charismatic and pentecostal communities that preach entire sanctification, assurance, and holy living.

A personal, vocational memorandum may help some readers to get in touch with my autobiographical motivation for doing this study. I feel called to help lead the Wesleyan family of churches, and evangelicals generally, back to their vital historic roots. This is why I write. It is not merely an incidental part of my vocation, nor disrelated to that aspect of my vocation that has focused in recent years on post-modern orthodoxy and classical consensual Christianity.[11] For the past ten years I have been working steadily on my systematic theology, pledging to my reader that I am seeking only to present ancient Christian ecumenical teaching rather than a denominational treatise.[12] That task now complete, I turn not to the root but to a particular branch of *the same tree, classical Christianity*. Now I want to show how a particular branch, Wesleyan theology, has grown out of the same root of ecumenical teaching that I have sought to expound in three volumes of Systematic Theology. I do not see these two tasks as conflicted, but complementary. Both projects are close to the center of my vocation: the rediscovery of ancient ecumenical theology, and the recovery of classical Christianity within my own evolving Wesleyan tradition.[13]

METHOD OF EXPOSITION

Rather than squeezing the thought of the texts into a rigid, preset systematic order, I have asked what order the texts themselves demand. I prefer to think of this method more as inductive than deductive, beginning with the texts, and asking whether they offer a cohesion worthy of the label "systematic." The ensuing sequence of argument is determined far more by Wesley's own text and language than by a set of predisposing topics imposed upon the text.

The way Christian doctrine was taught by eighteenth-century Anglican divines was largely through published teaching sermons, not rococo tomes on specific doctrines. Wesley was immersed in this Anglican homiletic teaching tradition. Those who ask of an Anglican writer a scholastic pattern of organization are sadly self-destined to be always disappointed. Some of the neglect of Wesley by the Reformed tradition hinges precisely on this point of mistaken and disappointed expectations.

---

[11]As a small town boy with the dust of the Oklahoma plains still under my eyelids, I now find myself thrust into a nexus of history that feels decisive for the human future. Working in the shadow of the prototype international cosmopolis, New York, at a time when my nation, now the world's leading superpower, arguably at the apex of its international influence, is languishing in desperate social crisis, I find myself located in the heart of Protestantism's second-largest denomination, teaching in one of its leading academic institutions. Inwardly this feels to me to be some sort of hidden providence beyond mere human artifice, placing upon me a weighty challenge.

[12]I have promised my reader that I would not foist off Arminian or Wesleyan or even Protestant thinking in my Systematic Theology, but that the reader could count on me for a fair exposition of classic Christian teaching, especially as defined in its first five centuries. I have worked especially hard not to be dismissed as a particularist trying to make my own personal tradition universal or clothe a concealed exclusivism in an ecumenical garb. I have bent over backward to quote ancient writers instead of Reformation or modern writers in order to establish that point.

[13]I do not want my reader to draw the unwarranted conclusion that I have suddenly abandoned my ecumenical patristic classical effort in focusing on my own tradition. Nor do I want my reader to have any reason to imagine that the Systematic Theology effort was a hidden ploy to draw others toward my own particular tradition.

In his address to readers of his collected works of 1771, Wesley himself made a preliminary attempt at a rough sequential organization of his instructional homilies: "I wanted to methodize these tracts, to range them under proper heads, placing those together which were on similar subjects, and in such order that one might illustrate another . . . there is scarce any subject of importance, either in practical or controversial divinity, which is not treated of more or less, either professedly or occasionally."[14] This is the systematic design we will build upon and seek to refine.

A CASE STUDY IN INTRATEXTUAL THEOLOGY

Two reference points are constantly correlated in what follows: the text itself and our contemporary language situation to which I believe the text still speaks. Where I have taken some restrained poetic license in interpreting Wesley for a contemporary audience, I have sought to offer a dynamic equivalency translation of his own views in plain modern English. If I have intruded my own views inordinately upon Wesley I have failed my deeper intention.[15] My aim is to offer a present-day interpretation and exposition of Wesley's teaching in contemporary language, deliberately seeking to be expressly accountable to his own text.

If the method is inductively expository, the order is systematic. My modest task is merely to arrange and explicate Wesley's texts in the prevailing classic order of the ancient Christian writers, but with the special imprint of Wesley's own colloquialisms, idioms, and predilections.[16] By classic order I mean the chain of theological reasoning generally found in the tradition from Irenaeus and Cyril of Jerusalem through John of Damascus and Thomas Aquinas to Calvin and John Pearson.[17]

I have deliberately focused upon primary sources in this study, leaving it to others, especially those with more historical than systematic

---

[14]Preface to the Third Edition, I:iii.

[15]For those spoiling for a fight with Wesley, or those who seek ammunition for a sustained critique of Wesley, this method is bound to be disappointing. My long range intention is not to disappoint the critic unremittingly, however, since in the last volume of this series, I will offer some of my own admonitions to the reader concerning traps and entanglements in Wesley to be avoided. Most of these points, I confess, were anticipated or answered by Wesley himself in his many decades of controversy. Stephen Gunter has probed the issues of Wesley's controversies better than any I know. A major portion of the pastoral volume of this series will focus on the issues of Wesley's irenics and polemics in defense of the evangelical revival.

[16]There is surprisingly little repetition in Wesley when the sequence is viewed economically in this traditional order. As editor he was a stickler for economy of style.

[17]Neither Albert Outler, Frank Baker, or Richard Heitzenrater has ever attempted anything of this sort, nor were they ever the slightest bit interested in it. Of those who have tried to provide a general account of Wesley's theology, neither Cell, Cannon, Williams, Mickey, or Harper approaches the comprehensiveness of these pages, partly because they were not working out of the Bicentennial edition. Though thorough, Deschner has restricted his interest primarily to Christology, and Lindström and Collins to soteriology.

interests, to pursue developmental questions concerning Wesley's theological and biographical transformations in their social contexts.[18] However intriguing the psychohistorical, social history, and historical critical approaches may be to me, they have a track record of not yielding profound theological insights, which require bringing to bear tested methods of systematic theology—exegesis according to the analogy of faith, the criteria of internal coherence, unity and continuity of canonical testimony, and conciliation. My hermeneutic method is to work more with the intratextual theological truth of the primary text itself than with the history of its development.[19]

This method necessarily collides with some Reformed evangelicals who without reading Wesley may tend easily to caricature him as semi-Pelagian or lacking a sound doctrine of grace; with some Lutherans who cannot imagine that he has in fact covered the key loci of systematic theology as thoroughly as Melanchthon; with some Anglicans who remember only one thing about Wesley and that is that he caused the separation of Methodism from the Church of England, forgetting that he himself remained Anglican all his life and resisted precisely that separation with all his might; and most of all with credulous Wesleyans who so sentimentalize and idealize his pragmatic skills that he is not taken seriously as an independent thinker. For those who look for a rigorous critique of Wesley's teaching, that too will be included in the final volume of the series.

WHETHER A SYSTEMATIC STUDY OF WESLEY IS NEEDED

This study stands in a singular relation of appreciation to the work of my incomparable mentor, Albert C. Outler—complementary, sympathetic, and grateful, not following but rather presupposing his method, seeking rather a method of its own. I have spent most of my professional life as a systematic theologian. Outler spent his as a historical theologian. My method is primarily systematic, Outler's historical. The following attempt seeks to order Wesley's thought systematically, a task Outler never aspired to do, and in fact looked upon somewhat disdainfully.

Outler's vocation was to provide an exhaustive placement of Wesley in his historical context, showing his sources, and accurately describing his thought in its historical-autobiographical development, which he did in an exemplary way. My attempt presupposes his work, and the work of other historians in this recent period that he described as the "Third Phase" of

---

[18]Several other scholars are currently making significant inquiries into Wesley's theology (notably Randy Maddox, Kenneth Collins, and Theodore Runyon). They are skilled in and intent upon entering into the vast arena of secondary literature on Wesley, to assess its adequacy—an arena I cheerfully leave to them.

[19]Though I commend the work of other colleagues who prefer to engage the secondary literature, the more I read it, the more I have come to see that a study is required that focuses deliberately on the primary texts themselves.

Wesley studies, a phase whose methods have been brilliantly dominated by historians but have noticeably failed to connect with systematic theologians.[20]

I have never been a historian in the sense that Frank Baker, Richard Heitzenrater, Timothy Smith, Paul M. Bassett, Stephen Gunter, Ted Campbell, and company are primarily historians. I straightforwardly am a systematic theologian, and work unapologetically according to the methods of systematic theology.[21] If historians sometimes assume that such a task is implausible or even impossible, my purpose is to offer an example of its viability.[22] Albert Outler made Wesley accessible to Wesleyans as a folk theologian. I seek to make Wesley accessible to non-Wesleyans as a systematic theologian.

Without denying or ignoring the intriguing question of how Wesley's theology developed and changed over time, the systematician's question is fashioned differently: To what degree, if any, does the gist of the whole of Wesley's theological contribution admit of consistent cohesion, or general representation as a viable, organic conception and design?[23] If you begin by insisting that the percentage is zero, then you have no responsibility such as that proposed in this volume, and you can cheerfully turn to other tasks. If the percentage is anything above zero, then the burden of proof rests upon the systematician to show textually that there indeed is in the primary text a solid core of cohesive teaching.[24] That is my assignment.

[20]I am restless both with historians who cannot take Wesley seriously as a theologian, and with theologians who refuse to see him in his historical-intellectual context.

[21]If some may misinterpret my intent as claiming too much for Wesley as systematician, let me refine the point more modestly that Wesley was an evangelical preacher whose intellectual temperament exhibited a steady concern for cohesion and consistency grounded in a wide data base. On this score I think Wesley is not so overtly systematic as Thomas Aquinas or Calvin or Barth, but moreso than Luther or Newman, and equally so with Cranmer and Edwards.

[22]Historians delight in caricaturing systematicians as always prematurely jumping to conclusions, overleaping piles of evidence, missing developmental complexities, overlooking contextual influences. Systematicians in turn caricature historians as always fixated upon picking up thin pieces of evidence but never grasping the larger picture, always too hesitant to make any judgments about how the changing views of a living person cohere through their mutations, so fixated on the specifics of the context that the substantial contribution of a person or period becomes diffused and lost. Each of these caricatures is to some degree justifiable. I admit my disposition from the outset as tending toward the systematic side, although I do admire the excellent work of rigorous historians such as Outler, Baker, and Heitzenrater.

[23]The most systematically ignored aspect of the secondary literature on Wesley's teaching is the triune frame of his theology, embracing his ordering of discipline, sacrament, pastoral practice, and moral reasoning. In the section on Trinity, I will show how important this is to him, and how triune reasoning is saturated throughout the entire enterprise, in his doctrines of God the Creator, God the Son, and God the Holy Spirit. This indeed, I will argue, is the pervasive principle of systematic cohesion of the whole corpus.

[24]Focal questions to be pursued are: Does Wesley's teaching illuminate the evangelical pastoral task today? How fully developed are his doctrines of creation, providence, the triune God, theological method, sin and grace, justification and sanctification, Word and sacraments, and eschatology? It is commonly acknowledged that Wesley gave explicit attention to selected areas of theology such as soteriology and ecclesiology, and the work of

Wesley has been prematurely dismissed as unsystematic on the ground that his writings were largely occasional, and not ordered in a methodical, systematic manner.[25] My objective is to show that all of his occasional writings indeed had a systematic core, and that core is textually available to anyone who cares to examine it fairly.

My training and temperament lead me to be far more interested in pastoral than historical questions as such. In this sense, Wesley is a special sort of systematic theologian—his cohesive reflections emerge directly out of his wide range of active pastoral relationships. This is especially noticeable in his letters, where pastoral and moral advice and spiritual admonition abound, yet integrate into a connected pattern of deliberate reflection. Readers who look for a systematic theologian strongly grounded in pastoral care will find it more in Wesley than in Schleiermacher or Barth, who ostensibly might otherwise appear to be "more systematic." The entire second volume of this series in fact will be devoted to the *pastoral*, and the third to the *moral* sides of Wesley's teaching.

One further whimsical note: Though Wesley is often imagined to be unduly sober and humorless, I have found many engaging passages where he radiates brilliant sparks of wit and comic perception.[26] Rather than merge them into a separate section on humor, I have decided to let them lie quietly in the text, awaiting the reader's unanticipated discovery. There is no other motive greater in my mind than proactively sharing with you the steady *joy* I have found in reading Wesley, which centers in taking pleasure in the good news of God's own coming.

It is customary in a Preface to set forth the ways in which the study ahead has practical utility or moral relevance—this book, for example, will be practically used for topical sermon preparation, for devotional reading, or as a reference work for identifying Wesley's ideas and opinions on ecological recovery, moral relativism, enthusiasm, catholicity, experience, paradise, final justification, providence, and countless other topics that will intrigue the curious or inspire the devout, or give courage to those weary in well doing. It awaits being fruitfully applied to numerous pressing issues of contemporary society such as addictive behaviors, the feminization of poverty, and punk nihilism. Instead, I prefer to alert you to what you are likely to enjoy most from these pages: good sense, practical

---

the Holy Spirit, but to what extent did Wesley attend sufficiently to the wider range of theological questions so as to be rightly regarded as a reliable guide to Christian doctrine as a whole? Is it possible to sort out Wesley's essays, sermons, and occasional writings in terms of the categories of classical doctrines of systematic theology, and survey them generally in a brief scope?

[25]It should not count against the systematic competence or cohesive thought of a writer that he is capable of occasional writings in which specific challenges are answered, provided those occasional writings are consistent with the larger literary whole. It should not count against relevance or contextualization to work out of a consistent systematic core, which is then capable of responding situationally to specific challenges.

[26]If typographers could insert a smile-face in the margins each time one of these sparks flies, the margins would be well-supplied.

wisdom, nonspeculative earthy realism. I am at a tardy point in my life where I most want to offer something beautiful and delightful to my reader, not merely a heavier moral burden. I hope that what follows will be assessed as much by aesthetic as moral or religious criteria. Since there is so much to be relished and enjoyed in Wesley, it seems deadly to think of this endeavor only in terms of what one ought to do in relation to it.

FURTHER READING

Overviews of Wesley's Theology

Burwash, Nathaniel. *Wesley's Doctrinal Standard*. Introduction. 1881. Reprint. Salem, Ohio: Schmul, 1967.

Cannon, William R. *Theology of John Wesley: With Special Reference to the Doctrine of Justification*. Nashville: Abingdon, 1946.

Cell, G. C. *The Rediscovery of John Wesley*. New York: Henry Holt, 1935.

Collins, Kenneth. *Faithful Witness*. Wilmore: Wesleyan Heritage Press, 1993.

—————. *Wesley on Salvation*. Grand Rapids: FAP, Zondervan, 1989.

Harper, Steve. *John Wesley's Message for Today*. Grand Rapids: FAP, Zondervan, 1983.

Lee, Umphrey. *John Wesley and Modern Religion*. Nashville: Cokesbury, 1936.

Mickey, Paul. *Essentials of Wesleyan Theology*. Grand Rapids: FAP, Zondervan, 1980.

Norwood, Frederick A. *The Story of American Methodism*. Nashville: Abingdon, 1974, chap. 3 on the "Roots and Structure of Wesley's Theology."

Outler, Albert C. "John Wesley as Theologian: Then and Now." MH 12, No. 4 (1974): 64–82.

—————. "Toward a Reappraisal of John Wesley as Theologian." *Perkins School of Theology Journal*, 14, no. 2 (1961): 5–14.

—————. , ed. *John Wesley*. Introduction, pp. 3–33, Library of Protestant Theology, New York: Oxford, 1964.

Slatte, Howard A. *Fire in the Brand: Introduction to the Creative Work and Theology of John Wesley*. New York: Exposition, 1963.

Sugden, Edward H. *Wesley's Standard Sermons*. London: Epworth, 1921; see Introduction and annotations.

Watson, Philip. *The Message of the Wesleys*. New York: Macmillan, 1964.

Williams, Colin W. *John Wesley's Theology Today*. Nashville: Abingdon, 1960.

Systematic Theologies Largely Based Upon Wesley's Theology

Banks, John S. *A Manual of Christian Doctrine*. 1st Am. ed., J. J. Tigert, ed. Nashville: Lamar & Barton, 1924.

Binney, Amos. *Theological Compend Improved*. With Daniel Steele. New York: Phillips and Hunt, 1875.

Burwash, Nathaniel. *Manual of Christian Theology*. 2 vols. London: Horace Marshall, 1900.

Gamertsfelder, S. *Systematic Theology*. Harrisburg: Evangelical Publishing House, 1952.

Merrill, Stephen M. *Aspects of Christian Experience*. New York: Methodist Book Concern.

Miley, John. *Systematic Theology*. Peabody, Mass.: Hendrickson, 1989. Reprint.

Miner, Raymond. *Systematic Theology*. 2 vol. Cincinnati: Hitchcock and Walden, 1877–79.

Outler, Albert C. *Theology in the Wesleyan Spirit*. Nashville: Tidings, 1975.

Pope, William Burt. *A Compendium of Christian Theology*. 3 vols. London: Wesleyan Methodist Book-Room, 1880.

Ralston, Thomas N. *Elements of Divinity*. New York: Abingdon, 1924.

Summers, Thomas O. *Systematic Theology*. 2 vols. Ed. J. J. Tigert. Nashville: Methodist Publishing House South, 1888.

Tillett, Wilbur. *Personal Salvation*. Nashville: Barbee and Smith, 1902.

Watson, Richard. *Theological Institutes*. 2 vols. New York: Mason and Lane, 1836, 1840; ed. John M'Clintock. New York: Carlton & Porter, 1850.

Weaver, Jonathan. *Christian Theology*. Dayton: United Brethren Publishing House, 1900.

Wynkoop, Mildred Bangs. *Foundations of Wesleyan-Arminian Theology*. Kansas City: Beacon Hill, 1967.

The Relation of Wesley's Theology to His Biography

Clarke, Adam. *Memoirs of the Wesley Family*. London: J. & T. Clarke, 1823.

Coke, Thomas and Henry Moore. *The Life of the Rev. John Wesley, A.M.* London: G. Paramore, 1792.

Gambold, John. "The Character of Mr. John Wesley." MM 21, 1798.

Green, Vivian H. H. *The Young Mr. Wesley*. London: Edward Arnold Ltd., 1961.

Heitzenrater, Richard P. *The Elusive Mr. Wesley*. 2 vols. Abingdon, 1984.

_____. *Mirror and Memory: Reflections on Early Methodism*. Nashville: Abingdon, 1989.

Schmidt, Martin. *John Wesley: A Theological Biography*. 2 vols. in 3. Nashville: Abingdon, 1963–73.

Tuttle, Robert. *John Wesley: His Life and Theology*. Grand Rapids: FAP, Zondervan, 1978.

Tyerman, Luke. *The Life and Times of the Rev. John Wesley*. 3 vols. New York: Harper, 1872.

Bibliographical Resources

Baker, Frank, comp. *A Union Catalogue of the Publications of John and Charles Wesley*. Durham: Duke University, 1966.

_____. "Unfolding John Wesley: A Survey of Twenty Years' Study in Wesley's Thought." QR, 1, no. 1 (1980).

Bassett, Paul M. "Finding the Real John Wesley." *Christianity Today* 28, no. 16 (1984).

Green, Richard. *The Works of John and Charles Wesley: A Bibliography*. 2d ed, New York: AMS Press, 1976.

Jarboe, Betty M. *John and Charles Wesley: A Bibliography*. Metuchen, N. J.: Scarecrow, 1987.

Jones, Arthur E. *A Union Checklist of Editions of the Publications of John and Charles Wesley: Based upon the "Works of John and Charles Wesley: A Bibliography" by Richard Green*, Madison, N. J.: Drew University, 1960.

Rowe, Kenneth E. *Methodist Union Catalogue*. Metuchen, N. J.: Scarecrow, 1975ff.

Humor in Wesley

Crawford, Robert C. "John Wesley's Humour." MM 157 (1934): 313–15.

Foster, Henry J. "Wesley's Humour." WMM 126 (1903): 446–49.

Page, W. Scott. "Wesley and the Sense of Humour." MR, 1906, 13.

Perkins, J. P. "The Humour of John Wesley." WMM 143 (1920): 697–98.

1

God

Wesley is seldom classified as one who reflected profoundly or passionately on the nature and existence of God. Yet in a series of homilies from his mature years, he entered into a meticulous, detailed consideration of the divine attributes, especially the eternity, omnipresence, and unity of God. Though spare, they freight ample argument sufficient to indicate the main lines of Wesley's doctrine of God.

ATTRIBUTES OF GOD

Non-Wesleyan evangelical readers will find Wesley to be particularly close to classic Protestant sources on the knowledge and attributes of God, while not ceasing to build bridges with the ancient Christian writers and pre-Constantinian eastern Christian orthodox theology.

Wesley summarized key points of his doctrine of God in his renowned "Letter to a Roman Catholic": "As I am assured that there is an infinite and independent Being and that it is impossible there should be more than one, so I believe that this one God is the Father

of all things," especially of self-determining rational creatures, and that this One "is in a peculiar manner the Father of those whom he regenerates by his Spirit, whom he adopts in his Son as co-heirs with him."[1]

On Eternity

Ps. 90:2: "From everlasting to everlasting thou art God." [Homily #54 1789 B2:358–72 J#54 VI:189–98]

As immensity is boundless space, so eternity is "boundless duration."[2] As omnipresence refers to God's relation to space, as sovereignly present in every location, eternity refers to God's relation to time as intimately present in every moment.

Eternity Past and Future

There was no time when God was not. There will be no time when God will not be.[3] If eternity is from everlasting to everlasting, it can be thought of as distinguishable in two directions: *eternity past* is that duration that reaches *from everlasting*, eternity before creation, time viewed as before,

---

[1]"A Letter to A Roman Catholic," JWO 494.
[2]#54 "On Eternity," sec. 1, 2:358.
[3]#54 "On Eternity," sec. 3, 2:359; JWO 455.

the eternity that precedes this now and all past nows (*a parte ante*). Then there is the *eternity yet to come*, the duration that reaches *to everlasting*, which will have no end, the whole of time after now, everything eternally on the future side of now (*a parte post*).[4]

Time viewed synoptically is a "fragment of eternity broken off at both ends."[5] The eternity of God embraces and surrounds time. Time is that portion of duration that begins when the world begins and ends when the world ends. We do not see all of time, but only a momentary glimpse, which we call the present.[6]

Eternity as Decision Now

For those who stand before God as if accountable eternally, everything is changed, all relationships reshaped, reborn, reformed. Social change and ethical accountability come from the change of heart of each person one by one, in due time affecting the structures of political order and economic life. Only the renewed, whole person serious about eternity is fitted to work effectively to transform society, not the broken, guilty, anxious, bored, narcissistic, time-enslaved.

Wesley offers a practical, nonspeculative way of thinking personally about the eternity of God by placing his hearer imaginatively on the brink of a here and now decision: Think of yourself as deciding now for or against eternal life. Each hearer is invited to enter now into an unending relation with the Eternal by choosing a happy eternity, a life of eternal blessedness, or the misery of missing what is eternally good and worthy of worship. This is the choice being offered in the emerging reign of God.

This decision is being made implicitly every temporal moment. It is hidden tacitly in every discrete human experience of time. This continuing choice has profound consequences for human happiness. It is no exaggeration to view human existence as deciding every moment toward the joy of eternal life or toward the despair of eternal emptiness.[7] Only when one thinks of oneself as standing on the edge of either a happy or pitiable eternity does present life become meaningful and serious. "The Creator bids thee now stretch out thy hand either to the one or to the other."[8]

Just take the exercise as a pragmatic hypothesis: Suppose it might be the case that your personal life will continue beyond bodily death in eternity. What does that do to behavior, to social accountability? Wesley thought that the bare hypothesis alone had the latent power of transforming human relationships.

Time

Every moment of the whole of time has the fleeting character of beginning and ending. That is what characterizes it as time.[9] It is not a sad thought that time, which had a finite beginning in God and which has a fleeting present, will have a consummate ending in God, who in God's own time is in process of duly completing and fittingly refinishing the good but fallen creation. Nothing

---

[4]#54 "On Eternity," sec. 7, 2:362; cf. #120 "The Unity of the Divine Being," proem, 4:61.

[5]#54 "On Eternity," sec. 3, 2:360; #58 "On Predestination," sec. 5; Augustine, *Confessions* XI–XII.

[6]#69 "The Imperfection of Human Knowledge," i.3, 2:570; VI:339.

[7]#124 "Human Life a Dream," 4:108–19; VII:318–25.

[8]#54 "On Eternity," sec. 17–19, 2:368–71.

[9]B2:360.

that happens within the distortions of history has power to undo God's long range eternal purpose within time.[10]

Just as we experience our living souls only as embodied within space, so we experience eternity only from within time. This is why we who are so enmeshed in temporal life, so permeated with finitude, have such great difficulty in grasping the very concept of eternity. Our human awareness, being a creature of fleet time, can form a veiled idea of eternity only by fragile analogy. As God is immense beyond any conceivable finite immensity, so eternity is infinite beyond any imaginable duration of time.[11]

Time remains for temporal minds an ever-flowing mystery. There is no nontemporal moment or place for the finite mind to step away, as if apart from time, to think transtemporally about time. Time is an uncommon mystery difficult to get our minds around precisely because we are creatures lodged in time. We are called within this temporal sphere to understand ourselves within the frame of reference of eternity, living life in this world as if accountable to the giver of time.[12]

God in the Now

What divides past and future is now, the infinitely fleeting moment that can never be possessed as a fixed entity. One can never capture or hold a moment except in the tenuous form of memory. This is why temporal life is rightly compared to a dream.[13]

What we call "now" keeps on vanishing, eluding our grasp, changing its face. Yet it is the only position from which anyone can ever know or see the world, through the tiny keyhole of this constantly disappearing moment we call now. This fleeting present lies "between two eternities"![14] The moment I say "now" I have already lost the now in which I just said "now." We have this little splinter of ongoing time, which itself is a continuing refraction of the eternal.[15]

God meets us in time, but as the incomparable Creator of time God is not bound by time. Only One who is simultaneously present with every moment of time can fully know the future and past reaches of eternity.[16] That One we call God.

Knowing Time From Within Time

God is radically different from creatures in that God inhabits all eternity, whereas creatures inhabit only fleeting successive temporal moments. Since God has a present relation to all past and future moments, God can know the temporal flow beyond our knowing. God's complete memory and foreknowledge of time do not coercively predetermine events to come or arbitrarily undo events that have occurred.[17] God's relation to the future and past is entirely different from ours.

Time-drenched minds have some vulnerable access through memory to their personal past and to their future through imagination. Meanwhile, the

[10]B2:358–70, 420–24; 3:196–97.
[11]#54 "On Eternity," sec. 4–5, 2:360.
[12]#54 "On Eternity," sec. 4–6, 2:360–61.
[13]#124 "Human Life a Dream," sec. 1–9, 4:109–14.
[14]#54 "On Eternity," sec. 4, 2:360.
[15]The Platonic idea that time is the unfolding expression of eternity is taken captive to Christ in the Incarnation. It is a powerful idea, that what we are experiencing right now is precisely eternity entering time, as seen archetypally in the nativity of the Son. Cf. Kierkegaard, *Philosophical Fragments*.
[16]#54 "On Eternity," sec. 14–18, 2:366–70.
[17]#54 "On Eternity," sec. 3, 2:359.

eternal God is always already present to the past, embracing its entirety. Harder to conceive is the premise that God is present to all future moments, a premise essential to the Christian teaching of the eternal God—that God already knows the future because eternally present to all moments. "Strictly speaking, there is no 'fore'knowledge, no more than 'after'knowledge with God: but all things are known to Him as present from eternity to eternity."[18]

This does not mean that God determines the future so as to ignore or arbitrarily overrule human freedom. Divine foreknowledge does not imply predetermination. It simply means that God knows what outcomes the freedom of creatures will bring, and how the free choices of creatures will interplay with incalculable contingencies. God has become paradoxically revealed in history as having already secured final outcomes that are still in process of unfolding in the decisions of free creatures in time.[19]

Whether Spiritual Creatures Have a Beginning in Time

Human soul (*psuche, anima*) is the living aspect of human existence in time. Through conception and birth we are entrusted with soul, which is to say a life, an enlivening of flesh. The soul is generated in sexual procreation as a gift of God. Once given, *psuche* continues to exist beyond death as a relation with the eternal Life-giver. Jewish and Christian Scriptures promise that the soul will be reunited with the body in the resurrection on the last day. The soul (*psuche, anima*) is created, hence not eternal in time past, but having been created, does not finally come to nothing in death.

If you think of a corpse, you have a body without life, without soul. Death is defined as the separation of life (that which God breathes into the body) from the body. When the motion of the body ceases, its cardiovascular movement ceases, the life or soul leaves the body, but thereby does not simply end, but awaits a final reckoning. That end-time event is called the resurrection. What happens at the end of history is the mystery of bodily resurrection, in a glorified body that transcends simple physicality, yet a resurrection of the same body. Death does not end the life of the soul or even finally of the body, since in the resurrection body and soul are reunited.[20]

Whether Material Creation Is Eternal

Matter is not eternal, since matter is created. Yet matter once created will not be annihilated but finally transformed so as to mirror once again the beauty and goodness of the original creation. Once God makes matter, God permits it continually to change, but not to be exterminated. The Almighty has sufficient power, of course, to annihilate atoms, but no reason to do so.[21]

Wesley argued for the durability of atomic matter through whatever possible cosmic changes. Though creatures may lose their present form, every subparticle of every atom endures, even while being transmuted, under one form or other, to the fulfillment of time in eternity. Even diamonds, the hardest of physical substances, may under extreme heat be turned to dust, yet as dust they continue.[22] No creature shares with God unbeginningness or eternal

---

[18]ENNT on 1 Peter 1:2; #58 "On Predestination," sec. 15, 2:420.
[19]#54 "On Eternity," sec. 4f., 2:360f.
[20]#54 "On Eternity," sec. 6, 2:361.
[21]#54 "On Eternity," sec. 7, 2:362.
[22]#54 "On Eternity," sec. 7, 2:362.

aseity, "yet there is no absurdity in supposing that all creatures are eternal *a parte post*. All matter indeed is continually changing . . . but that it is changeable, does in nowise imply that it is perishable. The substance may remain one and the same, though under innumerable different forms."[23]

The promised new creation does not imply eradication of the old, but its transmutation. There is promised to be a new heaven and new earth where nothing has been destroyed, a full renovation without annihilation. It "will melt" but "*not perish.*"[24] As matter changes in form but with its substance remaining through different forms, so in the case of the soul does life remain after death, yet in a different spiritual form.[25]

How Faith Transforms Temporality

The remedy for the despair over ever-decomposing temporality is faith that trusts in the trustability of the eternal One who gives life. The eternal happiness or self-alienation of the soul hinges on the choice of whether one trusts in the trustworthiness of God who comes before and after all things. Faith walks continually in the awareness of the unseen eternal One, meditating daily on that One who does not pass, who puts all things temporal in fitting proportion and perspective.[26]

God presides over each and every individual life as patiently as over the whole universe. Each of us has a short time to live in a bodily sense, perhaps a few decades at most, perhaps no time at all, since even the young and healthy are vulnerable to accident and illness. But no one, however vulnerable, is deprived of meditating upon the meaning of one's own temporal life, regardless of how short. The decisive frame of reference in which to understand one's own brief life is eternity, a thought both sobering and exhilarating.[27]

How Faith Requires Decision

This vision of eternity calls each hearer to a here and now choice with eternal consequence.[28] Rather than offering a speculative theory of eternity, Wesley entreats his hearer personally and earnestly: If your life is indeed cast within time, which stands always in relation to the eternal, what are you choosing to do with it? Eternity places a decisive challenge before your life, calls you to a specific decision: a relation of eternal happiness with the eternal life giver, or a relation of eternal misery in turning away from that eternal happiness. You are a rational creature and have the power to choose. How you live out your life in this sphere is decisive for eternity.[29]

Evangelical preaching leads to a single point: Each one is now making a decision about eternity. Now, after all, is the only moment we concretely experience. There is a great difference between the soul that lives forever happily glorifying God even amid the loss of creaturely goods, and the soul that mourns forever the loss of creaturely goods and resents the Giver for those losses.[30]

No one becomes eternally happy or

[23]#54 "On Eternity," sec. 7, 2:360.
[24]#54 "On Eternity," sec. 7, 2:361, italics added.
[25]#54 "On Eternity," sec. 7, 2:361–63.
[26]#54 "On Eternity," sec. 17, 2:368–72.
[27]#54 "On Eternity," sec. 17–19, 2:368–71.
[28]B1:549; 2:286, 296f.; 4:327, 402.
[29]#93 "On Redeeming the Time," 3:322–32; cf. Charles Wesley, "Awake, Thou That Sleepest," 1:142–58.
[30]#54 "On Eternity," sec. 17–20, 2:368–72.

miserable except by one's own choice.[31] There is no divine decree that condemns one to unhappiness or determines one absolutely to happiness so as to circumvent human freedom.

Those who participate by faith in the eternal life of God through the Son are taken up into a blessed eternity. If the "happy life" is to share in the creative willing and working of God in history, the miserable life is its opposite, separated from God's own life, alienated from it entirely. When one chooses temporal values over the source and end of all values, then one's life becomes miserable because ill-timed, out of proper focus, off target. In consequence of the primitive fall of humanity, this off-centeredness has become our pervasive condition and will remain our human condition till nature is changed by grace.[32]

The Omnipresence of God

Jer. 23:24: "Do not I fill heaven and earth?" [Homily #118 1788 B4:39–47 J#111 VII:238–44]

Finite minds are incapable of fully grasping God's omnipresence because the knower remains finitely localized in each and every perception.

Whether God Is Present Everywhere

Even when fleeing from God I find myself meeting the One from whom I flee (Ps. 139). "There is no point of space, whether within or without the bounds of creation, where God is not."[33] Wesley challenged deistic rationalists who argued that God first created then abruptly abandoned the world to its own devices, leaving the Creator functionally absent from the world.

God's holiness addresses and pervades the whole of creation—spiritual and physical: " '*Do not I fill heaven and earth?' declares the LORD*" (Jer. 23:24). As Jonah discovered, there is no place to hide from the presence of the One who creates and sustains all spatial locations.[34] To affirm that God is in heaven is not to deny that God is everywhere else present, but to celebrate metaphorically the abode of God as transcending and embracing all time and space.[35]

Take a grain of sand in your hand. Compare its magnitude not just with a sand dune but with the whole of space. Compared to the boundlessness of God, this world of space stands in the same relation as the millionth part of a grain of sand stands to known space. Yet even with such immensity, the cosmos remains measurable and bounded. All its physical expressions are finite, hence next to nothing in relation to the infinite.[36] Time and space are transcended by the boundlessness of God.

The Giver and Measurer of space cannot be measured by spatial quantities. The root word for immensity is measurelessness, not great measure. However one might imagine the cosmic immensity, God is present at every discrete point, from the smallest speck, the tiniest sparrow, every niche of time and space, to the uttermost parts of the seas and heavens, and unknown galaxies.[37]

Whether There Are Other Universes

Are other universes possible? Whether space is filled with matter we

---

[31]#54 "On Eternity," sec. 20, 2:372.
[32]#54 "On Eternity," sec. 17–20, 2:368–72.
[33]#118 "On the Omnipresence of God," i.1, 4:42.
[34]#118 "On the Omnipresence of God," i.1, 4:42.
[35]LJW 5:300; B1:123f.; 2:502, 538f., 569f.; 4:39–50.
[36]#118 "On the Omnipresence of God," i.2, 3, 4:42; cf. quotation from Cyprian, #103 "What is Man," Ps. 8:3, 4; ii.3, 3:458.
[37]#69 "The Imperfection of Human Knowledge," i.2, 2:570; VI:338.

do not know empirically, but we can know by the analogy of faith that whatever space exists is forever accompanied by God the Creator, who "fills everything in every way" (Eph. 1:23).

Suppose one imagines a space beyond knowable spaces. Wesley toyed with the fantasy as to whether some hypothesized "space beyond space" might be conceived. Suppose one could imagine the entire extent of the whole cosmos—would there then be any space outside the cosmos? If there is, that too would be bounded by the boundlessness of God, for God as singular Creator transcends all conceivable worlds.

Even if we posit a myriad of other creations about which we know nothing, the same reasoning applies. The one God is present to all possible creations imaginable. God is not merely the Creator of the universe we see, but of all that can be conceived. Otherwise, God would not be that necessary One than which no greater being can be conceived. No created order is conceivable without positing a creator, no cosmic design without a designer.[38]

The omnipresent God is as attentive to and enabling of the tiniest atomic element, as of the whole cosmos, sustaining each and governing all, influencing the aggregate uncoercively, without destroying the free will of rational creatures. When God gives freedom, it is neither an abandonment to stark nature or an artifice that only pretends to but does not offer viable self-determining freedom.[39]

Whether God Can Be Conceived as Without the World

To posit a world without God is to posit nothing, for one cannot have an effect without a cause. So the world minus God comes entirely to nothing, while God minus the world remains completely God. Nothing has been subtracted from God by the absence of a particular world. God's existence is not dependent on the world's existence, otherwise some creature would become weirdly necessary to the Creator.[40]

Suppose one fantasizes the premise that only God exists and not any world. That of course is a dream that could only be dreamed by a free personal agent in an actual world. We can entertain such fantasies only because a tangible world has indeed been created and sustained. But even granting such a fantastic premise, God would remain incomparable Creator still able to choose to create or not create any such conceivable world, which would remain dependent in every moment of time and space upon the sustaining power of the Creator.[41]

This radically distinguishes the Judeo-Christian naming of God from all pantheisms, which presume a source of being continuous with or inseparable from the world or reducible to the world so that God is the world, or the world God, or the world viewed as God's body. This is not merely a conceptual error or intellectual mistake but a profound sin of the mind that at root is a distorted act of idolatrous willing.[42] All notions of the self-sufficiency of matter or of the oozing or emanating of matter from God are notions foreign to the Hebrew Bible and the New Testament. All conceivable reductions of God to creaturely being, whether by skeptical naturalism or animistic nativism or

[38]#118 "On the Omnipresence of God," ii, 4:42–43.
[39]#118 "On the Omnipresence of God," ii, 4:42–44.
[40]#118 "On the Omnipresence of God," ii, 4:43–44.
[41]#118 "On the Omnipresence of God," 4:44; cf., 2:13.
[42]Letter to William Law, Jan. 6, 1756, LJW 3:343–45.

earth mother vitalism or philosophical pantheism are sharply repudiated.[43]

Some cannot imagine God without a world. They insist that since God's overflowing love is by some external necessity bound to be creative, God cannot be conceived except in relation to a creation. Wesley answers that a supposed "creator" who from the outset remains dependent upon the world thus "created" (so to speak) is not the Creator attested in Scripture who created "heaven and earth"—the creedal way of pointing synoptically to all that has been created. "Where no creature is, still God is there. The presence or absence of any or all creatures makes no difference with regard to him."[44] It is this precise point that puts Wesley in tension with views that later would be called process theology. Those who view the world as the body of God, those nativists who wish to exalt nature by viewing it as identical with God rather than creature, or who bind the world and God intrinsically together according to the analogy of body and mind, find few affinities with Wesley's tenet of divine omnipresence.[45]

Whether God Can Be Almighty Without Being Omnipresent

To imagine any space entirely beyond God's influence is to deny the witness of Scripture and creed to God the Father Almighty. To confess "God almighty" is to acknowledge at the same time the omnipresence of God.[46] There can be no serious affirmation of unsurpassable divine power that does not at the same time imply that God is pervasively present in the world. No one can act where not present.[47]

Empiricists may want to look at God as an object, as if analogous to chemical components or biological structures. But God does not yield to flat observation because God is Spirit, transcending materiality and natural causality. The study of creation is not a mode of inquiry in which facts can be established in the same way that empirical conclusions can be drawn by using scientific method substantiated through experimentation with repeatable physical measurements.

Those who behold God do so with spiritual senses. The Creator gives rational creatures not only our familiar physical senses,[48] but also by providence through the means of grace a spiritual sensibility, a capacity to receive God's self-disclosure. This sensibility grows through prayer, sacrament, sacrificial service, the reading of Scripture, and spiritual discipline.[49]

Moral Consequences of Divine Omnipresence

No one can speak rightly of the attributes of God while ignoring their moral implications. The teaching of divine omnipresence has powerful consequences for interpersonal relationships. It shapes our dealings with others. The very thought of God's omnipresence calls us to moral attentiveness to what we are currently saying and feeling, as if being held up before the all-seeing, all knowing One who fills even secret spaces.

If we live out our lives daily in the presence of God, that presence im-

[43]Letter to William Law, Jan. 6, 1756, LJW 3:332–42.
[44]#118 "On the Omnipresence of God," ii.3, 4:43; VII:240–41.
[45]#118 "On the Omnipresence of God," ii, 4:42–45.
[46]LJW 3:343f.; 5:365; 8:153; B1:589; 2:540f.; 4:320f.
[47]#120 "The Unity of the Divine Being," sec 3-4; LJW 6:49.
[48]Concerning the empirical knowledge derived from senses, see B4:29f., 49–51, 200; 11:56f.
[49]#118 "On the Omnipresence of God," ii, 4:42–45.

pinges powerfully upon each discrete moral choice. The serious beholder of space, whether in macrocosm or microcosm, acknowledges with awe that God meets us in every meeting, each moment, each twinkling of the eye, every millimeter of space—God is with us.[50] Emmanuel, the song of the Incarnation, is the grand historical illuminator of the blunter rational idea of omnipresence.

The very idea of the omnipresence of God draws each beholder toward a lively awareness of God's personal presence with us, toward the enjoyment of the reconciled divine companionship, accompanied by the wonder of being a responsibly free human agent in a world in which God accompanies every moment of time and space. Each believer is called to "take captive every thought to make it obedient to Christ" (2 Cor. 10:5), rejoicing in God's continuing presence accompanying each present moment.

The consequent moral implication: Measure each moral choice in relation to the simple fact of the eternal divine presence. Behavior is transformed, speech reshaped, thinking reconfigured in relation to this omnipresent Companion. God gives himself to us to make life again happy, as once again rooted in its true center instead of transient idolatries. The believer is called to "spare no pains to preserve always a deep, a continual, a lively, and a joyful sense of God's gracious presence."[51]

Those in Wesley's connection of spiritual formation may reasonably infer salient aspects of other divine attributes from these substantive discussions of omnipresence and eternity.[52]

The Unity of the Divine Being

Mark 12:32: "There is one God" [Homily #120 1789 B4:61–71 J#114 VII:264–73]

The Derivative Unity of Humanity

The idea of the unity of humanity is a consequence of the premise of the unity of God. It is only because God is one that we can glimpse the oneness of rational creatures amid the vast diversities of human cultures.

The personal and ethical expression of that centeredness is the love of the tangible, definite, particular one nearby (the neighbor) as oneself in response to the love of God. Where many gods are worshiped, one can be sure that neither the true God is worshiped nor the unity of humanity grasped.[53]

The guiding text on the unity of God is Mark 12:32, where a detractor having asked Jesus about the most important commandment, heard his reply from Hebrew Scripture: " 'Hear, O Israel, the Lord our God, the Lord is one. Love the Lord your God with all your heart and with all your soul and with all your mind and with all your strength.' The second is this: 'Love your neighbor as yourself.' There is no commandment greater than these" (Mark 12:29–31; Deut. 6:4, 5).

Unity of the Divine Attributes

God is known by God's acts in history. God is known from what God does. We discover God's character by recalling the long story of the disclosure of God's character in history.[54]

Though the divine unity is manifested by complementary attributes, all unite and cohere in God's own life. God is eternal without ceasing to be omnipres-

---

[50] #67 "On Divine Providence," 11, 2:539; VI:316.
[51] #118 "On the Omnipresence of God," iii.6, 4:47.
[52] CH 7:370.
[53] #120 "The Unity of the Divine Being," sec. 1–3, 4:61.
[54] #120 "The Unity of the Divine Being," sec. 1–3, 4:61.

ent, omnipresent without ceasing to be empathic, all-knowing without ceasing to engender freedom. Each divine attribute is complementary to other divine attributes.[55]

The Divine Necessity

Some attributes can be ascribed only to God and not in any way to creatures. Other divine attributes are said to be relational because they pertain to the relation God has with creation, as omnipresent, omnipotent, and omniscient.[56] The attributes of divine necessity and unbegottenness cannot be simply conveyed or unilaterally transferred to finite, dependent, prejudiced mortals, hence are called incommunicable.[57] Finite minds and bodies can never be in themselves necessary, since contingent on their creation. The divine attribute of aseity (underivitiveness or self-sufficiency) cannot be relocated or communicated or made analogous with anything that characterizes radically derived, dependent human existence.[58]

Divine Attributes Pertaining to God's Relation With Creatures: Goodness, Mercy, and Holiness

All creatures have their being in time within narrow bounds marked by birth and death. God transcends time by experiencing eternal simultaneity with all events of time. God alone is omnipresent to all other presents, so as to be aware of all conceivable pasts, in all conceivable aspects, and all conceivable futures.[59]

Being God is incommunicable to finite minds, who cannot know as God knows. Only God knows how to be God. God alone is omniscient, knowing not simply the part as we know the part, but knowing intensively and extensively the whole of what has occurred, is yet to occur, and is occurring in any moment of time and space. That premise does not rule out human freedom but speaks of an infinitely free One as human freedom's companion and enabler, foreknowing but not foreordaining all free acts of will.[60]

Among communicable divine attributes—those in which finite creatures may share and that can be communicated to others—are veracity, compassion,[61] justice,[62] and spirituality.[63]

The mercy of God is a characteristic of God that God wishes to share with us and calls us to share with others.[64] God alone is infinitely good, the giver of other goods, in a goodness beyond finite bounds, abundant in beneficence, as incomparable in goodness as in power and knowing. No less than seventeen hymns from the 1780 *Collection of Hymns for the Use of the People Called Methodists* are focused upon "Describing the Goodness of God."[65] The most fitting response to the goodness of God in creation is a grateful life of communicating goodness to others.[66]

---

[55]#120 "The Unity of the Divine Being," sec. 2–9, 4:61–64.
[56]LJW 3:343f.; 5:365; 8:153; B1:589; B2:540f.; 4:320f.
[57]LJW 2:71; 5:231.
[58]#120 "The Unity of the Divine Being," sec. 2, 4:61.
[59]#120 "The Unity of the Divine Being," sec. 3, 4:61.
[60]#120 "The Unity of the Divine Being," sec. 3–6, 4:61–62.
[61]B1:274f.; 2:422–35; JWO 226f., 385f., 469f.
[62]LJW 3:345; B1:344f.; 2:12f.; 4:285f.; JWO 435–37, 451f.
[63]#120 "The Unity of the Divine Being," sec. 7–11, 4:62–65.
[64]B2:411, 424, 434; 4:62f.
[65]CH 7:107–28.
[66]LJW 8:153.

God alone is incomparably holy.[67] It is understandable that in the presence of this Holy One, we who have abused our freedom feel intensely any hint of unholiness in our lives. The Holy One who is incomparably merciful calls us to be merciful.[68]

God is Spirit

The basic hebraic analogy for "Spirit" is wind moving without being seen, yet knowable by the spiritual senses. God is not seen as other objects are seen, yet is proximately knowable just as the wind is knowable even if not seen.

To affirm with Scripture that God is Spirit is to deny that God can be reduced to matter. As Spirit, God is not an object visible to our eyes, not reducible to finite causality or corporeal matter or material determinants. While sustaining nature in time, God is not reducible to nature. While making natural causality reliable, God remains the ground and premise of its reliability.[69]

God creates not only all matter, but also the whole range of spiritual creatures that transcend matter, all living beings in heaven and on earth, including the whole of angelic creation, humanity and human history with all its variable possibilities. God creates persons with the proximate capacity to refract God's own being, unity, mercy, justice, spirituality, and love.[70]

Happiness

There is a practical moral focus in Wesley's reasoning about each divine attribute. Its proper contemplation always aims practically at human happiness, a notion prominently accented in Wesley's instructional homilies, and a conspicuous feature of his teaching.[71]

God intends from the beginning to enable the happiness of creatures to that full extent to which each is capable. The moral order is provided for the happiness of creatures.[72] The purpose of creation is the sheer joy of God in creating companionable creatures to share his own goodness to the full extent that creatures are capable of sharing.[73] It is our skewed freedom that absurdly distorts and upsets that order. God does not create the world for the sake of the damnation or alienation of rational creatures.[74]

God exceedingly enjoys the work of creation. Its whole aspect elicits God's approbation and redounds to God's glory.[75] God "made all things to be happy." Our freedom is made to be happy in God. God created companionate free self-determining personal beings in order that God's own freedom might be shared in and enjoyed. This happiness is God's intention for every creature, even as wise parenting seeks the true happiness of the family.[76]

How Idolatry Misplaces Happiness

What stands in the way of happiness? We treat the finite goods of creation as if absolute goods. Idolatry is the disordering of human choice, the twisting of human intentionality away from its ordered good toward its disordered fall

[67]#120 "The Unity of the Divine Being," sec. 5–6.
[68]#120 "The Unity of the Divine Being," sec. 7, 4:62.
[69]#118 "On the Omnipresence of God," ii.8, 4:45.
[70]#120 "The Unity of the Divine Being," sec. 8, 4:63.
[71]B4:209.
[72]B1:35, 223f.; 2:195f.; 3:533f., 4:300f., 305.
[73]Varying degrees of happiness are proportional to degrees of faith active in love. B4:286.
[74]#120 "The Unity of the Divine Being," sec. 9, 4:63.
[75]B9:39f.; JWO 450f.
[76]#120 "The Unity of the Divine Being," sec. 9–11, 4:63–65.

from goodness.[77] An idol is any good creature or relation that we take and pretend to be absolute. We take these created goods and worship and adore them in the place of the Giver of all things.[78]

This seemingly irreversible problem that emerges everywhere in human history is summarized in the code term "sin." Those who are proffered freedom have a disastrous history of being prone to barter it away.[79]

God does not make things badly or prone innately to evil. Only good comes from God's hand as created. We receive these good gifts freely and then pretend that the creation itself is the source of our goods. We love the creature more than the Creator. That sin is prone to evil is a result, not of its having been created thus, but of its being willed as idolatrous freedom would have it.[80]

Human nature is simultaneously a composite of opposites: finitude and freedom capable of transcending finitude; living souls housed in dying bodies; spirit contending with flesh. We are given freedom out of the divine goodness, with the capacity to exercise our powers responsibly. That capacity becomes distorted either downwardly in the direction of sensuality or exalted in the direction of pride. In my sensuality I become weighted down with body, as if to pretend that I had no self-transcending spirit.[81] In my pride I pretend that I am the center of the universe, as if I had no body, no grounding finitude. These goods, which

are intended for ordered human happiness, become through the exercise of freedom idolatrously disordered toward sensuality and pride.[82]

Three Forms of False Religion

Even our religious sensibilities and our native proneness to worship enter into an implacable rivalry with the incomparable One, giver of all goods, who is jealous on behalf of our deeper human vocation. Religion of some sort is as native to the human condition as digestion or sex. It is endemic to the human situation always to be prone to adore some object of worship whether genuine or spurious. Of all the idolatries we are prone to create, the most subtly nuanced is religion itself.

False religion only moves us further away from real happiness. It may appear as *dead conventional religion of opinions* or "*of barely outward worship*," which has the form but not the power of godliness.[83] One who talks a good God game or attends services obsessively may fail entirely to receive the grace and embody the love of the revealing God. In speaking sometimes harshly of dead orthodoxy, Wesley was not opposing classic Christian orthodoxy, except as its true teachings have been falsely reduced to dead opinions without behavioral consequence.[84]

Or false religion may appear as *a servile religion of works righteousness* in which we hold ourselves up before God pretending, "Look, Lord, how wonderful," expecting to be received

---

[77]Worldly happiness is constituted by all those forms of fleeting, proximate happiness that rest anxiously in or are prone to idolatries, B1:253, 624–26, 636f.; 3:97f., 105–13, 234–36; 4:123–26, 206f.

[78]#120 "The Unity of the Divine Being," sec. 9–11, 4:63–65.

[79]#78 "Spiritual Idolatry," 3:103–5; VI:435–44.

[80]#28 "Upon Our Lord's Sermon on the Mount, VIII," 1:612–32; V:361–77.

[81]FA Part II, ii.16-20, 11:228-34; VIII:161-64.

[82]Kierkegaard, *Sickness Unto Death*; Reinhold Niebuhr, NDM I.

[83]#120 "The Unity of the Divine Being," sec. 15, 4:66.

[84]Letter to Charles Wesley, Jr., May 2, 1784, LJW 7:216–17, concerning Samuel Wesley who had "changed his religion" and become a Roman Catholic.

on the basis of our good deeds or services rendered or merits achieved. We conjecture that our own moral acts or religious works are the final good that we offer to God, turning our backs upon trusting in the incomparably good work of God for us.[85]

Finally, false religion may appear as an arid *practical atheism* that nonetheless continues unawarely to adore some finite object of worship. Wesley was less interested in theoretical than practical atheism, by which we actually live as though God does not exist.[86]

True Religion as Grateful Benevolence

True religion has two interconnected dimensions, like two halves of a whole: gratitude toward God and benevolence toward humanity. In contrast to all idolatries, true religion is expressed as a life of *gratitude for God's good gifts and benevolence toward the needy neighbor in response to God's gifts.*[87] True religion lives daily out of praise for the gifts of God in creation and redemption, grateful for life and finite freedom, and when freedom falls, the restoration of freedom to its deeper grounding in God.[88]

True religion reaches out to the wounded neighbor with goodwill in response to the good willing of God toward our wounded humanity. We are called to share the mercy of God with those who hunger for mercy, the goodness of God with the dispossessed, the love of God with the homeless.[89]

Those who try to develop a religious sensibility that has nothing in it of the neighbor's good have missed at least half of religion: benevolence toward others. Those who try to reduce religion to humanistic ethics lose the other half: the personal self-giving of God who invites and enables unfettered responsiveness to the neighbor.[90]

The Father is revealed through the Son as love. The love of God is shed abroad in our hearts by the Holy Spirit. The full response of faith and love to this one God is the ground of true human happiness and true religion. Such religion is rare in a history drenched with sin.

Those who most deeply are freed to love the neighbor are those who have no other gods before them than the One who is "eternal, omnipresent, all-perfect Spirit, is the Alpha and Omega, the first and the last. Not his Creator only, but his Sustainer, his Preserver, his Governor; yea, his Father, his Savior, Sanctifier, and Comforter. This God is his God, and his all, in time and eternity."[91]

Wesley explicitly identifies the threat to religion that comes from the great Enlightenment apostate "triumvirate, Rousseau, Voltaire, and David Hume,"[92] who extolled "humanity . . . as the very essence of religion . . . sparing no pains to establish a religion which should stand on its own foundation, independent of any revelation whatever." Even when fashionable, it is "neither better nor worse than

---

[85]#6 "The Righteousness of Faith," i, 1:204–9.
[86]#120 "The Unity of the Divine Being," sec. 15, 4:66; "On Living Without God," 7, VII:351.
[87]#120 "The Unity of the Divine Being," sec. 16–17, 4:67.
[88]B2:548f.
[89]#120 "The Unity of the Divine Being," sec. 16–18, 4:66–68.
[90]#120 "The Unity of the Divine Being," sec. 16–17, 4:67.
[91]"The Unity of the Divine Being," sec. 24, 4:71.
[92]#120 "The Unity of the Divine Being," sec. 18, 4:68. For Wesley's references to Hume see B11:460; JJW 5:458, 491, 523; on Rousseau, see B4:60, 69; JJW 5:352f.; 6:23; on Voltaire see JJW 4:45, 157; 6:211; 7:13; LJW 5:199; 6:123, 332, 338.

Atheism," putting asunder what God has joined together—love of God and neighbor. Wesley could smell the approach of Nietzsche, Marx, and Freud in his critique of William Wollaston's *The Religion of Nature Delineated*, of Jean-Jacques Burlamaqui's *Principles of Natural Law*, and especially of Francis Hutcheson's *Conduct of the Passions*, who "quite shuts God out" of moral reflection by regarding it as "*inconsistent with* virtue . . . if in doing a beneficent action you expect God to reward it. . . . It is then not a virtuous but a selfish action."[93] The beast of modernity was already slouching toward Bethlehem, where the center would not hold.

The Wisdom of God's Counsels

Rom. 11:33: "O the depth of the riches both of the wisdom and knowledge of God!" [Homily #68 1784 B2:551–66 J#68 VI:325–37]

Divine wisdom and power work together to revitalize freedom when it falls, to redeem it from its follies.[94] God's providence encompasses means as well as ends, shaping consequences as well as antecedents of human choosing. Faith views all things as so adapted by divine wisdom to the ends for which they were designed, that taken together, creation is even yet seen as *very good*. The wisdom of God's counsels saturates the human story despite all transitory recalcitrance.[95]

God's Wisdom Works Differently in Nature Than Human Freedom

God's guiding hand is present in the realm of the human spirit in a different way than amid nature. In nature, the creation is ordered by an unbending physical causality.[96] In the moral order, freedom itself shapes causality. Natural causality is reliable, but within the dependable chains of natural causality there appears a history shaped by self-determined willing. This freedom that flows within causal determinants is itself a co-determinant.

If in nature there is no freedom, hence no opposition to God's will, in history there is constant opposition. God's wisdom therefore is more conspicuous in the arena in which evil must be counteracted without violating the nature of freedom.[97]

Why would an all-wise God make a vulnerable finite freedom that could stand in defiance of God? Here the mystery of God's wisdom is profound. God enables human freedom, drawing it by grace constantly toward the good, but when freedom falls, as it so often does, God's redemptive grace is constantly working to raise it up again.[98]

God's Wisdom in Providence Has a History

This redemptive activity has a history converging on God's own covenant with a special people, Israel. That history comes to a new beginning, like a seed that is planted, preserved and grows, in the events surrounding the resurrection of Jesus and the coming of the Spirit at Pentecost. After Pentecost, the community of the resurrection grew through hazardous and challenging circumstances, persecutions, defections and apostasies, and violent attempts to resist faith.[99]

93#120 "The Unity of the Divine Being, sec.18, 4:68.
94#68 "The Wisdom of God's Counsels," sec. 2, 2:552.
95LJW 3:380; B2:540f., 552f.; 4:62, 523.
96#68 "The Wisdom of God's Counsels," sec. 3, 2:552.
97JWO 450f.
98#68 "The Wisdom of God's Counsels," sec. 4, 2:553.
99#68 "The Wisdom of God's Counsels," sec. 5, 2:553–54. For references to heresy, see LJW 3:182, 200; 7:4–16, 21; B2:555f.; 3:62f.; 4:394f., 409f.

The accurate, descriptive beholding of church history is itself an exercise in witnessing the unfolding of God's providence in history. Wesley knew well the history of the church, realizing that it was not simply a sentimental fabrication, but a real history of men and women of faith willing to risk their lives for their witness to the truth. The seeds of martyrs did not grow without trial or peril. Church history evidences almost every imaginable kind of hardship in its successive periods of struggle.[100] Wesley reflected upon providence not merely in nature or general history, but more powerfully within the frame of reference of the evangelical revival in which he himself had been intensely engaged. In no period of church history is the Christian community fully responsive to the work of the Spirit, though in some periods, such as the apostolic and the ante-Nicene and in the early Reformation and the evangelical revival, the community is much more responsive.

However apostate, the church by grace survived. "The gates of hell did never totally prevail against it. God always preserved a seed for himself, a few that worshipped him in spirit and in truth," whom "rich . . . Christians, who will always have number as well as power on their side," sometimes stigmatized as "heretics. Perhaps it was chiefly by this artifice of the devil . . . that the good which was in them being evil spoken of, they were prevented from being so extensively used as otherwise they might have been. Nay, I have doubted whether that arch-heretic, Montanus, was not one of the holiest men in the second century." Even while the views of the "arch heretic of the fifth century," Pelagius, cannot be affirmed, he surely was not as bad as made out by Augustine, "Augustine himself—a wonderful saint! as full of pride, passion, bitterness, censoriousness, and as foul-mouthed to all that contradicted him as George Fox himself."[101]

God's Wisdom in the Revival of Religion

Wesley was not one to idealize church history. He thought it had gone through long periods of relative alienation, as in medieval scholasticism. Just at the point at which the church became overspread with iniquity, "the Lord lifted up a standard against it."[102] He saw Luther as a consequential renewer of evangelical faith, yet too few fruits and many ambiguities were produced by his preaching, whose hearers too often remained worldly, forgetting that "to be friends with the world means to be at enmity with God" (James 4:4, TCNT).[103]

In his own time Wesley was convinced that there was a significant revival of religion occurring, in which God's special providences were being manifested.[104] He thought that God's providence was working in the revival, mending what had become broken, repairing God's creation where fallen, filling the earth with the knowledge of

---

[100]#68 "The Wisdom of God's Counsels," sec. 8–11, 2:555–57.

[101]#68 "The Wisdom of God's Counsels," sec. 9, 2:555–56; cf. letters to Alexander Coates, July 7, 1761, and John Fletcher, Aug. 18, 1775. Wesley thought that the real reason Pelagius offended some was "neither more nor less than this, the holding that Christians may by the grace of God (not without it; that I take to be a mere slander), 'go on to perfection.' "

[102]#68 "The Wisdom of God's Counsels," sec. 10, 2:556.

[103]#68 "The Wisdom of God's Counsels," sec. 10–17, 2:556–62.

[104]#66 "The Signs of the Times," 2:521–33.

the glory of God.[105] In Britain Wesley marked its beginning as 1627 with the flowering of Puritan revivalism.[106] The seeds of the eighteenth-century evangelical revival were sewn with the teachings of John Owen, Jeremy Taylor, William Law, and others, marked especially by a recovery of the resolution to become radically responsive to the Spirit, and with the revival led by Jonathan Edwards in North America.[107]

The astonishing method of divine wisdom in these revivals is to use ordinary persons, even ignorant and unlettered minds, to confound the wisdom of the world, and make God's strength known through human weakness. These providences call the faithful to set aside inordinate worldly securities and freely seek the treasures of the coming reign of God.[108]

God endows many with the Spirit only to see them fall by the wayside, by neglect or temptation. Even amid the worst apostasies God does not cease to pour out his Spirit to call humanity to repentance and full responsiveness to grace. If at first few fruits are borne, and if the danger of laying up treasure on earth arises anew in each generation, God always supplies new witnesses as the old fall away.[109] Young persons are especially important instruments of God. When older witnesses "die in the Lord, or lose the spiritual life which God had given them, he will supply . . . others that are alive to God, and desire only to spend and be spent for him."[110] Nothing is impossible with God. All can return if they choose.[111] Temptations can be rejected. Earnest prayer can protect from temptation.

The First Article: On God

Everything necessary for confessing the Christian teaching of God was for Wesley concisely summarized in the First Article of Religion, which retained its sixteenth-century language: "There is but one living and true God, everlasting, without body or parts, of infinite power, wisdom, and goodness; the maker and preserver of all things both visible and invisible. And in unity of this Godhead there are three persons, of one substance, power, and eternity— the Father, the Son, and the Holy Ghost."

No appraisal of Wesley's teaching of God is complete without examining this First Article of the twenty-four Wesley commended to the Christmas Conference of American Methodists in 1784. It is consensually held by those in Wesley's connection to express the essential features of biblical teaching on God. This language stands constitutionally in Wesleyan-tradition teaching as that doctrine of God handed down from the apostolic faith through ancient conciliar, Anglican, and Reformation traditions to all who would choose to stand subsequently in Wesley's connection of spiritual formation.[112] Those who scan Wesley's doctrine of God craving for something unique or individualistically original set themselves up for disappointment.

That God is "without body or parts" means that God is incorporeal, hence

---

[105]#63 "The General Spread of the Gospel," 13–27, 2:490–99.

[106]#68 "The Wisdom of God's Counsels," sec. 11, 2:557n; cf. Gillies, *Historical Collections*, regarded by Wesley as the forerunner of various charismatic movements before the eighteenth-century Evangelical Revival.

[107]#68 "The Wisdom of God's Counsels," sec. 12, 2:558.

[108]#68 "The Wisdom of God's Counsels," sec. 13, 2:558–59; B1:496f., 637f., 697.

[109]#68 "The Wisdom of God's Counsels," sec. 14–16, 2:559–61.

[110]#68 "The Wisdom of God's Counsels," sec. 19, 2:563.

[111]#68 "The Wisdom of God's Counsels," sec. 21–24, 2:564–66.

[112]Cf. LJW 4:25, 60, 115, 131, 149, 295.

not to be investigated as empirical objects are. If something can be reduced to empirical investigation, then you know right away that this is not God. That is what is meant by *via negativa*— pointing to the existence of God by first setting aside all those things that are not God. Those who view the world as God's body run counter to the teaching that God is without body. Those ideas that God can be divided into components or phases or periods of development run counter to classic Christian teaching that God is one, hence indivisible.[113] Rejected by this article are all pantheisms, all limitations of divine power excepting self-limitation, all views that imply that fate controls history—all of which are wearisome, familiar lunacies of contemporary popular culture.

The negative attributes of God (those typically beginning with, in- or im-) imply absence or denial, and thus assume an apophatic (*apophasis*, denial) or negative argument concerning the existence of God, that God is not finite, not deficient in power, and not lacking in justice or wisdom, not visible as an object.[114] In this way the *via negativa*, the negative way of reasoning about God, is written centrally into the Wesleyan tradition of teaching of God.

If some ingenious *novum* were asserted as Wesley's distinctive contribution to the doctrine of God, he would be first to deny it. He was a receiving conveyor of a well-established hebraic-apostolic recollection of God's action in history. It was far from his intention to invent an improved doctrine of God's power or love. He appealed to Scripture, to the three creeds (Apostles', Nicene-Constantinopolitan, and *Quicunque* [i.e., "Athanasian"] creeds), as a reliable summary of scriptural teaching.[115]

Those under Wesley's spiritual guidance confessed faith in one God, Creator, Sovereign, and preserver of all things visible and invisible. The divine attributes—unity, aliveness, truth, and eternality—are expressed in the divine actions of creating, governing, and preserving all things. The One who is infinite in power, wisdom, justice, goodness and love, rules with gracious regard for the well-being of humanity. God's power, wisdom, and love provide a plan and a means for the salvation of humanity. God is incomparably capable of accomplishing the divine purpose, consummately powerful, knowing, and good.

Unsurpassably just, it is inconceivable to Christian confessors that God would act unjustly.[116] God is infinite love, overflowing with goodness. We learn of divine love precisely through the palpable history of its self-disclosure, especially on the cross. The same One revealed on the cross is Creator, provider of all things, who exercises providential guidance and cares about all that happens in creation. One God is Father, Son, and Spirit: Creator, Redeemer of what is fallen in creation, who awakens in our hearts a response to his love, mercy, and grace.[117]

God has infinite power, knowledge, and goodness beyond that which any finite mind can conceive. The one living and true God is maker and preserver of all, providing for the continuity and sustenance of all that is.[118] God is not only the source and ground of all things that we can see and empirically investi-

---

[113]As in the classic rejection of modalism and Sabellianism.
[114]B4:45.
[115]Art. 1; cf. JJW 4:424; 8:332.
[116]LJW 3:382.
[117]LJW 4:321; 5:213, 294.
[118]B1:580f., 690.

gate, but of spiritual, incorporeal creatures. Everything that exists has been created by this one living true God whom no finite mind can know exhaustively, yet the just, loving and merciful character of God has been sufficiently disclosed in the history of revelation to allow trust and belief.[119]

What does it mean to say that if "your heart is as my heart, give me your hand"? Embedded in the crucial homily "Catholic Spirit" is a series of personal questions assumed to be affirmatively answered by anyone whose life is hid in Christ: "Is thy heart right with God? Dost thou believe his being, and his perfections? His eternity, immensity, wisdom, power; his justice, mercy, and truth?"[120] How could one's heart be right with God who distrusts God's eternity, wisdom, and goodness?

FURTHER READING ON GOD

Burtner and Childs, CWT, "God," 41ff. Collins, Kenneth. FW, 15-34.

Reddish, Robert O. *John Wesley, His Way of Knowing God.* Evergreen, Colo.: Rorge Publishing Co., 1972.

Truesdale, Albert. "Theism: The Eternal, Personal, Creative God." Chap. 4 in *A Contemporary Wesleyan Theology*, ed. Charles W. Carter. Grand Rapids: FAP, Zondervan, 1983, 103–43.

THE THREE-IN-ONE GOD

On the Trinity

1 John 5:7: "There are three that bear record in heaven, the Father, the Word, and the Holy Ghost." [Homily #55 1775 B2:373–86 J#55 VI:199–206]

The Triune Root
of All Vital Religion

One cannot read the New Testament, Wesley thought, without constantly hearing of the sending of the Son by the Father and the Spirit's enabling and fulfilling of the mission of the Son. Triune teaching is a way of bringing together the witness of the apostles within a cohesive premise.

God is one as Father, Son, and Spirit, not three gods, but one God in three persons. The Father is God, the Son is God, and the Spirit is God. Yet the Father is distinguishable from the Son, and the Son is distinguishable from the Spirit. The Son is sent by the Father, the Spirit fulfills and consummates the mission of the Son. These three are one in being, one in power, eternally God.[121] There is a community of discourse within the Godhead of persons who are equally the one God, coeternal and distinguishable as Father, Son and Spirit. The persons of the Trinity can be distinguished, but not separated as if one might consider the mission of the Son apart from the mission of the Spirit.[122] This is the baptism into which we have been baptized.

Since the ancient ecumenical Christian tradition so firmly assents to triune teaching as to make it definitive of orthodoxy, the triunity of God cannot be a point of indifference.[123] Wesley was a traditional Anglican in trinitarian belief and practice. He prayed daily with the prayer book to God the Son and God the Spirit who are together with the Father the one eternal God. Triune teaching is the heart of classic

---

[119]Letter to William Law, January 6, 1756, LJW 3:343–49.

[120]#39 "Catholic Spirit," i.14, 2:88.

[121]Art. 1-2.

[122]#55 "On the Trinity," sec. 1-3, 2:374–76.

[123]In a letter to Mary Bishop, April 17, 1776, Wesley commended William Jones' *The Catholic Doctrine of the Trinity*, 1756, as "more clear and more strong than any I ever saw. . . . If anything is wanting, it is the application . . . but this is abundantly supplied by my brother's Hymns," LJW 6:213.

Christian teaching, "the root of all vital religion."[124]

The Triune Fact and Triune Language

Triunity is a mystery to be sacrally affirmed, not empirically explained. Should anyone propose exhaustively to tame and decipher the triune mystery, the hearer does well to discount the pretended explanation. We can know *that* God is triune, not *how or why*. The central point of the homily on the Trinity is the modest conviction that God's triune life is hidden from rational-empirical inspection.

Wesley spoke of the Trinity as a *fact*, but not one that can yield to laboratory or objective analysis. He did not attempt to render any definitive linguistic account of the triune mystery. The *manner* in which God is three in one can be left to honest, humble adoration and celebration as a mystery of faith.[125] That God is Father, God is Son, and God is Holy Spirit stands unassailably as the central feature of orthodox Christian teaching of God.[126]

The history of exegesis is strewn with numerous opinions as to how best to express the central fact of the triune mystery. The New Testament text merely reveals the triune God, it does not explain it or theorize about it or provide a language for construing it.[127] Wesley did not think it obligatory to side with "this or that explication" of the texts attesting the triune mystery, but rather only to celebrate "the direct words, unexplained, just as they lie in the text."[128]

The Debate Over 1 John 5:7

The first letter of John throughout insists that Jesus Christ is truly God as well as truly human. At the point of this text, the writer was showing that this God-man was baptized and died. Jesus was Son of God not only at his baptism but at his death. Had he died as one with human nature only, his sacrificial death would not have been sufficient to reconcile the guilt of the whole history of human sin. It is the Holy Spirit who testifies that Jesus is the Son of God the Father by descending on him at his baptism, and by remaining with him through his death, empowering his resurrection.[129]

If the main text Wesley chose to attest the triune mystery were not replete with textual difficulties, his position would be stronger, but the textual impediments remain. The Authorized text reads: "*There are three that bear record in heaven, the Father, the Word, and the Holy Ghost, and these three are One*" (1 John 5:7). The same text in the NRSV reads: "There are three that testify: the Spirit and the water and the blood, and these three agree" with the accompanying footnote on manuscript variants: "A few other authorities read (with variations) "*There are three that testify in heaven, the Father, the Word, and the Holy Spirit, and these three are one.*"

Wesley offered an explicit hypothesis

---

[124]#55 "On the Trinity," sec. 17, 2:384.

[125]According to Peter Browne, "The mystery does not lie in the fact 'These Three are One,' but in the manner, the accounting how they are one. But with this I have nothing to do. I believe the fact. As to the manner (wherein the whole mystery lies) I believe nothing about it," i.e., not in the sense of disbelieving the mystery, but not trying to assign specific language to it. Letter to Miss March, Aug. 3, 1771, LJW 5:270.

[126]#55 "On the Trinity," sec. 1–2, 2:376; #117 "On the Discoveries of Faith," 4:27–38; 1:220.

[127]#55 "On the Trinity," sec. 3, 4, 2:376–78.

[128]#55 "On the Trinity," sec. 5, 2:378.

[129]#55 "On the Trinity," sec. 5, 2:378.

for why this text is present in some but absent in other manuscripts, though he did not want to press his theory of manuscript variations upon others. His suspicion was that the post-Constantinian Arian heretics wanted to omit or redact trinitarian texts. He hypothesized that Arian transcribers so disliked the text that they amended or omitted it. Acknowledging that the text is missing in some early manuscripts, Wesley countered by reasoning "(1) That though it is wanting in many ancient copies, yet it is found in more, abundantly more, and those copies of the greatest authority. (2) That it is cited by a whole train of ancient writers from the time of St. John to that of Constantine. . . . (3) That we can easily account for its being after that time wanting in many copies when we remember that Constantine's successor was a zealous Arian, who used every means to promote his bad cause . . . in particular the erasing this text out of as many copies as fell into his hands."[130]

Though this hypothesis is doubtful, it offers an intriguing glimpse into Wesley as textual critic. We learn from Wesley not to be afraid of rigorous historical textual criticism, provided it is responsible and thorough. Even if his hypothesis is dubious, it signals that he is inviting those in his spiritual connection to enter into responsible textual critical inquiry, asking what is to be made of the differences among available manuscripts. Those who disagree with his technical conclusion can hardly disagree with his intent.

Classic Triune Language Affirmed and Limited

Wesley affirmed the specific triune language of the three creeds: Apostles', Nicene, and Athanasian, but did not wish to promote a particular interpretation of them, or to be locked into some specific language considered necessary for their explication. The best traditional explication of the Trinity was in Wesley's view the Athanasian Creed (*Quicunque vult*), though he confesses to be uneasy with its prologue, which holds that those who do not assent to it "shall without doubt perish everlastingly."

Wesley admitted that he himself had "for some time scrupled subscribing to that creed, till I considered, (1), that these sentences only relate to *willful*, not involuntary unbelievers—to those who, having all the means of knowing the truth, nevertheless obstinately reject it; (2), that they relate only to the *substance* of the doctrine there delivered, not the philosophical *illustrations* of it."[131] On these grounds he came to accept the Athanasian Creed as the best classic statement of triune teaching. But he is aware that any explication takes place in the linguistic context of some philosophical worldview, which he was not willing to allow to dominate over the wonder of the triune mystery.

Given the importance to Wesley of the triune teaching of the Athanasian Creed, it seems fitting that I here quote it directly:

> We worship one God in Trinity, and trinity in Unity; Neither confounding the Persons; nor dividing the Substance. For there is one Person of the Father, another of the Son, and another of the Holy Ghost. But the Godhead of the Father, of the Son and of the Holy Ghost, is all one: the Glory equal, the Majesty co-eternal. Such as the Father is, such is the Son: and such is the Holy Ghost. The Father uncreate, the Son uncreate: and the Holy Ghost uncreate. The Father incomprehensible, the Son incomprehensible: and the Holy Ghost incomprehensible. The Father eternal, the Son eternal: and the Holy Ghost eternal. And yet they are not

[130]#55 "On the Trinity," sec. 5, 2:379.
[131]#55 "On the Trinity," sec. 3, 2:377; cf. LJW 4:125.

three eternals: but one eternal. As also there are not three incomprehensibles, nor three uncreated, but one uncreated, and one incomprehensible. So likewise, the Father is Almighty, the Son is Almighty: and the Holy Ghost Almighty. And yet they are not three Almighties: but one Almighty.[132]

Wesley urged that no belabored insistence be made regarding particular words in the classic formulations, such as *ousia* and *hupostasis*. However authoritative the Athanasian Creed, it does not provide the one and only definitive explanation of the mystery of the Trinity. Some tender minds may even be made unbelievers by a particular explication of it, or by having a philosophical language imposed that they either do not fully understand or to which they do not inwardly consent. Wesley did not want sincere questioners or doubters to be unnecessarily troubled or disabled or precipitously cast out of the circle of faith by excessive fondness for some specific reading of the New Testament text.

Though Wesley set forth a position with indeterminate boundaries, it was not his intention to welcome a wildly latitudinarian accommodation to any interpretation or to commend obscurantism. He echoed Augustine's view that we do not speak of the Trinity because we can speak of it adequately, but because we must not be silent.[133]

Wesley urged neither silence nor detailed explication, but simple affirmation of the biblical texts and the ecumenical creeds.[134] What remains sufficient is the apostolic testimony itself, not subsequent accretions of interpretations that have been added in different cultures with various philosophical languages over diverse centuries.[135]

Living Within Mystery

Those who believe nothing but what they comprehend are immobilized by skepticism if consistent. We still live as a body-soul interface even when we do not fully understand that interface in practice. So it is with the Trinity. Since we have the benefit of the revealed text, let us receive it even while not pretending once for all definitively to grasp its mystery.

To those who make the counterclaim that we cannot believe what we cannot comprehend, and therefore should omit the triune confession altogether, Wesley rejoined that there are many things we practically believe in that we do not comprehend: We do not understand the energy of the sun yet live in its warmth. We walk by light and breathe without understanding light and respiration. We live within gravitational fields but do not fully comprehend their characteristics. We stand upon the earth but our standing does not depend upon our understanding of it.[136]

By similar reasoning: "I believe this fact . . . that God is Three and one . . . I believe just so much as God has revealed, and no more. But this, the manner, he has not revealed."[137] Yet "I do not see how it is possible for any to have vital religion who denies that these three are one."[138]

Those who truly believe and confess the Trinity find their lives transformed by it. This stands as an incisive pragmatic argument for its truth. The Christian community has in many historical

---

[132]This version quoted from the BCP.
[133]Augustine, *On the Trinity*, I; #55 "On the Trinity," sec. 5, 2:378.
[134]On the ecumenical spirit of Wesley, see JWO 90f., 498f.
[135]#55 "On the Trinity," sec. 5, 2:378.
[136]#55 "On the Trinity," sec. 6–13, 2:379–83.
[137]#55 "On the Trinity," sec. 15, 2:384.
[138]#55 "On the Trinity," sec. 18, 2:386.

situations relied upon a gloriously mysterious teaching that has repeatedly brought it life and energy. The tenacious life of this community under persecution is historically unthinkable without the triune teaching.[139]

In commending Jonathan Swift's sermon "On the Trinity," Wesley approved the view that the Trinity is a mystery so far exceeding reason as to be altogether above rational explanation, in contrast to others who argued that the Trinity was rationally demonstrable.[140] Wesley did not pretend to make any original contribution to the interpretation of the Trinity.[141] There is a gentle spirit of toleration and patient trust that is at work here, yet without losing the central energy and substance of classic Christian triune thinking.

That Wesley earnestly confessed the triune teaching is clear from the first four of the essential Articles of Religion he commended to his connection: "There is but one living and true God," and *"in the unity of this Godhead there are three persons of one substance, power and eternity—the Father, the Son, and the Holy Ghost."* The Son is *"the Word of the Father, begotten from everlasting of the Father, the very and eternal God, of one substance with the Father."* The Holy Spirit, *"proceeding from the Father and the Son, is of one substance, majesty, and glory with the Father and the Son, very and eternal God."*

Triune Baptism in the Spirit

No one is rightly baptized only in the name of the Father, or only in the name of the Son, but in the name of the triune God, Father, Son, and Spirit. This is the baptism into which we are baptized.

Triune reflection is simply a way of ordering the whole gospel of God into an arrangement or exegetical economy consistent with the apostolic testimony and baptismal faith. Historically, all the ecumenically received expressions of the rule of faith (as expressed prototypically in the three creeds) emerged as baptismal formulae and confessional statements made at baptism which seek to declare what is happening in baptism. The creed is thus a summary way of talking of all that is crucial to the Christian faith. There is no topic of belief that does not fit into that pattern in some way. It is the Spirit who awakens our attentiveness to this Word spoken in baptism and Holy Communion.

Spiritual Worship—
On Triune Spirituality

1 John 5:20: "This is the true God, and eternal life." [Homily #77 1780 B3:88–102 J#77 VI:424–35]

Lively Communion
With the Triune God

In John's first epistle, the author focuses not directly upon faith as Paul had done, or on inward and outward holiness as in Paul, James, and Peter, but rather on "the foundation of all, the happy and holy communion which the faithful have with God the Father, Son, and Holy Ghost."[142] The very structure of the tract forms around communion with the Father (1 John 1), communion with the Son (1 John 2 and 3), and communion with the Spirit (1 John 4). The recapitulation of the whole argument is found in 1 John 5:18ff., and includes the guiding text of homily #77, Spiritual Worship, 1 John 5:20, This

---

[139]# "On the Trinity," sec. 15-18, 2:384–86.
[140]Cf. J. Trapp, *On the Trinity*, 1730; Wesley, #55 "On the Trinity," sec. 3, 2:377.
[141]B1:220; 2:101, 373–86; 4:31f., 37.
[142]#77 "Spiritual Worship," proem.2, 3:89–90.

triune One *"is the true God and eternal life."*[143]

To commune with the triune God, the true God, is to know him as one God over all, Father, Son, and Spirit.[144] In the Son we meet the Father.[145] The Son was with God from the beginning and was God. Wesley wrote to Mrs. Cock, November 3, 1789: "Do you still find deep and uninterrupted communion with God, with the Three-One God, with the Father and the Son through the Spirit?"[146]

Creator, Supporter, Preserver, Author, Redeemer, Governor of All

The triune God is "the only Cause, the sole *Creator* of all things," and as true God "the *Supporter* of all the things that he hath made," sustaining all created things by the word of his power, "by the same powerful word which brought them out of nothing. As this was absolutely necessary for the beginning of their all existence, it is equally so for the continuance of it: were his almighty influence withdrawn they could not subsist a moment longer. Hold up a stone in the air; the moment you withdraw your hand it naturally falls to the ground. In like manner, were he to withdraw his hand for a moment the creation would fall into nothing."[147]

As *Preserver* of all, he "preserves them in that degree of well-being which is suitable to their several natures. He preserves them in their several relations, connections, and dependencies,

so as to compose one system of beings, to form one entire universe."[148] "By and in him are all things compacted into one system."[149]

Whatever moves, moves by a mover. As primal *Author* of all motion in the universe, the true God has given to free spiritual creatures (angelic and human beings) "a small degree of self-moving power, but not to matter. All matter. . . is totally inert . . . and whenever any part of it seems to move it is in reality moved by something else."[150] When Isaac Newton spoke of the stars moving or attracting each other in proportion to the quantity of matter they contain, Wesley wanted to clarify the more fundamental premise that "they are continually *impelled* toward each other. Impelled, by what? 'By the subtle matter, the ether, or electric fire,' " but even this remains inert matter, consequently "as inert in itself as either sand or marble. It cannot therefore move itself; but probably it is the first material mover, the main spring whereby the Creator and Preserver of all things is pleased to move the universe."[151]

As *Redeemer* of all humanity, the incarnate God "tasted death for every man," that "he might make a full and sufficient sacrifice, oblation, and satisfaction for the sins of the whole world."[152] It is this triune God who is *Governor* of all, "Lord and Disposer of the whole creation," who presides "over each creature as if it were the universe, and over the universe as over

---

[143]#77 "Spiritual Worship," proem.1, 3:89–90.
[144]In a Letter to Hester Ann Roe, Feb. 11, 1777, Wesley recounted the ecstatic experience of triune spirituality reported by Charles Perronet, LJW 6:253; cf. to Lady Maxwell, July 4, 1787, LJW 7:392.
[145]B1:578f., 692.
[146]LJW 8:183.
[147]#77 "Spiritual Worship," i.2, 3, 3:91.
[148]#77 "Spiritual Worship," i.4, 3:91.
[149]Wesley's translation of Col. 1:17.
[150]#77 "Spiritual Worship," i.5, 3:92.
[151]#77 "Spiritual Worship," i.6, 3:92–93.
[152]BCP eucharistic prayer of consecration.

each individual creature," yet caring especially for those most responsive to his revealed grace, who are the apple of his eye, whom he hides under the shadow of his wings.[153] Christianity celebrates the triune God as *Consummator* of all things: "Of him [as Creator], and through him [as Sustainer], and to him [as End], are all things" (Rom. 11:36, KJV).[154]

Eternal Life Is Life in the Son Beginning Now With Faith

In all these ways the Son is truly God, with the Father and the Spirit. But how is he eternal life? The triune God invites us to eternal life. First, those faithful unto death *will receive* the crown of life purchased by God the Son.

Secondly, eternal life is far more than a future life. It is communion with what God the Son "is now." This triune God, made incarnate in the Son, is "now the life of everything that lives in any kind or degree," whether of *vegetable* life, "the lowest species of life . . . as being the source of all the motion on which vegetation depends," or of *animal* life, the power by which the animal heart beats, or of *rational* life, source of all that moves and all that is enabled to move itself according to its intelligence.[155]

Whoever has the Son has life eternal. This is the testimony that God has given us, "not only a title to but the real beginning of 'eternal life,'"[156] commencing when the Son is revealed in our hearts, enabling us to call him Lord, and live by faith in him.[157]

The Happiness of Experienced Triune Spirituality

The fullest happiness is eternal life. It begins with faith in the love of God shed abroad in our hearts, "instantly producing love to all mankind: general, pure benevolence, together with its genuine fruits, lowliness, meekness, patience, contentedness in every state; an entire, clear, full acquiescence in the whole will of God."[158] We are happy when God takes "full possession of our heart; when he reigns therein without a rival, the Lord of every motion there," which is what is meant by the kingdom of God,[159] wherein we are made "complete in him" (Col. 2:10, KJV).

As the triune God is one, so there is only one happiness for creatures, whose hearts cannot rest until they rest in God.[160] The vigor of youth may seem a kind of happiness, when "our blood dances in our veins; while the world smiles upon us and we have all the conveniences, yea, and superfluities of life," but in time it "flies away like a shadow."[161] "Give a man everything that this world can give," and still, as Horace knew, "something is always lacking to make one's fortune incomplete. . . . That *something* is neither more nor less than the knowledge and love of God without which no spirit can be happy."[162]

Wesley recalls his own experience as a child, "a stranger to pain and

[153]#77 "Spiritual Worship," i.8, 3:93–94.
[154]#77 "Spiritual Worship," i.19, 3:94–95.
[155]#77 "Spiritual Worship," ii.1–3, 3:95.
[156]#77 "Spiritual Worship," ii.4, 3:96.
[157]#117 "On the Discoveries of Faith," 7, 4:31–32; VII:233.
[158]#77 "Spiritual Worship," ii.5, 3:96.
[159]#77 "Spiritual Worship," ii.6, 3:96.
[160]#77 "Spiritual Worship," iii.1, 3:97; from Augustine, *Confessions*, I.i; see #3 "Awake, Thou That Sleepest," ii.5.
[161]#77 "Spiritual Worship," iii.1, 3:97.
[162]#77 "Spiritual Worship," iii.1, 3:97–98; Horace, *Odes* III.xxiv.64.

sickness, and particularly to lowness of spirits (which I do not remember to have felt one quarter of an hour since I was born), having plenty of all things . . . still I was not happy!," lacking the knowledge and love of God.[163]

"This happy knowledge of the true God is only another name for *religion*; I mean *Christian religion*,"which consists not in outward actions or duties or concepts, but more directly "in the knowledge and love of God, as manifested in the Son of his love, through the eternal Spirit."[164] No one who has turned aside from this grace is happy, even if surrounded with every possible aesthetic delight, as was Solomon, who teaches us plainly what happiness is not, more than what happiness is: It is "not to be found in natural knowledge, in power, or in the pleasures of sense or imagination."[165]

FURTHER READING ON THE TRIUNE TEACHING:

Cannon, William. *Theology of John Wesley*, 204–14.

Collins, K. FW, 58-62.

Mickey, Paul. *Essentials of Wesleyan Theology*, ch. 2, "The Holy Trinity," 29–44.

Williams, Colin. *John Wesley's Theology Today*, 93–97.

---

[163] #77 "Spiritual Worship," iii.2, 3, 3:98. Here Wesley anticipates Kierkegaard's aesthetic pseudonyms: "Look forward on any distant prospect: how beautiful does it appear! Come up to it; and the beauty vanishes away. . . . Just so is life!"

[164] #77 "Spiritual Worship," iii.4, 3:99.

[165] #77 "Spiritual Worship," iii.5, 3:99–100; cf. Matthew Prior, "An English Padlock."

2

Theological Method
The Authority of Scripture Understood in the Light of Tradition, Reason, and Experience

The Theological Method Best Enabling Knowledge of God

The quadrilateral method (the authority of Scripture understood in the light of tradition, reason, and experience) may be seen at work in the early part of *The Doctrine of Original Sin*, and in the *Appeals*, and most explicitly in the homily "On Sin in Believers."[1]

Those who wish to examine Wesley's systematic theological method are well advised to investigate the homilies on "Catholic Spirit," "A Caution Against Bigotry," "The Case of Reason Impartially Considered," "The Promise of Understanding," "The Imperfection of Human Knowledge," "A Clear and Concise Demonstration of the Divine Inspiration of Holy Scripture," and the argument of the *Appeals* (*Earnest Appeal* and *Farther Appeal to Men of Reason and Religion*).

SCRIPTURE
A Man of One Book

Wesley's primary appeal is to Scripture and only derivatively to tradition, reason, and experience. As early as 1730 he attested his determination to become " 'a man of one book,' regarding none, comparatively, but the Bible."[2]

It was Wesley's lifelong habit to rise early in the morning for prayer and Bible study, a poignant account of which he offers in his Preface to the Sermons: As "a creature of a day, passing through life as an arrow through the air," "just hovering over the great gulf, till a few moments hence I am no more seen—I drop into an unchangeable eternity! I want to know one thing, the way to heaven—how to land safe on that happy shore. God himself has condescended to teach the way: for this very end he came from heaven. He hath written it down in a book. O give me

---

[1]#13 "On Sin in Believers," i.5, 1:318–19; alternatively Wesley lists Scripture, reason, and experience as doctrinal norms, as in #14 "The Repentance of Believers," i.2, and on other occasions "Scripture, reason, and Christian antiquity," as in his Preface to his collected works, I, 1771.
[2]*Plain Account of Christian Perfection*, 10, XI:373.

that book! At any price give me the Book of God! I have it. Here is knowledge enough for me. Let me be *homo unius libri*."[3]

Should anything appear confusing in the sacred text, it is never impossible to pray for grace to the One who said: " 'If any be willing to do thy will, he shall know.' I am willing to do, let me know, thy will. I then search after and consider parallel passages of Scripture, comparing spiritual things with spiritual."[4] "If any of you lacks wisdom, he should ask God, who gives generously to all without finding fault, and it will be given to him" (James 1:5).

In describing himself as *homo unius libri*,[5] a man of one book,[6] he did not imply that there were no other books to be usefully read, but that all others were best read in relation to this revealing book.[7] To those who propose to read only the Bible, Wesley retorted: "If you need no book but the Bible, you are got above St. Paul. He wanted others too, 'Bring the books,' says he, 'but especially the parchments.' "[8] Wesley himself was editor of some four hundred books. He was a lifelong omnivorous reader for whom horseback was a moving library.[9]

Normative Authority of Scripture

It is "the faith of Protestants" to "believe neither more nor less than what is manifestly contained in, and provable by, the Holy Scriptures." "The written word is the whole and sole rule of their faith, as well as practice."[10] "We believe the Scripture to be of God."[11] We are asked to "be not wise above what is written. Enjoin nothing that the Bible does not clearly enjoin. Forbid nothing that it does not clearly forbid."[12] "I allow no other rule, whether of faith or practice, than the Holy Scriptures."[13] There is no hidden or screened canon within the canon, due to the plenary extent of scriptural inspiration.[14]

Wesley did not deny that there were forms of human agency in the writing, transmission, and hearing of Scripture, for "as God has made men the immediate instruments of all those revelations, so evangelical faith must be partly founded on human testimony."[15] Otherwise, Paul's idiomatic language would not differ from John's and Luke's, which it does.

The Spirit works not only in the mind of the sacred writer, but of the attentive reader: "All Scripture is inspired of God—The Spirit of God not only once

---

[3]*Sermons*, 1746, Pref. 5 1:105.
[4]*Sermons*, 1746, Pref. 5 1:106; John 7:17.
[5]LJW 6:30, 130.
[6]*Sermons*, Pref. 5 1:105.
[7]LJW 5:215, 221; 8:192; B1:57, 71; 4:93.
[8]"Minutes of Several Conversations," Q33, VIII:315.
[9]LJW 1:20, 65.
[10]#106 "On Faith," Heb. 11:6, i.8, 3:496; cf. #5 "Justification by Faith," sec. 2. Wesley repeatedly held "the written word of God to be the only and sufficient rule both of Christian faith and practice"; see "The Character of a Methodist," sec. 1, VIII:340.
[11]EA 13, 11:19.
[12]Letter to John Dickins, Dec. 26, 1789, LJW VIII:191–92; cf. #12 "The Witness of Our Own Spirit," sec. 6, 1:303.
[13]Letter to James Hervey, Mar. 20, 1739, LJW I:285; cf. B9:33f., 527.
[14]"I make the Word of God the rule of all my actions," Wesley wrote to the bishop of London, Edmund Gibson, and "no more follow any *secret impulse* instead thereof than I follow Mahomet or Confucius," LLBL 4–5 II:337.
[15]*Compendium on Natural Philosophy* II:447.

inspired those who wrote it, but continually inspires, supernaturally assists, those that read it with earnest prayer."[16]

Sensus Literalis *and Context*

Wesley held to the *plain or literal sense unless irrational or unworthy of God's moral character.*[17] We are to look for its plain, literal, historical sense *(sensus literalis)*, unless it has a metaphorical level or intent, and even in that case we consider the metaphor in its plainest sense. We read Scripture for its straightforward, unadorned sense, without pretentious speculations on hidden or allegorical meanings. We are "never to depart from the plain, literal sense, unless it implies an absurdity"![18]

To quote text against context is to fail to see the way in which the Holy Spirit intends its use. "You depart ever so little from . . . *the plain, literal meaning of any text, taken in connection with that context.*"[19]

Scripture can be warped for purposes of private interest. "Any passage is easily perverted, by being recited singly, without any of the preceding or following verses. By this means it may often seem to have one sense, when it will be plain, by observing what goes before and what follows after, that it really has the direct contrary."[20]

Scripture is composed of sentences. Each text seeks constantly to connect with our experience, in whatever specific cultural setting we find ourselves. We have this book, its sentences originally written in Hebrew and Greek. If we are to come into contact with that text, we must study.[21] Those who come seriously to the service of the Word do well to learn the original language of the text. Wesley was willing to engage in textual analysis, and to search among the available manuscripts for the most reliable text. He offered numerous corrections to the Authorized Version in his *Explanatory Notes Upon the New Testament.*

How the Analogy of Faith Tempers an Oversimplified Literalism

Each particular text of Scripture is best read by analogy with other correlated passages of Scripture and the whole course of scriptural teaching, and in relation to the history of its consensual interpretation by the great teachers of Scripture. By this means one allows the *clear texts to illuminate obscure texts.*

This is the principle of the analogy of faith, *analogia fidei*, which, in accord with classic Christian exegesis, Wesley constantly sought to employ. Scripture is the best interpreter of Scripture.[22] One begins to accumulate through the study of Scripture a sense of the wholeness of faith as one text illuminates another. "The literal sense of every text is to be taken, if it be not contrary to some other texts; but in that case the obscure text is to be interpreted by those which speak more plainly."[23] Scriptural wisdom comes out of a broadly based dialogue with the *general*

---

[16]ENNT 794, 2 Tim. 3:16.
[17]ENOT Preface; cf. XIV:266.
[18]#74 "Of the Church," sec. 12, 3:50.
[19]*Plain Account of Christian Perfection*, Q33, XI:429, italics added; cf. "Cautions and Directions Given to the Greatest Professors in Methodist Societies," 1762; see also Outler, 1:473n; R. Larry Shelton, "Wesley's Approach to Scripture in Historical Perspective," WTJ 16 (1981): 23–50.
[20]#137 "On Corrupting the Word of God," 7:470.
[21]B3:192f.
[22]B1:58f., 106; 2:102f.; 4:5f.; 11:169, 504; 9:201, 353.
[23]Letter to Samuel Furly, May 10, 1755, LJW III:129.

sense of the whole of Scripture, not a single set of selected texts. In the worshiping community, we bring previous memories of Scripture's address to each subsequent reading.

Wesley stated his design in the *Explanatory Notes Upon the Old Testament*: "To give the direct, literal meaning, of every verse, of every sentence, and so far as I am able, of every word in the oracles of God. I design only, like the hand of a dial, to point every man to this: not to take up his mind with something else, how excellent soever: but to keep his eye fixt upon the naked Bible, that he may read and hear it with understanding. . . . It is not my design to write a book, which a man may read separate from the Bible: but barely to assist those who fear God, in hearing and reading the Bible itself, by shewing the natural sense of every part, in as few and plain words as I can."[24]

"The Church is to be judged by the Scripture, not the Scripture by the Church. And Scripture is the best expounder of Scripture. The best way, therefore, to understand it, is carefully to compare Scripture with Scripture, and thereby learn the true meaning of it."[25] "Scripture interprets Scripture; one part fixing the sense of another."[26] This enables the Christian reader of the Old Testament to view the moral commands as covered promises. The Hebrew Bible is earnestly studied by Christians in relation to its having been fulfilled in Jesus Christ.[27]

There is a strong pragmatic element in Wesley's exegesis that focuses upon its practical application in walking in the way of holiness.[28] In this way Christian experience becomes confirmatory of wise and balanced forms of scriptural interpretation, while acting as a corrective to rash and imbalanced interpretations.[29] Reason and experience in this way become servants, not master, of the believer's understanding of revelation history.[30]

"Whosoever giveth his mind to Holy Scriptures with diligent study and burning desire, it cannot be that he should be left without help. For either God will send him some godly doctor to teach him or God himself from above will give light unto his mind and teach him those things which are necessary for him. Man's human and worldly wisdom or science is not needful to the understanding of Scripture but the revelation of the Holy Ghost who inspireth the true meaning unto them that with humility and diligence search."[31]

Spirit and Scripture

"The Scriptures are the touchstone whereby Christians examine all, real or supposed, revelations."[32] Scriptures are not to be pitted against the Spirit. Scripture can be understood only through the same Spirit whereby it is given.[33] The Scriptures, inspired by the Spirit, form the written rule by which the Spirit thereafter leads us into all

---

[24]ENOT Pref. 15, viii.
[25]"Popery Calmly Considered," i.6, X:142.
[26]"Address to the Clergy," i.1, X:482.
[27]B1:381f., 386f., 394f.; 2:514.
[28]William Arnett, "John Wesley—A Man of One Book," Drew Univ. diss., 1954, 89–96.
[29]B4:246f.; 11:509; 9:378f.
[30]B3:5, 16, 200f.; 4:198f., 219.
[31]Preface to the Reader, "The Doctrine of Salvation, Faith and Good Works Extracted From the Homilies of the Church of England," JWO 123; B1:381f., 386f., 394f.; 2:514.
[32]Letter to Thomas Whitehead, Feb. 10, 1748, LJW II:117.
[33]Arnett, "Man of One Book," 97.

truth.[34] *"The historical experience of the church, though fallible, is the better judge overall of Scripture's meanings than later interpreters."*[35]

To attest the work of the Spirit, one does well to mine the textuary of the Spirit's work, dig those jewels of instruction out of the hard rock of the written word.[36] "Every good textuary is a good divine," and "none can be a good Divine who is not a good textuary." Interpretation at times may be handicapped "without knowledge of the original tongues."[37]

If God the Spirit is the one who calls forth Scripture, then one has good reason to assume that God will be present in our reading of Scripture. Scripture is a means of grace by which God the Spirit leads sinners back to the love of the Father manifested in the Son.[38] The received canon is sufficient for faith, and fully adequate to teach the truth.[39]

"Though the Spirit is our principal leader, yet He is not our rule at all; the Scriptures are the rule whereby He leads us into all truth." A rule implies "something used by an intelligent being" so as to make everything "plain and clear."[40]

Scripture, Conscience, and General Revelation

The history of God's disclosure illumines all other forms of knowing. Special revelation does not on the whole run counter to general revelation but elucidates it.[41] God is present in the entire book of nature and history, for that is what Scripture itself teaches: "The heavens declare the glory of God; the skies proclaim the work of his hands. Day after day they pour forth speech" (Ps. 19:1–2a). Those who try to understand the ways of God in history and the love of God for fallen humanity do well to study diligently the history of divine self-disclosure.[42] It is in history through events that God has made known his holy self-giving love, particularly in Jesus Christ.[43]

Scripture does not override the private sphere of conscience, but points to it. Conscience is the internal witness testifying to moral rightness present within every human being. "Every man has a right to judge for himself, particularly in matters of religion, because every man must give an account of himself to God."[44]

Adequacy, Clarity, and Sufficiency of Scripture

Holy Scripture is "that 'word of God which remaineth for ever'; of which, though 'heaven and earth pass away, one jot or tittle shall not pass away.' The Scripture, therefore, of the Old and New Testament, is a most solid and precious system of divine truth. Every part thereof is worthy of God; and all together are one entire body, wherein is no defect, no excess. It is the fountain of heavenly wisdom, which they who are able to taste prefer to all writings of

---

[34]LJW II:117; 3:496.
[35]Outler, Intro. 1:58–59.
[36]CH 7:185–87, 474f.
[37]"Address to the Clergy," 1.2, X:482.
[38]#16 "The Means of Grace," 1:386–88; V:192–94.
[39]#137 "On Corrupting the Word of God," 7:470f.
[40]Letter [to Thomas Whitehead?], Feb. 10, 1748, LJW 2:117; B1:302f.; 9:114f., 198.
[41]#85 "On Working Out Our Own Salvation," proem. 1, 2, 3:199–200.
[42]B2:536; 1:420f.; 2:54f., 588, 591f.; 3:496, 504.
[43]B4:18.
[44]"Address to the Reader," 1771 edition of collected works, quoted in Preface to the Third Edition, I:iv.

men, however wise or learned or holy."[45]

"I try every church and every doctrine by the Bible."[46] "The Scripture, therefore, being delivered by men divinely inspired, is a rule sufficient of itself: So it neither needs, nor is capable of, any further addition."[47] "If there be any mistakes in the Bible, there may as well be a thousand. If there be one falsehood in that book, it did not come from the God of truth."[48] If any way "be contrary to Scripture, it is not good, and the longer we are in it so much the worse."[49]

"The language of his messengers, also, is exact in the highest degree: for the words which were given them accurately answered the impression made upon their minds; and hence Luther says, 'Divinity is nothing but a grammar of the language of the Holy Ghost.' To understand this thoroughly, we should observe the emphasis which lies on every word; the holy affections expressed thereby, and the tempers shown by every writer."[50]

Principles of Interpretation

In the Preface to the *Notes Upon the Old Testament*, Wesley set forth five constituent elements of serious, meditative Scripture study:

● Set apart a specified daily time for Scripture study.

● Read the Hebrew Bible in conjunction with the New Testament, reading both "with a single eye to know the whole will of God, and a fixed resolution to do it."

● "Have a constant eye to the *analogy of faith*, the connection and harmony there is between those grand, fundamental doctrines, original sin, justification by faith, the new birth, inward and outward holiness."

● Let your reading be surrounded by earnest prayer, "seeing 'Scripture can only be understood through the same Spirit whereby it was given.'"

● Pause frequently for honest personal self-examination.[51]

The Inspiration of Holy Scripture
XI:484ff.

A Clear and Concise Demonstration
of the Divine Inspiration
of Holy Scripture

This brief essay is hardly intended to elaborate a hermeneutic, but it does offer a striking glimpse into Wesley's view of Scripture. It is deceptively short. Almost silly. The first time you read it you think: This is theology? Too simple. The second time you read it, you begin to ponder whether something might be hidden there, but wonder just what. Later a light begins to dawn. Here is the argument:

There are four grand and powerful arguments that strongly induce us to believe that the Bible is from God. They are the arguments from miracle, the argument from prophecy, the argument from the intrinsic moral goodness of scriptural teaching, and the argument from the moral character of those who wrote it. Each argument has both inductive and deductive features. Wesley

---

[45]ENNT Pref. 10.
[46]LJW III:172.
[47]"Popery Calmly Considered," 1.3, X:141.
[48]JJW VI:117.
[49]Letter to James Lowther, Oct. 28, 1754, LJW III:122. "I build upon no authority, ancient or modern, but the Scripture. If this supports any doctrine, it will stand; if not, the sooner it falls the better." Cf. Arnett, MOB 113f.
[50]ENNT Pref. 12.
[51]ENOT Pref. 18, I; ix; cf. B1:58f., 106; 2:102f.; 4:5f., 246f.; 11:169, 504, 509; 9:201, 353, 378f.

first looks inductively at empirical evidence of the inspiration of Scripture.

Inductive Arguments for the Inspiration of Scripture

If miracles are attested, they must be true or false. If truly attested, they must flow from God's own power. Miracle requires the premise of one incomparably powerful and wise—God.

If prophecies are attested, they must be either true or false. If truly attested, either they have been fulfilled or are in the process of being fulfilled. If so, they must flow from God's unbounded knowing. Prophecy requires the premise of the wisdom of God. You cannot have fulfilled prophecy without positing God's eternal wisdom revealed.

The teachings of Scripture must be either morally good or evil. If the doctrines of Scripture are good, they of necessity flow out of the goodness of God. The goodness of the teaching requires the beneficence of God.

If the moral character of the authors of Scripture corresponds with their teaching, even under persecution and torture, they must premise some source and ground of moral character. The holiness of lives lived out in relation to the events attested in Scripture points to the holiness of God.[52]

Thus inductively, out of Scripture itself comes a series of intertextual arguments for the power, wisdom, goodness, holiness of God. The infinite power, omniscience, incomparable moral excellence, and righteousness of God must be posited as the ground of these visible consequences of scriptural testimony to miracle, prophecy, moral teaching, and holy lives lived.[53]

Deductive Arguments for the Inspiration of Scripture

Wesley then proceeds to develop a pithy deductive argument. Concisely he seeks to demonstrate that the Bible must be either the creation of:

> good human beings
> or angels,
> or bad human beings,
> or devils,
> or God.

These are the exhaustive alternatives.[54]

First, the Bible could not have been written merely by good persons because good persons would have been lying when they wrote, "Thus saith the Lord," for if it were not the Lord, but actually only the finite person speaking, just his own psychology or history or reason, he would be lying. No good person (and the same argument applies to good angels) would write or attest such a statement unless it was the Lord who called it forth. So *we can be sure that Scripture is not inspired by the good human beings, or even good angels, for they would not lie.*[55]

But could the Bible have been written by deceivers, by evil persons or fallen angels? *We can be sure that Scripture is not inspired by evil persons because a bad person or bad angel could not have invented such good doctrine.* Evildoers could not have invented a set of writings so wholly contrary to their own character.

Having thus eliminated all of the alternatives: inspiration by good men, good angels, bad men and bad angels, as authors of the Scripture, there is no other conclusion to draw than that it can only be breathed out as God's own

---

[52]JWO 89f., 181f., 225f., 375f.
[53]LJW 2:62, 69, 90, 104.
[54]"A Clear and Concise Demonstration of the Divine Inspiriation of Holy Scripture," XI:484.
[55]"A Clear and Concise Demonstration of the Divine Inspiration of Holy Scripture," XI:484; cf. B2:310f.

Word. God's speech to us, of course, is written and addressed through human persons, with human language, within different historical contexts, but its author and inspirer is God.[56] One can then take it for granted in reading the testimony of the prophets and the apostles that this is God's own self-communication[57] to be taken with utter seriousness as reliable divine address.[58]

Wesley as Commentator on Scripture

In writing his *Explanatory Notes Upon the New Testament*, Wesley's purpose was to make Scripture accessible in inexpensive format to Christian laity, especially in his connection of spiritual formation, who had neither the means nor time to read through highly technical commentaries. The cost of books was enormous in his day. He was producing these commentaries at extremely marginal cost, so it is not inaccurate to view his *Notes* as Bible study for the unlearned underclass of his day.

He focused especially on application of spiritual truth to ordinary living.[59] He sought to adapt the best commentators of his day for a general reading audience. He gratefully acknowledged that he worked freely out of Matthew Henry[60] and William Poole[61] in his Old Testament *Notes*, and from John A. Bengel, John Heylyn's *Theological Lectures*,[62] John Guyse's *Practical Expositor*,[63] and Philip Doddridge's *The Family Expositor*.[64] He broadly let Bengel speak for himself, especially in the commentary on Revelation. "All I can do is partly to translate, partly abridge the most necessary of his observations; allowing myself the liberty to alter some of them, and to add a few notes where he is not full."[65]

The *Notes* "were not principally designed for men of learning, who are provided with many other helps; and much less for men of long and deeper experience in the ways and Word of God. I desire to sit at their feet and learn from them. But I write chiefly for plain, unlettered men, who understand only their mother tongue, and yet reverence and love the Word of God, and have a desire to save their souls."[66]

"I have endeavored to make the notes as short as possible, that the comment may not obscure or swallow up the text; and as plain as possible, in pursuance of my main design, to assist the unlearned reader. For this reason I have studiously avoided, not only all curious and critical inquiries, and all use of the learned languages, but all such methods of reasoning and modes of expression as people in common life are unacquainted with."[67]

The *Notes Upon the Old Testament*[68] were intended to be "delivered weekly to subscribers" in sixty numbers, beginning April 25, 1765, but actually extended to 110 numbers, price sixpence each, with the final manuscript

---

[56]LJW 2:62–69, 90, 100, 104; 5:245.
[57]LJW 2:148; 3:127; B11:291, 504.
[58]"A Clear and Concise Demonstration of the Divine Inspiration of Holy Scripture," XI:484.
[59]LJW 4:93, 125; 8:67.
[60]*Exposition of the Old and New Testament*, used especially in Genesis.
[61]*Annotations on the Holy Bible*.
[62]London: Westminster Abbey, 1749–61, 2 vols.
[63]London: 1739–52, 3 vols.
[64]ENNT Pref. 8.
[65]ENNT 932.
[66]ENNT Pref. 3, 6; JJW 4:91f., 361; 7:345.
[67]ENNT Pref. 6, 7.
[68]JJW 5:112, 115.

dated December 24, 1766, the whole being later bound in three hefty volumes.[69] He recommended that each society subscribe, allowing "two, four, or six might join together for a copy, and bring the money to their leader weekly."[70]

Wesley was highly selective in his borrowing. His distinctive style shows through even amid heavy editing. The *Notes* are "an artful blending of the best of other scholars' work into the stream of his own theological perspectives."[71] He took liberty in refining and adopting edifying words of others to fit his own ministry of witness.

On Corrupting the Word of God

2 Cor. 2:17: "We are not as many who corrupt the Word of God." [Homily #137 1727 4:243–51 J#136 VII:468–73]

Those who corrupt the Word of God are contrasted with those utterly sincere in preaching it. Wesley thought an obsessive hermeneutic of suspicion[72] reflected poorly on its practitioners: "The honester any man is, the less apt is he to suspect another. . . . Would not any man be tempted to suspect his integrity who, without proof, suspected the want of it in another."[73]

Three Marks of Corrupters
of the Word

Three "marks of distinction" betray those prone to *corrupt* the Word of God. First, the corrupters are predisposed to blend Scripture with political interests, economic motives, or various human admixtures, diluting the divine word either with the errors of others, or the fancies of their own brain, usually without any awareness of their own self-deception.[74]

A second type of corrupter perverts the sense of a passage of Scripture, taking it out of context, "repeating the words wrong," or "putting a wrong sense upon them . . . foreign to the writer's intention" or even contrary to it. "Any passage is easily perverted" by neglecting its context.[75]

Third, others corrupt the Word not by adding to but subtracting from it. They "take either of the spirit or substance of it away, while they study to prophesy only smooth things, and therefore palliate and colour what they preach, to reconcile it to the taste of their hearers," washing their hands of "those stubborn texts that will not bend to their purpose."[76]

Sincerity in Hearing and
Speaking the Word

Sincere hearers of the Word of God attest it "genuine and unmixed," without unnatural interpretations. They do not take away from the Word, daring neither to say more or less than that which the Word addresses to that audience. They preach the whole counsel of God, and are willing to meet the resistances of hearers. They speak "with

---

[69]Bristol: Wm. Pine, 1765–66; reprint, Salem, Ohio: Schmul, 1975.

[70]LJW IV:312.

[71]Editor's Preface, *John Wesley's Commentary on the Bible*, ed. G. Roger Schoenhals (Grand Rapids: FAP, Zondervan, 1990), 7.

[72]The defensive assumption in relation to the text or the hearer that would begin *ad hominem* by questioning the arguer's motives or social location as determinative of its content. This sort of critique was later developed explicitly by the tradition of Marx, Freud, Jacques Derrida, and Paul Ricoeur.

[73]#137 "On Corrupting the Word of God," Pref. 2, 3, 4:246.

[74]#80 "On Friendship With the World," 3:126–40.

[75]#137 "On Corrupting the Word of God," i.2, 4:247.

[76]#137 "On Corrupting the Word of God," i.3, 4:247–48.

plainness and boldness," not softening the challenge of the Word.[77] One who preaches with sincerity, and finds only rejection need not fret, for he has done his duty as a watchman (Ezek. 33:1–9).[78]

Such sincerity is a crucial criterion of effective preaching. It enables the hearer to trust that the preacher has no end in view but the clear and accurate address of the Word.[79] When it comes from the heart, sincere communication has a capacity to "strangely insinuate into the hearts of others."[80] The hermeneutical center is, "Let the hearers accommodate themselves to the Word," not the Word to the hearers.[81] *"Unlike so many, we do not peddle the word of God for profit. On the contrary, in Christ we speak before God with sincerity, like men sent from God"* (2 Cor. 2:17).

FURTHER READING ON WESLEY'S SCRIPTURAL HERMENEUTIC

Arnett, William M. "John Wesley and the Bible," WTJ 3 (1968): 3–9.

_____. "John Wesley, Man of One Book," Drew Ph.D., Diss., 1954.

Artingstall, George. *A Man of One Book.* London: Epworth, 1953.

Clemons, James T. "John Wesley—Biblical Literalist." RL 46 (1977): 332–42.

Ferguson, Duncan S. "John Wesley on Scripture: The Hermeneutics of Pietism." MH 22 no. 4 (1984): 234–45.

Källstad, Thorvald. *John Wesley and the Bible: A Psychological Study.* Stockholm: Nya Bokförlags, 1974.

Hilderbrandt, Franz. *Christianity According to the Wesleys.* London, Epworth, 1956, 9–27.

McCown, Wayne G. "Wesley's Suggestions for Study of the Bible." In *A Contemporary Wesleyan Theology,* ed. C. W. Carter. Grand Rapids, FAP, Zondervan, 1983.

Mullen, Wilbur H. "John Wesley's Method of Biblical Interpretation." RL 47 (1978): 99–108.

Oswalt, John N. "Wesley's Use of the Old Testament." WTJ 12 (1977): 39–53.

Pellowe, Wm. C. S., "John Wesley's Use of the Bible." MR 106 (1923): 353–74.

Scoggs, Robin. "John Wesley as Biblical Scholar." JBR 38 (1960): 415–22.

Shelton, R. Larry. "Wesley's Approach to Scripture in Historical Perspective." WTJ 16 (1981): 23–50.

Smith, Timothy L. "John Wesley and the Wholeness of Scripture." *Interpretation—Jnl of Bible and Theol.* 39 (1985): 246–62.

Turner, George Allen. "John Wesley as an Interpreter of Scripture." In *Inspiration and Interpretation,* ed. J. F. Walvoord, 156–78. Grand Rapids: Eerdmans, 1957.

Yates, Arthur S. "Wesley and His Bible." MR (1960): 8.

Wesley's Hermeneutic Sources

Bengel, J. A. *Gnomon of the New Testament.* Grand Rapids: Baker, n.d.

Guyse, John. *Practical Exposition of the Four Gospels.* London, 1739.

Henry, Matthew. *A Commentary on the Holy Bible.* 6 vols. New York: Revell, 1935.

Heylyn, John. *An Interpretation of the New Testament.* London, 1749, 1761.

Wesley's *Explanatory Notes*

Arnett, William M. "A Study in John Wesley's Explanatory Notes Upon the Old Testament." WTJ 8 (1973):14–32.

Earle, Ralph. "John Wesley's New Testament." AS 14 no. 1 (1960): 61–67.

Laws, C. H. "Wesley's Notes on the New Testament." PWHS 18 (1931): 37–39.

Schoenhals, G. R., ed. *John Wesley's Notes on the Bible.* Grand Rapids: FAP, Zondervan, 1987.

Simon, John S. "Mr. Wesley's Notes Upon the New Testament." PWHS 9 (1914): 97–105.

---

[77]#137 "On Corrupting the Word of God," i.3, 4:248; cf. LJW 6:276.
[78]#137 "On Corrupting the Word of God," iii.1, 4:250.
[79]B1:281, 683f.; 4:365.
[80]#137 "On Corrupting the Word of God," Pref. 2, 4:245.
[81]#137 "On Corrupting the Word of God," ii.4, 4:250.

Smith, Timothy L. "Notes on the Exegesis of John Wesley's Explanatory Notes Upon the NT." WTJ 16 no. 1 (1981):107–13.

TRADITION

In the Preface of his collected works, Wesley sought to present thoughts "agreeable, I hope, to Scripture, reason and Christian antiquity."[82] *Antiquity* in this case refered to *"the religion of the primitive church*, of the whole church in the purest ages,"* with special reference to "Clemens Romanus, Ignatius, and Polycarp . . . Tertullian, Origen, Clemens Alexandrinus,[83] and Cyprian[84] . . . Chrysostom,[85] Basil,[86] Ephrem Syrus,[87] and Macarius[88]."[89] "We prove the doctrines we preach by Scripture and reason, and if need be, by antiquity."[90]

No thinking persons will easily dismiss or "condemn the Fathers of the Church," whose views are "indispens-ably necessary" for the practice of ministry. There is no excuse for "one who has the opportunity, and makes no use of it," to fail to read the Patristic texts. There is no warrant for "a person who has had a University education" yet has bypassed the ancient Christian writers.[91]

Wesley recalled that his own father had early given him the model of "reverence to the ancient church" when he was a student at Oxford.[92] This would prepare him later to debate in detail with learned patristic interpreters like Richard Smalbroke and Conyers Middleton on specific patristic references and translation nuances of the works of Irenaeus,[93] Minucius Felix,[94] Origen,[95] Didymus of Alexandria,[96] Eusebius,[97] Athanasius,[98] Epiphanius,[99] Gregory of Nyssa,[100] Gregory Nazianzen,[101] Augus-

---

[82]Wesley's Preface to the 1771 edition of his works, quoted by Jackson in his Preface to the third edition, March 1771, sec. 4, I:iv; cf. #13 "On Sin in Believers," iii.1–10.

[83]For other references to Clement of Alexandria, see LJW 2:327–28, 342, 387; 5:43; 6:129; cf. B9:31; B3:586; 4:402; JJW 5:197.

[84]For Wesley's extensive references to Cyprian, see B2:461–62; 3:196–97, 450–51, 458–59, 469–70; LJW 1:277, 323; 2:320, 333–37, 361, 373, 387; B11:437; JWO 42f., 126, 195, 264, 309, 328; JJW 1:416; 2:263; 4:97.

[85]For further references to John Chrysostom, see FA 11:156–62, 175; B11:155–59, 381–453; 2:113; 3:586; 4:402; JWO 131f., 264, 328; see also the Drew Univ. Ph.D. diss. by Kelley Steve McCormick on a comparative study of John Chrysostom and John Wesley.

[86]LJW 4:176; B11:8.

[87]JJW 1:276, 279, 284f., 294f.; 3:284; 4:457–59.

[88]For notes on the identity and view of "Macarius the Egyptian," see JWO ix, 9, 31, 119, 252, 274f.; JJW 1:254; LJW 2:387.

[89]#112 "On Laying the Foundation of the New Chapel," 1777, ii.3; 3:586; LJW II:387.

[90]FA Part III iii.28; B11:310.

[91]"Address to the Clergy," 1.2; X:484.

[92]Thirty years prior to his writing to William Dodd, March 12, 1756, LJW III:172, hence probably around 1726.

[93]For further references to Irenaeus, see LJW 2:319, 332, 387; JJW 1:356.

[94]LJW 2:332, 348.

[95]For further references to Origen, see LJW 2:91f., 100, 105, 324, 332, 353, 362, 387; 3:137; 4:176; B4:33n.

[96]Didymus Alexandrinus (the blind), JWO 129.

[97]LJW 2:331.

[98]FA 11:162–63, 175; LJW 1:367; B2:397.

[99]LJW 2:360.

[100]B1:75, 188n; JWO 9f., 31, 119.

[101]JWO 130.

tine,[102] Jerome,[103] Pachomius,[104] Theophylact,[105] Pseudo-Dionysius,[106] John of Damascus,[107] and others.[108]

Wesley understood the Methodists from the beginning as "orthodox in every point," the criterion of which was "firmly believing . . . the Three Creeds."[109] "Were you to recite the whole catalogue of *heresies* enumerated by Bishop Pearson it might be asked, 'Who can lay any one of these to their [the Methodists'] charge?' "[110]

The Ancient Christian Writers as Scriptural Exegetes

The Fathers are "the most authentic commentators on Scripture, as being both nearest the fountain, and eminently endued with the Spirit by whom all Scripture was given. . . . I speak chiefly of those who wrote before the Council of Nice. But who would not likewise desire to have some acquaintance with those that followed them? with St. Chrysostom, Basil, Jerome, Austin [Augustine]; and above all, the man of a broken heart, Ephraim Syrus?"[111] Typi-

cal of the Father's reliance on Scripture was Cyril of Jerusalem, who wrote in his Fifth Catechetical Lectures: "It behoveth us not to deliver, no not so much as the least thing of the holy mysteries of faith without the holy Scripture."[112]

Wesley was quick to concede that the ancient Christian writers made many occasional "mistakes, many weak suppositions, and many ill-drawn conclusions." Nonetheless, "I exceedingly reverence them as well as their writings . . . because they describe true, genuine Christianity."[113] "Some of these Fathers, being afraid of too literal a way of expounding the Scriptures, leaned sometimes to the other extreme. Yet nothing can be more unjust than to infer from hence 'that the age in which they lived could not relish or endure any but senseless, extravagant, enthusiastic, ridiculous comments on sacred writ.' "[114]

The exegesis of the church fathers[115] is especially helpful in "the *explication* of a doctrine that is not sufficiently explained, or for *confirmation* of a

---

[102]The bulk of Wesley's references to Augustine (St. Austin) are to be found in the letters, LJW 1:45; 2:60, 70; 3:171; 4:176; 6:175; 7:58, 333; see also B2:548, 566; B11:236, 492; JWO 124–26, 131f., 409; JJW 5:118.

[103]LJW 2:353; B2:113; 3:62n; FA 11:156, 159.

[104]B9:354.

[105]B4:6.

[106]JJW 2:365.

[107]B11:189n.

[108]FA Part I v.16–22; II:155–63.

[109]Nicene, Athanasian (Quicunque), and Apostles'; #112 "On Laying the Foundation of the New Chapel," i.3, 3:582. For various comments on "orthodoxy," see B1:220, 694; 3:582, 587; 4:50, 57, 146, 175, 398; 2:415–16; B11:22, 39, 477f.; LJW 3:183, 203; 4:347, 364.

[110]FA Part II i.9 11:277.

[111]"Address to the Clergy," i.2, X:484; cf. Dailie's treatise on patristic writers noted, JJW 3:390.

[112]"Roman Catechism, and Reply," i.Q8,, X:91; cf. "Popery Calmly Considered," i, X:141.

[113]Letter to Conyers Middleton, Jan. 4, 1749, iii. 11–12, LJW II:387. For Wesley's somewhat idiosyncratic views on Montanus, Augustine, and Pelagius, see #68 "The Wisdom of God's Counsels," sec. 9, 2:556.

[114]Letter to Conyers Middleton, Jan. 4, 1749, LJW II:362, quoting Middleton's "Free Inquiry," 1748.

[115]JWO 62, 119, 182, 195, 307, 336, 365, 375; see also "Manners of the Ancient Christians."

doctrine generally received."[116] When Wesley appealed alternatively to "reason, Scripture, or authority," the third of these criteria meant the ancient ecumenical creeds and councils and consensually received classical Christian writings.[117]

On the relation of Scripture and tradition: "The Scriptures are a complete rule of faith and practice; and they are clear in all necessary points. And yet their clearness does not prove that they need not be explained; nor their completeness, that they need not be enforced. . . . The esteeming the writings of the first three centuries, not equally with, but next to, the Scriptures, never carried any man yet into dangerous errors, nor probably ever will."[118] "*The historical experience of the church, though fallible, is the better judge over-all of Scripture's meanings than later interpreters.*"[119]

Wesley as Editor
of Classic Christian Writings

Wesley wrote grammars in seven of the eight foreign languages he knew (Hebrew, Greek, Latin, French, German, Dutch, Spanish, and Italian).[120] His lifelong fascination with the learning of languages rightly should put to rest the caricature of Wesley as an uneducated, non-scholarly, Bible-thumping "enthusiast." He read comfortably in more languages than Luther, Calvin, Jonathan Edwards, Joseph But-

ler, or Immanuel Kant. He also published a compendium of logic, considerable poetry, some in his own translation, a general history of Christianity and a history of England, a library of Christian classics, a system of natural philosophy, and a general commentary on Scripture.

The wide range of Wesley's work as an editor of the spiritual tradition is seen in the Prefaces of the various works he edited, abridged, published, and in some cases translated, the collection of which may be found in the Jackson edition, *Prefaces to Works Revised and Abridged from Various Authors.*[121] The 118 works listed show his tireless enterprise in making available to the common reader, and especially his Societies, the best literature of spiritual formation in plain, economic format.

He was particularly interested in presenting personal histories and testimonies to the holy life. In addition to hagiographies like Foxe's *Acts and Monuments of the Christian Martyrs*, Wesley added his own recensions of more recent Protestant hagiography,[122] along with collected letters of Joseph Alleine and Samuel Rutherford.

In some cases he presented materials with which he partly disagreed, yet in which he found sufficient merit to publish it nonetheless, as in the case of *An Extract from the Life of Mr. Thomas Firmin*, a "pious man" even if his

---

[116]"A Roman Catechism, With a Reply," Preface, X:87, italics added; cf. B1:74–76; JJW 1:367.

[117]FA Part I v. 31; II:176.

[118]LCM X:14.

[119]For Wesley's implicit use of the Vincentian canon, see Outler's Introduction, B1:58–59; cf. B1:324n, 550n.

[120]In addition to an English grammar, he wrote grammars in Hebrew, Greek, Latin, French, and Dutch. He also studied German in some detail, translated German poetry, and compiled a dictionary and grammar of German, JJW 1:110–12, 133f., 209f., 278, 295, 300, and a Spanish grammar, JJW 1:237f., 299; and for a time studied Italian, JJW 1:354. He was by his own acknowledgment far more accomplished in Greek and Latin than in the others.

[121]XIV:199–318.

[122]As in *An Extract of the Life and Death of Mr. Thomas Haliburton*, (1741), *Thomas Haliburton*, (1741), and *David Brainerd, Missionary to the Indians* (1768).

"notions of the Trinity were quite erro-neous,"[123] and *An Extract of the Life of Madam Guion* (1766) who "was actually deceived in many instances; the more frequently, because she imagined herself to be infallible,"[124] who resisted being "guided by the written word," and who exaggerated the efficacy of suffering for spiritual formation. Yet even with these limitations Wesley found in her "a pattern of true holiness."[125]

His special interest in the biographies of holy women is seen in his editions of the letters of Jane Cooper, and the lives and spiritual journals of Mary Gilbert (1769), and Elizabeth Harper (1772), and many others.

He found in *An Extract of Mr. Richard Baxter's Aphorisms of Justification* (1745) a "powerful antidote against the spreading poison of Antinomianism."[126] Each edition of the *Arminian Magazine* (1778–91) contained accounts and letters of pious persons, sacred poetry, lives of saints, and classic essays defending the universal offer of free grace.[127]

That he was interested in what today is called the practice of holistic medicine, and the analysis of the body/soul interface, is evident from his popular series of advisories on health matters: *Advice with Respect to Health* (1769, based on a work by Dr. Tissot), *An Extract from Dr. Cadogan's Dissertation on the Gout, and all Chronic Diseases* (1774), and his much reprinted *Primitive Physic: Or, An Easy and Natural Method of Curing Most Diseases* (23d edition, 1791), containing "safe, cheap, and easy medicines."[128] As to works on the natural sciences, in addition to his five-volume *Compendium of Natural Philosophy: A Survey of the Wisdom of God in the Creation* (1784), he wrote *The Desideratum: Or, Electricity Made Plain and Useful* (1759).[129]

His fascination with history[130] and its importance in spiritual formation is seen in his editions of *A Short Roman History* (1773), *A Concise History of England* (1776), *An Account of the Conduct of the War in the Middle Colonies* (1780), and *A Concise Ecclesiastical History* in four volumes (1781).[131]

The Christian Library

In the fifty volumes of *A Christian Library: Consisting of Extracts from, and Abridgments of, the Choicest Pieces of Practical Divinity which have been Published in the English Tongue* (1749–55),[132] he edited and published "such a collection of English divinity, as (I believe) is all true, all agreeable to the oracles of God; as is all practical, unmixed with controversy of any kind, and all intelligible to plain men; such as is not superficial, but going down to the depth, and describing the height, of Christianity; and yet not mystical, not obscure to any of those who are experienced in the ways of God."[133]

Since his defining editorial aim was to "preserve a consistency throughout"

[123]XIV:293.
[124]XIV:176.
[125]XIV:278.
[126]XIV:216.
[127]XIV:280.
[128]XIV:312.
[129]LJW 4:123, 166; 5:176, 342; JJW 3:320; 4:190; 5:247.
[130]JJW 3:499; 6:96; B3:108; 2:451.
[131]Redacted from the M'Laine translation of the work of J. L. von Mosheim.
[132]JJW 1:425; 3:391–92; 4:91, 94.
[133]CL Preface, XIV:222.

so that all writers would "conspire together to make 'the man of God perfect, thoroughly furnished unto every good word and work,'" he felt himself "at full liberty" not only to abridge but to add his own comments and corrections.[134] He felt that one could spend one's whole life reading the classical Christian writers and still "not read all." "This very plenty creates a difficulty," an information overload. So his editorial purpose was to make a fit selection, avoiding those that focus unnecessarily on controversy, that would more "tend to promote vain jangling, than holiness." He eschewed writings so mystical that they "find hidden meanings in everything," seeking "mysteries in the plainest truths, and make them such by their explications." He circumvented writers that make things unintelligible, "a fault which is not easy for men of learning to avoid."[135] Acknowledging rich varieties within the Christian tradition, he remained convinced that "the genuine religion of Jesus Christ has been one and the same from the beginning."[136]

He began his *Christian Library* with a "Preface to the Epistles of the Apostolical Fathers," in which he presents and commends the writings of Clement of Rome,[137] Ignatius,[138] and Polycarp[139] as those who delivered "the pure doctrine of the Gospel; what Christ and his Apostles taught, and what these holy men had themselves received from their own mouths."[140] Having "the advan-

tage of living in the apostolic times, of hearing the holy Apostles and conversing with them," and having been chosen by them for leadership in the nascent church, we "cannot with any reason doubt of what they deliver . . . but ought to receive it, though not with equal veneration, yet with only little less regard than we do the sacred writings of those who were their masters and instructors" and "as worthy of a much greater respect than any composures which have been made since."[141] As "persons of consummate piety; adorned with all those Christian virtues which they so affectionately recommend to us," they were "in all the necessary parts of it . . . so assisted by the Holy Ghost, as to be scarce capable of mistaking."[142]

When criticized by Roland Hill that he had "embowelled ['poor John Bunyan'] to make him look like Mr. Wesley," Wesley admitted that he had excised some of Bunyan's Calvinism to try to make him amenable to Wesley's audience—"However, those that are fond of his bowels may put them in again, and swallow them as they would the trail of a woodcock."[143]

FURTHER READINGS

The Christian Library

Dodge, Reginald J. *John Wesley's Christian Library*. London: Epworth, 1938.

"Wesley's Christian Library." WMM 50 (1827): 310–16.

---

[134]CL Preface, XIV:222.
[135]CL Preface, XIV:221.
[136]CL Preface, XIV:223.
[137]See also LJW 2:330; 3:137; B3:586.
[138]For further references to Ignatius, see LJW 2:327f., 387; 3:137; B1:36; 3:5; JJW 2:467f.; 3:65; B11:437.
[139]LJW 2:327–30, 362, 387; 3:137.
[140]CL XIV:223.
[141]CL XIV:223–25.
[142]CL XIV:224–25.
[143]Some remarks of Mr. Hill's "Review of All the Doctrines Taught by Mr. John Wesley," X:387.

The Freedom to Learn From Tradition

Harkness, Georgia. "The Roots of Methodist Theology." In *The Methodist Church in Social Thought and Action.* Nashville: Abingdon, 1964.

Shelton, R. Larry. "Wesley on Maintaining a Catholic Spirit." PM 53 no. 4 (1978):12, 13.

Wesley and Christian Antiquity

Campbell, Ted. *Wesley and Christian Antiquity.* Nashville: Abingdon, 1991.

McCormick, K. Steve. "John Chrysostom and John Wesley." Drew University Ph.D. diss.

Meeks, Douglas M., ed. *The Future of the Methodist Theological Traditions.* Nashville: Abingdon, 1985.

Orcibal, Jean. "The Theological Originality of John Wesley." In *A History of the Methodist Church in Great Britain.* London: Epworth, 1965.

Outler, A. C. "John Wesley's Interests in the Early Fathers of the Church." In *The Wesleyan Theological Heritage, Essays,* edited by T. Oden and L. Longden. Grand Rapids: FAP, Zondervan, 1991.

Petry, Ray C. "The Critical Temper and the Practice of Tradition." *Duke Div. School Review* 30 (Spring):1965.

Southgate, W. M. *John Jewel and the Problem of Doctrinal Authority.* Cambridge, Mass., 1962.

Stoeffler, F. Earnest. *The Rise of Evangelical Pietism.* Leiden: E. J. Brill, 1965.

Comparative Studies

Baker, Frank. *John Wesley and the Church of England.* Nashville: Abingdon, 1970.

————. "John Wesley and William Law." PWHS 37 (1970): 173–77.

Brantley, Richard E. *Locke, Wesley and the Method of English Romanticism.* Gainsville: Univ. of Florida Press, 1984.

————. *Wordsworth's 'Natural Methodism.'* New Haven: Yale Univ. Press, 1975.

Brigdon Thomas E. "Pascal and the Wesleys." PWHS 7 (1909): 60–63, 84–88.

Church, Leslie F. "Port Royal and John Wesley." LQHR 175 (1950): 291–93.

Cragg, Gerald R. *The Church and the Age of Reason.* Baltimore: Penguin, 1966.

Glasson, T. Francis. "Jeremy Taylor's Place in John Wesley's Life." PWHS 36 (1968): 105–7.

Green, J. B. *John Wesley and William Law.* London, 1945.

Hooper, Henry T. "Wesley and St. Francis." WMM 143 (1920): 527f.

Howard, Ivan. "Wesley Versus Phoebe Palmer." WTJ 6 (1971): 31–40.

Hughes, H. Trevor. "Jeremy Taylor and John Wesley." LQHR 174 (1949): 296–404.

Hutchinson, F. E. "John Wesley and George Herbert." LQHR 161 (1936): 439–55.

Leach, Elsie A. "Wesley's Use of Geo. Herbert." *Huntington Libr. Q* 16 (1953): 183–202.

Lloyd, A. K. "Doddridge and Wesley." PWHS 28 (1951): 50–52.

Marriott, Thomas. "John Wesley and William Wilberforce." WMM 68 (1945): 364–65.

McDonald, Frederick W. "Bishop Butler and John Wesley." *Meth Recorder* (1896): 142, 156, 172.

Moore, Sydney H. "Wesley and Fenelon." LQHR 169 (1944): 155–57.

Pask, A. H. "The Influence of Arminius on John Wesley." LQHR 185 (1960): 258–63.

"Pusey and Puseyism: Wesley and Methodism." *Meth Recorder.* (1882).

Reist, Irwin W. "John Wesley and George Whitefield: The Integrity of Two Theories of Grace." *Evangelical Q* 47 no. 1 (1975): 26–40.

Simon, John S. *Wesley or Voltaire.* London: C. H. Kelly, 1904.

Taylor, A. E. "St. John of the Cross and John Wesley." *Jnl of Th Studies* 46 (1945): 30–38.

Thomas, Gilbert. "George Fox and John Wesley." *Meth Recorder* (1924): 11.

Tyson, John R. "John Wesley and William Law: A Reappraisal." WTJ 17 no. 2 (1982): 58–78.

Watchhurst, Percy L. "Francis of Assisi and John Wesley." WMM 128 (1905): 484–86.

Weaver, Sampson. "Wesley and Wordsworth." WMM 127 (1904): 835–37.

Wiseman, Frederick Luke. "Herbert and Wesley." *Meth Recorder* (1933): 14.

Assessments of Wesley's Place in Church History

Baker, Frank. "Unfolding John Wesley: A Survey of Twenty Years' Studies in Wesley's Thought." QR 1 (1980).

Heitzenrater, Richard P. "The Present State of Wesley Studies." MH 22 (1984): 221–31.

_____. "Wesley Studies in the Church and the Academy." *Perkins Journal* 37 no. 3 (1984): 1–6.

Langford, Thomas. *Practical Divinity: Theology in the Wesleyan Tradition.* Nashville: Abingdon, 1982.

Minus, Paul. *Methodism's Destiny in an Ecumenical Age.* New York: Abingdon, 1969.

Outler, A. C. "Methodism's Theological Heritage." In *The Wesleyan Theological Heritage, Essays,* edited by T. Oden and L. Longden. Grand Rapids: FAP, Zondervan, 1991, pp. 189–211.

Rack, Henry D. *The Future of John Wesley's Methodism.* London: Lutterworth, 1965.

Rowe, Gilbert T. *The Meaning of Methodism.* Nashville, Cokesbury, 1926.

Rowe, Kenneth, ed. *The Place of Wesley in the Christian Tradition.* Metuchen: Scarecrow, 1976.

Urlin, R. D. *John Wesley's Place in Church History.* London: Rivington, 1879.

Wilson, Woodrow. *John Wesley's Place in History.* New York: Abingdon, 1915.

REASON

The faithful are urged not to "despise or lightly esteem reason, knowledge, or human learning."[144] "To renounce reason is to renounce religion," for "all irrational religion is false religion."[145] Religion is hobbled when reason is neglected: "It is impossible, without reasoning, either to prove or disprove anything."[146]

Reason is God's gift: "In all the duties of common life, God has given us our reason for a guide. And it is only by acting up to the dictates of it, by using all the understanding which God hath given us, that we can have a conscience void of offence towards God and towards man."[147]

In his letter to Dr. Rutherforth of Cambridge, Wesley rejected the view that "human learning is an impediment to a divine." "I do not depreciate learning of any kind." He defended his traveling preachers as "not ignorant men," who though they do not profess to know languages and philosophy, yet "some of them understand them well . . . better than great part of my pupils at the university did."[148]

Reason and Scripture, far from being pitted against each other, are linked intimately in the attempt to find "the plain scriptural rational way."[149] "Passion and prejudice govern the world, only under the name of reason. It is our part, by religion and reason joined, to counteract them all we can."[150] "You cannot but allow that the religion which we preach and live to be agreeable to the highest reason."[151] His main dissatisfaction with "mystic divines" was their tendency to "utterly decry the use of reason."[152] He admitted "no method of bringing any to the knowledge of the truth, except the methods of reason and persuasion."[153] "Christianity requires our assent to nothing but what is plain and intelligible in every proposition. Let every man first have a full conviction of the truth of each proposition in

---

[144]*Plain Account of Christian Perfection*, sec. 25, XI:429.
[145]Letter to Dr. Rutherford, Mar. 28, 1768, LJW V:364.
[146]"A Dialogue Between an Antinomian and His Friend," X:267.
[147]#70 "The Case of Reason Impartially Considered," ii.10, 2:592.
[148]B9:376–80, "A Letter to the Rev. Dr. Rutherford," ii.1–9.
[149]#37 "The Nature of Enthusiasm," sec. 26, 2:55.
[150]Letter to Joseph Benson, Oct. 5, 1779, LJW V:203.
[151]EA sec. 22, 11:53.
[152]EA sec. 30, 11:55.
[153]#112 "On Laying the Foundation of the New Chapel," ii.11, 3:588.

the gospel, as far only as it is plain and intelligible, and let him believe as far as he understands."[154] "So far as he departs from true genuine reason, so far he departs from Christianity."[155]

Yet reason alone cannot pass easily "from things natural to spiritual. . . . A gulf is here!"[156] "Let reason do all that reason can; Employ it as far as it will go," realizing that it is "utterly incapable of giving either faith, or hope, or love; and consequently of producing either real virtue, or substantial happiness."[157]

FURTHER READING

On Editing, Education, Books, Scholarship, and Culture

Herbert, T. W. *John Wesley as Editor and Author.* Princeton: Princeton Univ. Press, 1940.

Jackson, F. M. "A Bibliographical Catalogue of Books Mentioned in John Wesley's Journals." PWHS 4 (1902–4): 17, 47, 74, 107, 134, 173, 203, 232.

Joy, James R. "Wesley: A Man of a Thousand Books and a Book." RL 8 (1939): 71–84.

Lawton, George. *John Wesley's English: A Study of His Literary Style.* London: Allen and Unwin, 1962.

Lewis, Tho. H. "John Wesley as a Scholar." MQR 73 (1924): 648–58.

Mathews, Horace F. *Methodism and the Education of the People, 1791–1851.* London: Epworth, 1949.

Rogal, Samuel J. "A Journal and Diary Checklist of John Wesley's Reading." *Serif* 11 no. 1 (1974): 11–33.

Wesley on Science and Medicine

Collier, Frank. *John Wesley Among the Scientists.* New York: Abingdon, 1928.

Hill, A. *John Wesley Among the Physicians.* London: Epworth, 1953.

Hunter, Richard A. "A Brief Review of the Use of Electricity in Psychiatry with Spe-

cial Reference to John Wesley." *Brit Jnl of Physical Medicine* 20 no. 5 (1957): 98–100.

Pellowe, Wm. C. S. "John Wesley's Use of Science." MR 110 (1927): 394–403.

Rogal, Samuel J. "Pills for the Poor: Wesley's Primitive Physick." *Yale Jnl of Biology and Med* 51 (1978): 81–90.

Stewart, David. "John Wesley, the Physician." WTJ 4 (1969): 27–38.

Stillings, Dennis. "John Wesley: Philosopher of Electricity." *Medical Instrumentation* 7 (1973): 307.

Sweet, W. W. "John Wesley and Scientific Discovery." *Chr Cent* 40 (1923): 591–92.

Turrell, W. J. "Three Electrotherapists of the Eighteenth Century: John Wesley, Jean Paul Marat and James Graham." *Annals of Medical History* 3 (1921): 361–67.

The Case of Reason Impartially Considered

1 Cor. 14:20: "Brethren, be not children in understanding: howbeit in malice be ye children, but in understanding be men." [Homily #70 1781 2:587–600 J#70 VI:350–60]

Reason remains useful in its own proper sphere, but apart from that sphere is often either overvalued or undervalued. Reason must neither be exalted to presume to be an ultimate judge of revelation, nor ignored as a critic of emotive excess.[158] The medium between these two extremes has been generally anticipated by "that great master of reason, Mr. Locke," but with inadequate applications.[159] Wesley fought a twofold battle against both unreasonable charismatic enthusiasts who overstressed emotive spirituality, and excessive rationalists who wanted to impose hyperskeptical criteria on the inquiry into Christian truth.

---

[154]"Compendium of Natural Philosophy," II, 448–49.
[155]EA sec. 27 11:55.
[156]EA sec. 35 11:57.
[157]#70 "The Case of Reason Impartially Considered," ii.10, 2:600.
[158]B1:271f.; 2:591–95.
[159]#70 "The Case of Reason Impartially Considered," Pref. 1–5, 2:587–88.

On Not Undervaluing Reason

Those who wrongly consider reason as an enemy of religion are viewed as enthusiasts who tend to substitute their own dreams and emotive life for rational analysis. They also tend to substitute their own imagination for the written word, the reliable revelation of God. In reckless malice we are called to be undeveloped, but in rational understanding mature. So *"stop thinking like children. In regard to evil be infants, but in your thinking be adults"* (1 Cor. 14:20).

Those who desire to find some deprecation of reason by Wesley must look hard. He was never attracted to anti-intellectual fidism. Though not a rationalist in the reductionist sense, he valued the place of reason in its own proper sphere.[160]

Faith is not to be pitted against reason. Growing faith searches for the best reasons available for its grounding in revelation. Faith invites the best modes of argument it can find to account for its own depth.[161] It is pathetic stewardship not to use what God gives. What God gives to humans as distinguished from brute creation is some modest capacity for reasoning.[162]

On Not Overvaluing Reason

Others make the opposite mistake of overvaluing the omnicompetence of finite reasoning, admitting too few limits, imagining that reason can be trusted to analyze the truth with complete impartiality, as if the reasoning subject was not at the same time an egocentric sinner. The human capacity for finite reasoning thus is expected to carry more than its poor powers allow. This opens the door for finite reason to overextend itself as a censor of divine revelation.[163]

Reason in this way becomes oppressive in its relation to the testimony of revelation. Sin-drenched reasoning mistakenly fantasizes itself as an omnicompetent, autonomous guide that needs neither the embrace of divine forgiveness or the light of revelation. Thus some rationalists have failed to be grasped by the mystery of God's self-disclosure in history, having little patience with talk of revelation, unable to get their minds around it, so they want to reduce incarnation and resurrection to natural events or flat causal explanations.[164]

Wesley searched for a right balance fitting to the real but limited competencies of reasoning. He sought a middle ground that would neither over- or underestimate reason's proficiency. He pursued the middle way by first defending reason in two aspects: When viewed either as argument or understanding, reason has a significant role in the nurture of true religion.

On Reason as Argument

Reason viewed as argument is that capacity of human intelligence to account for the route by which one comes to conclusions. Reason serves logical and sequential argument by moving from premise to conclusion smoothly without a leap in logic.[165] The function

---

[160]EA 20–25, XIII:8–10.

[161]JWO 396f.

[162]#70 "The Case of Reason Impartially Considered," Pref. 1–5, 2:587–88.

[163]Letter to Dr. Robertson, Sept. 24, 1753, LJW 3:104–10.

[164]In his letter to Joseph Benson, Sept. 27, 1788, LJW 8:89–90, Wesley reported how he had been plunged into "unprofitable *reasonings*" by Isaac Watts's speculations on the glorified humanity of Christ.

[165]Wesley, who published a *Compendium of Logic* (1750) B2:547, a translation of Dean

of reason is to unpack one's assertions and show the layers of judgment that lie behind them.[166]

That Wesley was an old hand at analyzing argument, having taught logic at Oxford, is seen especially in his writings with a polemical edge.[167] With Isaiah, he invited his partners in dialogue to "Come now, let us reason together" (Isa. 1:18). When you make statements, give me your reasons, and I will give you mine. Those in his connection of spiritual formation were expected to be prepared to give reasons for their conclusions, a duty owed to all with whom one enters into discourse. "If you denounce against me all the curses from Genesis to Revelation they will not amount to one argument."[168] That is what he meant by reason as argument, which we today recognize as a left-brain (linear) function. But reason also has what we today would call a right-brain (intuitive) function.[169]

On Reason as Understanding

Reason has another, a deeper and more intuitively diffuse task: *as understanding,* reason is that faculty of human consciousness that has a capacity to apprehend, organize complex data, and name experiencing; to make judgments on the basis of evidence as to whether statements agree or disagree, distinguishing one judgment from another. Reasoning subjects can discourse, dialogue, and interact with each other to inquire into the truth of various arguments being set forth.

Reason as understanding assumes the capacity to empathize with another sufficiently that one understands what another is saying. On this ground intelligible discourse is possible, where two minds have the possibility of being of one mind.

In these diverse ways reason remains an important resource for human existence generally, and more particularly for the Christian life, insofar as the reading of Holy Writ, discerning its meaning, and living together meaningfully in a community, requires understanding.[170]

What Reason Can Do

Some things reason does better than others. Wesley plainly sets forth the competencies of reason in the realms of physical, religious, and moral reflection:

First, reason is singularly useful in ordering the physical world, searching for plausible evidences and explanations of causes of effects. Horticulture, music, seamanship, and the healing arts proceed by reason, as do all the sciences, mathematics, philosophy, grammar, logic, law, magistracy, and metaphysics.[171] Reason uses sensory experience and logic to understand how the world works, how effects are caused.[172] There is hardly a trace of antiscientific prejudice in Wesley. He was keenly interested in experiment and often dis-

---

Henry Aldrich's *Logic* for use at the Kingswood School, JJW 3:459, highly commended the learning of logic to all in leadership in his connection, JJW 3:391, 285.

[166]B4:21f.; 2:589f.

[167]When chided for his tendency to press logical points so as to "distinguish them away," Wesley retorted: "When men tack absurdities to the truth of God with which it hath nothing to do, I distinguish away those absurdities and let the truth remain"; LJW 2:90; March 25, 1747, to John Smith.

[168]FA Part I iv.7 11:138.

[169]#70 "The Case of Reason Impartially Considered," i.1, 2:589–90; cf. B1:59f., 613f.

[170]#70 "The Case of Reason Impartially Considered," i.2, 2:590.

[171]On mathematics, see LJW 3:104; on metaphysics, see B3:108f., 235.

[172]B2:587–88, 599–600.

played an investigative attitude toward the world. Scientific inquiry—observing, testing, hypothecating, analyzing, discovering—Wesley found appealing, not appalling.[173]

Secondly, reason has a key role to play in religion, both with regard to its foundation and its coherence. As to its foundation, reason is useful in making an intelligible *reception of revelation*. One uses one's rational capacity critically to understand what Scripture is saying, to analyze its language, its historical setting and moral consequences. The translation of meaning from one language to another requires rational capacities. This evangelical Oxford don was a practiced classic linguist who read Latin and Greek as quickly as he read English.

In the sphere of religion, good reasoning offers help in providing a critique of religious conceptualities, organizing thinking, seeking to clarify the basis of faith. It tries to tell the truth about its evidences and make proper distinctions. Reason seeks to provide order and cohesive structure to the teaching of the truth.[174] Reason helps organize disparate empirical data into cohesive reflections.[175] One cannot give counsel or attest intelligibly without rational reflection. What is said about human existence must correspond consistently with what is said about creation, the course of human history, the predicament of the will, and the future of humanity. Reason is in these ways a critical companion to the life of faith.[176]

Thirdly, reason recognizes moral consequences of ideas, helping each moral agent to understand what conscience is inwardly saying. Conscience needs rational deliberation to clarify itself. Conscience is the witness of moral self-awareness within ourselves that either accuses or excuses us. We hear ourselves constantly assessing ourselves morally. Reason helps us discern that assessment accurately.[177]

What Reason Cannot Do

If these are services reason can render, what can reason not do? Reason is powerless to elicit faith or hope or love—the theological virtues.

First, reason cannot produce *saving faith*. It cannot of itself bring one to a firm conviction of that which is not seen. It cannot bring one to trust in God. One can put beliefs to the tests of rational analysis, but one will never derive saving faith from a sequence of reasoning as such. For faith is a decision, a choice one makes to trust Another. You may find reasons that will lead you toward an act of faith, but reason as such lacks the capacity to take the risk-laden step of faith. It is difficult to engender trust without shifting into a narrative mode, without telling a story. We learn by listening to a history of revelation that the Life-giver is personally trustworthy, as known by God's own personal coming in the incarnate, crucified Lord.[178]

Nor can reason elicit *hope*. What reason can do is analyze the conditions under which hope can be grasped. But hope emerges only out of faith. No matter how much evidence is piled

---

[173]#70 "The Case of Reason Impartially Considered," i.3, 2:590–91.
[174]LJW 5:357.
[175]In reference to Peter Browne, "On Human Understanding," see JJW 4:192; LJW 1:56–58; 6:113.
[176]EA 11:37–95; VIII:1–45.
[177]#70 "The Case of Reason Impartially Considered," i.7, 2:592.
[178]#70 "The Case of Reason Impartially Considered," ii.1, 2:593.

layer upon layer, that does not of itself, without faith, elicit hope.[179]

Above all reason by itself cannot *love*. No one loves because one has come to that conclusion on the basis of rational argument.[180]

So reason is inadequate at these most crucial points. Reason can define, think about, conceptually order ideas of the virtues, but it cannot produce the actual behavioral excellences of wisdom, courage, temperance, justice, hope, or love on which the blessed life depends.[181] This means that reason cannot make us happy, unless rightly related to the ground of happiness, faith that loves all in God and God in all.[182]

The proper and modest use of reason does not pretend omnicompetence. Those who belittle reason do not honor God because they fail to acknowledge God's own gift of reasonable reflection. Those who fail to see the limits of reason compound reason's difficulties by imagining that reason itself can elicit faith, hope and love.[183]

The Imperfection
of Human Knowledge

1 Cor. 13:9 "We know in part." [Homily #69 1784 B2:567–86 J#69 VI:337–50]

From this tiny window of time, we grasp only slivers, not the whole of reality. How little we know, mused Wesley. We see society and history and nature from our slender nexus of this moment of time and space.

Nonetheless, the desire to know remains as immeasurable as time and space, and as universal as it is irrepressible. There is no circumference to our desire to know, but on every hand we find our knowledge limited, suggesting that human meaning is pointed toward some future state in which our knowledge shall be complete.[184]

However limited and subject to distortion, the desire for knowing is intrinsic to human consciousness. It is difficult to imagine a human being without a hunger to know that reaches beyond its grasp.[185] While this desire has no bounds, our actual range of knowing does.[186] No matter how wise, we only *"know in part"* (1 Cor. 13:9).[187]

Cosmology Reveals the Austere
Limits of Human Knowing

Realistic deliberation places human knowing within a vast cosmic scale of being, within which it is possible to some degree to know the physical world, living things, and to some degree ourselves, but to a far lesser degree the Ground and Giver of all knowing.[188] Even the wisest know in part. Who knows the extent of the universe, or the structure of light? How little we know of such elementary constituents as air, earth, fire, and water. How little we know about the depths of the sea, the

---

[179]#70 "The Case of Reason Impartially Considered," ii.5–7, 2:595–97.

[180]#70 "The Case of Reason Impartially Considered," ii.3, 8, 2:598.

[181]Reason offers "dim light," B2:172, for that which leads to enduring happiness; B1:60, 258; 2:593–99.

[182]#70 "The Case of Reason Impartially Considered," ii.10, 2:598–600.

[183]#70 "The Case of Reason Impartially Considered," ii.10, 2:598–600; See letter to Elizabeth Morgan, Jan. 1, 1779, LJW 6:335.

[184]#69 "The Imperfection of Human Knowledge," Pref. 1, 2:568.

[185]EA VIII:18–20.

[186]#69 "The Imperfection of Human Knowledge," Pref. 1–4, 2:568–69.

[187]B2:100–103, 568–86; 4:287f.

[188]#69 "The Imperfection of Human Knowledge," i.2–13, 2:570–77.

dynamics, structure, and function of vegetable and animal life.[189]

When we trudge through the thought worlds of astronomy and physics asking about the extent of the universe and the nature of physical bodies, how little we know. Is light composed of waves or particles? Of what are chemical particles made up? In geology, what lies beneath the earth's surface?[190] In biology and botany we are confronted constantly by the mysteries of microscopic organisms and plant life. Up and down the line of this protracted chain of being we find that the more we study the less we know.

From the study of creation, we can reason barely that God exists, but beyond that little is known, except by revelation, of the divine attributes. We can hypothesize divine characteristics such as justice, eternity, aseity, and omnipresence, even from natural reasoning without revelation. These are amenable to some preliminary rational analysis, but always only with a heavy residue of mystery.[191]

We learn of God from God's creation, but only indirectly, from within our fragile sensory apparatus. And even among believers, whatever is known of God's atoning grace within time tends to underscore our deeper ignorance of God's eternal counsels before time.[192]

We may speak of creation, but no one was there when it happened. We have a small window of finite fleeting time in which to view this sweeping natural order.[193] This makes it all the more fitting for us "to adore the wisdom of God who has so exactly proportioned our knowledge to our state!"[194]

The Study of Providence and Suffering Yields Only Partial Knowledge of God

How little we know of ourselves, of providence, of God's design, of suffering. Profound mystery is not only present in God but also in ordinary history. We often do not know why we suffer. We all suffer. Suffering is one of the most pervasive of human experiences. There we find how intimately one human life is connected with others. My sin affects you. Your sin affects me. My grandparents' sin affects me, and I affect my grandchildren yet unborn. Suffering is wrapped in mystery.

Providence is that understanding which reaches out beyond the mystery, and affirms that it is being held in the hands of God even if in present ways empirically unknowable. It remains beyond the comprehension even of the most faithful why, if two people thirst for the knowledge of salvation, one would be answered immediately and the other left to struggle for a long time.[195]

Knowledge of our ignorance may teach us the first steps toward dealing with our suffering. Though we may know some of the psychogenetic and social causes of our suffering and of others, we never know them exhaustively. That belongs only to God. The very recognition that we do not know the causes of our suffering thrusts us

---

[189]#69 "The Imperfection of Human Knowledge," i.5–7, 2:572–73.
[190]#69 "The Imperfection of Human Knowledge," i.8–9, 2:573–74.
[191]B11:268f.
[192]#69 "The Imperfection of Human Knowledge," i.1–4, 2:569–71.
[193]#69 "The Imperfection of Human Knowledge," i.10–13, 2:574–75. See also his conclusion to "Compendium of Natural Philosophy," reprinted as "Remarks on the Limits of Human Knowledge," XIII:488–99.
[194]Conclusion to his "Compendium of Natural Philosophy," reprinted as "Remarks on the Limits of Human Knowledge," XIII:498.
[195]#69 "The Imperfection of Human Knowledge," ii.2, 3, 2:578.

into a relation in which we are being freed to trust Another who does understand.[196]

Even if we may grasp the general outlines of providential ordering, how little we know of its particulars: why great nations are "now swept away," why so many in the "populous empire of Indostan" live in poverty "as the dung of the earth," why Africans are "continually driven to market and sold, like cattle, into the vilest bondage," why "American Indians, that is, the miserable remains of them" are slaughtered, and why myriads of Laplanders and Siberians must live under freezing conditions, and why "many, if not more . . . are wandering up and down the deserts of Tartary."[197]

Why isn't the medicine of the gospel sent to every place where the contagion of sin is found? Why is there "little more mercy or truth to be found among Christians than among Pagans," and why are "many called Christian . . . far worse than the Heathens?" Why does the antidote of Christianity at times become grievously adulterated, and so mixed with poisonous ingredients that it retains little of its original virtue, and at times "adds tenfold malignity to the disease which it was designed to cure"?[198]

Even the Study of God's Grace Yields Only Fragmentary Knowledge of the Wisdom of God's Counsels

The limits of human knowing apply to revealed religion as well as natural religion.[199] How can we explain why "a Hottentot, a New-Zealander, or an inhabitant of Nova-Zembla" does not have an equal chance at a decent education? [200] The profundity of these mysteries tends to drive some beyond a suspension of theoretical judgment and toward the decisive choice between atheism and saving faith. The force of such enigmas is so strong that they cannot be avoided "but by resolving all into the unsearchable wisdom of God, together with a deep conviction of our own ignorance, and inability to fathom his counsels."[201]

"Even among us . . . to whom are entrusted the oracles of God . . . there are still many circumstances in his dispensations which are above our comprehension. We know not why he suffered us so long to go on in our own ways . . . or why he made use of this or the other instrument. . . . It is enough that God knoweth . . . God undoubtedly has reasons; but those reasons are generally hid from the children of men."[202]

What We Learn From Our Own Ignorance

The greatest lesson we learn from the study of human consciousness is of our own ignorance. Each hearer is being taught humility, trust, and resignation precisely by these limits. The very shallowness of our knowing elicits:

● *Humility.* The knowledge of our imperfection teaches us to be a little less proud and assertive about how inclusive is our knowing.

● *Trust.* To learn most profoundly from our ignorance is to learn to trust God's incomparably adequate knowing of us and so awakens and engenders faith. The

---

[196]#69 "The Imperfection of Human Knowledge," iii.4, 5, 2:578–79.
[197]#69 "The Imperfection of Human Knowledge," ii.1–6, 2:578–80.
[198]#69 "The Imperfection of Human Knowledge," ii.8, 2:581.
[199]Cf. Wesley's remarks on Lord Kames in "Morality and Natural Religion," JJW 6:21; B3:493; 4:151; JJW 6:21; B3:493; 4:151.
[200]#69 "The Imperfection of Human Knowledge," iii.1, 2, 2:582–83; cf. B3:348f.
[201]#69 "The Imperfection of Human Knowledge," iii.2, 2:583; cf. 7:247.
[202]#69 "The Imperfection of Human Knowledge," iii.3–5, 2:583–84.

abysmal nature of our ignorance moves us ever closer to the personal decision to trust in God. "A full conviction of our own ignorance may teach us a full trust in his wisdom."[203]

• *Resignation.* To learn from our ignorance is to develop a yielding spirit, as Jesus in Gethsemene.[204] Our limits as human beings are finally brought to deepest awareness in the reality and fact of death. There we come absolutely to terms with our finitude. There we are given the most complete opportunity to learn to say: "Yet not my will, but yours" (Luke 22:42).[205]

"As thinking is the act of an embodied spirit, playing upon a set of material keys, it is not strange that the soul can make but ill music when her instrument is out of tune." Aware that "finite cannot measure infinite . . . there always will be something incomprehensible, something like Himself, in all his dispensations. We must therefore be content to be ignorant, until eternity opens our understanding."[206]

Of the Gradual Improvement of Natural Philosophy

Survey of the Wisdom of God in the Creation, or a Compendium of Natural Philosophy

In his Introduction to the *Compendium of Natural Philosophy*[207] (later published under the title "Of the Gradual Improvement of Natural Philosophy"), Wesley distinguished two phases of natural philosophy: "speculative philosophy ascends from man to God; practical descends" from God to creatures. The issues of natural philosophy "ascend from the consideration of man through all the order of things, as they are farther and farther removed from us, to God the center of all knowledge."[208]

Wesley consistently challenged the modern prejudice that assumed all significant scientific discoveries are recent, and the ancients had little knowledge of the natural world. The arts of genetics, chemistry, and glassmaking were studied and "in some measure known long ago. But . . . cultivated in our age, with far greater accuracy." The microscope could not have been a recent invention; rather it should be regarded as a reinvention. The evidence for this is a tiny fifteen-hundred-year-old seal of France," which to the naked eye presents only a confused group; but surveyed with a microscope, distinctly exhibits trees, a river, a boat, and sixteen or seventeen persons."[209] "It is commonly supposed that our age has a vast advantage over antiquity" in the study of the human body. "But this will bear a dispute. For . . . the chief of our hypotheses are not new, but known long ago," and in truth the modern studies often "terminate in mere conjectures."[210]

There are two ancient traditions of inquiry: the Hebraic, which views the visible world in relation to its Creator; and the Greek, which seeks to discover "the material causes of natural

[203]#69 "The Imperfection of Human Knowledge," iv., 2:585; CH 7:96f.
[204]#69 "The Imperfection of Human Knowledge," iv. 2:584–86.
[205]#69 "The Imperfection of Human Knowledge," iv.2, 3, 2:585–86.
[206]Letter to Mrs. Elizabeth Bennis, Oct. 28, 1771, LJW 5:284.
[207]1777, following the work of Charles Bonnet of Geneva, 3d American edition, notes by B. Mayo, 2 vols. (New York: N. Bangs and T. Mason, 1823; cf. B1:60, 90–91; 3:108, 272; B1:91f.; 2:362–65, 394, 571–76.
[208]"Of the Gradual Improvement of Natural Philosophy," 1, XIII:482.
[209]"Of the Gradual Improvement of Natural Philosophy," 11–19, XIII:485–86.
[210]"Of the Gradual Improvement of Natural Philosophy," 23, XIII:487.

things."[211] Among Greek schools, the subject of divinity became the special preoccupation of the Platonists, logic of the Paripatetics, morality the Stoics, and sensuality the Epicureans. The medieval scholastics neglected what was commendable in Aristotle, and tended "to obscure and pollute all philosophy with abstract, idle, vain speculation. Yet some of them, after the Arabians had introduced the knowledge of chemistry into Europe, were wise above the age they lived in," notably the thirteenth-century Franciscan Roger Bacon, and the Dominican Albertus Magnus.[212]

Later Francis Bacon (1561–1626) grasped "the defects of the school philosophy, incited all lovers of natural philosophy to a diligent search into natural history . . . by many experiments and observations."[213] From this followed William Harvey's seventeenth-century discovery of the circulation of the blood, John Pecquet's study of the thoracic duct, and other experiments in genetics and blood transfusion. Physicians have made such discoveries concerning the human body as to provide a providential reason to theodicy even for diseases: "In diseases themselves, the wonderful wisdom of the Author of nature appears; and by means of them many hidden recesses of the human frame are unexpectedly discovered."[214]

The divisions of natural inquiry may be conveniently seen in relation to the elements of air (as in the discovery of the barometer, thermometer, and air-pump), earth (geology, telescopy, the study of sunspots, planet motions, and the Milky Way, and various cosmic theories from Ptolemaic to post-Copernican), fire (as in the discovery of gunpowder and phosphorus), and water (as in the diving bell and submarine, and attempts to convert salt water into freshwater uses).[215]

In the attempted ascent of philosophical reflection from humanity to spiritual creation and finally to God, "we can neither depend upon reason nor experiment," but do well ultimately to turn to the wisdom of Scripture. "Here, therefore, we are to look for no new improvements; but to stand in the good old paths; to content ourselves with what God has been pleased to reveal."[216]

On Human Understanding

Remarks Upon Mr. Locke's Essay on Human Understanding, 1781

"For some days I have employed myself on the road in reading Mr. Locke's *Essay*," a "solid, weighty treatise" that shows evidence of a "deep fear of God." When compared to "the glittering trifle of Montesquieu," Locke is like gold.[217] "That all our ideas come from sensation or reflection, is fully proved."[218]

The following *mistakes of Locke*, upon which the Remarks focus, Wesley

---

[211]"Of the Gradual Improvement of Natural Philosophy," 2, 3, XIII:482.
[212]"Of the Gradual Improvement of Natural Philosophy," 4, 5, XIII:483.
[213]"Of the Gradual Improvement of Natural Philosophy," 6, XIII:483; cf. JJW 7:162; LJW 3:5n.
[214]"Of the Gradual Improvement of Natural Philosophy," 11, XIII:484.
[215]"Of the Gradual Improvement of Natural Philosophy," 18–21, XIII:486.
[216]"Of the Gradual Improvement of Natural Philosophy," 24, XIII:487.
[217]"Remarks Upon Mr. Locke's Essay on Human Understanding," XIII:455–56; cf. Richard E. Brantley, *Locke, Wesley, and the Method of English Romanticism* (Gainesville: Univ. of Florida Press, 1984). For more of Wesley's reflections on Locke, see JJW 3:179; 4:192; B2:571n, 589n; 3:361–62; LJW 1:136; 2:314; 7:228.
[218]"Remarks Upon Mr. Locke's Essay on Human Understanding," XIII:455–56.

thought to be compensated by many useful reflections.[219]

Aristotle's simpler threefold division of the mind into apprehension, judgment, and discourse is a more accurate account than Locke's account of perception, judgment (which includes discerning, comparing, compounding, and abstracting), and memory. Pleasure determines the will as often as pain. Desire must be distinguished both from the enjoyment of pleasure and the avoidance of pain.

Locke wrongly argued that a person's body undergoes dramatic changes within a lifetime that essentially obscure the person's continuing identity. Rather, it is the soul of man that gives animation and unity to the body. "I call Cato the same person all his life, because he has the same soul. I call him the same man, because he has the same body too, which he brought into the world."[220] Wesley disagreed with Locke's inference that "Socrates asleep and Socrates awake is not the same person." Absurdly, "Mr. Locke thinks, 'consciousness makes personal identity;' that is, knowing I am the same person, makes me the same person. . . . Does knowing I exist, make me exist? No; I am before I know I am."[221]

Locke's "grand design was . . . to drive Aritsotle's Logic out of the world, which he hated cordially, but never understood."[222] Wesley doubted that Locke ever read the fifteenth- and sixteenth-century "Schoolmen" against whom he railed. He too readily abandoned the usefulness of logic, judging its use by its abuse. Rightly used logic is the best means "to prevent or cure the obscurity of language. To divide simple terms according to the logical rules of division, and then to define each member of the division according to the three rules of definition, does all that human art can do, in order to having a clear and distinct idea of every word we use."[223]

The Present Times

The Hubris of Modernity

In "An Estimate of the Manners of the Present Times," Wesley presciently anticipated the spirit of modernity by describing a world without God. "See here the grand cause (together with intemperance) of our innumerable nervous complaints!" "How many, even young, healthy men, are too lazy either to walk or ride! . . . They waste away in gentle activity." Our "luxury increases sloth, unfitting us for exercise either of body or mind . . . And how many does a regular kind of luxury betray at last into gluttony and drunkenness; yea, and the lewdness too of every kind?"[224]

If there is a God, according to reductive naturalism, he " 'set this whirligig a-spinning,' he left it, and everything therein, to spin on its own way. Whether this is right or no, it is almost the universal sentiment of the English nation. . . . They do not take God into their account; they can do their whole business without him. . . . They take it for granted, that the race is to the swift, and the battle to the strong . . . [and] impute all to natural causes. . . . We talk indifferently on everything that comes in the way; on everything—but God. If any one were to name him in good company, with any degree of seriousness, suppose at a Gentleman or

---

[219]"Remarks Upon Mr. Locke's Essay on Human Understanding," XIII:455.
[220]"Remarks Upon Mr. Locke's Essay on Human Understanding," XIII:459.
[221]"Remarks Upon Mr. Locke's Essay on Human Understanding," XIII:458.
[222]"Remarks Upon Mr. Locke's Essay on Human Understanding," XIII:460.
[223]"Remarks Upon Mr. Locke's Essay on Human Understanding," XIII:462.
[224]"An Estimate of the Manners of the Present Times," 1, XI:156.

Nobleman's table, would not they all stand aghast? Would not a profound silence ensue, till some one started a more agreeable subject?"[225]

In his "Thoughts Upon Baron Montesquieu's Spirit of Laws," 1781, Wesley challenges Montesquieu's self-admiration, faddism, and rationalistic "air of infallibility, as though he were the Dictator not only of France, but of Europe." [226] Aesthetically, he "touches none of the passions," "gives no pleasure . . . to a thinking mind." "The more I study, the less I comprehend . . . I verily believe he did not comprehend [his own words] himself." Worse, he takes "every opportunity to depreciate the inspired writers."[227] "Other talents he undoubtedly had; but two he wanted—religion and logic." Compared to Pascal, Malebranche, or Locke, Montesquieu is infantile.[228]

Natural History

[*Arminian Magazine, 1782, V:546–48]*

Many of Wesley's critical thoughts on geological and natural history are found in his "Remarks on the Count de Buffon's 'Natural History,' " 1782.[229] Decades before Darwin's research, Wesley agreed with the Count that many parts of the earth were once covered with the sea for many ages; that strata were formed; and that stones were once a soft paste.[230]

Yet Wesley argued pithily against the hypotheses that the earth is "only a slice of the sun, cut off from it by the stroke of a comet"; that the inner core of the earth is glass; and that the sea covered *the whole earth* for many ages ("I think this is highly improbable; though it has doubtless covered many parts of it for some time"); that there is no final cause or purpose in natural history; that in most beings there are fewer useful or necessary organs than those that are useless or redundant; that there is no essential difference between vegetables and animals; that the world existed from eternity; and that the world was created by chance. On these grounds he ranked the Count "far beneath Voltaire, Rousseau, and Hume, (all of whom acknowledge the being of a God) in religion as in understanding."[231]

Natural Religion: An Assessment of Hinduism

In his "Remarks on Mr. H.'s 'Account of the Gentoo Religion in Hindustan,' " 1774,[232] Wesley offered a critique of a romanticizing admirer of Hindu religion. He was especially skeptical regarding the extreme antiquity claimed for Hinduism. It should be remembered that consequent upon his Georgia mission, Wesley could plausibly take on the role of having some practical expertise in comparative religion.[233] Who else among his readers had dealt hands on with the noble savage? "Are these twelve articles of his creed 'the fundamental points of [natural] religion?'. . . I never met with an Amer-

---

[225]"An Estimate of the Manners of the Present Times," 13–16, XI:160–61.
[226]"Thoughts Upon Baron Montesquieu's Spirit of Laws," XIII:415.
[227]"Thoughts Upon Baron Montesquieu's Spirit of Laws," XIII:415.
[228]"Thoughts Upon Baron Montesquieu's Spirit of Laws," XIII:416.
[229]B2:588n.
[230]"Remarks on the Count de Buffon's 'Natural History,' " XIII:448–51.
[231]"Remarks on the Count de Buffon's 'Natural History,' " XIII:455.
[232]Cf. LJW 6:118; B2:381n.
[233]JJW 1:156–62, 236–39, 248–50, 297f., 346, 406–9; 3:449; 4:52; 5:226, 496; 8:289, 317; LJW 1:201-3; 8:24; B11:502.

ican Indian who believed half of them."[234]

The fantasy of metempsychosis,[235] the transmigration of souls through extensive regions of purification, and the account of the creation (with the earth sitting on the head of a snake on the back of a tortoise)[236] shows that "They that do not believe the Bible will believe anything."[237] The lack of external verification suggests that these claims are to be ranked with the fairy tales.[238] It is circular reasoning to argue that the antiquity of the writing is proved by the tradition that they were perpetuated in antiquity.

Whereas once the Wesleys had held the "Mystic Divines . . . in great veneration, as the best explainers of the gospel . . . we are now convinced, that we therein greatly erred, not knowing the Scriptures, neither the power of God."[239] The Mystics would edify us by a "solitary religion," not troubling about outward works, but only "to work virtues in the will. . . . Directly opposite to this is the gospel of Christ. Solitary religion is not to be found there. 'Holy solitaries' is a phrase no more consistent with the gospel than holy adulterers. The gospel of Christ knows of no religion, but social; no holiness but social holiness."[240]

FURTHER READING

Mystical Experience and the History of Religions

Brigden, Thomas E. "The Wesleys and Islam." PWHS 8 (1911): 91–95.

Turner, E. E. "John Wesley and Mysticism." MR 113 (1930): 16–31.

van Valin, Howard F. "Mysticism in Wesley." AS 12 no. 2 (1958): 3–14.

Wilson, David D. "John Wesley's Break with Mysticism Reconsidered." PWHS 35 (1965): 65–67.

————. "John Wesley, Gregory Lopez and the Marquis de Renty." PWHS 35 (1966): 181–84.

————. "John Wesley and Mystical Prayer." LQHR 193 (1968): 61–69.

Reason and Authority

Cragg, C. R. *Reason and Authority in the Eighteenth Century.* Cambridge Univ. Press, 1964.

Frost, Stanley B. *Authoritäteslehre in den Werken John Wesleys.* München: Ernst Reinhardt, 1938.

Lacy, H. E. "Authority in John Wesley." LQHR 189 (1964): 114–19.

Stoeffler, F. Ernest. "The Wesleyan Concept of Religious Certainty—Its Prehistory and Significance." LQHR 33 (1964):128–39.

"Wesley's Epistemology." WTJ 10 (1975): 53–55.

Wesley and Philosophical Wisdom

Barber, F. L. "Wesley's Philosophy." *Biblical World.* 54 (1920): 142–49.

---

[234]"Remarks on Mr. H.'s Account of the Gentoo Religion in Hindustan," XIII:407.
[235]LJW 2:279.
[236]"Remarks on Mr. H.'s Account of the Gentoo Religion in Hindustan," XIII:404.
[237]"Remarks on Mr. H.'s Account of the Gentoo Religion in Hindustan," XIII:408.
[238]"Remarks on Mr. H.'s Account of the Gentoo Religion in Hindustan," XIII:405.
[239]HSP 1739 Preface, 1, XIV:319; see also his "Thoughts Upon Jacob Behmen (Boehme)," 1780, IX:509–14, and "A Specimen of the Divinity and Philosophy of the Highly-Illuminated Jacob Behmen," IX:514–19, on the limits of speculative mysticism; cf. LJW 3:332–38; 5:105–6; JJW 3:17, 282; 4:411; 5:46, 521; SS 1:240; B2:48n.
[240]HSP 1739 Pref. 4, 5, XIV:321. For Wesley's ambivalent reflections on mysticism, see LJW 1:289, 243; on kinds of mysticism, see JWO 252; on Quietism, see LJW 1:276; on the poison of mysticism, see JJW 5:28; JWO 45f., 63, 375f., 394. On the French mystical writers, see comments on Madame Guyon, JJW 3:18; 5:382f.; 6:130; 7:319; LJW 5:341f.; 6:39, 42–44, 125, 233; 8:18; on Madame Antoinette Bourignon, see LJW 7:66, 126; JJW 1:170, 191f.; 2:15f.; 6:11; 8:277; and Marquis Gaston de Renty, see B1:36, 61, 75, 344; 3:166f., 627; JJW 1:414, 450; LJW 4:184, 264, 293, 321; 5:129, 268, 271; 7:127.

Cannon, Wm. R. "Methodism in a Philosophy of History." MH 12 no. 4 (1974): 27–43.

Eayrs, George. *John Wesley: Christian Philosopher and Church Founder*. London: Epworth, 1926.

Eckhart, Ruth Alma. "Wesley and the Philosophers." MR 112 (1929): 330–45.

Fox, Harold G. "John Wesley and Natural Philosophy." *University of Dayton Review* 7 no. 1 (1970): 31–39.

Matthews, Rex D. " 'Religion and Reason Joined': A Study in the Theology of John Wesley." Th.D. diss., Harvard University, 1986.

_____. " 'We Walk by Faith, not by Sight': Religious Epistemology in the Later Sermons of John Wesley." Paper privately circulated.

Outler, A. C. *Theology in the Wesleyan Spirit*. Chap. 1 "Plundering the Egyptians," Nashville: Tidings, 1975, pp. 1–23.

Shimizu, Mitsuo. "Epistemology in the Thought of John Wesley." Drew Ph.D. diss., 1980 (revised for publication in Tokyo, 1993).

Thorsen, Donald. WQ, 169–201.

EXPERIENCE

Through experience one may "observe a plain, rational sense of God's revealing himself to us, of the inspiration of the Holy Ghost, and of a believer's feeling in himself the mighty working of the Spirit of Christ."[241]

The Necessity and Limits of Experience in Religious Affirmations

"And here properly comes in, to confirm this scriptural doctrine, the experience of the children of God—the experience not of two or three, nor of a few, but of a great multitude which no man can number. . . . It is confirmed by *your* experience and *mine*. The Spirit itself bore witness to my spirit that I was a child of God, gave me an evidence hereof, and I immediately cried, 'Abba, Father!' And this I did (and so did you) before I reflected on, or was conscious of, any fruit of the Spirit."[242]

In the Aldersgate experience, Wesley reported: "I felt my heart strangely warmed. I felt I did trust in Christ, Christ alone for salvation. And an assurance was given me, that he had taken away *my* sins, even mine, and saved me from the law of sin and death."[243]

In the events leading to the Aldersgate experience, Wesley's dialogue with Peter Böhler focused upon the close interconnection between "Scripture and experience." When Böhler argued that true faith would have "two fruits inseparably attending it, 'dominion over sin and constant peace from a sense of forgiveness,' " Wesley looked for it first in Scripture, where he found this abundantly attested. Yet he did not feel it inwardly. In this situation he was "forced to retreat" to the criterion of experience, not admitting it to be true " 'till I found some living witnesses of it.' He replied he could show me such at any time; if I desired it, the next day. And accordingly the next day he came again with three others, all of whom testified, of their own personal experience, that a true living faith in Christ is inseparable from a sense of pardon," and that this faith was "the free gift of God; and that he would surely bestow it upon every soul who earnestly and perseveringly sought it."[244]

The criterion of experience[245] pertains especially to the inner testimony of the assurance of salvation. No words "will adequately express what the children of God experience . . . an inward

---

[241]FA I, v.24, 11:167.

[242]#11 "The Witness of the Spirit," II, iii.6, 1:290.

[243]JJW 24 May 1738, sec. 14, I:475.

[244]JJW 24 May 1738, sec. 12, I:471–72.

[245]For further reference to Christian experience, see B1:154, 293, 297, 323; JWO 79f., 191–94, 209–19; 387f., 392f.; CH 7:3.

impression on the soul, whereby the Spirit of God directly witnesses to my spirit, that I am a child of God . . . a consciousness of our having received, in and by the Spirit of adoption, the tempers mentioned in the word of God. . . . A consciousness that we are inwardly conformed, by the Spirit of God, to the image of his Son."[246] This consciousness is offered as a birthright for all believers.[247]

Wesley witnessed in his own experience the truth of Christian doctrine: "I now am assured that these things are so: I *experience* them in my own breast. What Christianity (considered as a doctrine) promised is accomplished in my own soul."[248] Experience is more modestly viewed as the *appropriation of scriptural authority,* than the source of authority,[249] as in some forms of pietism.[250]

Wesley's critique of Francis Hutcheson focused on his inability to make intercorrelations with the multiple criteria of "Scripture, reason, and experience."[251] "That it *is* the Divine Spirit 'who worketh in us both to will and to do of his good pleasure,' of this, *experience, and reason, and Scripture* convince every sincere inquirer," which is God's "particular method of working."[252]

On Spiritual Senses

Spiritual knowledge is discerned with spiritual senses.[253] "Our ideas are not innate, but must all originally come from our senses." But there are *two types of senses: natural senses and spiritual senses,*[254] the latter "to discern spiritual good and evil. It is necessary that you have the *hearing* ear and the *seeing* eye . . . that you have a new class of senses opened in your soul, not depending on organs of flesh and blood, to be 'the *evidence* of things not seen,' as your bodily senses are of visible things, to be the avenues to the invisible world, to discern spiritual objects, and to furnish you with ideas of what the outward 'eye hath not seen, neither the ear heard.' And till you have these internal senses, till the eyes of your understanding are opened, you can have no apprehension of divine things, no idea of them at all . . . as you cannot reason concerning colours if you have no natural sight . . . so you cannot reason concerning spiritual things if you have no spiritual sight."[255]

Wesley argued that *"a great work of God"* was underway in the revival on the basis of "common sense. I know it by the evidence of my own eyes and ears. I have seen a considerable part of it; and I have abundant testimony, such as excludes all possible doubt, for what I have not seen."[256]

---

[246]#10 "Witness of the Spirit," I, i.6, 7, 1:273–74.

[247]#18 "Marks of the New Birth," ii.3, 1:423.

[248]Letter to Conyers Middleton, Jan. 4, 1749, ii.12, LJW II:383; italics added.

[249]C. Williams, JWTT, 33, italics added; cf. LJW 1:172; 3:137; 5:17; 6:129, 132, 136; SS 2:349.

[250]For Wesley's visit to Halle to meet the son of August Herman Francke, "whose name is indeed as precious ointment, Oh may I follow him, as he did Christ," see JJW 2:58; 2:16f.; cf. JJW 1:116, 121, 124.

[251]JJW V:382, Dec. 17, 1772, in reference to Hutcheson's *Essays on the Passions*; see also B3:279–81, 483f.; 4:158f.

[252]#140 "The Promise of Understanding," i.3, 4:284, italics added.

[253]On Wesley's spiritual theory of perception, see JWO 190f., 209f., 293–95, 395f.; B11:46f.

[254]For Wesley's physical theory of perception, see JWO 284f., 475f., 487f.

[255]EA sec. 32, 11:55–56.

[256]Letter to the author of *The Enthusiasm of Methodists and Papists Compar'd* (Bishop George Lavington), sec. 32, II:374; cf. B2:526–31; 3:452–53.

"I do not undervalue traditional [rationalistic apologetic] evidence. . . . And yet I cannot set it on a level with this"—the inner witness of the Spirit with our spirits that we are children of God. "Traditional evidence is of an extremely complicated nature, necessarily including so many and so various considerations that only men of strong and clear understanding can be sensible of its full force. On the contrary, how plain and simple is this! And how level to the lowest capacity! Is not this the sum? 'One thing I know: I was blind, but now I see.' An argument so plain that a peasant . . . may feel its force."[257]

On Living Without God

Eph. 2:12: "Without God in the world." [Homily #130 1790 B4:169–76 J#125 VII:349–54]

The Parable of the Toad

Wesley developed a curious, almost comic, metaphor of a creature receiving renewed capacity to see and hear the world: The plight of the person "without God in the world" is compared to the condition of a very large toad discovered inside the core of an ancient oak tree. When the tree was split open, the frog inside was found sightless, having never had any sensory experience whatever of the visible world.

The sensory deprivation of the ungodly life is set forth by analogy with such a creature who indeed possesses eyes, but has no sight, and no exercised practice of seeing; who has senses such as hearing, but has remained totally destitute of any actual sensations.

Lacking sensation, there is no reflection, memory or imagination.[258]

The parallel is between this sequestered creature and the person who is living "without God in the world," having no sense of God.[259] Like the toad who was "shut up from the sun, moon, and stars, and from the beautiful face of nature; indeed from the whole visible world, as much as if it had no being,"[260] such a person has no experience whatever of the invisible world upon which to reflect, no memory or imagination concerning any spiritual reality. Such is the deprived condition of the sensory apparatus in which the spiritual senses have remained entirely undeveloped, as in the practical atheists, who have "not the least sight of God, the intellectual Sun, nor any the least attraction toward him,"[261] who have never once had "God in all their thoughts."[262] Like the toad, the atheist—without God in the world—lives as though the spiritual world had no being. "He has not the least perception of it; not the most distant idea."[263]

The Receiving of Spiritual Senses in the New Birth

New life in the Spirit is like receiving a new sensory capacity, so that one can see with newly opened eyes that he has "an Advocate with the Father," can hear the voice of one who is the Resurrection, *feel* the love of God "shed abroad in his heart."[264]

The moment the Spirit strikes his heart, God breaks the hardness of the heart, like the splitting of the oak tree. All things become new. The sun of

---

[257] Letter to Conyers Middleton, LJW II:383–84.
[258] #130 "On Living Without God," sec. 5, 4:179.
[259] #130 "On Living Without God," sec. 5–7, 4:170.
[260] #130 "On Living Without God," sec. 3, 4:170.
[261] #130 "On Living Without God," sec. 8, 4:171.
[262] #130 "On Living Without God," sec. 7, 4:171.
[263] #130 "On Living Without God," sec. 8, 4:171; LJW 4:60; 7:263.
[264] #130 "On Living Without God," sec. 11, 4:173.

righteousness appears, revealing "the light of the knowledge of the glory of God in the face of Jesus Christ" (2 Cor. 4:6).[265] Like being born, his eyes now see, his ears now hear. He is able to taste how gracious the Lord is, how "Jesus' love is far better than wine."[266] He is consumed with the ecstatic joy of enjoying and using his entire sensory apparatus to soak up knowledge and love of God through all available means: reason, nature, and above all the history of revelation.[267]

"This change from spiritual death to spiritual life is properly the new birth,"[268] which empowers such a fundamental change of heart (not merely a conceptual shift of ideas) that the entire sensory apparatus is awakened to a new way of living and sensing the reality at hand. The new birth and the filling of the Spirit are like the splitting open of the ancient tree, while the old closed-down self is seen by analogy to the ensconced condition of the sinner, withdrawn from the exercise of all capacities of the spiritual senses.[269] To respond in faith to grace is to become a new creature in Christ.[270] One moves from the spheres of natural appetite and tedious morality to new life in the Spirit.[271]

Experiential Excess

That there are dangers in overemphasizing experience was made clear in "Thoughts on the Writings of Baron Swedenborg," where Wesley directly disputed many ideosyncratic ideas of that popular writer that were troubling

some in his societies: that God cannot be angry; that creation was not *ex nihilo*; that those who die go through three states before they enter either heaven or hell, providing instruction and discipline for reprobates; that angels were once human beings; that hell is merely symbolic; that there is still time for repentance in hell; that Scripture is full of blasphemy; that all who believe in the Trinity are possessed of the devil; that the Nicene Creed gave "birth to a faith which has entirely overturned the Christian church."[272]

The grand error of Baron Swedenborg was in his rejection of the triune teaching in favor of his own private experiencing. All of this is best explained in relation to Swedenborg's own account that "in the year 1743 the Lord was pleased to manifest himself to me in a personal appearance . . . to enable me to converse with spirits and angels; and this privilege I have enjoyed ever since."[273]

As if this were not enough to cast doubt on Swedenborg, Wesley wryly added an account of the "very serious Swedish Clergyman," Mr. Mathesius, who reported an incident when Swedenborg became "totally delirious . . . ran into the street stark naked, proclaimed himself the Messiah, and rolled himself in the mire. I suppose he dates from this time his admission into the society of angels."[274]

The Nature of Enthusiasm
Acts 26:24: "Paul, thou art beside thyself." [Homily #37 1750 B2:44–60 J#32 V:467–79]

[265] #130 "On Living Without God," sec. 9, 4:172.
[266] #130 "On Living Without God," sec. 9–11, 4:172–73.
[267] Letter to Elizabeth Ritchie, Jan. 17, 1775, LJW 6:136.
[268] #130 "On Living Without God," sec. 11, 4:173.
[269] #130 "On Living Without God," sec. 9–11, 4:172–73.
[270] #130 "On Living Without God," sec. 12, 13, 4:173–74.
[271] #130 "On Living Without God," sec. 14–16, 4:174–76.
[272] "Thoughts on the Writings of Baron Swedenborg," XIII:429.
[273] "Thoughts on the Writings of Baron Swedenborg," XIII:425.
[274] "Thoughts on the Writings of Baron Swedenborg," XIII:426.

"A religion of form . . . performed in a decent, regular manner" will not provoke others to say, as they said of Paul, "Much religion hath made you mad." The religion of the heart where one is "alive to God, and dead to all things here below" may prompt others to pass the sentence: *Thou art beside thyself.*[275]

"Enthusiasm" is a term sometimes used to refer either to a divine impulse that for the moment suspends reason and sense,[276] or to an uncommon ability in which the natural faculties are elevated to a higher degree than normal, rather than suspended.[277] It is more popularly viewed as a disorder of the mind that shuts the eyes of the understanding, which greatly hinders the exercise of reason, as a species of madness where one draws right conclusions from wrong premises.[278]

While true religion manifests the spirit of a sound mind, enthusiasm is "a religious madness arising from some falsely imagined influence or inspiration of God; at least, from imputing something to God which ought not to be imputed to him, or expecting something from God which ought not to be expected from him."[279] Enthusiasm talks loosely as if God were acting directly within the self without any correctives of scripturally informed reasoning.[280] Enthusiasts "undervalue the experience of almost every one in comparison" with their own.[281]

Types of Enthusiasm

Wesley distinguished four sorts of enthusiasts:

- "Those who imagine they have grace which they have not," so as to result in pride, excessive sentimentality, and distance from the mind of Christ. The imaginary Christian with a distempered brain may think himself as the champion of faith. He must be encountered directly and admonished about his self-deception.[282]

  He warned them, "Ah, poor self-deceivers! Christians ye are not. But you are enthusiasts in an high degree. Physicians, heal yourselves. But first know your disease: your whole life is enthusiasm, as being all suitable to your imagination."[283] He warned Thomas Maxfield against "overvaluing feelings and inward impressions . . . and undervaluing reason, knowledge, and wisdom in general."[284]

- Among other enthusiasts are "Those who imagine they have such gifts from God as they have not" and feel they are "directed by the Spirit when they are not." Some think they can defy laws of nature or prophesy the literal future, or feel that God is dictating the very words they say when they are carrying out their own private wars, as sometimes seen in faith healers, mediums, sorcerers, and fortune-tellers, who imagine they are receiving particular directions from God even in the most trifling circumstances of life. Meanwhile, God has given us reason as a guide, though never excluding the

[275]#37 "The Nature of Enthusiasm," sec. 1, 2:46; Acts 26:24; Rom. 6:11.
[276]#37 "The Nature of Enthusiasm," sec. 8, 2:48.
[277]#37 "The Nature of Enthusiasm," sec. 9, 2:49.
[278]#37 "The Nature of Enthusiasm," sec. 10–11, 2:49; JJW 2:130; B1:267–68; 2:587–88; 2:44-60; 1:269–70; FA 11:96–98; cf. 11:354–56, 361–74, 382–83; 468–81, 491–95; LJW 2:204–6; CH 7:199.
[279]#37 "The Nature of Enthusiasm," sec. 12, 2:50.
[280]Answer to Thomas Church, VIII:405–13; LJW 2:204–11, 241f.
[281]Letter to Mrs. Ryan, June 28, 1766, LJW 5:17–18. Cf. Wesley's comments on Montanus, B1:76, 268; 2:461, 555; LJW 2:357, 360; 4:133, 327–29, 336.
[282]#37 "The Nature of Enthusiasm," sec. 13–17, 2:50–52.
[283]#37 "The Nature of Enthusiasm," sec. 17, 2:52.
[284]Letter to Thomas Maxfield, Nov. 2, 1762, LJW 4:193.

quiet assistance of the Holy Spirit to aid the understanding. Christians pray for the Spirit to illumine their perception of the will of God by the power of the Spirit.[285]

- Then there are those enthusiasts "who think they attain the end without using the means, by the immediate power of God." Some imagine they can understand Scripture without studying it. They are often found speaking in public without any premeditation.[286]

- Finally, there are those enthusiasts who fantasize effects as acts of providence, which are not, meanwhile often ignoring the general providence that is available to all.[287]

The Steady Weeding of Emotive Excess

Several practical inferences follow: Each one should examine his own life for signs of excess.[288] Enthusiasm breeds pride and self-deception. It may block persons from the actual grace of God, and from seeking the good counsel of faithful friends.

It is best not even to use the volatile word "enthusiasm" unless one has studied to understand the psychological dynamics of self-deception.[289] "Think before you speak." Do not label others unfairly as enthusiasts.[290] Apply "the plain Scripture rule, with the help of experience and reason, and the ordinary assistance of the Spirit of God" to discern the will of God, using the "ordinary channels of his grace,"[291] expecting to grow daily in pure and holy

religion, so as to be deserving of the charge of enthusiasm in a positive sense, and avoiding the sort of enthusiasm that is "merely nominal Christianity."[292]

Whether Inward Feelings Confirm Saving Faith According to Scripture

In "A Letter to Dr. [Thomas] Rutherforth," Regius Professor of Divinity at Cambridge, March 28, 1768 (B9:373–88, J XIV, 347–59, LJW V, 357–69), Wesley replied to Anglican charges that Methodists reject the aid of human learning, exaggerate inward feelings and divine assurances. Wesley argued that his sentiments on Christian experience during the "last thirty years" (1738–68) had been consistent, with "few, if any, *real* contradictions," though there may have been "some *seeming* contradictions, especially considering I was answering so many different objectors."[293]

Wesley's position: (1) "Few, but very few, Christians have an *assurance* from God of *everlasting salvation*," apostolically termed the "plerophory, or full assurance of hope." (2) "More have such an *assurance* of being *now in the favour of God* as excludes all doubt and fear." (3) "A *consciousness of being in the favour of God . . .* is the common privilege of Christians." "Yet I do not affirm, there are no exceptions to this general rule. Possibly some may be in the favour of God, and yet go mourning. . . I have not for many years

---

[285]#37 "The Nature of Enthusiasm," sec. 18–26, 2:52–56.
[286]#37 "The Nature of Enthusiasm," sec. 27, 2:56; *Plain Account of Christian Perfection*, XI:429–30.
[287]#37 "The Nature of Enthusiasm," sec. 28, 2:56.
[288]Letter to Bishop Warburton, LJW 4:358–59.
[289]Wesley himself had been charged with "enthusiasm," see B9:114–21, 182–83, 196–213, 228–29, 304–6.
[290]#37 "The Nature of Enthusiasm," sec. 39, 2:59.
[291]#37 "The Nature of Enthusiasm," sec. 38–39, 2:59.
[292]#37 "The Nature of Enthusiasm," sec. 39, 2:60.
[293]Letter to Dr. Rutherforth, LJW i.3, 9:375.

thought a consciousness of acceptance to be essential to justifying faith."[294]

Then he summarized the position he had held for "above these forty years" (at least since 1728) on the role of "*inward feelings*"[295] in religious knowledge: "(1). The fruit of [the Spirit's] *ordinary influences* are love, joy, peace, long-suffering, gentleness, meekness. (2). Whoever has these, *inwardly feels* them. And if he understands his Bible, he discerns from whence they come. Observe, what he inwardly feels is *these fruits themselves; whence they come* he learns from the Bible."[296] "By 'feeling' I mean being inwardly conscious of."[297] "I look upon some of these bodily symptoms [in reference to fits and tears] to have been preternatural or diabolical, and others to have been effects which in some circumstances naturally followed from the strong and sudden emotions of mind . . . springing from gracious influences."[298]

Wesley appealed to Article XVII of the Thirty-nine Articles, which teaches that "godly persons *feel in themselves the working of the Spirit* of Christ, mortifying the works of the flesh . . . and drawing up their mind to high and heavenly things."[299]

Whether Scriptures Are Subordinate to Private Revelation

In "A Letter to a Person Lately Joined with the People called Quakers,"[300] 1748, Wesley states his objection to the teaching of the premier Quaker theologian Robert Barclay that private revelations "are not to be subjected to the examination of the Scriptures," and that "the Scriptures are not the principal ground of all truth," but are secondary and "subordinate to the Spirit."[301] Rather "the Scriptures are the rule whereby [the Spirit] leads us into all truth. Therefore, only talk good English: call the Spirit our guide, which signifies an intelligent being, and the Scriptures our rule, which signifies something used by an intelligent being."[302] The Scriptures are the measuring rod for examining all, real or supposed, revelations.

The inordinate focus upon private revelation may tempt toward "flat justification by works,"[303] toward antipathy toward reasoning, toward a form of worship that is reduced to quietism, toward neglect of the singing of psalms, toward the complete elimination of visible signs in baptism and the Lord's Supper, toward ordination without the laying on of hands, and toward prohibitions against swearing before magistrates, and any form of kneeling or bowing. Those who have "an honest heart, but a weak head," are called to abandon such trifles, and return to "spiritual, rational, scriptural religion."[304]

FURTHER READINGS ON EXPERIENCE

Bence, Clarence L. "Experimental Religion." *Preacher's Magazine.* 56 no. 1 (1980): 50–51.

---

[294]Letter to Dr. Rutherforth, LJW i.4, 9:375–76.

[295]Cf. B11:399, 492; EA 11:35; LJW 4:359; 6:18.

[296]Letter to Dr. Rutherforth, LJW iii.1, 9:381.

[297]FA Part I, V.2, 11:139–40.

[298]Letter to Dr. Rutherforth, LJW iii.12, 9:387.

[299]Art. XVII, Thirty-nine Articles, DSWT 117; italics added, 9:384.

[300]For further reference to Quakers, see LJW 2:116–28; 4:123; B2:265; 3:257, 260, 589; FA 11:171f., 254–60, 290.

[301]A Letter to a Person Lately Joined with the People called Quakers, 3, X:178.

[302]A Letter to a Person Lately Joined with the People called Quakers, 3, X:178.

[303]A Letter to a Person Lately Joined with the People called Quakers, 7, X:179.

[304]A Letter to a Person Lately Joined with the People called Quakers, 15, X:187.

Brown, Robert. *John Wesley's Theology: The Principle of Its Vitality and Its Progressive Stages of Development*. London: Jackson, Walford and Hodder, 1865.

Dieter, Melvin. "John Wesley and Creative Synthesis." AS 39 no. 3 (1984): 3–7.

Dreyer, Frederick. "Faith and Experience in the Thought of John Wesley." *Am Hist. Rev.* 88 no. 1 (1983): 12–30.

Garrison, R. Benj. "Vital Interaction: Scripture and Experience." RL 25 (1956): 563–73.

Gunter, W. Steven. *The Limits of Divine Love: John Wesley's Response to Antinomianism and Enthusiasm*. Nashville: Kingswood, Abingdon, 1989. Chap. 1 "Enthusiasm"; chap. 5 "Quest for Certainty"; chap. 9 "John Wesley as Improper Enthusiast"; and chap. 10 "More Heat Than Light."

Langford, Thomas. *Practical Divinity: Theology in the Wesleyan Tradition*. Nashville: Abingdon, 1982. "Theology of Experience"; chap. 8 "Brightman to Rall."

Lindström, Harald. *Wesley and Sanctification*. Nashville: Abingdon, 1946. "Experience in Wesley's Theology," 1ff.

Monk, Robert C. *John Wesley: His Puritan Heritage: A Study of the Christian Life*. Nashville: Abingdon, 1966. "Experience," 70ff.

Starkey, Lycurgus. *The Work of the Holy Spirit*. Abingdon, 1962. "Freedom of the Holy Spirit and Authority of Christian Faith," 140ff., also 15ff.

Williams, Colin. *John Wesley's Theology Today*. Nashville: Abingdon, 1960. "Authority and Experience," 23ff.

THE CATHOLIC SPIRIT

The Premise of Tolerance: Heart Ecumenism

Catholic Spirit

2 Kings 10:15: "Is thy heart right?" [Homily #39 1749 B2:79–96 J#34 V:492–504 JWO:91ff.]

Can Christians be of one heart even if they have differing opinions? The text for the homily on the catholic spirit is *"If your heart is as my heart then give me your hand"* (2 Kings 10:15), regarding the meeting between the ruthless Jehu and the religious fanatic Jehonadab. Sensing that Jehonadab might be a valuable asset, Jehu asked: "Are you in accord with me, as I am with you?" When Jehonadab[305] answered: "I am," Jehu replied: "If so, give me your hand" (2 Kings 10:15). Wesley was not here concerned with the mixed motives of Jehu, but the form of reconciliation of human estrangement that is due not to intellectual agreement, but goodwill, a "right heart." The major thesis is that we may be of one heart, even though not of one opinion.[306] Human barriers are overcome by the love of God and humanity, which reaches beyond human antipathies and cultural differences.

Honoring Legitimate Freedom to Hold Diverse Opinions

However dissimilar may be our cultural, moral, or religious opinions, persons of goodwill may become united by grace in trusting affection. Partisan disputation usually fails to grasp how hearts can be knit together despite conceptual, cultural, political, and economic differences. Persons holding divergent opinions and shaped by different modes of thinking and worship may still be joined in love, warmth, and mutual affection. Wesley's teaching on this text offers a decisive clue to the affectionate-tolerationist ethos of the Methodist movement.[307]

As inveterate sinners, we are forever prone to shortsightedness in the formation of our opinions. The knowing process is shaped by our social location, our

---

[305]With whom Wesley had good reason to identify. Jehonadab was the biblical type of one who had vowed to live always in tents away from a corrupt civilization, abstain from wine and strong drink, and struggle against idolatry, SS I:128.
[306]JJW 3:178–80; B9:31–34, 125f., 254f., 285f.; LJW 2:110.
[307]LJW 3:35, 180–83.

way of looking at the world from a highly particular historical and class status. Thinking emerges always out of highly circumstantial and culture-specific contexts. This is always how we think—out of a specific egocentric, ethnocentric history. None of us can know with full adequacy just how much our social prejudices shape our present vision. Conceptual and social differences in religion are an unavoidable consequence of our finitude, dullness of human understanding, and lack of empathy. There is in Wesley an unremitting critique of petty prejudice and social bias. He was aware that Christian teaching is always expressed through changing, variable social memories.

By "opinions" he meant ideas nonessential for Christian teaching, adiaphora neither commanded nor forbidden by Scripture that could be matters of free interpretation without straining the limits of genuine Christianity.[308] From his mother, Wesley had inherited a Puritan resistance to inflexible use of religious language; from his father a stubborn Anglican loyalty to the ancient Christian consensus of faith. However deeply committed to classic Christian essentials,[309] he resisted the notion that they could be captured in a single unalterable linguistic form. As lifelong editor he was tempted to revise any sentence he read, even those he himself had earlier written, a habit that suggests

he did not view any particular expression excepting the original sacred text as final or absolute.

Love the Core of True Religion

The essential core of true religion is "as I have loved you, so you must love one another" (John 13:34).[310] "This is love: not that we loved God, but that he loved us and sent his Son as an atoning sacrifice for our sins" (1 John 4:10).[311] "True religion is right tempers toward God and man. It is, in two words, gratitude and benevolence: gratitude to our Creator and supreme Benefactor, and benevolence to our fellow creatures. In other words, it is the loving God with all our heart, and our neighbour as ourselves."[312]

There remain "grand, general hindrances" to the practice of such love: "We can't all think alike" hence do not walk alike.[313] "So long as 'we know' but 'in part,' " all of us "will not see things alike," as an "unavoidable consequence of the present weakness and shortness of human understanding."[314] It is characteristic of human finitude that every one "necessarily believes that every particular opinion which he holds is true (for to believe any opinion is not true is the same thing as not to hold it)."[315] "But although a difference in opinions or modes of worship may prevent an entire external union, yet

---

[308]WQ 161.

[309]Stated clearly in #7 "The Way to the Kingdom," i.6; and his Letter to a Roman Catholic, 1749. For his distinction between opinion and essential (or fundamental) Christian teaching, see LJW 5:224; 4:297; 2:110; 7:216; 8:47; B1:175, 508; 2:374–76; 3:588; 4:146; JWO 77f., 99f.; JJW 3:178–80; B9:31–34, 125f., 254f., 285f.

[310]Correlated definitions of true religion include the mind of Christ, B9:527, and the restoration of the image of God in humanity, B9:255.

[311]B1:530; 3:389, 313, 448, 585f.; 4:57, 66f.; B9:502.

[312]#120 "The Unity of the Divine Being," sec. 16; cf. EA sec. 1, 11–45.

[313]#39 "Catholic Spirit," proem.3, 1:82.

[314]#39 "Catholic Spirit," i.3, 1:83.

[315]#39 "Catholic Spirit," i.4, 1:83–84.

need it prevent our union in affection?"[316]

Wesley's golden rule of toleration: "Every wise man therefore will allow others the same liberty of thinking which he desires they should allow him."[317] We do well to hold opinions in good conscience but not impose them unilaterally upon one another as if to make every minor opinion a test case of religious principle.[318]

Respect for Conscience

Wesley was appealing to the freedom to hold opinions, even peculiar ones, that do not dislodge the heart of Christian teaching. It is possible to embrace another affectionately who has a different persuasion. Amid the multiplicity of sentiments and inclinations there remains room for the address of conscience, for each one finally must stand before God.[319]

No one should seek to rule the conscience of another. I must not impose upon your conscience what my conscience is attesting to me. Better, rather, to seek inwardly a heart of sincerely penitent faith, leaving plenty of room for candid consultation, the free interplay of ideas, and a tolerance for alternative pathways. "Everyone must follow the dictates of his own conscience in simplicity and godly sincerity . . . then act according to the best light he has."[320] "I dare not therefore presume to impose my mode of worship on any other. I believe it is truly primitive and apostolical. But my belief is no rule for another."[321]

From this there follows a spirit of proportional tolerance that has become deeply written into the Wesleyan evangelical ethos. On matters of opinion, "we think and let think."[322] This tradition helped establish and refine the Anglican tradition of toleration, and the Reformation achievement of "the right of private judgment,"[323] especially in its pietistic phase, where sincerity of the heart became just as highly valued as detailed confessional agreement. The bands and societies did not come together on the basis of strict doctrinal concurrence, but active repentance.

Challenging Latitudinarianism

The catholic spirit must not be confused either with latitudinarianism on the one hand or partisan bigotry on the other. Wesley was concerned about valid argument and defensible exegesis concerning classic consensual teaching, which he called the old catholic faith, but less intent upon specific doctrinal definition of minutiae that do not come from the heart of faith.[324]

This does not imply that anything goes, or that doctrine is diminished in importance. Wesley strongly resisted the indifferentism that he termed "speculative latitudinarianism"—an indifference to all opinions,[325] "the spawn of hell, not the offspring of heaven," "being 'driven to and from, and tossed about with every wind of doctrine.'" That is "a great curse, not a blessing;

---

[316]#39 "Catholic Spirit," i.4, 1:82.
[317]#39 "Catholic Spirit," i.6, 1:84.
[318]JJW 7:389.
[319]EA 11–19, VIII:6–8, 124–28, 206–7.
[320]#39 "Catholic Spirit," i.9, 1:85; 2 Cor. 1:2; cf. Letter to Rev. Mr. Potter, Nov. 4, 1758, IX:88–89.
[321]#39 "Catholic Spirit," i.11, 1:86.
[322]B2:59, 341, 376; 4:145; JJW 7:389.
[323]#39 "Catholic Spirit," i.10, 1:86; cf. V:136.
[324]Letter to Adam Clarke, Sept. 10, 1756, XIII:213–15.
[325]B2:92f.; B4:312; JWO 101f., 306.

an irreconcilable enemy, not a friend to true catholicism. A man of a truly catholic spirit has not now his religion to *seek*. He is fixed as the sun in his judgment concerning the main branches of Christian doctrine," though "always ready to hear and weigh whatsoever can be offered against his principles." Some think they have a catholic spirit but only have "a muddy understanding; because your mind is all in a mist; because you have no settled, consistent principles, but are for jumbling all opinions together. . . . Go first and learn the first elements of the gospel of Christ, and then shall you learn to be of a truly catholic spirit."[326]

Nor is the catholic spirit a practical latitudinarianism—an indifference as to public worship.[327] Anglican "latitudinarians" appealed to an age weary of religious controversy. While remaining in the Church of England, they attached minimal importance to distinct doctrinal definition, sacramental practice, and church discipline, appealing to reason and toleration, and promoting only irenic pluralism. They formulated Christian teaching always in minimalist terms. This was a view that Wesley sharply distinguished from the catholic spirit.

How the Sincerity of the Catholic Heart Is Tested

There is a brilliant device in the homily on the Catholic Spirit by which Wesley tested sincerity of the catholic heart. It is a series of questions asking whether one has become personally accountable to the core of Christian teaching, paragraphs i.12–18. Pivotal to the structure of the homily, it includes fifty-three questions to be put soberly

not to the head but to the heart. How do I assess whether "my heart is as your heart"? Instead of a confessional approach that would say, "Here are confessional definitions on which we must agree," Wesley calmly addressed the hearer with a powerful series of highly personal questions, treating the uprighted heart as a matter of intense personal self-examination. This is a different approach to theological truth-telling than is typical in the more confessionally focused Reformed traditions.

These self-examination questions have a triune structure and sequence: The first series of issues for self-appraisal deals with God the Father, the second with Christ and salvation, and the third with the work of the Holy Spirit. Questions are raised from the heart to the heart. First concerning God the Father, each one is to ask himself inwardly: Is God experienced by me as eternal? Incomparably just and merciful?[328] Secondly, concerning God the Son, am I justified by faith in his atoning action on the cross, or do I expect my own works to justify me?[329] Thirdly, concerning God the Spirit, am I receptive to God's own working to bring justifying grace to a full personal expression of maturity?[330]

Having one's heart right before God is not simply an emotive matter that can brush aside scriptural doctrine, but requires pressing these questions with inward intensity and honesty. Wesley was arguing for doctrinal purity manifested in "catholic love," not for doctrinal pluralism.[331]

It is only by answering accountably a cascade of fifty-three profoundly doctrinal and personal questions that one

---

[326]#39 "Catholic Spirit," iii.1, 2:93, italics added.
[327]#39 "Catholic Spirit," iii.1, 1:92.
[328]#39 "Catholic Spirit," i.12, 1:87.
[329]#39 "Catholic Spirit," i.13, 1:87.
[330]#39 "Catholic Spirit," i.14–18, 1:88–89.
[331]#39 "Catholic Spirit," i.14–18, 1:88–89; Hymns and Spiritual Songs, 21st ed., 1777, Preface, XIV:338–39.

comes to discover whether one's heart is right with God and rightly prepared for the openness of faith active in love. Each question is asked in God's presence as attested by the inner court of conscience. What matters is less getting a correct objective answer than whether one's conscience attests a serious, probing self-appraisal.[332]

An Invitation to True Catholicity

If your heart, thus defined, is right with God, then extend to me your hand. This is an invitation to fellowship not based on moral rules or opinions, but inward self-examination of the rightness of one's heart in the presence of God.[333] If your heart is as my heart, we are invited by the Spirit to be joined together into a bonded society of persons whose lives are committed to radical accountability to God. Though some read the catholic spirit as if to imply that doctrinal standards [334] are minimized, or that there are insignificant confessional boundaries in this life that we share with God in Christ, this is hardly the intention of Wesley's text. By "give me your hand," "I mean, first, love me" with a "very tender affection," "closer than a brother," as a "companion in the kingdom." "Love me with the love that 'is not provoked' either at my follies or infirmities, or even at my acting (if it should sometimes so appear to thee) not according to the will of God. Love me so as to 'think no evil' of me." Love me with "the love that 'covereth all things,' " that " 'believeth all things,' that is

always willing to think the best, to put the fairest construction on all my words and actions," hoping "to the end that whatever is amiss will, by the grace of God, be corrected."[335]

One whose heart is in accord with another will show his care by interceding for the other that shortcomings may be amended to better fulfill God's will, by stirring the other to good works, to acts of mercy, and loving not in word only but in deed and truth.[336] Such is the catholic spirit, not a spirit that seeks first to identify right doctrine, though assuming it, but that seeks to reach out in dialogue,[337] good conscience, faith, and fervent intercession for the partner in dialogue. "With open arms the world embrace, but cleave to those who cleave to thee."[338]

To a Roman Catholic

In "A Letter to a Roman Catholic," Wesley gives us a model of what is meant by the catholic spirit. Himself often accused of being a papist by those who viewed his doctrine of sanctification as too close to the Council of Trent,[339] Wesley shared typical Anglican anxieties about Rome as a foreign power intent upon curbing English liberties. Yet he became aware during his Irish visits of 1747 and following that Catholics showed up frequently in Methodist preaching services, and were ready to hear. This letter seeks to go beyond Catholics and Protestants "looking on the other as monsters."[340] Even "allowing both sides to retain our own opinions," he asked for "the soft-

---

[332]Minutes, May 13, 1746, VIII:288–89.
[333]#39 "Catholic Spirit," ii.1, 1:89.
[334]For a fuller discussion of Wesleyan doctrinal standards, see Oden, *Doctrinal Standards in the Wesleyan Tradition* (Grand Rapids: FAP, Zondervan, 1988); cf. JJW 4:32; 8:70–71.
[335]#39 "Catholic Spirit," ii.3, 4, 1:90–91.
[336]#39 "Catholic Spirit," ii.5–7, 1:91.
[337]LJW 3:180.
[338]Charles Wesley, "Catholic Love," *Poetic Works*, VI:71–72.
[339]Cf. LJW 4:140; 6:371; 7:7; JJW 2:469; 3:409.
[340]A Letter to a Roman Catholic, X:80; JWO 492.

ening [of] our hearts toward each other." "I do not suppose that all the bitterness is on your side. I know there is too much on our side also. So much that I fear many Protestants (so-called) will be angry at me, too, for writing to you," thinking you deserve no special treatment. "But I think you do . . . deserve the tenderist [sic] regard I can show, were it only because . . . the Son of God has bought you and me with his own blood."[341]

"I am not persuading you to leave or change your religion, but to follow after that fear and love of God without which all religion is vain."[342] "A true Protestant believes in God" and "loves his neighbour (that is, every man, friend of enemy, good or bad) as himself, as he loves his own soul, as Christ loved us. . . . This, and this alone, is the old religion. This is true primitive Christianity. O when . . . shall it be found both in us and you?"[343] "Then if we cannot as yet *think alike* in all things, at least we may *love alike* . . . let us resolve, first, not to hurt one another . . . secondly . . . to speak nothing harsh or unkind of each other. The sure way to avoid this is to say all the good we can, both of and to one another . . . thirdly, resolve to harbour no unkind thought, no unfriendly temper towards each other . . . fourthly, endeavour to help each other on in whatever we are agreed leads to the Kingdom."[344]

A Caution Against Bigotry

Mark 9:38: "We saw one casting out devils in thy name." [Homily #38 1750 B2:61–78 J#33 V:479–92]

Why Bigotry Is an Offense Against the Catholic Spirit

Wesley vividly envisioned a demonic element in human divisions and tendencies to dissociation. He spoke with unnerving realism about the Adversary's efforts to divide human beings into enemy camps. Who but the devil could so enjoy needling, segregating, disjoining, and alienating? The catholic spirit wants to reach out, mend, transcend difference, include, welcome and embrace. Its opposite, the spirit of bigotry, is divisive, exclusive, and self-righteous.[345]

Alert to tragic deficits in his own English culture, Wesley was also aware of the ingrained egocentricity that pervades all human cultures. He himself had been through culture shock, having spent two years[346] in frontier polyglot America, and knew something about cross-cultural dialogue. He beheld bigotry in every society he knew. He had an especially vivid memory of the slave trade in Savannah and of the custom of native American Indians in Georgia in roasting their prisoners to death.[347]

He was deeply concerned about the genocides of his time. He specifically speaks of the extermination of whole nations not only by pagans and Muslims, but supposedly Christian Spanish, Dutch, and English. He did not have an Anglo-centric, but rather a cross-cultural, conception of bigotry. He was deeply aware that it pervaded the English and American cultures in which he himself had ministered. Surveying the barbarity of his own society, Wesley cited a long list of the ways in which

---

[341] A Letter to a Roman Catholic, JWO 493–94.
[342] A Letter to a Roman Catholic, sec. 13, JWO 496.
[343] A Letter to a Roman Catholic, sec. 14, JWO 498.
[344] A Letter to a Roman Catholic, sec. 13–17, JWO 496–99. For other references to Roman Catholic teaching, see B1:77–79, 87, 128f., 508; 2:292, 374f., 581; 3:450f.
[345] #38 "A Caution Against Bigotry," i.2, 1:64; cf. LJW 1:200; 2:300; 4:367.
[346] Feb 5, 1736–Dec. 22, 1737.
[347] #38 "A Caution Against Bigotry," i.9, 1:67.

this disease had contaminated his own national environment.[348]

Prejudice Reproved: Do Not Stop the Well-doer

Wesley made an ardent plea for reconciling narrowly embittered partisanships.[349] The *bigot* is defined as one who has too strong an attachment to or fondness of his own party, opinion, church, in–group, race, or religion.[350] Bigotry is excessive partisanship, an inordinate sense of the rightness of one's own causes and interests, based on too sharp a distinction between us and them, of an in-group and out-group, which tempts constantly toward prejudice.[351] It is an inveterate, diabolical proneness to narrow partisanship. The bigot mercilessly views the other party in the worse light.[352]

The problem of incipient bigotry among the faithful is that they hesitate to admit that others who have widely different opinions could also have the same faith and be recipients of the same Spirit. Thus bigotry is seen as an offense against the catholic spirit and as a counterindication of catholicity.[353] The text for this homily is the episode in which the disciples discovered a man *"driving out demons in your name and we told him to stop, because he was not one of us"* (Mark 9:38)—"us" meaning not one of the Twelve, though apparently a believer, acting in Jesus' name, and accomplishing what the disciples had been unable to do. "Casting out demons" becomes in this homily a broad metaphor for any concrete, helpful, redemptive activity.[354]

Remember that it was Jesus' own disciples in this case who were the bigots, saying hysterically: "They are not following us; they are so different from us."[355] Wesley deplored the frequency with which the we/they, in-group/out-group momentum distorts human perceptions. We see things from the vantage point of *us*, from the vantage point of maleness or femaleness. Nationals see the truth from the nexus of special national values and memories. Long before Marx, Wesley recognized that social location remains a constant temptation to bias. He was keenly aware of the obstacles to transcending one's own special economic interests.[356]

How the Spirit of Bigotry Is Tested

If this is how human egocentricity reasons, how does the Lord reason? How are we rightly to respond when we see demons cast out by one whose opinions are politically incorrect or biased or ill-informed? Wesley insists that we must first become aware of our own

---

[348]#38 "A Caution Against Bigotry," i.10, 1:67.

[349]Having been charged by Anglicans with excessive zealotry and disregard for parish boundaries, Wesley replied to Bishop Joseph Butler: "I am a priest of the church universal. And being ordained a Fellow of a College, I was not limited to any particular cure, but have an indeterminate commission to preach the word of God in any part of the Church of England." Henry More, Wesley, I:465; 1:61n. Arguing that valid ministry should be measured by its fruits rather than merely by its form, on March 28, 1739, he wrote: "I look upon *all the world as my parish*," 25:616.

[350]#38 "A Caution Against Bigotry," iv.1, 1:76.

[351]Especially, in his setting, prejudices with respect to plausible experiential evidences of the work of God in the revival, B2:84; 3:515; FA 11:280–81, 515f.

[352]#38 "A Caution Against Bigotry," i.1–14, 1:64–68.

[353]"A Plain Account of the People Called Methodists," v, VIII:257.

[354]#38 "A Caution Against Bigotry," proem.1–3, 1:63–64; cf. #33 "Sermon on the Mount XIII," 1:687–92, a caution against false prophets; and LJW 2:351; 3:348.

[355]#38 "A Caution Against Bigotry," ii.1, 1:69, paraphrased.

[356]#38 "A Caution Against Bigotry," i.3–14, 1:65–68.

bigotry, of the ways in which we ourselves are often unwilling to allow the benefit of the doubt to others who view the world from a different history of valuing.[357]

Jesus' injunction: Do not hinder others from using whatever power God has given them. Do not be quick in judgment. When you and I differ, you pray for me that my gift may be used of God, and I will pray that yours will. " 'Do not stop him,' Jesus said. 'No one who does a miracle in my name can in the next moment say anything bad about me, for whoever is not against us is for us. I tell you the truth, anyone who gives you a cup of water in my name because you belong to Christ will certainly not lose his reward' " (Mark 9:39–41).

Those who belonging to Christ offer acts of mercy in his name, who are being led by the Spirit who elicits faith active in love, will not go badly wrong with their words if their hearts are right.[358] So do not think it your major business to undermine a miracle done in Christ's name by one out of your own fold. Do not dump out the water of mercy offered in Christ's name because a different language is used. Look carefully toward the correspondence between others' behavioral outcomes and their doctrinal teachings. Insofar as they correspond, the rule of Gameliel applies, that God is at work in the correspondence. Let God be the judge of it.[359]

One's Own Bigotry Examined

The homily concludes with a thoughtful self-examination seeking to track the steps of one's own bigotry. Wesley asks tough, personal questions: Are you sorry when God blesses someone who holds erroneous views? Suppose you were to see a Roman Catholic or Unitarian offering a cup of cold water in Christ's name so as to cast out the demonic spirit of human egocentricity. Insofar as the fruits of the Spirit are manifested through constructive personal change, you do well not to forbid him lest you sentence yourself as guilty of bigotry.[360]

The best exercise in transcending bigotry is to pray for the one different from you. Rejoice in his gifts. Enlarge his good work. Speak well of the different one. Show him kindness.[361]

Even if you must bear the brunt of another's bigotry, do not be bigoted in return. Do not imagine that another's intolerance justifies your own. Let him have all the bigotry to himself. If he speaks evil of you, speak all manner of good of him. Do not be phony or pretend to like what you do not like, but look for whatever is truly good in the one who is dissimilar.[362]

This spirit of proximate toleration is deeply written into the Wesleyan evangelical revivals, which like the Anglican ethos was more a culture of consent than dissent. Its successors have not manifested a tradition dominated by church trials or petty divisiveness or constant ideological combat. It is a rich jewel forever subject to becoming misplaced.[363]

FOR FURTHER READING

Theological Method

Coppedge, Allan. "John Wesley and the Issue of Authority in Theological Pluralism." In

---

[357]#38 "A Caution Against Bigotry," iii, 1:73–75.
[358]Letter to John Newton, April 9, 1765, LJW 4:293.
[359]#38 "A Caution Against Bigotry,' " iii.1–10, 1:73–75.
[360]#38 "A Caution Against Bigotry," iv.2–4, 1:77.
[361]#38 "A Caution Against Bigotry," iv.5, 1:77.
[362]#38 "A Caution Against Bigotry," iv.6, 1:78; cf. 1:253; 3:315, 588.
[363]"Advice to the People Called Methodists," 1745, 9:123–31; VIII:351–59.

A Spectrum of Thought. Wilmore: Francis Asbury Publishing Co, 1982.

Dunning, Ray. "Systematic Theology in a Wesleyan Mode." WTJ 17 no. 1 (1982): 15–22.

Maddox, Randy L. "Responsible Grace: The Systematic Perspective of Wesleyan Theology." WTJ 19 no. 2 (1984): 7–22.

Matthews, Rex D. " 'Religion and Reason Joined': A Study in the Theology of John Wesley." Th.D. diss., Harvard University, 1986.

Moore, Robert L. *John Wesley and Authority: A Psychological Perspective.* Missoula: Scholars Press, 1979.

Outler, A. C. *The Wesleyan Theological Heritage, Essays.* Edited by T. Oden and L. Longden, Grand Rapids: FAP, Zondervan, 1991.

Reddish, Robert O. *John Wesley, His Way of Knowing God.* Evergreen, Colo.: Rorge Publishing Co., 1972.

Shimizu, Mitsuo. "Epistemology in the Thought of John Wesley." Ph.D. diss., Drew University, 1980.

Thorsen, Donald A. D. *The Wesleyan Quadrilateral: Scripture, Tradition, Reason, and Experience as a Model of Evangelical Theology.* Grand Rapids: FAP, Zondervan, 1990.

Doctrinal Standards

Beet, Joseph Agar. "The First Four Volumes of Wesley's Sermons." PWHS 1913, 9:86–89.

Collins, Kenneth. *John Wesley on Salvation.* Grand Rapids: FAP, Zondervan, 1989. "On Reading Wesley's Sermons: The Structure of the Fifty-three Standard Sermons, Ordo Salutis Displayed in the Sermons," 129–39.

Cushman, Robert E. *John Wesley's Experimental Divinity: Studies in Methodist Doctrinal Standards.* Nashville: Kingswood, Abingdon, 1989.

Davies, Rupert E. "Our Doctrines." Chap. 5 in Vol. 1 *A History of the Methodist Church in Great Britain.* 147–79. London: Epworth, 1965.

————. "The People of God." LQHR 184 (1959): 223–30. On Methodist doctrines.

Heitzenrater, Richard. *Mirror and Memory: Reflections on Early Methodism.* Nashville: Kingswood, Abingdon, 1989.

Hughes, Henry Maldwyn. *Wesley's Standards in the Light of Today.* London: Epworth, 1921. Also in *London Q Rev.* 128 (1917): 214–34.

Lockyer, Tho. F. "What Are 'Our Doctrines'?" *London Q Review* 134 (1920): 46–63.

Neely, Thomas. *Doctrinal Standards of Methodism.* New York: Revell, 1918.

Oden, Thomas C. *Doctrinal Standards in the Wesleyan Tradition.* Grand Rapids: FAP, Zondervan, 1988.

Ogden, Schubert M. "Doctrinal Standards in the United Methodist Church." *Perkins Journal* 28 (Fall 1974).

Redd, Alexander. *Problem of Methodism Reviewed: or, John Wesley and the Methodist Standards Defended.* Mt. Sterling, Ky.: Advocate Publishing Co., 1893.

Rowe, G. Stringer. "A Note on Wesley's Deed Poll." PWHS 1 (1897): 37, 38.

Simon, John S. "John Wesley's Deed of Declaration." PWHS 12 (1919): 81–93.

Warren, Samuel. "Statement of the Principal Doctrines of Wesleyan Methodism." In Vol. 1 of *Chronicles of Wesleyan Methodism,* 3–30. London: John Stephens, 1827.

West, Anson. "The Doctrinal Unity of Methodism." In *The Methodist Episcopal Church in the U.S.,* 245–55. New York: Phillips and Hunt, 1885.

Catechetics

MacDonald, James A., ed. *Wesley's Revision of the Shorter Catechism.* Edinburgh: Geo. A. Morton, 1906.

McGonigle, Herbert. "Wesley's Revision of the Shorter Catechism." PM 56 no. 1 (1980): 59–63.

The Articles of Religion

Blankenship, Paul F. "Wesley's Abridgment of the Thirty-nine Articles as Seen From His Deletions." MH 2 no. 3 (1964): 35–47.

Harmon, Nolan B., and John W. Bardsley. "John Wesley and the Articles of Religion." RL 22 (1953): 280–91.

Wheeler, Henry. *History and Exposition of the Twenty-five Articles of Religion of the Methodist Episcopal Church.* New York: Eaton and Mains, 1908.

3

Creation, Providence, and Theodicy

THE GOODNESS OF CREATION

Wesley's teachings on creation and providence are concentrated in his homilies on "God's Approbation of His Works," "Of Divine Providence," "The Wisdom of God's Counsels," a discourse "On God's Sovereignty," and a series on spiritual creatures. They serve as his extended comment on that article of religion that confesses that God is *"maker and preserver of all things, both visible and invisible."*[1]

Admittedly, Wesley is seldom remembered as one who had momentous reflections on creation or providence. My modest purpose is to show that he did in fact deal with these loci responsibly, and in some ways astutely.

God's Approbation of His Works

Gen. 1:31: "It was very good." [Homily #56 1782 B2:387–99 J#56 VI:206–15]

Everything is created "good in its kind." Viewed potentially and developmentally, each creature as created is "suited to the end for which it is designed; adapted to promote the good of the whole, and the glory of the great Creator."[2]

God's Enjoyment of the Goodness of Primordial Creation

What is created, insofar as given by God, is truly good in every way. *"God saw all that he had made, and it was very good"* (Gen. 1:31). The creation is not by design constitutionally prone to perversion. It becomes distorted only through the exercise of freedom. Wesley evidenced no temptations toward either Manichean or Neoplatonic anti-materialism. There is nothing that resembles gnostic fantasies of creation itself as incorrigibly dragging the soul downward. Creation is good. God heartily approves of his own work in giving time, space, and life proportionally to diverse creatures.[3]

Creation Fallen

Scripture distinguishes sharply between the good of creation before sin and the fallenness of creation after sin.

---

[1] Art. 1.
[2] #56 "God's Approbation of His Works," proem.1, 2:387; cf. B1:513–16; 2:387–99, 437–50, 537f., 552f.; 4:25f., 42f., 63f., 69f., 153f., 307f.
[3] #56 "God's Approbation of His Works," 2:387–99; LJW 6:91.

As created, each creature is fit to promote the good of the whole.[4] *As fallen*, the good of the whole has become grossly skewed and scrambled. We live out of a lengthy history of sin that has taken this good creation and brought it to the lost condition in which human history is now enmeshed.[5]

No one now lives in that original unsullied creation. Sadly, we meet created being always in broken, fragmented ways, never in undefiled primal goodness. We live in a creation originally given as good yet now fallen through a history of idolatry, pride, sensuality, and twisted imagination.[6]

Fallenness comes logically and chronologically only after creation, not as if embedded within creation or necessitated by creation. Creation as such remains good insofar *as created*, even after the Fall.

Since no finite creature was there at the creation, all creatures with physical eyes have a limited understanding of creation. We can nonetheless hypothesize the goodness of original creation based upon its fragmented forms of goodness in the present order of experience. We can believe in that hypothesized original goodness because it is clearly attested in Scripture.[7]

We who now behold fallen creation are always already entangled in a protracted history of sin. Each discrete creature is always more prone to see his or her own private good more clearly than goods of the whole or the infinite Source of the whole good. Our perception of the created order is thus forever limited not merely because we are creatures, but creatures configured by a grim history of sin.

Unpolluted Air, Earth, Water, and Energy: An Ecological Axiom

We find in Wesley an uncommonly high doctrine of the original goodness of unfallen physical creation. Original creation as such is "very good," having no admixture of evil, insofar as received from the hand of God.

Using arguments from both reason and revelation, Wesley surveyed the knowable created order in a way that encompassed its basic constituent physical elements—the subtle combinations and variations of earth, air, fire, and water—comprising all forms of the created order in their specific permutations.[8] Each and all together were regarded as good as originally given, "all essentially distinct from each other, and yet so intimately mixed together in all compound bodies that we cannot find any, be it ever so minute, which does not contain them all."[9]

By *earth* the ancients symbolically pointed to all palpable matter, all physical, non-liquid, non-gaseous creation. We are given the physical environment as a gift for our stewardship. As created the earth is filled with unadulterated, untainted creaturely goods. As such, it is beautiful, though when distorted by sin it can be terrifying.[10] There was originally no pollution in the *air*, and

---

[4]LJW 3:333–35.

[5]"Doctrine of Original Sin," IX:191f.

[6]*A Collection of Hymns for the Use of the People Called Methodists*, The Goodness of God, 7:107–29.

[7]B2:387–99, 437–50, 537f.; 4:25–26, 42–43, 63–64.

[8]B2:383–90, 504–8, 573–74; 4:136–37.

[9]#56 "God's Approbation of His Works," i.1, 2:388.

[10]B2:389–90, 506–8, 573–74; LJW 4:282–87; cf. L. Starkey, *The Work of the Holy Spirit*, "The Order of Creation," 39f.

the *water* supported abundant forms of sea life.[11]

By *fire* we point to all of the diverse particles of energy present in creation. There is a splendid balance of light and fire in the created order. The specific distance between the sun and the earth is a spectacular example of how God has offered the earth light and fire in exquisite proportion. The sun is a precisely balanced source of good for creatures who need light and heat in specific congruity and equilibrium. The relation of earth and light elicits a veritable celebration of God's goodness in the created order.[12]

Wesley goes much further. He ruminates almost ecstatically on the created excellence of all biological forms, vegetable and animal, sometimes embracing curious ideas about their original goodness. Reasoning out of scriptural testimony, he posited an untrammeled innocence in the unfallen natural order in its original perfection (lacking weeds and unpleasant insects, for example, where animals do not prey on one another). A world without sin is a place of incomparable happiness, since not spoiled by the slightest hint of twisted self-assertiveness.[13] By sleep,[14] which faintly refracts the primal condition belonging "to innocent human nature," "the springs of the animal machine were wound up from time to time."[15]

The Disordering of Creation

Intellectual elites often make the naïve mistake of assuming "that the world is now in the same state it was at the beginning." So the King of Castile imagined: "If I had made the world, I would have made it better," to which God replies: I "did not make it as it is now."[16]

This paradise became lost and fallen through idolatry, vanity, sensuality, and alienated imagination.[17] Human pride imagines that it could have done a far better job than God in ordering creation, and so fantasizes a reordering of all things according to its sinful imaginings. Out of this pretended improvement comes all manner of evil.[18]

The created world thus becomes distorted by intergenerational sin, as symbolized by the lengthening history of the progeny of Adam and Eve. The world we now see is not the originally good creation, but a world grossly distorted by the evil that freedom has collectively chosen and rechosen. God did not unilaterally insert this evil into the world, but freedom absurdly elected it. God gives freedom, and freedom absurdly debauches the goodness of creation.

The Free-Will Defense

The "free-will defense" stands staunchly against the pretense that God is the author of evil. World history is an accumulation of decisions in which each period affects subsequent periods, layer upon layer. "God made man upright," but man " 'found out to himself many inventions' of happiness independent of God."[19] We as a human species have outrageously worsened

---

[11]#56 "God's Approbation of His Works," i.2–5, 2:389–91; B2:390f., 505f.
[12]#56 "God's Approbation of His Works," i.7, 2:392.
[13]#56 "God's Approbation of His Works," i.8–14, 2:393–96.
[14]On sleep, see B2:134, 392; 3:267, 322–24; 4:110.
[15]#56 "God's Approbation of His Works," i:7, 2:392. In a letter to Hester Ann Roe, June 2, 1776, Wesley asked: "Do you commune with God in the night season? Does He bid you even in sleep, Go on? And does He 'make your very dreams devout'?" LJW 6:223.
[16]#56 "God's Approbation of His Works," ii.1, 2:397.
[17]B1:208; 2:561; 3:183f.; 4:341.
[18]#132 "On Faith," 4:190–97.
[19]#56 "God's Approbation of His Works," ii.3, 2:399; Eccl. 7:29.

creation through the licenses taken by idolatrous freedom. Consequently, the whole creation, the cosmos, the natural order now groans in travail. We have caused the cosmos to suffer.[20]

Manichaeans posited one good god who caused all goods, opposed by another evil god who caused all evils, with history viewed as the arena of eternal conflict of these two. There is not a hint of a Manichaean flavor in Wesley, for whom the creation as such was unambiguously *good*. Only after the fall of freedom, when creatures by their own self-determining freedom, bent toward pride and idolatry, fall, does a train of disastrous effects follow. Soame Jenyns wrongly assumed that "evil must exist in the very nature of things."[21] "It must, *in the present nature* of things, supposing man to have rebelled against God. But evil did not exist at all in the original nature of things."[22]

The fundamental goodness of creation remains despite all historical absurdities. God does not take away human liberty altogether, but allows it to play itself out in judgment, addressing it patiently with the call to repentance within the limits of time. Just because human freedom has botched and muddled creation does not mean that God accedes to the disarray. God persists amid the fallenness of human history to permit this corrupted chronicle to continue, patiently offering the promise of redemption to all who are fallen. The biblical testimony of heavenly bliss at the end of history echoes the primal vision of the genesis of untainted good in divine creation.[23]

Countering William Law's Quasi-Manichean Speculations

(To William Law, Jan. 6, 1756, LJW 3:332–70; IV:466–509)

How Bad Philosophy Attracts Bad Divinity

William Law's early works on Christian spirituality, on *Christian Perfection* (1726), and *A Serious Call to a Devout and Holy Life* (1728), had decisively influenced the young Wesley and his colleagues in the Oxford Holy Club. By 1735, however, Law had begun to read Jacob Boehme and delve into various versions of Protestant mysticism of dubious orthodoxy, influenced by theosophic gnosticism through Paracelsus and the left wing of the Reformation. After a decade of quiescence during the 1740s, William Law began to publish his thoughts on mysticism in *The Way to Divine Knowledge, The Spirit of Prayer* (1749–50), and *The Spirit of Love* (1753–54), in which he denigrated the church's means of grace, and substituted a gnostic cosmology and universalist mysticism, attesting a "Spirit of Christ" deeply hidden within every natural human being.

Baffled by the follies of his former mentor, by 1756 Wesley determined to write an "Open Letter" to Law, respecting his former views, but admonishing him against his foolish turn toward "superfluous, uncertain, dangerous, irrational, and unscriptural philosophy," that is so "often flatly contrary to Scripture, to reason, and to itself."[24] Remembering that Law had once admonished Wesley about spoiling religion with philosophy, Wesley now turned the tables by showing this is what Law was doing: "Reverend Sir,— In matters of religion I regard no writings but the inspired. Tauler, Behmen [Boehme], and a whole army of Mystic authors, are with me nothing to St. Paul . . . At a time when I was in great

---

[20]#56 "God's Approbation of His Works," ii.1, 2:397.
[21]"Free Inquiry Into the Nature and Origin of Evil," 1757, pp. 15–17, 108–9.
[22]#56 "God's Approbation of His Works," ii.2, 2:398–99.
[23]#56 "God's Approbation of His Works," ii.1–3, 2:397–99.
[24]LJW 3:332–33.

danger of not valuing this authority enough, you made that important observation: '. . . So far as you add philosophy to religion, just so far you spoil it.' This remark I have never forgotten. . . But have not you?''[25]

Wesley criticized Law's *speculations* under four headings: nature antecedent to creation, creation, Adam in Paradise, and the Fall. In each case he precisely quotes and refutes Law point by point, largely on the basis of scriptural texts. As to Law's view that "nature as well as God is antecedent to all creatures," Wesley inquired: "Is then nature God? Or are there two eternal, universal, infinite beings?"[26] As to the fantastic notion that "God brought gross matter" out of the "sinful properties" the fallen angels had imparted to nature, Wesley asks him to explain how physical elements as such can have either sin or virtue.[27] As to how the earthly body of Adam might have contained latent evil, Wesley asks: "Was there evil in the world, and even in Adam . . . at his first creation?" Wesley thought Law, in his cosmological speculations, had taken unconscionable liberties with both revelation and reason, had gone far beyond the plain sense of Scripture, and offered weak, inconsistent proofs.[28]

Countering a Hermaphrodite Anthropology

In Law's conjectures, Adam "had at first the nature of an angel," hence was "both male and female." Wesley questioned whether "angels are hermaphrodites," challenging Law's curious speculations that "Eve would not have been

had Adam stood," that Adam would have brought forth the Second Adam, Christ, without Eve, and that "Christ was both male and female."[29] As to the notion that Adam "lost much of his perfection before Eve was taken out of him," Wesley asks for some shred of textual evidence on which to ground such speculation.[30]

"Bad philosophy has, by insensible degrees, paved the way for bad divinity."[31] Disastrous repercussions follow from Law's loose suppositions: "You deny the omnipotence of God" by asserting an inexorable degeneration of spiritual nature into material nature. God is limited both before and after creation.[32] There is Manicheanism lurking in the notions that "Matter could not possibly be but from sin" and the human body is "curdled spirit."[33]

SPIRITUAL CREATION

God is giver not only of physical but also spiritual creation. Incorporeal spiritual powers are also creatures, not coeternal with God, but contingent entirely upon the gift of their creation. There is a radical difference between any creature and its creator.

Of Good Angels

Heb. 1:14: "Are they not all ministering spirits?" [Homily #71 1783 B3:3–15 J#71 VI:361–70]

Wesley offered two teaching homilies on angelic powers. He was not fixated on this issue, but did find attested in Scripture a range of spiritual creation located in the chain of being between corporeal humanity and uncreated di-

[25]Letter to William Law, proem, LJW 3:332.
[26]Letter to William Law, i.1, LJW 3:333–34.
[27]Letter to William Law, i.2, LJW 3:335–36.
[28]Letter to William Law, i.3–4, LJW 3:338–43.
[29]Letter to William Law, i.3–4, LJW 3:338–42.
[30]Letter to William Law, i.3–4, LJW 3:338–43.
[31]Letter to William Law, ii.1, LJW 3:343.
[32]Letter to William Law, ii.1, LJW 3:343–44.
[33]*The Spirit of Love*, Part I:23.

vinity. It would be a stupendous gap in
the order of creation if the universe had
inorganic matter, plant and animal life,
and human life growing in complexity
and spirituality, and then vaulted
through the heavens all the way from
human existence to God in the highest.
It is more plausible to assume that there
must be something in between.[34]

"There is one chain of being, from
the lowest to the highest point, from an
unorganized particle of earth or water,
to Michael the archangel. And the scale
of creatures does not advance *per sal-
tum*, by leaps, but by smooth and gentle
degrees; although it is true that these
are frequently imperceptible to our imperfect faculties."[35]

He found solace in the text from
Hebrews 1:14, which asks: "*Are not all
angels ministering spirits sent to serve
those who will inherit salvation?*" We
have now come to the decisive juncture
of discussing these incorporeal agencies
in the created order—not as to whether
they empirically can be shown to exist
(a fruitless way of putting the question
with respect to invisible creatures), but
as to their ministry, what they do.

It would seem tempting to skip over
this discussion of good and bad angels,
but whenever I have ventured (against
Bultmann's advice) to discuss these
matters with modern audiences, they
have found them exceptionally intriguing (quite apart from the expectations of
guild biblical scholarship about how
modern audiences are supposed to be
bored by such matters). This may seem
at first to be a quaint corner of Wesley's
thinking, but when we ask our own
blunt questions of him, empathizing
with his vocabulary and entering seri-

ously into it, his language becomes
surprisingly capable of registering plausibly in contemporary life.[36]

The Idea of Angels in the History
of Religion and Philosophy

These ministering spirits were widely
known and recognized in ancient
Greco-Roman poetry, philosophy, and
religion, in the ancient literature of
Socrates, Hesiod, Plato and Aristotle,
and virtually all the classical writers of
Greek antiquity, from whom we hear
frequent testimony concerning them.
These primitive writings were "crude,
imperfect, and confused. . . fragments
of truth, partly delivered down by their
forefathers, and partly borrowed from
the inspired writings."[37] They offered a
preliminary attempt to understand the
unseen ministering spirits who were to
be more fully attested gradually in unfolding salvation history. Though many
have had various opinions of angelic
creation, it is only in the history of
revelation that we obtain a reliable
picture of their ministrations.

The only way to grasp the intention
of God with respect to these non-empir-
ical, non-corporeal creatures, is to attend very closely to the text of Scripture, which provides "a clear, rational,
consistent account of those whom our
eyes have not seen or our ears heard."[38]
Wesley's argument for superpersonal
spiritual creatures comes from reason
illumined by revelation, using the wisdom of historic tradition, and from his
own experience in the evangelical revival as supporting evidence.[39] He is
content to let others argue about angels
from strictly rationalist or empiricist
premises.

---

[34]#71 "Of Good Angels," 3:4–15.
[35]#72 "Of Evil Angels," Pref. 1 3:16; cf #56 "God's Approbation of His Works," i.14.
[36]#71 "Of Good Angels," 3:4–7.
[37]#71 "Of Good Angels," Pref. 1, 3:4.
[38]#71 "Of Good Angels," Pref. 4, 3:6.
[39]CH 7:511–12; cf. 4:346–49; JJW 6:229.

Scriptural Testimony to Ministering Spirits

God has the power to work either immediately or mediately (through other than direct means). Through ministering spirits God has chosen to work through incorporeal spiritual beings, using them to endear us to God and to one another. God has endued them with "understanding, will, and liberty, essential to, if not the essence of, a spirit."[40] Angels can read the thoughts of human beings because they see their "kindred spirit more clearly than we see the body."[41] Their ministrations are grounded in this ability, which, having existed since creation, has accumulated wisdom from "surveying the hearts and ways of men in their successive generations."[42]

God is capable of making "winds his messengers, flames of fire his servants" (Ps. 104:4). They do not need bodies or physical magnitude to serve the Lord.[43] They enjoy extraordinary vision, but without physical eyes, with what seems to us an almost unlimited sight and perception. They communicate, yet without the sound of speech.[44] They have an extraordinary capacity to see many things at a glance that we corporeal observers miss, or do not see well or wholly. With intuitive brilliance they see at one glance the truth presented to them, as distinguished from our crude and laborious reasoning and data gathering processes. They have immediate intellectual apprehension, and the ability to penetrate human hearts. They know the hearts of those to whom they minister. They have a high degree of wisdom compared to our finite faculties.[45]

The angels are not just individually active, but belong to an ordered community. Those unfallen angels who celebrate God's life are found to be continually and intentionally ministering to our souls. Care of souls is the work of these ministering spirits. Our pastoral care is a participation in their ministry. Good angels work to enable our goodness, as ministers of God the Spirit. They have a guardianship role, especially to the faithful.[46]

Ministering spirits attend our souls, addressing us in our fallen condition, never flatly overwhelming human freedom or dictating terms. They work as persuasive, not coercive agents. The premise is synergistic, not monergistic. They counter and thwart the destructive work of evil spiritual powers. They work to overturn the intentions and effects of evil in myriad unperceived ways.

They minister in ways analogous to the best ministries of human agents of reconciliation, yet with greater agility and subtlety. Think of the best caregivers you know and that is something like the work of the ministering spirits of God. They minister quietly through interpersonal relationships, even when persons remain unaware of their ministries. The good angels minister not merely to the righteous, but also to the unrighteous, calling them to repentance and accountability, assisting in the search for truth.[47]

They work through illness toward wholeness. They minister through dreams. The faithful need not fear these

---

[40] #71 "Of Good Angels," i.1, 3:6.
[41] #71 "Of Good Angels," i.2, 3:7; cf. 3:72; 4:229.
[42] #71 "Of Good Angels," i.3, 3:8.
[43] #71 "Of Good Angels," i.1, 3:6.
[44] #71 "Of Good Angels," i.2, 3:7.
[45] #71 "Of Good Angels," i.2–3, 3:7–8.
[46] #71 "Of Good Angels," ii, 3:11–12.
[47] #71 "Of Good Angels," ii.3–8, 3:12–14.

ministering spirits, for they are given for our good. Through them, God works in our hearts to elicit happiness and holiness. We cannot fully understand their ministrations on our behalf as long as we dwell in the body.[48]

Though not omnipresent, they have been given "an immense sphere of action,"[49] including governments and empires, political and economic orders, and cultural processes. But they work chiefly within the vast, silent reaches of the human heart, and through human relationships.[50] They have power to cause or remove pain, knowing all the intricacies of the human body.

Though good, they are not to be worshiped, for only God is worthy of worship, yet God does indeed work through them. The ministering spirits are not identical with the Holy Spirit, who remains the one uncreated God through whom these creaturely spirits are sustained.[51]

On Guardian Angels

Ps. 91:11: "He shall give his angels charge over thee, to keep thee in all thy ways." [Homily #135 1726 B4:224–35 (not in Jackson edition)]

Even amid wealth, power, or glory, it is scarcely possible to forget that human beings "are weak, miserable, helpless creatures," unequal to the dangers that surround us, riddled with guilt and disease. Our lives end "at length with a total dissolution. The meanest object of our scorn—a beast, an insect, nay, even things that themselves have no life—are sufficient either to take away

ours, or to make it a curse rather than a blessing."[52]

If life is so miserable, how can God be regarded as good? Evil is permitted "to humble our natural pride and self-sufficiency." However we may be tempted to be defeated by worldly powers, "unless by our own positive voluntary act, they 'shall have no advantage over us.'" The free-will defense circumvents any thought of injustice in God.

Whether Incorporeal Ministering Spirits Attend Us at Certain Times

"They are always ready to assist us when we need their assistance, always present when their presence may be of service, in every circumstance of life wherein is danger of any sort;"[53] they are to "keep us in all our ways" (Ps. 91:11). Whether in bodily pain or the temptation of our souls, whether we are aware of approaching evil or not, they make "their timely interposition."[54] Thus even amid afflictions, "we cannot doubt" God's goodness insofar as we "consider what peculiar care he hath taken" for our protection by giving "his angels charge over them, to keep them in all their ways."[55]

It would exceed the commission they have received, however, if they absolutely prevented evil, so as to circumvent the challenge of vice or the possibility of virtue. Their mission is not to deliver the soul from all temptation or bodily pain, as if to coerce choice, but to accompany choice, seeing that "where there is no choice, there can be no virtue. But had we been without

---

[48]#71 "Of Good Angels," ii.2, 3:11–12.
[49]#71 "Of Good Angels," i.6, 3:9.
[50]#71 "Of Good Angels," ii.7–9, 3:13–14.
[51]#71 "Of Good Angels," ii.10, 3:15.
[52]#135 "On Guardian Angels," Pref. 1, 4:225.
[53]#135 "On Guardian Angels," i.1, 4:226–27.
[54]#135 "On Guardian Angels," i.2, 4:227.
[55]#135 "On Guardian Angels," Pref. 3, 4:226.

virtue, we must have been content with some lower happiness than that we now hope to partake of."[56]

Whether Incorporeal Ministering Spirits Guard Us by Certain Methods

Excelling in strength and wisdom, they may alter "some material cause that else would have a pernicious effect: the cleansing [of] (for instance) tainted air."[57] They have power to raise or allay human passions. "That one immaterial being, by touching another, should either increase or lessen its motion, that an angel should either retard or quicken the stream wherewith the passions of an angelic substance flow, is not more to be wondered at than that one piece of matter should have the same effect on its kindred substance."[58] They may instill good thoughts in our hearts, keeping the righteous from spiritual dangers.[59]

"It is not improbable their fellowship with us is far more sensible than ours with them. Suppose any of them are present, they are hid from our eyes, but we are not hid from their sight. They, no doubt, clearly discern all our words and actions, if not all our thoughts too. For it is hard to think these walls of flesh and blood can intercept the view of an angelic being. But we have, in general, only a faint and indistinct perception of their presence, unless . . . by an internal sense, for which human language has not any name."[60]

Why This Intermediary Mission Is Assigned to Incorporeal Ministering Spirits

The omnipotent One does not arbitrarily use his own immediate power to accomplish his purpose, but uses these ministering spirits. Even if God's purpose in doing so is hidden in a "knowledge too wonderful for [us]" (Ps. 139:6 KJV), it "cannot be unlawful to extend our search as far as our limited faculties will permit."

God assigns mediated power to ministering spirits because they delight in finding such employment, in conducing others in the paths of happiness.[61] "In doing good to us they do good to themselves also," for "by exercising the goodness they have already they continually acquire more" by habituation.[62] "The greater goodwill they bear to men, the greater must be their joy when these men, in the fullness of time, are received into that glory appointed for them."[63]

Blessed are all who enjoy their protection! "No temporal evil shall befall him, unless to clear the way for a greater good!" "Let him but be true to himself, let him but fix his love on their common Creator, and nothing in the creation, animate or inanimate, by design or chance, shall have power to hurt him." God's own ministering spirits offer us "consolation among the numberless evils wherewith we are surrounded."[64]

Of Evil Angels

Eph. 6:12: "We wrestle against principalities." [Homily #72 1783 B3:16–29 J#72 VI:370–80]

---

[56] #135 "On Guardian Angels," i.4–5, 4:227–28.
[57] #135 "On Guardian Angels," ii.3, 4:229.
[58] #135 "On Guardian Angels," ii.6, 4:230.
[59] #135 "On Guardian Angels," ii.8, 4:231.
[60] Letter to Miss Bishop, June 12, 1773, XIII:24.
[61] #135 "On Guardian Angels," iii.1, 4:231–32.
[62] #135 "On Guardian Angels," iii.2, 4:232.
[63] #135 "On Guardian Angels," iii.3, 4:232.
[64] #135 "On Guardian Angels," v, 4:234–35.

Originally all angels were of the same nature: spirits with ordered affections. They had self-determining liberty by which they could choose to be loyal to God, yet they absurdly chose to be disloyal.[65]

Whether Incorporeal Spiritual Creatures Have Fallen From Grace

Leaving the original ordering of God, they abandoned all goodness and took on the opposite nature: pride, arrogance, self-exaltation, envy, rage against the divine order, and despair over their condition. They are diligent in the prosecution of their design, yet God has set limits on their power to destroy. They do not merely act individually, but are united to a common head, "the prince, the god of this world," Satan, the adversary, in whose kingdom a hierarchy exists, and specific tasks are assigned.[66]

Like human beings, angels may fall. Some have proved corruptible. That is a part of the risk of rational freedom. Evil angels have the same powers of intelligence, movement, and communication, but are fallen from grace.[67] There is a transpersonal struggle going on in the heavenly spheres between those incorporeal superpersonal agents who have fallen and those who are servants of God, doing what angels are created to do: praise God and increase the love of God in creation.[68]

The reasons for the apostasy, and the causes and precise effects of the fall of perhaps one-third of the angels, remain a mystery, perhaps owing to jealousy or perhaps owing to the decree of Psalm 2:6–7, concerning the "only begotten Son to be over all creatures," that elicits envy and pride in the first-born creatures. They like human beings later would say in their hearts, "I will raise my throne above the stars of God," "I will make myself like the Most High" (Is. 14:13, 14).[69]

By revelation we learn the truth about these incorporeal powers, that while all were created holy, some fell. Paul summarized the apostolic teaching of fallen angels in a single terse sentence: "*For our struggle is not against flesh and blood, but against the rulers, against the authorities, against the powers of this dark world and against the spiritual forces of evil in the heavenly realms*" (Eph. 6:12). Paul calls upon the believer to "put on the full armor of God, so that when the day of evil comes, you may be able to stand" (5:13). Our present wrestling is not finally against human ingenuity, evil appetites, or passions, but against powers with such superhuman force and competence that they are called in Scripture the "rulers of this world." Though some fallen angels remain in their citadel, others go about ruinously sowing evil.[70]

Their Employment

They seek constantly to govern the world, encouraging ignorance, unrighteousness, and error. Any weakness leaves us open to temptation, which they are clever to exploit. They attempt to extinguish the love of God when it inflames, to blind hearts to God's power and promise. They are ready to take advantage of circumstantial shortcomings and inattentiveness.[71]

---

[65]#72 "Of Evil Angels," i.1–4, 3:17–19.
[66]#72 "Of Evil Angels," ii.1–3, 3:20–21.
[67]On Satan's devices, see B2:138–51; 4:144–47.
[68]#72 "Of Evil Angels," i.1–3, 3:17–19.
[69]#72 "Of Evil Angels," i.3, 3:18.
[70]#72 "Of Evil Angels," i.6, 3:20.
[71]#72 "Of Evil Angels," ii.2–4, 3:21–23; cf. Letter to the Bishop of Gloucester 11:495–96.

Their most furious attacks are directed against the emergence of faith, hope, and love. They oppose the love of the neighbor as vigorously as the love of God, fomenting dissention, war, and conflict. They not only draw us toward doing evil, but seek to prevent us from doing good, infusing evil thoughts, eliciting doubt, subverting good motivations. When an evil thought occurs without any obvious or reasonable connection with a previous thought, there is reason to suspect the work of evil angels. They aggravate evil passions by "touching the springs of the animal machine," easily disturbing the vulnerable equilibrium of the body-soul interface.[72]

This is why Satan is constantly viewed in Scripture as tempter and arch deceiver.[73] Both believers and unbelievers are tempted to sin. The hosts of demonic powers are actively tempting and deceiving amid the symptoms of illness, anxiety, addictions, and psychological disturbances.[74] No good is done without the assistance of God, no evil without the tempting of the Adversary.[75]

Wesley conjectured that many illnesses of the psychosomatic interface, "both of the acute and chronical kind, are either occasioned or increased by diabolical agency; particularly those that begin in an instant." Merely describing these as nervous illnesses is a rationalization *ignotum per ignotius* (explaining something unknown by something even more unknown). "For what do we know of nerves them-selves? Not even whether they are solid or hollow!"[76]

The Combat of Faith

Scripture calls us to put on the whole armor of God in this conflict, having the mind of Christ, calling upon his name, walking the narrow way, avoiding offense, grasping the shield of faith to cast aside their fiery darts, wearing the helmet of salvation against doubt, remaining steadfast in faith even amid the roar of lions.[77] The faithful are urged to be wary of the time when Satan "transforms himself into an angel of light." Then "watch and pray that you enter not into temptation."[78]

When temptations come they are viewed by faith as "occasions of fighting that you may conquer. If there is no fight, there is no victory."[79] The trial continues daily: "Each day will bring just temptation enough and power enough to conquer it. . . . The unction of the Holy One is given to believers for this very end—to enable them to distinguish (which otherwise would be impossible) between sin and temptation. And this you will do not by any general rule, but by listening to Him on all particular occasions and by your consulting with those that have experience in the ways of God."[80]

God permitted Satan to tempt and deceive Job, because God knew Job would be given grace to resist temptation. God gives our freedom a wide range of operation, but hedges freedom at the point at which it becomes self-destructive.[81]

---

[72]#72 "Of Evil Angels," ii, 3:20–27.
[73]B1:187–88; 3:566; B9:385; FA 11:123–24.
[74]#72 "Of Evil Angels," ii.10, 3:24–25; cf. B9:218–20.
[75]#72 "Of Evil Angels," ii.9, 3:24; cf. B1:129–30; FA 11:120–21.
[76]#72 "Of Evil Angels," ii.12, 3:25–26.
[77]#72 "Of Evil Angels," iii.1–3, 3:27–29; CH 7:250–52, 785f.
[78]#72 "Of Evil Angels," iii.4–6, 3:28–29.
[79]Letter to Damaris Perronet, March 30, 1771, LJW 5:234.
[80]Letter to Elizabeth Briggs, April 14, 1771, LJW 5:237.
[81]#72 "Of Evil Angels," ii.14, 3:26.

The moral law functions to protect us from temptation. As a parent is gracious in instructing the child not to play near a precipice, so is God gracious in giving us the decalogue, which clearly states: "Thou shalt not." The good parent is a living partner who knows when to say no, and to say no out of love, and when to leave freedom room to play. The hedging of the Law is motivated by the shielding care of protecting love.

To those who asked why God bothers with these secondary incorporeal agencies, and why God does not simply act unilaterally and directly, Wesley appealed to Scripture, where there is specific testimony to these superpersonal agents. They remain an enduring fact of the history of revelation. God is working through good ministering spirits and spiritual powers against all residual evil spiritual powers toward a final consummation of his purpose in creation.[82]

In Earth as in Heaven

Matt. 6:10: "Thy will be done in earth, as it is in heaven." [Homily #145 1734 B4:346–50 (not in the Jackson edition)]

We are called to do the will of God on earth as the angels do it in heaven. The whole scope of obedience is implied in the text. Wesley's purpose is to show the extensive nature of angelic obedience as a pattern for the obedience of faith.[83] The prototype of all prayer is *"Thy will be done in earth, as it is in heaven"* (Matt. 6:10).

How the Obedience of Faith
Is Patterned After the Full Extent
of Angelic Obedience

There are three defining aspects in angelic obedience: doing *what* God will,

in the manner that God will, and with the *motive* God intends. The obedience of faith follows the same pattern. Negatively faith seeks "to do *nothing but* what is the will of God." Positively faith seeks "to do *all* that is the will of God: i.e., contained in the Scriptures," as interpreted by the ancient Christian writers, whether left to human reason for contextualization, or whether indirectly bidden by God in obedience to the "laws of the church and state." In any case we are called to do all that is God's will *as* he wills it, "in that measure and with that affection only," and with "right motive" . . . "because he wills it."[84]

"Angels do all that is the will of God, and that only," precisely *as God wills it*, "in that measure and with that affection only," and with the "right motive, i.e., that we do all, and do all thus, only because he wills it."[85]

Given these parameters, is such obedience possible for the faithful in this life? "Without idly disputing whether we can do thus or no, let us do what we can. And we can, if we will, make his will at least the *sine qua non* in all our actions. And if we do this, we shall in time do more."[86]

All who follow Christ are invited to say with him first "Not my will," and on this basis "but thine, be done" (Luke 22:42 KJV). "So far only as self goes out," and self-will is conquered, can God come in. We are being called to "do the will of God on earth as it is done in heaven."[87]

PROVIDENCE

On Divine Providence

Luke 12:7: "Even the very hairs of your head are all numbered." [Homily #67 1786 B2:534–50 J#67 VI:313–25]

---

[82]#72 "Of Evil Angels," iii, 3:27–29.
[83]#145 "In Earth as in Heaven," Pref., 4:348.
[84]#145 "In Earth as in Heaven," ii, 4:349, italics added.
[85]#145 "In Earth as in Heaven," 4:348–49.
[86]#145 "In Earth as in Heaven," ii.3, 4:349.
[87]#145 "In Earth as in Heaven," iii, 4:349–50.

Only the Divine Provider Can Give
a Full Account of Providence

Much in God's purposeful activity remains for finite creatures a mystery. Only an eternally omniscient One could offer a reliable account of God's "manner of governing the world." Only the eternally omnipresent One could adequately grasp the originating vision and goal and intermediary links and overall design of providence. Sufficient intimations of this governance, however, have been given in general outline in Scripture, which is viewed as the veritable "history of God."[88]

Though the Hebraic–Christian teaching of providence has been intuitively grasped by the wise of all ages from Cato to the Chickasaws, and indistinctly attested by ancient poets and philosophers, it awaited the history of Israel to become more explicitly understood.[89] Among the foremost classic Christian doctrines, "there is scarce any that is so little regarded, and perhaps so little understood" as providence.[90]

As sole creator who has "called out of nothing, by his all-powerful word, the whole universe, all that is," God daily sustains creation "in the being which he has given it."[91] The same One who created all, sustains all, as omnipresent participator in and omniscient discerner of all that is.[92] At every moment God sustains what God has created, even if miserably fallen.[93]

The guiding text of the homily on providence: "*Even the very hairs of your head are all numbered. Don't be afraid; you are worth more than many sparrows*" (Luke 12:7).

God's care extends not only to the macrocosmic design of the whole, but to every microcosmic expression, each discrete happening, as symbolized by a particular hair on a specific head. Every distinct aspect of creaturely being is quietly upheld in being by providence, for "nothing is so small or insignificant in the sight of men as not to be an object of the care and providence of God."[94] Though it is beyond "our narrow understandings" how all this works together, we may learn personally to trust the Orderer and Sustainer.[95]

The eternal, all-knowing One sees at each moment the mutual interconnections of each diverse creature, and of the whole as it works together.[96] This knowledge includes the "inanimate parts of creation," as well as plants, animals, incorporeal spirits, and humans with all their thoughts, feelings and conditions. God "sees all their sufferings, with every circumstance of them."[97] "His mercy is over all his works" (Ps. 145:9).[98]

"It is hard, indeed, to comprehend this; nay, it is hard to believe it, considering the complicated wickedness, and the complicated misery, which we see on every side. But believe it we must, unless we make God a liar; although it is sure, no man can comprehend it . . . Can a worm comprehend a man? How

---

[88]#67 "On Divine Providence," sec. 4, 2:536.

[89]#67 "On Divine Providence," sec. 1–4, 2:535–36; cf. FA, Part II, 11:227.

[90]#67 "On Divine Providence," sec. 7, 2:537.

[91]#67 "On Divine Providence," sec. 8–9, 2:537–38; cf. #77 "Spiritual Worship," 3:91.

[92]#67 "On Divine Providence," sec. 8–12, 2:537–39.

[93]B1:523–26; 2:534–50, 577–82; 3:595–608; 4:365f.; JWO 187f.

[94]#67 "On Divine Providence," sec. 6, 2:537.

[95]#67 "On Divine Providence," sec. 9–11, 2:538–39.

[96]Cf. "On Guardian Angels," 4:233–34; "The One Thing Needful," 4:356; LCM, X:70–71.

[97]#67 "On Divine Providence," sec. 12, 2:539; cf. #98 "On Visiting the Sick," 3:391.

[98]#67 "On Divine Providence," sec. 16, 2:542.

much less can it be supposed, that a man can comprehend God!''[99]

Whether Freedom and Moral Agency Are Consistent With Providence

Providence does not eliminate but rather guards freedom, even when freedom falls. Sin emerges as a toxic waste product of freedom. Free will does not contradict providence. Those given the gift of freedom must live with the consequences.[100]

Suppose one imagines that it would be better to have a world that has no freedom in it—only rocks, no choices. That is not the kind of world God has chosen to create, as is evident from the actual history of freedom. God creates free human beings both with the capacity to enjoy life with God and an aptitude for distorting the created world.[101]

It is theoretically conceivable that God could decree the peremptory and immediate destruction of all forms of evil, but if the possibility of vice were absolutely destroyed, so also would be the possibility of virtue, since virtue and vice are concomitant expressions of freedom. You cannot have it both ways: both freedom and the protection of freedom from all its potential follies. If you have a world in which freedom can exercise itself in the direction of virtue, you must allow those conditions in which freedom might fall into vice. God

does not *desire* to see freedom fall, but in the interest of freedom, *permits* the conditions in which freedom is able to fall. Otherwise one would be hard put to explain the obvious fact that freedom has indeed fallen in this world.[102] God does not permit any temporal evil that does not "clear the way for greater good."[103]

Had God abolished sin by fiat, God would be repudiating his own wisdom in creating free companionate beings. Providence is not viewed simply as the unilateral decree of God, but rather as working synergistically amid complex layers of causality.[104] It is God's way of working within the free dynamics of self-determination embedded in natural causality so as to elicit our free responses through grace.[105]

Human choosing is governed by its Orderer as having rational freedom, "not as stock or stone."[106] Providence acts not only through natural causality but amid a freewheeling, proximately indeterminate history, hedging and persuading and constraining human folly.

In responding to the constant permutations of freedom in history, God does not ever abdicate his own character or abandon his purpose in creation, for God cannot "deny himself . . . counteract himself, or oppose his own work."[107] God "has never precluded himself from making exceptions" to the laws of nature "whensoever he pleases."[108]

[99]#67 "On Divine Providence," sec. 13, 2:540.
[100]#67 "On Divine Providence," sec. 15, 2:541.
[101]#67 "On Divine Providence," sec. 14–15, 2:540–41.
[102]#141 "The Image of God," 4:294f. For an illustration of how God's providence permitted the independence of the American colonies to work itself out toward a greater end, see "The Late Work of God in North America," 3:594–608.
[103]#135 "On Guardian Angels," 4:234.
[104]For comments on Arminianism and synergism, see LJW 5:89; 6:331; 7:247; B9:65; JJW 2:473.
[105]#67 "On Divine Providence," sec. 12–13, 2:541; for a further distinction between creation and providence see "Thoughts Upon God's Sovereignty," X:361.
[106]#67 "On Divine Providence," sec. 15, 2:540–41.
[107]#67 "On Divine Providence," sec. 13–15, 2:539–41.
[108]#67 "On Divine Providence," sec. 22, 2:546.

Complementary Spheres of Providence

There are three concentric circles in which the providence of God is working with varied tempo and intention: all of nature and human history; all the baptized who have been claimed into the redemptive community; and all those who having confirmed and received their baptism, and having been justified are actively responding to sanctifying grace.[109] The last of these are those who worship the revealed God in spirit and in truth.[110]

First, the whole of nature and history is the widest arena of God's sustaining, providing, and caring action. God foresees the needs of all things. God, whose "love is not confined," does not simply create and abandon, but sustains, nurtures, and cares for the created order in that way that best suits the whole.[111]

This is what has been usually called "general providence,"[112] though Wesley had his mind trained upon seeing the general always in particulars: "God acts in heaven, in earth, and under the earth, throughout the whole compass of his creation; by sustaining all things, without which everything would in an instant sink into its primitive nothing; by governing all, every moment superintending everything that he has made; strongly and sweetly influencing all, and yet without destroying the liberty of his rational creatures."[113]

Second, this providential activity, which is generally present in all nature and human history, is more specifically and intensively effective in the *worshiping* community, where the Word is proclaimed and sacraments administered. This smaller circle of providence encompasses all who profess to believe in Christ, who by honoring God receive from God "a nearer concern for them."[114]

Third, the providence that is beheld generally in all of humanity, and more intensively within the worshiping community, is most powerfully discerned in those who actively and *intentionally share life in Christ*. Within this community we know that there are some who vitally live their faith, live out their daily walk in Christ, who most truly embody testimony to God's saving work everywhere. They are distinguished from those who are attached superficially to the covenant community but have not responded in faith to its word and sacrament. Within the baptized community there are wheat and tares.[115]

This more intimate third circle of providence circumscribes those who, having committed themselves radically to reorder their lives in relation to God's self-giving, have set themselves to a disciplined life in Christ—"real Christians" who "worship God not in form only but in spirit and in truth."[116] This community that embodies faith active in love is where the providential action of God is most emphatically witnessed and experienced. It is upon them that much of the ensuing discussion of providence is focused.[117]

Special Providence and Miracle

Wesley was suspicious of any notion of *general providence* that might implic-

---

[109]#77 "Spiritual Worship," 9, 3:94; VI:428.
[110]#67 "On Divine Providence," sec. 16–18, 2:541–42.
[111]#67 "On Divine Providence," sec. 16, 2:542.
[112]Cf. B2:56f., 544-8; FA 11:226f., 530f.
[113]#118 "On the Omnipresence of God," ii.1, 4:42–43.
[114]#67 "On Divine Providence," sec. 17, 2:542–43.
[115]#67 "On Divine Providence," sec. 18, 2:543.
[116]#67 "On Divine Providence," sec. 18, 2:543.
[117]#67 "On Divine Providence," sec. 18–19 2:543–44.

itly deny special providences.[118] *Special providence* refers to the caring of God in specific ways toward particular persons in specific situations. If God is to act in history to redeem what is lost, this must come to focus in actual concrete events, in unrepeatable times and places where that divine caring is made known and experienced.[119]

God does not neglect the whole in caring for the part, or the part in caring for the whole. A general providence that excludes particular providence is "self-contradictory nonsense."[120] One cannot reasonably posit God's provision of the general laws of nature, and then absolutely disallow that God may suspend a law for the special fulfillment of his will in particular situations.[121] "Either, therefore, allow a particular providence, or do not pretend to believe any providence at all. If you do not believe that the Governor of the world governs all things in it, small and great; that fire and hail, snow and vapour, wind and storm, fulfil his word; that he rules kingdoms and cities, fleets and armies, and all the individuals whereof they are composed (and yet *without forcing the wills of men, or necessitating any of their actions*;) do not affect to believe that he governs anything."[122]

The recognition of special providence is a highly personal form of knowing. Wesley was convinced that his own ministries were abundantly accompanied by special evidences of quiet providential ordering. Almighty God is free to break through the usually reliable arena of natural causality.[123] To construct a view of reality that imperiously omits any possibility of divine intervention is an arbitrary and unnecessary narrowing of reality.[124]

Wesley was intensely interested in investigating paranormal activities, special acts of providence, from healings to earthquakes, seeking to discern the contours of God's judgment and grace in history.[125] When he visited his bands, he asked each one how God was enabling and hedging their way, and how they were interpreting the providence of God in their personal experience.[126] This encouraged believers further to trust God's providing, and to become aware of each unfolding gift of providence. Believers are called to receive everything excepting sin as given by the hand of God.[127]

God's care for the world in general and the faithful in particular calls us wholly to trust the Sustainer of all things, to thank God for constant providential care, to walk humbly as we celebrate God's personal interest in creatures, and to use the means of grace

---

[118]#67 "On Divine Providence," 2:546; cf. FA Part II, 11:226–27; LCM X:71; "Wandering Thoughts," 2:132; *Journal*, July 6, 1781, IV:211. Wesley thought the idea of general providence could devolve into "a sounding word which means just nothing," #37 "The Nature of Enthusiasm," 2:56.

[119]#67 "On Divine Providence," sec. 23–26, 2:546–48; cf. B2:56f., 544–48; FA 11:226f., 530f.

[120]#67 "On Divine Providence," sec. 26, 2:548.

[121]"Principles of a Methodist Farther Explained," B9:207–22, 396f.; B11:147–53, 468f., 512–17.

[122]"An Estimate of the Manners of the Present Times," 13, XI:160, italics added.

[123]"Serious Thoughts Occasioned by the Late Earthquake at Lisbon," XI:1–13.

[124]#67 "On Divine Providence," sec. 22–25, 2:546–47.

[125]"Serious Thoughts Occasioned by the Late Earthquake at Lisbon," XI:3, 4.

[126]Cf. "The Providentially Protected Person," pp. 125–30 of *The Elusive Mr. Wesley: John Wesley His Own Biographer*, ed. R. Heitzenrater.

[127]#37 "The Nature of Enthusiasm," 2:56–57.

provided.[128] Those who obstinately turn their backs on providence make themselves vulnerable to despair. Those who order their lives around it are in that measure opened to unexpected blessings. A special form of happiness comes from knowing that God is caring for us even under conditions of adversity.[129]

If special providences are ruled out by overweening reason, then "the hairs of our head are no longer numbered, and not only a sparrow, but a city, an empire, may fall to the ground, without the will or care of our heavenly Father."[130] The general providing activity at times has special moments of dramatic clarification of the divine intentionality in discrete providential events.

Scripture maintains that "providence extends to every individual in the whole system of beings which [God] hath made; that all *natural causes* of every kind depend wholly upon his will; and he increases, lessens, suspends, or destroys their efficacy, according to his own good pleasure; that he uses *preternatural causes* at his will,— the ministry of good or of evil angels; and that he hath never yet precluded himself from exerting his own immediate power, from *speaking* life or death into any of his creatures, from *looking* a world into being or into nothing."[131]

Wesley was vexed that so "few persons understand" "the doctrine of a Particular Providence," "—at least,

not practically, so as to apply it to every circumstance of life." He particularly was irritated to hear God's "government of the world continually found fault with."[132] Yet at times an excessive or highly subjective stress on special providence caused Wesley to caution against "enthusiasm."[133]

On God's Sovereignty

(Thoughts Upon God's Sovereignty X:361–63)

God creates according to God's sovereign will, and governs justly all that has been created.[134] God does not overleap and displace human freedom by coercing human decision-making. Rather God supplies humanity with sufficient grace to which freedom can respond and for which freedom is accountable.

It is no diminution of the sovereign freedom of God to hold that human beings are morally free and responsible. Only an incomparably wise and powerful God could abide having vulnerable human freedom in a good universe. Wesley posited a divine freedom that transcends all human freedom while still preserving moral accountability.[135]

No finite creature is in a moral position to ask the Creator whether the creation was created justly or not, for creation is always sheer gift. There is no reasonable basis for the contingent

[128]#67 "On Divine Providence," sec. 27–29, 2:548–50.
[129]These same ideas of providence are embedded in the homily #39, "Catholic Spirit," 2:79f., in a series of personal questions assumed to be affirmatively answered by anyone whose life is hid in Christ: "Dost thou believe that he now 'upholdeth all things by the word of his power'? And that he governs even the most minute, even the most noxious, to his own glory, and the good of them that love him?"
[130]To those who allow "only a general Providence," Wesley confessed, "I do not understand the term," FA VIII:159.
[131]FA 11:227; VIII:159.
[132]Letter to Ebenezer Blackwell, Aug. 31, 1755, LJW 3:139.
[133]#37 "The Nature of Enthusiasm," 28–30, 2:56–57.
[134]JWO 435f., 452f., 486.
[135]X:361–62.

creature to lodge a complaint of injustice toward the sovereign Creator.[136]

Prior to creation, God is free to create as he pleases. Having created, as Governor God does not act by fiat as "a mere Sovereign . . . but as an impartial Judge, guided in all things by invariable justice," which presupposes "free-agency."[137] "In some cases, mercy rejoices over justice . . . God may reward more, but he will never punish more than strict justice requires." It belongs to the omniscient justice of God to reproach no one "for doing anything which he could not possibly avoid" or for "omitting anything which he could not possibly do."[138]

Whether Miracles Have Ceased

"A letter to the Rev. Dr. Conyers Middleton Occasioned by his late 'Free Inquiry,'" Jan. 4, 1749, X:1–79; LJW II:312ff. [last section in JWO, 181ff. First part reprinted as "A Plain Account of Genuine Christianity"].

The deist, Dr. Conyers Middleton of Trinity College, Cambridge, published in 1748 *A Free Inquiry into the Miraculous Powers which are supposed to have subsisted in the Christian Church, etc.,* in which he argued that no authenticated miracles took place after the time of the apostles.[139] His deeper motive was to discredit ante-Nicene sources altogether by tendentiously showing them to be already fomenting religious corruption. Wesley thought the essay important enough to cause him to cancel a planned trip to Holland and set immediately to answer it,

spending "almost twenty days in that unpleasing employment."[140]

Wesley narrowed the debate to the central point in dispute: "whether the testimony of the Fathers be a sufficient ground to believe that miraculous gifts subsisted at all after the days of the Apostles."[141] Wesley challenged each shred of proposed evidence presented by Middleton, who sought to prove that whatever miraculous powers might have been imparted to the apostles were withdrawn from the post-apostolic writers, who turned out to be "credulous and superstitious." Middleton offered only weak arguments that miraculous powers were withdrawn in the midst of intensely increasing persecution. Middleton had charged the patristic writers with encouraging the worst medieval corruptions such as monasticism, relic worship, and praying for the dead, yet his evidences were flimsy and his arguments disconnected.[142]

A devastating critique is offered of the scholarship underlying the five proposals of Middleton's *Free Inquiry.* Wesley showed that Middleton himself quotes numerous sources (Theophilus of Antioch, Tertullian, Minucius Felix, Origen, Cyprian, Arnobius, Lactantius) contradicting his own original assertion that miracles ceased after the time of the apostles. A very loose reading of Ignatius "convinces me you have not read . . . one page of it."[143] Meanwhile, "the farther you go, the more things you imagine . . . yourself to have proved."[144] Wesley defended the character and integrity of Clement of Rome, Polycarp, Justin Martyr, and Irenaeus

---

[136]X:361.
[137]X:362.
[138]X:363.
[139]LJW 1:235; 2:88, 101, 105f., 207, 210, 229, 362, 350.
[140]JJW 3:390.
[141]LCM X:5.
[142]LCM X:7–14.
[143]LCM X:19.
[144]LCM X:24.

as trustable writers willing to die for the truth.[145]

Middleton was naïvely fixated upon "gleaning up every scrap of heathen scandal and palming it upon us as unquestionable evidence."[146] So what if Celsus represented Christian wonder-workers as common cheats and Lucian viewed them as money-hungry con-artists, this does not constitute reliable evidence. Using bad translations, paraphrases, misquotations, wrong attributions, thrown-together selections, inconsistencies, and non sequiturs, Middleton had constructed his case tendentiously. Wesley, the itinerant preacher of the revival, was taking on directly a leading Cambridge teacher whom many regarded as an expert in patristic studies. "Poor Celsus had not a second; though he multiplies, under your forming hand, into a cloud of witnesses."[147] "You are resolved to draw out of the well what was never in it."[148]

The incidental inaccuracies of Justin and Irenaeus cannot be used to discredit all of their testimony to the miraculous in their times. That the Fathers studied demonic influences does not consign them to the "grossest credulity."[149] Middleton fantasizes superstitious jugglers and swindlers and charlatans at every turn, yet "there is no more proof of their ever existing, than of a witch's sailing in an egg-shell."[150]

Even if some of the early Christian writers were at times mistaken, that "by no means proves that they were all knaves together." Middleton had

"promised great things, and performed just nothing" with a "lame piece of work." "At every dead lift you are sure to play upon us these dear creatures of your own imagination . . . your tenth legion."[151]

Countering Naturalistic and Cultural Reductionism

Simplistic naturalistic reductions for various types of miracles struck Wesley as more implausible than the original reports. The casting out of demonic powers cannot be reduced to epileptic fits or ventriloquism.[152] The healing miracles reported in the post-apostolic period cannot be reduced to the natural efficacies of oils.[153] The serious historian does not select only those data that reinforce his predisposing prejudices. Admittedly the heathen as well as early Christians claimed miraculous cures, and oil may cure some diseases by natural efficacy, and we do not know the precise bounds of natural causality, yet "all this will not prove that no miraculous cures were performed . . . in the three succeeding centuries" after the apostles.[154] The visions and ecstasies of early-church writers were not of the same kind as those of the Delphic Pythia or the Cumaean Sibyl.[155]

There is no evidence that visions and prophecies were "contrived" by church leaders. In order to make his case, Middleton had to invent numerous "additions of his own" to the text "in order to make something out of

[145]LCM X:16–24.
[146]LCM X:25.
[147]LCM X:26–27.
[148]LCM X:29.
[149]LCM X:36.
[150]LCM X:37.
[151]LCM X:38.
[152]LCM X:44–46.
[153]LJW 1:235; 2:88, 101, 105f., 207, 210, 229, 362, 350.
[154]LCM X:41.
[155]LCM X:47.

nothing."[156] As to the gift of tongues, many cases may have gone unrecorded, but Irenaeus wrote that many in his day spoke with tongues. And it is simply "an historical mistake" to assume that "this gift has never once been heard of" since the Reformation, for "it has been heard of more than once, no farther off than the valleys of Dauphiny" less than fifty years ago.[157]

It is a futile effort to try to prove that martyr apologists were frauds. For "they were hated . . . And this very hatred would naturally prompt [opponents] to examine the ground of the challenges daily repeated by them they hated; were it only that, by discovering the fraud . . . they might have had a better pretense for throwing the Christians to the lions."[158] There is no room to "doubt of the truth of the facts therein asserted, seeing the apologists constantly desired their enemies 'to come and see them with their own eyes;'—a hazard which liars would never have run, had not the facts themselves been infallibly certain."[159]

FURTHER READING ON CREATION AND PROVIDENCE

Collins, FW, 25-29.

Lipscomb, Andrew A. "Providence of God in Methodism." In *Wesley Memorial Volume*, 383–403. Edited by J. O. A. Clark. New York: Phillips & Hunt, 1881.

"Piety and Providence." In Rack, RE, 420–71.

Slaatte, H. A. *Fire in the Brand*. New York: Exposition Press, 1963, 115ff.

Wood, R. W. "God in History. Wesley a Child of Providence." MQR 78 (1929): 94–104.

THEODICY

A theodicy offers reasoning about how evil and suffering are to be understood in relation to reasoning about divine justice, power, and love. In his homilies on "The Promise of Understanding" and "The General Deliverance," and in numerous letters, Wesley explicitly set forth a penetrating theodicy. At age twenty-six Wesley wrote to his father a searching theological reflection on evil:

Unde Malum?[160]

(Letter to his Father, Jan 15, 1731, on Archbishop William King's *Origin of Evil*, B25:264–67)

How came evil into the world?[161] The Manichean supposition of "two supreme, independent principles is next door to a contradiction in terms. . . . Nay, if there can be two essentially distinct absolute infinities, there may be an infinity of such absolute infinities."[162] "It is just as repugnant to Infinite Goodness to create what it foresaw would be spoiled by another as to create what would be spoiled by the constitution of its own nature . . . But if it could be proved that to permit evils in the world is consistent with, nay, necessarily results from, infinite goodness, then the difficulty would vanish."[163]

Why does God permit pain? "Pain is necessary to make us watchful against it, and to warn us of what tends toward

---

[156]LCM X:48.
[157]LCM X:54–56.
[158]LCM X:60.
[159]LCM X:60–61.
[160]Whence comes evil? A response to Archbishop William King's *De Origine Mali*, LJW 1:64, 68; 8:254; B2:434.
[161]"Evil is a deviation from those measures of eternal, unerring order and reason—not to choose what is worthy to be chosen . . . [thus] we may fairly account for the origin of evil from the possibility of a various use of our liberty," Letter to his Father, Dec. 19, 1729, on Humphrey Ditton's view of the origin of evil, 25:242.
[162]Paraphrasing Humphrey Ditton, in Letter to his Father, Dec. 19, 1729, 25:241.
[163]Letter to his Father, Jan. 15, 1731, 25:264–67; cf. B4:279–80, 285–86.

it, as is the fear of death likewise, which is of use in many cases that pain does not reach. From these all the passions necessarily spring . . . But if pain and the fear of death were extinguished no animal could long subsist. Since therefore these evils are necessarily joined with more than equivalent goods, then permitting these is not repugnant to, but flows from, infinite goodness. The same observation holds as to hunger, thirst, childhood, age, diseases, wild beasts, and poisons. They are all therefore permitted because each of them is necessarily connected with such a good as outweighs the evil."[164]

Why does God permit the free exercise of human liberty? "By liberty I mean an active, self-determining power, which does not choose things because they are pleasing, but is pleased with them because it chooses them . . . That man partakes of this principle I conclude, (1), because experience shows it; (2) because we observe in ourselves the signs and properties of such a power. We observe we can counteract our appetites, senses, and even our reason if we so choose; which we can no otherwise account for than by admitting such a power in ourselves . . . if, therefore, this be the noblest of all our faculties, then our chief happiness lies in the due use of" this liberty.[165]

This liberty sometimes yields "pain, namely when it falls short of what it chooses, which may come to pass if we choose other things impossible to be had, or inconsistent with each other, or such as are out of our power . . . And into these foolish choices we may be betrayed either by ignorance, negligence, by indulging the exercise of

liberty too far, by obstinacy, or habit; or lastly by the importunity of our natural appetites. Hence it appears how cautious we ought to be in choosing."[166]

Put yourself in God's place by asking what were God's options in allowing liberty to become abused. There are three ways by which God might have hindered his creatures from thus abusing their liberty:

● First, by *not creating any being free.* But had this method been taken, then,

(1) the whole universe would have been a mere machine;

(2) that would have been wanting which is most pleasing to God of anything in the universe, namely, the virtuous freedom of his reasonable creatures;

(3) his reasonable creatures would have been in a worse state than they are now; for only free agents can be perfectly happy, as without a possibility of choosing wrong there can be no freedom.

● The second way by which God might prevent the abuse of liberty is *by overruling this power,* and constraining us to choose right. But this would be to do and undo, to contradict himself, to take away what he had given.

● The third way by which God might have hindered his creatures from making an ill use of liberty is *by placing them where they should have no temptation* to abuse it. But this too would have been the same in effect as to have given them no liberty at all.[167]

Without allowing freedom to fall, God would deprive humanity of its most distinctive gift. Rather, God honored humanity by granting liberty the possibility of choosing wrongly, with its train of painful consequences.

[164]Letter to his Father, Jan. 15, 1731, 25:265.
[165]Letter to his Father, Jan. 15, 1731, 25:265–66, paraphrasing William King.
[166]Letter to his Father, Jan. 15, 1731, 25:266; for subsequent reference to the origin of evil see, B2:401–3, 434, 476; LJW 1:44, 64n, 68, 305, 309; 5:117; JJW 8:285.
[167]Letter to his Father, Jan. 15, 1731, 25:267, paraphrasing William King, italics added.

The Promise of Understanding

John 13:7: "What God does we know not, but shall hereafter." [140 1730 B4:279–89 (not in Jackson edition)]

How adequately can we know the purposes of God in permitting freedom to fall? Wesley found comfort in the eschatologically oriented New Testament text: *"You do not realize now what I am doing,"* Jesus said as he washed the feet of Peter who resisted him, *"but later you will understand"* (John 13:7). From this interchange, Wesley meditated upon the prevailing ignorance of human finitude.

The Desire to Know: Ordinate and Inordinate

Rightly bounded, the unfallen desire to know is pleasurable and fruitful. This desire prompts us to improve our reasoning, awakens curiosity, and readies us to receive knowledge. "So long as this is contained within proper bounds and directed to proper objects, there is scarce in the mind of man a more delightful or more useful inclination" than the desire to know. It is "one of the earliest principles in the soul." [168]

This pleasurable desire to know, which when bounded makes joyful the heart and enlightens the eyes, may become idolatrously fixed upon improper objects so as to elicit pain. When this desire overextends itself beyond its proper boundaries, the searching is never content, ever unsatisfied. [169]

Wesley is intrigued by the scriptural paradox that we are able to know so little in this life, yet promised full knowing at the final resurrection. No one can in this flesh "find out the Almighty to perfection," yet this is no intrinsic tragedy or evil, for we are scripturally promised that we shall adequately "know hereafter." [170]

The Present Lack of Knowledge of Nature

Wesley set forth a series of scriptural arguments on why finite minds cannot know how the infinite God has ordered the world, the heavens, heart, grace, or life in the Spirit; why it is impossible to say why evil is permitted a temporary place in creation; why God has not made humanity from the outset perfect; why inequalities are permitted among free creatures shaped by varied temperaments; and why God permits the noblest of creatures to remain so long in such wretched ignorance.

No finite mind can fully grasp how God has ordered the world, even if fragmentary evidences of this ordering abound "daily before our eyes." [171] From the far reaches of our cosmological ignorance to the inward depths of our self-ignorance, the liability is the same: We can know *that* cosmos and self are ordered, but not exhaustively *why*.

Newton's view theory of gravity was employed as an example: It is clear *that* there is an attraction, a "tendency in every natural body to approach to every other," that there is a secret chain by which all parts of the universe are meaningfully connected. But when we ask *how* this tendency has become universally balanced, and what the universal cohesion and spring of the whole of nature precisely is, we can appeal only to such rational concepts as a "law of nature" or to metaphors such as "the finger of God." At some point our knowledge of the "infinite variety" and

---

[168] #140 "The Promise of Understanding," Pref. 1, 4:281.
[169] B1:208; 2:561; 3:183f.; 4:341.
[170] #140 "The Promise of Understanding," Pref. 5, 4:282.
[171] #140 "The Promise of Understanding," i.1, 4:282.

"perfect regularity" of natural processes comes to its limit.[172]

Whether the Springs of Human Action Are Unsearchable

The psychosomatic interface is just as much a mystery to human knowing as is the heavenly panoply. "Who knows how the thought of his inmost soul immediately strikes the outmost part of his body? How an impression made on the outmost part of his body immediately strikes his inmost soul,"[173] as in the case of a blush, for example, or a prick of the skin? How is life knit with the body? In what way is spirit enclosed in matter? These are open to empirical inquiry. We are not without rational competencies to describe some aspects of this interface, but finally "man is all a mystery to himself. *That* God does work wonderfully in him he knows, but the *manner* of his working he cannot know; it is too wonderful for his present capacity. Whether he surveys his own hand or heart or head, he sees numberless footsteps of the Almighty, but vainly does he attempt to trace them up to their spring: 'clouds and darkness are round about it.' "[174]

Moreover the springs of grace are unsearchable. Effectual prayer avails much, "but how it avails we cannot explain. How God acts upon us in consequence of our friends' prayers . . . we cannot know."[175] All whys beg for eschatological reference.

Viewing Natural, Moral, and Penal Evil Eschatologically

Why and how God acts and hedges and opens and closes doors remains in this time and space unknowable, but is *promised to be known hereafter.* At present "we cannot say why God suffered evil to have a place in his creation; why he, who is so infinitely good himself, who made all things 'very good,' . . . permitted what is so entirely contrary to his own nature, and so destructive of his noblest works. 'Why are sin and its attendant pain in the world?' has been a question ever since the world began, and the world will probably end before human understandings have answered it with any certainty."[176]

Wesley's theodicy argued that

". . . all evil is either natural, moral, or penal; that natural evil or pain is no evil at all if it be overbalanced with the following pleasure; that moral evil, or sin, cannot possibly befall anyone unless those who willingly embrace, who choose it; and that penal evil, or punishment, cannot possibly befall any unless they likewise choose it by choosing sin. This entirely cuts off all imputation on the justice or goodness of God, since it can never be proved that it is contrary to either of these to give his creatures [the] liberty of embracing either good or evil, to put happiness and misery in their own hands, to leave them the choice of life and death."[177]

But "why did God give them that choice? It is sure, in so doing he did not act contrary to any of his attributes." But might God have compounded us in some other way? Suppose God had determined that humans could be happy completely apart from their own choice, "to have let him know only life," "to have tied him down to happiness, to have given him no choice of misery." Such choicelessness could hardly be termed human. "The All-wise could not

---

[172]#140 "The Promise of Understanding," i.1, 4:283; on gravitation see B3:93; 4:283.
[173]#140 "The Promise of Understanding," i.2, 4:283.
[174]#140 "The Promise of Understanding," i.2, 4:284; Ps. 97:2.
[175]#140 "The Promise of Understanding," i.4, 4:284.
[176]#140 "The Promise of Understanding," ii.1, 4:285.
[177]#140 "The Promise of Understanding," ii.1, 4:285.

do anything without sufficient motives. . . But what they are is hid from human eyes . . . reasons they are which the ear of man hath not heard, nor can it yet enter into the heart to conceive."[178]

Why Inequalities and Boundaries Prevail in Temporal Creation

Even among those that choose the blessed, holy walk, there are inequalities that none can explain. Even if we are given life within specific bounds, God has not "so bounded any of his rational creatures" but that they may obtain some degree of happiness. Such bounds elicit empathy and perseverance.

In much suffering we may "commonly trace the immediate reason of the suffering. We may commonly observe that [the] particular affliction under which a man labours either is pointed at the particular vice to which he naturally inclines, or is conducive to that virtue he particularly wants. But if we move one step further, we are lost again. We cannot tell why it was that he was suffered to be naturally inclined."[179] Even if I can identify that my suffering is due to pride, which has the good purpose of bringing me to humility, "yet the difficulty recurs—'But why did the good God suffer me to be so prone to pride?'" We are left to exclaim: "how unsearchable are his judgments, and his ways past finding out"! (Rom. 11:33, KJV).[180]

Why Ignorance of the Causes of Evil Remains Our Portion in This Life

Four arguments[181] are offered in defense of God in permitting human ignorance:

1. Such "ignorance may teach us the usefullest knowledge, may lead us to humility, that, conscious how little we can know of him, we may be the more intent upon knowing ourselves." By coming to terms with "our utter inability to understand . . . we may seriously apply to what we are able to understand—the manner and reasons of our own [acting]." *What else could teach us a more realistic assessment of ourselves* "than to have so many instances daily before us of the imperfection of our noblest endowment. If reason, boasted reason, be so imperfect, what must be the meaner parts of our frame?"[182]

2. By pride of knowing the angels fell, so lest human creatures also would fall by too much knowledge, "God peculiarly guarded" humanity against such profusion of knowledge that would tempt toward pride. Hence a blessing flows precisely from our ignorance, which we in our inexperience have difficulty grasping.[183] *By limiting our knowledge, God is thereby limiting our temptation to pride.* We are thus taught humility precisely by "the present weakness of our understanding," which calls us to acknowledge our limits more readily, hence points toward repentance.[184]

3. Between birth and death we are called to "*live by faith, not by sight*" (2 Cor. 5:7). God's central design is not

---

[178]#140 "The Promise of Understanding," ii.1, 4:285–86.

[179]#140 "The Promise of Understanding," ii.2, 4:286.

[180]#140 "The Promise of Understanding," ii.2, 4:286–87.

[181]They are divided by Wesley into three, with points one and two being held together in this passage as a single argument.

[182]#140 "The Promise of Understanding," iii.1, 4:287.

[183]B2:131–35; 3:172, 191f.; cf. B2:429–30; 4:344.

[184]#140 "The Promise of Understanding," iii.2, 4:288.

that we now see and know but freely believe, with "such an assent as we were free to give or withhold as depended wholly on our choice. And this intention of our Creator is excellently served by the measure of understanding we now enjoy. It suffices for faith, but not for knowledge. We can believe in God—we cannot see him."[185]

4. The most compelling apology for the justice of relative human ignorance is grasped only by being viewed eschatologically: *We shall know hereafter.* We are ignorant now in order to provide "an entertainment for heaven. And what an entertainment! To have the curtain drawn at once, and enjoy the full blaze of God's wisdom and goodness! To see clearly how the Author of this visible world fastened all its parts together . . . that amazing union between the body and the soul of man, that astonishing correspondence between spirit and matter, between perishing dust and immortal flame! . . . why he suffered sin and pain to mingle with those works of which he had declared that they were very good! What unspeakable blessings those are which owe their being to this curse; what infinite beauty arises from, and overbalances this deformity . . . fitly reserved for that state wherein, being clothed with glory and immortality, we shall be . . . pure and strong enough to see God!"[186]

On Natural Evil

("Serious Thoughts Occasioned by the Late Earthquake at Lisbon," 1755, XI:3–10)

Wesley found in the tragic occurence of a devastating earthquake in Portugal an occasion for calling England to come to its senses. The time for repentance is always limited.[187]

Among disasters that Wesley regarded as evidences of divine judgment and thus a merciful call to repentance were war, pestilence, severe storms, and, most stunningly, earthquakes.[188] He went to great lengths to inquire empirically into the causes of the fallen rock at Whitson Cliffs ("I walked, crept, and climbed round and over a great part of the ruins"), seeking natural causation, yet never being fully satisfied that the event could be reduced to "merely natural cause."[189]

Wesley would not leave romanticists in a false peace. "What think you of a comet? . . . The late ingenious and accurate Dr. Halley (never yet suspected of enthusiasm) fixes the return of the great comet in the year 1758 [three years hence]; and he observes that the last time it revolved, it moved in the very same line which the earth describes in her annual course round the sun," which would "set the earth on fire."[190]

Allowing that there are natural causes in disasters, "they are still under the direction of the Lord of nature; Nay, what is nature itself, but the art of

---

[185]#140 "The Promise of Understanding," iii.2, 4:288.

[186]#140 "The Promise of Understanding," iii.3, 4:288–89.

[187]The supposed cause of divine judgment in Lisbon's case was in Wesley's view probably the Portuguese Inquisition; cf. JJW 4:141; 5:40.

[188]Concerning earthquakes, see B2:390, 507; LJW 3:156; 6:150, 284; JJW 3:453–57; 4:117–20; CH 7:727.

[189]"Serious Thoughts Occasioned by the Late Earthquake at Lisbon," XI:3, 4; cf. XI:496–504.

[190]"Serious Thoughts Occasioned by the Late Earthquake at Lisbon," XI:9.

God, or God's method of acting in the material world."[191] Those who live in friendship with God need "not fear, though the earth be moved, and the hills be carried into the midst of the sea."[192]

[The Groaning of Creation And] The General Deliverance

Rom. 8:22: "The whole creation groaneth, and travaileth in pain together until now." [Homily #60 1781 B2:437–50 J#60 VI:241–53]

Toward a Philosophical Ecology

Closer to a philosophical ecology than anything else found in Wesley, the homily on "The General Deliverance" views plant and animal life in relation first to the original human condition prior to the Fall, then after the Fall, and finally in the light of the resurrection. The predicament of plants and animals and even of the inorganic world is viewed in the context of salvation history—creation, fall, the history of sin, and redemption.

The mercy of God is over all of God's works: rocks, plants, animals, humans, angelic creatures.[193] Therefore we are being called to express the same goodness and mercy toward creation that God has shown toward us, to be merciful in whatever sphere of responsibility we are given—not only with respect to our own human suffering, but nonhuman creation's suffering as well.

The Great Chain of Being

Wesley posited a great chain of being in which the One who is incomparably good brings forth a created order (not an emanation) that exhibits vast variety and complexity, wherein less conscious elements are ordered to benefit, enable, and serve more freely conscious elements.[194] As plants sustain and provide energy for animal life, so animals provide sustenance for human life.[195]

Inorganic matter[196] sustains and feeds organic matter, which in turn is the basis of a food chain that sustains animals, who in turn supply sustenance for human beings who live precariously in this curious juxtaposition of finitude and freedom, this special arena of creation with our roots in nature yet with astonishing capacities for imagination, reason, and self-determination. Humanity is the psychosomatic interface that straddles finitude and freedom, standing in the middle of creation, "a creature capable of God, capable of knowing, loving, and obeying his Creator."[197]

The Human Compositum Antecedent to the History of Sin

Human creation is viewed as a distinct compositum, a unique interfacing of body and spirit, finitude and freedom. Like animals, we have bodies, but unlike animals we have linguistic, rational, imaginative and spiritual capacities transcending brute creation. They do not have those competencies to the degree that we do. Human freedom has capacities for refracting the goodness and mercy of God that nonhuman creatures in various degrees lack.[198] "Man is capable of God" in far greater measure than nonhuman creation.[199] Like angelic

---

[191]"Serious Thoughts Occasioned by the Late Earthquake at Lisbon," XI:6, 7.
[192]"Serious Thoughts Occasioned by the Late Earthquake at Lisbon," XI:10; see also Charles Wesley: "The Cause and Cure of Earthquakes," VII:386–99.
[193]#60 "The General Deliverance," proem.1, 2:437.
[194]#60 "The General Deliverance," i.1f., 2:438–41; see also B2:396f., 436; 3:454.
[195]#60 "The General Deliverance," i.5, 2:441.
[196]B11:269.
[197]#60 "The General Deliverance," i.2, 2:439.
[198]#60 "The General Deliverance," i.2, 2:439.
[199]#60 "The General Deliverance," i.5, 2:441.

creation, we have spiritual capacities, yet unlike angelic powers we have physical bodies situated in time.

Before the history of sin began to unfold, humanity in its original condition had unfallen freedom, deathless life, and no guilt or anxiety.[200] Each creature reflects the divine glory in its own way, humans by imaging the moral nature of God,[201] and animals by their vital life.[202] In paradise humanity was perfectly happy, reflecting the image of God, with freedom of choice, without which he would have been "as incapable of vice or virtue as any part of the inanimate creation. In these, in the power of self-motion, understanding, will, and liberty, the natural image of God consisted."[203]

The Original Plant and Brute Creation

Humanity stood right at the cosmic center as steward and name-giver, being given responsible dominion over this created order.[204] No animal has ever received a name except by humans, who were thereby being given the task of stewardship of the whole plant and animal world.[205] Through humanity the blessings of God were intended to flow to other creatures. In this way nonhuman creatures have from the outset been dependent upon the destiny of humanity for their happiness.[206] Humanity's goodness lies in reflecting God's goodness. The creatures' goodness is in serving the whole of the created order in their appropriate

and proportional way. Every creature is gifted with some particular way of serving the whole. No creature serves the whole in the same way any other creature does. Brute creation prior to the Fall is viewed biblically as a garden in which there is plenty of food, no pain, pleasure, gratitude, and immortality.

What happened when humanity willed to disobey and broke this intended relationship? The consequences for the whole chain of being were disastrous. Through sin human life has made itself incapable of transmitting these blessings that were intended for the benefit of other creatures.[207] Here we can see the outlines of a primitive Wesleyan anticipation of environmental ethics.

The Creation Groaning in Travail: Rom. 8:19–22

In Romans 8 Paul compared the present sufferings of the cosmos to the glory to be revealed. The whole creation is groaning in travail, in pain waiting this manifestation.[208] "I consider that our present sufferings are not worth comparing with the glory that will be revealed in us" (Rom. 8:18). The glory to be revealed in us is the work of the Holy Spirit that is already in process but not yet complete. Paul had in mind the whole physical cosmos, including inorganic, organic, and animal life: "The creation waits in eager expectation for the sons of God to be revealed. For the creation was subjected to frustration, not by its own choice, but by the will of the one who subjected

---

[200]#60 "The General Deliverance," i.1. 2:438.

[201]#45 "The New Birth," i.1, 2:188.

[202]LJW 3:108; SS 2:230n.

[203]#60 "The General Deliverance," i.1, 2:438–39; cf. #62 "The End of Christ's Coming," i.3, 2:474.

[204]#60 "The General Deliverance," i.3, 2:440.

[205]On stewardship, see B1:548f.; 2:266f., 276–98; 3:231f., 239f.; 4:183f.

[206]#60 "The General Deliverance," i.3–5, 2:440–41.

[207]#60 "The General Deliverance," ii.1, 2:442.

[208]#60 "The General Deliverance," proem.2, 2:438.

it, in hope that the creation itself will be liberated from its bondage to decay and brought into the glorious freedom of the children of God. We know that the whole creation has been groaning as in the pains of childbirth right up to the present time" (Rom. 8:19–22).[209]

That means that the physical cosmos with all its living creatures await the resurrection. It is worth paying particular attention as to how this correlates with the present ecological crisis. Wesley developed a distinctive notion of the inchoate hunger of animal creation for the resurrection. The whole cosmos is awaiting this final manifestation of divine mercy, which is already in the process of coming.[210]

The Failure of Humanity to Communicate Divine Blessings to Brute Creation

Much unnecessary suffering and pain in the biosphere is due to human sin. For this reason the creation was subjected to frustration not by its own choice—these animals did not get a chance to choose, but were subjected by the wills of those who subjected them, namely, humanity once splendid but then absurdly fallen. The history of sin subjected other nonhuman life forms to the human fate.[211] So when human beings fall by their own choice the animal and plant world suffer for our collective intergenerational human choices.

The history of sin thus forms the definitive juncture, a hinge for the subsequent conveyance of design and meaning between Creator and brute creation.[212] "As all the blessings of God

in paradise flowed through man to the inferior creatures; as man was the great channel of communication, between the Creator and the whole brute creation; so when man made himself incapable of transmitting those blessings, that communication was necessarily cut off."[213]

Human sin comes to have devastating effects upon plant and animal life. Because we have lost the source of our blessedness, we are no longer able to be a source of blessing for the plant and animal world. In this way plant and animal life to some degree share the lost blessedness and operative misery of humanity.[214] The biosphere has come to depend upon the capacity of the human mind and spirit to reflect the holiness and goodness of God, and to suffer when this fails to occur.[215]

The Wesleyan Ecological— Eschatological Theodicy for Brute Creation

In our inattentiveness to our true good, we, as warned, fell and lost our holiness and blessedness, and destined the body toward death. When we lose our original trust-filled liberty, the beasts lose their more limited spheres of enfranchisement. They are deprived of their proximate blessedness by the human fall. So animal and plant life on this vulnerable earth has become profoundly implicated in the history of sin. There is suffering not only in human history but in the whole of the natural order as a result of our sin.[216]

If the Creator of all things does not despise anything that has been made, and wills that all creatures be happy, how has it happened that there is so

---

[209]LJW 3:107.
[210]#60 "The General Deliverance," i.1f., 2:438f.
[211]#60 "The General Deliverance," ii.1, 2:442.
[212]#60 "The General Deliverance," i.5, 2:441.
[213]#60 "The General Deliverance," ii.1, 2:442.
[214]In this way misery is the "daughter of sin," B:2:410; 4:299.
[215]#60 "The General Deliverance," proem.2, 2:438.
[216]#60 "The General Deliverance," ii, 2:44 2–5; cf. B2:400, 428f., 509; 4:285.

much travail in natural creation? Why do so many evils oppress and overwhelm creatures (plants, animals, humans)?

The answer cannot be given within the bounds of history, but only in relation to the end of history. There is no adequate answer to the question of theodicy except in eschatological reference. We get no adequate purchase on the problem of suffering without seeing it in relation to the last judgment.

Suffering now must be understood in relation to a gradually unfolding process which is only now being revealed. Those who demand immediate rational answers to why we suffer rule themselves out of this eschatological perspective. In Wesley's view, the sufferer's suffering cannot be understood apart from its social history. Each sufferer has identity only within a particular social matrix. You cannot pluck me from my time, or detach me from my history, which is a very long and complicated history involving free agents who sin, whose sins affect other choices and subsequent chains of sin in succeeding generations. Sin is not a simple problem to be solved individualistically. The history of sin has a devastating impact upon human nature.[217]

The Groaning of Fallen Creation: On Animal Pain

We are talking about the crisis of the plant and animal world. We and they live in a fallen world, the only world we have ever seen. "We" in the corporate, representative, Adamic sense were once in the garden, but "I" as an individual was not born in that time. You and I were born into a world in which animals are deprived of their original condition by the human fall. Intuitively most animals know this, and instinctively flee from humans. Humanity is the common enemy of the birds, beasts, fish, plants. The hunting of animals is viewed as *prima facie* evidence of the fallenness of humanity. The human shark has become the prototype predator in this strangely deformed order.[218]

Wesley thought that a few domesticated animals have regained some capacity to refract their original disposition.[219] Even those "friendly creatures," the "generous horse," toward which Wesley had deep lifelong affection, "that serves his master's necessity or pleasure with unwearied diligence," and "the faithful dog, that waits the motion of his hand, or his eye"—they too suffer enormously from the fate of human freedom. Much of the rest of the animal world is filled with savagery and cruelty. They live by destroying each other. They have lost their original beauty and splendor. Though lacking the guilt and anxiety that characterize human freedom, they experience many other forms of bodily pain.[220]

The whole creation groans under the power of sin. It is groaning as if in the pains of childbirth, right up to the present time. Meanwhile we ourselves groan inwardly, awaiting eagerly for our adoption as children of God. We look toward the consummation of a process of redemption of our bodies that is begun but yet not complete. In this hope we are saved.[221]

The General Deliverance

Will brute creation always remain in its present condition? Judged empirically, apart from God's promises, we can

[217]#60 "The General Deliverance," ii, 2:442–45.
[218]#60 "The General Deliverance," ii.2–4, 2:442–44.
[219]#60 "The General Deliverance," ii.2, 2:442.
[220]#60 "The General Deliverance," ii.3, 2:444.
[221]#60 "The General Deliverance," iii.1, 2:445.

only imagine that it always will remain as it now is. But on the basis of scriptural revelation, a general deliverance is promised for all creation. The animal creation is destined to be restored when and to the extent that human existence is restored to its original creation of imaging the moral goodness of God.[222]

Wesley is a different kind of ecologist who is trying to place ecological reflection in the context of the history of sin, the divine–human reconciliation, and the eschatological vision of general deliverance. There follows an extended, almost surreal, vision of what the restored creation will be like in its recovered beauty, liberty, true affections, and original vigor. This is not an argument for animal rights, but rather an argument for eschatological theodicy that affects brute creation. The future of animal and plant life is seen in relation to the beginning and the end, especially the resurrection. The deliverance of plant and animal life is contingent upon the restoration of the fallen human will, which itself has caused the fallenness of the plant and animal life.[223]

Creation itself will be liberated from its bondage to decay. Paul is here speaking not only about the liberation of human history, but by it the liberation of the cosmos and all its creatures, who will be included and brought into the glorious freedom of the children of God. The restoration of the freedom of the children of God will have spectacular influence upon the cosmos itself.[224]

Justice of God Amid the Alienation of Creaturely Life

We are now called to understand our present ecological accountability within creation as a final accountability to which we will be called on the last day. God's mercy will finally extend over all God's works. God's justice continues in the midst of the alienation of creaturely life, and will eventually work itself out.[225] Meanwhile, we are encouraged to be merciful as God is merciful.

The promise of general deliverance softens our hearts to the hearts of those little ones for whom the Lord cares. It enlarges our heart toward those whom God does not forget. It reminds us that we are different from nonhuman creatures, yet even in our differences akin to them, and are given a mediating role in relation to them. It encourages us to hope, to look forward to the time of deliverance that God has prepared.[226]

Brute creation has something at stake in the future hope that is proclaimed in the gospel—to be delivered from its present bondage, and to share in the recovery of the glorious liberty of the children of God.[227] In the final redemption of humanity, God may raise brute creatures higher in their scale of being than was their primitive condition before the Fall. If human consciousness in the glorious resurrection will rise to a new level of agility and spirituality like the angels, so may an analogous transmutation occur in animal life:[228] "May I be permitted to mention here a conjecture concerning the brute creation? What if it should please the all-wise, all-gracious Creator to raise them higher in the scale of beings?" so that "something better remains after death for these poor creatures"—would not that nullify the objections to the lack of

[222]#60 "The General Deliverance," iii.1, 2:445.
[223]#60 "The General Deliverance," iii, 2:444–48.
[224]#60 "The General Deliverance," iii.1–5, 2:445–47.
[225]#60 "The General Deliverance," iii, 2:445–48.
[226]#60 "The General Deliverance," iii.5–8, 2:447–9.
[227]#60 "The General Deliverance," iii.1, 2, 2:445.
[228]#60 "The General Deliverance," iii.6, 2:448.

divine justice in the matter of animal pain?[229]

As God is in time turning the Fall toward the final advantage of the whole creation, and not of merely human history, so in the general deliverance God promises to enhance the glory of nonhuman creatures in a way that will transcend their original condition.[230] Here we have a wonderful vision of animals being blessed by the recovered holiness, happiness, and goodness of humanity, now by grace made more able to reflect the holiness and goodness of God. The original garden existence will be restored, in which there is no sorrow or pain or death and where there is order, freedom, harmony, celebration, and incomparable beauty.[231]

In this way, the doctrines of creation and eschaton become intimately tied together. Eschatology requires a universal vision of history. That essentially is what eschatology is, a panoramic view of universal history as seen from its end. It is an attempt to see present history in relation to the end of history, and the end in relation to its beginning. A Christian understanding of history from beginning to end is an eschatology.[232]

FURTHER READING ON THEODICY

Bowmer, John. "John Wesley's Philosophy of Suffering." LQHR 184 (1959): 60–66.

Collins, Kenneth, FW, 29-34.

Hubbartt, G. F. "The Theodicy of John Wesley." AS 12, 2 (1958): 15–18.

Walls, Jerry. "The Free Will Defense: Calvinism, Wesley and the Goodness of God." *Christian Scholar's Review* 13:19–33 (1983).

---

[229]#60 "The General Deliverance," iii.6, 2:448.
[230]Cf. #15 "The Great Assize"; #59 "God's Love to Fallen Man."
[231]#60 "The General Deliverance," iii.2, 3, 2:445–46.
[232]#4 "Scriptural Christianity," iii, 1:169–72.

4

Human Existence
Created, Fallen, and Redeemed

The self cannot be understood as if abstracted out of that history in which selfhood is *given by God, fallen into sin, and redeemed by grace.* To understand my human existence, I must see my individual existence in relation to my social history, a history of sin.

Wesley's anthropology constantly returned to this threefold social–historical interpretation of human existence: created in the image of God, fallen by its own volition, restored and reclaimed by God's mercy. It is most tightly summarized in the language of the Articles of Religion and Doctrinal Minutes, and set forth more fully in selected teaching homilies, especially "The Image of God," "What Is Man?" (two discourses), "Heavenly Treasure in Earthen Vessels," "Human Life a Dream," "The Deceitfulness of the Human Heart," "On the Fall of Man," "Spiritual Idolatry," and "The One Thing Needful." It is fully elaborated in his major extended theological treatise, *The Doctrine of Original Sin.*

THE ANTHROPOLOGY OF THE ARTICLES OF RELIGION

Far Gone From Original Righteousness and Inclined to Evil Continually

What God gives in human nature is good as created, but becomes distorted by intergenerational human decision into a condition of corporate wretchedness and misery. The seventh of the Twenty-five Articles of Religion rejects the romantic optimism that holds to the Pelagian view of humanity (that it was by the moral example of Adam that distortions in consciousness came to be learned). The article sets forth the Pauline–Augustinian–Reformation teaching of sin, rejecting Pelagianism as not sufficiently attentive to the corporate and historical nature of sin, for "*Original sin standeth not in the following of Adam (as the Pelagians do vainly talk).*"[1]

Biblical teaching holds that sin east of Eden "*is the corruption of the nature of every man, that naturally is engendered of the offspring of Adam, whereby man is very far gone from original righteousness, and of his own nature inclined to*

---

[1]XXV Art. 7; cf. LJW 2:23; 4:158; 6:175.

evil, and that continually." Present human existence is far gone from that unblemished integrity. We do not merely stumble or fall inconsequentially, so we might voluntarily backtrack and correct it at any moment. That is not the way history works. Rather, it is as though humanity has already voluntarily fallen down a huge cliff and cannot get back up to the starting place, the Eden of original righteousness.[2]

This fallen creature is *"of his own nature inclined to evil, and that continually."* Insofar as human nature resists prevenient and sustaining grace, it is incessantly drawn by a persistent *yetzer hara* (inclination to evil), which is evidenced in the actual history of idolatry, pride, and sensuality so characteristic of human history. Later we will see how persistently Wesley emphasized prevenient grace as always working to redeem what has become fallen, but that is a doctrine of redeeming grace, not fallen human nature.

Note that Wesley like Augustine and Calvin used the term *human nature* dialectically in two different ways: human nature *as created* and human nature *as fallen*. The created nature of man is capable of reflecting the goodness of God, but has become disastrously fallen into syndromes of sin that have become repeatedly reinforced by personal choice and passed on persistently from one generation to the next, through families, social structures, and economic orders, interpersonal relationships, and through each sinner's own individual free will. Evil has become invasive of the very nature of fallen humanity—unremitting, continuous, ubiquitous.

This is why sin is universal in human history. Sin has been transmitted to all descendants of Adam and Eve so as to become a kind of "'second nature" to human progeny. The result is a disastrous practical impairment but not complete destruction of the original righteousness given in creation. The ravages of sin are manifested in the continuous proneness of the will to fall ever again into sin. This is an exceedingly serious conception of human fallenness. Human existence is alienated not only on the scale of the individual person, but as a whole federal history, a socio-historical type under the head, Adam.

Free Will After the Fall (Article 8)[3]

"The condition of man after the fall of Adam is such that he cannot turn and prepare himself by his own natural strength and good works to faith and calling upon God; wherefore we have no power to do good works, pleasant and acceptable to God, without the grace of God preventing us that we may have a good will, and working with us when we have that good will." Apart from grace it is not possible not to sin (*non posse non peccare*) after the Fall. Once caught in this intergenerational syndrome of sin, the sinner as social creature does not escape its determinants and consequences. By our own natural strength, without grace, there is no way to happiness, in the absence of grace-enabled faith, hope, and love. The human spirit is entangled in a maze of self-deceptions.

The resultant impairment: we are unable to change ourselves, to reverse our fallen trajectory; hence when considered apart from grace, "There is no one who does good, not even one" (Rom. 3:12, from Ps. 53:1).[4]

---

[2]B1:118, 495f.; cf. CH 7:213, 652, 691.

[3]Anglican Article X became the eighth article of Wesley's twenty-four.

[4]Wesleyan anthropological assumptions are rehearsed pithily in the Article of the Confession that humanity is "fallen from righteousness and, apart from the grace of our

Fallen men and women cannot turn to repent without grace preceding them. There is no way to get back to the original condition of righteousness by dint of their own earnest moral calisthenics or social enterprise or political fortitude. Whatever natural strength we might seem to have had to do good works has become radically blemished, unable to call upon God, execute or even envision a good work. There is no way for the sinner to achieve a good will or sustain it without grace preceding.

Only on these terms (grace-enabled faith active in love) may sinners will that which is good and pleasing to God. Insofar as the sinner has a good will, it emerges only through cooperation with divine grace moving ahead of us, with and through our fallen freedom.

"Supposing a man to be now void of faith and hope and love, he cannot effect any degree of them in himself by any possible exertion of his understanding and of any or all his other natural faculties, though he should enjoy them in their utmost perfection. A distinct power from God, not implied in any of these, is indispensably necessary before it is possible he should arrive at the very lowest degree of Christian faith or hope or love . . . he must be created anew."[5]

THE IMAGE OF GOD

In His Own Image

Gen. 1:27: "God created man in his own image." [141 1730 B4:290–303 (not present in the Jackson edition)]

If made in the image of God, "whence flow those numberless imperfections that stain and dishonor" human nature? Human beings are so prone to sickness, pain, ignorance, and unruly passions that it may seem far more plausible to many to think they are rather made in the image of animal or demonic creation.[6]

" 'God created man upright; in the image of God created he him; but man found out to himself many inventions.' Abusing the liberty wherewith he was endowed, he rebelled against his Creator, and wilfully changed the image of the incorruptible God into sin, misery, and corruption."[7]

Whether Humanity Was Originally Made Righteous in the Image of God

Man and woman were originally made in the image of God able to distinguish truth from falsehood, able to perceive things as they were, able to judge justly and swiftly, able to name things congruently with sufficient *understanding*, "not arbitrarily, but expressive of their inward natures." In these ways they resembled and refracted God's own wisdom and justice.[8]

Along with clear understanding, man and woman were originally given "a *will* equally perfect" so long as it "followed the dictates of such an understanding." Hence all the *affections* of man and woman, under the conditions of original righteousness, were rationally ordered around a single affection: "Love. Love filled the whole expansion

Lord Jesus Christ, is destitute of holiness and inclined to evil. Except a man be born again he cannot see the kingdom of God. In his own strength without divine grace man cannot do good works pleasing and acceptable to God. We believe however that man influenced and empowered by the Holy Spirit is responsible in freedom to exercise his will for good."

[5]LJW 2:71, to "John Smith," June 25, 1746.
[6]#141 "The Image of God," proem.1–3, 4:292.
[7]#141 "The Image of God," proem.4, 4:293, conflating Gen. 1:27 and Eccl. 7:29; 4:294–303; B11:269.
[8]#141 "The Image of God," i.1, 4:293–94; cf. #5 "Justification by Faith," i.1, 1:184. On humanity as originally "capable of God," see B2:439–41, 448f.

of his soul; it possessed him without a rival. Every movement of his heart was love."[9]

"What made his image yet plainer in his human offspring" was "the liberty he originally enjoyed; the perfect *freedom* implanted in his nature, and interwoven with all its parts." He could either "keep or change his first estate: it was left to himself what he would do, his own choice was to determine him in all things. The balance did not incline to one side or the other unless by his own deed."[10]

As a result of an "unerring understanding, an uncorrupt will, and perfect freedom," man and woman were *happy,* for their "understanding was satisfied with truth," their will with good, and they were "at full liberty to enjoy either the Creator or the creation; to indulge in rivers of pleasure, ever new, ever pure from any mixture of pain."[11]

A Conjecture on How the Death of Original Righteousness Occurred Gradually as Through Heart Disease

"The liberty of man necessarily required that he should have some trial, else he would have had no choice." The tree of knowledge of good and evil was prohibited. The consequence of eating from it was clearly stated: "You will surely die" (Gen. 2:17). "Yet man did eat of it, and the consequence accordingly was death to him and his descendants, and preparatory to death, sickness and pain, folly, vice, and slavery."[12]

Wesley offered a specific conjecture on the transition of the psychosomatic interface from its original to its fallen condition. As "compound of matter and spirit," it was ordained that "neither part of the compound should act at all but together with its companion." The body had been prepared for immortality, with the vessels containing the bodily juices "ever clear and open." By merely eating of the forbidden fruit "whose deadly nature he was forewarned seems to have contained a juice, the particles of which were apt to cleave to whatever they touched." Entering his body, they were prone to "adhere to the inner coats of the finer vessels, to which again other particles that before floated loose in the blood, continually joining, would naturally lay a foundation for numberless disorders." Every day they "lose something of their spring. . . . The smaller channels would gradually fill up," leading to death.[13] Deadly lipid buildup in arterial vessels causing heart disease were here being intuitively described with considerable accuracy. The arterial disease that Adam and Eve got from the forbidden fruit, slow in coming, could have been avoided.

The Consequences of the Fall for Human Understanding, Will, Liberty, and Happiness

With the psychosomatic "instrument being now quite untuned," four consequences ensued: (1) The *understanding* "mistook falsehood for truth," perceiving as if "through a glass darkly," followed by doubt, error, confusion and slowness, now "unable to trace out fully" the nature of things once understood so well.[14]

(2) The *will*, its guide blinded, became "*now* seized by legions of vile affections. Grief and anger and hatred and fear and shame, at once rushed in

[9]#141 "The Image of God," i.2, 4:294–95.
[10]#141 "The Image of God," i.3, 4:295, italics added.
[11]#141 "The Image of God," i.4, 4:295, italics added.
[12]#141 "The Image of God," ii, 4:296; #5 "Justification by Faith," i.5, 1:185.
[13]#141 "The Image of God," i.1 4:296–97.
[14]#141 "The Image of God," ii.2, 4:298.

upon it . . . Nay, love itself, that ray of the Godhead, that balm of life, now became a torment. Its light being gone, it wandered about seeking rest and finding none; till at length" resorted to "the guilded poison of earthly enjoyments."[15]

(3) *Liberty* "went away with virtue." "The subject of virtue became the slave of vice."[16]

(4) "The consequence of his being enslaved to a depraved understanding and a corrupted will could be not other than the reverse of that *happiness* which flowed from them when in their perfection." Thus it was "not the good God but man himself made man what he is now."[17]

Whether the Image of God May be Recovered

The *understanding* must be brought by humility to repentance, true self-knowledge, and faith. The will then must be redirected by the renewed understanding toward charity, "to collect the scattered beams of that affection which is truly human, truly divine," forgiving as we have been forgiven. By being restored "first to knowledge, and then to virtue," we are delivered to "*freedom* and *happiness* . . . that liberty which not only implies the absence of all pain, unless what is necessary to future pleasure, but such a measure of present happiness as is a fit introduction to that which flows at God's right hand for evermore!"[18] This restoration is available to all who will gladly receive the means of grace.[19]

The One Thing Needful

Luke 10:42: "One thing is needful." [146 1734 B4:351–59 (not in the Jackson edition)]

The One Thing Needful: The Restoration of the Fallen Image

Though humanity was created in the image of God, sin has profoundly effaced that image, as evidenced by the loss of freedom, now so bound by "heavy chains" of "vile affections" that it is not possible even to "lift up an eye, a thought to heaven." "The whole head is faint, and the whole heart sick."[20]

The one thing needful: "To recover our first estate . . . to be born again, to be formed anew after the likeness of our Creator . . . to re-exchange the image of Satan for the image of God, bondage for freedom, sickness for health . . . to regain our native freedom."[21] This is "our one great business," "the one work we have to do."

The One End of Our Creation

"*The one end of our creation*," is that we might love God supremely and all things in God, for *love* is perfect freedom, the very image of God. "Love is the health of the soul, the full exertion of all its powers, the perfection of all its faculties."[22]

The one end of our redemption is that we be restored to health and freedom, that every spiritual sickness of our nature might be healed. This is the purpose of the incarnation, life, death and resurrection of Christ: to proclaim

---

[15]#141 "The Image of God," ii.3, 4:298.
[16]#141 "The Image of God," ii.4, 4:298–99.
[17]#141 "The Image of God," ii.5, 4:299; for further reference to the consequences of the Fall see B1:185–87; 2:189–90, 400–412, 467–68, 476f., 508–9; 4:162–63, 295–99; LJW 3:340, 373.
[18]#141 "The Image of God," iii.1–3, 4:299–300.
[19]B2:482f.; 4:299–301, 354f.
[20]#146 "The One Thing Needful," i.3, 4:354; Isa. 1:5.
[21]#146 "The One Thing Needful," i.5, 4:355; cf. 2:483.
[22]#146 "The One Thing Needful," ii.1, 2, 4:355, italics added.

liberty to captives, to enjoin what is necessary for our recovery and forbid what is obstructive of it.[23] *The one end of all God's providential dispensations* is "solely our sanctification; our recovery from that vile bondage, the love of his creatures, to the free love of our Creator."[24] *The one end of the operations of the Spirit in us* is to do this one thing needful, "to restore us to health, to liberty, to holiness."[25]

THE HUMAN COMPOSITE OF FINITUDE AND TRANSCENDENCE

What Is Man? Psalm 8:3, 4: (Discourse i)

Ps. 8:3, 4: "What is Man?" [Homily #103 1787 B3:454–63 J#103 VII:167–74]

Of the Finite Magnitude of Human Existence in the Universe as Viewed Physically

Wesley sought to view the stature of moral, corporeal, rational creatures in comparison to the whole cosmos and eternity. However important human life is to us, when temporally and physically viewed it takes up only a small speck of space and fleeting streak of time in an immense cosmos.

The location of human existence within time and space in this vast universe was being more adequately understood in Wesley's experimentally oriented century than before. "What is the space of the whole creation, what is all finite space that is, or can be conceived, in comparison of infinity?"[26] Reason, when taken alone, suggests "that so diminutive a creature would be overlooked" by the "One that inhabi-

teth eternity," especially when we consider duration.[27]

The Duration of Human Existence in the Universe as Viewed Temporally

As to duration, humans at best may live about fourscore years, but what does that add up to against the actual cosmic scale? The brevity of human life is viewed by Wesley not merely in relation to prehistoric time, but more so in relation to the infinite duration of eternity. So he took as his text: "*When I look at your heavens, the work of your fingers, the moon and the stars that you have established; what are human beings that you are mindful of them, mortals that you care for them? Yet you have made them a little lower than God, and crowned them with glory and honor. You have given them dominion over the works of your hands*" (Ps. 8:3–6a NRSV).

From Cyprian he refashioned this comparison: "Suppose there was a ball of sand as large as the globe of earth, and suppose one grain of this were to be annihilated in a thousand years; yet that whole space of time where this ball would be annihilating . . . would bear . . . infinitely less proportion to eternity, than a single grain of sand would bear to that whole mass."[28] Augustine marveled that sinful humanity is allotted any portion at all of space and time. Even when viewed against the immensity of creation, "so small a portion" it is.[29]

On the Greatness of the Human Soul Within Space and Time

So small and brief is human life that it may seem inconsequential. Viewed ma-

---

[23]#146 "The One Thing Needful," ii.3, 4:356.
[24]#146 "The One Thing Needful," iii.4, 4:356–57.
[25]#146 "The One Thing Needful," ii.5, 4:357.
[26]#103 "What is Man?" Psalm 8:3, 4, i.6, 3:457.
[27]#103 "What is Man?" Psalm 8:3, 4, i.7, 3:458; Isa. 57:15.
[28]#103 "What is Man?" Psalm 8:3, 4, ii.3, 3:458.
[29]Confessions, I.1, 3:459n.

terialistically, this can only lead the most glorious of all creatures to despair over the human condition.[30]

Only when humanity is beheld in relation to God, who cares infinitely for sinners, does the true greatness of the human appear.[31] The value of even a single soul is so great that it exceeds the whole of the material order. "The body is not the man," who is "not only a house of clay, but . . . an incorruptible picture of the God of glory, a spirit that is of infinitely more value than the whole earth, or more value than the sun, moon, and stars, put together, yea, than the whole material creation," since "not liable either to dissolution or decay."[32] That is not intended to be a diminution of matter, but an exaltation of the true value of the soul,[33] of every individual soul to whom God's mercy is graciously offered in Jesus Christ, to whom the good news of God's coming is continuously addressed. That which makes the body alive is valuable beyond compare, because God acts graciously first to offer life, then to justify the life of the sinner when fallen, and finally to sanctify the life of the justified. The living soul of the human person is of a higher order than physical creation, and more durable.[34]

So humanity is a subject of intense interest to God.[35] To eliminate any remaining shadow of fear, God gave his Son to suffer death on the cross "for us men and for our salvation."[36]

Suppose There Were Other Worlds

Wesley approached again the puzzling question of the possible plurality of inhabited worlds, "a favorite notion with all those who deny the Christian Revelation" because it seems to afford them a plausible critique of divine justice.[37] It was being debated in his time as to whether other worlds might exist in the cosmic expanse, and how that might affect Christian testimony. One leading speculator, Christian Huygens, hypothesized that the moon might be populated, and maybe that there were other unknown worlds in the cosmos. But even Huygens, "before he died, doubted of this whole hypothesis."[38]

Resisting the temptation to speculate on matters about which little evidence was available, Wesley argued from the key theological premise that the creation is one creation of the one God, leaving it as a matter of empirical inquiry as to whether other unknown spaces within creation exist or are populated. It would be as easy for God to "create thousands or millions of worlds as one."[39] Whether one or many, the same comparison prevails, the whole of human history is infinitely shorter in time than eternity, and of less magnitude in space than infinity.[40]

What Is Man? Psalm 8:4 (Discourse II)

Ps. 8:4: "What is Man?" [Homily #116 1788 B4:19–27 J#109 VII:225–30]

---

[30]#103 "What is Man?" Psalm 8:3, 4, ii.4–5, 3:459–60.
[31]B2:284, 289f, 382; 4:22–25, 30–31, 292, 298.
[32]#103 "What is Man?" Psalm 8:3, 4, ii.5, 3:460.
[33]B2:284, 289f., 382; 4:22–25, 30–31, 292, 298.
[34]Cf. Augustine on The Greatness of the Soul; Tho. Aquinas, *On the Soul.*
[35]#103 "What Is Man?" Psalm 8:3, 4, ii.5–8, 3:460–61.
[36]BCP, Communion, Nicene Creed.
[37]#103 "What is Man?" Psalm 8:3, 4, ii.9, 3:461.
[38]#103 "What is Man?" Psalm 8:3, 4, ii.11, 3:462.
[39]#103 "What is Man?" Psalm 8:3, 4, ii.12, 3:462.
[40]#103 "What is Man?" Psalm 8:3, 4, ii.8–14, 3:461–63.

I Find Something in Me That Thinks

I am doubtless "a curious machine, 'fearfully and wonderfully made,'" but there is far more to me.[41] There is no denying that "the human body is composed of all the four elements [air, earth, fire, water] duly proportioned and mixed together . . . whence flows the animal heat."[42] But "who am I" goes beyond the reductionist explanation of human existence that had wide circulation in Wesley's day. All such reductionisms fail to understand the relation of soul and body, by reducing soul to body. Such attempts were constantly emergent in the tradition of British empiricism (as represented by the traditions following Hobbes and Hume).[43]

Thus when we seriously ask anew the ancient psalmist's question—who am I, or "*What is man?*" (Ps. 8:4), what is the constitutional nature of human existence?—the inquiry remains perennially pertinent amid the continuing challenges of reductive naturalism and materialism.

So what am I besides mud and bones? "I find something in me that *thinks*; which neither earth, water, air, fire, nor any mixture of them, can possibly do," and something that perceives objects by the senses,[44] "forms inward ideas of them. It *judges* concerning them . . . *reasons* . . . reflects upon its own operations. . . . endued with imagination and memory."[45] My passions and affections are "diversified a thousand ways. And they seem to be the only spring of action in that inward principle I call the soul."[46]

On Human Liberty

The human self, having *liberty*, is capable of determining itself freely within the constraints of natural causality, according to its perceived good. We are capable of using our freedom to determine ourselves responsively or nonresponsively in relation to the grace offered. We are not flatly determined by external circumstances.[47] The soul is free, hence capable of shaping itself in response to different contingencies.[48] Human liberty has both the power of choosing either to do or not to do (liberty of contradiction) or to do this or the contrary (liberty of contrariety).[49] Contrariety is the ability to choose, while contradiction is the ability to act on that choice or to refrain from the exercise of choice.[50]

The purpose of human life is to love and enjoy God and serve the Creator through the full use of one's redeemed powers. The human problem is that we have rebelled against this intended way of ordering our lives. The felicity for which our life is fashioned is thwarted by our own freedom, intergenerational-

---

[41]#116 "What is Man?" Psalm 8:4, sec. 1, 4:20; cf. B3:9, 24; LJW 3:336.

[42]#116 "What is Man?" Psalm 8:4, sec. 2, 4:20.

[43]B4:29f., 49-51, 200; B11:56f.

[44]B1:409; 2:285, 288f., 294; 4:21; on animal senses, see B2:394f.

[45]#116 "What is Man?" Psalm 8:4, sec. 5, 4:21.

[46]#116 "What is Man?" Psalm 8:4, sec. 7, 4:22.

[47]On chance, see LJW 1:103; 6:339; 7:45.

[48]#63 "The General Spread of the Gospel," 9–12, 2:488–90.

[49]TUN iii.9, X:468–69; cf. B1:130n, 576n. "I am full as certain of this, that I am free . . . to speak or not . . . to do this or the contrary, as I am of my own existence. I have not only what is termed a 'liberty of contradiction'—a power to do or not to do; but what is termed, a 'liberty of contrariety,'—a power to act one way, or the contrary," #116 "What is Man?" Psalm 8:4, sec. 11, 4:24; see also #62 "The End of Christ's Coming," i.4–5; and "Thoughts Upon Necessity," iii.9.

[50]#116 "What is Man?" 11, 4:24; cf. #62 "The End of Christ's Coming," i.4, 5; "Thoughts Upon Necessity," iii.9.

ly and socially conceived. We humans are an unhappy lot as long as the purpose of our lives remains obstructed and unfulfilled. The way to happiness is holiness, whereby we are enabled again to reflect God's image as holy.[51]

The Psychosomatic Interface

Human existence is characterized by a continuing dialectical struggle between this earthly natural body and the living self's capacity for reason, conscience, and imagination. This is what we mean by the body-soul composite.[52] Soul enlivens body, awakens body to life, transcends sheer corporeality. Soul is not dependent upon body for its life, rather body is dependent upon soul for its life. Body and soul are intimately united in human freedom, each affecting the other so profoundly and constantly that sickness can at times be brought on through demoralization. One can overcome some forms of illness by acts of spiritual insight, courage, and will. The body, lacking soul, has no capacity for self-motion.[53]

From the enlivening Spirit, "the source of all the motion in the universe," my soul has "an inward principle of motion, whereby it governs at pleasure every part of the body," excepting those involuntary motions "absolutely needful for the continuance of life" such as blood circulation, inhaling and exhaling. "Were it otherwise, grievous inconveniences might follow," like losing one's life through inattention.[54]

That "*I* am something distinct from my body," is evident from the fact that "when my body dies, I shall not die."[55] Though human existence is rooted in the body and nature, it is yet capable of transcending that rootedness by reason, imagination, and consciousness. Death is the separation of soul and body, in which the body dies, and the soul lives on. Only God knows precisely when death occurs, but in general terms death occurs when life (*psuche*, soul) leaves the body.[56] In the resurrection, the unity of soul and body is recovered in its intrinsic psychosomatic interface in a glorified body.

For one end only is life given to the body: To prepare for eternity. "You were born for nothing else . . . you were not created to please your senses," but "by seeking and finding happiness in God on earth, to secure the glory of God in heaven."[57]

Human Life a Dream

Ps. 73:20: "Even like as a dream when one awaketh; so shalt thou make their image to vanish out of the city." [Homily #124 1789 B4:108–19 J#121 VII:318–25]

This homily springs out of a single penetrating metaphor—the relation of dream life and real life. Temporal life is like a dream. When one wakes up, what one was dreaming about is not there anymore. It has vanished. The analogy is between the transiency of life and the durability of eternity. Real life is eternal. Human life is like a dream in relation to eternal. It is ephemeral,

---

[51]#116 "What is Man?" Psalm 8:4, sec. 11, 4:24.
[52]B4:279–83; cf. 2:129–34, 382–83, 405–6, 438–39.
[53]Cannon, *The Theology of John Wesley*, 177–79.
[54]#116 "What is Man?" Psalm 8:4, sec. 8, 9, 4:22–23.
[55]#116 "What is Man?" Psalm 8:4, sec. 10, 4:23.
[56]Whether precisely at the point of the ending of respiration, or circulation of blood, or rigor mortis, we cannot say. #116 "What is Man?" Psalm 8:4, sec. 10–12, 4:23–25.
[57]#116 "What is Man?" Psalm 8:4, sec. 15, 4:26.

passing. The life that awaits is everlasting.[58]

As long as the psalmist meditated on the "prosperity of the wicked," the arrogant scoffers whose "hearts overflow with follies," he was wearied by this thought of the temporality of creatures, "until I went into the sanctuary of God; then I perceived their end. Truly you set them in slippery places; you make them fall to ruin." For they can be swept away in a moment. *"They are like a dream when one awakes; on awakening you despise their phantoms"* (Ps. 73:6–20 NRSV).[59] The psalmist's thoughts show "how near a resemblance there is between human life and a dream."[60]

The Ephemeral Quality of Dreaming

Wesley offered some intriguing observations on the origin of dreams.[61] Few human phenomena are more mysterious. Whence come dreams? From diverse strata of causal determinants: one's body and physical condition; through the recollected passions of the previous day; perhaps even through incorporeal spiritual powers that should not be ruled out as having potential effect upon the shaping of dreams.[62] Though God may at times speak through dreams, we are always susceptible to misjudge God's address in dreams, instances of which are abundantly attested in Scripture.[63]

The more interesting question is whether one can know one is dreaming while still in the dream state. Rather, the dream is best recognized only in relation to the contextual real life in which it is occuring. "It is a kind of parenthesis, inserted in life, as that is in a discourse, which goes on equally well either with it or without it." By this we may know a dream: "by its being broken off at both ends," by its radical contingency in relation with the real things that flow before and after.[64]

God who sees everything in simultaneity, sees creation in something like the manner in which we see in a dream, with many things happening simultaneously, not merely linearly, but all at once. The dream thus signals some remnant of the eternal in human life. Wesley is here comparing dreaming to time, not eternity, but even dreaming holds some affinity to eternity in the sense that it is a fleeting reflection of eternity still existing within the conditions of the history of sin.[65]

The Resemblance of Human Life to a Protracted Illusion

Wesley's real interest is neither in the origin nor interpretation of dreams, but on the dream as an archetype of illusion, and human life in this fallen world as a protracted illusion.[66] Though this may sound at first as if it resonates with the Eastern religions' view of maya, Wesley's stronger motive is present awakening, while time remains, to the decisive conditions of this worldly reality, so as to be prepared for eternity.[67]

A dream is a condition in which imagined events are presented to our

---

[58]#124 "Human Life a Dream," sec. 1–2, 4:109–10; cf. CH 7:398.

[59]#124 "Human Life a Dream," sec. 1, 4:109–10.

[60]#124 "Human Life a Dream," sec. 2, 4:110.

[61]See also B2:54, 130, 289, 577; 4:108–19; B11:496–97.

[62]Cf. JJW 4:229–30; 6:495–96.

[63]#124 "Human Life a Dream," sec. 3–5, 4:110–11. Dreams are "not simply to be relied upon without corroborating evidences," JJW 2:226.

[64]#124 "Human Life a Dream," sec. 5, 4:111.

[65]#60 "The General Deliverance," 2:436–50.

[66]#124 "Human Life a Dream," intro., 4:109.

[67]B4:112–18.

minds in sleep, but which have no palpable being except in the imagination. The dream state is a fantasy, a play with the energies of human experiences. Precisely that ephemeral—as passing as a dream—is temporal life compared to eternity.

One awakens from temporal life into eternity.[68] The resemblance is between the fleeting nature of the dream, and the infinite continuation of eternal life.[69] In such an awakening, one would perceive one's old life and world with entirely new eyes. You have no more to do with those poor transient shadows. Now you see, hear, feel, but without that body of clay. Now you are all eye, all ear, all perception.[70] In this new world of spiritual realities in eternity, the matters of this visible world would not be taken with absolute seriousness or finality.[71] Wesley is not demeaning the value of current life in this analogy, but elevating it by placing it in its eternal context.

On Connecting Dream Life and Real Life: Temporality and Eternity

The vital question: where would you stand if your "dream of life" were unexpectedly to end now? How would you value your earthly treasures and accomplishments? To know real, eternal life, is far more consequential than to be great in the eyes of the world while spiritually dead.[72] Will our affections be so turned to those things above that when we awake from the dream of earthly life, we will relish life in the light of God? Or will our affections be so fixated on those transitory shadows of this dream life that when we awake we

will want to flee the light of heaven? How different will be the awakening of those who yearned for eternity as opposed to those who yearn now for earthly things.[73]

At some point, each one must awaken from dream life to real life, from temporality to eternity. Religion provides the foundation and means for correlating these two worlds and lives: temporal and eternal. The good news that God is with us brings eternal life already into the sphere of temporality in the Incarnate Lord.[74] We retain a constant sense of the connection between heaven and earth when we remember that our present life is but a dream and that soon we will awake to real life.[75] The homily ends with a fervent plea to take time seriously, hence this life seriously, in relation to eternal life. For the dream of corporeal life will be over soon. Perhaps tonight your soul may be required of you.

Heavenly Treasure in Earthen Vessels

2 Cor. 4:7: "We have this treasure in earthen vessels." [Homily #129 1790 B4:161–67 J#124 VII:344–48]

Man has long been a "riddle to himself," a vexing mixture of "nobleness and baseness." The deeper one's self-exploration proceeds, the more mysterious one may become to oneself.[76]

The biblical account is clarifying: The reason for human greatness is that humanity is made in the image of God; the reason for human baseness is that freedom has fallen. By juxtaposing the *creation* with the *fall* of humanity, "the

---

[68]JJW 1:245; 5:68, 229.

[69]#124 "Human Life a Dream," sec. 6–7, 4:112.

[70]#124 "Human Life a Dream," sec. 7, 4:112–13.

[71]#124 "Human Life a Dream," sec. 8, 4:113.

[72]#124 "Human Life a Dream," sec. 9–10, 4:113–15.

[73]#124 "Human Life a Dream," sec. 12–13, 4:115–17.

[74]#124 "Human Life a Dream," sec. 14–16, 4:117–18.

[75]#124 "Human Life a Dream," sec. 16–18, 4:118–19.

[76]#129 "Heavenly Treasure in Earthen Vessels," proem.1, 4:162.

greatness and littleness, the dignity and baseness, the happiness and misery, of his present state, are no longer a mystery, but clear consequences of his original state and his rebellion against God. This is the key that opens the whole mystery, that removes all the difficulty," by showing the difference between what God originally made, and "what man has made himself."[77]

Though fallen into a dismal history of sin and rebellion against God, the human self is being made capable by grace of reflecting to a greater or lesser extent the image of God. This is the mystery of human existence, its grandeur and misery, its glory and shame. This is the wonderful *compositum* of *humanum*— the human capacity for reflecting the goodness of God precisely while rooted in the natural causality and time, and prone to sin. This is what we are made up of, a tautly nuanced conflation of opposites, a blend of God's grace working within distorted human freedom, made in the image of God yet fallen into a history of sin. I not only have a body, but more so am a body, subject to the vicissitudes of history.[78]

The Treasure We Now Have

Paul provided the prevailing metaphor for grasping this compositum of opposites: *"We have this treasure in jars of clay to show that this all-surpassing power is from God and not from us"* (2 Cor 4:7). The "we" is first considered as "all humanity," and then

as those born anew through saving faith.

The treasure in which all humanity now already shares is the "remains of the image of God": First the treasure of *liberty*: a spiritual nature with free will, characterized by understanding, liberty, self-moving, and self-governing power.[79] And secondly all have been given the treasure of a *natural conscience* able roughly to discern between good and evil. Conscience, that form of consciousness that accuses and excuses us, bears testimony to the splintered image of God in us, even though forever being diluted and distorted by willed sin and quasi-conscious self-deception. These treasures of liberty and conscience are found among Muslims, pagans, and "the vilest of savages."[80] They indicate the remnant of the divine image still remaining even amid fallen human history. "Such treasure have all the children of men, more or less, even when they do not yet know God."[81]

The treasure which Christian believers have received is the fullness of *justification by faith*, whereby believers are born anew from above. The love of God is shed abroad in their hearts. In them is being renewed the whole image of God, not merely a remnant.[82] They have faith in God's working in them, "a peace which sets them above the fear of death," a "hope full of immortality."[83] The treasure of the reborn is God the Son forming in them—a spiritual nature capable of refracting divine goodness,

---

[77]#129 "Heavenly Treasure in Earthen Vessels," proem.2, 3, 4:162–63; B2:188f., 540f.; 4:293–95.

[78]#129 "Heavenly Treasure in Earthen Vessels," i.1, 4:163.

[79]LJW 7:16.

[80]#129 "Heavenly Treasure in Earthen Vessels," i.1, 2, 4:163. When Wesley speaks of the honesty of the heathen, B1:131f., 135, 669, their proximate justice, B1:500f., 655f., their sincerity, B1:263, 307, their structures of morality, 1:488f.; 2:66f., 472f.; 3:199f., and of preparatory virtues of refined heathen, LJW 8:219, he is assuming the crucial premises of liberty and conscience as preparation for the gospel.

[81]#129 "Heavenly Treasure in Earthen Vessels," i.1, 2, 4:163.

[82]#129 "Heavenly Treasure in Earthen Vessels," i.2, 3, 4:163–64.

[83]#129 "Heavenly Treasure in Earthen Vessels," i.3, 4:164.

always placed within natural causal determinants, yet graciously made capable of attesting God in time.

In Earthen Vessels

This treasure we have in earthen vessels. We are mortal, corruptible, and in fact corrupted as an entire human history.[84] We are capable of taking this treasure and grossly distorting it. The treasure is lodged within brittle, vulnerable bodies subject to sickness, error, and death. Not only is the body debased and depraved, but the mind, by which the direction of the soul is guided, is also disordered toward error "in ten thousand shapes."[85]

God permits such a treasure still to be lodged in such poor earthen vessels in order "to show that this all-surpassing power is from God and not from us" (2 Cor. 4:7).[86] The main design of God is to keep the vessel humble, so that whatever comes—limitation, weakness, affliction—we shall by our weakness learn where our strength lies.[87]

Human reason, will, and memory, however distorted, remain a transcript of the triune God:

You, whom he ordained to be
Transcripts of the Trinity. . .

You, of reason's powers possessed,
You, with will and memory blest:
You, with finer sense endued,
Creatures capable of God;
Noblest of his creatures, why,
Why will you for ever die?[88]

And when we rise in love renewed,
Our souls resemble thee,

An image of the Triune God
To all Eternity.[89]

On Necessity

("Thoughts Upon Necessity" X:457–74; and "A Thought on Necessity," X:474–80)

Wesley was especially interested in the analogies between pseudo-religious monergistic reductionisms such as predestination, and pseudoscientific materialistic monergisms such as those of David Hartley and Lord Kames—people who in Wesley's day were saying what the B. F. Skinners and Bertrand Russells have asserted in our time.

Wesley could not believe "the noblest creature in the visible world to be only a fine piece of clock work." Rather, the human person is a free agent, "self-determined in action," not determined by another. Adam's prototypical sin was to plead other-determination: "It is true, I did eat; but the cause of my eating, the spring of my action, was in another."[90]

Types of Naturalistic Reductionism: Ancient, Scientific, and Religious

Among leading ancient theories of necessity were the Manicheans who made a whole dualistic system of such a denial, and the Stoics who saw human action fatefully bound up in an indissoluble chain of causes and effects.[91] David Hartley argued that all our thoughts depend upon vibrations in the brain, from which proceed reflections, passions, dispositions, and actions.[92] If so, all behavior would then be deter-

---

[84]B1:177f.; 2:406–8; 3:195f., 456–60.
[85]#129 "Heavenly Treasure in Earthen Vessels," ii.1, 2, 4:164–66; on total depravity see #6 "The Righteousness of Faith," i.4–6, cf. SS 1:141n; LJW 5:231.
[86]#129 "Heavenly Treasure in Earthen Vessels," ii.4, 4:166–67.
[87]#129 "Heavenly Treasure in Earthen Vessels," ii.4–7, 4:166-67.
[88]CH 7:88, cf. 390, 395, 527.
[89]CH 7:390.
[90]TUN i.1, X:457.
[91]TUN i.2, X:457; cf. B1:76n, 386n; 2:130n, 285n; 3:493n.
[92]*Essay on Man.*

mined by causes external to the self. Even virtues and vices are hypothesized as being caused by vibrations of the brain.[93]

Similarly Lord Kames described the universe as an immense machine, an amazing piece of clock-work, consisting of innumerable wheels fitly framed, into which are squeezed human beings. Persons think they are free but are not.[94] Amid all supposed "rational" schemes, reason itself remains impotent as it considers free will.[95]

Predestinarians are partly responsible for setting a disastrous pattern for scientific inquiry in their assertion that "Whatever happens in time, was unchangeably determined from all eternity . . . The greatest and the smallest events were equally predetermined . . . It follows, that no man can do either more or less good, or more or less evil, than he does."[96] Wesley sought to refute both scientific and religious determinisms.

Countering Naturalistic Reductionism

If people were governed by materialistic causes wholly external to themselves (whether physical, psychological, sociological, or economic), then there could be no moral good or evil, no virtue or vice, hence no judgment to come, contrary to the biblical view of human accountability.[97] Absurdities necessarily follow from the scheme of necessity.

"It is not easy for a man of common understanding . . . to unravel these finely woven schemes. . . . But he knows, he feels, he is certain, they cannot be true; that the holy God cannot be the author of sin."[98] Even Hartley admits that "upon this scheme, all the moral constitution of our nature is overturned . . . man is no longer a moral agent."[99] With human freedom misplaced, human dignity is lost.[100]

"If I cannot believe what I feel in myself, namely, that it depends on me, and no other being, whether I shall now open or shut my eyes, move my head hither and thither, or stretch my hand or my foot, if I am necessitated to do all this, contrary to the whole both of my inward and outward sense, I can believe nothing else, but must necessarily sink into universal skepticism."[101]

Jonathan Edwards seems to have found a way to maintain both necessity and moral culpability. Yet "Edwards' whole mistake," in Wesley's view, is that the will on this "supposition, is irresistibly impelled; so that they cannot help willing thus or thus. If so, they are no more blameable for that will, than for the actions which follow it. There is no blame if they are under a necessity of willing. There can be no moral good or evil, unless they have liberty as well as will."[102]

Against naturalistic determinisms, Wesley argued that people can resist their motives at times, even when they want to proceed with an action. It is not the case that "choice must be determined by that motive which appears best upon the whole," for people evi-

---

[93]"A Thought on Necessity," X:474–75.
[94]Henry Home Kames, *Essay on Liberty and Necessity*; see Wesley, "A Thought on Necessity," X:474–80.
[95]"A Thought on Necessity," X:477–78.
[96]TUN i.7, X:459.
[97]TUN iii.1–2, X:463–64; cf. B3:493, 498f.; 4:50.
[98]TUN iii.1, X:463.
[99]TUN iii.3, X:465.
[100]B2:486; 4:151.
[101]"Thoughts Upon Necessity," iv.3 X:472.
[102]TUN iii.7, X:467.

dently choose at times against their better motives. The very thing I desire most to do, I do not. People are not passive in receiving all sensory impressions. Human judgments may be changed. The mind has the intrinsic power of cutting off the connection between the judgment and the will. One's outward actions do not necessarily follow one's will.[103]

Rather, God created human beings with understanding, will, and liberty. The understanding needs the will to execute its decisions, and the will needs liberty to determine itself. To deny liberty is to deny the essence of the human spirit. God does not necessitate humans to be happy any more than to be miserable. That depends on what they do with their freedom, by grace.

FURTHER READINGS ON THE HUMAN CONDITION

Barker, Joseph. *A Review of Wesley's Notions Concerning the Primeval State of Man and the Universe.* London, ca. 1855.

Collins, Kenneth. FW, 105-24.

Matsumoto, Hiroaki. "John Wesley's Understanding of Man." In *Japanese Contributions to the Study of John Wesley* (Macon, Ga.), 1967; 79–96. Also in WQR 4 (1967): 83–102.

Outler, A. C. *Theology in the Wesleyan Spirit.* Chap. 2 "Diagnosing the Human Flaw: Reflections Upon the Human Condition," 23–45.

Prince, John W. *Wesley on Religious Education.* New York: Methodist Book Concern, 1926, "Theory of Human Nature," 13ff.

Reist, Irwin W. "John Wesley's View of Man: Free Grace Versus Free Will." WTJ 7 (1972): 25–35.

Shelton, R. Larry. "Wesley's Doctrine of Man." PM 55 no. 4 (1980): 36, 37.

Vogel, John Richard. "Faith and the Image of God." DePauw University Master's thesis, 1967.

Walls, Jerry. "The Free Will Defense: Calvinism, Wesley and the Goodness of God." Christian Scholar's Review 13 (1983): 19–33.

---

[103]TUN iv.3, X:472; on the distinction between inward and outward sin, see B1:239–40, 245f., 336–44; 2:215f.

5

Sin

THE DECEITFULNESS OF THE HUMAN HEART

Jer. 17:9: "The heart is deceitful above all things, and desperately wicked: Who can know it?" [Homily #128 1790 B4:149–60 J#123 VII:335–44]

Why Optimists Forever Misjudge the Human Heart

Inordinate optimism about progress in history was a characteristic of Wesley's age. Many believed that people are naturally good, virtuous, wise, and happy, and far from being prone to sin. The cultured despisers of his day engaged in "labored panegyrics" on the dignity of human nature, and absence of sin.[1] After such deep drafts of optimism, it seems that the wise men of this age might have learned a little more than the pagans of old.[2]

We remain captive to extravagant illusions about our autonomous human potential. The pious Lord Kames and the skeptical David Hume were more inclined to blame God for sin than human willing. The fault seems to be with the Creator for creating the problem in the first place.[3] Some plead psychological determinations: "I often act wrong, for want of more understanding"; others plead somatic determinations: "I frequently feel wrong tempers," but do not regard this as a sin, "for it depends on the motions of my blood and spirits, which I cannot help."[4] Others argue sociological determinations, that individual human beings cannot be blamed for the evil so widely evident and disbursed in the world. Others go so far as to exaggerate demonic determinations, that it is Satan that "*forces* men to act as they do; therefore they are unaccountable."[5] Even Satan never uttered such a blasphemy.

Toward Scriptural Realism About the Human Heart: Why Desperately Wicked?

The scriptural view of the origin of sin gives an entirely different account:

---

[1] #128 "The Deceitfulness of the Human Heart," proem.1–3, 4:150–51.
[2] #128 "The Deceitfulness of the Human Heart," proem.3, 4:149-51.
[3] #128 "The Deceitfulness of the Human Heart," proem.3, 4:151.
[4] #128 "The Deceitfulness of the Human Heart," proem.3, 4:151.
[5] #128 "The Deceitfulness of the Human Heart," proem.4, 4:151.

"The heart of man is deceitful above all things and desperately wicked. Who can know it?" (Jer. 17:9 KJV). The subject is the heart of man, described first as desperately wicked; secondly, as deceitful above all things; and thirdly, it is so much so that no one can know oneself apart from grace.

What is this desperate wickedness? We do well not to focus too quickly upon particular sins that are "no more than the leaves, or, at most, the fruits" that spring from the root of sin: pride and self-will, inordinately loving the creature above the Creator, a centering of one's valuing upon oneself, judging everything by how it affects me, my interest, my passion, my destiny.[6] We love created goods so excessively that we exalt their limited finite values to ultimacy. In doing so we fail to stand accountably before the source and ground and giver of the world, and hence the whole cosmos suffers from our spiritual disorder.[7]

It is this heart of sin that gives rise to individual acts of sin.[8] All species of sin have their center in "idolatry, pride, either thinking of themselves more highly than they ought to think, or glorying in something which they have received, as though they had not received it . . . seeking happiness out of God."[9]

Despite differing in a thousand ways, everyone is like everyone else in "enmity against God."[10] Such is the universal human condition: "no crime ever prevailed among the Turks or Tartars, which we cannot parallel in every part of Christendom."[11]

To this is added another frightful dimension: the attested world of super-personal, noncorporeal, disembodied intelligences determined to usurp divine power. That is what the Arch-deceiver and his affiliated powers seek to do. We do not hear a lot of loose canon talk of Satan by Wesley, but the demonic distortion of legitimate power stands as background noise in any serious discussion of sin.[12] When Satan transfused his self-will and self-pride into human history, the history of sin was launched, and soon covered the whole world, infecting every facet of the human cognition.

Why Deceitful Above All Things?

As a result, it is folly to think that persons who earnestly seek self-understanding achieve it handily. For their hearts are deceitful. If " 'every imagination of the thought of man's heart is evil,' only evil, and that continually," self-knowledge is hard to come by.

This deceit leads us to imagine that we are much wiser and better than we show evidence of being. It leads us to deceive not only ourselves but others who depend upon our truth-telling. Often truth-seekers do not even recognize their own untruthfulness. Wesley was as intensely interested in the psychology of self-deception as were Kierkegaard and Freud later.[13] "Who can discover it in all the disguises [sin] assumes, or trace it through all its latent mazes?"[14] How artfully we conceal from others, and from ourselves.

Why are so few conscious of this? We might have learned long ago from

---

[6]On self-will see B1:337f.; 3:353–55; 4:152–54.
[7]#128 "The Deceitfulness of the Human Heart," i.1, 4:152.
[8]#128 "The Deceitfulness of the Human Heart," i.1, 4:152.
[9]#128 "The Deceitfulness of the Human Heart," i.4, 4:154.
[10]#128 "The Deceitfulness of the Human Heart," i.4, 4:155; Gen. 6.5.
[11]#128 "The Deceitfulness of the Human Heart," ii.4, 4:156.
[12]#128 "The Deceitfulness of the Human Heart," i.3, 4:154.
[13]B3:98f.; 4:149–60.
[14]#128 "The Deceitfulness of the Human Heart," iii.5, 4:157.

Scripture that the heart is deceitful "in the highest degree, above all that we can conceive. So deceitful, that the generality of men are continually deceiving both themselves and others . . . not knowing either their own tempers or characters, imagining themselves to be abundantly better and wiser than they are." None is "willing to know his own heart" except those humbly taught of God, who comes as Servant Messiah.[15]

Socrates extolled knowledge of oneself, assuming that the unexamined life is not worth living. Wesley wondered about the extent to which we are able of ourselves adequately to know ourselves, because we see ourselves constantly from the vantage point of our own narrow self-interests and egocentricities. This tends to trap us in layered self-deceptions.[16]

Toward the Mending of the Self-Deceived Will

Even this desperate state can be overcome through saving faith. In those born of God the "heart is 'renewed in righteousness and true holiness.'" Yet "the heart, even of a believer, is not wholly purified when he is justified. Sin is then overcome, but it is not rooted out; it is conquered, but not destroyed. Experience shows him, first, that the roots of sin, self-will, pride, and idolatry remain still in his heart. But as long as he continues to watch and pray, none of them can prevail against him. Experience teaches him secondly, that sin . . . cleaves to his best actions."[17]

No one can know one's heart except the One who made it. Nothing can cure except convicting, justifying, and sanctifying grace. Only grace can reverse these illusions. Without the help of grace, I remain a mystery to myself. Only through the disclosure of God's love can a sinner know himself rightly.

How desperate we are without God. "He that trusteth in his own heart is a fool."[18] One most wise in one's own eyes is most foolish. "At what distance from wisdom must that man be who never suspected his want of it? And will not his thinking so well of himself prevent his receiving instruction? . . . no fool is so incapable of amendment as one that imagines himself to be wise."[19] The one who most assuredly thinks he is standing alone is on the slipperiest ground.[20] The faithful can only cry to God to search their hearts, and lead them into the way of understanding.

Wesley echoed cautiously the realistic hopes for modest improvements of the human condition through scientific inquiry and technological innovation. He was not resistant to the natural sciences of his day, and saw them as an attempt to understand God's providential ordering of nature and history, however addictively prone to distortions of pride and carnality.[21]

Christ came to enable us to know ourselves utterly. However desperately wicked human pride may be, it is constantly being addressed by divine forgiveness. It is the self-assertive sinner to whom God reaches out to reconcile, pardon, redeem, and sanctify inside out.[22]

---

[15]#128 "The Deceitfulness of the Human Heart," ii.1, 4:155.
[16]LJW 6:139; on delusions of the senses see B3:538.
[17]#128 "The Deceitfulness of the Human Heart," ii.5, 4:157.
[18]#128 "The Deceitfulness of the Human Heart," iii.1, 4:159.
[19]#128 "The Deceitfulness of the Human Heart," iii.2, 4:159.
[20]#128 "The Deceitfulness of the Human Heart," iii.3, 4:160.
[21]#128 "The Deceitfulness of the Human Heart," iii, 4:159–60.
[22]A Collection of Hymns for the Use of the People Called Methodists, Exhorting and Beseeching to Return to God, 7:79–94.

On the Fall of Man

Gen. 3:19: "Dust thou art, and unto dust thou shalt return." [Homily #57 1782 B2:400–412 J#57 VI:215–24]

Why Does God Allow Misery and Heartache in the World?

"Why is there *pain* in the world, seeing God is 'loving to every man, and his mercy is over all his works?' Because there is sin. Had there been no sin, there would have been no pain. But pain (supposing God to be just) is the necessary effect of sin. But why is there sin?"[23] Because man and woman, having spirit, will, reason, and liberty, akin to God, nonetheless "chose evil." This is Scripture's "plain, simple account of the origin of evil." Without it man remains an "enigma to himself."[24]

Sin began with Eve's unbelief and Adam's idolatry, with Eve believing the Tempter rather than God, and Adam loving creatures idolatrously more than God.[25] The pain and curse of childbearing and labor followed this free choice of evil. The loss of innocence meant the loss of happiness. Prior to the Fall there was no inequality of women, and no hard labor for men.[26]

The Consequence of Sin for the Psychosomatic Interface of Dust and Spirit

God did not make man as "mere matter, a piece of . . . clay; but a spirit, like himself, although clothed with a material vehicle."[27] Man is not merely dust, but dust shaped by living spirit.

When trapped in syndromes of rebellion, this holds many possibilities for stumbling and falling. Given the momentum of the history of sin, soon "every child of man is in a thousand mistakes, and is liable to fresh mistakes every moment," not merely out of ignorance, but the will to err.

The psychosomatic equilibrium easily tilts out of kilter. The living soul plays itself out "upon a set of material keys," and cannot "make any better music than the nature and state of its instrument allows." Thinking becomes distorted by the passions of the corruptible body, which "hinders the soul in its operations: and, at best, serves it very imperfectly. Yet the soul cannot dispense with its service."[28]

To Dust You Shall Return

"We are all traveling toward death." Death comes to all humans.[29] The execution of the decree of death is built into the very nature of the human body after the Fall, which consists of "innumerable membranes exquisitely thin," that are filled with circulating fluids, which reach their full measure of functioning in youth and early adulthood, by middle age acquire some stiffness and stenosis, and after sixty years or so, "wrinkles show the proportion of the fluids to be lessened," there is a diminution of the juices, "finer vessels are filled up," and in "extreme old age the arteries themselves . . . become hard," and "death naturally ensues." From the outset of life, "we are preparing . . .

---

[23]#57 "On the Fall of Man," 2:400; cf. LJW 1:88, 97, 102.
[24]#57 "On the Fall of Man," proem.1, 2:401; cf. LJW 3:375–87.
[25]#57 "On the Fall of Man," i.1, 2:401–3.
[26]#57 "On the Fall of Man," i.2–3, 2:403–5.
[27]#57 "On the Fall of Man," ii.6, 2:409.
[28]#57 "On the Fall of Man," ii.2, 2:403.
[29]#57 "On the Fall of Man," ii.4, 2:407. Excepting special biblical examples of those who so walked with God that they may not have died—Enoch, Elijah, and John the apostle—the sentence of death for sin is passed on all of Adam's and Eve's posterity.

to return to the dust from whence we came!"[30]

Yet God does not despise the work of his hands, but provides a remedy for all who are fallen, by bearing our sins in his body on the tree.[31] As God is just in punishing sin, so God is merciful in providing a universal remedy, in his Son through his Spirit, for a universal evil. The righteousness of One suffices as justification for all.[32]

Spiritual Idolatry

1 John 5:20, 21: "Keep yourselves from idols." [Homily #78 1781 B3:103–14 J#73 VI:435–44]

To make an idol first requires something good, some gift of the creaturely order that we then take to be better than it is and elevate it to a pretended deity. An idol is anything that tempts the heart away from centeredness in God, any good thing in the creaturely environment that is capable of being adored,[33] anything good enough in this world to seem worthy of worship out of twisted desire, shaped by the figments of imagination and pride.[34]

"Spiritual idolatry" is sharply distinguished from triune "spiritual worship."[35] Wesley entreats: "*Keep yourselves from idols*" (1 John 5:21). Our idols become implacable "rivals of God." Though innumerable, they may be sorted out in three forms as objects of *sense, pride, and imagination*,[36] as seen in the *triplex concupiscentia* of 1 John 2:16: "For everything in the world—the *cravings* of sinful man, the *lust* of his eyes and the *boasting* of what he has and does—comes not from the Father but from the world."[37]

Idolatry in the Form of Sensuality

The proximate goodness of sensuality tempts one to be dragged down into the false imagination that what life really amounts to is one's own sensory experience and physical satisfactions, of which we seem never to get enough.[38] *The idolatry of sense* feeds off of the desire of the flesh, "the cravings of sinful man," ("all that panders to the appetites," 1 John 2:16, NEB). We may idolatrize good things like sex, food, security, money, or any material good. We are sensory beings so we love these good things. The consequent problem is that we may love them in such a way that instead of seeing them in relation to their Giver, we pretend that they are good in and of themselves. That is the sensual side of the problem of idolatry.

We worship sensory objects linked with the fulfillment of bodily appetites. We idolatrize those things that make our lives temporally more comfortable or pleasant. Sensuality is prone to become a spiritual disease of both rich and

---

[30]#57 "On the Fall of Man," i.5, 2:407–8; cf. 3:269–70.

[31]#57 "On the Fall of Man," ii.8, 2:410.

[32]#57 "On the Fall of Man," ii.9, 2:411–12.

[33]See also #44 "Original Sin" ii.7; #128 "The Deceitfulness of the Human Heart" i.4; and #127 "On the Wedding Garment," sec. 12, on the theme of idolatry.

[34]#120 "The Unity of the Divine Being," 12–18, 4:65–67; VII:267–69.

[35]Written on the same text, 1 John 5:20–21, at the same time, Christmas season of 1780, and published together in the *Arminian Magazine*.

[36]These three forms of idolatry are also considered in #78 "Spiritual Idolatry."

[37]Italics added. Wesley concurred with Augustine that "all sins may be included within these three classes of vice," *Enarratio in Psalmum*, viii.13, MPL 36:115; #7 "The Way to the Kingdom," ii.2, and #2 "The Almost Christian," ii.1, 1:137n; cf. B1:409; 3:89, 282, 351, 534f.; 4:65, 182f.

[38]#120 "The Unity of the Divine Being," sec. 11–13, 4:64–66.

poor, either of whom can become inordinately attached to worldly things.[39]

Idolatry in the Form of Pride

If the idols of sensuality exploit our capacity for bodily and corporeal life, the idols of pride exploit our capacity for self-transcendence.[40] While sensuality pulls us inordinately downward, pride raises us inordinately upward, beyond our limits and competence. Pride tends toward the pretension that we have no limitations.[41]

In my pride I absurdly imagine my egocentric self to be the center of all other values, so that I myself become adversary to the true God, by boasting of who I am and what I do. By *the pride of life* I seek my happiness through the praise of others. I exalt my finitude to the comic pretense that other values revolve around me.[42]

Prototypical pride is seen in the demonic aspiration of the fallen angels who desire despairingly to be God. From this absurdity springs the lie that has saturated human history,[43] the pretense that creatures can feign being God. As a result, I assess each value only in relation to its value for me.[44]

The Idols of Imagination

Pulled apart by pride and sensuality, these two conflicting directions are intensified by the exercise of the idolatrous imagination.[45] Idolatry escalates the objects of fancy by the devices of the imagination. We fantasize finite creatures as God. We prolifically imagine that which is not God as if it were truly God.

Imagination is a marvelous human faculty capable of engaging in a relation with possibility.[46] But when imagination takes over inordinately and becomes controlled by idolatrous sensuality and pride, anxiety and guilt intensify. The escalated imagination of sensory ecstasy or egocentric pride tends through imagination toward compulsive addictions to lust and hubris.

The wonderfully created capacity of imagination in this way falls increasingly into distortions as great as those powers. By imagination we come to love more that which is less worthy of love than God. Sensuality and pride, when intensified by the idolatrous imagination, are basic ingredients in the oft-repeated, ever-unfolding fall of human history.[47] The idolatry of imagination feeds off of *the desire of the eye*, in finding gratification in grand and beautiful objects, apparel, furniture, and amusements.

A key feature of Wesley's psychological analysis of imagination is the crucial function of novelty in the idolatrizing process. The aesthetic imagination is constantly hungering for something new to enjoy, so it is immersed in diversions and amusements, and the pleasure that is taken in seeking curiosities. Novelty heightens the pleasure of

---

[39]#120 "The Unity of the Divine Being," sec. 12, 4:65.

[40]B3:350, 419f.; 1:125f., 338; 2:179.

[41]Idolatry as sense, imagination and pride is also discussed in #120 "The Unity of the Divine Being."

[42]#95 "On the Education of Children," 5–16, 3:348f.; VII:89–94; FA VIII:141.

[43]On the spiritual pride of the English, see B11:238f., of ancient Israel, see B11:2008f., of the Methodists see B11:387–89. In these passages Wesley counters the common modern complaint that religious discussions of pride are characteristically neglectful of social self-criticism, and of one's own social location or tradition.

[44]#120 "The Unity of the Divine Being," sec. 12, 4:65.

[45]LJW 4:305; 5:336; B1:338f.; 3:106f., 183f., 524f.; 4:123f.; 11:128.

[46]On the right use of imagination, see B2:294.

[47]#120 "The Unity of the Divine Being," sec. 12–14, 4:65–66.

music, poetry, and philosophy. Wesley was well aware of the intimate connection between education superficially conceived and idolatry. Academics are "so far from suspecting" this relationship that "they seriously believe it is a matter of great praise to 'give ourselves wholly' " to the quest for novel ideas.[48]

Inordinate Love of Money and Sex

The inordinate love of the world is most clearly seen in the human fixation on the *love of money*, not merely money functionally understood, but the obsession with money, seeking money for its own sake, and thus placing happiness precisely in acquiring or possessing it. This is "effectually to renounce the true God, and to set up an idol in his place."[49]

Even more compulsively the inordinate love of the world may appear in *sexuality*, in fixing our love upon beloved human creatures, not with a pure heart grounded in enduring covenant love, but by lustfully making of another an immediate object of pleasure for oneself. Wesley admonished spouses not to "put a man or a woman in the place of God . . . let this be carefully considered, even by those whom God has joined together."[50] Idolatry, always looking better than it is, never elicits happiness.[51]

Whether Penitent Faith Can Break the Bondage of Idolatry

We keep ourselves from idols first by becoming deeply convicted that no idol can bring the happiness it promises.[52] Idolatry is initially combatted by praying for the grace to become aware of one's own temptations, and then the grace to trust in God instead of the gods.[53] One does not overcome idolatry without coming to one's senses, awakening from sleep, choosing the better way, and resolving to seek happiness in the true ground of happiness.[54]

No idolatry can be overcome without *repentance*, which becomes filled with consciousness of one's own impotence, guilt, and the madness of idolatry. So "Cry for a thorough knowledge of yourself . . . Pray that you may be fully discovered to yourself; that you may know yourself as also you are known."[55] Only on the basis of such realistic awareness of one's own impotence to change one's idolatries can they be overcome by grace through the *faith* that exclaims: "Lord, I would believe! Help thou my unbelief. And help me now!"[56]

ORIGINAL SIN

The Doctrine of Original Sin According to Scripture, Reason, and Experience

(1756–57 IX:191–465)

Why Wesley Wrote His Longest Treatise on Sin

Nothing in human history is more original than sin. The underlying reason for giving so much attention to the study of original sin is not a fixation on sin itself, but on theodicy and redemption. A solid doctrine of original sin is required, first, to free God of the charge of being responsible for man's sinful condition, and then to exalt the gospel

---

[48]#78 "Spiritual Idolatry," 1.7–14, 3:106–9.
[49]#78 "Spiritual Idolatry," 1.17, 3:110.
[50]#78 "Spiritual Idolatry," 1.18, 3:111.
[51]#78 "Spiritual Idolatry," i.17–18, 3:110–11.
[52]#78 "Spiritual Idolatry," ii.1, 3:111.
[53]PW 7:194.
[54]#78 "Spiritual Idolatry," ii.3, 3:113.
[55]#78 "Spiritual Idolatry," ii.4, 3:113.
[56]#78 "Spiritual Idolatry," ii.5, 3:114.

of justification, new birth, and especially transforming, sanctifying grace.[57]

For these reasons Wesley wrote only one full-length systematic treatise, and it happened to be on a perennially unpopular topic—original sin.[58] It comprises most of the eleventh volume of the Jackson edition, a large tome, with almost three hundred packed pages devoted to exhaustive exegetical analysis. The few who have carefully read it discover the side of Wesley most frequently ignored by his modern romantic sycophants and by those who imagine him to be Pelagian. The secondary literature has focused so much more on his soteriology and ecclesiology that it has almost totally ignored his most detailed treatise—on original sin. This extensive dissertation is among the most demanding and intricate of Wesley's writings. The reader must pay astute attention to the quotation marks to identify who is quoting or refuting whom. There are profuse quotations without the benefit of modern stylistic conventions.[59]

Though some of the material of Part I of *The Doctrine of Original Sin* found its way into one of the standard sermons, Homily #44 "Original Sin,"[60] one should not assume that it is merely a summary of the longer treatise.

Though Wesley liked to write with a tight economy of style and scale, in *The Doctrine of Original Sin* he was determined to go into whatever length required to nail down his historical, exegetical, and ethical points. Here he functions more than elsewhere as a deliberate systematic theologian reflecting upon all the ancillary issues relating to the depth of the human predicament.[61]

However closely argued, this inquiry is addressed less to the academic world than to the leadership of those in his direct connection of spiritual formation—his societies and bands,[62] as a caveat against diluted views of sin. And he still is capable of making contact with minds seeking his counsel in modern times.

But why so extensively? He saw the problem of sin as a profound dilemma requiring probing, untiring analysis. Here he was less than ever willing to suffer fools gladly.

Even today it is not unusual to hear Wesley or Wesleyans polemically dismissed as romantic, naturalistic, humanistic Pelagians, despite all disclaimers. It is sometimes imagined that Wesley espoused an optimistic view of human nature. This treatise deserves to be read by anyone thinking such foolishness. Temperamentally, Wesley was indeed turned toward the possibilities of grace, rather than boringly bemoaning the endless consequences of fallen human nature. He was engaged in the lifelong act of reconstruction of the human condition, both personal and social. He did not hesitate to seek the complete reformation of the human character. Amid the characteristic opti-

---

[57]DOS Pt. II, ii, IX:273–85.

[58]For references to original sin apart from DOS, see JJW 3:374; 4:199; B1:64f., 185–89, 211–13, 225–29; 2:170–85; 4:152–55; 9:50–52; 11:163f., 519f.; LJW 4:48, 67.

[59]The annotated Bicentennial edition of the treatise on *Original Sin* (not yet available at this date of publication) will make it easier for the reader to discern the difference between Wesley's own views and those numerous points where he is quoting others either favorably or unfavorably.

[60]#44 1759, 2:170–85; VI:54–65.

[61]DOS Pt. I, Pref. 5, IX:194.

[62]Though he often speaks in first person to Taylor, and though the argument is couched in an academic format, more so than usual for Wesley, it is nonetheless a moral admonition for those who might otherwise be led astray.

mism of his period, however, he appears as a realistic and tough-minded analyst of sin, and at times a grieving observer of inexorable human fallenness.[63]

We will not penetrate far into Wesley's theology until we take seriously his doctrine of original sin.[64] It is, he admitted, a dismal subject, but one that must be presupposed in any effort to understand other essential Christian doctrines such as incarnation, justification, and redemption. One who has no way to grasp the perplexity, depth, and recalcitrance of human sin, has little need to speak of Christ on the cross. One cannot get to atonement or redemption until one takes seriously the predicament to which Christ is an answer. It is a foundational locus of theology.

Whether the Origin of Sin Is a Fit Subject for Serious Inquiry

What we are most averse to in worship is confessing, especially our sins. Sometimes in common worship we have tended to circumvent entirely the act of confession—one of the least Wesleyan aspects of Wesley's modern progeny. The subject of original sin so avidly neglected by modern Christianity was not neglected by Mr. Wesley. Few liberal Protestants have ever heard a sermon on original sin, except in the guise of political jeremiad against economic injustice or war or racism or social oppression.

Wesley anticipated modern analyses of the dynamics of the psychogenetic transmission of neurotic patterns and intergenerational consequences of injustice. Modern psychologically oriented Christians familiar with the ideas of repression, the unconscious, and neurotic behavior, who know much about how psychological dysfunction gets passed on from parents to children, often know almost nothing about classic Christian understanding of intergenerational transmission of evil.[65]

Sin as a Socially Transmitted Disease[66]

The dynamics of social and class transmission of economic oppression are well known to modern Christians who refuse to take original sin seriously. Yet these modern views of social location and class conflict were astutely anticipated by classical Christianity generally and by Wesley in particular during the early phase of the industrial revolution, and are reflected with special discernment in Wesley's teaching of original sin.[67] Long before Marx or Lenin or Niebuhr or Gutierrez, Wesley and others before him (notably John Chrysostom, Gregory the Great, Francis of Siena, and Thomas Aquinas) were speaking of social location, economic interest, and class conflict as basic distorting influences on our perception of everything, falsifying our capacity to see the common good.

The implicit intergenerational doctrine of sin that became secularized in Marx and Freud was explicitly anticipated by Wesley. These familiar modern categories of interpretation are still proximately useful in explicating the Christian doctrine of original sin, yet finally inadequate, refusing as they do to understand the human condition as voluntary alienation standing in final relation to the ground and source of life,

---

[63]DOS Pt. I, Pref., IX:193–95.
[64]Wesley viewed original sin as a "grand doctrine," LJW 4:146, 153, 237; 5:327; 6:49, among the doctrinal essentials.
[65]Albert C. Outler, *Theology in the Wesleyan Spirit*, chap. 1.
[66]On sin as disease, see B1:404, 586; 2:184, 342; 3:134–35, 533f.; 4:86f.
[67]DOS Pt. I, ii.1–15, IX:208–38.

even though they achieved certain insights into the human condition. This is worth noting in a preliminary way so that some readers may make contact with Wesley's view of original sin in a way they might not otherwise be able to recognize.

We imagine that our modern psychological analyses of the human predicament are unprecedented in their accuracy and acumen. Freud had a complex analysis of the etiology of neurosis especially as it emerged out of relations with primary persons, key voices that shape the growth of individual consciousness. Long before Freud the classic Christian tradition had understood that sin is socially and interpersonally transmitted, that parental inputs affect neurotic responses, yet never unilaterally and never without the collusion of our freedom. The intergenerational transmission of distorted sexuality is another way of talking about original sin.[68]

Similarly we imagine that our modern sociological analyses of the human predicament are unprecedented. Marx offered a complex economic analysis of the etiology of social conflict, as it emerged especially out of class consciousness and oppressive economic patterns. Centuries before Marx the classic Christian tradition had understood that sin is socially and economically transmitted, that class biases misshape the truth of our relations with each other. Our location in a socioeconomic order powerfully shapes our ways of thinking about moral judgments and ideas. We become natively biased in relation to our own class. The intergenerational transmission of unjust economic and class oppressions is a surrogate speech for original sin.

Consciousness raising was for Marx the raising of the consciousness of the underclass to the injustices of class oppression, calling upon people to unite and break their chains of economic bondage through revolution. Now we find that this revolution was a poverty machine which itself has required a free market resolution. Such is the history of sin. Rightly understood, original sin is not alien to modern consciousness. Even when we hear nothing of sin from modern pulpits, it is a deeply familiar modern theme.

Wesley shied away from theorizing about a single glib unilateral explanation of the transmission of sin: "The fact I know, both by Scripture and by experience. I know it is transmitted; but how" precisely it is transmitted is shrouded under "the mystery of iniquity."[69]

Modernity does not use the term *sin* to talk about sin, but sin nonetheless remains an intense modern preoccupation. One cannot open one's eyes without seeing how deeply our society is in trouble, our cities, our sexuality, our compulsions. Our sense of sin is deepgoing. Wesley regarded the doctrine of original sin as the first line of defense against the deadly optimisms of the Enlightenment. To the extent that he failed, the task must again be undertaken in our time.[70]

The question: "What is the real state, with regard to knowledge and virtue, wherein mankind have been from the earliest times? And what state are they in at this day?"[71]

[68]B1:533–41; SS 1:382.
[69]Letter to John Robertson, Sept. 24, 1753, 3:107; cf. #61 "The Mystery of Iniquity," 1:32–34; 2:466–68; CH 7:115–17.
[70]DOS Pt. I, ii.12–15, IX:230–38.
[71]DOS Pt. I, IX:196.

*Combating the Deist Denial
of Original Sin: A Searching
Response
to John Taylor*

Wesley never imagined that he was doing any original thinking in his explication of the traditional doctrine of original sin. Rather he thought of himself merely as defending the received faith against crypto-Arians of his time, as represented by a leading deist, John Taylor (1694-1761) of Norwich, a proto-Unitarian who had written a popular book in 1740 on *The Scripture-Doctrine of Original Sin, Exposed to Free and Candid Examination*,[72] in which he challenged the basic premise of original sin. Wesley thought that Taylor was working out of a deistic theism, a Pelagian anthropology, a reductionist Christology, a work-righteousness ethic, and a universalist eschatology, all of which were undermining substantive Christian teaching.[73] Wesley considered Taylor's unitarianism as tending toward antinomianism, toward the trivializing of Christ's work on the cross, the weakening of Christ's deity, and finally the impugning of God's character by making God responsible for present human sinfulness.[74]

Taylor viewed sin benignly as an imbalance of appetites propagated by habit, following the classical Greek view of habituated vice.[75] It was an "old Deism in a new dress; seeing it saps the very foundation of all revealed religion, whether Jewish or Christian . . . If, therefore, we take away this foundation . . . the Christian system falls at once."[76]

All of these tendencies to which Wesley was trying to respond remain epidemic in popular modern Christianity. If so, it may be that this least-read treatise on original sin is among his most relevant for contemporary audiences.[77]

Wesley considered these views as a deadly toxin being diffused insidiously throughout the church, to which an antidote was urgently needed. "I verily believe no single person since Mahomet has given such a wound to Christianity as Dr. Taylor," whose books "have poisoned so many of the clergy, and indeed the fountains themselves—the universities in England, Scotland, Holland, and Germany."[78] In the absence of an adequate rejoinder by others, Wesley "dare not be silent any longer." He considered it his solemn pastoral duty to admonish and amend these misunderstandings on behalf of all who looked to him for spiritual counsel.[79]

---

[72]London: J. Waugh, 1740; a second edition in 1741 contained a Supplement replying to Jennings and Watts; the 3d ed. appeared in 1746, eleven years before Wesley entered the fray.

[73]John Taylor, *The Scripture-Doctrine of Original Sin, Exposed to Free and Candid Examination*, London: 1740; his other works include *The Scripture Doctrine of Atonement*, and *The Lord's Supper Explained Upon Scripture*.

[74]LJW 3:180, 208; B1:461; 3:474; 4:100, 151n, 522.

[75]Opposing all federalist interpretations of Adam's sin, and viewing all guilt as personal and nontransferable, Taylor concluded: "If we come into the world infected and depraved with sinful dispositions, then sin must be natural to us; and if natural, then necessary; and if necessary, then no sin," 129.

[76]DOS Pref. 4 IX:194.

[77]DOS Pref. IX:192–94.

[78]Letter to Augustus Toplady, Dec. 9, 1758.

[79]DOS Pref. 2 IX:193. In his journal of Aug. 28, 1748, Wesley notes that he had encountered at Shackerley some "disciples of Dr. Taylor; laughing at Original Sin, and consequently, at the whole frame of Scriptural Christianity." When he returned to Shackerley on April 10, 1751, "Being now in the very midst of Mr. Taylor's disciples, I

Wesley's refutations were complemented by David Jenning's *Vindication*[80] and John Hervey's dialogue, *Theron and Aspasio*, as well as careful studies of original sin by Isaac Watts,[81] Samuel Hebden,[82] and Thomas Boston.[83]

All this is by way of preface, to put Wesley's treatise in its setting. It reveals the Anglican evangelist in a complex theological debate in which he sincerely thought that the integrity of Christian teaching was decisively at stake. In so far as the presupposition of original sin is misplaced, all else becomes more difficult to understand in theology.[84]

Evidences of Sin in the History of Sin

Human History Attests the Universality of Corruption

We see Wesley's quadrilateral theological method more consciously unfolding here than anywhere else in his writings. We see him first working with historical arguments, then experiential and sociological arguments, and finally with early patristic and scriptural arguments.

Wesley began with historical testimony to original sin, setting forth massive layers of historical evidence for the universality of human misery and sin.[85] It was this first portion of *The Doctrine of Original Sin* that Wesley reprinted

separately in 1762 under the comic-pathetic title of *The Dignity of Human Nature*.

It would be foolish to expect that an eighteenth-century mind could have already grasped in detail the psychological and social analyses of the nineteenth and twentieth centuries. We do not expect persons to know methods and worldviews that emerge only after they die. Yet those who dismiss Wesley often do so on such absurd grounds. From the vantage point of our modern chauvinism, our recent sense of the moral superiority of modernity over all pre-modern modes of consciousness, we tend to view Wesley's historical arguments as quaint and dismissible, at times even humorous. There is no reason not to enjoy that humor so long as it does not block us from hearing the text.

It requires a deeper empathy than modern chauvinist contempt for antiquity to get back into his frame of reference so as to grasp what he was seeing about the universal evidences of corruption. Only those who survey the human condition from its earliest times see the depth of its predicament, with its perennial tendency to misjudge the attainability of knowledge and virtue.[86]

Whether Human Corruptibility and Misery Are Found Universally

With the primordial fall of freedom into corruption, the consequences have

---

enlarged much more than I am accustomed to do on the doctrine of Original Sin; and determined, if God should give me a few years' life, publicly to answer his new gospel."

[80]*A Vindication of the Scripture-Doctrine of Original Sin*, London: 1740.

[81]*The Ruin and Recovery of Mankind*, London: 1740.

[82]Hebden (1692?-1747), (independent minister of Wrentham, Suffolk), *The Doctrine of Original Sin, as laid down in the Assembly's Catechism, explained.*

[83]*Human Nature in its Fourfold State*, 10th ed., Edinburgh: 1753, extracted in Pt. VII of DOS. Jonathan Edwards did not publish *The Great Christian Doctrine of Original Sin Defended* until 1758.

[84]DOS Pref. IX:193–95.

[85]Note the full title: *The Doctrine of Original Sin According to Scripture, Reason, and Experience*. The role of tradition, particularly patristic tradition, is here viewed as an ancillary aspect of Scripture, namely, as part of the history of exegesis. In another sense tradition is rightly viewed under "experience," inasmuch as it attests the experience of the historic Christian community, particularly in its classical consensual phase.

[86]DOS Pt. I, I.1, IX:196.

pervaded everything that happen subsequently in the intensely interconnected story of human history, where each one's personal decisions affect the succeeding flow of interpersonal and social sin. The wonderful capacity for imagination becomes distorted by pride and sensuality, turning the heart toward thinking and doing evil continually so that all flesh becomes adulterated. Total depravity does not mean that there is nothing good in human creation, but that sin taints every corner and aspect of human choosing.

Story after story reveals this corruption. The primary scriptural text Wesley was working out of was Gen. 6:5: *"And God saw that the wickedness of man was great in the earth, and that every imagination of the thoughts of his heart was only evil continually"* (KJV). Already "the contagion had spread itself through the inner man; had tainted the seat of their principles, and the source of their actions."[87]

Wesley's survey of the history of sin is hardly a cheery argument, for its very purpose is to prove historically the universality of pride and sloth, not just among pagans, but among those also to whom saving grace has come, yet who have turned again to apostasy and fallenness. When Wesley thinks about the whole course of human history, the biblical narrative forms the core of it, though not its entirety. He was far better educated in classical Hellenistic and Roman literary sources in their original Greek and Latin than standard guild academics today.[88]

The story of Noah offers a synoptic and typic way of talking about the general corruption of history, the radical deterioration of God's gift of accountable freedom. When Plan A (Paradise) degenerated to rebellion, Plan B (expulsion from Paradise) was put in effect. When Plan B failed, Plan C was required—a flood, a new beginning, a rainbow covenant, and a new promise. Noah attests not only the negation of the old but a new beginning, a new covenant with all humanity, not just with a particular people.[89]

After the flood, the relentless story of corruption continues, scene upon scene: The account of the tower of Babel typifies the universality of the corruption of language. Human speech becomes confused, twisted, and contaminated. That idolatrous human beings do not communicate well with each other remains a profound evidence of the general fallenness of humanity.[90] There is no hint in the earliest accounts of ancient history that primitive humanity was ever pervasively reformed. Sodom, having not even ten righteous persons, was destroyed by fire and brimstone. In Canaanitic culture, sin is attested at every hand. War, torture, and exploitation abound.[91]

The calling of Abraham offered a new beginning for the covenant people, but again sin came to reign even among the progeny of Israel. Though one might have expected them to excel in virtue because of God's law and promises, they behaved much like those who had never known God. The covenant of law was given to bless the people and offer the promise of happiness, but they repeatedly neglected it and returned inveterately to sin.[92] The syndrome of idolatry led to Babylonian captivity, which should have corrected it, but did

---

[87]DOS Pt. I, I.1, IX:197, quoting John Hervey, *Theron and Aspasio*, Dialogue 11; cf. LJW 6:121.

[88]DOS Pt. I, I.1-2, IX:196–7.

[89]DOS Pt. I, I.3, IX:197.

[90]DOS Pt. I, I.3, IX:197.

[91]DOS Pt. I, I.8, IX:200.

[92]DOS Pt. I, I.4, IX:198.

so only temporarily. Captivity had the redemptive intent of bringing the faithful back to the covenant promise. Faith was recovered in captivity, only to be lost again in idolatry and national waywardness.[93]

The story of actual human history apart from grace is a story of sin winning again and again. Jesus himself set forth a dismal picture of the persistent deteriorations of history. He viewed the religious leaders of his time as whited sepulchres full of dead men's bones, displaying every imaginable stench of uncleanness.[94]

Paul offered the definitive text for original sin in Romans 1 and 2: We are given human existence as good, but worship the creature rather than the Creator. Out of our persistent idolatries, all other forms of human distortion emerge, from the collapse of natural sexuality to every other imaginable offense.[95]

Wesley then turned to Greco-Roman history, asking the same questions of Hesiod, Homer, Aeschylus, and all of the ancient historians, poets, and tragedians. These lead to the same dismal conclusion, that no society recorded in ancient history comes even close to moral accountability or happiness. Even the best of societies are attended by painful human costs. Even the best of persons lived within profoundly distorted histories. The supposed virtues of Rome were given the lie by the cruelty of its most noble citizens such as Cato and Julius Caesar. Than Pompey "a less amiable character is not easy to find."[96]

Infant exposure was in Wesley's mind a particularly horrid example of an accepted unjust social practice in Rome. To this he added the torture of victims in war, and numerous abusive political and sexual practices. Wesley was a sensitive moral historian who hated injustices, a good classical scholar who had read Thucydides and Tacitus and Cicero from early school days in their original Greek and Latin. He found no part of the story they told untainted by sin. The universality of sin is evident to anyone who reasonably looks at the evidence.[97]

We see this especially when we view human history lengthening out over many generations. Original sin implies that no one can enter history as if starting with an absolutely clean moral slate, as if nothing unseemly had ever happened before. Previously distorted human history happened before I got here. I am not personally responsible for the choices of others, but those choices affect me. That history has entered into my history. My parents' experience has entered decisively into my history.

In this way human fallenness has a social and historical character. Whole societies can affect the form sin takes in a given period. Modern individuals think of themselves under a radically individualistic premise. But Scripture thinks corporately about human life. Sin has vast incalculable intergenerational effects.[98]

Sociological and Experiential Evidences of the Universality of Human Corruption

The Universality of Sin in Non-theistic Cultures

If it seems that Wesley was functioning as an amateur social anthropologist,

[93]DOS Pt. I, I.8–10, IX:200–201.
[94]DOS Pt. I, I.11, IX:201; Mt. 23:27.
[95]DOS Pt. I, I.12, IX:202–3.
[96]DOS Pt. I, I.12–13, IX:202–4.
[97]DOS Pt. I, I.12–18, IX:202–8.
[98]DOS Pt. I, I.1f., IX:196f.

and not a very good one, it is only fair to remember that the methods of field anthropology had not yet been invented in the modern sense. The term *heathen* referred to those who did not share the premises of western theism.[99] Wesley inquired first into the moral happiness of nontheistic cultures, then of theistic. Wesley followed Brerewood's population geography in concluding that if the world were divided into thirty parts, nineteen would be heathen, six Islamic, and only five Christian.[100] A disturbing percentage of those formally viewed as baptized Christians obviously would fall far short of the mark of moral accountability.[101]

Wesley's intention in Part I.ii of *Original Sin* was to make a multicultural survey of human societies, asking whether any have surmounted the outrageous effects of sin. He ranged widely in remarking on cultures about which he had more information: native American culture, which he had experienced to some degree firsthand, then African and Asian. No one today would consider Wesley to be a normative or even reliable interpreter of these great cultures, as he shared many stereotypes common to his generation. But it is evident that he was interested in bringing into his theological analysis what he knew of these cultures, even though limited by what we today would regard as a relatively small data base.[102]

Among native American cultures with whom he had some immediate experience,[103] he observed as evidence of sin their constant intertribal warfare. He was especially disturbed by their practice of torturing defenseless vic-

tims. As one of the few English writers of his day who had actually spent time in the immediate environment of native American Indians, Wesley did not share the distantly conceived inflated picture of the noble savage that prevailed among enlightened French literati of the eighteenth century. Wesley punctured this picture mercilessly, providing a graphic depiction of how these natives were as deeply embedded in sin as the avaricious colonial British.[104]

Turning to Asia, Wesley was disturbed by what appeared to him as the complete immobility of Chinese society, unable to yield to any significant changes, trapped in cultural prejudices and oddities, such as the crippling of women by the binding of their feet, and their 300,000–character alphabet, which he thought not only amusing, but debilitating to social progress, and a means of social control by knowledge and power elites. He suspected that the aristocratic class benefitted from this immobility, often in absurd and demeaning ways, being fed by servants, having feces preserved, etc.[105]

Wesley's picture of eighteenth-century black African culture, shaped by contemporary stereotypes of primitive animists, was keenly aware of the constant warfare between tribes and the lack of intertribal justice, yet he was capable of appreciation of many aspects of native African culture. Above all he was implacably opposed to slavery, which he had personally observed in Savannah, as radically demeaning all who touched it.

His purpose in all of this was to show that not just a small slice of human

[99]LJW 1:188, 225, 286; 4:67; 5:327.
[100]Edward Brerewood, *Enquiries touching the Diversity of Languages,* 1614.
[101]DOS Pt. I, ii.2, IX:210.
[102]DOS Pt. I, ii.1, IX:208f.
[103]See his *Journal* accounts of interactions with native Americans of Georgia, JJW 1:156–62, 236–39, 248–50, 297f., 406–9.
[104]DOS Pt. I, ii.3, IX:210–13.
[105]DOS Pt. I, ii.4, 5, IX:213–15.

history, but the whole of it is thoroughly saturated with corruptions analogous to those described summarily in Genesis 3 and Romans 1–2. There is, he thought, a cohesion in the biblical description of sin that is illustrated at every turn of subsequent so-called secular human history.[106]

In "Thoughts on a Late Publication," 1789, a critique of a report by W. Wilson and G. Keate on their travels to the Pelew Islands, Wesley took strong exception to the romantic hypothesis that the natives of Pelew constituted "a nation who are by nature free from sin, without any ill tempers, without anything blamable either in their words or actions."[107] Even this report shows that they murdered prisoners in cold blood, and practiced polygamy and theft. "I have conversed, in fourscore years, (between forty and fifty of which I have, at an average, travelled four thousand miles a year,) with more persons than these two gentlemen[108] put together; and many of them Indians of various nations, Creeks, Cherokees, Chickasaws, and no ways infected with Christianity: But one such man as" described in the Pelew account "I have not found."[109] "If mankind are faultless by nature, naturally endued with light to see all necessary truth, and with strength to follow it . . . revelation is a mere fable."[110] Homer fantastically supposed that the Ethiopians were similarly unblamable, but even Homer did little justice to humankind if the account of the Pelew natives be true. If true, of course, the scriptural account of the universal fall of humanity would have to be false.

The Universality of Sin in "Theistic" Cultures

If these problems pervade the nontheistic history of humanity, to what degree are they mitigated in the theistic world, as one might expect? He addressed first the Muslim world as he knew it, again by certain exaggerated caricatures, but keep in mind his purpose—to show the universality of corruption and misery, not to show that Muslims are more corrupt than Christians and animists, but equally prone to be so.[111] He decried Islamic holy wars undertaken with religious rhetoric disguising economic motivations. They have earned their reputation as "wolves and tigers to all other nations." He viewed the rigid attachment of Islamic followers to an untranslatable Koran as the height of immobile irrationality. He warned of the tendencies to fanaticism in Islamic determinism, whose exponents are prone to "beat each other's brains from generation to generation!"[112]

Wesley's dated views of alternative cultures are not to be taken as normative for our time. What we are seeking to grasp is his fundamental point of view toward the general corruptibility of human nature, and how it correlates with the human condition everywhere.

The Universality of Sin in "Christian" Cultures

Having addressed the universality of sin in nontheistic and theistic cultures,

---

[106]DOS Pt. I, ii.1–5, IX:208–15.
[107]"Thoughts on a Late Publication," XIII:411.
[108]Captain W. Wilson and George Keate, *An Account of the Pelew Islands*; JJW 7:464; 8:29; Arminian Magazine (1790): 545, (1791): 38f.
[109]"Thoughts on a Late Publication," XIII:412.
[110]"Thoughts on a Late Publication," XIII:413.
[111]For further reference to Islam see LJW 1:277; 5:250; 6:118, 123, 371; JJW 5:242; 1:311f.; CH 7:608.
[112]DOS Pt. I, ii.6, IX:215–16.

he then proceeded to speak about the special forms of sin prevailing in supposedly Christian cultures, first Greek Orthodox, and then Roman Catholic, leaving his most devastating disapproval for Protestants. With both the Orthodox and Roman traditions, he is quick to see the superstitious imagination as demoralizing. The Counter-Reformation inquisition revealed the pretentious hypocrisy pervasive in Roman canon law.[113]

Given the withering power of his censure of these traditions, one might expect him then to be a little softer on Protestantism, but again the optimists are to be disappointed. For in none of the preceding cultural criticisms would he be more stringent than in his own. He aimed squarely at the irascible Protestant tendency toward divisiveness, its failure to be a tradition of continuing reform, and especially its failure to reform its own social environments. Among key examples of the perennial injustices of societies shaped by Protestant religion: poverty, war, social oppression, prostitution, and litigiousness, with "villains exalted to the highest places."[114]

The court itself, sworn to uphold justice, becomes the instrument for perverting justice. Honesty among lawyers is very thinly spread.[115] "If my neighbor has a mind to my cow, he hires a lawyer to prove that he ought to have my cow from me. I must hire another to defend my right, it being against all rules of law that a man should speak for himself. In pleading, they do not dwell on the merits of the cause, but upon circumstances foreign thereto."[116]

His point: Sin is everywhere an empirical fact, even where civilized virtues attempt to shine brightest. Wherever you see the human will at work, you see its miserable products. There is nowhere to look in human history where one will not find a history of injustice, a dismal account of the social and interpersonal transmission of sin and misery.[117]

Whether War Is the Primal Prototype of Social Sin

His most recurrent example of social sin is *war*. He examined realistically what happens when leaders become inordinately ambitious for power. Innocents are killed. He was stunned by the myriad ways we deceive ourselves, pretending in our nationalism that we are exceedingly advanced morally—rational and well-intentioned, all while promoting the enterprises of institutionalized horror.

"Now, who can reconcile war, I will not say to religion, but to any degree of reason or common sense?. . . Here are forty thousand men gathered together on this plain. What are they going to do? See, there are thirty or forty thousand more at a little distance. And these are going to shoot them through the head or body, to stab them, or split their skulls, and send most of their souls into everlasting fire as fast as they possibly can. Why so?. . . They do not so much as know them . . . What a method of proof! What an amazing way of deciding controversies!" "All our declamations on the strength of human reason, and the eminence of our virtues, are no more than the cant and jargon of pride and ignorance, so long

---

[113]DOS Pt. I, ii.7-9, IX:217–19.
[114]DOS Pt. I, ii.9, IX:219–21.
[115]DOS Pt. I, ii.11, IX:228–30.
[116]DOS Pt. I, ii.9, IX:219–21; quoting Abraham Cowley.
[117]DOS Pt. I, ii.12–15, IX:230–38.

as there is such a thing as war in the world."[118]

Experiential Self-Examination

As if this indictment were not enough, Wesley invites each reader to "survey" her or his own behavior. Whatever may be the objective situation in human history, the question may be asked even more personally and inwardly by any serious person: Am I pleased with my own behavior? The last time I made a resolution, how long did it take actually to correct my behavior? Each hearer is called to press such questions in the most candid way directly home to the scenes of daily decisions.[119] How long has it been since my conscience tells me that I did something contrary to justice? Who has not entertained "unreasonable desires" one knows are wrong? Who has not taken one's anger farther than the cause required?[120] Only the hearer can answer in the depths of inwardness.[121]

Anyone with any remaining doubt about original sin does well to examine himself or herself in complete honesty, scrutinizing skewed motives and the bad consequences of good intentions. Wesley probes relentlessly into whether one has made promises that remained unfulfilled, whether one's spouse is treated fairly, what one's children think of one's fairness, how those closest to you judge your trustability, when guilt occasionally creeps in and one wonders where it comes from, whether one is consistently fair with people with whom one works daily, whether the needy neighbor is attended to as vigorously as

oneself. We resolve to change but remain the same. We say things contrary to truth or love that we later regret.[122] If all were honest, would written receipts be required? In any serious self-examination, those who look at their behavior know how far below the mark they fall.

Long before sociologist Erving Goffman spoke of impression management, Wesley was observing that "The generality of men do not wear their worst side outward. Rather, they study to appear better than they are, and to conceal what they can of their faults." We conceal parts of ourselves that others may not see the whole. Our modes of impression management always make us put on a face better than the reality.[123] For Wesley all such sociological truisms stand as empirical testimony to the universality of human corruption.[124]

Guilt plays an important proximate role in bringing us to ourselves by helping us to see where we are failing to reflect the goodness of God in human relationship. Guilt functions positively to call us to ourselves in God's presence. Conscience is that universally experienced human awareness that relentlessly notices whenever we fall short of the image of God trying to shine throught our human finitude.[125] Wesley was not trying artificially to create more guilt, but to deal pastorally with the already existent level of guilt created by sin.

Humanity Is Universally Unhappy Because it Is Unholy

"Universal misery is at once a consequence and a proof of this universal

---

[118]DOS Pt. I, ii.10, IX:221–23.
[119]SS 2:215.
[120]This stands in the Puritan tradition of penitential self-examination of conscience, B1:299; 2:215, 511; 3:124n.
[121]DOS Pt. I, ii.15, IX:236–38.
[122]DOS Pt. I, ii.12, IX:231–34.
[123]DOS Pt. I, ii.13, IX:234.
[124]C. Williams, JWTT, 56.
[125]B1:301–4; 3:479–90.

corruption. Men are unhappy (how very few are the exceptions!) because they are unholy . . . 'Pain accompanies and follows sin.' ''[126] As long as "vicious tempers" rule the heart, peace has no place there. "Sin is the root of trouble, and it is unholiness which causes unhappiness." Unhappiness is neither attributable to economic hardship nor prevented by frugality or abundance.[127]

No moment of human history is left unaffected by this misery. The ground of our misery is our lack of actually reflecting the holiness of God, the image of God originally given in human creation. We do not exercise our original capacity for proximately reflecting or imaging God. Our persistent unholiness is the basis for our unhappiness.

After layered centuries of sin, human history is not rightly described as rather a bit unhappy. Much stronger terms are required: wretchedness, misery. "Sin is the baleful source of affliction; and consequently, the flood of miseries which covers the face of the earth,— which overwhelms not only single persons, but whole families, towns, cities, kingdoms,—is a demonstrative proof of the overflowing of ungodliness in every nation under heaven."[128] All of the above we can learn rationally and experientially, from the study of history, society, and self.

Scriptural Evidences of Original Sin As Received by Ecumenical Tradition

Although Wesley found evidences for original sin in historical, sociological, and experiential inquiries, it was chiefly from Scripture that he sought to counter the deistic[129] arguments against intergenerational guilt, and spiritual death as a result of the history of sin.

From the Beginning

Original means first. Original sin is the form of sin in human history that dates back to its beginning. That sin is original which is the archetype of subsequent sin, derivative from the first sin, and being configured from the fallen human condition becomes the formative pattern for other sins in history.

No sooner did God give humanity freedom than we managed to corrupt and adulterate it. This is what human beings have been doing from the origins of human history. That is essentially what original sin means. Fallen human history has been molded by sin in ways that influence all subsequent communication.

The biblical way of portraying and corporately signifying the radical fallenness of humanity is by rehearsing the account of Adam and Eve.[130] They fell from holiness and happiness in a way that has decisively impacted the entire subsequent history of freedom.[131]

Each of us has become involved in their story, the human story, the history of sin. Their story is ours. What they did has consequences for us, just as what we do has consequences for all who follow us. Alienated freedom makes noises that rumble endlessly toward the future. The consequences of my sin do not end with me, but impact others after me whom I will never see.

---

[126]DOS Pt. I, ii.14, IX:235, *culpam poena premit comes.*

[127]DOS Pt. I, ii.15, IX:237; cf. B1:197f.; 4:287f.

[128]DOS Pt. I, ii.14–15, IX:235–38.

[129]For Wesley's comments on deism, see B3:452, 494, 499; FA 11:175–76; LJW 2:75, 96, 313; 7:263–65; JJW 1:357; 3:433.

[130]B4:366.

[131]In Pt. IV of *The Doctrine of Original Sin*, Wesley developed this point by including a substantial extract from Isaac Watts' response to Taylor, *The Ruin and Recovery of Mankind*, 1741; DOS iv, IX:397–415.

Whether One Suffers
From Another's Sin?

The evil lodged at the heart of human history cannot be explained merely in terms of having followed a bad example or being cursed by a bad upbringing. It requires the more searching scriptural premise of the corrupted and corrupting will.[132]

The first scriptural evidence of original sin is that after Adam and Eve sinned they were filled with shame, eliciting a sense of nakedness, fear and guilt, and loss of the graces they had earlier received. And even their shame in the presence of the holy God was deceptively covered up because of their pride, which refused to acknowledge their guilt.[133]

Scripturally, the consequence of Adam's sin was death not only for Adam but all his progeny.[134] In Adam all die as the result of the disobedience of one.[135] It is false to assert that Adam's posterity could not be justly punished for the transgression of the prototypical human sin. For that would be to deny the corporate character of human history, including the evident fact that we suffer with and for each other. "So we do in fact suffer for Adam's sin, and that too by the sentence inflicted on our first parents. We suffer death in consequence of their transgression. Therefore we are, in some sense, guilty of their sin. I would ask, What is guilt, but an obligation to suffer punishment for sin? Now since we suffer the same penal evil which God threatened to, and inflicted on, Adam for his sin . . . Therefore we are all in some way guilty of Adam's sin."[136]

Distinguishing Death Temporal
From Death Spiritual

Taylor had argued individualistically that the only result of the Fall was physical death for Adam, and that it had no vast consequences for the corruption of human nature socially. Wesley responded that death in Adam implies far more than the loss of his own personal bodily life. The death expressed in the original admonition and pronounced upon humanity, included a judgment upon all evils that affect the temporal body: "death temporal, spiritual, and eternal," both a temporal death (dissolution of the body) and a spiritual death (loss of eternal life).[137]

The result of original sin was a continuing propensity to sin, which itself resulted in actual sins of individuals in human history. Taylor could not grasp how a just God could hold progeny accountable for their parents' sin. Wesley appealed to the corporate anthropology of the scriptural principle that the sins of the fathers are visited upon their posterity.[138]

Whether Redemption in Christ Makes
Up for Losses Suffered in Adam

By one man sin entered the world. The punishment threatened to Adam is now inflicted upon all humanity, so that all are deemed sinners in the presence of God. By one offense death reigned in human history. All of us are involved in this single judicial sentence. All of us are constituted sinners by Adam's sinning so as to be liable for punishment.

As by the offence of one many are dead, by one grace is extended to all humanity. In one, Adam, many are

---

[132]DOS Pt. II, i.1, IX:238–39.
[133]DOS Pt. II, i.4, IX:241–42; cf. B1:442f.
[134]SS 1:157.
[135]DOS Pt. II, i.3, IX:240–41; Gen. 2:17.
[136]DOS Pt. II, i.5, IX:242–43, with reference to Jenning's *Vindication*.
[137]DOS Pt. II, i.6, IX:244–45; on physical and spiritual death, see B1:142–47, 227–28.
[138]DOS Pt. I, i.6–7, IX:244–46.

made dead. In one, Christ, many made alive. What is lost by one is restored by the other. Through our relation with Adam we all suffer; through our relation with the second Adam, all are offered new life and all who believe effectively receive new life.[139]

Though all humanity died spiritually in Adam,[140] humanity has nonetheless gained in more blessings through Christ than it frittered away in Adam. Where sin abounds, grace more abounds.[141] The benefit we attain through Christ far surpasses what we lost in Adam, for Christ removes all sin, and not original sin only. Christ raises believers to a far happier state than that which Adam enjoyed in paradise.[142]

Exegesis of the Westminster Catechism's Scripture Texts on Original Sin

A detailed exegetical inquiry ensues into principal passages of Scripture on original sin, particularly those cited by six propositions on original sin of the Larger Catechism of Westminster,[143] which formed a useful structure upon which to organize his exegetical study, though Wesley added: "To this I never subscribed, but I think it is in the main a very excellent composition, which I shall therefore cheerfully endeavour to defend, so far as I conceive it is grounded on clear Scripture."[144]

Taylor opposed all six propositions because he thought they (1) demeaned human freedom and moral agency, and (2) intensified the impasse of theodicy. Wesley answered both objections. Original sin does not imply that humanity lacks moral choice, for through grace God has restored a measure of free will to all. By common or prevening grace, not by nature, rational moral agents are capable of performing acts of moral accountability.

Sufficient prevening grace is given to all humanity to enable them to pray for the grace further necessary to repent and believe.[145] Since God acted to redeem humanity, providing "a Savior for them all . . . this fully acquits both his justice and his mercy."[146] Thus the tension created for theodicy by the doctrine of original sin is resolved not by logic, but by action—the redeeming action of God's grace on the cross through the Son, and in our hearts through the Holy Spirit. A high doctrine of original sin is the premise and companion of a high doctrine of grace. Since the whole of humanity is involved in guilt and punishment, having no possibility of self-salvation, each one must cast himself solely on the grace offered in Christ.

Adam as Public Person: On Federal Headship

Wesley defended Westminster Proposition 1: "The covenant being made with Adam not only for himself, but for his posterity, all mankind descending from him by ordinary generation, sinned in him, and fell with him, in his first transgression."[147] Original sin best explains the universality of sin. All alternative explanations—example, custom, education, or the passage of time—are inept insofar as they skip over the decisive first cause, thus failing

---

[139]DOS Pt. II, i.16, IX:255–57.
[140]DOS Pt. II, i.17–18, IX:257–61.
[141]DOS Pt. II, i.14, IX:253–55.
[142]DOS Pt. II, i.5–7, IX:242–46.
[143]DOS Pt. II, ii.i, IX:261–88.
[144]DOS Pt. II, ii.1, IX:261.
[145]DOS Pt. II ii.9, 10, IX:273
[146]DOS Pt. II, ii.18, IX:285.
[147]COC III:679; DOS Pt. II, ii.2, IX:262.

to grasp why sin is so pervasive in human history.

Adam stands at the head of human history as a "public person." His forensic position is predicated on his biological position.[148] The divine command to "not eat" and the deadly consequence of its neglect were not addressed merely to Adam personally, but to all humanity corporately.[149]

Neither representative or federal head are scriptural terms, hence for Wesley hardly worthy of lengthy disputation. Nonetheless, he argues that both Adam and Christ are in Scripture representatives of all humanity. Adam as a "public person" was an anticipative type or figure of Christ, for as all juridically die in Adam, all are by grace made alive in Christ. As God laid on all the iniquities of Adam, God laid on Christ the iniquities of us all.[150]

The Consequence of Adam's Fall for Subsequent Human History

Wesley defended Westminster Proposition 2: "The fall brought mankind into an estate of sin and misery."[151] Adam's disobedience brought guilt and spiritual death to all, not just physical suffering and death to Adam. Humanity as a whole was swept into a corporate state of sin and suffering, making them corrupt and guilty, and subject to punishment.[152] In the Fall the image of God in all humanity was gravely damaged, though not entirely obliterated (Gen. 5:3; Eccl. 7:29). Romans 5 and 1 Corinthians 15 describe the situation as one of spiritual death. Before the Fall Adam was perfect, but his perfection was not absolute, since he could grow and change and alter his future by his own decision. He was temptable as a result of his natural liberty. In response to Taylor's interpretation of death not as a punishment for sin but as a benefit to all humanity intended to increase the vanity of earthly things and abate their force to delude us, the Scripture counters constantly that it is a punishment.[153]

Wesley defended Westminster Proposition 3: " 'Sin is any want of conformity to, or transgression of, the law of God,' given as a rule to the reasonable creation."[154] By the Fall, such sin comes to be "of our nature," or a kind of second nature to all who share in human history. We are described as having a law of sin in our members (Rom. 7:23), being dead in sin (Eph. 2:1).

The Abyss into Which Humanity Plunged

Wesley defended Westminster Proposition 4: "The sinfulness of that estate whereinto man fell, consists in the guilt of Adam's first sin, the want of original righteousness, and the corruption of his whole nature, which is commonly called original sin; together with all actual transgressions which proceed from it."[155] "The Lord saw how great man's wickedness on the earth had become, and that every inclination of the thoughts of his heart was only evil all the time" (Gen 6:5). "Now the earth was corrupt in God's sight and was full

---

[148]LJW 4:98, 155.
[149]DOS Pt. II, ii.2, IX:262.
[150]DOS Pt. III, vi, IX:332–34.
[151]DOS Pt. II, ii.3, IX:263; COC III:679.
[152]DOS Pt. I, ii.3, IX:263.
[153]DOS Pt. II, i.18, IX:258–59.
[154]DOS Pt. II, ii.4, IX:264, quoting Westminster Shorter Catechism, Q 14, COC III:678.
[155]COC III:679; DOS Pt. II, ii.5, IX:264; on sin as indebtedness, see B1:586.

of violence" (Gen. 6:11).[156] It is not fitting to hedge with elaborate excuses the clear biblical description that "our very nature exposed us to the Divine Wrath, like the rest of mankind" (Eph. 2:3 TCNT, so that we "were by nature the children of wrath," KJV).[157] "The mind of sinful man is death . . . Those controlled by the sinful nature cannot please God" (Rom. 8:6,8).[158] "Without supernatural grace we can neither will nor do what is pleasing to God."[159]

Wesley corroborated David Jennings' subtle argument in response to Taylor's view that if sin is natural, it is necessary. "If by sin is meant the corrupt bias of our wills, that indeed is natural to us, as our nature is corrupted by the fall; but not as it came originally out of the hand of God . . . A proud or passionate temper is evil, whether a man has contracted it himself, or derived it from his parents." If by sin is meant those sinful actions to which this corrupt bias of the will inclines us, it is not self-evident that these are necessary, hence not culpable. "If a corrupt bias makes sin to be necessary, and consequently, to be no sin, then the more any man is inclined to sin, the less sin he can commit . . . And so the man, instead of growing more wicked, grows more innocent."[160]

"Is God the cause of those sinful motions? He is the cause of the motion . . . [but] of the sin, he is not . . . otherwise you make God the direct author of all the sin under heaven." This view of original sin has ancient ecumenical conciliar assent, being held in the Greek East and the Latin West, and ecumenically, "so far as we can

learn, in every church under heaven."[161]

Distinguishing Original From Actual Sin

Wesley then defended Westminster Proposition 5: "Original sin is conveyed from our first parents to their posterity by natural generation, so as all that proceed from them in that way are conceived and born in sin."[162] Actual sins spring from within the context of original sin. Evil works proceed from an evil heart. We choose to follow a natural inclination to sin.

"Surely I was sinful at birth, sinful from the time my mother conceived me" (Ps. 51:5). Otherwise the work of saving grace in Christ would hardly be necessary, were there no depth of captivity in the human predicament. Wesley finds empirical evidence for this in the primitive egocentricities of neonates, and in the fact that some sin without even being tempted, which he thought to be confirmation of an internally rooted rebelliousness against the giver of good.

One person's sin and its consequent punishment are in fact visited upon others. This is the solemn principle of the social and corporeal nature and consequence of sin in human history. For progenitors' sins, descendants in fact often must suffer. This is a part of the high price we pay for the precious gift of freedom.

But by grace we can conquer this primordial inclination.[163] Even though we were "conceived in sin and shapen in iniquity," there is always sufficient grace to remove whatever sin has been

[156]DOS Pt. II, ii.9, IX:272.
[157]DOS Pt. II, ii.6, IX:266–69.
[158]DOS Pt. II, ii.8, IX:271.
[159]DOS Pt. II, ii.10, IX:273.
[160]DOS Pt. II, ii.10, IX:273, in reference to D. Jennings, *Vindication*, 68.
[161]DOS Pt. II, ii.11, IX:274.
[162]DOS Pt. II, ii.13, IX:275.
[163]DOS Pt. II, ii.12, IX:275.

willed. That "my mother conceived me" does not refer flatly to sexual copulation, but to the general history of sin in which my physical conception took place. Eve is the mother of us all.[164] "Who can bring what is pure from the impure? No one!" (Job 14:4).[165] Yet no one can plead being without excuse simply by an appeal to another's depravity.

The Intergenerational Sociality of Sin

The premise of the sociality of sin is a deeply held hebraic assumption. It goes directly against the stream of naïve individualism, which assumes that I am responsible only for my private, individual actions, not for others or for how my behavior touches others. Hebraic consciousness passionately held to the social nature of human existence. Wesley shared that assumption of relational humanity, and translated it into eighteenth-century terms, controversies, and moral choices.

Your sin can affect me; my sin can affect my grandchildren; my grandfather's sin can affect me in ways difficult to understand exhaustively, yet to some degree subject to empirical analysis. These causal chains are not wholly mysterious, or beyond inquiry, yet there remains a stubborn element of the mystery of iniquity in all human freedom, since these causal chains are often hidden in the complex history of freedom's outcomes.

Sin's effects reverberate from person to person and from generation to generation. Wesley ruled out an individual conception of sin populated only by two parties, me and God. The individualistic fantasy is that my foibles do not affect anybody else, or if so, surely not all that seriously, or if seriously, surely not eternally. Wrong. Wesley viewed the human predicament as radically bound

together in social covenant. This was ultimately symbolized by the notion of the federal headship of Adam representing humanity, and all whose life and breath derive finally from Eve, the mother of all living.

Their choices, free choices, were not fated, not determined, but chosen and these preferences were permitted by God as giver and valuer of human self-determination. God does not want sin, but permits sin in the interest of preserving free, companionate, self-determined persons with whom to communicate incomparable divine love and holiness.

Beginning with Adam and Eve a corruption moves steadily from one generation to the next, inexorably. It is predictable that my generation is going to have its good and bad effects upon the next generation, and the next on the next. No one begins with a clean slate because all finite freedom lives in an actual history, not a fantasy world, in which we truly affect the destinies and possibilities of others. This is a highly realistic assumption about the moral consequences of human choices. Wesley found this doctrine of sin clearly attested throughout Scripture, Genesis to Revelation, especially in the prophetic and apostolic witnesses, and in no voice more definitely than Jesus'.

All other less realistic hypotheses for explaining sin are deficient. Some hypothesize a crafty escape hatch from responsibility in the notion that sin occurs exhaustively by social determination, that since we learn by example, custom, and social processes, sin is transferred *without our willing it*. Wesley answered that social processes obviously transfer sin, but not without our willing it. Each of us reinforces and relives the history of Adam and Eve's fallenness.

---

[164]DOS Pt. II, ii.13, IX:275–79.
[165]DOS Pt. II, ii.14–15, IX:279–80.

Whether Loss of Communion With God Sharpens the Sting of Theodicy

Wesley defended Westminster Proposition 6: "All mankind by their fall lost communion with God, are under his wrath and curse, and so made liable to all the miseries in this life."[166] "The faded glory, the darkness, the disorder, the impurity, the decayed state in all respects of this temple, too plainly show the Great Inhabitant is gone."[167]

God originally created our natures pure. Evil is the absurd corruption of nature brought on by Adam's free choice under God's permissive will. Otherwise God would be guilty of authoring evil. God is the *primum mobile*, the spring of all motion throughout the universe, thus the first cause of every vegetable, animal, and human activity. Yet sin is not God's will, but man's. That we are conceived in sin is not God's responsibility, but comes as a result of human pride, envy, and rebelliousness. God "who this moment supplies the power by which a sinful action is committed is not chargeable with the sinfulness of that action."[168]

To those who challenge the justice of God in allowing the history of sin, Wesley has an eschatological answer: The provision of "a Saviour for them all; and this fully acquits both [God's] justice and mercy."[169]

Whether There Remains a Natural Propensity to Sin

Are we now in worse moral circumstances than Adam? Yes, if by *moral circumstances* one means the decline of religion and virtue. No, if by *moral circumstances* one is referring to some provision of spiritual improvement, for in that case we are far better off than Adam, due to the history of grace.[170]

We derive from Adam a natural propensity to sin, within the permissive will of God, but this does not make God the source, only the permitter, of wrongful acts of human freedom. All have "a natural propensity to sin. Nevertheless, this propensity is not necessary, if by necessary you mean irresistible. We can resist and conquer it too, by the grace which is ever at hand."[171] In response to Taylor's arguments against a natural propensity to sin, which assumes that we are sinners because we commit acts of sin, Wesley contends: we commit sinful acts because we are sinners: "I (and you too, whether you will it or no) am inclined, and was ever since I can remember antecedently to any choice of my own, to pride, revenge, idolatry."[172]

Do the vices of parents in fact often infect their children? The most common observation shows that they do. This cannot stand as a charge against the justice of God. Lacking the premise of original sin it remains difficult to account for the fact that children begin so soon to sin. As soon as their faculties appear, they appear to be disordered. The use and abuse of reason grow up together.[173]

Human freedom has always shown itself prone in time to this fallenness. The social history of sin inclines personal freedom toward harmful habituation. The inclination to evil appears inevitably to accompany the unsullied

[166]COC III:679–80; DOS Pt. II, ii.17, IX:282.
[167]DOS Pt. II, ii:20, IX: 288; quoted from John Howe, *The Living Temple*, London: Parkhurst, 1703.
[168]DOS III, vii, IX:335.
[169]DOS Pt. II, ii.18, IX:285.
[170]DOS Pt. II, iii, IX:289.
[171]DOS Pt. II, iii, IX:284.
[172]DOS Pt. II, iii, IX:294.
[173]DOS Pt. II, iii, IX:295.

gift of freedom. Individual self-determining freedom finds its own distinctive ways further to distort the history of sin, and subtly collude with temptations to choose the lesser good.

Whether Guilt May be Imputed From One to Another

As guilt was imputed to the scapegoat in hebraic sacrificial liturgy, so are our sins borne by Christ on the cross. It is true that no just God would punish the innocent, but "God does not look upon infants as innocent, but as involved in the guilt of Adam's sin," and at times suffering mightily from their parents' sins, even as they may benefit from their parents' righteousness.[174] Though the mercy of God extracts numberless blessings from punishments, they are punishments still, imputed corporately for societal sin.[175]

That all are under the curse of sin is evident from the fact that all suffer. Suffering may result even where there is no personal individual sin, but only indirect corporate sin. Brutes and infants may suffer even without exercising their wills sinfully as individuals, because their lives are framed in the context of corporate sin.[176] Human toil and pain in childbirth are the prototype scriptural evidences that progeny suffer for the sins of their parents. However great their sufferings, "the best of men cannot be made unhappy by any calamities or oppressions whatsoever," for they have learned to be content in every possible state, rejoicing and giving thanks.[177]

The teaching of human nature as radically fallen does not indicate that one despises humanity, "since, whatever we are by nature, we may by grace be children of God, and heirs." Even when sinners have lost the power to perform their duty by nature, they still by grace may perform it, and thus it does not cease to be their duty.[178]

The Link Between Redemption and Original Sin

Original Sin and New Birth

Regeneration does not mean autonomously "gaining habits of holiness," for that would locate it as a natural change, while it is a change enabled by supernatural grace. "The new birth is not, as you supposed, the progress, or the whole, of sanctification, but the beginning of it; as the natural birth is not the whole of life, but only the entrance upon it. He that is 'born of a woman,' then begins to live a natural life; he that is 'born of God,' then begins to live a spiritual."[179]

"There is no possibility of the power of godliness" without a serious understanding of original sin. "No man truly believes in Christ, till he is deeply convinced of his own sinfulness, and helplessness. But this no man ever was, neither can be, who does not know he has a corrupt nature."[180]

Original sin, far from being a threat to moral endeavor, is a spur to the repentance that readies the will for faith active in love. Far from turning people away from God in moral disgust, it turns sinners toward God in the more radical sense of trusting in grace. "The doctrine, that we are by nature 'dead in sin,' and therefore 'children of wrath,' promotes repentance, a true knowledge of ourselves, and thereby leads to faith

---

[174]DOS Pt. III, i, IX:316.
[175]DOS Pt. III, ii, IX:317–19.
[176]DOS Pt. III, iii, IX:320–26.
[177]DOS Pt. III, iii, IX:324–26.
[178]DOS Pt. III, iv, IX:327.
[179]DOS Pt. II, iii, IX:310.
[180]DOS Pt. II, iii, IX:313.

in Christ, to a true knowledge of Christ crucified. And faith worketh love; and by love, all holiness both of heart and life. Consequently, this doctrine promotes (nay, and is absolutely, indispensably necessary to promote) the whole of that religion which the Son of God lived and died to establish."[181] In the new birth, believers put on "the new man" (Col. 3:9 KJV) by a real inward change, a renewal of the soul in righteousness and true holiness, a renewal of the image of God in us—where God's love governs the senses, appetites, and passions, as was the case in the pre-fallen Adam.[182]

Refixing the Pivot

Wesley's views still haunt the present inheritors of the Wesleyan tradition, though they inhabit a society in which these assumptions seem easily dismissable.[183] Those who preach can no longer assume that average modern Protestant audiences understand the premise of original sin around which other biblical teachings pivot.

To refix the pivot must then become a part of our teaching task. The responsibility to enter this arena falls to those to whom the teaching task is committed. They have a duty to teach this profound hebraic assumption as well as they can, even and especially while the culture is resisting it. To do so requires an insurgency against the romanticist optimism of a modern cultural momentum that appearing sweet has gone sour.

We have watched drug abuse spread, trapping seeming innocents before they know they are caught in a syndrome they can hardly escape, feeling they must supply their habit, colluding with mixed motives, doing violence to remain addicted. This describes original sin. The key terms above are "seeming," "hardly," "feeling," and "colluding." They are not wholly innocent due to their collusions with evil, and their feeling of bondage is not absolutely unaffected by their choices.

Wesley intuited (as Reinhold Niebuhr would later state explicitly) that the only Christian doctrine supported by extensive empirical evidence is original sin: "Original sin . . . is no play of imagination, but plain, clear fact. We see it with our eyes and hear it with our ears daily. Heathens, Turks, Jews, Christians, of every nation, as such men as are there described. Such are the tempers, such the manners, of lords, gentlemen, clergymen, in England, as well as of tradesmen and the low vulgar. No man in his senses can deny it; and none can account for it but upon the supposition of original sin."[184]

What is today ironically called "news" sets forth this perennial evidence anew each day. The media function constantly as guilt-creating machines and anxiety-eliciting devices seeking to sell papers and soap. But few think of this as original sin.

Wesley did not think the problem of sin could be solved politically, but rather only by a drastic change of heart, one by one. Many economic problems emerge out of sin, but are not resolvable economically without a new birth made possible only by response to the merciful love of God the Son who enters our human scene and offers himself on the cross. To share that new birth is to affect the entire circumference of our lives. Though original sin is

---

[181]DOS Pt. II, iii, IX:312.

[182]DOS Pt. III, viii, IX:339–45.

[183]Robert Chiles, *Theological Transition in American Methodism*, argues that the trend of the Methodist theological tradition has been to move away from original sin, from free grace to free will.

[184]Letter to Samuel Sparrow, July 2, 1772, LJW 5:327.

a massive subject stretching from the beginning to the end of human history, rightly understood it brings each sinner to a personal decision, a change of heart, an opportunity for repentance.[185]

There is no way to explain the universal extent of sin if humanity has remained upright by nature. The only plausible explanation for the extent and depth of sin is the biblical account of original sin.[186] Our sinning, though the result of our fallen nature, is still our responsibility. We are responsible for sin's continuance, even if not personally responsible for its primal origin.

In the appendices to *Doctrine of Original Sin*, there are substantial extracts from Isaac Watts' response to Taylor, *The Ruin and Recovery of Mankind*, 1741 (Part IV); Samuel Hebden's tracts in response to Taylor (Parts V and VI);[187] and Thomas Boston's *Fourfold State of Man* (Part VII).

In a concluding letter to Taylor, Wesley speaks of his deep motivation: "Were it not on a point of so deep importance, I would no more enter the lists with Dr. Taylor, than I would lift my hand against a giant . . . I am grieved for you . . . O Sir, think it possible that you may have been mistaken! that you may have leaned too far, to what you thought was the better extreme! Be persuaded once more to review your whole cause, and that from the very foundation."[188]

FURTHER READING ON SIN

Arnett, William. "The Wesleyan/Arminian Teaching on Sin." In *Insights Into Holiness*, edited by Kenneth Geiger. Kansas City: Beacon Hill, 1962, pp. 55–72.

Bainbridge, W. and M. Riggall. "Wesley and Dr. John Taylor of Norwich." PWHS 16 (1928): 69–71.

Baker, Frank. "Wesley and Arminius." PWHS 22 (1939): 118, 119.

Blaising, Craig. "John Wesley's Doctrine of Original Sin." Dallas Theological Seminary diss., 1979, microfilm.

Burtner and Childs, *Compend*, 107ff.

Collins, Kenneth. FW, 110-24.

—————. *John Wesley on Salvation*. Grand Rapids: FAP, Zondervan, 1989. Chap. 1 "Prevenient Grace and Human Sin."

Cox, Leo George. "John Wesley's Concept of Sin." Bulletin of ETS 5 (1962): 18–24.

Fletcher, John. *An Appeal to Matter of Fact and Common Sense: A Natural Demonstration of Man's Corrupt and Lost Estate*. Bristol: William Pine, 1772.

Hannah, Vern A. "Original Sin and Sanctification: A Problem for Wesleyans." WTJ 12 (Spring 1977): 47–53.

Harper, Steve. *John Wesley's Theology Today*. Grand Rapids: FAP, Zondervan, 1983. Chap. 2, 27–30.

Joy, James R. "Wesley: A Man of A Thousand Books and a Book." RL 8 (1939): 71–84.

Keefer, Luke L., Jr. "Characteristics of Wesley's Arminianism." WTJ 22 (Spring 1987): 88–100.

Lindström, H. *Wesley and Sanctification*, op. cit., on original and personal sin, 19ff.: on Wesley's view of man and free will, 50ff.

Outler, Albert C. *Theology in the Wesleyan Spirit*. Nashville: Tidings, 1975, "Diagnosing the Human Flaw," 23–45.

Payne, George. *The Doctrine of Original Sin*. London: Jackson and Walford, 1845.

Rose, Delbert. "The Wesleyan Understanding of Sin." In *Distinctive Emphases of Asbury Theological Seminary*, 7–30.

Slaate. FB, 115ff.

Smith, H. Shelton. *Changing Conceptions of Original Sin*. New York: Scribners, 1955.

Starkey. WHS, 53ff.

Willliams, Colin. *John Wesley's Theology Today*. "Original Sin," 47ff.

Williams, N. P. *The Ideas of the Fall and of Original Sin*. London, New York, 1927.

Wynkoop. FWAT, 102ff.

---

[185]CH 7:513, 550, 560.
[186]DOS Pt. II, ii.20, IX:286–88.
[187]"Man's Original Righteousness," "Baptismal Regeneration Disproved," and "The Doctrine of Original Sin," 1740–41.
[188]DOS Pt. VI, IX:431–33.

6

The Incarnate Crucified Lord

Wesley prayed that the people in his connection of spiritual formation might be saved from supposed "improvements" upon the apostolic testimony or presumed Christological innovations.[1] Wesley at no point hinted that there is a needed purification, progression or remodeling of ancient ecumenical Christological definitions.[2] There is very little of that in Protestantism, whose Reformers gladly accepted ecumenical definitions of the ancient church, in whose steps Wesley seasonably followed.

CHRISTOLOGY

The Person of Christ

In Wesley's view, it is precisely in Christology that we meet the "inmost mystery of the Christian faith," where "all the inventions of men ought now to be kept at the utmost distance" to allow Scripture to speak of the one mediator who has "become the guarantee of a better covenant" (Heb. 7:22).[3] "I do not know how any one can be a Christian believer . . . till God the Holy Ghost witnesses that God the Father has accepted him through the merits of God the Son; and having this witness, he honours the Son, and the blessed Spirit, 'even as he honors the Father.' "[4]

Two Natures: Truly God, Truly Human

Wesley effortlessly employed the language of Chalcedon in phrases like "Real God, as real man,"[5] "perfect, as God and as man,"[6] "the Son of God and the Son of Man" whereby one phrase is "taken from his divine, and the other from his human nature."[7]

The Son's unity with the Father is a unity of divine essence, nature, substance, and glory, as well as a unity of

---

[1]Wesley was distrustful of novelty in theology generally, but most of all respecting Christology; see B2:181, 550; 3:106–9, 193, 235, 524f.; 4:183, 394.

[2]LJW 5:334.

[3]To William Law, ii.3, LJW 3:354–55, in reference to Anna Maria van Schurmann; cf. B2:379–85, 421.

[4]#55 "On the Trinity," sec. 17, 2:385; John 5:23.

[5]ENNT 730, on Phil. 2:6; 4:98; #123 "On Knowing Christ After the Flesh," 4:98–101.

[6]ENNT 815, on Heb. 2:10.

[7]ENNT 291, on Luke 22:70; cf. WC 15; 3:90–95; 4:97–106.

perfections or attributes (omniscience, omnipresence, and omnipotence) and operations or actions. "I am one with the Father in essence, in speaking, and in acting."[8] The Father is his Father "in a singular and incommunicable manner; and ours, through Him, in such a kind as a creature is capable of."[9] Though inseparably united with the Father, the Son is a distinguishable voice from the Father as a person, yet always understood emphatically within their unity of essence.[10] The Son is worthy of worship, since "Christ is God."[11]

Arguments Concerning
the Divinity of Christ

Wesley often called Jesus simply "God,"[12] or ὁ ὤν, the One who is of Romans 9:5, " 'He that existeth, over all, God blessed for ever': the supreme, the eternal, 'equal with the Father as touching his Godhead, though yielding to the Father as touching his manhood.' "[13] In the Sermon on the Mount Jesus speaks as 'ὁ ὤν," the One who *incomparable is*, "the being of beings, Jehovah, the self-existent, the supreme, the God who is over all."[14] He claims the divine name, "I am," of Exodus 3:14 (John 8:24, 27–28, 58). His eternal generation distinguishes him from all creatures. "He has all the natural, essential attributes of his Father . . . the entire Divine Nature."[15]

To the Son are ascribed "all the attributes and all the works of God. So that we need not scruple to pronounce him God of God, Light of Light, very God of very God, in glory equal with the Father, in majesty coeternal."[16] The Incarnation is necessary to reveal the harmony of God's attributes, especially the subtle interfacing of God's justice, which must discipline the sinner, and God's mercy, which reconciles the sinner—a reconciliation that occurs out of divine love as an event in history on the cross.[17] Through incarnation and atonement, we learn "that not sovereignty alone, but justice, mercy, and truth hold the reins."[18]

Arguments Concerning
the Humanity of Christ

"In the fullness of time He was made man, another common Head of mankind, a second general Parent and Representative of the whole human race."[19] In becoming "flesh," God becomes fully human, not simply body but all that pertains to humanity.[20] He is a "real man, like other men," even "a common man, without any peculiar excellence or comeliness," who becomes weary, who weeps, who is tempted as we are yet without sin, who increases in wisdom "as to his human nature," who passes through stages of development like other human beings,

---

[8]ENNT 365, on John 14:10.
[9]ENNT 386, on John 20:21.
[10]ENNT on John 1:1; 8:16–19.
[11]ENNT on Rev. 20:6; 1 Thess. 3:11; 5:27; 1 Cor. 1:2.
[12]ENNT, *passim*, cf. Col. 1:17; Rev. 1:4; John 12:41.
[13]#20 "The Lord Our Righteousness," i.1, 1:452; cf. #21 "Upon Our Lord's Sermon on the Mount I," intro., 9; Athanasian Creed, BCP.
[14]#21 "Upon Our Lord's Sermon on the Mount I," proem.9, 1:474; cf. B4:61; CH 7:121–26, 403–4.
[15]*Compend of Natural Philosophy*, V:215; LJW 1:118; 2:67; cf. CH 7:313, 316, 382, 386, 391.
[16]#77 "Spiritual Worship," i.1, 3:91.
[17]ENNT on 1 John 4:8; Rom. 3:25–26; see also B1:186; 2:479; CH 7:235, 534, 707.
[18]PCC X:235; ENNT on Rom. 9:21 and Mark 3:13.
[19]#5 "Justification by Faith," i.7, 1:185–86.
[20]ENNT on John 1:14; cf. 3:201–2.

who as man lives within limitations of time, finitude, and the restrictions of contextual knowing.[21] Wesley anticipated the nineteenth-century historicist's interest in the biography of Jesus, commenting freely on his temperament, psychological dynamics, interpersonal relationships, and courage, yet without displacing the theandric (God/man) premise. In all this there is no hint of a docetic (flesh-repudiating) tendency in Christology.[22] Above all his humanity is seen in his death and burial. "He did not use His power to quit His body as soon as it was fastened to the cross, leaving only an insensible corpse to the cruelty of His murderers; but continued His abode in it, with a steady resolution."[23] In the bodily ascension, God "exalted Him in his human nature."[24]

The Assumption of Human Nature by the Son in the Virgin Birth

"I believe that he was made man, joining the human nature with the divine in one person, being conceived by the singular operation of the Holy Ghost and born of the Blessed Virgin Mary."[25] "Christ, the Second Person, had a being, before he was born of a virgin,"[26] but it was the being of the *preexistent Son*,[27] not a preexistent human flesh—an idea that Wesley thought "exceeding dangerous" since it tended to compromise the Son's coequality and coeternality with the Father.[28]

In the *virginal conception* "The power of God was put forth by the Holy Ghost, as the immediate divine agent in this work."[29] "As Christ was to be born of a pure virgin, so the wisdom of God ordered it to be of one espoused; that, to prevent reproach, He might have a reputed father according to the flesh."[30] Mary who was "as well after as before she brought him forth, continues a pure and unspotted virgin."[31] The nativity hymns of Charles Wesley attest the virgin conception and Christmas theology more splendidly than anything written by John.

Yet the angelic salutation "gives *no room for any pretense of paying adoration* to the virgin."[32] "She rejoiced in hope of salvation through faith in Him, which is a blessing common to all true believers, more than in being His mother after the flesh, which was an honour peculiar to her . . . In like manner he

---

[21]ENNT on Phil. 2:7–8; Heb. 2:17; John 4:6; Luke 2:40, 43, 52; Mark 6:6; cf. 1:337; 3:273; LJW 8:89–90.

[22]ENNT on gospels, *passim*; cf. WC 27, 28.

[23]ENNT on Matt. 27:50; Deschner conjectures that "somewhere in the background of Wesley's thought there must lie an attitude toward human nature, as such, which forbids him from taking with final seriousness the idea that the incarnation means an affirmation of human nature, not simply subjection to it," or perhaps his "concern for practical holiness required an idealization of Christ's human nature," WC 32.

[24]ENNT on Eph. 1:20; Luke 24:51.

[25]Letter to a Roman Catholic, sec. 7, JWO 494.

[26]*Compend of Natural Philosophy*, V:215.

[27]CH 7:505.

[28]#62 "The End of Christ's Coming," ii.2, 2:478–79, a tendency Wesley found in Isaac Watts, who pleaded with God not to be displeased because he "cannot believe him to be coequal and coeternal with the Father," in Watts, *A Solemn Address to the Great and Ever Blessed God*, 1745; cf. WC 29.

[29]ENNT 203 on Luke 1:35.

[30]ENNT 202 on Luke 1:27.

[31]Letter to a Roman Catholic, sec. 7, X:81; JWO 495; ENNT 18 on Matt. 1:25.

[32]ENNT 203 on Luke 1:28.

has regarded our low estate; and vouchsafed to come and save her and us."[33]

The Mystery of the Personal Union

Insofar as the theandric mediator shares our humanity, he does not know or need to know the time of the day of judgment, for "as man He was no more omniscient than omnipresent," whereas according to his divine nature "He knows all the circumstances of it."[34] Wesley explicitly affirmed the classic principle of *perichoresis*,[35] "the communication of properties between the divine and human nature: whereby what is proper to the divine nature is spoken concerning the human; and what is proper to the human is, as here, [John 3:13] spoken of the divine."[36] When Wesley speaks, for example, of "the blood of the only begotten Son of God," the assumption is that the human properties of the man Jesus have been shared participatively with the one person of the God-man, Jesus Christ[37]—an "amazing union!"[38] It is this union that David Lerch in *Heil und Heiligung bei John Wesley* regards as the Christological key to Wesley.[39]

The personal union of one who is truly God and truly human *theanthropos*—"the God-man,"[40] is at once "man and Mediator." God is "His Father, primarily, with respect to His divine nature, as his only-begotten Son; and, secondarily, with respect to His human nature, as that is personally united to the divine."[41] He is "*without father*, as to His human nature; *without mother*, as to His divine."[42] It is not subordinationist to say with Scripture that "As He is man, the Father is doubtless 'greater than the Son,'" according to his humanity. As fully human he "bids His disciples also to pray" to his Father, "but never forbids their praying to Himself" as eternal Son.[43]

The Christology of the Articles of Religion

God and Humanity in Personal Union

The obvious place to focus a textual study of Wesley's Christology is Article 2 of the Articles of Religion on the Son of God. Its two clauses distinguish the *person* from the *work* of Christ. In one spare sentence we have the summary teaching of the Son as the Word of God, preexistent logos with the Father, the address of the Father, sent by the Father, truly God, of one substance with the Father, truly eternal who becomes incarnate assuming human nature, born of the Blessed Virgin, one person with two natures, truly human

---

[33]ENNT 204 on Luke 1:47.
[34]ENNT on Mark 13:32; #40 "Christian Perfection," i.6, 2:103.
[35]In Latin *communicatio idiomatorum*.
[36]ENNT 312.
[37]ENNT 479 on Acts 20:28.
[38]ENNT 330 on John 6:57.
[39]Zürich: *Christliche Vereinsbuchhandlung*, 1941, 70. A similar point is made by Franz Hildebrandt, *From Luther to Wesley*, London: Lutterworth, 1951, 40.
[40]ENNT 435 on Acts 10:36.
[41]ENNT 702 on Eph. 1:3.
[42]ENNT 827 on Heb. 7:3, which Deschner regards as a "mis-exegesis," since elsewhere Wesley teaches that "God is also father of Jesus Christ in his human nature," WC 42. Yet Wesley is correct to regard Christ as "*without father*, as to His human nature," consistent with the ancient ecumenical tradition, cf. WL 109–10, and especially the Eleventh Council of Toledo, where it is confessed that "He was begotten from the Father without a mother before all ages, and in the end of the ages He was generated from a mother without a father," *The Christian Faith*, Neuner and Dupuis, 170; cf. SCD para. 282–86, 110–11.
[43]Letter to Samuel Sparrow, Oct. 9, 1773, LJW 6:46.

and truly divine, undivided. The Son is the Word of the Father, not less God than the Father, of one substance [*homoousios*] with the Father. He took human nature in the womb of Mary so that in him two whole and perfect natures, God and humanity, became one person. In this one person we have not half God or half man, not an Arian-like almost God, not part God, but, according to the teaching of the ancient Christological tradition, Godhead and humanity joined together in one hypostatic union of two natures in one person never to be viewed as separable.[44]

The Work He Came to Do

If this is *who* he is, *what* did this unique person do that evidences his divine Sonship, and *why*? This theandric mediator did something for each one of us sinners. His work is consummated in his atoning action in which he *suffered for us, was crucified for us, died for us, was buried* (XXV Art. 2). This descent theme points to the length to which God goes to show his love for us by sharing our humanity, and by his death and resurrection to bridge the alienation between the holiness of God and fallen humanity.

The work of his life is consummated in the atoning deed of his death, to be a sacrifice not only covering and redeeming our primordial guilt inherited from the history of sin, but also the actual sin resulting from our own free decisions and collusions.[45]

Why? *To reconcile his Father to us.*[46] The focus is neither on reconciling us to the Father, or on reconciling us to each other as if that could occur apart from

his reconciling his Father to us, but on God's own incomparable act of reconciling his Father to us. He who is truly God became truly human and truly suffered. Patripassianism is thereby rejected, for the Father did not suffer, but the Son suffered as Incarnate Lord, was crucified for us, dead and buried.[47] This is a shorthand way of speaking about salvation from all sin, inherited and acquired, social and personal, primordial and historical. No individual act of natural freedom can excise itself from this distorted, despairing human condition. All who are born enter a history burdened by sin. In addition to that inherited burden, each of us has made our actual personal self-determined additions to that history of sin.

The Son's atonement is addressed to and sufficient for every individual sinner who shares in the tragic history of sin. For those who reach the age of responsibility, it is effective for their salvation when they repent and believe. For those who have not reached the age of accountability or who are unable to take responsibility for themselves, sufficient grace works preveniently to draw them toward the means of grace that would enable their salvation, provided they use the available means of grace.

The Resurrection

The third Article confesses the resurrection as the decisive event that makes sense out of his death: "*Christ did truly rise from the dead and took again his body with all things appertaining to the perfection of man's nature, wherewith he ascended into heaven and there*

---

[44]Council of Chalcedon, CC, 35–36; XXV Art., art. 2; #77 "Spiritual Worship," i, 3:90–95.

[45]Nicene Creed, BCP.

[46]In its spareness the Christological article mentions nothing at all about Jesus' baptism, earthly ministry, preaching, teaching, prophetic work, or miracles.

[47]LJW 3:353f.

sitteth until he returns to judge at the last day" (XXV Art. 3).

The first clause attests the central truth of the history of our salvation, that Christ indeed rose from the dead in a real body, a glorified body, experiencing all things that pertain to human nature. It is this one who represents sinners in the presence of the Father, who having ascended into heaven, sits in session at the right hand of the Father and intercedes on our behalf and will return on the last day.[48] This is the central salvation occurrence that vindicates the whole work of Jesus in his earthly ministry and on the cross.[49]

The Descent Motif

Despite the absence of the phrase "descent into hell" in the Sunday Service, there is strongly evident elsewhere in Wesley's Christology a radical descent[50] theme; from eternal Logos of the Father to incarnation to death to burial; and only then is there a mighty reversal: Christ raised from the dead, ascended to heaven, sitting on the right hand of God the Father, and promised to come again with glory to judge the quick and the dead, whose kingdom shall have no end. To understand each of these phases of descent and ascent is to grasp the essence of Wesley's Christology.

That Christ descended into hell was omitted in the 1784 Sunday Service that Wesley sent to the churches in America. Among the Thirty-nine Articles is Article III, "On the Going Down of Christ into Hell": "As Christ died for us and was buried, so also is it to be believed that he went down into hell."

Wesley excised that Article in his liturgical advice to American Methodists. All he did was strike the phrase from the Service, offering no detailed explanation of this omission or its motives or implications.

It is likely that the main reason Wesley did not include the descent of Christ into the netherworld is that it was even in his time a highly contested and controversial hypothesis. In narrowing the thirty-nine to twenty-four articles, he was trying to make as spare a statement as possible of necessary affirmations of faith. We cannot conclude from that omission that Wesley disregarded the Scripture texts that arguably attest the descent into hell, but he saw a nest of exegetical problems embedded in them that he did not want to be a burden to his shortened form of confession. On Acts 2:27 he noted that "it does not appear that ever our Lord went into hell. His soul, when it was separated from the body, did not go thither, but to paradise (Luke 23:43)."[51] "His body was then laid in the grave and his soul went to the place of separate spirits."[52] Deschner speculates that his motive was that he was "loath to teach anything suggesting a second chance for those who resisted repentance in this life."[53] So the "descent to hell" theme, unobtrusively stricken, without any divisive attempt to controvert it, has remained largely absent from the Wesleyan tradition of worship until recent years. In the 1989 hymnal published by the United Methodist Church, the phrase reappeared in transmuted form as "He descended to the

---

[48]CH 7:155, 696; cf. 1:121.

[49]B4:102f.

[50]On the divine *kenosis* see B3:201f.; CH 7:315f., 323.

[51]ENNT 399.

[52]Letter to a Roman Cathoilic, sec. 8, JWO 495.

[53]WC 51. It should be noted, however, that one of the key texts Deschner relied upon, Sermon J#141, "On the Holy Spirit," is now known to be not Wesley's but John Gambold's; cf. 4:547.

dead" rather than "went down into hell."[54]

Ascension, Session, and Intercession

The Son who has descended to us to share our life, having completed his atoning mission, ascended to the heavenly presence of the Father to intercede for us. The purpose of ascension is intercession, and the due reception of legitimate authority in the emerging governance of God. The reign of God is already inaugurated, to be completed on the last day. The worshiping community expects the return of Christ on the last day to judge all acts of human freedom.

The Articles of Religion remain a doctrinal standard in the American Wesleyan connection,[55] unamendable constitutionally save by a highly unlikely process of amendment of the constitution itself.[56] The soteriological homilies yet to be discussed deal more explicitly with the relevance of Christ's work for personal salvation, fully explicating the themes of justification, assurance, new birth, and sanctification.

Article Twenty on Atonement

If sin has become a kind of second nature to us, and we are far fallen from our original righteousness, what has God done that has the effect of saving

us? The answer is found most concisely in Article Twenty,[57] which speaks of an "offering of Christ, once made," for which no other satisfaction is either possible or necessary. What happened on the cross is not the death of a good man only, but the death of God the Son who comes to us in mission to reconcile the Father to us.[58] Only one who was truly human could become the representative of humanity before God the Father. Only one who was truly God could offer a fitting sacrifice for the sins of all humanity.[59]

From the self-offering of this unique theandric person comes "the perfect redemption, propitiation and satisfaction." It is entirely adequate to save from sin. It is a perfect and complete sacrifice, a wholly sufficient conciliation of the divine rejection of sin, and satisfaction of divine justice.[60] We are mercifully clothed in the Son's own righteousness. God's holiness at the heavenly throne is met by God's love on the cross so that sinners can be reconciled to God by the holy love of God. Those who are intent upon looking for the language of *liberation* in the Articles of Religion will find it embedded in Article Twenty, for in the cross we have redemption of humanity from bondage to sin.[61] The atoning act is intended "for all the sins of the whole

---

[54]United Methodist Hymnal, 7; cf. 4:189.
[55]With a few exceptions, see DSWT 81–173.
[56]The Evangelical United Brethren Confession similarly combines all key affirmations of Wesley's Christology: "We believe in Jesus Christ, truly God and truly man, in whom the divine and human natures are perfectly and inseparably united. He is the eternal Word made flesh, the only begotten Son of the Father, born of the Virgin Mary by the power of the Holy Spirit. As ministering Servant he lived, suffered and died on the cross. He was buried, rose from the dead and ascended into heaven to be with the Father, from whence he shall return. He is eternal Savior and Mediator, who intercedes for us, and by him all men will be judged."
[57]Cf. Art. XXXI of the Thirty-nine Anglican Articles, Of the One Oblation of Christ Finished Upon the Cross.
[58]LJW 2:320.
[59]#62 "The End of Christ's Coming," ii, 2:478–80.
[60]#85 "On Working Out Our Own Salvation," proem, 3:199–202; Letter to William Law, Jan. 6, 1756, LJW 3:353.
[61]Cf. LJW 6:89, 94.

world," not for the elect only, though not all accept its conditions by responding in faith active in love.

This once-for-allness is contrasted with the medieval teaching of repeated sacrifice. When the Anglican Article was written, the sixteenth-century Anglican tradition was trying to set itself apart from deteriorating aspects of the medieval scholastic teaching in which the sacrifice of Christ was presumed to be offered repeatedly in the Mass. What was being protested was the notion that the very operation of the Mass was regarded as a renewal of the sacrifice of Christ, a view rejected by the Augsburg Confession and Anglican Articles. "Wherefore the sacrifice of masses in which it is commonly said that the priest doth offer Christ for the quick and the dead, to have remission of pain or guilt, is a blasphemous fable and dangerous deceit." It may seem embarrassing to Protestants in an ecumenical age that there is found in the Article such a heavy polemic against medieval Catholic sacramentalism. Thus we find a helpful ecumenical clarification of the intent of the Articles in the United Methodist *Discipline* following 1968, that in the present time these Articles are to be read in the light of their historic context and biases, and in relation to current ecumenical realities.[62]

Article Nine on Justification

God was in Christ reconciling the world to himself. The ninth Article, on justification, confesses that "We are accounted righteous before God, only for the merit of our Lord and Saviour Jesus Christ, by faith, and not for our own works or deservings. Wherefore, that we are justified by faith only is a

most wholesome doctrine, and very full of comfort."[63] We are uprighted in the presence of the Father by the merit of the Son on the cross. The favor of the Father is received only for the merit of the Son. Justification is by grace through faith.

Those who know how tainted by self-interest is their best work are free to celebrate the unmerited goodness of God in coming to us in the flesh on the cross. The gospel teaches us to despair over our own fulfilling of the law apart from grace, and to trust in God's own fulfilling of it for us. The privilege of every believer is freedom from bondage to the law, freedom from guilt and anxiety, from all, not some, sin, contritely confessed and bearing fruits meet for repentance. The righteousness of Christ is imputed to all humanity. All are cleared juridically from the guilt of Adam's sin.

This is a "most wholesome doctrine," edifying and strengthening the penitent, enabling spiritual health, as opposed to the heavy legalism that hammers people down with the law. After 1738 Wesley strongly advocated classic Reformation teaching of *sola fide, sola gratia*, with the special emphasis upon the premise that unfeigned faith is always active in works of love, a theme found abundantly in Luther and Calvin.[64]

The Celebration of Nicene Christology

The Wesleyan tradition, like the Anglican and the ancient ecumenical tradition, has relied liturgically upon the Nicea-Constantinopolitan Creed as a prototype of classic Christological

---

[62]A Resolution of Intent of the General Conference of 1970, *Journal*, 254–55; Book of Resolutions, 1968, 65–72.

[63]XXV Art. 9.

[64]"Principles of a Methodist," 2–7, VIII:361–63.

teaching.[65] Wesley recited and revered the creed regularly as an Anglican priest in his daily offices. For this reason it cannot be regarded as a diversion of Wesleyan studies if we make reference to the major loci of the creed, which confesses faith in one Lord Jesus Christ, the only Son of God, eternally begotten of the Father. Not a creature, the Son is eternally the Son of the Father, Light from Light, True God from True God, begotten not made, of one being with the Father, through whom all things were made. For us and our salvation he came down from heaven (the descent/humiliation motif), was incarnate of the Holy Spirit by the Virgin Mary, became truly human. We are not speaking of a demi-god who never quite became a part of our human nature but a fully human person who does not cease being God, true God, who for our sakes was crucified under Pontius Pilate, suffered death and was buried and on the third day arose again in accordance with the Scripture. He ascended into heaven and is seated at the right hand of the Father, and he will come again in glory to judge the living and the dead, and his kingdom will have no end.[66] Each phrase of the creed was repeatedly confirmed in the prayers and homilies of Wesley.

The Christology of the Eucharistic Liturgy

There is perhaps no shorter route to the core of Wesley's Christology than an examination of Wesley's Order for the Administration of the Lord's Supper in the 1784 service. It is edifying to scrutinize the Wesleyan eucharistic liturgy as a concentrated statement of

Christological reasoning, asking: Who is the Mediator who was acting on our behalf? What has God the Son done for us? Why did God suffer for us?

The Wesleyan form of Eucharist, following the Book of Common Prayer, begins with an invitation to those who truly and earnestly repent of their sins. The address of Communion is not to the unserious or those who have only superficially examined their lives, or to the impenitent, but precisely to those who are already bringing themselves through a penitential process to a point of spiritual readiness and contrite expectation of the presence of Christ.[67]

Holy Communion is offered to those, who repenting, are seeking to live in love and charity with their neighbor, intending to lead a new life, following the commandments of God, walking from henceforth in his holy ways. Such are they who are called to draw near with faith and take this sacrament to their comfort, making their confession to God meekly kneeling upon their knees.[68]

The confession is addressed to Almighty God, recalling that our minds have misconceived our true good, our mouths misspoken the truth, our deeds and hands worked mischief.[69] These sins are beheld in relation to the holy God, for they are committed not merely against our better selves or the offended neighbor, but "against thy divine majesty."[70]

Christ's forgiveness is addressed to all, but those prepared to receive that forgiveness must be attentive to those penitential disciplines that take forgiveness seriously. The gospel gives "assurance of pardon to the penitent, but to no

[65]B2:256n; 3:91n, 460f.; 4:33, 63, 199; cf. CH 7:387n, 661n.
[66]BCP; CH 7:155, 584, 696.
[67]SSM 131.
[68]SSM 131.
[69]LJW 3:327.
[70]SSM 132.

one else.''[71] Those who come thirsting to the Lord's Table come with contrite hearts, asking God to have mercy, praying for forgiveness of all that is past, seeking grace that we may ever hereafter serve and please God in newness of life. With that confession, we are readied by grace for the petition for pardon—to ask forgiveness for all them that with hearty repentance and true faith are turning to God, who pardons and delivers sinners from sins and strengthens the penitent in all goodness.[72]

The act of absolution occurs in the comfortable words of Scripture announcing the forgiveness of God, whose reliable word is conveyed through the ordained elder: "If anyone sins, we have an advocate with the Father, Jesus Christ the righteous," the expiation on behalf of our sins. In this substitution metaphor, one life is being given for another. The reception of forgiveness is conditional upon faith: "If we confess our sins, he is faithful and just and will forgive our sins and cleanse us from all unrighteousness" (1 John 1:9).[73]

Holy Communion

The prayer of humble access moves us one step closer to the moment of lively communion with the resurrected Lord. Think of this as an eschatological banquet table in which the risen Lord is present in the life of the church, and we invited personally to his table. We do not presume to come to this feast trusting in our own righteousness, but in God's manifold and great mercies. We are of ourselves not worthy to gather up the crumbs under that table.

But it belongs to God's character always to have mercy. Each recipient is called to walk in newness of life and evermore dwell in him. To commune with Christ is to receive his shed blood and share in his broken body. Our sincere self-offering occurs in response to God's offering to us.[74]

From this follows a prayer of consecration that gives thanks for the tender mercy of God the Father who offers his only Son in complete giving, suffering on the cross for our redemption.[75] It is this mighty salvation event that he offered in instituting the Supper, and commanded us to continue a perpetual memory of his costly death until his coming again. We celebrate this self-offering as a sufficient sacrifice for us and for the sins of the whole world.[76]

In Holy Communion we pray for the grace to share as partakers of the divine nature through him, remembering his passion, death and resurrection. Communion is not merely an act of remembrance of his life, death, and resurrection, but also a participation in his divine nature.[77] Bread and wine are consecrated as the body and blood of Christ, given for us, as blood of the new covenant.[78]

This 1784 service of Communion, received with minimal amendments from the Book of Common Prayer, brings us as close to Wesley's Christology as anything he published for his connection of spiritual formation. He commended that it be received by us as often as possible. It has been celebrated the world over with scant revision by those who have stood in Wesley's connection.

---

[71]Letter to his Mother, Feb. 28, 1730, LJW 1:48.
[72]SSM 131–35.
[73]SSM 132–33.
[74]SSM 135.
[75]CH 7:107–11, 113, 228f., 269f., 337f.
[76]SSM 136.
[77]B1:56, 73, 75, 99, 150, 398f., 498.
[78]SSM 136–37.

The Crux of Wesley's Christology

In his Letter to a Roman Catholic, Wesley summarized the classic three-fold teaching of the work of the messianic Savior as prophet, priest, and king: "I believe that Jesus of Nazareth was the Saviour of the world, the Messiah so long foretold; that being anointed with the Holy Ghost,

- he was a *prophet*, revealing to us the whole will of God;
- that he was a *priest*, who gave himself a sacrifice for sin, and still makes intercession for transgressors;
- that he is a *king*, who has all power in heaven and earth, and will reign till he has subdued all things to himself."[79]

It is useful here to recall the searching Christological questions embedded in the sermon "Catholic Spirit":[80]

- Having absolutely disclaimed all thy own works, thy own righteousness, hast thou "submitted thyself unto the righteousness of God," "which is by faith in Christ Jesus"?
- Art thou "found in him, not having thy own righteousness, but the righteousness which is by faith"?
- And art thou, through him, "fighting the good fight of faith, and laying hold of eternal life"?
- Dost thou believe in the Lord Jesus Christ, "God over all, blessed for ever"?
- Is he "revealed in" thy soul?
- Dost thou "know Jesus Christ and him crucified"?
- Does he "dwell in thee, and thou in him"?
- Is he "formed in thy heart by faith"?

Intensely personal questions, they cannot be answered perfunctorily. These questions were to be seriously asked and answered affirmatively as the prevailing assumption of joining hands in Christian koinonia.

The Priestly Work of Christ: Atonement

Christ's work is understood as the payment of ransom or satisfaction. The sinner is up to his neck in debts that can never be paid. Christ's work pays all the debts. He suffered for all humanity, bore our punishment, paid the price of our sins for us. Thus we have nothing to offer God but the merits of Christ. This follows the Anglican Homily of Salvation in which the work of the Son atones to satisfy God's justice, following the Latin idea of atonement found in Tertullian, Cyprian, and more fully developed by Anselm of Canterbury.[81] This same substitutionary Christology can also be viewed from another angle as Christ's victory over the powers of evil, for in the Atonement he binds up the power of the strong man, sin.[82]

Both the humanity and divinity of Christ are active in Christ's atoning work. Christ is "our great High-priest, 'taken from among men, and ordained for men in things pertaining to God': as such, 'reconciling us to God by his blood,' and 'ever living to make intercession for us.'"[83] The subject of the Atonement is "one Christ, very God and very man."[84] The crucified one is the theandric mediator, seen especially "from the perspective of His divine nature, but provided with a human nature as a necessary instrument for

[79]Letter to a Roman Catholic, sec. 7, JWO 494; cf. 1:121; 2:37–38, 161; 4:433, bullets added.
[80]#39 "Catholic Spirit," i.13, 2:87, bullets added.
[81]WC 56–70.
[82]#9 "The Spirit of Bondage and of Adoption"; cf. Aulen, *Christus Victor*, 20–24.
[83]#36 "The Law Established Through Faith, II," i.6, 2:37; Heb. 5:1; Rom. 5:9–10; Heb. 7:25; CH 7:114f., 364, 529–31.
[84]XXV Art. 2; ENNT on Phil. 2:8.

His atoning work, which consists primarily in His death."[85] Wesley paraphrased John 14:19: "Because I am the Living One in My divine nature, and shall rise again in My human nature, and live for ever in heaven: therefore, ye shall live the life of faith and love on earth, and hereafter the life of glory."[86]

GOD'S LOVE
TO FALLEN HUMANITY
God's Love to Fallen Man

Rom. 5:15: "Not as the transgression, so is the free gift." [Homily #59 1782 B2:422–35 J#59 VI:231–49]

Felix Culpa

If God foresaw the consequences of Adam's fall, why would it not have been wiser of God to have prevented that fall altogether? We are tempted to imagine in our pride that God blundered and that even we could have done better.

But would it have been a better universe if human history had been entirely and absolutely prevented from falling? Wesley answered emphatically that God, foreknowing the Fall, also knew that the good that would come out of the redemption following the Fall would be greater than the evil to be suffered. Looking backwards we can now see that it is only through the history of fallenness that another history, that of redeeming grace, becomes meaningful.[87]

Wesley followed that view of creation and atonement that asserts that the Fall was an ironically felicitous fall, a *felix culpa, a happy fault,* a blessed

disaster, when seen in the light of its resolution in redemption.[88] For out of its misery came a redemption not possible without the absurd history of humanity turning its back upon God's goodness and grace. While it was formally within the power of God to prevent human disobedience, he did not choose this way by simple fiat. God knew that it was best to allow estranged freedom to play itself out in disobedience, which God did not prefer or will but permitted, knowing that he could redeem whatever consequences would emerge. God permitted the Fall in order that something more sound and advantageous would come from it—the redemption of humanity.[89]

The foreknowing God knew that "the evil resulting" from the Fall was "not worthy to be compared with . . . the good resulting from" salvation, and "to permit the fall of the first man was far best for mankind in general," so that "by the fall of Adam, mankind in general have gained a capacity . . . of attaining more holiness and happiness on earth than it would have been possible for them to attain if Adam had not fallen."[90]

Without premising a history of sin there would have been "no occasion" for "such 'an Advocate with the Father' as 'Jesus Christ the righteous,'" or for the Son's "obedience unto death," and "no such thing as faith in God thus loving the world," hence no justification, no redemption.[91] Without Adam's fall we "might have loved the Author of our being . . . as our Creator and Preserver. . . . But we

---

[85]Deschner, WC 167.

[86]ENNT 366.

[87]#59 "God's Love to Fallen Man," proem, 2:423–24.

[88]The ancient Latin Easter hymn celebrated *O felix culpa quae tantum ac talem meruit habere redemptorem*; cf. T. Oden, *The Word of Life,* San Francisco: HarperCollins, 1990, 115.

[89]B2:424–35; 4:26.

[90]#59 "God's Love to Fallen Man," proem, 2:424.

[91]#59 "God's Love to Fallen Man," i.1, 2, 2:425–26; cf. 3:201–2.

could not have loved him as 'bearing our sins in his own body on the tree.' "[92]

"We see, then, what unspeakable advantage we derive from the fall." The imperative, "If God SO loved us, how ought we to love one another!" would have been "totally wanting if Adam had not fallen."[93]

How God Brings Good From Evil

"How much good does [God] continually bring out of this evil! How much holiness and happiness out of pain!"[94] "What are termed afflictions in the language of men are in the language of God styled blessings." "Had there been no pain, [Christianity] could have had no being. Upon this foundation . . . all our passive graces are built . . . What room could there be for trust in God if there was no such things as pain or danger." "Had there been neither natural nor moral evil in the world, what must have become of patience, meekness, gentleness, longsuffering? . . . The more they are exercised, the more all our graces are strengthened."[95] "As God's permission of Adam's fall gave all his posterity a thousand opportunities of *suffering*, and thereby of exercising all those passive graces which increase both their holiness and happiness; so it gives them opportunities of *doing good* in numberless instances . . . And what exertions of benevolence, of compassion, of godlike mercy, had then been totally prevented!"[96]

"Unless in Adam all had died . . . every child of man must have personally answered for himself to God." "Now who would not rather be on the footing he is now? Under a covenant of mercy?"[97]

The universality of grace is correlated in Romans 5 with the universal consequences of Adam's fall. Lacking a universal predicament, there would have been no universal remedy. Had Adam not fallen, Christ would have been unnecessary. If the wrongdoing of one brought death upon all, that is happily exceeded by the grace of God in the one man Jesus Christ. That God primordially wills the salvation of all from the beginning does not imply that God prevents our freedom from being tempted. Election is universal in the primordial sense that God is willing that all be saved; but all are not saved by virtue of the voluntary sin that pervades human history, for which we humans are corporately responsible. "And none ever was or can be a loser but by his own choice."[98]

"Justification sometimes means our acquittal at the last day. But . . . that justification where our Articles and Homilies speak [means] present pardon and acceptance with God; who therein declares His righteousness and mercy, by or for the remission of the sins that are past."[99] Thus "the justification whereof St. Paul and our Articles speak, is one only . . . Yet I do not deny that there is another justification

---

[92]#59 "God's Love to Fallen Man," i.3, 2:427; 1 Peter 2:24; cf. Samuel Hoard, "God's Love to Fallen Mankind," 1633, extracted in the *Arminian Magazine*, 1778, Vol. 1.
[93]#59 "God's Love to Fallen Man," i.5, 2:428; cf. CH 7:517–18, 530–31.
[94]#59 "God's Love to Fallen Man," i.5, 6, 2:428.
[95]#59 "God's Love to Fallen Man," i.7, 8, 2:429–30.
[96]#59 "God's Love to Fallen Man," i.9, 2:430.
[97]#59 "God's Love to Fallen Man," ii.12, 2:432–33.
[98]#59 "God's Love to Fallen Man," ii.15, 2:434.
[99]Letter to Thomas Church, Feb. 2, 1745, LJW 2:186; B1:121; 2:156.

(of which our Lord speaks) at the last day."[100]

FURTHER READINGS

Christology

Collins, Kenneth. *John Wesley on Salvation*. Grand Rapids: FAP, Zondervan, 1989. Chap. 2 " Convincing Grace and Initial Repentance."

Mason, C. E. "John Wesley's Doctrine of Salvation." Master's Thesis, Union Theological Seminary, 1950.

Schilling, Paul. "John Wesley's Theology of Salvation." Chap. 2 in *Methodism and Society in Theological Perspective*, 44–64. Nashville: Abingdon, 1960.

Deschner, John. *Wesley's Christology*. Dallas: SMU Press, 1960 (Zondervan reprint with Foreword, 1988).

Harper, Steve. *John Wesley's Theology Today*. Grand Rapids: FAP, Zondervan, 1983. Chap. 4 on converting grace.

Hildebrandt, Franz. "Wesley's Christology." PWHS 33 (1962): 122–24.

Lerch, David. *Heil und Heiligung bei John Wesley*. Zürich: Christliche Vereinsbuchhandlung, 1941.

McIntosh, Lawrence. "The Nature and Design of Christianity in John Wesley's Early Theology." Drew Univ. Ph.D. diss. 1966.

Outler, A. C. *Theology in the Wesleyan Spirit*. Nashville: Discipleship Resources, 1975. Chap. 2 " 'Offering Christ,' The Gist of the Gospel," 35–65.

Rack. "Aldersgate and Revival." RE, 137–81.

Rattenbury, J. E. *The Evangelical Doctrines of Charles Wesley's Hymns*. London: Epworth, 1941.

Scott, Percy. *John Wesleys Lehre von der Heiligung vergleichen mit einem Lutherisch-pietistischen Beispel*. Berlin: Alfred Töpelmann, 1939.

Smith, Harmon L. "Wesley's Doctrine of Justification: Beginning and Process." LQHR 189 (1964): 120–28; also Duke Div. School Bull. 28 (1963): 88–98.

Tavard, George. *Justification*. New York: Paulist, 1983.

Verhalen, Philippo A. *The Proclamation of the Word in the Writings of John Wesley*. Rome: Pontificia Universitas Gregoriana, 1969.

Wilson, Charles R. "John Wesley's Christology." In *A Contemporary Wesleyan Theology*, edited by C. W. Carter, Grand Rapids: FAP, Zondervan, 1983, 342–50.

Wesley's Christological Antecedents and Developments

Fowler, James W. "John Wesley's Development in Faith." Chap. 6 of *The Future of the Methodist Theological Traditions*. Nashville: Abingdon, 1985.

Green, V. H. H. *The Young Mr. Wesley*. London, 1961.

Heitzenrater, R. P. "John Wesley's Early Sermons." PWHS 31 (1970): 110–28; also in *Mirror and Memory*, 150–62.

Hildebrandt, Franz. *From Luther to Wesley*. London: Lutterworth, 1951.

Knox, Ronald. *Enthusiasm*. New York: Oxford, 1950.

Outler, Albert C. JWO, 1964.

Sermons and Homilies Appointed to be Read in Church in the Time of Queen Elizabeth of Famous Memory (1547–71). Oxford: Clarendon, 1802.

Wood, A. Skevington. *The Burning Heart: John Wesley, Evangelist*. Exeter: Paternoster, 1967.

THE SCRIPTURE WAY OF SALVATION

Salvation by Faith

Eph. 2:8: "By grace you are saved through faith." [Homily #1 1738 B1:117–30 J#1 V:7–17]

The "standard sermons," entitled *Sermons on Several Occasions* (first four volumes of the original series), are the key teaching homilies. The first of these homilies is "Salvation by Faith," whose text is, *"By grace you are saved through faith"* (Eph. 2:8). Preached at St. Mary's, Oxford, it was written only

---

[100]Some remarks on Mr. Hill's "Farrago Double-Distilled" X:430; on final justification see LJW 3:244, 250. "No good works can be done before justification. Yet I believe (and that without the least self-contradiction) that final salvation is 'by works as a condition,' " in the sense of good works flowing out of faith, works meet for repentance: "Whatever you did for one of the least of these brothers of mine, you did for me!" (Matt. 25:40), X:432.

eighteen days after Aldersgate. Deeply affected by the power of that experience, its theological nucleus is: *"Grace is the source, faith the condition of salvation."* [101] All else in all the standard sermons turns on this pivot: Salvation is a free, unmerited divine gift, rightly received by trusting the self-giving Giver.

Defining Faith Negatively by What It Is Not

Saving faith is best characterized by first distinguishing it from what it is not. The way is then clearer to show what it is. Saving faith is differentiated from the general faith of natural humanity, from despairing demonic recognition of Christ's lordship, [102] and from that insight that results from empirical or historical inquiry. [103]

1. Wesley distinguished saving faith from the *general form of faith present in natural human moral consciousness* ("the faith of the heathen"), the faith that is evidenced by the sincere and conscientious practice of moral virtue in natural humanity. Not necessarily a demeaning term, "heathen" was commonly employed in eighteenth-century preaching in the Hebrew sense of *goi* and the Greek sense of *ethnos*—those who do not worship the God of Israel or of Jesus Christ, but may have access to rational knowledge of the being and attributes of God, and a hope of future judgment. They may show behavioral evidences of justice, love, and mercy.

These evidences even in fallen humanity of natural human trust and hope are anticipative of (but fall short of) the faith that is emergent in Israel and realized in Jesus Christ, which is saving faith. [104]

2. Nor is saving faith the *despairing demonic recognition* of Christ's lordship described by theologians as "the faith of the devils," who not only know what the heathen know of God, but also unbelievingly know that "Jesus Christ is the Son of God, the Christ, the Saviour." [105] The demonic powers rightly identify Christ but do not assent to his lordship. They know intensely and desperately *that* Jesus is the Christ. That is precisely why they are afraid of the revelation he bears: it will do them in. When the demons come upon Christ, they distinguish him immediately and scatter, knowing that the Son of God has appeared. They are cast into swine who bolt abruptly into the sea. [106] Such demonic recognition is still an enormous leap away from the actual welcoming relationship in which one personally trusts another so as to cast one's whole lot upon the truth of his Word. Simple recognition that Jesus is the Christ is hardly the same as the renouncing of all other gods and trusting in this incomparably trustable One. [107]

3. Saving faith is not the same as *the recognition that results from empirical or historical inquiry*. Though faith is attentive to the acts of God in history, it

---

[101] 1:118, #1, prologue 3.

[102] The convicted despair felt by the demonic energies upon recognizing that the Messiah would end their power—the closest the demonic can get to faith, a kind of convicted but despairing persuasion of the truth.

[103] #106 "On Faith, (Heb. 11:6)," i, 3:493–95.

[104] #2 "The Almost Christian," i.1–3, 1:131–32.

[105] 1:119, #1 "Salvation by Faith," i.2; #7 "The Way to the Kingdom," i.6.

[106] Mark 5:12–17; cf. Kierkegaard, *The Concept of Anxiety* on Demonic Dread.

[107] "Even the devils believe that Christ was born of a virgin, that He wrought all kinds of miracles, that for our sakes He suffered a most painful death to redeem us from death everlasting . . . and yet for all this faith, they be but devils." Letter to Thomas Church, June 1746, LJW 2:269.

does not hinge directly upon establishing events as objectively historical, for that is always an approximate undertaking. Hence resurrection faith is not to be taken in the embryonic sense of the preresurrection faith that some of the apostles had during Jesus' earthly ministry while he was physically walking with them.[108] Though they had left all to follow him, preaching the coming kingdom, and healing diseases, before the resurrection, some did not thoroughly experience saving faith, except in the form of hope and anticipation. For in saving faith one trusts not merely in the earthly Jesus of history, but the crucified, resurrected Christ. Nor is saving faith "barely a speculative rational thing, a cold, lifeless assent, a train of ideas in the head, but also a disposition of the heart."[109]

What Then Is Saving Faith?

Faith is a fully trusting response to grace. To imagine that faith elicits grace is to turn the order of salvation on its head. Rather, grace enables faith. Grace comes before faith. Faith is the disposition of the whole heart, mind, strength, will to receive grace joyfully. In apostolic preaching, faith is the sole condition of salvation. Those who have faith are saved.[110]

"Christian faith is then not only an assent to the whole gospel of Christ, but also a full reliance on the blood of Christ, a trust in the merits of his life, death, and resurrection; a recumbency upon him as our atonement and our life, as *given for us* and *living in us*."[111] It is a "sure confidence which a man hath in

God, that through the merits of Christ *his* sins are forgiven, and *he* reconciled to the favour of God; and, in consequence hereof, a closing with him and cleaving to him as our 'wisdom, righteousness, sanctification, and redemption,' or, in one word, our salvation."[112]

Saving faith is this total trust, casting one's whole life upon the truth manifested in the resurrected Christ. It is a disposition of the heart to embrace and hold fast the merit of the Son dying on the cross. We are saved by grace through this active reliance and recumbency.[113]

The Three Tenses of Turning Away From the Death of Sin and Toward the Life of Faith

So faith saves, but from what? Note the tenses: Faith saves from the guilt of past sin, from fear of future punishment, and from the power of present sin, thus *from all sin*.[114]

1. God's pardoning act saves the believer now *from the present power of sin*,[115] whether (a) *habitual sin*, which no longer reigns in the believer, though it may remain; or (b) from *willful sin*, insofar as the will while abiding in faith is "utterly set against all sin, and abhorreth it as deadly poison," or from *the compulsive desire to sin*, for grace is undermining the emergence of unholy desire in us. Thus one born of God is being freed not to sin habitually, or by compulsive desire, or even by (c) *willful concurrence with human infirmities*.[116] Lacking concurrence of the will, infirmities and evidences of finitude "are not properly sins." We are pres-

---

[108] #43 "The Scripture Way of Salvation," ii.3.
[109] #1 "Salvation by Faith," i.4, 1:120.
[110] #106 "On Faith (Heb. 11:6)," i.10–13, 3:497–98.
[111] #1 "Salvation by Faith," i.5, 1:121.
[112] #1 "Salvation by Faith," i.5, 1:121; cf. "An Earnest Appeal," sec. 59, 11:68–69.
[113] #1 "Salvation by Faith," i.5–ii.2, 1:121–22.
[114] #1 "Salvation by Faith," ii, 1:121–25; cf. B1:383; 3:179; 4:26.
[115] #1 "Salvation by Faith," B1:121; cf. 2:156.
[116] #1 "Salvation by Faith," i.6, 1:124.

ently saved from the reign of sin even though the remnants of sin remain in a history of sin that has continuing fall-out.[117]

2. Saving faith saves *from the guilt of past sin*. For Christ has "blotted out the handwriting that was against us"—the verdict, the sentence of death, "nailing it to the cross." Forgiven, we enter into a new relation with our past, having no need to carry it around as a burden of guilt.[118]

3. Saving faith saves *from the fear of future punishment*, from all anxiety over God's withering judgment of our sin, or about God's anger against the corruption of the goodness of creation that we feel in ourselves. Those who walk by faith are not paralyzed by fear of the final sentence of divine judgment, for they behold God as a Father who brings a reconciling peace from which nothing can separate them.[119] "They are also saved from the fear, though not from the possibility, of falling away from the grace of God."[120] Assuming these premises, "We know that those who are born of God do not sin; but the one who was born of God protects them, and the evil one does not touch them (1 John 5:18 NRSV). Sin has no power over one who walks daily in faith. Though the believer cannot say "he *hath not sinned*, yet now '*he sinneth not*'" insofar as he remains faithfully responsive to grace.[121] Now is the only moment in which it is imperative not to sin. All past and future moments can be left to grace.

Salvation is not just a theoretical or juridical position but an experienced and behavioral deliverance from all sorts of sin, actually sufficient to change our lives now and into the future. This is a radical understanding of the extent of God's saving work in us. Justification denotes "a deliverance from guilt and punishment, by the atonement of Christ actually applied to the soul of the sinner now believing on him, and a deliverance from the power of sin, through Christ 'formed in his heart.'"[122]

Salvation for Life in Christ

Being born again of the Spirit into a new life "hid with Christ in God" (cf. Col. 3:3), one gladly receives "the sincere milk of the word, and grows thereby" (cf. 1 Peter 2:2), "from faith to faith," "from grace to grace," until at length—eschatologically viewed, he comes to receive the inheritance of full salvation—"he comes unto a perfect man, unto the measure of the stature of the fullness of Christ" (Eph. 4:13; 6:10; Rom. 1:17).[123]

From this new birth one may grow in faith by grace toward perfect love, receiving strength from God by being fed by the Word. God's saving activity intends to transform the whole self from willful sinning, sinful desiring, and habitual sinning toward wholly trusting in God, so as to reshape the whole life of the believer away from the idolatry of the world, and toward the reception of the gifts God wishes to give.[124]

Salvation Begun, Continued, and Completed

The sum of salvation is stated in the Doctrinal Minutes: "In asserting salvation by faith we mean this: 1. That pardon (salvation begun) is received by

---

[117]#1 "Salvation by Faith," i.5–7, 1:121–23.
[118]#1 "Salvation by Faith," i.1–3, 1:121–22.
[119]#1 "Salvation by Faith," i.4, 1:122.
[120]PCC sec. 74; #76 "On Perfection," prologue; cf. LJW 3:100f.
[121]#1 "Salvation by Faith," ii.6, 1:124.
[122]#1 "Salvation by Faith," ii.7, 1:124; CH 7:290–92.
[123]#1 "Salvation by Faith," i.7, 1:124.
[124]#1 "Salvation by Faith," iii, 1:125–30; cf. #77 "Spiritual Worship," ii.5, 6, VI:430.

faith producing works; 2. That holiness (salvation continued) is faith working by love; 3. That heaven (salvation finished) is the reward of this faith."[125]

In the Preface to the 1740 *Hymns and Sacred Poems*, the Wesleys distinguished salvation from and salvation for: It is a salvation *from fear*, knowing the believer has peace with God; from *doubt*, aware of the Spirit's witness of assurance, and from *sin* so as to become servants of righteousness, according to the promise "That the true child of God does not sin; he is in the charge of God's own Son and the evil one must keep his distance" (1 John 5:18 PHILLIPS). Freed from self-will, they desire nothing but the will of God. Free from evil thoughts, there is "no room for this in a soul which is full of God." Free from "that great root of sin and bitterness, pride," they "feel that all their sufficiency is from God." "Not that they have 'already attained' all they shall attain, either 'are already,' in this sense, 'perfect.' But they daily go on 'from strength to strength: Beholding now as in a glass the glory of the Lord, they are changed into the same image, from glory to glory.'"[126]

Whether Salvation by Faith Stimulates License

Everything not of faith, since unresponsive to God, hence tending to be contemptuous of God's gifts, is unacceptable to God. God wishes us to come to him by the way he has illumined. God wishes us to trust his own costly plan of salvation, not invent another imagined to be better.[127]

For those who do not begin at this point, all that follows is likely to be tainted. The sinner who at heart remains corrupt cannot atone for his own sinfulness through his own works. There is no merit in any work when considered apart from grace. "All who preach not faith do manifestly make void the law . . . 'We establish the law,' both by showing its full extent and spiritual meaning; and by calling all to that living way, whereby 'the righteousness of the law may be fulfilled in them.'"[128]

We cannot rightly fulfill even any part of the law without trusting what God has done for us on the cross. Justifying faith does not void but fulfills the law, so that the law becomes rightly established through faith.[129] Some who have this faith may be tempted to continue in sin that grace may abound, yet God's grace when rightly understood leads to repentance and deeds of mercy, not license.[130] When faith becomes the occasion for resting easy or refusing to do good works, it ceases to be faith.[131]

True faith always produces good works fitting to its circumstances. The thief on the cross, whose faith brought a promise of paradise, did all the works of mercy possible for him hanging on a cross. Any one grounded in faith will be out there manifesting good works, living an accountable and useful life. Law and gospel are to be preached together so that one does not reduce the gospel to license.[132]

---

[125]Minutes, 1746, May 13, Q3, JWO 159.
[126]HSP 1740, Pref. 4–7, XIV:323–25.
[127]#1 "Salvation by Faith," iii, 1:125–30.
[128]#1 "Salvation by Faith," iii.2, 1:125; cf. LJW 6:122.
[129]#34 "The Original, Nature, Properties, and Use of the Law," iv.23, 2:16.
[130]"Dialogue Between an Antinomian and His Friend," X:266–84.
[131]#1 "Salvation by Faith," iii.4, 1:126–27.
[132]Minutes, Aug. 2, 1745, VIII:284–85. As Luther ("that champion of the Lord of hosts") discovered; #1 "Salvation by Faith," iii.9, 1:129. Only eighteen days before, Wesley had

Whether Salvation by Faith Induces Pride and Despair

Even the best of human motivations are prone to pride. That saving faith that constantly seeks to become active in love, however, is a tonic against pride, or any boasting in ourselves. Justifying faith glories only in the gracious gift that has transforming power to change our pride.[133] We come to the Lord's Table humbly, and if not humbly, not truly or efficaciously.[134]

Repentance in one sense may bring us temporarily to despair over our own competencies, our own natural abilities to save ourselves, so as to lead more fully to trust in God's saving work. "For none can trust in the merits of Christ, till he has utterly renounced his own."[135] There is thus a redeeming aspect in this constructive kind of despair, which points toward deeper faith.[136] No one is prepared to trust in God's righteousness until he has come to despair of his own.[137]

Some worry that justification is a humiliating, uncomfortable, even masochistic doctrine, lowering self-esteem. Justifying faith is better understood as a reversal of low self-esteem. It at last offers a firm basis for genuine self-affirmation and the recovery of self-worth. For we are being actively loved by the One most able to love and worthy of being loved. It is profoundly comforting inasmuch as it is primarily a doctrine about God's mercy and forgiveness to sinners.[138]

But should such a volatile and dangerous teaching be preached indiscriminately to neophytes? Wesley answered that it must be preached precisely to sinners, namely, to "every creature," and especially to the poor who "have a peculiar right to have the gospel preached unto them."[139] "Never was the maintaining this doctrine more seasonable than it is at this day. . . . It is endless to attack, one by one, all the errors" of the church, "but salvation by faith strikes at the root."[140] "For this reason the adversary so rages whenever 'salvation by faith' is declared."[141]

The Scripture Way of Salvation

Eph. 2:8: "Ye are saved by faith." [Homily #43 1765 B2:153–69 J#43 V:43–54]

The End, Salvation; The Means, Faith

Christianity is that plain and simple religion that teaches that the sublime goal of human life, salvation, can be obtained only by the means, faith.[142] "The end is, in one word, salvation; the means to attain it, faith,"[143] by which "we see the *spiritual world*, which is all round about us, and yet no more discerned by our natural faculties than if it had no being."[144] "It is by this faith . . . that we *receive Christ* . . . in all His

"felt his heart strangely warmed" while listening to the reading of the introduction to Luther's commentary on Romans. Later, in 1749, Wesley published a life of Luther.

[133]#119 "Walking by Sight and Walking by Faith," 16–19, 4:56–58.
[134]#1 "Salvation by Faith," iii.3, 1:126.
[135]#1 "Salvation by Faith," iii.5, 1:127.
[136]#86 "A Call to Backsliders," 3:210–26.
[137]#1 "Salvation by Faith," iii.5, 6, 1:127–28.
[138]Thirty-nine Articles of Religion, xi.
[139]#1 "Salvation by Faith," iii.7, 1:128.
[140]#1 "Salvation by Faith," iii.8, 1:128–29.
[141]#1 "Salvation by Faith," iii.9, 1:129.
[142]B1:120–21, 138–39; 3:497–98.
[143]#43 "The Scripture Way of Salvation," proem.1, 2:156.
[144]#43 "The Scripture Way of Salvation," ii.1, 2:160–61.

offices, as our Prophet, Priest, and King."[145]

"Faith necessarily implies an assurance," an appropriation of evidence, that I am a child of this Abba. Note that this evidentiary assessment of grace "goes before the confidence. For a man cannot have a childlike confidence in God till he knows he is a child of God."[146] "By this faith we are saved, justified, and sanctified."[147] Faith is "the only condition of justification,"[148] which is God's verdict demonstrating willingness to pardon sinners. "We are sanctified as well as justified by faith."[149]

"Both repentance, and fruits meet for repentance, are, in some sense, necessary to justification. But they are not necessary in the *same sense* with faith, nor in the *same degree*. Not in the *same degree*; for those fruits are only necessary *conditionally*; if there be time and opportunity for them . . . Not in the *same sense*; for this repentance and these fruits are only *remotely* necessary, necessary in order to the continuance of his faith, as well as the increase of it; whereas faith is *immediately and directly* necessary to sanctification" as it is to justification.[150]

Expect It Now!

Justifying faith "may be *gradually* wrought in some . . . in this sense, they do not advert to the particular moment wherein sin ceases to be. But it is infinitely desirable," and hence possible, "that it should be done *instanta-neously* . . . in a moment, in the twinkling of an eye,'' as it in fact did usually occur in the context of the revival.[151]

"By this token you may surely know whether you seek [salvation] by faith or by works. If by works you want something to be done *first, before* you are sanctified . . . If you seek it by faith, you may expect it *as you are* . . . there is an inseparable connection between these three points,—expect it *by faith*, expect it *as you are*, and expect it *now!*''[152]

Distinguishing the Pardon of the Son From the Power of the Spirit

There is a gradual work of sanctification taking place that enables the believer to put to death the deeds of the sinful nature. This process waits upon entire sanctification, full salvation, and the perfection of love, which so fills the heart that there is no more room for sin.[153]

"At the same time that we are justified, yea, in that very moment, sanctification begins."[154] Justification refers to a relational change whereby God accepts us into a new relation of sonship and daughterhood; sanctification refers to a real change whereby we are "inwardly renewed by the power of God."[155] "From the time of our being born again, the gradual work of sanctification takes place. We are enabled 'by the Spirit' to 'mortify the deeds of the body,' of our evil nature; and as we are more and more dead to sin, we are more and more alive to God. We go on

---

[145]#43 "The Scripture Way of Salvation," ii.2, 2:161; CH 7:314–15.
[146]#43 "The Scripture Way of Salvation," ii.3, 2:161–62.
[147]#43 "The Scripture Way of Salvation," ii.4, 2:162.
[148]#43 "The Scripture Way of Salvation," iii.2, 2:163.
[149]#43 "The Scripture Way of Salvation," iii.3, 2:163.
[150]#43 "The Scripture Way of Salvation," iii.2, 13, 2:163, 167.
[151]#43 "The Scripture Way of Salvation," iii.18, 2:168–69, italics added.
[152]#43 "The Scripture Way of Salvation," iii.18, 2:169.
[153]#43 "The Scripture Way of Salvation," iii, 2:162–69.
[154]#43 "The Scripture Way of Salvation," i.4, 2:158.
[155]#43 "The Scripture Way of Salvation," i.4, 2:158.

from grace to grace."[156] "No man is sanctified till he believes; every man when he believes is sanctified."[157] To the extent that he unreservedly believes, though subject to lapses, he is made the temple of God by grace.

Sin is not unequivocally destroyed in the new birth, but its power is "suspended." "Temptations return, and sin revives, showing it was but stunned before, not dead. They now feel two principles in themselves, plainly contrary to each other: 'the flesh lusting against the spirit,' [fallen] nature opposing the grace of God."[158] Meanwhile, the witness of the Spirit attests that one is a child of God. "How exactly did Macarius, fourteen hundred years ago," understand that neophytes in faith "presently imagine they have no more sin," while the more experienced and prudent in faith realize that even after concupiscence may have "withered quite away . . . for five or six years . . . yet after all, when they thought themselves freed entirely from it, the corruption that lurked within, was stirred up anew."[159]

"There is a repentance consequent upon, as well as a repentance previous to, justification." "The repentance consequent upon justification," being "widely different from that which is antecedent to it," is "a conviction wrought by the Holy Ghost, of the *sin* which still *remains* in our heart; of the *phronema sarkos, the carnal mind,* which 'does still remain,' (as our Church speaks,) even in them that are

regenerate, although it does no longer *reign*; it has not now dominion over them."[160]

The faith by which "we are sanctified, saved from sin, and perfected in love" is a divine evidence and conviction that God has promised this way in Scripture, that what God has promised he is able to perform, that God is able and willing to do it now, and that he indeed "doth it."[161] "Of all the written sermons, this one had the most extensive history of oral preaching behind it," according to Outler, and remains "the most successful summary of the Wesleyan vision of the *ordo salutis.*"[162]

JUSTIFICATION

Justification by Faith

Rom. 4:5: "To him that worketh not, but believeth on Him that justifieth the ungodly, his faith is counted for righteousness." [Homily #5 1746 B1:181–99 J#5 V:53–64]

This more than any other of Wesley's homilies sets forth the classic Reformation teaching of justification, the verdict expressed in God the Son's self-sacrificing action on the cross. Justification is first viewed in relation to the history of sin leading to the cross, then in relation to sanctification, its recipients, and sole condition.[163]

*The Salvation History Setting:
Creation, Fall, and the Promise
of Redemption*

Our original condition is not alienation from God, but divine-human en-

---

[156]#43 "The Scripture Way of Salvation," i.8, 2:160.
[157]#43 "The Scripture Way of Salvation," iii.3, 2:164.
[158]#43 "The Scripture Way of Salvation," i.6, 2:159; Gal. 5:17.
[159]#43 "The Scripture Way of Salvation," i.7, 2:159; see 159n, from *The Spiritual Homilies of Macarius the Egyptian,* 1721, translation "by a presbyter of the Church of England."
[160]#43 "The Scripture Way of Salvation," iii.6, 2:165.
[161]#43 "The Scripture Way of Salvation," iii.13-17, 2:166-68.
[162]Outler, Introduction, #43 "The Scripture Way of Salvation," 2:154.
[163]On justification, see LJW 1:248; 2:107; B1:182–99, 320f.; CH 7:11, 80, 142; cf. LJW 5:96; 6:296; JJW 5:194.

counter, personal dialogue, and unsullied refraction of the divine goodness.[164] Humanity was made in the image of God: holy, dwelling in love, as God is love, knowing no evil. To uncorrupted humanity, God gave a perfect law requiring radical obedience, with no allowance for falling short, "man being altogether equal to the task assigned, and thoroughly furnished for every good word and work."[165]

But of course, from that first primitive condition, freedom has gone awry in a sordid story of disobedience and fallenness into a history of sin in which humanity becomes alienated from God. Guilt and death come to pervade this fallen human condition.[166] This history sets the context, the "general ground," for the teaching of justification, without which the doctrine is meaninglessly dehistorized.[167]

Into this fallen human condition God sends his Son as a sacrifice for the sins of the world. God the Son on the cross is embodying an incomparable word of divine pardon, apart from any act or merit of our own, which invites us to be reconciled again to the Father and brought back into our original condition of holiness and happiness. This reconciling act of God is our justification, our being uprighted in the presence of God, not by anything we have done on our own but by what God has done for us on the cross. If one "*does a piece of work, his wages are not 'counted' as a favour; they are paid as debt. But if without any work to his credit he simply puts his faith in him who acquits the guilty, then his faith is indeed 'counted as righteousness'*" (Rom. 4:4, 5 NEB). The sinner is uprighted by atoning grace declared on the cross, by God's own righteousness, which is the work of Christ for us, a juridical act that occurs through an event, the cross. As in Adam, "the common father and representative of us all," death passed upon all men, "even so, by the sacrifice for sin made by the second Adam, as the representative of us all, God is so far reconciled to the world, that He hath given them a new covenant."[168]

Justification is already completed on the cross and not something for me to complete. Saving faith is our trusting response to this divine deed of justification in which we are counted righteous. God the Spirit works in the heart to transform our behavior so that it bears fruit.[169]

Distinguishing Justification and Sanctification

Justification is "what God *does for us* through his Son." Sanctification is what God "*works in us* by his Spirit."[170] God's work for us through the Son prepares the ground for God's work in us through the Spirit, the new birth of receiving justifying grace. Having been born anew in Christ's love, we are freed to grow in sanctifying grace.[171]

Justification is a forensic declaration, a verdict credited in our favor, God's act for us. That does not instantly make the hearer behaviorally or actually righteous in terms of behavioral change. That behavioral change is the work of

[164]#141 "The Image of God." Salvation is the restoration of the image of God; #1 "Salvation by Faith," para. 1; #44 "Original Sin," iii.5.
[165]#5 "Justification by Faith," i.1–3, 1:184.
[166]#56 "God's Approbation of His Works," ii.1, 2:397–98.
[167]#5 "Justification by Faith," i.1–9, 1:184–87.
[168]#5 "Justification by Faith," i.5–9, 1:185–87; CH 7:120, 210.
[169]#5 "Justification by Faith," i.7–9, 1:186–87; cf. B1:642.
[170]See #45 "The New Birth," sec. 1, 2:187; #19 "The Great Privilege of Those That Are Born of God," i.1.
[171]#5 "Justification by Faith," ii.1, 1:187.

the Holy Spirit who works to perfect what is given in justification. The Spirit's work in us seeks the complete and mature embodiment of the life of faith.[172]

While sanctification is the "immediate *fruit* of justification," it remains nevertheless "a distinct gift of God," and distinguished from justification just as growth is related to but distinguishable from birth. Wesley knew that in rare instances Scripture used the term *justification* in a generic sense "so as to include sanctification also, yet in general use they are sufficiently distinguished from each other both by St. Paul and the other inspired writers."[173]

Justification is the objective ground of regeneration, the beginning of a birthing process. If justification enables a new birth, sanctification enables a steadily growing process. Nobody grows until he or she is born. Nobody enters into this process of sanctification except by being born by justifying grace.[174]

There is a triune premise underlying this, which is worth grasping since it is a pivotal Wesleyan distinction: Justification is the work of the Son, sanctification of the Spirit. They are integrally connected since God is one, and inseparable because "the Lord . . . is the Spirit" (2 Cor. 3:17), yet distinguishable because the mission of the Spirit is to bring to full expression the ministry of the Son.

Justification does not dismantle conscience or the just address of the moral law. "Least of all does justification imply that God is deceived in those whom he justifies" or that God pretends that sinners are what they are not.[175]

Rather, "the plain scriptural notion of justification is pardon, forgiveness of sins. It is that act of God the Father whereby, for the sake of the propitiation made by the blood of his Son, he 'showeth forth his righteousness (or mercy) by the remission of the sins that are past' " (cf. Rom. 3:25, 1:189n).[176] To those justified by faith "God 'will not impute sin' to his condemnation" (Rom. 4:7, 8, 1:189n). All his past sins "in thought, word, and deed, 'are covered,' are blotted out; shall not be remembered or mentioned against him, any more than if they had not been. God will not inflict on that sinner what he deserved to suffer, because the Son of his love hath suffered for him."[177]

Whether Only Sinners Are Justified

To whom is this justifying grace addressed? Only to the ungodly! Only sinners have the need or occasion for pardon.[178] The shepherd responds urgently to seek and save the one who is lost.[179] The physician comes to heal not those already healthy but those struggling mightily with the sickness of the history of sin.[180]

This has structural consequences for the way we order theological reflection:

[172]JWO 201f.
[173]#5 "Justification by Faith," ii.1, 1:187.
[174]#5 "Justification by Faith," ii, 1:187–90.
[175]#5 "Justification by Faith," ii.4, 1:188.
[176]In a letter to John Newton, May 14, 1765, he wrote: "I think on justification just as I have done any time these seven and twenty years—and just as Mr. Calvin does. In this respect I do not differ from him a hair's breadth." Calvin, however, as Outler notes, asserts that "in justification, faith is merely passive" (Inst. 3.20.5), whereas "Wesley understood justifying faith as 'active,' " 1:189n.
[177]#5 "Justification by Faith," ii.5, 1:189–90.
[178]#5 "Justification by Faith," iii.1, 1:190.
[179]#5 "Justification by Faith," iii.3, 1:191.
[180]#5 "Justification by Faith," iii.3, 4, 1:191–92.

justification comes before sanctification, just as the work of the Son on the cross makes way for the mighty work of the Spirit in Pentecost and following. This ordering must not be turned on its head, so as first to require sanctification, as if only the saints are justified. It is not that one must first become holy so as to be worthy of being justified.[181] That in fact was what Wesley, in his Georgia period, seemed close to believing, that one had best seek to be holy to ready oneself for justifying grace.[182] But by the time he preaches this sermon it is clear that the order is reversed: Justification is the premise of any work of sanctification, and any response to sanctifying grace.[183]

William Law, Wesley's earlier mentor, had viewed religion primarily as sanctification, conformity to the life of Christ, bearing the cross, mortification as the essence of piety, and the necessary condition of justification.[184] Writing to Law in May of 1738, Wesley recognized that Law's way was a deadly capitulation to legalism, and that faith in Christ's work of atonement was the only necessary condition of justification. Sanctification is "not the cause, but the effect" of justification.[185]

The Terms Upon Which Saving Grace Is Received

What is the condition of receiving this justification? Only one word can express it: faith, understood as trust, (*pistis*), confidence in the truthfulness of God's word addressed on the cross. Faith is the divine evidence or conviction of the truth of things not seen by our bodily eyes.[186] Justifying faith hinges not merely on the conceptual conviction that God was in Christ, but more so on the sure personal trust that Christ died for my sins[187]—the *pro me* theme so prominent in Luther is rediscovered here. The surprising awareness that this gift is truly "for me" is written decisively into the language of the Aldersgate narrative—even to me!

Faith is strictly speaking "the sole condition of justification,"[188] and in fact "the *only necessary* condition" of justification.[189] Without faith one is still under the curse of the law. Faith is counted to the believer as righteousness.[190]

"The terms of acceptance for fallen man are, repentance and faith. 'Repent and believe the gospel.'"[191] Repent and believe. Repentance turns away from sin, faith turns toward grace, so as to view this as a single turning. "Infants indeed our Church supposes to be justified in baptism, although they cannot then either *believe* or *repent*. But she expressly requires both *repentance* and *faith* in those who come to be baptized when they are of riper years. As ear-

---

[181]#5 "Justification by Faith," iii.2, 1:191.

[182]The holy living tradition of Jeremy Taylor had stressed that "repentance and works meet for repentance" (Acts 26:20, KJV) were ordinarily required as evidences of readiness for justification, especially when understood as final justification on the last day. See Taylor, *Unum Necessarium*, chap. ix, *Works*, II:598f.

[183]Thirty-nine Articles, xii; "The Doctrine of Salvation, Faith and Good Works," ii.6.

[184]William Law, *Serious Call to the Devout and Holy Life*, 112f., 165, 219; WS 56.

[185]*Hymns and Sacred Poems*, 1739, Preface 2; XIV:320. For further comments on William Law, see B1:34f., 476f.; 3:328–30, 504–7; LJW 1:161; 3:215, 332, 370.

[186]#5 "Justification by Faith," iii.2, 1:191.

[187]#5 "Justification by Faith," iv.2, 1:194.

[188]#5 "Justification by Faith," iv.6, 1:197. Elsewhere he conjoins with faith repentance: #14 "The Repentance of Believers," ii.6; Minutes, 1745; "Principles of a Methodist Father Explained," vi.4.

[189]#5 "Justification by Faith," iv.4, 5; 1:195–96

[190]#43 "The Scripture Way of Salvation," 2:153–69.

[191]Letter to James Hervey, LJW 3:375.

nestly therefore as our Church inculcates justification by faith alone, she nevertheless supposes repentance to be previous to faith, and 'fruits meet for repentance'; yea, and universal holiness to be previous to final [eschatological] justification.''[192]

Righteousness is given at the moment of faith, when the sinner casts himself upon the mercy of God, in an act of trust that occurs only by grace. Who can doubt in such a complete yielding that he is completely forgiven at that moment?

Justification is a legal metaphor by which it is said we are counted as if upright in the presence of God due to the act of the Son on the cross to take upon himself the sin of the whole world. It is for all even though some do not respond to it fully. This judicial act of justification grants full pardon,[193] a complete release from the penalty of sin to all who believe in Jesus Christ and receive Him as Lord.[194]

God chose faith to combat pride, so that we cannot come before God claiming our goodness but only ready to refract God's own goodness.[195] Sinners are urged not to try to plead their own righteousness lest they destroy their own soul, but rather to look solely to the cross, which takes sin away. ''Thou ungodly one, who hearest or readest these words! thou vile, helpless, miserable sinner! I charge thee before God the Judge of all, go straight unto Him, with all thy ungodliness. Take heed thou destroy not thy own soul by pleading thy righteousness, more or less. Go as altogether ungodly, guilty, lost, destroyed. . . . Thou art the man! I want thee for my Lord! I challenge *thee* for a child of God by faith!''[196]

The Doctrinal Minutes on Justification

Wesley established a yearly conference, the first of which was held in 1744 where Methodist leaders were brought together for substantive colloquy on doctrine and discipline. Wesleyan theology was hammered out in dialogue, through a process of conversation with embattled frontline advocates. The outcome of this dialogical process is seen in the Larger Minutes, often called the Doctrinal Minutes, of the first three years of annual conferences, 1744–47. The record of those conversations became key reference points for doctrinal preaching among all early Methodist preachers, the core of what was later to be known as ''our doctrines'' in subsequent *Disciplines*. These were published under the title: ''Minutes of Some Late Conversations between the Rev. Mr. Wesley and Others.''[197] The intent was to clarify key points of doctrine and practice in the emerging revival movement, especially justification, assurance, and sanctification. The Minutes were recorded in the form of questions asked and answered. Wesley consulted with his colleagues in the connection, who engaged earnestly in dialogue, but their joint decisions, assuming their consent, were strongly influenced by Wesley.

Justification is there defined as: ''to be pardoned and received into God's favor; into such a state, that if we continue therein, we shall be finally saved.''[198] Faith is the sole ''condition

[192]FA Part I, ii.4, 11:111.
[193]LJW 3:371; B1:189, 585–87; 2:157f.; JWO 197, 202, 273.
[194]See the Articles of Religion on the Holy Spirit and soteriology.
[195]#45 ''The New Birth,'' i.4, 2:190.
[196]#5 ''Justification by Faith,'' iv.9, 1:198–99.
[197]VIII:275–98.
[198]Minutes, 1744, June 25, Q1, JWO 137.

of justification."[199] Works meet for repentance imply obeying God, forgiving others, doing good, attending upon the ordinances of God.[200]

"Faith, in general, is a divine supernatural *elenchos* of things not seen, i.e. of past, future, or spiritual things. 'Tis a spiritual sight of God and the things of God. Therefore, repentance is a low species of faith, i.e. a supernatural sense of an offended God. Justifying faith is a supernatural inward sense or sight of God in Christ reconciling the world unto himself."[201]

His letters confirm that justification is the gracious act of God by which he grants full pardon of all guilt and complete release from the penalty of sins committed, so that penitent sinners are accepted as righteous.[202] "Pardon and acceptance, though they may be distinguished, cannot be divided."[203] All who believe on Jesus Christ and receive Him as Lord and Savior are saved. Sincerity of intention toward God is a necessary but not sufficient condition for salvation. The sole sufficient condition for justification is clear: penitent faith. Thus, repent and believe. Repentance consists of conviction of sin, and faith in the conviction that God showed his love by dying for me, the premise of all holiness and good works.[204]

Consciousness of pardon is central to the whole Methodist ethos. This represented a shift of consciousness from the discipline-focused pre-Aldersgate Holy Club of Oxford to the grace-saturated revival movement after 1738. At Oxford there was a strong resolution and total commitment to the holy life. But what was missing was a radical appropriation of justification by grace through faith, which only after 1738 became rightly grasped and profoundly appropriated. This does not mean that justification teaching was absent altogether before Aldersgate, but it did not yet have the personal experiential force and emotive power that it was soon to have. The joyful awareness of pardon would become the central energy of the revival. "Wherein does our doctrine now differ from that we preached when at Oxford? Chiefly in these two points: We then knew nothing of the righteousness of faith in justification, nor of the nature of faith itself as implying consciousness of pardon."[205]

Adam's sin is imputed to all humanity in the sense that in Adam all die. "By the merits of Christ all men are cleared from the guilt of Adam's actual sin," and through "the obedience and death of Christ . . . believers are re-united to God and made partakers of the divine nature."[206]

Wesley held that there is "no merit, taking the word strictly, but in the blood of Christ . . . salvation is not by the merit of works," yet following Christ's own teaching, "we are rewarded *according to* our works . . . this differs from *for the sake of* our works," for "numberless words in all languages . . . may be taken either in a proper or improper sense. When I say, 'I do not grant that works are meritorious, even

---

[199]Minutes, 1744, June 25, Q2, JWO 137.
[200]Minutes, 1744, June 25, Q3, JWO 137.
[201]Minutes, 1744, June 25, Q4, JWO 137.
[202]In his "Conversation with the Bishop of Bristol," 1739, Wesley concisely defined "justifying faith" as "a conviction wrought in a man by the Holy Ghost, that Christ hath loved him, and given himself for him; and that, through Christ, his sins are forgiven," XIII:499.
[203]Letter to James Hervey, LJW 3:377.
[204]Minutes, 1744, June 25, Q4–7, JWO 137f.
[205]Minutes, 1746, May 13, Q4, JWO 160.
[206]Minutes, 1744, June 25, Q16, JWO 139; LJW 3:379.

when accompanied by faith,' I take that word in a proper sense. But others take it in an improper, as nearly equivalent with rewardable.' "[207]

The Righteousness of Faith

Rom. 10:8: "The word is nigh thee, even in thy mouth, and in thy heart; that is, the word of faith which we preach." [Homily #6 1746 B1:200–216 J#6 V:65–76]

The sixth of the standard teaching homilies, "The Righteousness of Faith,"[208] is textually focused on Romans 10:5–8, which contrasts the righteousness that is by the law with the righteousness that is by faith.[209]

The Despair That Arises From Trusting in the Righteousness That Is of the Law

The law is a harsh taskmaster. Wesley is relentless in describing the requirement of the law as such. The law makes radical demands, with no allowance for falling short.[210] If we decide we are going to live our lives under God's command only, not by the mercy of God, we have to do it consistently and completely. The covenant of works requires that one fulfill every manner of righteousness, not only in perfect degree but without interruption.[211] Anything less brings a conscience permeated with offence. The law required the alternative: "Obey or die. It required no man to obey and die too. If any man

had perfectly obeyed, he would not have died."[212] The law brings us to despair over our own righteousness and gives us readiness to trust in God's righteousness. We cannot possibly fulfill the law. Why preach it then? Because the law teaches us not to trust in our own righteousness but in God's. Wesley admitted in *A Farther Appeal* that "it is my endeavour to drive all I can into what you may term another species of 'madness', . . . which I term 'repentance' or 'conviction' " as preparatory to saving grace.[213] Yet Wesley looked with disfavor upon deliberate efforts to manipulate persons toward despair in order to bring them to faith.[214]

Wesley like Luther argued that those who attempt to live by the law with utter seriousness, live always on the edge of despair, always aware of radical inadequacies. It is folly to live that way, when God desires to offer us forgiveness through his Son.[215]

The Wisdom of Anchoring Oneself in the Righteousness of Faith

If that is folly what is wisdom? Wisdom is to live by faith in God's own righteousness declared. It is receiving the assistance of the Spirit which by grace wants to call us into trusting Christ's righteousness for us.[216] The covenant of grace requires no work prior to justification, but only that one believe in God's work done for us on

---

[207]"Some Remarks on Mr. Hill's 'Farrago Double-Distilled,' " X:434.

[208]In preaching on this text from his father's tombstone in Epworth, "several dropped down as dead; and among the rest such a cry was heard of sinners groaning for the righteousness of faith as almost drowned my voice," JJW June 12, 1742.

[209]B1:127, 196, 201–16, 592; 2:28f.; cf. LJW 3:82, 375; 5:222–23, 263.

[210]LJW 3:82, 375; 5:222–23, 263.

[211]The covenant of law too self-assuredly tends to assume that a perfected perfection is theoretically possible for fallen humanity. #35 "The Law Established Through Faith, I," ii.3, 4.

[212]Letter to James Hervey, LJW 3:277.

[213]FA Part I, vii.12, 11:196.

[214]#106 "On Faith (Heb. 11:6)," i.11, 12; cf. B11:196–99.

[215]SS 1:131–34; 2:65.

[216]SS 1:138–39.

the cross. The moment one believes in Jesus as Lord, one is saved from condemnation, guilt, and punishment for prior sin, and is given the power to serve God in true holiness from that time forward. Faith is the condition by which humanity may recover the favor and image of God, receive the life of God in the soul, and be restored to the knowledge and love of God.[217]

The covenant of grace presupposes that fallen humanity lives in despair, dead to God's righteousness, unholy and unhappy,[218] not the unblemished condition of humanity prior to the Fall. Only grace illumines the folly of trusting in the righteousness that is of the law, which fundamentally misconceives the human condition as if unfallen, when humanity was alive to God, and capable of fulfilling the command of God.[219]

The law was never designed to recover God's favor once lost. The only way to recover the favor and image of God, once lost, is through trusting the gift of the revealed righteousness that comes by faith.[220]

"By 'the righteousness which is of faith,' is meant that condition of justification (and in consequence of present and final salvation, if we endure therein unto the end), which was given by God to *fallen man* through the merits and mediation of his only begotten Son. This was in part revealed to Adam soon after his fall, being contained in the original promise made to him and his seed concerning the seed of the woman, who would 'bruise the serpent's head.' "[221]

False Starts Through Legal Obedience

Those who desire to be reconciled to the favor of God do not say in their hearts: " 'I must *first do this*. I must *first* conquer every sin, break off every evil word and work, and do all good to all men; or I must *first* go to Church, receive the Lord's Supper, hear more sermons, and say more prayers.' " For to do so would be to remain insensible to the righteousness of God, still " 'seeking to establish thy own righteousness' as the ground of thy reconciliation. Knowest thou not that thou canst do nothing but sin till thou art reconciled to God? Wherefore then dost thou say, I must do this and this *first*, and then I shall believe? Nay, but *first believe*."[222]

It is a non-starter to insist, "I can't be accepted yet because I am not *good enough*." No one is good enough to merit God's atoning love. It is equally ruinous to say "I must *do* something more before I come to Christ," or "wait for *more sincerity*," for "if there be anything good in *sincerity*, why dost thou expect it *before* thou hast faith?— seeing that faith itself is the only root of whatever is really good and holy."[223]

---

[217]#1 "Salvation by Faith."
[218]Never lacking, however, the prevenient grace that underlies conscience. J#85 iii.4.
[219]#127 "On the Wedding Garment," sec. 19; Minutes, May 13, 1746; *Notes* on Heb. 8:8.
[220]#45 "The New Birth," iii.1.
[221]#6 "The Righteousness of Faith," i.7, 1:205. Here Wesley is assuming a "double justification" received first by faith in the atoning work on the cross, and finally confirmed in final justification on the last day. #5 "Justification by Faith," ii.5; letter to Thomas Church, Feb. 2, 1745.
[222]#6 "The Righteousness of Faith," iii.1, 1:214.
[223]#6 "The Righteousness of Faith," iii.2–5, 1:214–16. Cf. #2 "The Almost Christian," i.9.

Extractions From the Edwardian Homilies

The Doctrine of Salvation, Faith, and Good Works (Extracted From the Edwardian Homilies)

Having recently returned from Georgia, Feb. 1, 1738, Wesley set about to publish an extract from the Anglican Homilies (variously called Cranmerian or Edwardian or Elizabethan Homilies), which were the official teaching of the Church of England during the period of Edward VI, largely written by Thomas Cranmer (except for one by John Harpsfield and another by Edmund Bonner), to which twenty-one further homilies (by John Jewel and others) were added in the period of Queen Elizabeth.[224] Wesley abridged these homilies for use within his connection of spiritual formation. According to prevailing protocols of the eighteenth-century popular editor (contrary to twentieth-century assumptions) he edited texts functionally in relation to his purpose of informing and instructing his connection.

This series of homilies in Wesley's version became widely read in the eighteenth century, reprinted through nineteen editions. He himself appealed to these homilies frequently in his preaching, pastoral care, and irenics. He insisted that his own teaching of salvation, justification, faith, and good works was not different from the ancient ecumenical consensual, catholic teaching upheld by the Church of England. He did not want his detractors to imagine that he was inventing some cleverly fashioned new doctrine of justification.

Of the Salvation of Humanity

The premise of justifying faith is God's grace, Christ's atoning work on the cross, to which we are enabled to respond by grace in lively faith. There is a triune premise in this sequence: God the Father is gracious toward us; God the Son manifests that grace on the cross; God the Holy Spirit enables our reception of that gracious work for us by faith.[225]

One is not justified by one's repentance, nor by one's good works, nor by the act of faith as such as if without grace—for faith quintessentially is the reception of grace.[226] It is not my seizing justification by my act of faith that justifies me. It is God's mercy through the atoning work of Christ that justifies me and faith is my reception of that justification.

To embrace the promise of God's personally addressed Word does not mean that simply by intellectually assenting to God's promises we are saved, or by accepting a set of propositions.[227] Rather, it means personally meeting and trusting the Word of this incomparable One, the word of forgiveness spoken to us on the cross, that it is a true word not a deception.[228]

Of True Christian Faith: The Complementary Teachings of James and Paul

The homilies then focus upon the relation of faith and works, correlating Paul's doctrine of justification through grace by faith alone and James's doctrine that faith without works is dead. Wesley remained determined to hold those themes tightly together. The Cranmerian Homilies gave him the

---

[224]CC 230–65; *Certain Sermons or Homilies, Appointed to be read in churches in the time of the late Queen Elizabeth*; cf. B1:139, 193n; B11:443f., 451–53; JJW 2:101, 275.
[225]DSF sec. 1–5, JWO 124–25; cf. B4:24; 1:349f.
[226]DSF sec. 6–9, JWO 125–27.
[227]DSF sec. 14, JWO 128.
[228]DSF sec. 7–14, JWO 126–29.

clearest statement of their intimate correlation. Without good works faith is not true and vital faith.[229] Anyone who is living the life of faith is going to be actively engaged in the love of the neighbor, manifesting the love of God by loving one's neighbor, demonstrating our faith by our work.[230] Justification, whose sole condition is penitent faith, is never lacking in fruits of faith, by which the believer is assured that the Spirit is working within.[231]

Wesley is meticulous in showing that Paul and James do not contradict each other: "St. Paul speaks of that justification which was when Abraham was seventy-five years old, more than twenty years before Isaac was born; St. James, of that justification which was when he offered up Isaac on the altar ... St. Paul speaks of works that precede faith, St. James, of works that spring from faith."[232]

Without faith there is no good work that can be performed.[233] Those who "shine in good works without faith are like dead men who have goodly and precious tombs."[234] We do not do good works prior to faith. Good works are the fruit and outgrowth of faith. Among good works that faith brings forth are obedience to God's commandments, reading of the Word, giving oneself totally to God, loving God in all things and loving all persons in relation to the love of God, obeying duly constituted authority.[235]

The "whole tenor" of the Anglican liturgy, Articles, and Homilies was deftly summarized by Wesley: "(1). That no good work, properly so called, can go *before* justification; (2). That *no degree* of true sanctification can be previous to it; (3). That as the *meritorious cause* of justification is the life and death of Christ, so the *condition* of it is faith, faith alone; and (4). That both inward and outward holiness are consequent on this faith, and are the ordinary, stated conditions of final justification."[236]

The Lord Our Righteousness

Jer. 23:6: "This is the name whereby he shall be called, The Lord Our Righteousness." [Homily #20 1765 B1:444–65 J#20 V:234–46]

Christ's Active and Passive Obedience

Jesus' obedience implied not only an incomparably good *doing* (active obedience), but also an incomparably patient *suffering for others* (passive obedience), his "suffering the whole will of God from the time he came into the world till 'he bore our sins in his own body upon the tree.' " "But as the active and passive righteousness of Christ were never in fact separated from each other, so we never need separate them at all, either in speaking or even in thinking," and this is what

---

[229]LJW 7:302; JJW 2:354–56; B1:689, 695; 2:164–66; 3:400–5; 9:94–99, 318f., 325–28, 357f.

[230]DSF sec. 8, JWO 131.

[231]B11:456f.

[232]Minutes, 1744, June 25, Q14, JWO 138.

[233]DSF sec. 9, JWO 132.

[234]DSF sec. 11, JWO 132.

[235]DSF sec. 12, 13, JWO 133, 272f., 362, 365, 373f.

[236]FA Part I, ii.8, 11:115; on the *sola fide* theme, cf. LJW 3:321 in response to Lavington, and 3:351 quoting Anna Marie van Schurrman's *Journal* in response to William Law. On the distinction between the formal and meritorious causes of justification, see FA 11:112–15; cf. 11:447–48; B1:78, 80–83, 382f., 455–60; 2:157f.

we mean when we speak of "the Lord our righteousness."[237]

Christ's work required an active obedience by which he actively fulfilled the law, and a passive obedience by which he suffered for sinners in order to enable their fulfillment of the law.

The Believer Clothed in a Righteousness Not His Own

In receiving God's justifying grace we are receiving an imputed gift, offered freely on our behalf. Imputation is a juridical metaphor, and as such not yet more than the embryo of a behavior-reconstructing process. If the judge says in a court room, "You are free," and bangs the gavel, that is an imputation whereby one is declared free from offense to the law. But that declaration does not in itself determine that the behavior that follows will be responsible.

That Christ's righteousness is imputed means that "all believers are forgiven and accepted, not for the sake of anything in them, or of anything that ever was, that is, or ever can be done by them, but wholly and solely for the sake of what Christ hath done and suffered for them."[238] "This is the doctrine which I have constantly believed and taught for near eight and twenty years. This I published to all the world in the year 1738, and ten or twelve times since."[239] It is not that faith as such is imputed for righteousness, but that "faith in the righteousness of

Christ" is so imputed that the believer is clothed in a righteousness not his own, a glorious dress that enables and calls him to "put off the filthy rags" of his own righteousness.[240]

Christ's righteousness is imputed to us when we believe, as soon as we believe, so that "faith and the righteousness of Christ are inseparable."[241] Believers may vary greatly in their ways of expressing this while still remaining unified in their sharing experientially in Christ's righteousness.[242]

Distinguishing Christ's Divine and Human Righteousness

John Deschner provided this systematic outline-analysis of "The Lord Our Righteousness":[243]

Christ's righteousness consists of two parts:
1. His divine righteousness [God's essential righteousness].
2. His human righteousness: this is imputed as a whole to man.

It consists of two parts:
  a. Internal human righteousness: Christ's human image of God.
  b. External human righteousness: Christ's obedience.

This in turn, consists of two parts:
  1) Active obedience: what Christ did. Two aspects can also be distinguished here:
     a) Negative active obedience: He did no sin.

---

[237]#20 "The Lord Our Righteousness," i.1–4, 1:452–53.

[238]#20 "The Lord Our Righteousness," ii.5, 1:455; cf. LJW 3:248f., 373, 385; 5:5; JJW 4:103; 6:173; B2:153.

[239]See his abridgment of the Anglican Homilies, "The Doctrine of Salvation," "Faith and Good Works," i.5; #5 "Justification by Faith," i.8; and his abridgment of John Goodwin's Treatise on Justification; cf. B9:406, 410.

[240]#20 "The Lord Our Righteousness," ii.11, 1:458.

[241]#20 "The Lord Our Righteousness," ii.1; cf. B1:567–71; 4:219.

[242]Even with the dying Bellarmine "it is safest to trust in the merits of Christ," and who would argue that "notwithstanding his wrong opinions, he had no share" in Christ's righteousness? #20 "The Lord Our Righteousness," i.1–4, 1:452–53.

[243]Deschner, WC 157–58.

b) Positive active obedience: He did God's will perfectly.

2) Passive obedience: what Christ suffered.

Accordingly, Christ's divine righteousness is identical with the essential righteousness of God, since the Father and Son are one. Christ's human *imago* is a copy or transcript of Christ's own divine righteousness, and a prototype for the progressive conformity of humanity to God's righteousness.[244] "When Christ's sacrifice re-establishes the law, it is *this* representation of the law, i.e., Christ's humanity, which, crucified and risen, stands as the decisive definition of all law. The new commandment is not only love in the abstract, but that love which is defined by Christ's suffering humanity . . . In Christ the law itself, as Christ's human *imago*, dies and rises again . . . [hence] the law, i.e., Christ's risen humanity, confronts believers as the consequence and promise, not the condition, of justification . . . the oral law turns its promissory face to man, so to speak, in the risen humanity of Christ, imputed to believers in the form of participation in Christ's corporate Body."[245]

The righteousness belonging to the mediator may be viewed either as an *internal* righteousness (the image of God stamped on every power and faculty of his soul, without any defect or admixture of unholiness) or an *external righteousness*, (knowing no outward sin, viewed negatively, and doing all things well, viewed positively).[246]

How Imputed Righteousness Becomes Implanted Righteousness

Wesley was especially interested in the implanting process that manifests itself behaviorally following the received imputation.[247] "I believe that God implants righteousness in everyone to whom He has imputed it."[248] Implanting is a lively horticultural metaphor, as distinguished from a declarative, juridical metaphor.[249] It requires daily nurturing, not a simple bang of a gavel. It is the fruit of our acceptance with God, not the ground of it.[250]

To speak of the imputation of Christ's righteousness is not to argue that his divine nature as immutable holiness is unambiguously imputed to us. Rather it is the righteousness that belongs to him as *theanthropos*, as unique mediator between God and man that is imputed to us. This in classical dogmatics is sometimes called the human righteousness of the theandric Son, to distinguish it from that righteousness

---

[244]#20 "The Lord Our Righteousness," i.2; cf. Deschner, WC 158–59.

[245]Deschner, WC 159–60.

[246]#20 "The Lord Our Righteousness," i.1–4, 1:452–53.

[247]In 1765 Wesley published an extract of John Goodwin's treatise on justification, *Imputatio Fidei*, 1642, which he found especially edifying; see LJW 4:274, 279f., 287; B1:83n; 4:7n.

[248]#20 "The Lord Our Righteousness," ii.12; on imputed righteousness, see B1:63, 294, 445, 452–63; 4:142f.; HWI 217, 274, 347f.

[249]See also the metaphor of imparted righteousness, B1:63, 80, 643; 4:144; JWO 217f., 274, 348.

[250]"Neither do I deny *imputed righteousness*, #20 "The Lord Our Righteousness," ii.14, 1:458. In this respect Wesley distinguishes his view from that of Robert Barclay and the Quakers, ii.16, 1:460; but who would dare to suggest that all who are unclear in their opinions about imputed righteousness "are void of all Christian experience?" ii.16. On matters of opinion regarding the use of language, it is best to "think and let think," ii.20, 1:464. Cf. #7 "The Way to the Kingdom," i.6.

that belongs to the divine nature *in se*.[251] In this way, through the Atonement, God's own righteousness becomes God's righteousness *in us* as a gift by which humanity is made righteous (Rom. 1:17).[252]

Those to whom the righteousness of Christ is imputed are by the work of the Spirit being made righteous not in conjecture only but by grace actually being behaviorally uprighted. They are being renewed in the image of God in a lifelong process that seeks to manifest God's own holy love behaviorally, both inwardly in a regenerated attitude and outwardly in the works of love.[253]

Holiness of heart and life is "not the cause, but the effect of" justification. "The sole cause of our acceptance with God . . . is the righteousness and the death of Christ, who fulfilled God's law, and died in our stead."[254]

*Caveat on the Excessive Use
of the Imputation Metaphor*

Some who are "otherwise well-meaning . . . have been deluded and hardened, at least for the present, chiefly, if not merely, by the *too frequent* and improper use of the phrase *imputed righteousness*."[255] Those who overstress the imputed character of God's righteousness with the particular spin that it has minimal implication for my personal behavior change, tend toward antinomianism.[256] The imputed righteousness of Christ must not be used as an excuse or "a cover for . . . unrighteousness."[257]

For some in Wesley's day began to get nervous any time anyone began to mention good works, fearing that good works might be thought to precede justifying faith.[258] Wesley agreed with them on their concern that good works flow from faith and do not precede it. But if the focus of preaching turns toward the Son's saving action on the cross so as to neglect the work of the Spirit in our hearts and behavior processes, the balance of Scripture metaphors has been overturned.[259]

**On the Imputed Righteousness
of Christ**

Thoughts on the Imputed Righteousness of Christ [X:312–16] and Letter to James Hervey, Oct. 15, 1756 [LJW 3:371–88][260]

---

[251]#85 "On Working Out Our Own Salvation," sec. 4. In response to Roland Hill's criticism, he acknowledged that "by Christ's human righteousness," he meant "that mediatorial righteousness which was wrought by God in the human nature." "Some Remarks of Mr. Hill's 'Review of All the Doctrines Taught by Mr. John Wesley,' " X:384.

[252]ENNT on Rom. 1:17; Phil. 3:9.

[253]It is this implanting and growth process that Wesley calls by the name of "inherent righteousness."

[254]HSP 1739, Pref. 2, XIV:320.

[255]Letter to John Newton, Feb. 28, 1766, LJW 5:5.

[256]JWO 301f., 377f.; LJW 3:248f, 373, 385; 5:5; JJW 4:103; 6:173; B2:153.

[257]#20 "The Lord Our Righteousness," ii.19, 1:462.

[258]This sermon (#20) served as a response to his former student, James Hervey, whose *Theron and Aspasio* set forth the differences between Arminians and Calvinists, for whom the imputed righteousness of Christ was the central feature of justification. Outler recognizes this as a "landmark sermon" in which Wesley, fending off charges of Jesuitism and Bellarminism, draws careful lines between Arminian and Calvinist nuances of soteriology. It marks the beginning of the mature Wesley as a theologian who has decided to set forth his differences with Calvinist evangelicals.

[259]See #34–36 "The Original, Nature, Properties, and Use of the Law," and "The Law Established Through Faith, I and II."

[260]This letter is included in the Preface to a "Treatise on Justification," extracted from Mr. John Goodwin, X:316–46.

How Imputed Righteousness May Become Exaggerated Toward Antinomianism

In the gospel "the righteousness of God is revealed" (Rom. 1:17). "God made him who had no sin to be sin for us, so that in him we might become the righteousness of God" (2 Cor. 5:21). "The righteousness of God" in these cases means "God's method of justifying sinners."[261]

However, Wesley did not find in Scripture the specific phrase "imputed righteousness of Christ." Hence "I dare not insist upon, neither require any one to use [it]. . . I am myself the more sparing in the use of it, because it has been so frequently and so dreadfully abused; and because the Antinomians use it at this day to justify the grossest abominations."[262]

"Is temperance imputed only to him that is a drunkard still: or chastity, to her that goes on in whoredom?" In this perverse way, according to Zinzendorf, obedience becomes "a proof of unbelief, and disobedience a proof of faith!" Rather: "Nay, but a believer is really chaste and temperate. And if so, he is thus far holy" inwardly.[263]

Wesley thought that the troublesome "*particular phrase*, 'the imputed righteousness of Christ'" was prone to misinterpretation, and had been used as a ruse to avoid any effort actually to walk in the way of holiness, and hence had inadvertently "done immense hurt."[264] This particular "*mode of expression* . . . is always dangerous, often fatal."[265] "O how deep an aversion to inward holiness does this scheme naturally create!"[266]

Wesley affirmed that Christ is "our substitute as to penal sufferings" but not as a substitute for our personal acts of obedience.[267] That we are "complete in him" refers also to our sanctification by cooperating grace, not merely justification by grace operating. "God, through [Christ], first accounts, and then makes us righteous."[268] Hence we should never talk an easy game of imputation without taking seriously the process of behavioral sanctification.

Christ tasted death for every man, but Wesley thought it "vain philosophy" to so stretch the point that the righteousness that justifies us is already in every sense behaviorally "carried on, completed . . . wrought out" so that "the nice, metaphysical doctrine of imputed righteousness leads not to repentance, but to licentiousness."[269] Rather, the righteousness of God "signifies God's method of justifying sinners."[270] "He alone is truly righteous, whose faith worketh by love."[271]

The singular condition of our reception of justifying grace is "repent and believe." Christ does not repent for us or enact our belief without us. Those who say that invite antinomianism to "come in with a full tide."[272] When Hervey contended that believers could

---

[261]"Thoughts on the Imputed Righteousness of Christ," X:313.
[262]"Thoughts on the Imputed Righteousness of Christ," X:315.
[263]"An Extract from A Short View of the Difference Between the Moravian Brethren, (so Called,) and the Rev. Mr. John and Charles Wesley," X:203.
[264]LJW 3:371–72.
[265]Letter to James Hervey, LJW 3:381.
[266]Letter to James Hervey, LJW 3:384.
[267]LJW 3:373.
[268]Letter to James Hervey, LJW 3:384.
[269]LJW 3:373.
[270]Letter to James Hervey, LJW 3:382.
[271]LJW 3:375.
[272]Letter to James Hervey, LJW 3:379.

remain "notorious transgressors in themselves," yet at the same time "have a sinless obedience in Christ," Wesley mused: "O syren song! Pleasing sound to James Wheatley, Thomas Williams, James Relly!" (leading antinomian defectors from Methodism).[273] "We swarm with Antinomians on every side. Why are you at such pains to increase their number!"[274] "The very quintessence of Antinomianism" is the easy premise that Christ has behaviorally and ethically "satisfied the demand of the law for me."[275] It is a return straight to Zinzendorf's "Antinomianism without a mask" to say that all the claims of the law are behaviorally answered in Christ.[276]

The End of Christ's Coming

1 John 3:8: "For this purpose was the Son of God manifested, that he might destroy the works of the devil." [Homily #62 1781 B2:471–84 J#62 VI:267–77]

For the dilemma of sin, rational philosophy can offer only "broken reeds, bubbles, smoke!" "Nature points out the disease; but nature show us no remedy."[277]

To Destroy the Works of the Devil

Humanity is created in the moral image of God originally capable of righteousness and holiness,[278] and in the natural image of God capable of free self-determination.[279] Humanity in its

created condition was "capable of mistaking, of being deceived, although not necessitated to it."[280] Now full of sin, unholy and unhappy, humanity has virtually lost the moral image of God.

The final end of Christ's coming is to destroy "sin and the fruits of sin," and all of the works of the adversary.[281] By making of himself a full, perfect, and sufficient sacrifice and satisfaction for the sins of the whole world, the incarnate Son has already begun to bind the power of evil.[282] The Spirit is enabling faith to become active in love, and thereby restore the moral image of God in holiness and righteousness.[283]

Full Salvation: Restoration of the Image of God

The saving activity of the triune God goes beyond simply a juridical declaring of freedom from guilt and punishment of sin. It also includes the promise of freedom from the "power and root of sin," by the offer of sanctifying grace, which looks toward a process of behavioral reflection and embodiment of the way of holiness. The steps by which this renewal occurs are familiar to gospel preaching. Faith trusts that God was in Christ reconciling the world to himself. This strikes at the root of pride and self-will, enabling repentance and faith.[284]

But this is not a simplistic argument for the complete and easy renovation of humanity from all sin immediately, or

---

[273]LJW 3:379; cf. JWO 235, 377f.
[274]Letter to James Hervey, LJW 3:385.
[275]Letter to James Hervey, LJW 3:386.
[276]Hervey argued that "Our present blessedness does not consist in being free from sin." Wesley replied: "I really think it does," according to the apostolic teaching that "You have been set free from sin and become slaves of righteousness" (Rom. 6:18), LJW 3:380.
[277]#62 "The End of Christ's Coming," proem.3, 2:473.
[278]#62 "The End of Christ's Coming," i.7–9, 2:475–76.
[279]#62 "The End of Christ's Coming," i.3–6, 2:474–75.
[280]#62 "The End of Christ's Coming," i.3, 2:474.
[281]#62 "The End of Christ's Coming," ii.1, 2:478; CH 7:410, 443–44; LJW 4:122.
[282]#62 "The End of Christ's Coming," ii.1–5, 2:478–79.
[283]#62 "The End of Christ's Coming," ii. 6, 7, 2:480.
[284]#62 "The End of Christ's Coming," iii, 2:480–84.

the destruction of evil without a struggle. The combat of flesh and spirit remains in all the faithful. The Son "does not destroy the whole work of the devil in man, as long as he remains in this life. He does not yet destroy bodily weakness, sickness, pain, and a thousand infirmities incident to flesh and blood. He does not destroy all that weakness of understanding, which is the natural consequence of the soul's dwelling in a corruptible body," all of which are destroyed in death, which itself is overcome in the resurrection.[285]

"Real religion" is "a restoration, not only to the favour, but likewise to the image of God, implying not barely deliverance from sin, but the being filled with the fulness of God." Yet how little this is in "this enlightened age, wherein it is taken for granted, the world is wiser than ever it was from the beginning. . . . Among all our discoveries, who has discovered this?" It is discovered by viewing Scripture "in one connected chain. And the agreement of every part of it, with every other," viz., by means of the analogy of faith that works by love toward "all inward and outward holiness."[286]

God is able and willing to destroy all sin in all that believe. Sin is not intrinsic to humanity as created by God, but a malformation, a disease of humanity that God is in the process of correcting.

FURTHER READINGS ON JUSTIFICATION

Bolster, Geo. R. "Wesley's Doctrine of Justification." *Ev. Quarterly* 24 (1952): 144–55.

Brockwell, Ch. W., Jr. "John Wesley's Doctrine of Justification." WTJ 18 no. 2 (1983): 18–32.

Cannon, W. R. *The Theology of John Wesley: With Special Reference to the Doctrine of Justification.* New York: Abingdon, 1946.

Collins, Kenneth. *John Wesley on Salvation.* Grand Rapids: FAP, Zondervan, 1989. Chap. 3 "Justification by Faith."

Cushman, R. E. "Salvation for All." In *Faith Seeking Understanding.* Durham: Duke Univ. Press, 1981, 63–74.

Gunter, W. Steven. *The Limits of Divine Love, John Wesley's Response to Antinomianism and Enthusiasm.* Nashville: Abingdon, Kingswood, 1989. Chap. 4 "Via Salutis: Wesley's Early Steps"; chap. 6 "Faith Alone," and chap. 7 "Faith Alone Misunderstood."

Hildebrandt, Franz. *From Luther to Wesley.* London: Lutterworth, 1951.

Koerber, Carolo. CSSR. *Theology of Conversion According to John Wesley.* Rome: Gregorian University, Neo-Eboraci, 1967, on Justification, 1–37.

Lindström. WS, 105ff.; atonement, justification, 55ff.; the law, 75ff.; justification and sanctification, 83ff.

Monk, R. JWPH. "Justification by Faith," 75ff.

Prince, J. W. *Wesley on Religious Education.* "Repentance" and "Justification by Faith and Regeneration," 44ff.

Rees, A. H. *The Doctrine of Justification in the Anglican Reformers.* London, 1939.

Smith, L. Harmon. "Wesley's Doctrine of Justification: Beginning and Process." *Duke Div. School Review* 28 (May 1963).

Starkey, L. WHS. "Order of Redemption," chap. III "'Justification and Faith."

Wynkoop. FWAT. "The Function of Faith," 222ff.

COUNTERING CHRISTOLOGICAL DISTORTIONS

On Knowing Christ After the Flesh

2 Cor. 5:16: "Henceforth know we no man after the flesh; Yea, though we did know Christ after the flesh, yet now henceforth know we him no more." [Homily #123 1789 B4:97–106 J#107 VII:291–97]

Finding no definitive treatises on this important theme, Wesley felt that this text had been grossly misconstrued by some forms of pietism. His own transla-

---

[285] #62 "The End of Christ's Coming," iii.3, 2:482.
[286] #62 "The End of Christ's Coming," iii.5–6, 2:482–84; cf. B1:118, 495f.

tion of the preceding passage is: "He died for all, that they who live might not henceforth live unto themselves [seek their own honour, or profit, or pleasure] but unto him. So that we from this time [we that know him by faith] know no one after the flesh." The NIV translation reads: "*So from now on we regard no one from a worldly point of view*" — in a merely human fashion, based on their outward lives by worldly standards. "*Though we once regarded Christ in this way, we do so no longer. Therefore, if anyone is in Christ, he is a new creation*" (vv. 16b–17). Wesley commented: "This uncommon expression . . . seems to mean: We regard no man according to his former state,—his country, riches, power, or wisdom. We consider all men only in their spiritual state." If we merely behold Christ "after the flesh . . . loving him as a man, with a natural affection," we miss his divinity, for Christ is God.[287]

The heretical prototypes of knowing Christ after the flesh are the Arians who viewed "Christ as inferior to the Father," and the Socinians who denied the Atonement and did "not allow him to be the supreme God." This tendency is seen in the unitarian John Taylor, who inadvertently demeaned Jesus by treating him "with great civility" as a "very worthy personage" while denying his divinity. Especially odious to Wesley was a sentimentalist hymnody that tended to deal with Christ overfamiliarly, neglecting his deity.[288] Wesley urged the avoidance of "every fondling expression," and especially the impertinent use of the word "dear" as ad-

dressed to God, which is "one particular word, which I never use myself either in verse or prose, in praying or preaching . . . I have sometimes almost scrupled singing, (even in the midst of my brother's excellent hymn,) 'That dear disfigured face,' or that glowing expression, 'Drop thy warm blood upon my heart.' "[289]

Christ's Lordship is debased when treated with excessive fervor or emotive display, by "loud shouting, horrid, unnatural screaming, repeating the same words twenty or thirty times, jumping two or three feet high, and throwing about the arms or legs, both of men and women, in a manner shocking not only to religion, but to common decency!"[290] One wonders just what these people were doing. In any event, Wesley thought it showed "improper familiarity with God."

Since Wesley presupposed the patristic teaching of *perichoresis*, the interpenetrating of the two natures in one person, he found the pietistic sentimentality and overfamiliarity one-sided. The antidote to all this is a rigorous traditional Christology whereby we " 'honour the Son even as we honour the Father.' We are to pay him the same worship as we pay to the Father. We are to love him with all our heart and soul; and to consecrate all we have and are, all we think, speak, and do, to the THREE–ONE GOD, Father, Son, and Spirit."[291]

On Preaching Christ

Letter to an Evangelical Layman, Dec. 20, 1751 [B26:482–89][292]

---

[287]#123 "On Knowing Christ After the Flesh," sec. 1–3, 4:98–99.

[288]#123 "On Knowing Christ After the Flesh," sec. 4–7, 4:100–101; Wesley found this tendency in the Moravian hymnody, and even in Isaac Watts's *Horae Lyricae*.

[289]#123 "On Knowing Christ After the Flesh," sec. 8–10, 4:101–3.

[290]#123 "On Knowing Christ After the Flesh," sec. 11, 4:103.

[291]#123 "On Knowing Christ After the Flesh," sec. 16, 4:106.

[292]This is the same document as that which appears in Jackson's and Outler's editions

Countering Antinomianism in the Preaching of the Righteousness of Faith

The law-gospel correlation is central to this letter. Those who have read Bonhoeffer on "cheap grace" will understand instantly the bent of antinomianism against which Wesley struggled. Some were preaching Christ without a cross, the gospel without any consequent requirement, forgiveness without response, pardon without perseverance, the mercy of God without ever mentioning human accountability in response to pardon.[293]

Wesley recognized the dangers of such antinomianism and considered them undermining of faith itself.[294] Those who preach the gospel must counter the false imagination that we are thereby being called to relax morally or flaunt the law or duties to God, self, and neighbor. There are great dangers in turning preaching into "soft words," so they "vitiate their taste, so that they cannot relish sound doctrine; and spoil their appetite, so that they cannot turn it into nourishment; they, as it were, feed them with sweetmeats, till the genuine wine of the kingdom seems quite insipid to them."[295]

Gospel and Law Dialectically Correlated in Every Evangelical Testimony

Law and gospel are instead to be preached as intertwined, with the requirement of God clarified in the context of the gospel.[296] "Some think, preaching the law only, others, preaching the gospel only. I think, neither the one nor the other; but duly mixing both, in every place, if not in every sermon."[297] "The first and great command" is "Believe on the Lord Jesus Christ."[298]

This was the preaching of all the Methodists until James Wheatly, who began congratulating himself that he preached "only Christ" by neglecting the dialectic between law and gospel, doing incalculable harm, causing preachers to leave the ministry, and a demoralization of society membership, as at Newcastle. But in the societies of Yorkshire where the dialectic was held fast, Wesley found members "alive, strong, vigorous of soul, believing, loving, and praising God their Saviour," having heard the indicative-imperative: "Christ died for you; therefore die to sin." "The law thus preached both enlightens and strengthens the soul . . . both nourishes and teaches . . . is the guide, 'food, medicine, and stay' of the believing soul."[299]

To preach the gospel is to declare God's love to sinners.[300] To preach the law means to make clear God's requirement resulting from the gospel.[301] This moral address of God is heard prototypically, first in the Decalogue, and most fully in the Sermon on the Mount. Those who would preach the commands and not the gospel fall into the grip of legalism. Those who preach the gospel without divine requirement implicit in it risk falling down the slippery

---

under the title "Letter on Preaching Christ," JWO 232–37; XI:486–92, written to an anonymous individual who had denounced Wesley as a legalist.

[293]"A Dialogue Between an Antinomian and His Friend," X:266–76.
[294]B9:370–72.
[295]LPC 26:487; XI:491.
[296]B1:304f., 551–55; 2:20–43; JWO 232–37.
[297]LPC 7, 26:483; XI:486.
[298]LPC 18, 26:485; XI:489, Acts 16:31.
[299]LPC 18, 26:485; XI:489.
[300]LJW 1:158; 5:259, 292; B1:229, 1:347–50.
[301]LJW 3:82.

slope of antinomianism.[302] Wesley, like Luther, was trying to protect the laity from both distortions. Preaching that too hastily reassures of God's love and pardon may result in only a slight healing of the wound of sin. It is chiefly in personal, one-on-one pastoral counsel with a "thoroughly convinced sinner that one should be preaching nothing but the gospel."[303]

Rightly understood in the light of the gospel, the law of the Lord converts the soul, makes us wise, rejoices the heart, and opens our eyes morally (Ps. 19:7–9). A proper balance of law and gospel was the basis for edifying the societies. When the gospel is preached in a proper dialectical balance with the divine requirement, there follows a deeper expression of faith active in love, a greater sense of disciplined intentionality in the community.[304] He thought that this was being empirically validated through the very communities he himself was responsible for guiding.[305]

We Preach Christ Crucified

1 Cor. 1:23–24: "But we preach Christ crucified, unto the Jews a stumblingblock, and unto the Greeks foolishness; but unto them which are called, both Jews and Greeks, Christ the power of God, and the wisdom of God." [Attributed to Wesley as transcribed by Mr. Williamson, on the opening of a new preaching-house at Wakefield 1774 4:519–24 (Appendix)]

To preach Christ crucified is to preach in the closest connection "*justification* by faith in his blood," whereby "faith is counted for righteousness," with *sanctification*, whereby one being born again from above finds that "as

great a change must pass upon us as when we were born at first. All our nature must be changed by the operation of the Holy Ghost and then be made alive, receive a new life (which is hid with Christ in God), and so, being born again, . . . go on from grace to grace, till we appear at last before him."[306]

To the self-righteous, this message is a stumbling block. To those who imagine themselves reasonable, it is foolishness. But to those called, it is the power and wisdom of God:

First, to the self-righteous, it appears as a stumbling block. Such preaching of justification and sanctification together appears as an impediment to those who (to use Paul's characterization of certain Jews of his day) "have an outside righteousness" and on that account despise others," thinking they have sufficient righteousness of their own to justify themselves, desiring to be justified by their own works. Taken in that symbolic sense, there remain an abundance of works-righteousness advocates "in every Christian country."[307]

Second, to those who imagine themselves reasonable, this seems foolishness. Such preaching of justification and sanctification in closest connection is disregarded by those who "pride themselves in their own wisdom" and who attempt to "understand everything by their own reason," even when they cannot begin to explain the psychosomatic interface or the ground of moral accountability. Talk to anatomist William Hunter or proto-Unitarian John Taylor about such things and see how these teachings are regarded as foolishness. Taylor will tell you, "In pro-

---

[302]B1:347, 554f.; 2:125; 4:220.
[303]LPC 9, 26:483; XI:487.
[304]Letter to Ebenezer Blackwell, Dec. 20, 1752, 3:79–85.
[305]LPC 26:482–88; XI:489–92.
[306]"We Preach Christ Crucified," 4:521.
[307]"We Preach Christ Crucified," 4:521.

cess of time, I will mend," and Hunter will say, "a man can never be justified by the righteousness of another."[308]

To those called, however, the preaching of justification and sanctification in closest connection is experienced as the *wisdom of God*, whereby "all his attributes and perfections harmonize: justice and mercy meet together." Such preaching is also experienced as the *"power of God* with regard to sanctification." "You then found that sin had no more dominion over you. Then, my brethren, this was the moment of your sanctification. Then you were endowed with power from on high, and from that time you had power to mortify the deeds of the body and subdue all love to the world. Then the kingdom of heaven was like a grain of mustard seed," looking to grow toward the time when "nothing may dwell in your hearts but love alone."[309]

Anyone who has experienced any "remarkable turn of providence, either in prosperity or adversity" is thereby being *"outwardly called"* to forsake sin and turn to God. Anyone who has experienced "a wish that you may die the death of the righteous" is thereby being *inwardly called.* Anyone who is being given the present opportunity to receive the forgiveness of sins is thereby being *effectually* called by God's grace.[310]

Challenging Mystic Speculations on the Atonement

Letter to William Law, Jan. 6, 1756 [LJW 3:332–70; IV:466–509]

Refuting the Denial of the Necessity of Christ's Death

Atonement according to William Law in his later phase was in Wesley's view merely the subjective comfort of inner illumination, as if "the one only work of Christ as your redeemer is to raise into life the smothered spark of heaven in you."[311] Lacking, as Law had, any premise of the capacity of God for disciplining his children, there can be "no scriptural doctrine of justification."

"If the Son of God did not die to atone for our sins, what did He die for?"[312] In advancing the penal satisfaction view of atonement, Wesley argued that Christ's death is necessary. By this time Law seemed "not even to know what the term 'justification' means." Wesley commended Anna Maria van Schurmann's plain account of the Atonement in her *Journal*[313] and letter in *Eukleria*,[314] to establish these five crucial Christological points:

1. Christ has acquired for us a right to eternal life "by His satisfaction and merits alone. Neither our repentance nor amendment can be any satisfaction for sin." It is only "through His blood that we have redemption" (Eph. 1:7). He "sent His Son to be the propitiation for our sins" (1 John 4:9–10). The Lord is "our righteousness" (Jer. 23:6), who "gave Himself a ransom for all" (1 Tim. 2:6). It was impossible for the sinner to satisfy God "by a partial and imperfect obedience. Neither could he merit anything from Him to whom he owed all things. There was need, therefore, of a Mediator who could repair the immense wrong he had done to the

---

[308]"We Preach Christ Crucified," 4:522.
[309]"We Preach Christ Crucified," 4:523–24.
[310]"We Preach Christ Crucified," 4:523.
[311]Letter to William Law, ii.3, LJW 3:351.
[312]Letter to William Law, ii.2, 3, LJW 3:345–57.
[313]Anna Maria van Schurmann, *Journal*, I:435d.
[314]Anna Maria van Schurmann, Part II:118; Letter to William Law, ii.3, LJW 3:353–56.

THE INCARNATE CRUCIFIED LORD

Divine Majesty . . . suffer in the place of His people, and merit for them pardon, holiness and glory."[315]

2. The imitation of Christ lies primarily in faith in Christ crucified, who "leaving you an example that you should follow in his steps" (1 Peter 2:21), "died for us" that we might be "justified by his blood" (Rom. 5:8, 9).[316]

3. "The origin and cause of our redemption is the ineffable love of God the Father, who willed to redeem us by the blood of His own Son; the grace of the Son, who freely took our curse upon Him, and imparts His blessing and merits to us; and the Holy Spirit who communicates the love of the Father and the grace of the Son to our hearts."[317]

Just here we stand at the "inmost mystery of the Christian faith," where "all the inventions of men ought now to be kept at the utmost distance" to allow Scripture to speak of the one Mediator who has "become the guarantee of a better covenant" (Heb. 7:22), who "took up our infirmities and carried our sorrows," who was "pierced for our transgressions, he was crushed for our iniquities; the punishment that brought us peace was upon him, and by his wounds we are healed." "The Lord has laid on him the iniquity of us all," who was "led like a lamb to the slaughter," who was "cut off from the land of the living; for the transgression of my people he was stricken. He was assigned a

grave with the wicked," "though he had done no violence" (Isa. 53:4–9). Yet all this "was only the prelude of a glorious victory" where through his resurrection he raised us up with him, and having born "the sin of many . . . made intercession for the transgressors."[318]

4. Christ is not only a pattern, but principally the "surety of the new covenant, yea a sacrifice and a victim for the sins of his people."[319] "God presented him as a sacrifice of atonement, through faith in his blood . . . so as to be just and the one who justifies those who have faith in Jesus" (Rom. 3:25, 26). "We have been made holy through the sacrifice of the body of Jesus Christ once for all . . . because by one sacrifice he has made perfect forever those who are being made holy" (Heb. 10:10–14). "In all the ancient types and figures, 'without shedding of blood there was no remission': which was intended to show there never could be any without the blood of the great Antitype, without that grand propitiatory sacrifice which (like the figure of it) was to be offered 'without the gate.' "[320]

5. In this way the suffering Messiah atones for the sins of the people and restores them to God's favor. "Christ redeemed us from the curse of the law by becoming a curse for us" (Gal. 3:13). "He himself bore our sins in his body on the tree, so that we might die to sins and live for righteousness" (1 Peter 2:24). This is just what is denied by the

---

[315]Anna Maria van Schurmann, quoted by Wesley in a letter to William Law, ii.3, LJW 3:335; cf. FA B111:108; B1:608f.

[316]Anna Maria van Schurmann, quoted by Wesley in a letter to William Law, ii.3, LJW 3:354.

[317]Anna Maria van Schurmann, quoted by Wesley in a letter to William Law, ii.3, LJW 3:354.

[318]Anna Maria van Schurmann, quoted by Wesley in a letter to William Law, ii.3, LJW 3:354–55; cf. CH, 7:290–92.

[319]Anna Maria van Schurmann, quoted by Wesley in a letter to William Law, ii.3, LJW 3:355–56.

[320]Anna Maria van Schurmann, quoted by Wesley in a letter to William Law, ii.3, LJW 3:356.

Socinians who "rob Christ of the principal part of His priestly office, and leave Him only that of interceding for us by prayer."[321] In a similar way Law's Christology has dwindled into "the very essence of Deism."[322]

Resisting Mystical Misunderstandings of the New Birth, Baptism, and Faith

Law diminished regeneration to "nothing else but the regaining of our first angelic spirit and body," and faith to merely "a desire of coming to God," echoing the mystical longing for union with God. Wesley pounced on the term "desire": "I know the contrary from experience. I had this desire many years before I even knew what saving faith was."[323] Faith is rather "an *elenchos*, an 'evidence,' or 'conviction' (which is totally different from a desire) 'of things not seen,' a supernatural, a divine evidence and conviction of the things which God hath revealed in His Word . . . that the Son of God hath loved me and given Himself for me. Whosoever hath this faith is born of God."[324]

It is precisely such a subjectivist distortion of faith that led to Law's curious views on fervor and coldness in prayer, by which the soul seeks highest union with God through fervor, and then inconsistently seeks a still higher union through coldness. While Law contended that "coldness in one's spiritual journey can be beneficial," Wesley maintained that such spiritual coldness puts the believers "at the peril of their souls."[325]

Countering Mystical Universalism and the Denial of the Means of Grace

Letter to William Law, Jan. 6, 1756 [LJW 3:332–70; IV:466–509]

Whether "Christ-in-Everyone" Universalism Induces Spiritual Inertia

Reflecting the mystical tradition, Law argued complaisantly for the presence of Christ in every human spirit, "lying there in a state of insensibility and death." Wesley wondered how Christ could be both alive, "knocking at the door of the heart," and yet be dead. This leads to a soft universalism (the idea of "Christ in everyman")[326] so as to make people "easy who never believed at all," so that "Jews, Mohametans, Deists, Heathens, are all members of the Church of Christ! Should we not add devils too?" Catholicity now magnanimously "takes in all the world."

"I cannot find in the Bible when that was, when 'God spoke Christ into Adam.' " "There can hardly be any doctrine under heaven more agreeable to flesh and blood; nor any which more directly tends to prevent the very dawn of conviction" than to say to the one asleep in sin: Christ is already in your heart; you have now the inspiration of the Spirit. "As soon as you have sewed this pillow to his soul, he sinks back into the sleep of death."[327]

Whether the Outward Means of Grace Are Inconsequential

The deeper problem of William Law was a romantic, self-sufficient view of the individual, which Wesley perceived

---

[321]Anna Maria van Schurmann, quoted by Wesley in a letter to William Law, ii.3, LJW 3:356; CH 7:441–42.
[322]Letter to William Law, ii.3, LJW 3:357.
[323]Letter to William Law, ii.4, LJW 3:359; cf. Cell, RJW 94–129.
[324]Letter to William Law, ii.4, LJW 3:359.
[325]Letter to William Law, ii.4, LJW 3:359–61.
[326]Letter to William Law, ii.5, LJW 3:361.
[327]Letter to William Law, ii.5, LJW 3:361–64.

as a danger to faith. Wesley recognized clearly that Law had offered too simplistic a way of salvation, "a way so plain that they who follow it need no Bible, no human teaching, no outward means whatever, being everyone able to stand alone, everyone sufficient for himself." Wesley needled Law for his "easy way to salvation," "by the mere turning of your mind," as if "easily and immediately," all of which was "liable to ten thousand delusions,"[328] especially his advice to "Stop all self-activity; be retired, silent, passive, and humbly attentive to the inward light." Such a mixture of works-righteousness and quietism would be spiritually incendiary.[329]

If Law is correct that we always have embedded within natural human consciousness "a Priest, a church, and an altar," then there is no need for the church: "no other supper, worship, priest, or altar." Rather, "There is but one scriptural way wherein we receive inward grace, through the outward means which God hath appointed."[330]

Against Law's tendency to place Christ and Scripture in flat opposition to each other, Wesley affirmed the classical Protestant view that the revealed and written word work concurrently: "Both by the Bible and by experience we know that his Word and his Spirit act in connexion with each other."[331]

---

[328]IV:502.
[329]Letter to William Law, ii.6, LJW 3:364–68; cf. B1:376.
[330]Letter to William Law, ii.6, LJW 3:367.
[331]Letter to William Law, ii.6, LJW 3:367; IV:505.

7

The Holy Spirit

In "A Letter to a Roman Catholic," Wesley astutely summarized his credo concerning the person and work of the Holy Spirit: "I believe the infinite and eternal Spirit of God, equal with the Father and the Son, to be not only perfectly holy in himself, but the immediate cause of all holiness in us:

enlightening our understandings,
rectifying our wills and affections,
renewing our natures,
uniting our persons to Christ,
assuring us of the adoption of sons,
leading us in our actions,
purifying and sanctifying our souls
and bodies to a full and eternal
enjoyment of God."[1]

God the Spirit "acts on the wills and affections of men; withdrawing them from evil, inclining them to good, *inspiring* (breathing, as it were) good thoughts into them."[2]

INDWELLING

Scriptural Christianity

Acts 4:11: "And they were all filled with the Holy Ghost." [Homily #4 August 24, 1744[3] B2:159–80 J#4 V:37–52]

"Scriptural Christianity" is the last sermon Wesley preached at Oxford. All who read it know why. Keep in mind that he knew his audience well. He had been among Oxford students and faculty for many years, and yet at this point he wrote: "I preached, I suppose the last time, at St. Mary's. Be it so. I am now clear of the blood of these men. I have fully delivered my own soul."[4]

You can hear the vexation in Wesley's voice, disheartened that Oxford had not proved the arena where his vision of Christian community could come alive. So he was washing his hands of Oxford. When he preached this sermon, he did not intend it for publication, but to counter "false and scurrilous accounts" a printed version

---

[1]Letter to a Roman Catholic, sec. 8, JWO 495; spaces added.
[2]FA Part I, i.6, 11:108.
[3]The festival of St. Bartholomew, on which occurred the Massacre of Paris, 1572, and the Great Ejectment of the Nonconformists in England in 1662, in which both of Wesley's grandfathers had suffered rejection.
[4]"Short History of the People Called Methodist," sec. 30; *Journal* I:470, Aug. 24, 1744.

was produced, so volatile was its language. As Ezekiel was called "to warn the people, then if anyone hears the trumpet but does not take warning and the sword comes and takes his life, his blood will be on his own head" (Ezek. 33:3–4), so Wesley admonished his Oxford colleagues.

At this point in his life Wesley was making an irreversible vocational decision no longer to be an Oxford don, but instead to enter into the work of an itinerant evangelist. It was clear by this time that the university was not his calling. His parting shot to the university is sermon 4 of the Standard Sermons. The analogy is drawn between the reality of the early church being filled with the Spirit and what was then happening in the Evangelical Revival, the work in which he was becoming so deeply invested, in contrast to Oxford, which had the form but not the power of godliness.

Spirit-Filled Christianity: On Being Filled With the Spirit

The text is Acts 4:31, which recounts that after Pentecost the disciples were "all filled with the Holy Spirit and spoke the word of God boldly" (cf. 2:4). The gifts given with and following Pentecost are given for all and are "essential to all Christians in all ages": the mind of Christ, the fruits of the Spirit, the life Christ lived. It is typical for the life of the believer to be filled with the Holy Spirit.[5] That is scriptural Christianity in all ages.[6] Wherever the church is being filled with the Spirit, scriptural Christianity is coming alive. Where the mind of Christ is bearing the fruits of the Spirit and people are actually walking in the way of faith, there is scriptural Christianity.[7] This life begins with individuals and spreads by testimony and example through persecution, so as to cover the earth, looking finally toward the consummate victory of the sovereign God in and beyond history.[8]

The filling of all the faithful with the Spirit was not primarily to manifest extraordinary gifts, but simply for bestowing the mind of Christ upon all so as to elicit the fruits of the Spirit in all (Gal. 5:22–24). What happened at Pentecost does not happen only occasionally, but ordinarily and normatively within the faithful community of the baptized. Wesley urged all in his connection of spiritual formation to proceed "without busying ourselves, then in curious, needless inquiries, touching those extraordinary gifts," and focus instead on ordinary gifts.[9]

It is thus characteristic for ordinary believers to be "filled with the Holy Spirit." That is what the life of this community is all about. Wesley argued that the gifts of the Spirit are still being distributed to the church, and the work of the Spirit is still capable of transforming the community of faith in ways analogous to the experiences reported in Acts.

Scriptural Christianity in Its Rise: Beginning With Individuals

All who responded in faith to the good news of Peter's preaching were emboldened to attest the witness of the Spirit within, having faith, and love of God and humanity, victory over temptation, and zeal for good works. The self-offering of the Holy Spirit is for the

---

[5]#4 "Scriptural Christianity," proem.3, 1:160.

[6]Letter to Conyers Middleton, Jan. 4, 1749.

[7]#10 "The Witness of the Spirit, I," ii.12, 1:283; CH 7:508–9.

[8]#4 "Scriptural Christianity," proem.5, 1:161.

[9]#4 "Scriptural Christianity," proem.5, 1:160; see #J89 "The More Excellent Way," sec. 2; cf. B3:263–66; B9:353f.

"more excellent purpose" of proffering to sinners the mind of Christ, that by inward renewal they might by grace be enabled to "fulfill all outward righteousness," so that from new birth there would be integral and comprehensive behavioral transformation.[10] The love of God is shed abroad in our hearts by the Holy Spirit given to us (Rom. 5:5).[11]

Those who receive God's love, love each other in word, deed, and truth. They are not puffed up.[12] They are meek and long-suffering. With this love shaping their lives, they would knowingly harm no one. One who receives this Spirit knows that it is not enough merely to abstain from doing evil, but one must do good continually.[13]

It is the ordinary work of the Spirit to awaken individuals to God's pardon and power. This happens through a social process, within a community, yet one by one to individuals within that community. The individual never hears the testimony of the gospel apart from some community of testimony.

This Word comes to us one by one. The Spirit works patiently one by one. This does not imply that this one-by-one meeting lacks social consequences. There will be social consequence if there is deep inward transformation of the individual. Wesley was neither an individualistic evangelist who neglected the worshiping community and its context, nor a social determinist who demeaned individual decision.

The method of social change in scriptural Christianity moves steadily from individual conversion to social conversion, rather than presuming to change the world by rationalistically setting up a logical strategy hoping that people will be well-motivated enough to fall in line. A decisive historical difference between the French Enlightenment and the Evangelical revival tradition hinges upon this point: The French Revolution was an immediatist, rationalistic, idea-oriented uprising, in which the revolutionaries were trying first to get the right idea of an ideal society. The British and American evangelical revivals proceeded not so much by means of a deductive revolutionary rationalism, but with a historically formed, organic, incremental, personal understanding of social change. Wesley understood historical change from this more incremental, organic one-by-one model that he found in the preaching of the Acts of the Apostles.[14]

The beginning place for the Holy Spirit is personal conversion focusing on prevenient grace, conviction, repentance, receiving the good news of God's grace, trusting in the Word of God spoken in Christ, which brings the newly born believer into the family of God. This amounts to a new birth, a regeneration of spiritual life that places one's feet on the way toward holiness and happiness. The Spirit of adoption into this family of God leads toward an assurance of the forgiveness of sins and love of the neighbor, temperance, guilelessness, and vital community in the body of Christ, holding all things in common, in union with Christ (Gal. 2:20), and peace with God.[15]

This is how Christianity appeared in its inception. "Such was Christianity on its rise" with persons suddenly and immediately being filled with the Spirit, lifting up their voices boldly in one accord, with one heart and mind, cru-

[10]#4 "Scriptural Christianity," i.1–2, 1:161–62.
[11]#4 "Scriptural Christianity," i.4, 5, 1:163.
[12]#4 "Scriptural Christianity," i.6, 1:163.
[13]#4 "Scriptural Christianity," i.9, 1:164.
[14]#4 "Scriptural Christianity," ii.1–9, 1:161–64.
[15]#4 "Scriptural Christianity," i.2, 1:162.

cified to the world, feeding upon apostolic teaching, breaking bread, praying, sharing and lacking nothing.[16]

The Spread of Scriptural Christianity From One to Another

Persons effectively transformed by this good news felt called upon to attest it.[17] This good news spread from one to another in mission. All were exhorted to believe, to live out their belief in love, and thereby attest the ground of their belief. Love took the form of testimony. They sought to awaken those asleep, attend those awakened, and nurture all who enter the family of faith. They thundered to the careless, preached reconciliation to the convicted, reasoned with nonbelievers, encouraged believers, patiently engaged in works of mercy. Their labors were effective. They grew. They addressed each person individually as each had special needs.[18]

They became salt, light, and leaven within the world. This is scriptural Christianity. Rightly taught, it elicits transformed lives in mission, who manifest the compassion of God amid the misery of the world. The numbers were increasing of those who were beginning to turn the world upside down. Their labor was not in vain, since accompanied by the Spirit.[19]

By scriptural Christianity Wesley referred not simply to the proclamation of the gospel but the living out of the life of the gospel concretely. When he spoke of scriptural holiness, he was talking about that transformed life that is lived in dialogue with this word of Scripture, of those filled with the Holy Spirit, becoming contagious from person to person, meeting persecution and trouble and persevering suffering and finally covering the earth.[20]

But the world was offended. Those whose lives were inordinately attached to pleasure, reputation, acquisitive trade, and bigoted opinions, and especially men of religion (in the sense of self-satisfied worldly religionists who were seeking to use religion for their own purposes) were offended. So though Christianity spread in world history, yet, "how soon did the tares appear,"[21] wherever the wheat was sewn. How soon did the mystery of iniquity work even alongside the mystery of godliness. How soon did the arch-deceiver find a seat even in the temple of God. Yet despite corruptions the reign of God spread.[22]

Wherever the church proceeds in mission, it causes offense proportional to its success. As scriptural Christianity grew, so did the persecution of believers, but by their fidelity the kingdom was spread ever more widely, for "their sufferings spake to all the world." Wesley himself had only recently been through a period of persecution, with the Wednesbury riots in the back of his mind. As their labor grew mightily and prevailed, "so much the more did the offenses prevail also."[23]

The Mission of Scriptural Christianity: Covering the Earth

Greater things than what we have seen have been promised. The kingdom of God stands in prospect. Where God reigns, he subdues all things to himself,

[16]#4 "Scriptural Christianity," i.10, 1:165.
[17]#4 "Scriptural Christianity," ii.1, 165.
[18]#4 "Scriptural Christianity," ii.1–4, 165–67.
[19]#4 "Scriptural Christianity," ii.5, 1:167.
[20]CH 7:476–87.
[21]#4 "Scriptural Christianity," ii.9, 1:169.
[22]#4 "Scriptural Christianity," ii.5–7, 1:167–68.
[23]#4 "Scriptural Christianity," ii.5–7, 1:167–68.

causing every heart to overflow with love, and every mouth with praise.

This mission looks forward to the time when this testimony will cover the earth,[24] when the biblical hopes will be accomplished (Isa. 2:1–4; 11:6–12). The prospect is for peace, an end to poverty and oppression, a fulfillment of righteousness and final justice.

Scriptural Christianity first begins with individuals, spreads in committed, intensively disciplined communities, and reaches out to the whole suffering world. Individuals come together into intentional communities as intensive change agents and soon they in turn are quietly affecting society. In this way salvation is coming to the Gentiles—to all the nations.[25] There is no insurmountable obstacle or intrinsic reason why all cannot hear it. The hope is for a transformed creation, where all are blessed, where mercy accompanies justice, where there is no evil speaking, remembering that words offer a window upon the soul.[26] "Their 'love is without dissimulation'; their words are always the just expression of their thoughts, opening a window into their breast, that whosoever desires may look into their hearts and see that only love and God are there."[27] The mission of the church is to spread scriptural Christianity the world over.[28] They are happy who have the Lord for their God (Ps. 144:15).[29]

A Plain, Confrontative Application

At the end of this sermon he asks of those listening whether they think scriptural Christianity exists at Oxford. Here at Oxford, he said to his university audience, where you might expect to find the best of Christian culture's expression, Christianity does not exist.[30] Plain talk is required. Just as Kierkegaard would later ask: Does Christianity exist in Denmark, where everyone was already baptized, each one could produce a baptismal certificate, but none knew what it means? Modern readers are reminded of the spirit of Kierkegaard's *Attack on Christendom*, where he said Luther had his Ninety-five Theses but I have only one: to introduce Christianity to Christendom.

Wesley was convinced that there were few evidences of genuine repentance and faith and the filling of the Spirit in the audience he was addressing. He says even in the most educated, even in the most pious, even among clergy, there appears slim evidence of living faith.[31] The sermon thus intentionally ended on a combative note. He left Oxford with a strong note of confrontation.

Wesley fired a barrage of rhetorical questions to his stunned audience.[32] Is this a community filled with the Holy Spirit? He appealed directly to their conscience: You who are called and authorized to form the tender minds and consciences of youth, are you filled with the Spirit?[33] Are those called to ministry serving as a viable moral pattern to others in conversation, charity, spirit, faith, purity (1 Tim. 4:12)? Are the ordained taught of God, that they

---

[24]#4 "Scriptural Christianity," iii.1; V:45.
[25]#4 "Scriptural Christianity," iii.2, 1:169.
[26]#4 "Scriptural Christianity," iii.5, 1:171.
[27]#4 "Scriptural Christianity," iii.5, 1:171; cf. #90 "An Israelite Indeed," ii.10; #138 "On Dissimulation."
[28]#4 "Scriptural Christianity," iii.1–5, 1:169–71.
[29]#4 "Scriptural Christianity," iii.6, 1:172.
[30]#4 "Scriptural Christianity," iv.1–4, 1:172–74.
[31]#4 "Scriptural Christianity," iv.6, 1:175–76.
[32]#4 "Scriptural Christianity," iv.5, 1:175.
[33]Cf. JJW Feb. 8, 1736, conversation with Spangenberg.

may be able to teach?[34] Are they giving themselves wholly to their office? Are students teachable, willing to enter into a discipline of learning that would lead them to new life? Do university students have either the form or power of Christian godliness, so as to become devoted daily to prayer and good works?[35]

Or do we have a "generation of triflers, triflers with God, with one another, and with your own souls?"[36] The time given for repentance may be short. There is not an infinite amount of time given for finite persons to repent.

How can scriptural Christianity be restored? We have a right to look to ordained leadership. But lacking that, it may fall that Christianity will be "restored by young, unknown, inconsiderable men."[37] He is convinced that Oxford would not be ready for the alternative that the Holy Spirit had prepared. The renewal of scriptural Christianity is a work of God through instruments and means of God's own choosing. Establishment religiosity will be surprised at what God does, and the means God chooses.

Who can restore scriptural Christianity? Only God. If we grieve the Spirit, the change may come through cultural crisis, famine, or pestilence. Better now to bend our knees to the living God.[38] So ends the sermon on Scriptural Christianity.

DOCTRINAL STANDARDS ON PNEUMATOLOGY

The Holy Spirit in the Articles and Doctrinal Minutes

Another textual avenue of approach to the Wesleyan tradition's teaching on the Holy Spirit is by means of the Articles and doctrinal minutes.

Articles Two and Four

The Holy Ghost is truly God.[39] When we pray to the Spirit, we pray to God. God the Spirit, like God the Son, is nothing less than the eternal, all-wise, incomparably good giver of life. The Holy Spirit proceeds from and is one in being with the Father and the Son. The Spirit is of one substance with the Father, and of one substance (consubstantial) with the Son.[40]

The work of the Spirit is that of applying the ministry and mission of the Son to our hearts. The Holy Spirit is addressing us at close quarters to make clear to us what God has done for us in the Son. The Spirit is given to fulfill and consummate the work of the Son, which is offered on the cross juridically, but still requires a process in time for us to receive it and grow thereby. This is where the Spirit remains steadily at work. The Holy Spirit is God coming to us to transform our lives.[41] The Wesleyan teaching of the work of the Spirit focuses on how God the Spirit acts in drawing us toward full responsiveness to the grace manifested in the Son.

---

[34]#4 "Scriptural Christianity," iv.8, 1:177; BCP, Ordering of Priests.

[35]#4 "Scriptural Christianity," iv.9, 1:178; #150 "Hypocrisy in Oxford."

[36]#4 "Scriptural Christianity," iv.10, 1:179.

[37]#4 "Scriptural Christianity," iv.11, 1:179.

[38]#4 "Scriptural Christianity," iv.11, 1:179–80.

[39]CH 7:279f., 502f., 532–36, 623–25, 708f.

[40]Article 4 of Wesley's American prayer book confessed: "The Holy Ghost, proceeding from the Father and the Son, is of one substance, majesty, and glory with the Father and the Son, very and eternal God" (XXV Art.4). "And in unity of this Godhead there are three persons, of one substance, power and eternity, the Father, Son and Holy Ghost" (XXV Art.2).

[41]B1:75f.; 2:191; 4:284.

Spirit and Canon—Article Five

The work of the Spirit is addressed implicitly in the fifth Article of Religion on Scripture: "The Holy Scriptures containeth all things necessary to salvation, so that whatsoever is not read therein, nor may be proved thereby, is not to be required of any man, that it should be believed as an article of faith, or be thought requisite or necessary to salvation." The Spirit works to awaken responses to the apostolic testimony, and before that the Spirit is found eliciting the apostolic oral preaching, which later called forth written testimony. It is by the Spirit that the apostles were guided to testify, and empowered by the Spirit to attest accurately. The Holy Spirit in this way guarantees the sufficiency of the written Word. That is less an anthropological assertion than a pneumatological affirmation.

That Scripture is sufficient for salvation is not a conclusion that can be derived from historical arguments. It has the logical status of an *a priori* argument. The prior assumption is that God the Spirit is capable of witnessing sufficiently to salvation.

The working premise is that whatever is said of the Spirit will be consistent with Scripture, interpreted according to the analogy of faith in the community of faith. Scripture is nothing less than the Word of God written. Lacking scriptural grounding, the best hypothesis lacks authority for preaching. That is not to neglect reason, experience, or tradition, but to recognize that each of these sources of knowing are derivative, and exist in relation to the primacy of the divine self-disclosure as attested in Scripture, which is the central norm of Christian doctrine.[42]

God the Spirit summons into being the written word and attends it through a concrete history of consensual reception. The whole notion of the authority of canon and canonization is a pneumatological teaching. It asks how the Holy Spirit enables the written word to be accurately transmitted through the hazards of history. It is only the Spirit of God who guarantees the authenticity of the canon. How can we be sure we received a reliable canon? How do we know that it is not deeply flawed? We know because we trust that the Spirit of God who raised Jesus from the dead would not deliver to us a defective canon. The reliability of the canon cannot be answered without the premise of the tending work of the Spirit, shepherding the written word through time. There is no wooden language of inerrancy in the Articles. What we have is a trustworthy and sufficient testimony. We count on God the Spirit to make plain the truth of God's coming.[43]

The Spirit works not only to elicit the Scripture as rule and guide for faith and practice, but also to summon into being the life and mission of the interpreting community. The church exists because of the activity of the Spirit, anticipatively prior to Pentecost, and in a fulfilled way following Pentecost, and continuing through the recurring proclamation of the Word and the administration of the Sacraments, offering the means by which the living body of Christ is sustained. Every feature of the concept of authority is derivative from the grace of the Holy Spirit. We are now in the heartland of Wesleyan spiritual formation.

Those who look for the core of the Christian teaching of the personal and social empowerment of the laity will find it here in the work of the Holy Spirit, in his convicting, guiding, comforting, sustaining and persevering activity. The Spirit first brings us to a conviction of our sin, helping us to

---

[42]#74 "Of the Church," 3:45–57.
[43]Letter to "John Smith," March 25, 1747, LJW 2:90.

stand seriously under the law, under judgment, and in due time to an awareness of the gospel. The Spirit is guiding us through a path that leads us to a community of faith, requiring and enabling full responsiveness to the good news of the Son.[44] The Spirit sustains and empowers the faithful and guides them into all truth.[45]

The Work of the Spirit in the Doctrinal Minutes

The Minutes of the early Methodist preachers' conferences ("Minutes of Several Conversations Between the Rev. Mr. Wesley and others, from the year 1744 to 1789") attest the centrality of the witness of the Spirit.[46] They teach that the moment one exercises faith, trusting God's reconciling Word, one is justified by the Son, with the Spirit bearing assuring witness within. The Spirit is inwardly attesting the power of grace to cleanse from all sin, so as wholly to refashion broken lives.

The Methodist revival lived out of the awareness of the Spirit's power to assure the believer of the active presence of justifying and sanctifying grace. One can examine one's life to see if the evidences of the new life are present in the fruits of faith active in love. First, the "sinner is convinced by the Holy Ghost, 'Christ loved me, and gave himself for me.' " Secondly, "Immediately the same Spirit bears witness, 'Thou art pardoned; thou hast redemption in his blood.' "[47] "No man can be justified and not know it."[48] "The immediate fruits of justifying faith" are "peace, joy, love, power over all out-ward sin and power to keep down all inward sin."[49] Justifying faith brings with it a divine assurance that I, even I, am a child in the reconciled family of God.

Against those who hold that this is not the ordinary privilege of all believers, Wesley taught that it is the common entitlement of all who have faith, all who are adopted into the family of God. The Scriptures were written "that you may believe that Jesus is the Christ, the Son of God, and that by believing you may have life in his name" (John 20:31). Those who remain deeply ambivalent about whether they have received this witness of the Spirit, even though they may have good tempers and lead a decent moral life, may still be struggling to receive the prevenient grace that comes prior to justifying grace.

To sin willfully and impenitently subsequent to this new birth is voluntarily to throw away faith's benefits. Justifying faith is not consistent with willful sin. Those who willfully sin are thereby casting away their faith. Believers may enter a period of doubt without the loss of faith, but faith as such is not lost except by the lack of trust in God's righteousness, and then it may be regained by repentance, using the means of grace, eliciting a lively new reception of grace that elicits works of love.

THE WITNESS OF THE SPIRIT WITH OUR SPIRIT

A central feature of Wesley's pneumatology is the constant inner testi-

---

[44]B2:53–58; 4:288f., 357; FA 11:258f.; B9:199f.

[45]Those who come into Wesley's connection of spiritual formation stand under a restriction on their capacity to change, revise, or supposedly "improve" the received doctrine of the Holy Spirit. The Restrictive Rules limit subsequent legislative bodies from amending the Articles.

[46]LJW 3:136–37; 5:170, 202, 262; VIII:275–339.

[47]Minutes, 1744, June 25, Q4, JWO 137; cf. CH 7:195–96; B1:274f., 405.

[48]Minutes, 1744, June 25, Q5, JWO 137.

[49]Minutes, 1744, June 25, Q7, JWO 138.

mony of the Spirit in our hearts.[50] "The doctrine which it defends formed part of almost every sermon of Wesley's in these early years."[51] It is found in most concentrated form in the Standard Sermons, Discourses I and II on "The Witness of the Spirit," and a sequel discourse "The Witness of Our Own Spirit." (Note that two of the sermons relating to the Holy Spirit in the Jackson edition were erroneously attributed to Wesley: "On Grieving the Holy Spirit," by William Tilly,[52] and "On the Holy Spirit" by John Gambold.)[53]

The Witness of the Spirit
Discourse I

Rom. 8:16: "The Spirit itself beareth witness within our spirit, that we are children of God." [Homily #10 1746 B1:267–84 J#10 V:111–23]

The consequences of the work of the witnessing Spirit are evidenced in the new birth, assurance, fruits of the Spirit and radical yieldedness to God.[54] These do not proceed in chronological sequence, but belong together in intrinsic affinity.

The First Non-Starter: Privatistic Enthusiasm

By 1746 Wesley had seen enough revivalist excesses to realize that some who claim to have received the Spirit of God have only egoistic delusions of their own spirits. Lacking discernment, the enthusiast uncritically identifies as God's Spirit that which is merely welling up within as a nativistic expression of earthly hopes and despairs. The familiar " 'new' age" flakiness that we today call channeling, imaging, and psychic intuition are tired reruns of what Wesley once would have dubbed enthusiasm.[55]

Enthusiasts claim the Spirit as a private inspiration apart from the history of the Spirit's disclosure. Enthusiasts define the Spirit too emotively and privately with the result that the Spirit is not recognized as present in the larger community, or in historical and social processes.[56]

Enthusiasts may be thus deluded into a false assurance of saving grace by mistakenly identifying their own private spirit with God's own eternal Spirit, or even mistaking a demonic spirit with the Spirit of God. They take the energies of their own spirit and project them upon God as if divine. They prematurely assume they possess the Spirit, and so miss beholding and experiencing the full reach of the Spirit of God witnessing within the human spirit.

The Opposite Non-Starter: Rationalistic Skepticism

In the opposite corner are rationalist skeptics who doubt that anyone can adequately know God, and question whether reconciliation with the Father is even conceivable. They imagine that such matters are not subject to knowledge but only to rash speculation. If the skeptics are right, then even if God has saved humanity, no finite beholder could dependably perceive it, since such claims are intrinsically undemonstrable, hence unknowable. They are unready to credit God's Spirit with any assuring influence upon us, while being always too ready to reduce the fruits of the Spirit to naturalistic, psychological, sociological, or physical causes.

[50]CH 7:196f., 502.
[51]SS I:199.
[52]VII:485–92.
[53]VII:508–20.
[54]B1:194, 267–99; 2:160f., 206.
[55]#37 "The Nature of Enthusiasm," 2:44–60.
[56]#10 "The Witness of the Spirit, I," proem.1, 1:269.

Wesley sought to weave a fine path between these two hazards that still remain with us today—inordinate emphasis either upon our own individualistic personal experiences or on objectivizing reason. These two spurious reductionisms were so competing in his day as to appear to exhaust the alternatives.

The natural reductionists were warily assuming that all we have is ourselves talking to ourselves. The emotive reductionists oppositely tended to assume that my private experience is finally God talking to me regardless of what is said in the objective text, tradition, or community. Wesley resisted both the extreme skeptical rationalists who think that the Spirit does not address us personally, and the enthusiasts who speak too confidently of personal revelation apart from the history of revelation.[57]

God's Spirit Bearing Witness With Our Spirit

How do we know that we are children of God? First by the witness of our own spirit. "You undoubtedly know in your own breast, if, by the grace of God, it belongs to you. Your conscience informs you from day to day."

"Superadded to, and conjoined with," this internal self-witness is God's own witness that we are reconciled as children in the family of God. In Romans 8, Paul deliberately set forth the way God the Spirit attests our salvation by himself witnessing in our hearts. There is a concurrence between what God whispers to us by his Spirit directly witnessing within us, and what our own hearts say to us as a consequence. The central problem is how one discerns the Spirit of God working within one's own spirit without denying either the finitude of one's own perception or the transcendence of God's own Spirit.[58]

At what school do we learn that we have been adopted into this family, that we can live this new life, and enjoy this liberty? Within the community of faith, nurtured by the means of grace. It is not simply my spirit desperately trying to persuade myself of this truth. Nor is it simply God decreeing this as if to circumvent my rational and emotive responsiveness. Both sides are held in creative tension and mutuality.[59]

Romans 8:16 requires a distinguishing of voices, so as to discern what one's own spirit is saying and what God is saying through Scripture in the dialogue of the Spirit with the human spirit. At the core of the Wesleyan teaching of assurance is the question: Do these jointly confirm each other? Do they elicit a reliable inward impression on the soul that I am a child of God?[60]

God's Spirit always comes before the testimony of our own spirit, but permits and enables the reverberation of our own testimony to confirm it. God witnesses in our hearts and then we confirm this attestation. These two witnesses work together so that we can know that we are children of God, so much so that one "can no more doubt the reality of his sonship, than he can doubt of the shining of the sun."[61]

"Faith is one thing; the full assurance of faith another . . . Some Christians have only the first of these; they have faith, but mixed with doubts and fears. Some have also the full assurance of faith, a full conviction of present pardon; and yet not the full assurance of hope; not a full conviction of their

---

[57]#10 "The Witness of the Spirit," I, proem.2, 1:270.
[58]#10 "The Witness of the Spirit," I, i.7–9, 1:275–76.
[59]Letter to "John Smith," March 25, 1747, LJW 2:100–103.
[60]B2:153–54, 161–62; 9:374–76; CH 7:58; FA 11:132–37, 398–99.
[61]#10 "The Witness of the Spirit," I, i.12, 1:276.

future perseverance ... The faith which we preach as necessary to all Christians, is the first of these."[62] "There may be faith without full assurance. And these lower degrees of faith do not exclude doubts ... This *plerophory*, or full assurance, is doubtless wrought in us by the Holy Ghost. But so is every degree of true faith."[63]

Testing Whether the Spirit's Work Is Discernible

This inner dialogue lies at the heart of the meaning of assurance. Apart from the Spirit's assuring work, there is no way to invent a credible or durable feeling of assurance. But the Spirit attests and offers assurance as a gift. God's own self-giving *is* the gift.[64] The Spirit attests the gift which the Father offers through the Son.[65]

On this premise, we can then disclose this truth mutually with other members of the gathered, confessing, worshiping community.[66] We can use our own reasoning to try to discern the truth of Scripture and the truth of the testimony of friends and of one's own heart. The Wesleyan societies were intensive dialogical processes, interacting, interpersonally encountering, exceedingly self-disclosing, personally open.

A unique sort of spiritual reasoning occurs in such a setting: examining the witness of one's own spirit, accurately stated and articulated publicly through personal testimony. The objective written word of Scripture is at work to help correct privatistic exaggerations and illuminate what is happening within subjective experience. We learn about our own spirit by self-examination, by honest listening to conscience, and by talking with others whom we have learned are trustworthy.[67]

How do we know it is not some demonic power working within? By testing the competing spirits in the community of faith on the basis of Scripture, tradition, reason, and experience. We are not without an ecclesial laboratory for testing the spirits. The quadrilateral method is here being put practically to work.[68] Each partner in dialogue is checking out attestations of the witness of the Spirit in terms of these criteria, all of which appear prominently in this homily.[69]

In the community of faith one is given opportunity to attest both the witness of one's own spirit and the apostolic memory of God's self-attestation. Within this community of praise and reflection and disclosure, one may come steadily and assuredly to know that one is a child of God, reclaimed into the family of God. Wesley was confident that the Spirit would not disappoint when a believer follows these conditions and trusts these promises. This is not strictly speaking a natural or physical test but rather a dialogical, conversational test in which we are asked to discern the Spirit in the context of a community of faith, using Scripture as a guide and our own ratio-

---

[62]Second Letter to Bishop Lavington, sec. 20, 11:398; IX:32; cf. JWO 50–52, 159f., 165f., 188f., 363f.

[63]Letter to Richard Tompson, Feb. 5, 1756, LJW 3:161; on the distinction between the fullness of pardon and degrees of reception of full pardon, cf. LJW 3:374; on full assurance of faith see B2:153–54, 161–62; Letter to Dr. Rutherforth, B9:374–76; CH 7:58; FA 11:132–37, 398–99; B9:61, 100, 376; JJW 2:49.

[64]B1:149–55; 2:410, 2:268; 3:263–66; CH 7:583.

[65]#10 "The Witness of the Spirit," I, i.2–4, 1:271–72.

[66]B11:468.

[67]#10 "The Witness of the Spirit, I," i.1–6, 1:270–74.

[68]#10 "The Witness of the Spirit, I," i.1–6, 1:270–73.

[69]#10 "The Witness of the Spirit, I," ii.11–13, 1:282–83.

nal capacity as a hedge against inordinate egoism. Wesley was concerned that these points not be exaggerated so that egocentric adrenaline might claim to possess the Spirit unilaterally.[70]

Marks Against Presumption

The reciprocal witness of God's Spirit with my spirit in a community of dialogue is quite different from the privatistic, reclusive presumption of my natural mind. It is not that my spirit takes charge of the Spirit of God, but rather responds concurrently with the Spirit's advocacy.[71] There are reliable marks set forth in Scripture that one is becoming a child of God, signs of new life in the Spirit: repentance, behavioral reversal, a sense of serene joy, and obedient keeping of the commandments.[72]

When one truly *repents*, having been convicted of sin and in godly sorrow turned in faith to God, one need not wonder despairingly whether one is a recipient of God's saving love. Those who experience in themselves a syndrome of continual resistance to repentance cannot yet be said to enjoy the shared witness of the Spirit with our spirits.[73] Repentance elicits a fundamental *behavioral reversal*, a turning around of one's actual conduct in such a way that it bears fruit in the works of love. The joint witnesses are accompanied by palpable evidences of moral and behavioral change. One does not just keep on living as sinner. Anyone can ask: Have I undergone such a reversal of wretched behaviors that could be rightly described as a new birth of spirit? If not, pray for the grace of

repentance that enables readiness to receive the witness of the Spirit.[74]

The new life is further evidenced by the fruits of the Spirit, especially a yielding, humble, joyful spirit. Anyone can ask whether he or she is experiencing a *joyful sense of God's presence*, felicity in the Lord, precisely amid the keeping of the commandments. There has always been a focus in Methodist preaching on the joy of the reception of the Spirit. If absent, one of the marks of assurance is missing.[75]

The new life is a life of *obedience* that actively serves the neighbor in love. Anyone can ask how willingly one is keeping the commandments of Scripture: Am I walking according to the Decalogue, telling the truth, not worshiping false gods, not committing adultery? An honest negative points one back to square one—repentance.[76]

Rebirth *precedes* the witness of the Spirit; the joyful fruits of the Spirit *accompany* the witness, and the life of obedience *follows* the Spirit's witness. Admittedly we always remain subject to egocentric, self-deceptive temptations. But Wesley was confident that when we give ourselves these tests honestly within an accountable community of candid dialogue, they yield reliable knowledge. There is no reason for one to remain wholly in the dark about one's assurance of salvation. Such are the marks that one is becoming a child of God.[77]

The Witness of the Spirit Discourse II

Rom. 8:16: "The Spirit itself beareth witness with our spirit, that we are

[70]#10 "The Witness of the Spirit, I," i.7–12, 1:274–76.
[71]#10 "The Witness of the Spirit, I," i.11–ii.2, 1:275–77.
[72]#10 "The Witness of the Spirit, I," 1:277–84.
[73]#10 "The Witness of the Spirit, I," ii.4, 1:278.
[74]#10 "The Witness of the Spirit, I," i.6–12, 1:274–76.
[75]#10 "The Witness of the Spirit, I," ii.6, 1:279–80.
[76]#10 "The Witness of the Spirit, I," ii.7, 1:280.
[77]#10 "The Witness of the Spirit, I," ii.4–7, 1:278–80.

children of God." [Homily #11 1767 B1:285–98 J#11 V:123–34]

Two decades later Wesley wrote another discourse on the same text and the same theme—the conjoint witness of God's Spirit and our spirit. Here the witness of the Spirit is defined as the "inward impression on the soul whereby the Spirit of God immediately and directly witnesses to my spirit that I am the child of God, that Jesus Christ has loved me and given himself for me and that all my sins are blotted out and that I even I am reconciled to God."[78]

All who study holy writ know that there is an inward testimony of the Spirit whose mission is to bear fruit by engendering faith. What had not been adequately attested in earlier Protestantism is the correspondence between the testimony of the Holy Spirit and our own spirit.

The Entitlement of the Believer to Hear Reliable Testimony

It is a great privilege of those born of God to know assuredly that they are saved by grace. Every believer has a right to know that this inward testimony is being reliably heard, received, and existentially brought into appropriation in a felt process. This inner testimony can be known by conscience, analyzed by critical reason, confirmed by daily Scripture study, and by heartfelt examining of one's own experience. That they may know the salvation of God is the entitlement of all who unfeignedly believe.[79]

Wesley considered assurance so intrinsic to salvation that all who have repented and believed the gospel and trusted God's love are being enfran-

chised to know assuredly their reconciliation to God.[80] There is no need for believers to meander in the bewilderment of the wilderness state as to whether God's saving grace is being offered to them.[81]

Few who attest saving grace would disagree that there is an indirect witness of some kind, either through conscience, or rational reflection (as a "result of reason or reflection on what we feel in our own souls" based on Scripture and experience), or through the fruits of faith. But is there a personal direct testimony of the Spirit in the heart? Wesley thought so, but realized that one has to learn how to listen rightly for this consolation and summons.[82] It requires the disciplines of Scripture study, using means of grace, sacraments, and prayer. The Spirit is trying to get through to us by all these means. This homily seeks to help persons learn to listen for that inward testimony. No one can do this for another. Each must listen for himself.

Countering Aberrations and Falsifications

Even the Spirit's work of assurance can be falsified, counterfeited, and perverted. Wesley reminded his hearers that the internal testimony of the Spirit must be constantly tested against the written word of Scripture, and correlated with an honest examination of conscience.[83] Even this does not eliminate the possibility of self-delusion, though these checks are seeking to reduce its likelihood.[84]

God has given two witnesses to secure against delusion—a direct and an

---

[78]#11 "The Witness of the Spirit, II," ii.2, 1:287.
[79]#11 "The Witness of the Spirit, II," ii, 1:286–88.
[80]B9:61, 100, 376; JJW 2:49.
[81]EA VIII:22–25.
[82]#11 "The Witness of the Spirit, II," 1:287f.
[83]#129 "Heavenly Treasure in Earthen Vessels," 4:161–62; VII:345.
[84]Letter to "John Smith," March 25, 1747, LJW 2:100–105.

indirect witness.[85] Their purpose is to assure us we are children of God.[86] Individual experience alone is insufficient proof. Rather the function of experience in the Christian life is to confirm what is found in Scripture, not invent something wholly contrary to Scripture.[87] Though some may fancy they experience what they do not, this cannot stand as discounting testimony against those who have fully used these means of grace. A false profession does not invalidate a true profession of the witness of the Spirit.[88]

The true witness of the Spirit is known by the fruits of love, peace, and joy. Lacking these fruits, the testimony is likely to be unreliable or intermittent.[89] "Let none ever presume to rest in any supposed testimony of the Spirit which is separate from the fruits of it," and "let none rest in any supposed fruit of the Spirit without witness."[90]

The Imperative to Teach Assurance

With regard to the conviction of assurance, Wesley was convinced that "the whole Christian church in the first centuries enjoyed it. For though we have few points of doctrine explicitly taught in the small remains of the ante-Nicene Fathers, yet I think none that carefully reads Clemens Romanus, Ignatius, Polycarp, Origen, or any other of them, can doubt whether either the writer himself possessed it or all whom he mentions as real Christians."[91]

Methodists in particular need to be clear about this teaching "because it is one grand part of the testimony which God has given them to bear" to all humanity. Indeed through Methodists "this great evangelical truth has been recovered, which had been for many years well nigh lost and forgotten."[92] Many Wesleyan hymns were written on the theme of assurance. Wesley thought that the assuring witness of the Spirit was a doctrine that had not been sufficiently explicated in previous Protestantism. Since it had been misunderstood, he considered it the destiny of the Methodist societies to carry this revitalized teaching to the whole church.

The doctrine of the assuring witness of the Spirit is a quintessentially Wesleyan doctrine. Though hardly distinctive to this community, the doctrine of assurance is nevertheless one that Wesleyans in three successive centuries have thought exceedingly important, and often central to their teaching mission. This tradition of preaching sought to make clear that God not only gives us this juridical gift of justifying grace through the Son on the cross, but that God also works through the Spirit to attest the meaning of the Son's mission, and bring it to full actualization in us.[93]

This sense of empowerment was especially needed in an environment in which many were being taught that the eternal decree of election was pretemporally decided by God as if without any personal responsiveness required. The secularizing equivalent of this is naturalistic determinism. Advocates of predestination were admonishing believers not to get involved in a subjec-

[85]#11 "The Witness of the Spirit, II," iii, iv, 1:288–96.
[86]#11 "The Witness of the Spirit, II," v.2–3, 1:297.
[87]#11 "The Witness of the Spirit, II," ii.5–iii.5, 1:287–90.
[88]#11 "The Witness of the Spirit, II," v.1–2, 1:296–97.
[89]#11 "The Witness of the Spirit, II," v.3, 4, 1:297–98; so are false prophets known by their fruits, SS 2:16.
[90]#11 "The Witness of the Spirit, II," v.3–4, 1:297–98.
[91]Letter to Richard Tompson, July 25, 1755, LJW 3:137.
[92]#11 "The Witness of the Spirit, II," i.4, 1:285.
[93]B1:81; 3:210; CH 7:532, 535, 687.

tivist introverted monologue since the decision about their salvation had already been made before eternity, and since what happens within our own spirits is an entirely ancillary if not inconsequential matter.

Those who neglect this teaching may turn religion into a routine matter of going to church without that which makes the church meaningful: the experience of new life in the Spirit. Those who claim to have received this testimony yet remain uncharitable and arrogant, negate by their behavior what they attest in their words.

The Witness of Our Own Spirit

2 Cor. 1:12: "This is our rejoicing, the testimony of our conscience, that in simplicity and godly sincerity, not with fleshly wisdom, but by the grace of God, we have had our conversation in the world." [Homily #12 1746 B1:299–313 J#12 V:132–44]

Sustained reception of saving grace hinges upon that special form of evidence provided by conscience. A good conscience gives inner testimony of sincere responsiveness to prevenient and justifying grace. The ground of the Christian's joy is the serenity, faith, hope, and love that come out of the testimony of a good conscience, which assures us that we have been single-minded and sincere in God's sight, and have conducted ourselves in the world, not in the strength of carnal wisdom or worldly cunning or shrewdness, but by the grace of God.[94]

Natural Conscience

Conscience is that form of consciousness by which we excuse or accuse ourselves morally. By conscience "I mean that every person capable of reflection is conscious to himself, when he looks back on anything he has done, whether it be good or evil."[95] Everybody has it. No rational agent is without this capacity to discern whether one is doing right or wrong according to one's own lights. All rational beings have a mode of consciousness by which one says to oneself that what one is doing is proportionally acceptable or not morally. It is a moral sense, which according to Paul is universally given. Such awareness is intrinsic to consciousness, for it is simply the moral part of consciousness, that part of consciousness that makes a moral judgment about the decency, truth, and appropriateness of one's behavior.[96]

Scripture as the Rule of Christian Conscience

Christians like others know when their conscience says to them that something they are doing is not right. Conscience is a universal human function but Christians are attuned to conscience in a particular way—under the guidance of Word and sacrament. Conscience troubles everyone from time to time, but Christians it disturbs in special ways, because Christians have a consciousness shaped by the requirement and grace of God as revealed in history and attested in Scripture.[97]

"The Christian rule of right and wrong is the Word of God, the writings of the Old and New Testament . . . this is a lantern unto a Christian's feet . . . the whole and sole outward rule whereby his conscience is to be directed in all things."[98]

How does the conscience of the Christian function and how is it formed?

[94]#12 "The Witness of Our Own Spirit," sec. 1–4, 1:300–301.
[95]EA sec. 14, 11:49.
[96]#12 "The Witness of Our Own Spirit," sec. 3–5, 1:301–2.
[97]LJW 2:125; 3:11, 118.
[98]#12 "The Witness of Our Own Spirit," sec. 6, 1:302–3.

Christian conscience is shaped by the history of salvation. It is honed by a daily dialogue with Scripture. When Paul speaks of a good conscience void of offence he means a conscience decisively shaped by the address of God as attested in holy writ. No understanding of right and wrong is adequate to the Christian that has not been contoured by the attestation of Scripture to the Word of God in Jesus Christ.[99]

The Regenerate Conscience Void of Offence

A Christian conscience void of offence is a conscience living by faith on the sole foundation of Christ's atoning work,[100] instructed by the revealed and written Word, capable of self-examination, able without pretence to confess before God one's sin, which attests that one's actual moral behavior is consistent with one's heartfelt beliefs.[101]

Conscience is transformed when it comes under the influence of Christ, Scripture, the community of faith, Word, and sacraments. There is a sharp functional distinction in Wesley's mind between natural conscience, which everyone has, and Christian conscience, which is instructed by Scripture, grace, and God's saving work. In this redeemed community we share our faith and experience, disclose to others the ways the Spirit is working in us, use our reason, and listen to Scripture better to discern the divine address.[102]

The regenerated, Christ-shaped conscience does not let us off cheaply. It tells us the truth about ourselves. When we listen to it with sincerity, we either hear it acquitting or accusing us. Paul would not have commended a conscience void of offence if that were wholly impossible. Conscience is a mode of consciousness intrinsic to the witness of our own spirit to ourselves. Our own spirit bears witness within an accountable community of faith that it is not offending against the holiness of God.[103]

By Grace a Conversation in the World

Either you have a conscience void of offence or you have a conscience that keeps on offending you. Paul is proposing a day-by-day walk without offence to the law of God, assuming that one's behavior is constantly being embraced by the atoning work of God. There is no way to have a good conscience without the Atonement. No Christian can enjoy a conscience void of offence without God's forgiving word, but that must not become an open door for antinomian license or pretending that one is above the law.[104]

We are called to conduct ourselves in the world, and in this community of prayer and moral accountability, not with fleshly wisdom, but by the grace of God. Our conversation within the world—our daily movement through the world is a walk by grace, a conversation that may attest simple purity of heart, godly sincerity, relying upon God's holy atoning love, with a heart focused single-mindedly on accountability to God.[105]

The Ground of Christian Joy

The ground of Christian joy is grace. The faithful are drawn to a single intention: becoming answerable to God in

---

[99]LJW 6:19.
[100]#12 "The Witness of Our Own Spirit," sec. 8, 1:304–5.
[101]LJW 7:209; SS 1:226.
[102]SS 1:221.
[103]B1:270–74, 299–313.
[104]LJW 7:209; cf. LJW 6:19; SS 1:226.
[105]B3:271–72; 4:375–76.

daily behavior.[106] That is what it means to live the *simple life*. Even though it may complicate our life in the world, it simplifies things profoundly if one is simply being accountable to God.[107] Simplicity has "a single intention of promoting his glory and doing and suffering his blessed will."[108]

Purity of heart is an expression of this simplicity. It is to desire God in all things, loving nothing more than God. This results in a walk of *holiness*, reflecting the holiness of God, which occurs by godly sincerity, and thereby recovering the moral image of God.[109] *Godly sincerity* is doing all to the glory of God, referring all one's aspirations to God, with unblemished intentionality.[110]

"Simplicity regards the intention itself, sincerity the execution of it . . . as actually hitting the mark which we aim at by simplicity . . . that all our actions flow on in an even stream, uniformly subservient to this great end; and that in our whole lives, we are moving straight toward God, and that continually."[111] "Seek one thing, and you will be far less troubled with unprofitable reasonings."[112]

This results in a life of joy even amid suffering, a gladness that emerges out of a life of obedience.[113] What the Spirit through conscience wants to do for us is take us step by step through a life of receptivity of grace by which our resistances to grace are day by day being overcome.

Holiness and happiness are thereby intrinsically joined. Those who want to live the happy life do well to realize that it is precisely this life of day-by-day resisting temptation and living with radical accountability before God, that bears the fruit of human happiness. Wesley had a very uncomplicated notion of happiness: holiness.[114]

The joy that we have in the Christian life is in part based upon the testimony of our own conscience. The Christian's conscience keeps on witnessing not just of the law but of the gospel, not just of God's judging requirement upon us but of Christ's love that enables us to fulfill those requirements.

Happiness is not premised upon the basis of economic or psychological ("fleshly") wisdom but upon the basis of the inner testimony of the Spirit confirmed by conscience.[115] Only on this ground can we enter into this joy. It is by the grace of God we have had our conversation in the world, not by virtue of a natural joy, of a joy arising out of a seared, callous conscience, but a joy in obedience, elicited by grace, a joy the world is not capable of inventing.[116]

The First-fruits of the Spirit

Rom. 8:1: "There is therefore now no condemnation for those who are in Christ Jesus, who walk not after the flesh but after the Spirit." [Homily #8 1746 B1:233–47 J#8 V:87–97]

---

[106]#125 "On a Single Eye," 4:120–30.
[107]#12 "The Witness of Our Own Spirit," sec. 11–13, 1:306–8.
[108]#12 "The Witness of Our Own Spirit," sec. 12, 1:307; #148 "A Single Intention," 4:371–77.
[109]#90 "An Israelite Indeed," ii.4, 3:286.
[110]#12 "The Witness of Our Own Spirit," sec. 16, 1:309–10; B1:134–35, 263f., 288f., 207f., 3:286.
[111]#12 "The Witness of Our Own Spirit," sec. 12, 1:307.
[112]Letter to Miss Bishop, June 12, 1773, XIII:24.
[113]CH 7:94f., 308–98, 494–96.
[114]#12 "The Witness of Our Own Spirit," sec. 16–20, 1:309–13.
[115]#12 "The Witness of Our Own Spirit," sec. 14, 1:308.
[116]#12 "The Witness of Our Own Spirit," sec. 17–20, 1:310–13.

Those Who Walk After the Spirit

Those engrafted in Christ, dwelling in him, united with him, *walk not after the flesh*, which "signifies corrupt nature."[117] Having "crucified the flesh with its affections and lusts," even if they "feel the root of bitterness in themselves, yet are they endued with power from on high to trample it continually," so that they are no longer bound to sin.[118] "They are led into every holy desire, into every divine and heavenly temper, till every thought which arises in their heart is holiness unto the Lord," speaking "always in grace, seasoned with salt," and doing "only the things which please God," so "in the whole course of their words and actions" bear "the genuine fruits of the Spirit of God, namely, 'love, joy, peace, long-suffering, gentleness, goodness, fidelity, meekness, temperance.'"[119]

The recipient is redeemed, bought back from bondage. The redeemer pays the debt for the enslaved. Having been crucified with him, those who live in him have been resurrected with him, and so walk after the Spirit and bear the fruits of the Spirit.[120]

For Them There Is No Condemnation

There is now no condemnation for those who are in Christ — no condemnation either of past or present sin, or for inward sin, defects, infirmities or involuntary failings. The six imperatives that follow this indicative are summarized in the schema on page 239.

If Freed From Past Sin, Away With Guilt

There is no condemnation for any past sin. Those whose life is hid in Christ no longer have to bear the dismal burden of compulsively recollecting their former value negations. Nothing that freedom has distorted is beyond this divine reconciling activity. All guilt-eliciting value-diminutions are taken up into the pardon of God. Since God remembers our past sins no more, we are invited to quit remembering them. We are called and enabled to feel no condemnation, "no sense of guilt, or dread," having the peace of God ruling in our hearts.[121]

So long as one believes and walks after the Spirit one is not condemned either by God or by one's own heart. Condemnation is no longer the fitting category for those who live by faith in God's redeeming love and share by faith Christ's death and resurrection. As we trust in God's revealed righteousness, faith wipes away all past moral marks against the self.[122]

If Freed From Present Sin, Then Do Not Commit New Sin

"It is for freedom that Christ has set us free. Stand firm, then, and do not let yourselves be burdened again by a yoke of slavery" (Gal. 5:1). The moral imperative not to commit sin derives from the evangelical indicative that God has freed us from sin.

To the extent that we recalcitrantly decide to continue to collude with temptation, we return by choice once again to live under condemnation. Insofar as

---

[117] #8 "The First-fruits of the Spirit," i.2, 1:235; B1:153–55.

[118] #8 "The First-fruits of the Spirit," i.2, 3, 1:236–37.

[119] #8 "The First-fruits of the Spirit," i.4–6, 1:236–37; Zech. 14:20–21; Col. 4:6; Gal. 5:22–23.

[120] #8 "The First-fruits of the Spirit," i, 1:235–37; cf. FA 11:292; B1:233–47; 1:160–65, 283–88; B11:171f., 178, 197.

[121] #8 "The First-fruits of the Spirit," ii.1, 2, 1:237; JJW 2:250.

[122] #8 "The First-fruits of the Spirit," iii, 1:243–44.

FOR THOSE WHO WALK AFTER THE SPIRIT

If There Is No Condemnation for:	Therefore, the Imperative Is:
Past Sins	Away With Guilt
Present Sins	Avoid Committing New Sins
Inward Sin, Though Natural Corruption Remains	Be Not Afraid to Know All the Evil of Your Heart
Defects That Drive One Closer to God	Do Not Despair of Defects
Sins of Infirmity	Let Satan Gain No Advantage
Anything Not in One's Power to Change	If You Sin, Take It to the Lord

we continue in sin, we are called to pray anew for the grace of repentance.[123]

No Condemnation for Inward Sin Though Natural Corruption Remains

The roots of sin are being dug up, uprooted. We are being radically called by new life in Christ to go to the very underpinnings of our old sinful life and change those behaviors and intentions, both inwardly and outwardly, that they may more closely reflect the love and goodness of God.

It is "too plain to be denied" that the corruption of nature "does still remain, even in those who are the children of God by faith," who still have remaining in them "the seeds of pride and vanity, of anger, lust and evil desire."[124] Of these Paul speaks as "babes in Christ" (1 Cor. 3:1). Still they are not condemned. Though they grow "more sensible day by day that their 'heart is deceitful and desperately wicked'; yet

so long as they do not yield thereto, so long as they give no place to the devil . . . God is well-pleased with their sincere though imperfect obedience."[125]

The corresponding imperative: "fret not thyself because of ungodliness, though it still remain in thy heart. Repine not because thou still comest short of the glorious image of God." "Be not afraid to know all the evil of thy heart, to know thyself as also thou art known."[126] God's desire is that we know ourselves accurately.

> Show me, as my soul can bear,
> The depth of inbred sin:
> All the unbelief declare,
> The pride that lurks within![127]

To be the child of this Father is to be invited to trust that God "will withhold from thee no manner of thing that is good," so do not fear looking deeply into your own failings, provided you do

---

[123]#8 "The First-fruits of the Spirit," ii.4, iii.3, 1:238, 244.
[124]#8 "The First-fruits of the Spirit," ii.5, 1:239.
[125]#8 "The First-fruits of the Spirit," ii.6, 1:240; Jer. 17:9.
[126]#8 "The First-fruits of the Spirit," iii.4, 1:245.
[127]Charles Wesley, *Hymns and Sacred Poems*, 1742, p. 209, *Poetic Works*, II.263.

not let the shield of faith be torn away from you.[128]

There Is No Condemnation for Defects That Drive One Closer to God

Even when the believer is "continually convinced of sin cleaving to all they do," "yet there is no condemnation to them still, either from God or from their own heart. The consideration of these manifold defects only gives them a deeper sense that they have always need" of the crucified Advocate who ever lives to make intercession for them. "So far are these from driving them away from him in whom they have believed, that they rather drive them the closer."[129]

If There Is No Condemnation for Sins of Infirmity, Let Not the Adversary Gain an Advantage

"By 'sins of infirmity' I would mean such involuntary failings as the saying a thing we believe true, though in fact it prove to be false; or the hurting our neighbour without knowing or designing it, perhaps when we designed to do him good." Though deviations from the perfect will of God, they "do not bring any guilt on the conscience of 'them which are in Christ Jesus.' "[130]

Even those being made "perfect in love . . . still need his Spirit, and consequently his intercession, for the continuance of that love from moment to moment. Besides, we should still be encompassed with infirmities, and liable to mistakes . . . even though the heart was all love . . . as long as he remains in the body, the greatest saint may say,

'Every moment Lord, I need
The merit of thy death.' "[131]

The corresponding imperative: Do not let the Adversary gain an advantage from your keen awareness of your infirmities. Do not let your weakness or folly shake your "filial trust in God . . . Do not lie there, fretting thyself and bemoaning thy weakness . . . Leap and walk."[132]

There Is No Condemnation for Anything Not in One's Power to Change

" 'There is no condemnation' to them for anything whatever which is not in their power to help, whether it be of an inward or outward nature, and whether it be doing something or leaving something undone . . . There is no guilt, because there is no choice."[133]

Sins of surprise are those in which I am quietly or unconsciously overtaken. Wesley argued that to the extent I collude or cooperate or concur in a behavioral pattern that leads to sin, then I am to that extent accountable. Then I must return to petition for forgiveness. This is why the Christian life is a life of daily repentance, even while it is going on toward full maturity.[134] Even when "surprised into what [your] soul abhors," if you are "overtaken in a fault, then grieve unto the Lord . . . Pour out thy heart before him."[135]

FURTHER READING ON THE WORK OF THE SPIRIT IN ASSURANCE

Banks, Stanley. "Witness of the Spirit." AS 14 1 (1960): 48–60.

---

[128]#8 "The First-fruits of the Spirit," iii.4, 1:245–46.
[129]#8 "The First-fruits of the Spirit," ii.7, 1:240; Heb. 7:25.
[130]#8 "The First-fruits of the Spirit," ii.8, 1:241.
[131]To James Hervey, LJW 3:380.
[132]#8 "The First-fruits of the Spirit," iii.5, 1:246–47.
[133]#8 "The First-fruits of the Spirit," ii.9, 1:241.
[134]#8 "The First-fruits of the Spirit," ii.11, 1:242.
[135]#8 "The First-fruits of the Spirit," iii.6, 1:247.

Burtner and Chiles. CWT, 89ff., 168ff.

Collins, Kenneth. FW, 57–82.

_____. *John Wesley on Salvation.* Grand Rapids: FAP, Zondervan, 1989. Chap. 5 "New Birth and Assurance."

Howard, Ivan. "The Doctrine of Assurance." In *Further Insights Into Holiness,* edited by K. Geiger. Kansas City: Beacon Hill of Kansas City, 1963.

"John Wesley on the Witness of the Spirit." *Quarterly Chr. Spectator* 8 (1836): 353–68.

Langford, Thomas. *Practical Divinity: Theology in the Wesleyan Tradition.* Nashville: Abingdon, 1982. Chap. 6 "Holiness Theology."

McDonald, William. *John Wesley and His Doctrine.* Boston: McDonald and Gill, 1893.

McGonigle, Herbert. "Pneumatological Nomenclature in Early Methodism." WTJ 8 (1973): 61–72.

Noll, Mark. "John Wesley and the Doctrine of Assurance." *Bibliotheca Sacra* 132 (1974): 195–223.

Oswalt, John N. "John Wesley and the Old Testament Concept of the Holy Spirit." RL 48 (1979): 283–92.

Slaate, H. FB, chap. 7.

Smith, Timothy L. "The Doctrine of the Sanctifying Spirit in John Wesley and John Fletcher." PM 55 1 (1979): 16, 17, 54–58.

_____. *Whitefield and Wesley on the New Birth.* Grand Rapids: FAP, Zondervan, 1986.

Starkey, Lycurgus M. WHS. "The New Birth." Chaps. 3–4.

Watkin-Jones, Howard. *The Holy Spirit From Arminius to Wesley.* London: Epworth, n.d.

Williams, Colin. JWTT. "New Birth and Assurance," 98ff.

Wynkoop, Mildred Bangs. FWAT, 302ff.

_____. "Theological Roots of Wesleyanism's Understanding of the Holy Spirit." WTJ 14 1 (1979): 77–98.

Yates, Arthur S. *The Doctrine of Assurance, with Special Reference to John Wesley.* London: Epworth, 1952.

8

On Grace and Predestination

GRACE

Defining Prevenient Grace

Prevenient grace is the grace that begins to enable one to choose further to cooperate with saving grace. By offering the will the restored capacity to respond to grace, the person then may freely and increasingly become an active, willing participant in receiving the conditions for justification.

Freedom grows through stages. Prevenient grace is the lowest gear in the drive train of grace that enables one to move from inertia so that one may gradually be brought up to speed. It is the grace that brings initial recognition that a more decisive new stage may be possible, even if only vaguely imaginable.

Prevenient grace elicits the inception of the good will, while cooperating grace works within the constricted settings of broken human freedom to turn it around, redeem, and enable the will to be responsive to God's own good will. There is no adequate understanding of the depth of sin without affirming at the same time the constant winsomeness of the grace of God drawing sinners always toward ever more appropriate and fitting responses to the holy love that constantly works to open up the possibility of repentance. But of itself the fallen will cannot simply turn itself around and will to do good.[1] The sinner is at liberty to resist grace, but not to initiate grace.

Since the fall of freedom no one spiritually dead is able to choose that which is his truest good. Nonetheless, persons still have a "degree of liberty" that allows them to be self-governing, "otherwise we were mere machines, stocks and stones."[2] This autonomy, however, does not enable persons to turn to God by means of their own resources.

No fallen creature has power to do good work pleasing to God "without the grace of God by Christ *preventing* us," (*nos praeveniente*)—going before us.[3] Grace is always to be found working way out ahead of us, and only then

---

[1]Praying for a Blessing, *A Collection of Hymns for the Use of the People Called Methodist*, 7:178–88.
[2]#129 "Heavenly Treasure in Earthen Vessels," i.1, 4:163.
[3]XXV Art.8.

"working with us when we have that good will," that we may cooperate with ever-fresh new offerings of grace. Today we use the term *prevent* to mean obstruct, hinder, or stop. But in eighteenth-century usage it meant to prepare, make ready, to go before (Lat.: *prevenire*).

The title of the eighth Article, "On Free Will," might more accurately be entitled "Grace and Free Will": *"The condition of man after the fall of Adam is such that he cannot turn and prepare himself, by his own natural strength and works, to faith, and calling upon God; wherefore we have no power to do good work, pleasant and acceptable to God, without the grace of God by Christ preventing us, that we may have a good will, and working with us, when we have that good will."* The grace that precedes freedom is that grace that helps us to receive more grace, which prepares our will so that we may become first of all aware of our predicament, so as to come to that repentance that is prior to that faith that is lived out in love to God and neighbor.[4]

On Working Out Our Own Salvation

Phil. 2:12–13: "Work out your own salvation with fear and trembling, for it is God which worketh in you both to will and to do of his good pleasure." [Homily #85 1785 B3:199–209 J#85 VI:506–13]

Prevenient grace plays a crucial role in Wesleyan evangelical teaching.[5] There is no single treatise where this important teaching is concentrated, but it is found pointedly in the homilies "On Working Out Our Own Salvation," and "On Conscience."

The most important homily that touches upon prevenient grace takes for its text Philippians 2:12–13: *"Work out your own salvation with fear and trembling; for it is God who is at work in you, both to will and to work for his good pleasure"* (NRSV). God working in us enables our working and co-working with God. What appears to be a contradiction (that grace elicits freedom) is a call to action that attests the ground of its action. *We can work because God is working in us.*[6]

God's prevenient grace works everywhere, since the Holy Spirit is present to all, though most powerfully among a vital community of believers. "No one sins because he has not grace, but because he does not use the grace he hath."[7] All are called to be ready to stir up whatever grace is in them that more grace will be given.

Prevening grace works sufficiently in every domain in which original sin is working. The deficiencies of human willing do not negate the sufficiency of grace offered. Assuming the depth of the human predicament as spelled out in "The Doctrine of Original Sin," it is impossible without grace to make the least motion toward God.[8]

God Works in Us

That God works in us both *to will and to do* his good pleasure, "removes all imagination of merit from man . . . God breathes into us every good desire, and brings every good desire to good effect."[9] Inward religion (holiness of heart) is grounded in God's work in us

---

[4]PCC 43–47, X:228–31.

[5]"This grace prompts our first wish to please God, our first glimmer of understanding concerning God's will, and our 'first slight transient conviction' of having sinned against God." UM *Discipline*, 1988, para. 68, 46.

[6]#85 "On Working Out Our Own Salvation," proem, 3:199–201.

[7]#85 "On Working Out Our Own Salvation," iii.4, 3:207.

[8]#85 "On Working Out Our Own Salvation," i, 3:202–3.

[9]#85 "On Working Out Our Own Salvation," i.1, 2, 3:202–3.

"to will" (*to telein*, to desire, wish, love, intend), and outward religion (holiness of life) is grounded in God's giving us the energy "to do" (*to energein*, to energize, execute, actualize) his good pleasure.[10] Energy from God "works in us every right disposition, and then furnishes us for every good word and work."[11]

Paul's call to "work out your own salvation" does not Pelagianly imply that one may work *without* the prevening grace of God, but rather only *with* it. Yet the co-working (*sunergia*, cooperation) design of grace asks for our responsive willing, through which it is God who is working concurrently in us to will and do God's own good pleasure.[12]

No stage of saving faith, not the slightest motion, is a matter of merited goodness. God comes our way not when we merit it, but before we merit it, precisely while we are yet sinners. God is helping us come to the desire to do the good through prevening grace, then to enable a result of good action from that good will.[13]

God comes personally to humanity in the form of a servant.[14] This calls each hearer of the gospel to have that mind that was also in Christ Jesus, who though he was in the form of God counted not equality with God as something to be grasped (Phil. 2:1–6). This is the mind in which we are called to share. This pivotal Christological passage concludes with the imperative, which calls us to *work out our own salvation*, not that salvation is our work but that it involves our free response to

grace. We are to work because it is God who is working in us to enable our working.

How Are We to Work?

We are called in response to work out our own salvation *with fear and trembling*, taking with utter seriousness what God is doing for us.[15] This responding is to be done constantly and completely. For each particular hearer this remains a personal, individuated task. It is, after all, your own personal salvation. You have your own salvation to work on. It does not occur by simple, unilateral, absolute fiat, as if to ignore whether one is cooperating or not.[16]

God is at work in us, operating in us, actively present in our inner lives, enabling our outward acts. Grace works inwardly to convert our passions so as to transform and reorder them in relation to the love of God and humanity. Out of that reordering, the fruits of faith emerge in good works.[17]

God Works, Therefore You Can Work

Since God is working in you, you are called to share responsively in the working out of your own salvation. God asks us to respond as fully and situationally as we are proportionally able. This is a matter of our willing, which God does not coerce, but seeks to draw forth by illuminating, wooing the will, inwardly convicting.[18]

"Faith is *the work of God*; and yet it is *the duty of man* to believe. And every man may believe *if* he will, though not *when* he will. If he seek faith in the

---

[10]#85 "On Working Out Our Own Salvation," i.1–2, 3:202.
[11]#85 "On Working Out Our Own Salvation," i.3, 3:203.
[12]#85 "On Working Out Our Own Salvation," i, 3:202–3.
[13]#85 "On Working Out Our Own Salvation," i.2, 3:202–3.
[14]CH 7:468.
[15]B4:523; LJW 5:257; 6:258.
[16]#85 "On Working Out Our Own Salvation," ii.2, 3:204–5.
[17]#85 "On Working Out Our Own Salvation," i, 3:202–3.
[18]#85 "On Working Out Our Own Salvation," ii, 3:203–6.

appointed ways, sooner or later the power of the Lord will be present, whereby (1) God works, and by His power (2) man believes."[19]

God Works, Therefore You Must Work

The indicative of grace requires the imperative of obedience. If God is for us, therefore we ought to work in response to God's work in us. God is working; we are called to work. What God is doing enables us to do. God works in us, so we ought to co-work with his working in us.[20] We are to work with "singleness of heart . . . utmost earnestness of spirit, and with all care and caution, and secondly, with the utmost diligence, speed, punctuality, and exactness"[21]

Wesley did not have a passive, idle, lethargic, quietistic notion of saving grace. Its reception requires energetic work, earnest prayer, spirited study of Scripture, and active good works. It is not as if God zaps us with grace apart from our responsive cooperation. Every subsequent act of cooperating with grace is premised on God's preceding grace, which elicits and requires free human responsiveness.[22]

The Fourfold Sequence of the Work of Saving Grace

The well-designed order of the work of grace was once familiar to Wesley's connection of spiritual formation: prevening, convicting, justifying, and sanctifying grace. This order is drawn from and found abundantly in the post-Augustinian ecumenical tradition. We have fallen from our original condition of uprightness, yet within this fallenness grace is at work ceaselessly to free us from guilt and sin. The diverse outworking of grace is phased in four dimensions, working contextually in each according to individuated need.[23]

1. Prevenient Grace. The saving work of God begins not by our being attentive to prevening grace, but by grace that attends us and awakens our attentiveness. The focus is not first of all upon our cooperative initiative by which we imagine ourselves coming early to God, pleading to cooperate. Rather, the initiative comes from grace prevening prior to our first awakening to the mercy and holiness of God.[24]

Prevenient grace elicits "the first wish to please God, the first dawn of light concerning his will, and the first slight transient conviction of having sinned against him."[25] Grace works ahead of us to draw us toward faith, to begin its work in us. Even the first fragile intuition of conviction of sin, the first intimation of our need for God, is the work of preparing, prevening grace, which draws us gradually toward wishing to please God. Grace is working quietly at the point of our desiring, bringing us in time to despair over our own righteousness, challenging our perverse dispositions, so that our distorted wills cease gradually to resist the gifts of God.

Grace works antecedently to conversion to convict freedom of its fallenness, and its need for a radical reversal, repentance, a reversal that is only possible in view of God's justifying grace, which meets us on the cross, of

[19]Letter to Isaac Andrews, Jan. 4, 1784, LJW 7:202.
[20]#85 "On Working Out Our Own Salvation," proem.4, 3:201.
[21]#85 "On Working Out Our Own Salvation," ii.2, 3:205.
[22]#85 "On Working Out Our Own Salvation," iii.7, 3:208.
[23]#85 "On Working Out Our Own Salvation," ii.1, 3:203; "Principles of a Methodist," 29, VIII:373–74.
[24]B1:35, 57, 74–76, 80f.; 2:156f.; 3:203f.
[25]#85 "On Working Out Our Own Salvation," ii.1, 3:203.

which we in time may become aware. At each stage we are called to receive and respond to the grace being incrementally given. Prevenient grace does not justify, but readies for justification, giving us the desire for faith, which is the one condition of justification.

The chief function of prevenient grace is to bring the person to a state of nonresistance to subsequent forms of grace. Prevenient grace is that grace that goes before us to prepare us for more grace, the grace that makes it possible for persons to take the first steps toward saving grace.[26]

2. Convicting Grace. Prevening grace leads toward convicting grace, which begins not with our self-initiated determination to repent but by the grace that elicits a determination to repent.[27] Prevenient grace brings one to the point of attentiveness to one's own sinfulness, asking for works meet for repentance. That does not mean that works evidencing repentance are justifying works, since no work justifies, but that the threshold of grace is being entered by penitence.[28]

Convicting grace enables one to grow toward repentance, toward greater knowledge of oneself as sinner, aware of how far away from God one is. Convicting grace brings one to despair over one's own righteousness under the law, and leads to repentance, which turns around one's intentionality.[29]

3. Justifying Grace. Wesley's distinction between justification and sanctification is: "By justification we are saved from the guilt of sin and restored to the favor of God; by sanctification we are saved from the power and root of sin, and restored to the image of God." Whoever grasps that one sentence, which is worth memorizing, has laid hold of the heart of Wesleyan soteriology.

The statement means: By justification God has worked for us to pardon us. Justifying grace calls us to trust the One who takes my sin upon himself on the cross.[30] God works through justifying grace for us to make us aware that his favor is addressed personally to us.[31] We respond in simple trust, which proceeds in a process of growth in responsiveness, which is sanctification.[32]

We cannot take grace seriously without taking seriously the depth, subtlety, and recalcitrance of the history of sin. In the Wesleyan tradition, however, we do not just talk about how bad things are, how deeply enmeshed in evil, but how God the Spirit is at work in human history to elicit responses by which that predicament can be transformed.[33]

4. Sanctifying Grace. By sanctifying grace our salvation is being brought to full moral and behavioral fruitfulness. If in justification we are saved from the guilt of sin, and restored to the favor of God, in sanctification we are *saved from the root of sin, and restored to the renewed image of God.* The best way of thinking of *imago* is as mirror, imaging or mirroring the goodness of God.

Sanctifying grace is not merely an awareness of God's pardon (the central concern of justifying grace). Rather it is further bent upon actively digging into and dislodging the roots of sin, cutting

---

[26]#85 "On Working Out Our Own Salvation," ii.1, 3:203–4.
[27]B1:200f., 291f., 350–52, 477–81; 2:22f.; CH 7:180–84, 210–34.
[28]B3:204; SS 1:185f.
[29]#85 "On Working Out Our Own Salvation," ii.1, 3:203–4.
[30]B1:381; 2:583f.
[31]LJW 5:103, 358.
[32]LJW 4:201.
[33]#85 "On Working Out Our Own Salvation," ii.1, 3:203–4.

those roots (gradually or quickly, whether by sawing or snipping) so as to enable the believer actually to live out the glorious liberty of the children of God.[34] It offers a new life in the family of God. The eviction of sin requires the rooting out of actual personally chosen habits of sin, as well as the complex history of sin, which is formally or juridically overcome in the grace of baptism with the gift of the Spirit.

In this way sanctifying grace seeks to go to the very root of sin behaviorally and practically to uproot the sin and bring one again to the way of holiness.[35] This is a defining Methodist doctrine. God does not leave us alone with justifying grace as if to tempt us to licentiousness, but wishes functionally to reclaim the whole of our broken lives. That has implications both for personal and social life.[36]

Since natural finitude and physical infirmities are not as such sin, which is willful negation of a known moral requirement, sanctifying grace does not have as its purpose the ending of either finitude or physical diseases and infirmities, which may become a means of increasing faith, hope, and love.

Whether Gradual or Instantaneous

Sanctifying grace works both by gradual and instantaneous means.[37] Wesley could not deny that some in the evangelical revival were apparently experiencing the Spirit's perfect work as coming to them in an instantaneous flood of consummating grace.[38] Knowing that grace could work powerfully to change life radically in a single sweep-

ing experience, he could not thereafter ignore it, for it had become a fact of revival history.[39]

Nor did he want to deny that grace works quietly and gradually and over a period of time, patiently within the recalcitrant confines of human freedom. He knew that many such as himself were involved in a lengthy process of receiving it gradually.

Meanwhile, believers learn to cooperate daily with grace by the means of grace: by searching the Scriptures, which attest the history of grace; by attending holy communion; by making use of the ordinances of God; by becoming attentive to conscience; by sharing in common prayer, godly admonition, and good counsel.[40]

Whether Freedom Is Causally Bound

It is a false placing of the question to ask whether we are free or bound by causal chains. Grace is working precisely amid natural causality to enable freedom.[41] This is an argument for human freedom. It would be more absurd if God had worked in a costly way to free us, yet we remained automatons or puppets.[42] God would not work in us to free us were we not created with the capacity for freedom, which though now fallen into sin, can be redeemed and reconstituted by grace.

The heart of Wesley's reasoning on the interface is: *God works in you, therefore you can work; God works in you, therefore you must work.* There is a moral imperative for us to work, to respond to the grace given. Justification comes to us as a radical gift, but having

[34]LJW 3:189; 7:152; 8:147.
[35]B2:582–84; 3:53f.
[36]#85 "On Working Out Our Own Salvation," ii.1, 3:203–4.
[37]LJW 2:280; LJW 7:267.
[38]B11:368–69; JJW 1:454f.; JWO 53f.; SS 1:298; 2:239.
[39]LJW 2:280; 7:267.
[40]#85 "On Working Out Our Own Salvation," ii.1, 3:204.
[41]"A Thought Upon Necessity," X:474–80,
[42]#128 "The Deceitfulness of the Human Heart, proem, 4:150–52.

been given as gift it calls for our radical response. If it is being made possible for us to cooperate with justifying and sanctifying grace toward our salvation, then we must do it. God does not by fiat save us, but wishes to save us with our willing, cooperative action. If God is working in us so that we can work, therefore we must work.[43]

Wesley concluded his homily by quoting Augustine: "He who made us without ourselves will not save us without ourselves."[44] God does not will to save us without our will. God wills to save us with our will cooperating.

Wesley was just as uptight about quietists and antinomians as blatant sinners. He had benefited immensely by dialogue with the Moravians, but when he got to know them well he realized that there was a slight pinch of it he stiffly resisted—a quietism that said God is going to do it for us so let us just sit back and do nothing. Wesley never sat anywhere very long. He was constantly on the move.

As God creates us *ex nihilo* without any cooperation of our own, for no one makes an application to be born, so God recreates our freedom to love from its fallen condition of unresponsive spiritual deadness. As birth is a radical gift, so is the new birth. God does not desire to bring us into this new birth without our cooperation.

Grace and Law

Prevenient grace breaks down our resistance to other forms of grace. It enables us to move toward more subtle and inclusive levels of reception of grace. Prevenient grace brings us to despair over our own righteousness under the law, teaching us that we cannot without grace perform the works of the law adequately.[45]

The law has three functions: First, the law curbs our native anarchic temptations. It says to human self-assertion: No, go no further. Intrude no further than this line on the well-being of the neighbor. Second, the law leads us to despair over our righteousness. If we had only the law without grace, we would be entirely miserable. Third, the law brings us into a fuller life of participation in Christ.[46] Prevenient grace works through the law, which fulfills all of these three functions, yet as contextually called for.[47]

Common Grace

"Some great truths, as the being and attributes of God, and the difference between moral good and evil, were known, in some measure, to the heathen world. The traces of them are to be found in all nations. So that in some sense, it may be said to every child of man, 'He hath showed thee, O man, what is good, even to do justly, to love mercy, and to walk humbly with thy God.' With this truth he has, in some measure, 'enlightened every one that cometh into the world.' "[48]

Here is a decisive point of contact with the history of religions and a theology of world religions. Wesley had read a translation of the Koran, some of the Vedas, and had a very rough precursory knowledge of Buddhism. But his views on comparative religion were largely shaped by Hebrew-Christian Scripture as received through patristic exegesis. The common and prevening grace working in other religions accord-

---

[43]#85 "On Working Out Our Own Salvation," iii.7, 3:208–9.
[44]#85 "On Working Out Our Own Salvation," iii.7, 3:208; Augustine, Sermon 169, xi.13.
[45]#85 "On Working Out Our Own Salvation," iii, 3:206–9.
[46]#34 "On the Origen, Nature, Properties, and Use of the Law," 2:4–19.
[47]#34 "On the Origen, Nature, Properties, and Use of the Law," 2:1–19.
[48]#85 "On Working Out Our Own Salvation," proem, 3:199, cf. ENNT on Acts 17:24 and Rom. 1:19–20.

ingly is understood not as something other than the grace of the One who meets us in the Incarnation, the same triune One working preveniently.

Common grace is present throughout the whole human condition. Grace is not stingy. It is present wherever human beings are present, to call freedom to repentance wherever human beings are, addressed to the will, working precisely amid the constant intergenerational and social transmissions of sin. Grace works every moment, both before and after the subjective dynamics of faith, both without and within the circle of faith. In this way common grace is found in all nations, in every child of man and woman, in all who love mercy.

Due to the diversity of gifts, all persons are not all being given the same specific graces at any moment, for the Spirit is distributing different gifts to different persons according to emergent needs and historical requirements.[49] God does not make us accountable for a grace not given to us. God makes us accountable only for that grace that in fact is given to us.[50]

Grace Not Nature

This is not a statement about natural ability, or about nature as such working of itself, but about grace working through nature. "The will of man is by nature free only to evil. Yet . . . every man has a measure of free-will restored to him by grace."[51] "Natural free-will, in the present state of mankind, I do not understand: I only assert, that there is a measure of free-will supernaturally re-stored to every man, together with that supernatural light which 'enlightens every man that comes into the world.' "[52]

Prevenient grace is sometimes pelagianly misunderstood as natural human ability. This makes Lutheran and Reformed evangelicals nervous, as if Wesleyans too might be inadvertently speaking of some universal natural capacity to do the good. They well know that "there is no one who does good, not even one" (Rom. 3:12b), apart from grace. They worry that Wesleyan talk of prevenience tempts us to think too forwardly about what we contribute to our salvation, how we cooperate with grace, and thus forget that it is precisely grace that enables our cooperation. This worry is wholly in accord with what Wesley himself was concerned about.

It is completely contrary to Wesley's intent to think of grace as natural to humanity, or inherent in our nature. Grace remains a radical gift wholly unmerited by us in our natural fallenness. Grace comes before any of our natural competencies or responses.[53]

Though not intrinsic to freedom, grace is constantly present to freedom as a gift. That does not reduce grace to an expression of nature. Grace remains grace. It is not something we possess by nature. It is given us. Yet grace is given abundantly to everyone—the paleolithic moundmakers of Georgia, the forest Hottentots of Africa, and the Islamic hordes.

Wesley was not arguing that human beings naturally have a good will, for

---

[49]B1:149–55; 2:410, 268; 3:263–66; CH 7:583.

[50]#85 "On Working Out Our Own Salvation," iii, 3:206–9.

[51]"Some Remarks on Mr. Hill's Review," xvi, X:392.

[52]PCC, sec. 45, X:229–30; similarly, Wesley asserted that both he and Fletcher "absolutely deny natural free-will. We both steadily assert that the will of man is by nature free only to do evil. Yet we both believe that every man has a measure of free-will restored to him by grace," "Some Remarks of Mr. Hill's 'Review of All the Doctrines Taught by Mr. John Wesley,' " X:392.

[53]#85 "On Working Out Our Own Salvation," i, 3:202–3.

that he has already named Pelagianism and rejected in his discourse on original sin. Rather, everywhere human beings exercise freedom, there grace is working to elicit out of the distortions of fallen human nature responses of faith, hope, and love. Prevenient grace remains a teaching that can be easily misunderstood as to imagine that Wesley was covertly affirming the very Pelagianism he had so frequently denied elsewhere. The confusion can be cleared by making clear that common grace is (as with Calvin) still grace, not nature.

Common grace bestows upon fallen man the conditions for experiencing some preliminary knowledge of the existence of God and his attributes. Common grace works to offer all humanity the possibility of reflecting on the fundamental fact that God is and is good and holy.[54] This does not constitute a saving knowledge of God as such, but only the opening of the door for the readiness to receive by faith saving grace in Jesus Christ.[55] One can be shaped by common grace and moved by prevenient grace and still know nothing yet of incarnation, cross, resurrection, repentance, faith, hope, and love. Prevenient grace offers knowledge about God, not personal knowledge of the revealed God.

The Relation of Prevenient Grace and Conscience

Conscience is "that faculty whereby we are at once conscious of our own thoughts, words, and actions, and of their merit or demerit, of their being good or bad, and consequently, deserving either praise or censure" (J VII 187). Conscience is a mode of consciousness, in which one is aware of the goodness or badness of one's own actions. All have that mode of consciousness. No sapient person is wholly lacking in the capacity to review morally one's own behavior. All who have consciousness have this facility of looking at oneself and saying that was passable, that was not so good.[56]

If you posited freedom without the conscience that is intrinsic to freedom, you would never have the capacity for freedom to assess itself. Conscience is the capacity to judge oneself, present in all human beings, regardless of how acculturated.

Prevenient grace works through conscience. Conscience is capable of being distorted, yet God works steadily and step by step to ready persons for further grace.

Conscience is universally present in common humanity not as a gift of nature but of grace that mercifully leads us back to our true selves. Conscience is not merely a natural function lacking in common grace, but rather "a supernatural gift of God, above all his natural endowments."[57] While prevenient grace is "vulgarly called 'natural conscience' . . . it is more properly termed 'preventing grace.' "[58] Through the prevening grace of moral awareness, persons are drawn toward repentance and clearer self-knowledge. To assign this function to a hypothesized "natural conscience" is a vulgar description of it because it fails to acknowledge conscience as the gift of grace refracted through the varieties of human cultures. This operation of conscience must be augmented by a

---

[54]#69 "The Imperfection of Human Knowledge," proem, 2:568–69.
[55]B1:118, 213.
[56]#85 "On Working Out Our Own Salvation," iii.4, 3:207.
[57]#105 "On Conscience," i.1–4, 3:481.
[58]#85 "On Working Out Our Own Salvation," iii.4, 3:207.

second "convincing grace" that leads to repentance.[59]

In conscience we experience not a natural liberty to do the good, but to hope for it. In this way Christ who is the end of the law is being inscribed ever anew on our hearts by the preliminary discernment of the difference between good and evil.

This teaching of prevenient grace served as a structural foundation for Wesley's teaching about baptism. Though he affirmed adult baptism, he also could view infant baptism as expressing the prevenience of grace, that grace is at work even before responsiveness or the age of accountability. The inclusion of the child in the community of faith corresponds to circumcision as an act of initiation bringing one initially into the community of faith.

The knowledge that stems from conscience does not necessarily include specific awareness of the Christian gospel, though it may also be formed by the history of revelation. Rather it involves "some discernment of the difference between moral good and evil," along with "some desire to please God, as well as some light concerning what does really please him, and some convictions when they are sensible of displeasing him."[60] "For though in one sense it may be termed natural, because it is found in all men; yet, properly speaking, it is not natural, but a supernatural gift of God, above all his natural endowments. No, it is not nature, but the Son of God, that is 'the true light, which enlighteneth every man that cometh into the world.'"[61] "For allowing that all the souls of men are dead in sin by nature; this excuses none, seeing there is no man that is in a state of mere nature;

there is no man, unless he has quenched the Spirit, that is wholly void of the grace of God. No man living is entirely destitute of what is vulgarly called natural conscience."[62]

FURTHER READINGS ON GRACE

Collins, Kenneth. *John Wesley on Salvation*. Grand Rapids: FAP, Zondervan, 1989. Chap. 1, "Prevenient Grace and Human Sin."

Dorr, Donal. "Total Corruption and the Wesleyan Tradition: Prevenient Grace." *Irish Theo. Q* 31 (1964): 303–21.

Harper, Steve. *John Wesley's Theology Today*. FAP, Zondervan, 1983. Chap. 3 "Prevenient Grace."

Langford, Thomas. *Practical Divinity: Theology in the Wesleyan Tradition*. Nashville: Abingdon, 1982. Chap. 2 "Wesley's Theology of Grace," 24–48.

Lawton, George. "Grace in Wesley's Fifty-three Sermons." PWHS 42 (1980): 112–15.

Nicholson, Roy S. "John Wesley on Prevenient Grace." *Wesleyan Advocate* (1976): 5, 6.

Nilson, E. A. "Prevenient Grace." LQHR 184 (1959): 188–94.

Smith, J. Weldon III. "Some Notes on Wesley's Doctrine of Prevenient Grace." RL 34 (1964): 68–80.

Williams, Colin. JWTT, "The Order of Salvation: Prevenient Grace," 39ff.

PREDESTINATION

Whether the Subject Matter Is Relevant to Preaching

The subject of predestination, if vexatious to approach, is even more arduous to master. Only two subjects in the Wesley literary corpus place serious intellectual burdens on the reader and this is one of them (original sin being the other). In both cases Wesley is enmeshed in a complex polemical engagement with preachers of the Puritan tradition who were exercising consider-

---

[59]#85 "On Working Out Our Own Salvation," ii.1, 3:204.
[60]#129 "Heavenly Treasure in Earthen Vessels," i.1, 4:169.
[61]#105 "On Conscience," i.5, 3:482.
[62]#85 "On Working Out Our Own Salvation," iii.4, 3:207.

able influence within Methodist societies. He could not afford simply to ignore the challenge.

Though predestination is hardly an urgent question today, one need only sample the literature of the late eighteenth and early nineteenth centuries to see how fiercely it was debated. It emerged (and even today remains) as a key theological difference between Anglican-Arminian-Wesleyan evangelicals and Reformed evangelicals (including many Baptists, with their special focus on eternal security).

Though predestination has an antiquarian ring to modern ears, the deeper issue remains profound for anyone who wishes to think scripturally about the power and knowledge of God, and the complex, puzzling relation of grace and freedom. It is tempting to ignore it altogether, though to do so would be ill-advised. It remains a theme that draws together a host of basic issues that still trouble the divided body of Christ. It yields a flood of light on correlated teachings upon human existence, freedom, divine sovereignty, and providence.

To the Very Edge of Calvinism

From the Minutes of 1745: "Q23. Wherein may we come to the very edge of Calvinism? A. (1.) In ascribing all good to the free grace of God. (2.) In denying all natural free will, and all power antecedent to grace. And (3.) In excluding all merit from man; even for what he has or does by the grace of God."[63]

In an unusually conciliatory mood in August 24, 1743, Wesley had attempted a doctrinal *eirenicon* with Whitefield in the following terms: "With regard to . . . Unconditional Election, I believe,

That God, before the foundation of the world, did unconditionally elect certain persons to do certain works, as Paul to preach the gospel: That He has unconditionally elected some nations to receive peculiar privileges, the Jewish nation in particular: that He has unconditionally elected some nations to hear the gospel. . . : That He has unconditionally elected some persons to many peculiar advantages, both with regard to temporal and spiritual things: And I do not deny (though I cannot prove that it is so), that He has unconditionally elected some persons [thence eminently styled 'The Elect'] to eternal glory. But I cannot believe, That all those who are not thus elected to glory must perish everlastingly; or That there is one soul on earth who has not, [nor] ever had a possibility of escaping eternal damnation."[64] Subsequent controversy would require more precise definition.

Wesley's Omission of the Predestinarian Article in the Twenty-five Articles

Wesley struck entirely Article XVII of the Anglican Thirty-nine, on Predestination and Election. This cannot imply that by omitting it he rejected all its aspects, for some phrases in the Article he would approve wholly, such as that "we must receive God's promises in such wise as they are generally set forth to us in Holy Scripture." But he had serious reservations about the Article's main contention that God before the foundation of the world had "decreed by his counsel, secret to us, to deliver from curse and damnation those whom he hath chosen in Christ out of mankind." This language was not considered sufficiently indisputable to be sus-

---

[63]Minutes, Aug. 2, 1745, VIII:285; JWO 347–50, 425–28, 447–50.
[64]JJW 3:85; cf. CH 7:134, 35, 701. For comments favorable to Calvin and Calvinism, see B1:453; LJW 6:146, 153, 210.

tained as a central confession for American Methodists.[65]

In his letter to James Hervey, Wesley argued that Article 17 of the Thirty-nine Articles "barely defines the term [predestination], without either affirming or denying the thing; whereas the Thirty-first totally overthrows and razes it from the foundation."[66] "Mr. Sellon has clearly showed, that the Seventeenth Article does not assert absolute predestination . . . I never preached against the Seventeenth Article, nor had the least thought of doing it. But did Mr. Hill never preach against the Thirty-first Article, which explicitly asserts universal redemption?"[67]

The omitted language is actually a moderate, not a radical, doctrine of election consistent with his *eirenicon* with Whitefield: Some are predestined to life by the everlasting purpose of God. Only the elect are brought to everlasting salvation, as vessels made to honor, having been called according to God's purpose by his Spirit working in due season. They by grace obey this calling, are justified freely, made sons of God by adoption. The elect are made like the image of Christ, walking in good works, and at length, by God's mercy, attain everlasting happiness. This teaching is said by the Anglican Article XVII to be "full of sweet, pleasant and unspeakable comfort to godly persons," because it establishes and confirms faith, fervently kindling love to God. Yet for "curious and carnal persons, lacking the Spirit of

Christ," they will "have continually before their eyes the sentence of God's predestination," so as to warn them against the "recklessness of most unclean living." Wesley's quarrel with double predestinarianism was not directed primarily against the Anglican formulary, but more so against the much harsher conceptions of the later Reformed tradition following Dort.

The Paradox of the Eternal Decree

Wesley affirmed that the eternal love of God motivated the Incarnation. Due to God's foreknowing of the history of sin, God decided from all eternity, before the foundation of the world,[68] that the Son should become man in order that all humanity might be offered the choice of believing or not believing in God's love, and as a result of that choice, eternal closeness or separation from God.[69] In Wesley's view a healthy teaching of predestination implies not unilaterally or monergistically "a chain of causes and effects," but a providential ordering of phases of the divine will in time, the incremental "method in which God works, the order in which the several branches of salvation constantly follow each other."[70]

The paradoxical idea of an eternal decree that presupposes the fall of freedom is possible on the premise of God's eternal foresight, wherein all events in time are viewed as eternally present by the all-knowing God. God does not need to wait till freedom decides to fall to envision a plan of

---

[65]LJW 1:23, 279; 2:69, 88, 192; 3:200, 249.

[66]LJW 3:379; Anglican Article XXXI is on "the One Oblation of Christ Finished Upon the Cross," which confesses that "there is none other satisfaction for sin but that alone," DSWT 122.

[67]"Some Remarks on Mr. Hill's 'Review of All the Doctrines Taught by Mr. John Wesley,' " X:383; cf. "Answer to Roland Hill's Tract," LJW 5:213, 329; 6:305f.; JJW 5:476; B1:206n; 4:7n; and "Remarks on Mr. Hill's Review," B1:206n, 451n, 643n; 4:7n; 9:402–15.

[68]#66 "The Signs of the Times," i.1, 2:521–23; ENNT on 1 Tim. 1:9.

[69]WC 19.

[70]#58 "On Predestination," sec. 4, 2:416; B1:87, 327, 375f., 413–21; 3:545–48; JWO 349f., 425f.

redemption, because God sees from eternity that man will fall, and hence the remedy can be envisioned from before the foundation of the world.[71] "Salvation remains conditional, but it is salvation with an eternally-grounded content." In resisting a wooden view of predestination, Wesley stressed God's foreknowledge of free choice of sin by persons; yet "when Wesley thinks of the fall in the context of sanctification, a supralapsarian motif can suddenly appear: God not only foresees the fall and provides a remedy; God decrees, foresees, and permits the creation, fall and incarnation in order to effect His overriding purpose, that man should be made holier and happier than Adam before the fall!"[72]

In a letter of May 14, 1765, Wesley wrote: "Just so my brother and I reasoned thirty years ago, 'as thinking it our duty to oppose predestination with our whole strength; not as an opinion, but as a dangerous mistake, which appears to be subversive of the very foundation of Christian experience, and which has, in fact, given occasion to the most grievous offenses.' "[73] He regarded double predestination as "the very antidote of Methodism . . . the most deadly and successful enemy which it ever had . . . a lie . . . [which does] strike at the root of Methodism, grieve the holiest of your friends, and endanger your own soul."[74]

Free Grace

Rom. 8:32: "He that spared not his own Son, but delivered him up for us all, how shall he not with him also freely give us all things?" [Homily #110 1739 B3:542–63; J#128 VII:373–86]

To those who may have wondered in what sense Wesleyan evangelicals are different from Calvinists, this homily offers the leading indicator. There are in fact only a few differences. Wesley was very close to Calvin in most ways, so much so that he could concede to John Newton that "the holding Particular Election and Final Perseverance is compatible" with "a love to Christ and a work of grace," stating that he never differed "from [Calvin] an hair's breadth."[75] But in this homily the distance from Dort to Oxford is prodigious. Those who grasp accurately this parting of the ways will see instantly why Wesleyans are so close to Calvinists in doctrinal instinct, yet so far in temperament.[76]

With the exception of a few traditional Calvinists, most contemporary Presbyterians have not followed double predestinarian teaching any more rigorously than Methodists have followed entire sanctification teaching. Admittedly, predestination remains a pariah doctrine today, even among traditions that once fought diligently for it. But there still remain today rhetorical echoes of this debate reverberating from the eighteenth century.

Central to the teaching task in the Wesleyan societies was the reformulation of the understanding of the relation of grace and freedom. This homily is addressed to Methodist societies, to warn of predestinarian entanglements, the first round of many on predestination, the commencing shot of a long battle.

There were in the societies some who strongly believed in predestination teaching. George Whitefield and Augus-

---

[71]WC 20; PCC X:237f.
[72]Deschner, WC 22.
[73]JJW 5:116.
[74]XIII:150.
[75]Letters, May 14, 1765, LJW 4:297; cf. B1:453; LJW 6:146, 153, 210.
[76]See also LJW 5:238, 250, 322, 344; 6:34–35, 75–76; and Letter to Thomas Maxfield, B9:422–23.

tus Toplady and others within the Methodist orbit held fiercely to the predestinarian hypothesis. Wesley's quarrel with Calvinists would rage intermittently from 1739 in the free grace controversy to 1778 and following with the defiant publication of the *Arminian Magazine*. By Arminianism he referred to a moderated Calvinism, tempered in the direction of synergism, over against absolute double predestination. Meanwhile, Wesley's theology retained most other standard features of Reformed exegesis excepting its hyperAugustinian elements.

Aware that this sermon would awaken controversy, he sought divine guidance by drawing lots on whether to restrict his attack on predestination to preaching, but received the lot "preach and print."[77] In his preface "To the Reader" he stated that he felt "indispensably obliged to declare this truth to all the world," hoping that responses would come "in charity, in love, and in the spirit of meekness."[78]

Universal Scope of God's Atoning Work

The Wesleyans and double predestinarians agreed that grace produces good fruit, and that works as such do not justify. The burning issue remained whether saving grace is offered to all or some. Wesley argued that the free sovereign grace of God is in all and for all.[79] Wherever humanity is struggling with sin, God's free grace is enabling, sufficient strength for that struggle.[80]

The beginning point is the sovereign freedom of God to share his mercy with all humanity. While we were yet sinners Christ died for the ungodly. While dead in our sins, God did not spare "his own Son, but delivered him up *for us all*" (Rom. 8:32, KJV, italics added). This is not a grace that is decreed to operate only in some, but *in all* (as in Calvin common grace operates in all). Grace, whether prevenient or cooperating, is offered sufficiently and freely *to all*. The atoning grace in Christ is freely given to all precisely *while we were yet sinners*. All humanity comes under the condemnation of sin, yet while we were dead in sins, God freely was giving us all things.[81]

Justifying grace does not depend upon any human merit, good works, tempers, good desires, good purposes, or intentions. Yet grace elicits a good willing that animates good works. Good works are the fruit of grace, not its root, the effects of grace, not its cause.[82]

The Dilemma of Double Predestination

The key premise of double predestination is that God ordained some to eternal salvation and some to eternal damnation, predestining both. Thus, "by virtue of the eternal, unchangeable, irresistible decree of God, one part of mankind are infallibly saved and the rest infallibly damned, it being impossible that any of the former should be damned, or that any of the latter should be saved."[83] In this view, there are two decrees of God, salvation for the elect and damnation for the damned.

Whoever holds to the premise of absolute pretemporal election of some individuals to life is hard put to grant the corollary premise that God pretem-

[77]Letters, to James Hutton and the Fetter Lane Society, April 30, 1739, 25:640. Outler judged Wesley unable to recognize his aggressive role in the controversy, 3:543.

[78]#110 "Free Grace," 3:544.

[79]B1:122.

[80]#110 "Free Grace," sec. 2–4, 3:544; B2:154, 292.

[81]#110 "Free Grace," sec. 3–5, 3:545–46.

[82]#110 "Free Grace," sec. 3, 3:545.

[83]#110 "Free Grace," sec. 9, 3:547.

porally elected some to death. Whatever one calls it—election, preterition, predestination, or reprobation—it all tends toward the same point: God before time decides all who will be elected and all who will be damned.[84] Wesley thought it delusive to imagine that one could take a harmless speculative taste of the predestinarian sedative and leave behind the rest. Either you buy into its all-encompassing dual premise, or not at all.[85]

Seven Arguments
Against Double Predestination

The price of double predestinarian exegesis is far too high not only for moral accountability but for theodicy, evangelism, the attributes of God, the goodness of creation, and human freedom. Wesley set forth a series of arguments to show that predestination could not be a scriptural doctrine of God:

1. Predestination *makes preaching unnecessary* and absurd. Why should one preach if it is already decided before time by divine decree that about which one is asked to decide? Preaching is vain if the decisive matter of human response to grace is already settled from the beginning of time.[86]

2. Predestination tends to *undermine holiness*. It takes away the primary motive to follow after the holiness commended in Scripture—"the hope of future reward and fear of punishment," so that hearers believe falsely that their lot is already invariably cast. It thereby undermines the desire for holiness and active cooperation with grace, which is the purpose of preaching the word and administering the sacraments.[87]

Suppose I am ill, and know that I am

destined to live or die, regardless of what is done, but I do not know which. I might plausibly conclude that I have no need of a physician because my lot is already cast. Similarly Wesley argued that a person who understood himself to be predestined is tempted to feel no need to grow in godliness.

3. Contrary to its claim, the predestinarian premise tends to *obstruct the consoling work of the Spirit* out of which the comfort of religion flows. Among those prone to realistic self-examination, the preoccupation inevitably tends to focus on despair. It is neither consoling nor morally challenging to assert that God decides who will be saved unilaterally apart from all human responsiveness.[88]

Not only reprobates but sincere questioners are left to despair. Whatever its intention, the doctrine refocuses attention subjectively upon whether or not I am elected, rather than whether God elects to love humanity in Christ. It tends to lead believers to pride and sinners to despair. It tends to minimize the importance of moment by moment dependency upon the witness of God's Spirit for assurance. Under this premise, admonition to the elect becomes superfluous, and admonition to the damned ludicrous.[89]

Predestination teaching has a dubious history of increasing sharp tempers and coldness of heart toward those thought to be excluded from grace, tending to thwart meekness and love. "Does it not hinder the work of God in the soul, feed all evil and weaken all good tempers?"[90] Wesley thought that evangelical testimony does better to stand empathically in the shoes of the reprobate, grasp the

[84]#110 "Free Grace," sec. 5–8, 3:545–47.
[85]#110 "Free Grace," sec. 4–10, 3:545–48.
[86]#110 "Free Grace," sec. 11, 3:548.
[87]#110 "Free Grace," sec. 12, 3:548–49.
[88]#110 "Free Grace," sec. 13–15, 3:549–50.
[89]#110 "Free Grace," sec. 13–14, 3:549.
[90]Letter to Lady Maxwell, Sept. 30, 1788, 8:95.

depths of his despair over fulfilling the requirements of the law, and there address to him the word of free grace.[91]

4. Predestination tends to destroy *zeal for works of mercy*, such as feeding the hungry. There is little incentive for clothing the naked or visiting the prisoner. Why bother to do good works if one is already securely elected, irreversibly right with God? Wesley had seen enough of acquisitive Puritans and mean-spirited Dissenters to be convinced that predestinarian arguments tend toward unintended antinomianism.[92] Though Calvin himself never intended to discourage good works, his followers at times have been tempted to conclude that if predestined, one's preferred position can be more easily rationalized, and injustices reinforced with a self-righteous demeanor. The doctrine invites a cheaper solution than the scriptural requirement for faith working in love.[93]

5. Predestinarian tenets have a tendency to undermine the need for any actual history of revelation by *trivializing historical revelation* so as to make it absurd and superfluous. Why does one really need any history of revelation if all is settled from the beginning?[94]

6. Furthermore, it is *bad exegesis*. The analogy of faith is the basis of interpreting Scripture, whereby one allows the clear teachings of Scripture to interpret and validate ambiguous or controverted teachings of Scripture in a balanced way. Those who take double predestinarian premises as the key to all other biblical testimony find it increasingly hard to state an apologetic for other crucial biblical teachings such as obedience, faith, hope, and love. They cite texts on election, but systematically ignore those on God's universal love for sinners. Wesley was convinced that the origin of this doctrine was not in Scripture but in a narrower unecumenical tradition of interpretation that does not account for the fuller witness of Scripture as received by the pre-Augustinian ancient church.

In this way the predestinarian premise wrongly ratchets Scripture toward seeming to contradict itself. For it is Scripture that so often appeals to responsible freedom, and calls all to respond to God's saving action. If God has monergistically decreed every detail from the beginning, it makes a sham out of those texts that emphasize decisive response to grace. Pitting Scripture against Scripture, predestination increases the difficulty of the exegete in making sense out of many biblical teachings.[95]

7. Predestination is prone to blasphemy, making of God a liar and Jesus a hypocrite, by dangling salvation before all, yet allowing only a tiny group of the elect to receive it, misrepresenting Christ as a deceiver in his promises to care for all. If the Father does not primordially intend that all should be saved, the Son's words to that effect are a mockery. It presents God as taunting his helpless creatures by offering that which he does not intend to make possible, by pretending a boundless compassion for all, which turns out to be restricted.[96]

By predestination teaching *the moral attributes of God are subverted*. The sovereignty of God is supposedly affirmed by destroying other moral attributes of God—mercy, compassion,

[91] #110 "Free Grace," sec. 13–17, 3:549–51.
[92] #110 "Free Grace," 3:550f.
[93] #110 "Free Grace," sec. 18, 3:551; cf. 1:481.
[94] #110 "Free Grace," sec. 19, 3:551–52.
[95] #110 "Free Grace," sec. 20–22, 3:552–54.
[96] #110 "Free Grace," sec. 23–30, 3:554–59.

truth, justice, and love. "This is the blasphemy for which (however I love the persons who assert it) I abhor the doctrine."[97] It makes the premise of the veracity of God difficult to defend. How can One be just or merciful who makes a decree to damn prior to any possible responsiveness? The merciful God appears as a capricious tyrant more deceptive and cruel than the devil himself, and the human person an automaton.

Double predestination makes the devil's work unnecessary. If true, God would be worse than the devil. While Scripture teaches that God's sovereignty is directed by his love, and views love as God's foremost attribute, absolute predestination disorders the primacy of God's love among the divine attributes.[98]

Wesley's Reconstruction of Positive Aspects of the Teaching of Predestination as Divine Foreknowing

God freely wills grace to all, but not all decide to receive this incomparable gift. Wesley did not reject altogether the scriptural teaching of God's electing love, but set forth a view of election that did not require the double decree premise.[99]

Accordingly, God's choice of us seeks our confirming choice of God. God sets before us life and death. The soul that chooses life shall live and the soul that chooses death shall die. The pivot is choice. Persons are not made reprobate because God wills them to be damned, but because they respond deficiently to sufficient grace.[100]

God offers grace freely to all who will receive it, forcing grace upon none.

Wesley followed a traditional eastern patristic, synergistic way of understanding the predestination texts: They point to God's foreknowledge of those who would believe, as those who are "elect according to the foreknowledge of God" (1 Peter 1:2).

On Predestination

Rom. 8:29–30: "Whom he did foreknow, he also did predestinate to be conformed to the image of his Son: whom he did predestinate, them he also called. And, whom he called, them he also justified; and whom he justified, them he also glorified." [Homily #58 1773 B2:413–21; J#58 VI:225–30]

Wesley did not deny every conceivable view of predestination, but only that late hyper-Augustinian view he thought unscriptural, unreasonable, and lacking ecumenical consent. Wesley's own predestinarian teaching is grounded textually in Romans 8:29–30: "*For God knew his own before ever they were, and also ordained that they should be shaped to the likeness of his Son, that he might be the eldest among a large family of brothers; and it is these, so fore-ordained, whom he has also called. And those whom he called he has justified, and to those whom he justified he has also given his splendour*" (NEB). Wesley gleaned from this text a carefully tempered doctrine of predestination that preserves grace-enabled freedom. While such passages should inspire humility, they tend instead among some to elicit uncharitable hubris. Theodore Beza's supralapsarian explication of this passage is the infelicitous logical outcome of an opinionated fixation upon divine sovereignty.[101]

---

[97]#110 "Free Grace," sec. 29, 3:558–59.
[98]PCC 45–48, X:229–31; 1 John 4:8b; on the doctrine of absolute decrees see B2:416; 3:545–47; cf. LJW 5:83; 6:296; 7:99.
[99]B2:417–24.
[100]#110 "Free Grace," sec. 14–30, 3:549–59.
[101]Acknowledging this as a difficult Pauline text, Wesley mused about whether Peter might

Whether God's Foreknowing Implies Predetermining

God's knowing differs from human knowing in time. God is simultaneously aware of all events in time, since only God is eternal and omniscient. God is already foreknowing of all who are responding negatively or positively to free grace. To God, all time is eternally present. Hence even our temporal notions of foreknowing and afterknowing are strictly speaking not the way God sees time, but only metaphorical expressions. From creation to consummation, God knows what is in the heart of everyone.[102] God has no need of planning. *It is precisely God's foreknowing that defines, interprets, clarifies, and explicates the otherwise obscure meaning of God's foreordaining will.*[103] Note the sequence: "whom he did foreknow, he also did predestinate to be conformed to the image of his Son (Rom. 8:29, KJV).[104]

One does not sin *because* God knows it in advance, but God knows it because the person is choosing to sin. God's foreknowing in no way necessitates human action, it simply foreknows human actions, their determinants and consequents. God's foreknowing recognizes our sin, but does not cause it. As one may know the sun is shining yet that knowledge does not cause the sun to shine, so God knows that a person sins.[105]

God's Will Cannot Be Temporally Bound to Linear Sequences

One can best discern the meaning of Romans 8:29–30 by rethinking its terms in reverse order from last to first—from glorification backward in time toward foreknowing. Among all those saved, there is not one who has not been purchased by the blood of Christ. No one is justified without being called, first with an outward call and then an inward call. No one is finally called without being conformed to the image of the Son. No one is sanctified by grace without this being foreknown by God. The moral image of God is thereby being freely expressed in the elect, by God's eternally foreknown plan,[106] so as to enable them to share in the eternal blessing.[107]

Thus the apostle is not in this text describing an unalterable series of cause-effect relationships with each layer building upon the previous one. For the sequence of the text is equally illuminating if read from back to front—from glorifying to predestining. Paul is not delineating "a chain of causes and effects . . . but simply showing the *method in which God works,*" the providential arrangement by which the order of salvation steadily unfolds, so the work of God may be considered "either forward or backward—either from the beginning to the end, or *from the end to the beginning.*"[108] God witnesses all

---

have had this text in mind when he noted that Paul's "letters contain some things that are hard to understand, which ignorant and unstable people distort, as they do the other Scriptures, to their own destruction" (2 Peter 3:16). Subsequently predestination became, in Wesley's view, a doctrine that "many of the most learned men in the world and not the 'unstable' only, but many who seemed to be well established in the truths of the gospel, have, for several centuries, 'wrested' to their own destruction," 2:415.

[102]#58 "On Predestination," sec. 5, 2:416–17.
[103]#58 "On Predestination," sec. 15, 2:420–21.
[104]#58 "On Predestination," sec. 7, 2:418.
[105]#58 "On Predestination," sec. 5, 2:417.
[106]On dispensations of grace within this plan, see B3:492–93; LJW 5:268.
[107]#58 "On Predestination," sec. 7–14, 2:418–20.
[108]#58 "On Predestination," sec. 4, 2:416, italics added. This is a salient anticipation of

eternity at once, observing everything in an "eternal now," innocent of the charge that his knowing makes him the direct causative agent of evil.[109] Double predestinarian exegesis binds God too tightly in a linear conception of time. Wesley amended this presumption by appealing to the transtemporal nature of God, for whom there is no before or after.

Sustaining Moral Accountability Within the Premise of Divine Foreknowing

God wills eternal life to the faithful according to God's foreknowledge. God's elect have been "chosen *according to* the foreknowledge of God, through the sanctifying work of the Spirit, for obedience to Jesus Christ" (1 Peter 1:2, italics added).

The burden of sin meanwhile rests squarely on the sinner, not God the giver of the freedom. The sinner absurdly turns away from God in sin. Lacking freedom, no one could be held morally responsible. Having freedom is what we mean by being a person.

God sees from eternity who will and will not accept his atoning work. God does not coerce the acceptance of his offer. The Atonement is available for all, but not received by all. Wesley was convinced that this reading of the Pauline text was to be found in the pre-Augustinian, orthodox patristic consensus, especially in the apostolic fathers, the ante-Nicene writers of the period of martyrdom, as well as Athanasius, John Chrysostom, and the early ecumenical conciliar tradition.[110]

The Destiny to Conform to the Son's Image

God's predestining will has as its goal to conform those whom he did foreknow "to the image of his Son" (or to be "shaped to the likeness of his Son," NEB). All who of any future time freely and truly believe in the Son are promised that they shall be conformed to the Son's image, saved from outward and inward sin, and enabled to walk in the way of holiness.

Those so foreknown and in this sense predestined are in time effectually called outwardly by the word of his grace, and inwardly by the Spirit, justifying them freely, and making them children of God. The divine decree is that "believers shall be saved, those whom he foreknows as such, he calls both outwardly and inwardly—outwardly by the word of his grace, and inwardly by his Spirit."[111]

Those called freely are offered justifying grace freely, and sanctifying grace to be received freely. Sanctification of the believing life occurs as the believer is conformed to the image of the Son. The conforming process, which aims in time toward the complete yielding of the will to God, comes to full fruition in glorification: "having made them 'meet to be partakers of the inheritance of the saints in light,' he gives them 'the kingdom which was prepared for them before the world began.' "[112]

"Whom he predestined" means those whom he foreknew to be believers who would respond to their effectual calling by grace. All who actually in time come to believe, God is

---

Pannenberg's view of proleptic eschatological reasoning, from the end to the whole, see *History as Revelation*.

[109]#58 "On Predestination," sec. 5, 2:417.

[110]DPF X:265; cf. Council of Ephesus, 431 A.D.; Second Council of Carthage, 529 A.D.; see my discussion of the interpreting predestination texts in *The Transforming Power of Grace*, Nashville: Abingdon, 1993.

[111]#58 "On Predestination," sec. 8, 2:418.

[112]#58 "On Predestination," sec. 10, 2:418–19.

foreknowing of their belief. From God's point of view the past tense is merely a way of speaking. For God's "fore"-knowing is an eternal now—"to speak after the manner of men: for in fact there is nothing *before* or *after* to God."[113]

The substance of this homily, preached in Ireland in 1773, echoes the letter of John Wesley's mother, Susanna, to John in his Oxford days: "I do firmly believe that God from eternity hath elected some to everlasting life. But then I humbly conceive that this election is founded on his foreknowledge, according to that in the 8th of Romans: . . . 'Whom in his eternal prescience God saw would make a right use of their powers, and accept the offered mercy . . . he did predestinate, adopt for his children, his peculiar treasure. And that they might be conformed to the image of his Son, he called them to himself, by his external Word, the preaching of the gospel, and internally by his Holy Spirit.' "[114]

In this way scriptural teaching is not inconsistent in asserting both that "He that believeth shall be saved; he that believeth not shall be damned," and that God wills to save all. "O that men would . . . be content with this plain account of it, and not endeavor to wade into those mysteries which are too deep for angels to fathom."[115]

Predestination Calmly Considered

[1752 JWO:427–72 X:204–59]

Wesley was not wholly lacking a reprobation teaching, but insisted that it not be monergistic or coerce human freedom. He held that God is just in passing by those who have freely rejected his gift of grace.

Nor did Wesley advise those in his

connection of spiritual formation to disdain predestination, but rather to wrestle with it circumspectly as to its scriptural grounding. In his most detailed essay on predestination, Wesley initiated the colloquy with predestinarian teaching by making an empathic point that showed his capacity to enter into dialogue with those different from himself.

The Experiential Ground of Irresistibility Teaching

Wesley offered an experiential explanation of the psychological tenacity of predestinarian teaching. He was convinced that the idea had profound roots in the experience of believers redeemed by the radical power of grace. Those who had experienced the compelling power of grace in themselves tend to infer that God always works irresistibly in every believer. Wesley thus credits predestination with a certain psychological plausibility and power: the feeling that God is calling one so powerfully to grace that it seems irresistible.[116] Under such circumstances it may seem that the posture of freedom is entirely passive, and that grace is simply and unilaterally filling the soul with mercy. Then one leaps to the controversial inference that grace has nothing to do with appealing to our freedom, so as to make us completely inert rather than cooperating agents working out our own salvation in fear and trembling to receive the grace given. This preemptive psychological deduction prematurely assumes that the only way to interpret what has happened to me is to suppose that God chose this path from the beginning before the foundation of the world, destining some to salvation and some to reprobation.

---

[113]#58 "On Predestination," sec. 7, 2:418.
[114]Aug. 18, 1725, 25:179–80.
[115]#58 "On Predestination," sec. 16, 2:421.
[116]PCC 1–4, JWO 427–28.

This premature experiential deduction then becomes systematized into a whole structure of exegesis and thought.[117] While Scripture rightly should shape experience, in much predestinarian exegesis, the texts have become overwhelmed precipitously by this bias in experience. Thus the tables have turned on the charge against pietism, that it is too experientially and emotively oriented, and this charge is now addressed directly to those most prone to make it.

There is no height or strength of holiness from which it is impossible to fall. But by grace anyone who has fallen may by repentance find forgiveness. Wesley admitted that God "*may* possibly, at *some times*, work irresistibly in *some souls*," but one cannot infer from that "that he *always* works thus."[118] The ordinary work of the Spirit is not coercive. That the Spirit can be resisted is evident from Acts 7:51. Paul would not allow that "God is so the whole worker of our salvation as to exclude man's working at all,"[119] since Paul speaks of the faithful as being "workers together with him" (1 Cor. 3:9).

Countering the Premature Systematization of a Falsely Simple Experiential Deduction

Wesley entered into a careful systematic review of predestinarian arguments, texts, and reasonings. I underscore *systematic* because Wesley is so often dismissed by detractors as an unsystematic experiential preacher who lacks the internal cohesion of a systematic thinker. A central purpose of this exposition is to show the interior coherence of his theological system to those who have not yet read the texts. "Predestination Calmly Considered" is not one of his typical brief teaching homilies, but a distinctly systematic treatise, which shows that the aging former Oxford don could engage in detailed doctrinal reflection and think economically in an orderly way when the occasion demanded.

At first glance it may seem as if the predestinarian system is more rationally ordered, and its opponents weak on argument. There is a prevailing logical clarity and moral certainty that permeates predestinarian thought. It is God who does all the deciding from the outset, and only then works out its consequences in unconditional reprobation, absolute election, irresistible grace, and eternal perseverance. Those who hunger for an uncomplicated account of the divine human relation, and a less nuanced theology, may have moral and psychological preferences for predestinarian reasoning. Especially if divine sovereignty is the solitary string on one's fiddle, one may tilt toward predestinarian exegesis. But those who seek to understand the intimate inward dialogue of grace and freedom look for a more complex and interactive field theory.

Wesley sought a more subtly harmonized explanation in which many more factors could be considered than simply God's omnipotent power. The grace/freedom interface requires more sophisticated forms of reasoning than the arguments of the absolute decrees. The covenant relation is dialogical not monological, dialectical not deductive, synergistic not monergistic (and today we would say analogical not digital). Hence the interactive reasoning of mutuality requires a more rigorous and intricate analysis, but at the end of the day is left with fewer absurdities than its simpler alternative, a predestinarian

---

[117]PCC 1–4, JWO 427–28.
[118]PCC 81, JWO 468; cf. LJW 5:83; B2:489f.; JJW 3:85f.; JWO 427f., 448ff., 469f.
[119]PCC 48, JWO 448.

system that only at first glance appears to be more consistent.[120]

Letting Predestinarians Speak in Their Own Words

Usually he preferred to let predestinarian sources speak for themselves: the Paris Confession of Faith of 1559, Calvin's *Institutes*, Dort's Decrees of 1618, Westminster's Confession of 1646.[121] When in an argumentative temperament, Wesley became very textually focused. In the heat of a polemical showdown, however, Wesley sometimes trimmed and edited the predestinarian voices so as to leave out crucial disclaimers, such as those that assert that God was not the author of sin, that free will is still preserved by the doctrine of election, so as to amount to a severe abridgment of the tradition of Dort.[122]

Wesley was faced with a strong, internally cohesive, predestinarian system, which finds its classic Reformed expression in Calvin's *Institutes*: "All men are not created for the same end, but some are fore-ordained to eternal life, others to eternal damnation. So according as every man was created for the one end or the other, we say he was *elected* (i.e., predestinated to life) or *reprobated* (i.e., predestinated to damnation)."[123] And Westminster: "By the decree of God, for the manifestation of his glory, some men and angels are predestinated unto everlasting life and others foreordained to everlasting death."[124]

Wesley defined the doctrine of double predestination as follows: "Before the foundations of the world were laid, God of his own mere will and pleasure fixed a decree concerning all the children of men who should be born unto the end of the world. This decree was unchangeable with regard to God, and irresistible with regard to man. And herein it was ordained, that one part of mankind should be saved from sin and hell, and all the rest left to perish for ever and ever, without help, without hope."[125]

That is the view Wesley was trying to make a fair account of and rebut with detailed textual analysis. Wesley's task was the formidable one of inquiring into how grace meets freedom and deals with human recalcitrance. To do this he had to ask whether the predestinarian's scriptural warrants were valid, and to what degree they end in undermining the divine attributes of justice, wisdom, love, and veracity.

At least it is clear that those who assert unconditional election are stuck logically also with unconditional reprobation.[126] If one maintains that only the elect are saved, then it follows that those whom God did not choose to elect are necessarily destined to be damned, even though only passively by the fact of nonelection. "Go now and find out how to split the hair between thy being reprobated and not elected."[127] Wesley appealed to Calvin's own logic that "election cannot stand without reprobation. Whom God passes by, those he reprobates."[128] "Unconditional election

---

[120]PCC 1–16, JWO 427–33; cf. B9:423, 520f.
[121]PCC 1–9, JWO 427–30.
[122]JWO 425–26.
[123]PCC 7, JWO 429; Calvin, *Institutes*, 3.21.5.
[124]PCC 7, JWO 429.
[125]PCC 14, JWO 432.
[126]JJW 2:353; 3:84–86.
[127]PCC 12, JWO 431.
[128]Inst. 3.23.1; PCC 9, JWO 430.

cannot appear without the cloven foot of reprobation."[129]

The Condition of Divine Election

In challenging this teaching it is necessary to distinguish two biblical senses of election:

(1) Election in Scripture may refer to *a personal divine appointment to accomplish a particular task*, such as God's election of Cyrus or Paul. This does not imply eternal happiness. Judas for example was called to be a disciple, yet not saved, holy, or blessed.[130]

(2) In other passages election refers to *election to eternal happiness*. Such election to eternal happiness is not unconditional, for it is conditioned upon its faithful reception.[131] Insofar as one has faith, one shares rightly in God's electing love. Lacking faith, one does not share in God's electing love. Subjectively viewed, the decisive factor is one's own choosing—always by grace alone through faith—in response to God's electing love for all.[132] As with the people of Israel, the full circle of an effective, actualized teaching of election calls for and requires human confirmation of the election of God.[133] In this way election in Scripture refers not exclusively to God's unilateral choice, but also to grace-enabled human responsiveness to God's choice.[134]

Eternal happiness in Scripture is not an absolute pretemporal divine choice. Rather, it is grounded in God's own choice to love all humanity, addressed freely to all, and awaiting the response of all. Wedding guests who fail to respond lose their invitation (Matt. 22:8). Those inattentive to wisdom find that she will spurn them (Prov. 1:23–29). Israel was instructed that "if you forsake him, he will forsake you" (2 Chron. 15:2). The people were given a choice of a blessing or a curse, depending upon how they keep the command of God (Deut. 11:26–28). God keeps his covenant love with those who love him and keep his commands (Deut 7:12). Only when we choose to build the house on the gracious rock provided do we find a place that does not fall (Matt. 7:26).[135]

To those who respond with horror that Wesley is making salvation conditional, he answered that it is not he who is setting limits, but the revealed Word of God that has explicitly defined what is necessary for the reception of the covenant.[136] "If you . . . are careful to obey my commands . . . I will keep my covenant with you." "If you reject my decrees . . . I will set my face against you" (Lev. 26:3, 9, 15, 17). God has "done all which was necessary for the conditional salvation of all mankind; that is, if they believe."[137] "I am justified through the righteousness of Christ, as the price; through faith, as the condition. I do not say . . . Faith is that *for which* we were accepted; but . . . Faith is that *through which* we are accepted. We are justified, we are accepted of

[129]PCC 15, JWO 432.
[130]PCC 16, JWO 433.
[131]PCC 17, JWO 433.
[132]JJW 5:116.
[133]JWO 433f.; cf. "Principles of a Methodist," B9:59–63.
[134]PCC 19, JWO 434.
[135]PCC 19, JWO 434.
[136]B11:108-17, 444–57; SS 1:128.
[137]"An Extract from A Short View of the Difference Between the Moravian Brethren, (so Called,) and the Rev. Mr. John and Charles Wesley," X:202.

God, for the sake of Christ, through faith."[138]

God's atoning act on the cross is not conditional. God's gift on the cross can not be finally obliterated by any particular person's disbelief. The gift of the Son and the Spirit is objectively given on the cross whether received or not. What happened on the cross is for all, yet only some respond in faith, hope, and love to the electing love of God.

Distinguishing Precognition From Preordination

It is only God, "to whom all things are present at once, who sees all eternity at one view," who can precognitively speak of believers freely responding to grace as the "elect from the foundation of the world."[139] God has prescient awareness of how our wills are going to respond, for God is eternal, omniscient, present to future time as well as past, who grasps the consequences of specific acts of freedom. But that does not imply that God unilaterally determines our acts of freedom.

God, who is incomparably capable of being the ground and giver of all things, could have made the world differently, but not in such a way that would be inconsistent with God's own intention as Creator. God has freely, omnipotently chosen to create this world, the one we see, a real world, not a fantasy. Within this world there are natural causes in a complex order of causality, and free beings in this world whose decisions are not reducible to external determinants alone, but due in part to self-determination within the webbing of causality.[140] The permission of freedom is within the range of the affirmation of God's omnipotence.[141]

Whether Unconditional Election Is a Scriptural Doctrine

Unilaterally decreed reprobation is not consistent with the scriptural teaching that all are invited to salvation, or that God primordially intends and is willing that all should be saved.[142] It is not God's will that any should be lost, but rather that all would repent (2 Peter 3:9). God bestows his riches upon all who call upon him (Rom. 10:13). As Adam's sin leads to the condemnation of all, so Christ's obedience leads to the reconciliation of all (Rom. 5:18, 19). The good news is to be proclaimed to all creation (Mark 16:15). Christ died for all (2 Cor. 5:15). Christ, the lamb who takes away the sins of the world (John 1:29), is the intended remedy not only for our sins, but for the sins of the whole world (1 John 2:2). Wesley patiently worked through the texts (Matt. 22:9; Luke 19:41ff.; John 5:16, 34, 40; Acts 17:24; 1 Tim. 2:3, 4; 4:10; James 1:5; 1 John 4:14) that show God came to save all, and died for all. All are atoned for. Christ is the propitiation for the sins of the whole world. What happened on the cross is not for some but all (Matt. 18:11; John 1:29; 3:17;

---

[138]"Some Remarks of Mr. Hill's 'Review of All the Doctrines Taught by Mr. John Wesley,' " X:390 (italics added).

[139]PCC 17, 18, JWO 433. This assumes a critical distinction between precognition and preordination. God has preknowledge of futurity based upon God's eternity. Only God knows how our freedom will spell itself out. But that does not deny that freedom is spelling itself out in self-determination. Wesley insisted that this freedom is not undermined but enabled by grace.

[140]JWO 474–76, 489f.

[141]PCC 120, JWO 432–34.

[142]PCC 19, JWO 434.

12:47; Rom. 14:15; 1 Cor 8:11; 2 Cor. 5:4; Heb. 2:9; 2 Peter 2:1).[143]

The eternal decree is that those who believe will be saved, not that those who are saved will believe. The parable of the potter and clay (Rom. 9:21) does not conclude for unconditional pretemporal reprobation, for "God has a right to fix the terms on which he will show mercy." God may show mercy to whoever meets the terms God defines for showing mercy regardless of previous privilege, even to the Gentiles if God so desires.[144]

The abridged code phrase, God "hardened his heart," upon deeper inspection actually means that God "permitted Satan to harden it."[145] God permits obstinate believers to harden in their unbelief. That "no man is able to pluck them out of my Father's hand" (John 10:28) assumes that some have freely chosen by grace to follow and obey.

Challenging the Justice of the Logic of Determinism

A false idea of divine justice is on trial amid claims that God could justly condemn a free person to eternal damnation totally apart from any opportunity for that person to cooperate. "Justice can have no place in rewarding or punishing mere machines."[146] In Scripture, "God is pleased to appeal to man himself touching the justice of His proceedings."[147]

How can God be regarded as a just judge if an eternal decree has been made that does not take into account any capacity to accept or reject grace? Why should the Spirit be active in our hearts to enable this response if it is already predetermined? God's justice does not damn anyone except those who refuse the grace being freely offered to them.[148]

If unconditional predestination to reprobation is true, then the sincerity of God's promises is put in question. For how could God be straightforward in his call to repent if repentance were impossible, or already absolutely negated by a pretemporal divine decree? One who is not given the power to do good cannot justly be condemned for not doing good. One cannot justly be condemned of sin if the means to escape sin are not present. Who could be justly condemned for doing evil if he could do only evil?[149] Unbelief could not be the basis of the condemnation of those who did not have the power to believe.[150]

God's sovereignty is manifested through free will, not undermined by it.[151] Predestination may be pressed in such a way as to exalt God by debasing human freedom.[152] Meanwhile it may actually demean God's justice, mercy, veracity, and sincerity, making absurd preaching aimed at repentance and faith. The sovereignty of God must be viewed not abstractly but in conjunction with God's other attributes.

---

[143]PCC 19–23, JWO 434–35.
[144]PCC 24–33, JWO 435–41.
[145]PCC 56, JWO 453–54.
[146]PCC 37, JWO 442.
[147]PCC 22, JWO 435; X:216.
[148]PCC 22, JWO 435; X:216.
[149]PCC 31, JWO 439; X:221.
[150]PCC 35–6, JWO 441; X:223.
[151]LJW 6:287; 1:184.
[152]Monotheletism is that heresy that viewed the Christ as having only one will. Orthodoxy speaks of two wills in the God–man, a human will and a divine will to which the human will is freely yielded in constant consecration. Wesley regarded hyper-Augustininan predestinarianism as a novel form of monotheletism, assuming that only one will is present in conversion and that is God's.

God's unchangeableness is expressed precisely through his constant, responsive love. God is unchangeable in his will to save those who respond in faith.[153] "God's unchangeableness with regard to his decrees is this: he has unchangeably decreed to save holy believers and to condemn obstinate, impenitent unbelievers." "Unchangeably he loveth faith and unchangeably hateth unbelief."[154] God is *unchangeable* precisely with regard to his decree to save those who respond to his love in faith. In his incomparable *faithfulness* God will perform what he has promised, will keep his covenants, which from the outset require and enable human responsiveness.[155]

The Responsive Wisdom, Justice, Mercy, Sovereignty, and Faithfulness of the Unchangeable God

The Incarnation shows that God comes to us humbly. The wisdom of God adapts itself to our human condition. God works not by duress, but gently in our hearts, reproving, grieving, wooing, like a lover trying to invite and draw and persuade the beloved. It is a wiser God who offers salvation to humanity without forcing salvation upon them, who enables human self-determination, and welcomes the free interactive play of human choice, than one who would simply create a closed world in which freedom is a cruel illusion.[156]

God by grace saves humanity first by enlightening everyone who comes into the world with an understanding of good and evil by means of common grace; then by convicting grace reproving when the will falls into evil; then by moving the will gently, not coercively, to respond cooperatively; then by wooing the will, by nurturing good desires into our hearts, by setting life and death before us, by seeking to persuade us to choose life.[157]

The human person is not a stone or a cannonball that does not act but is merely acted upon. No one holds a cannonball responsible for what it effects. Similarly one impelled by a force he cannot resist cannot be held accountable either for reward or punishment.[158] The best metaphors for grace eliciting freedom are not drawn from billiard-ball natural causality, but from the interpersonal, interactive, dialogical sphere in which one person addresses and appeals to another's freedom.

God's glory is not magnified by demeaning God's attributes. It is unconvincing that God's justice is glorified because in his sovereign will he has preordained persons to sin unceasingly. What would one say of a man who, though he could save millions with just one word, chooses rather to save only a few, refusing to save the others by saying: "I will not, because I will not"? Neither does it commend God's mercy to argue that God has acted in such an arbitrary way.[159] The sovereignty of God rightly appears "in fixing from eternity that decree, 'He that believeth shall be saved,'" in "all the general circumstances of creation," in "allotting the natural endowments" of humanity, and in "dispensing the various gifts of his Spirit," but not in whimsically damning some, while saving others.[160]

---

[153]PCC 58, JWO 455.
[154]PCC 58–59, JWO 455; X:238.
[155]PCC 59–78, JWO 455–67.
[156]PCC 51–52, JWO 449–50.
[157]PCC 52–54, JWO 450–52.
[158]PCC 37, JWO 442; X:224.
[159]PCC 52–53, JWO 450–51.
[160]PCC 53–56, JWO 451–53.

Free Will Defended

Wesley held to the freewill defense that God creates freedom, and freedom chooses evil in its own struggle against God, who is the author not of sin but of freedom, which is created good even if prone to fall. No creature capable of mirroring the image of God can be considered an automaton.

Human beings are created to reflect the freedom of God. Only through freedom can the goodness of God be consciously and rationally reflected, unlike inorganic matter, which can only refract God's goodness inertly, without speech or reason.[161]

Take away freedom and you take away the greatest expression of God's glory in creation. Scripture repeatedly calls each of us to choose between death and life, good and evil (Gen. 3:17; Deut. 7:9–12; Ps. 115:9; Matt. 7:26). Freedom is capable of glorifying and reflecting God in ways that inanimate life forms are incapable. Wesley took special delight in quoting back to Reformed advocates the language of the Westminster Assembly, which allowed that "God hath endued the will of man with that natural liberty that is neither forced, nor by an absolute necessity of nature, determined to do good or evil."[162]

Wesley's Rejection of Semi-Pelagianism

The hypothesis that God saves us without our freedom is not more exalting to God than that God saves us with and through our freedom. It is not more glorifying to God to save an automaton irresistibly than to save a free agent by such grace as one may either concur with or resist.[163]

Some argue that if human free will is given any power at all, such power is taken away from God, and thus God would not have the whole glory of the work of salvation, but some would fall to the human will. Wesley answered, against all hints of semi-Pelagianism, that the power "to work together with him" by grace is wholly from God. The creation of the human who may "work together with God" is the ground for the greater glorification of God, for such power to work has come from God. God does not exclude human freedom from cooperating with his grace, but rather creates, redeems, and newly enables human freedom.[164]

One could not cooperate with God had not the power and possibility of cooperating come from God. So it is no offense to grace to say that grace enables human freedom to cooperate with grace. The right use of freedom, far from detracting from the glory of God, enhances God's glory.

By synergism we do not imply that fallen freedom retains a natural capacity to reach out and take the initiative and establish a restored relation with God. Rather by synergism we mean that human freedom by grace is being enabled to cooperate interactively with God's saving plan.[165] It is the coworking by grace of human willing with the divine willing.[166]

Falling From Grace

Those who, having once truly believed and been endued with the faith that produces a good conscience, may later fall (Ezek. 18:24. 1 Tim. 1:18, 19).

161PCC 49, JWO 447.
162Westminster Confession, IX.1.
163PCC 49, JWO 448; X:231.
164PCC 43–49, JWO 446–48.
165JWO, Introduction, 13–16; cf. 119, 425.
166PCC 43–49, JWO 446–48.

Those once grafted into the good olive tree may later be broken off through willful unbelief (Rom. 11:16–22). Branches that "abide not" are cast forth and burned (John 15:6). Those having once known Christ can again become entangled in the world (2 Peter 2:20). Those who have been made partakers of the Holy Spirit and have produced fruits of the Spirit may nevertheless fall from grace back into former pollutions (Heb. 6:4–6; 10:29).[167]

Even those most actively receiving sanctifying grace may yet fall (Heb. 10:26–29). We share finally in Christ only if we hold to our first confidence (Heb 3:14). We are instructed to take care that we do not lose what we have (2 John 8), to hold fast so that no one seizes the crown (Rev. 3:11).[168] Grace is almighty but not irresistible.[169]

A Dialogue Between a Predestinarian and His Friend

[X:259–66]

Whether Sin Is Made a Necessity by Uncritical Views of Predestination

Addressed to predestinarians in a conversational style, Wesley is approaching them as a friendly but tough-minded partner in dialogue. The purpose of this dialogue is to answer predestinarians who in debate often claim that "that is not what predestinarians say." In order to counter this, Wesley uses direct quotes from leading Re-

formed writings (notably Zwingli,[170] Calvin,[171] the Westminster Catechism, Peter Martyr,[172] Zanchius,[173] Piscator,[174] and Twisse[175]) as a composite partner in dialogue.

He identifies the central premise of absolute predestination, according to its own key sources: that God from eternity ordained all that has come to pass, with no exceptions, extending also to human actions.[176] Calvin wrote: "The wills of men are so governed by the will of God that they are carried on straight to the mark which he has foreordained."[177]

The consequent trend of such an argument tends to make sin a necessity. According to this argument, God made Adam and Eve for the very purpose that they would be tempted and fall into sin. God's decree is grounded not in his foreknowledge but in his will. All but the elect are predestined by God to reprobation. Why does God call upon the reprobate to repent? Only that they may become more deaf and blind. If the number and identity of the reprobate are fixed before time, there can be no meaning in calling them to repentance.[178]

The predestinarian is left with three options: either to equivocate, or swallow all these assertions and honestly try to avow them, or renounce them all together, freely affirming free grace to all. Wesley had come to the conclusion

[167]PCC 68–79, JWO 458–68.
[168]PCC 73–78, JWO 463–67.
[169]PCC 81, JWO 468.
[170]Sermon on Providence.
[171]Inst. 1.16.3, 8; 1.17.5; 3.23.1–2, 6; 3.24.8, 12–13.
[172]Commentary on Romans.
[173]"On the Nature of God."
[174]"Disputation on Predestination."
[175]*Vindiciae Gratiae Potestatis et Providentiae Dei*, 3, 22.
[176]DPF X:260.
[177]Calvin, Inst. 1.16.8.
[178]DPF X:259–64.

that the first two required a sacrifice of both intellect and moral prudence.[179]

Wesley conceded that God foresaw the Fall, but not that he directly ordained it. God permitted, but did not mandate the Fall by divine decree. It would indeed be a "horrible decree" if God preordained Adam's fall, or caused sin, or diminished the glory of God in the creation of human freedom.[180] Absolute unconditional election and reprobation cannot be found in holy writ. It bears the dismal fruit of the burning of Michael Servetus.[181]

Wesley contrasted the permissive will of God, which places the responsibility for rebellion and possibility of obedience squarely on the human agent who willfully shuns or embraces the compassionate and universal offer of grace, with the predestinarian assertion of the irresistibility of God's will. If the Fall occurred "not only by the permission, but also by the appointment of God,"[182] then sin occurs by necessity.

Reclaiming the Pre-Augustinian Consensual Tradition

More subtle and more difficult to argue is the pre-Augustinian Eastern patristic teaching of free grace meeting free will. Wesley was not inventing this interpretation, but reincorporating it within the Protestant teaching of justification though grace by faith, which becomes active in love. The pre-Nicene teaching of grace gently coaxing freedom was reappropriated by Wesleyan evangelicalism as energetically as by any in Protestantism. Wesley realized that Protestants who resist the inconsistencies of predestination are likely to be stereotyped wrongly as semi-Pelagians,

but warned that those who are afraid of hard names are probably going to be averse to discipleship.

When Calvinists appealed to a hyper-Augustinian mode of anti-Pelagian exegesis, Wesley had ready a counter appeal to the Eastern church fathers before Pelagius. Those who wish to see where Christian theology is most mature and full must search in the sources prior to Augustine's belated fifth-century fight with Pelagianism.

The Pelagian challenge rightly required an astute rejoinder. Augustine answered it deftly. But for a broader corrective to less heinous excesses, we must look to the pre-Augustinian consensus of antiquity as stated by Irenaeus, John Chrysostom, Gregory of Nyssa, and Gregory Nazianzen. This was a form of argument familiar to the early Eastern and Western orthodox traditions, and especially valued by the Anglican tradition by which Wesley had been nurtured.

In its extreme form, the double decrees of predestinarianism as well as the modern determinists seemed to Wesley to have more affinity to Islamic doctrine than Augustinian. For the first four centuries of church history, the Eastern church was against all views of fixed determinism.[183] "Augustine speaks sometimes for [absolute double predestination] and sometimes against it. But all antiquity for the four first centuries is against [it], as is the whole Eastern Church to this day; and the Church of England, both in her Catechism, Articles, and Homilies. And so are divers of our most holy Martyrs, Bishop Hooper and Bishop Latimer in particular."[184]

---

[179]DPF X:260.
[180]DPF X:261–62; JJW 6:131.
[181]DPF X:266.
[182]DPF X:261, quoting Calvin, Inst. 3.24.8.
[183]LS Pt. 2.
[184]DPF X:265. According to Chrysostom, Judas had been earlier "a child of the kingdom"

The Consequence
of Predestinarian Excess

In "The Consequence Proved" Wesley responded to a tract written by predestinarian Augustus Toplady, which asserted that "One in twenty, suppose, of mankind are elected; nineteen in twenty are reprobated. The elect shall be saved, do what they will; the Reprobate shall be damned, do what they can."[185] When an outcry emerged "that no such consequence follows from the doctrine of absolute predestination," Wesley followed Toplady's argument through to its logical conclusion: "I calmly affirm, it is a fair state of the case; this consequence does naturally and necessarily follow" as stated by Toplady. If God's love is unconditional and immutable, and election is fixed, the non-elect cannot be reprobated for sins "they never had. . . . For it cannot be a sin in a spark to rise, or in a stone to fall."[186] If it was never "in their power to love God and their neighbor," how can they be held responsible? Unbelief cannot reasonably be turned "obstinate" if they never had a possibility of removing it. "How then can the Judge of all the earth consign them to everlasting fire, for what was in effect his own act and deed?"[187]

Wesley from youthful days had an intense allergic reaction to absolute predestination: "I never did believe it, nor the doctrines connected with it, no, not for an hour. In this, at least, I have been consistent with myself . . . I believe no decree of reprobation . . . I believe no decree of preterition . . . I do not believe . . . any such absolute election, as implies that all but the absolutely elect shall inevitably be damned . . . I do not believe the doctrine of irresistible grace, or of infallible perseverance . . . I do not believe salvation by works."[188]

Serious Thoughts Upon the Perseverance of the Saints

[1751 X:284–98]

Faith active in love is the sole condition for God's fulfillment of his covenant promise of salvation to the believer. Can a believer who has been justified return to a state of nature as if prior to justification, and annul the effects of justifying grace in his life? Answering too simply either yes or no presents "great difficulties."[189] The issue is resolved only by careful examination of texts that admit of debatable interpretations.

Whether a Believer Can Make
a Shipwreck of Faith

God's covenant with Israel was conditional on the people keeping God's law. The point is realistically stated in Ezekiel: "But if a righteous man turns from his righteousness and commits sin and does the same detestable things the wicked man does, will he live? None of the righteous things he has done will be remembered. Because of the unfaithfulness he is guilty of and because of the sins he has committed, he will die" (Ezek. 18:24).

Paul speaks of those who holding to faith and having had a good conscience, have made a shipwreck of their faith (1 Tim. 1:18, 19). Shipwreck is a meta-

who had received the promise from Jesus himself, "but afterwards he became a child of hell" by his own willful choice, so even Judas was not predestined to reprobation.

[185]"The Consequence Proved," X:370.
[186]"The Consequence Proved," X:372.
[187]"The Consequence Proved," X:373–74.
[188]"Some Remarks of Mr. Hill's 'Review of All the Doctrines Taught by Mr. John Wesley,'" X:379.
[189]"Serious Thoughts Upon the Perseverance of the Saints," X:285.

phor of total loss.[190] "He that believeth shall be saved" does not imply that one cannot cease to believe, having once believed. Those who believe and continue believing in faith active in love "shall be saved; he that believeth not," if he continue in unbelief, "shall be damned."[191]

The Falling Away of Believers

Wesley's argument on perseverance is based on his understanding of the *saint* (*chasid*), who loves the Lord (Ps. 31:23), whose way God preserves (Prov. 2:8), whose death is precious to the Lord (Ps.116:15). "Saint" in Greek is *hagios*, one set apart from the profane world, who being endued with the faith that purifies the heart, maintains a good conscience; who is grafted into the good olive tree, the church; who is a branch of the true vine, Christ; who so effectually knows Christ as to have escaped the pollutions of the world; who sees the light of the glory of God in the face of Jesus Christ; who having been made partaker of the fruits of the Holy Spirit, lives by faith in the Son, sanctified by the blood of the covenant.[192]

Such is the saint. But can such a saint fall away from faith? By falling away, he means that a believer may not only fall into occasional sin, but fall so far as to perish everlastingly.

Each of these above elements of the scriptural definition of the *hagios* is conditional upon faith, whose ground is sufficiently supplied by grace. One must continue in faith, not having faith just at one moment, but continually in time (1 Tim. 1:18, 19). God who alone is unchangeable, will carry out his prom-

ise to enable purity of heart to grow upon the condition of faith.

One who has been baptized into the church can fall away. One who has served splendidly as a branch of the true vine can be cut off (John 15:1–6). One who has begun responding to sanctifying grace can fall from that grace (Heb. 6:4, 6; 10:26–29). Wesley concludes that "a saint may fall away" having believed, so as finally to perish.[193] No promise of God is ever offered so unconditionally that the response one makes to it is irrelevant to honoring it. No promise can be claimed until the condition is met: "perform the condition, and the promise is sure. Believe, and thou shalt be saved."[194]

God's righteousness is not found exclusively in forensic and imputed metaphors, but also is at work through the nurturant metaphors, working behaviorally toward the making righteous of the believer, toward the fit maturation of those who believe. Wesley took the premise of grace much further into the dynamics of human freedom than did the continental Reformation, without relaxing a high view of God's sovereign grace or the depth of the human predicament.

Whether Grace Is Resistible

Jesus lamented Jerusalem's refusal of him (Luke 13:34). While the hyper-Augustinian tradition taught irresistible grace, the pre-Augustinian Eastern tradition insisted on human responsiveness to resistible grace. Otherwise Scripture could not meaningfully call the believer to avoid "an unbelieving heart that turns away from God" (Heb.

---

[190]"Serious Thoughts Upon the Perseverance of the Saints," X:287.
[191]"Serious Thoughts Upon the Perseverance of the Saints," X:288.
[192]"Serious Thoughts Upon the Perseverance of the Saints," X:285.
[193]"Serious Thoughts Upon the Perseverance of the Saints," X:285.
[194]"Serious Thoughts Upon the Perseverance of the Saints," X:290.

3:12). It was in this tradition that Wesley intentionally stood.[195]

"Not that I deny, that there are exempt cases, wherein 'The o'erwhelming power of saving grace' does, for a time, work as irresistibly as lightning."[196] In a *Journal* entry of August 24, 1743, Wesley writes lucidly on this point: "That the grace which brings faith, and thereby salvation into the soul, is irresistible at that moment: That most believers may remember some time when God did irresistibly convince them of sin: that most believers do, at some other times, find God irresistibly acting upon their souls. Yet I believe that the grace of God, both before and after these moments, may be, and hath been, resisted; and that, in general, it does not act irresistibly; but we may comply therewith, or may not."[197]

The promises of salvation and perseverance are conditional upon the continued reliance of the believer on prevenient, convicting, cooperating, and sanctifying grace. One forfeits the right to receive the promise when one ceases to have faith.[198] Wesley sought to preserve the scriptural teaching of the universal significance of the Atonement without leading to an unscriptural assertion of the universality of faithful obedience.[199]

Believers are assured of their perseverance as long as they do not neglect the condition of the promise, which is actively trusting in the promise.[200] It is not within human power to turn to God without grace, but it remains within human power to reject the grace offered.[201]

It is challenging enough for the infant to learn to walk, but more challenging for the youth to stay on the arduous path through many temptations. Few are willing to stay the long journey. On November 26, 1790, Wesley wrote to Adam Clarke: "To retain the grace of God is much more than to gain it; hardly one in three does this. And this should be strongly and explicitly urged on all who have tasted of perfect love. If we can prove that any of our local preachers or leaders, either directly or indirectly, speak against it, let him be a local preacher or leader no longer."[202] Wesley did not want anyone in leadership in his connection who had serious doubts about the power of the Spirit completely to reshape human life. The teaching remains the centerpiece of Methodist revivalism. Sanctifying grace is to be set forth explicitly to all who would be serious in the presence of God.

Why Unconditional Predestination
Puts Faith Active in Love
in Jeopardy

In a mature reflection of 1779, "Thoughts on Salvation by Faith," Wesley maintained that he and his brother had held to a fixed course for over forty years following Aldersgate on the centrality of "our constant theme": "By grace we are saved through faith" (Eph. 2:8). "It was our daily subject, both in verse and prose . . . we could hardly speak of anything else, either in public or private."[203] For this we were "stoned in the streets, and several times narrowly escaped with

---

[195]LJW 5:83; B2:489f.; JJW 3:85f.; JWO 427f., 448f., 468f.

[196]#63 "The General Spread of the Gospel," 12; 2:489.

[197]JJW 3:85.

[198]B1:233–34; 3:156, 169; B9:407; 11:398; SS 2:149.

[199]"Serious Thoughts Upon the Perseverance of the Saints," X:292–8.

[200]LJW 5:83.

[201]"Serious Thoughts Upon the Perseverance of the Saints," X:290–94.

[202]Letter to Adam Clarke, Nov. 26, 1790, LJW 3:633.

[203]"Thoughts on Salvation by Faith," XI:492–93.

our lives . . . and painted as unheard-of monsters.'' Yet because they so emphasized faith active in works of love they were accused of salvation by works. Wesley's steady purpose for forty years was to hold together salvation by grace through faith "so as not to contradict that other expression of the same Apostle, 'Without holiness no man shall see the Lord.' "[204] Without "personal holiness . . . none who is not himself conformed to the law of God here, 'shall see the Lord' in glory." This is apostolic testimony that "all the laboured evasions of Witsius" cannot invalidate.[205]

"I was in this perplexity" about the all or nothing tendency within predestination teaching "when a thought shot across my mind, which solved the matter at once: 'This is the key: Those that hold, "Every one is absolutely predestinated either to salvation or damnation," see no medium between salvation by works and salvation by absolute decrees.' It follows, that whosoever denied salvation by absolute decrees, in so doing (according to this apprehension) asserts salvation by works."[206] It would be a peculiarly myopic exegesis to conclude that anyone who denies predestination must be asserting salvation by works.

Wesley shrewdly reasoned that *if salvation is by absolute decree, it is not by works, but neither can it be by faith*, "for unconditional decree excludes faith as well as works."[207] If one admits

to the scriptural condition that "he that believeth shall be saved," then there must be an element of free, responsible cooperation in the work of grace, for there is no faith that does not work by love freely responding to grace.[208]

This is why "we must expect, all who hold unconditional decrees will say, we teach salvation by works," since their premise prevents them from conceiving a third alternative.[209] He concluded that "none shall finally be saved by any faith but that which worketh by love, both inward and outward holiness."[210] In this way classical Christian teaching "stands opposite to the doctrine of the *antinomians* on the one hand, and to that of *justification by works* on the other."[211]

FURTHER READINGS ON PREDESTINATION

Cell, George Croft. *The Rediscovery of John Wesley.* New York: Univ. Press of America. Reprint, 1935. Chap. 10 "The Very Edge of Calvinism," 242–72.

Gunter, W. Steven. *The Limits of Divine Love: John Wesley's Response to Antinomianism and Enthusiasm.* Nashville: Kingswood, Abingdon, 1989. Chap. 14, on conditional election, 227–67.

"Horrible Decrees" in Rack, RE, 420–71.

Pinnock, H. Clark, ed. *A Case for Arminianism.* Grand Rapids: Zondervan, 1989.

Shipley, David C. "Wesley and Some Calvinist Controversies." *Drew Gateway* XXV, no. 4 (1955): 195–210.

Walls, Jerry L. "The Free Will Defense: Calvinism, Wesley, and the Goodness of God." *Christian Scholar's Review* 13 (1983): 19–33.

---

[204]TSF XI:495.
[205]Letter to James Hervey, LJW 3:383.
[206]TSF XI:493.
[207]TSF XI:494.
[208]TSF XI:494.
[209]TSF XI:494.
[210]TSF XI:495.
[211]FA Part I, ii.4, 11:111.

9

Soteriology

Wesley neither sought nor pretended to make any novel contribution to a Christian theory of salvation. All key questions of salvation teaching were in his view apostolically defined and clarified ecumenically by consensus, having survived relatively intact through centuries of challenge. He resolved only to magnify experientially the moral, personal, and societal outworkings of the biblical calling of God to repentance and faith.

Step by step Wesley clarified how one estranged from God is drawn from natural through legal to evangelical existence. His first forty-four homilies (later designated Standard Sermons and considered normative for teaching in the Wesleyan connection of spiritual formation) focus explicitly upon the basic themes of salvation. He called for present, deliberate decision in response to God's gracious action.

NATURAL, LEGAL, AND EVANGELICAL EXISTENCE

The Spirit of Bondage and of Adoption

Rom. 8:15: "We have not received the spirit of bondage again unto fear; but we have received the Spirit of Adoption, whereby we cry, 'Abba, Father.' " [Homily #9 1746 B1:248–66; J#9 V:98–111]

Among the most important of Wesley's soteriological discourses, this one is worthy of painstaking study in order to grasp structurally the argument of a whole series of crucial teaching homilies on salvation. Much else will fall into place for readers who rightly grasp its core design.

The unconscious form of the spirit of bondage is the natural state, the conscious form is the legal state, and the spirit of adoption is the evangelical condition of being adopted into the family of God as child of the Father. The text, Romans 8:15, assumes a three-stage transit of human existence, the first of which is natural self, in which the bulk of humanity dwells.[1]

Learning as sinner to say from the heart, "Father," is central to the freedom of the Christian life. This personal address belongs to evangelical existence. But how does one make the unlikely move from the unconscious condition of sin through sin-con-

---

[1] #9 "The Spirit of Bondage and of Adoption," i.3, 1:250.

GRACE WORKS THROUGH THREE STAGES

NATURAL	LEGAL	EVANGELICAL
The Spirit of Bondage	The Spirit of Bondage unto Fear	The Spirit of Adoption
Aesthetic	Ethical	Religious
What I want to do	What I ought to do	What God does for me
Unaware of moral danger	Aware of bondage as if facing an abyss	Aware of bondage being transcended
Sleeping	Awakening	Reposing
Attempted avoidance of suffering	Tragic moral choices deepen suffering	Joy amid suffering
Lacking faith	Faith of the servant	Faith of the son or daughter
Autonomy	Heteronomy	Theonomy
Blameless lack of dread	Dreadful blame	Overcoming of dread by faith
Easy self-ignorance	Odious self-knowledge	Gracious freedom
False peace of the naturalized self	Internal war within the moral self	True peace of the reconciled self
Fantasized liberty	Bondage	True liberty
Wrestling in utter darkness	Seeing the painful light of hell	Beholding the joyous light of heaven
Neither conquers nor fights	Fights but does not conquer	Fights and conquers
Sins willingly	Sins unwillingly	Does not sin willingly
Prevenient grace	Convicting grace	Justifying grace
Neither loves nor fears God	Only fears God	Loves as God loves
Naïvete	Death of naïvete	New birth
Supposed freedom	Slavery to sin	Children of a new inheritance

sciousness to the joy of faith, hope, and love?[2]

The Human Condition

The organization of the homily follows a classic Pauline-Augustinian sequence of three basic phases of the maturation of the human condition: natural, legal, and evangelical (see chart on previous page).

Augustine had previously analyzed the threefold transition from the capacity of natural reason in its fallenness, to servitude under the divine requirement, to freedom in Christ.[3] *Luther* had similarly analyzed the passage from the natural fallen condition of unawareness of sin, to bondage under the law, to humanity under grace.[4]

Those who have had the privilege of reading *Kierkegaard* will recall his three basic stages along life's way: the aesthetic pleasure-principle stage, the ethical-choice stage, and religious consciousness, which deals primarily with the problem of suffering (with religious consciousness A as the pathos of the natural religion expressed by Socrates, and religious consciousness B as the evangelical consciousness of those whose life is hid in Christ).[5] Wesley preceded Kierkegaard in astutely analyzing the psychological dynamics of these transitions.

Tillich's language may be used to translate the same sequence, moving from autonomous human existence unaware of its estrangement to the heteronomous awakening of awareness of estrangement from oneself; and finally toward the theonomous capacity to enter into estrangement without being estranged, wherein one accepts one's

acceptance, grounding oneself in the ground of being, so that one is no longer estranged from oneself, even though the remnants of estrangement may continue.[6]

A century before Kierkegaard and two before Tillich, Wesley had developed his own version of the stages along life's way, or three states of human existence. It appears in many of his writings, but no place more clearly than in "The Spirit of Bondage and of Adoption." The same sequential structure is evident in "The Almost Christian" and the altogether Christian; the legalistic faith of the servant and the faith of the son adopted into the family of God; the righteousness of the law and "The Righteousness of Faith." It recurs in crucial sermons on salvation by grace through faith, "Scriptural Christianity," "Justification by Faith," "The Witness of the Spirit," and "The New Birth."

In all of these homilies, Wesley was working out of a Pauline-Augustinian exegetical tradition, grounded especially in Paul's letter to Rome. Each of these Protestant interpreters is operating out of an exegetical memory of Romans 1 and 2, which begins with the natural human condition, natural reason; then views the human condition under bondage to the law (Romans 2 and 3); then the transition in 3:24ff. into evangelical existence, with the remainder of Romans setting forth new life in Christ.

The Natural State of Fallen Humanity

The characteristic feature of the natural condition in which sin has come to

[2]#9 "The Spirit of Bondage and of Adoption," proem.1, 1:249.
[3]*The Spirit and the Letter.*
[4]Luther, *The Freedom of a Christian*, MLS:42–85; for further reference to Luther by Wesley see JJW 1:409, 467, 475; B2:78, 556f.; 3:335, 449, 505; 11:318f.; JWO 366f.
[5]Kierkegaard, *Stages Along Life's Way.*
[6]Tillich, *Systematic Theology.*

feel at home is a bondage that is unconscious of its plight, analogous to the state of moral sleep, or ethical unconsciousness—unawareness of any serious moral hazard.[7]

Think of a child playing near a cliff. Unawareness of the danger does not make the situation less dangerous, but more. This is the condition of the natural self. While one is playing perilously on the edge of a measureless moral abyss (final judgment), one remains totally unaware of it. The abyss is the righteousness of the requirement of God impinging on all actions.

A powerful series of metaphors (family alienation, legal condemnation, spiritual death) rhetorically illumine ways in which in actual history all human progeny have together fallen from their created nature into a relentless chronicle of sin.[8] By seeking only pleasure and evading any awareness of personal accountability, the falsely naturalized fallenness of the self follows hedonic criteria, remains morally unserious about oneself, not yet having come to any recognition of one's actual moral condition before God, or any serious realization of one's own self-deceptions.[9]

This falsely naturalized condition of the self reclines in complete unawareness of the judgment and claim of God, hence remains largely unaware of its very self. There is no dread of moral inadequacy, much less of divine justice, no anxiety about moral insolvency. One does not have enough understanding of oneself even to stand in awe of the divine claim. There is rather a lively fictive life in which the imagination fancies itself blameless. The prevailing presumption is of innate goodness, canopied under a self-congratulatory attitude that focuses upon one's own achievements.[10]

This "natural man" (or woman) remains ethically asleep, having no consciousness of moral jeopardy. This person experiences life as secure, peaceful, feeling nothing awry. There is no thought that one is harming anyone else, no awareness of any deep structural or familial or national or racial brokenness, no hint of any unretraceable lostness.[11]

This chronically fallen condition is rightly described as a condition of "ignorance" in which one is uninformed of oneself as a morally problematic being. Wesley thought that this ignorance never glares so strongly as in persons of learning, among whom he had spent so much of his life.[12] The ethos of the university tends to accentuate this ignorance inasmuch as it may be the least likely place to become aware of the depth of one's own moral bankruptcy. More education does not of itself offer a solution to this dilemma, but may reinforce its hubris. Nowhere are people more confident of themselves morally than in academia, where the imagination prevails that inveterate sinners are perfectly capable of thinking of themselves as having the unhindered capacity to talk rationally about their abilities and freedom, and their capacity to reason their way out of the human predicament through education, cleverness, and invention.

To "men of reason" Wesley spoke bluntly: "Your soul is utterly dead in sin, dead in pride, in vanity, in self-will, in sensuality, in love of the world. You are utterly dead to God. There is no

---

[7]B2:19; cf. Kierkegaard, *Sickness unto Death*, I.
[8]Cf. B1:250–55, 263–66, 401f., 433f., 2:76f., 4:171f.
[9]#9 "The Spirit of Bondage and of Adoption," i.2, 1:252.
[10]#9 "The Spirit of Bondage and of Adoption," i.2, 1:252.
[11]#9 "The Spirit of Bondage and of Adoption," i.1, 1:249.
[12]#9 "The Spirit of Bondage and of Adoption," i.4, 1:253.

intercourse between your soul and God . . . You have no spiritual 'sense exercised to discern spiritual good and evil' . . . My soul is distressed for you . . . you are 'seeking death in the error of your life.' "[13]

Such is "natural" humanity where dwells a chronic sense of deluded self-congratulation about human wisdom and goodness. The focus is on natural gratification, ego strength and self-affirmation, guided confidently by the pleasure principle and the avoidance of pain. One is likely to think of oneself at this stage as a good person, expecting others to think well of him.[14]

Wesley used biting irony to describe this natural character clothed in self-deceit, who understands himself to be free from vulgarity, prejudice, enthusiasm, bigotry, and superstition. He fancies himself as walking in a kind of natural liberty, as a freely self-actualizing person. Such are the imaginations of the natural self, largely unaware of the turbulent history of sin.

Put in terms of social-location categories, one remains quite unaware of one's social sin, racism, cultural prejudices, gender-centricity, or expressions of economic interest. One does not see how deeply enmeshed one is in these self-deceptions. There is no personal sense of alienation from the neighbor, much less the neighbor's Creator. If a serious or disturbing thought comes, one finds a way of bypassing it.[15] It never occurs to him that he himself is the person who is stumbling toward death.[16]

There is no striving against sin be-cause there is no recognition of oneself as sinner. Wesley thought this condition characterized the bulk of humanity—a state of moral numbness, of relative unconsciousness.

Such a person may be a nominally religious person, a quite decent sinner, a person who attends religious services and displays the form of godliness though not its power, whose consciousness of sin is so slight as to be unregisterable on any scale.[17] Consciousness-raising for Wesley is a radical movement from natural unawareness of sin toward growing moral awareness.[18] At this stage one neither loves or fears God.

How does it happen that the moral drifter moves toward becoming morally serious? Each person's story is unique.[19]

Legal Man: Life Under the Law

"By some awful providence, or by His word applied with the demonstration of His Spirit, God touches the heart of him that lay asleep in darkness and in the shadow of death." Something happens to shake the sleeper out of this moral stupor. The eyes of moral understanding are snapped open to how one is colluding with corruption, injustice, and inhumanity.[20]

A horrid light breaks in upon the soul, as if gleaming from a bottomless pit. Awareness of one's sin is magnified when understood in the presence of One whose holiness is a consuming fire. God's justice is first glimpsed, then relentlessly beheld as an all-encompass-

[13]EA 50–51 11:64; cf. JWO 49f., 128f., 405.
[14]#9 "The Spirit of Bondage and of Adoption," i.5, 1:253.
[15]#9 "The Spirit of Bondage and of Adoption," i.6, 1:253–54.
[16]#9 "The Spirit of Bondage and of Adoption," i.7, 1:254.
[17]B1:688–91; 3:313f.; 4:57f.; 11:63f., 237–40, 251f., 258–60, 483f.; CH 7:188–93, 194–200; FA 11:250f., 268, 273.
[18]B1:330n.
[19]#9 "The Spirit of Bondage and of Adoption," i.7–8, 1:254–55.
[20]#9 "The Spirit of Bondage and of Adoption," ii.1, 1:255; cf. 2:4, iv.1.

ing conflagration.[21] Once at peace, now errant freedom is increasingly grieved. This trouble is itself a maturation process. At long last moral awareness is making some headway. Having been lulled into a false peace, one is now impelled toward a consciousness of danger.

The possibility of repentance emerges. The need for vast change is dreadfully grasped. A hint of contrition is beginning to dawn by prevening grace. This may be a phlegmatic process or an abrupt event. The cycle is extremely variable, here in a moment, there by degrees. There is no way to predict how providence will move in one's life to spur one toward repentance. Not everyone makes the transition. Some who glimpse the edge of the precipice pretend they saw nothing.

The pith of legal consciousness: I behold each of my actions as if standing in the presence of the holy One who intends to render judgment according to my works on the final day for every idle word, for all the false imaginations of my heart. The most secret recesses of my soul are easily penetrated by God's holy knowing. Nothing is hidden from its light. It is a fearful thing to fall into the hands of the living God.

The gravity and magnitude of God's requirement is now grasped in a way that was never before recognized under the conditions of hedonic-natural dreaming. The law teaches what God requires, what we ought to do, without imparting the power to do it. Not only does the law require: "Thou shall not commit adultery" as an outward act, but inwardly in doing so is judging my lust. "Thou shall not kill" is intensified inwardly when it calls me to deal with the causes of my anger. The law itself, intended for good, in the hands of the sinner merely moves one into a deepened syndrome of self-alienation.

God is not fooled by the self-deception that has prevented me from seeing myself. I recognize that the whole self is sick, the whole heart faint.[22]

A floodlight is shining on my sin. It is not shining on God's mercy at this point. I feel myself to be naked, as if all things were open to him with whom I have to do, all pretenses cut through. Everything in me is exposed, open to the All-knowing One with whom no chicanery is possible. Whereas previously I had felt clothed in a kind of fantasy of innocence, now I experience radical vulnerability, with fig leaves stripped away.[23]

From this follows one of Wesley's most searching psychological descriptions of the dynamics of guilt. His most stunning visual metaphor of the law-judgment syndrome is his fantasy of himself as being *cleft asunder* as in a sacrifice, as if the piercing requirement of God were literally splitting him apart, opening up the whole self.[24]

Consciousness becomes trapped in a whirling entanglement of guilt and fear of punishment.[25] No matter how one strives to improve, one is drawn further into its vortex. Amid this anguish and guilt one senses with the psalmist that "there is no one who does good, not even one" (Ps. 14:3; Rom. 3:10). The law is breathing down our necks so heavily as to expose every recess of sin. It presses at every point, outwardly concerning our behavior and inwardly

---

[21]#9 "The Spirit of Bondage and of Adoption," ii.1, 1:255; cf. V:443.

[22]#9 "The Spirit of Bondage and of Adoption," ii.2, 1:255–56.

[23]#9 "The Spirit of Bondage and of Adoption," ii.2–3, 1:255–56.

[24]#9 "The Spirit of Bondage and of Adoption," ii.3, 1:256. As one who has been cleft asunder in open heart surgery, I find this an especially poignant metaphor.

[25]SS 2:246–48, 261.

concerning our motivations, never giving respite.

It is this condition that Paul called *the spirit of bondage unto fear*, where one is captive to the alienating forces of guilt and dread. One experiences paradigmatic guilt, where even some trivial value negation becomes symbolic of one's whole life-alienation, where some second-rate event reflects the total guilt that I feel in the cosmos. A small slice of experience serves as a window upon the vast burden of human history's piled-up guilt.

What has happened to the exultant freedom of will I once thought I had as my natural hedonic self? Aware of my imprisonment by my own will, I feel the anguish of a wounded spirit. The pleasures I once loved I take no delight in. They pall upon the taste. There is a nausea that pervades this syndrome of vulnerability, fear of punishment, fear of death, despair of lostness in the clutches of the demonic, sorrowing over blessings lost, the feeling of being cursed to remorse and despair. Now I feel condemned, despairing over any capacity to change myself, fearing final judgment of the just judge. Having fallen from the former blithe unawareness of sin, this intense awareness is felt as slavery to despair.[26]

This is legal consciousness, humanity under the law. Working out of Romans 7, Wesley does not hold back in his description of the human predicament under the law. Under bondage to the law, I am in a prison of my own making. The more I struggle against my fetters, the more I feel my bondage. I bite at the chains but do not break them.[27] I picture myself trying to climb out of this mo-

rass by following the law perfectly, to get myself back to square one of the original condition that was lost. But the law proves too encompassing. I never quite fulfill it. Before this One I am always inadequate—the same despair Luther described in "The Bondage of the Will."[28]

"O wretched man that I am! who shall deliver me from the body of this death? I thank God through Jesus Christ our Lord . . . There is therefore now no condemnation to them which are in Christ Jesus, who walk not after the flesh, but after the Spirit" (Rom. 7:24–8:1, KJV).[29]

Only now is one prepared to hear this good news, though one may have heard it prosaically declared a thousand times. Only at the point of feeling the depth of this personal condemnation is one ready to hear that God's good news is *for me*. Those who have not been through the pedagogy of this personal moral awakening, who have never stood under the judgment of God, are not yet sufficiently formed by grace to hear the gospel. Everything hinges upon readiness to hear the declaration of pardon, which can be heard only by sinners. The call is to repent and believe, and by this receive remission of sin.[30]

Evangelical Existence: Humanity Under Grace

The Spirit by convicting grace draws us toward justifying grace.[31] The possibility of repentance grows precisely as one takes seriously the depth of this alienation. At some point the needed grace of repentance is offered in a timely way. By pardon I am offered the

[26]#9 "The Spirit of Bondage and of Adoption," ii.6, 1:257; B:2:233–35; 3:211–26.
[27]#9 "The Spirit of Bondage and of Adoption," ii.6–9, 1:257–59.
[28]Luther, MLS:166–207; SS 2:255.
[29]#9 "The Spirit of Bondage and of Adoption," ii.8, 1:258.
[30]#9 "The Spirit of Bondage and of Adoption," ii.9–10, 1:268–60.
[31]B1:200f., 291f, 350–52, 477–81; 2:22f.; 3:204; CH 7:180–84, 210–34; SS 1:185f., 257.

possibility of cutting to the root of sin, going right to the source of it, by renouncing the whole premise of this former bondage and receiving by grace a new life.

By repentance we are offered the possibility of entering into a new mode of consciousness: life under grace. Only then is it possible for this bondage to end, so that one is no more trapped in the condemnation syndrome, but coming under grace—the condition of one who is finding the favor of God within God's own way of righteousness.[32]

How does it occur that one moves beyond this desperate pit into new life? God's justifying action reaches into the middle of this human condition. God takes responsibility for us in our sin, becoming sin for us in the sense that in his sacrifice on the cross he takes our sin upon himself. We share in that death, the death of Christ, and in his resurrection.

Faith is affirmative response, a yea saying to that grace given to all on the cross. What happens on the cross is a finished act. By the Spirit it becomes imparted by a grace-enabled free response. Trust in unmerited grace is the first step toward a full life of response to God.[33] It constitutes a new birth of spiritual life.[34]

The fallen and naturalized self neither loves nor fears God. The legal self only fears God. The evangelical self under grace can now love as God has loved us, becoming a child of God not merely a servant. The bondage is overcome by divine grace, whereby a new relation to God beyond law is made possible.

The Spirit of Adoption

Baptism means participation in the death and resurrection of Christ. By baptism the faithful enter into new life in the Spirit, as children of the Father and not merely servants in the Father's house, sharing in adoption as sons and daughters in the family of God. Baptism begins this life.

By receiving Holy Communion again and again this new life is nurtured. If baptism is analogous to birth, the Supper is analogous to a constant feeding of the reborn life, which bears the fruits of the Spirit.

Adoption and assurance are closely connected teachings of the Wesleyan evangelical revival. The Spirit does not fail to attest our sonship and daughterhood when we receive justifying grace by faith. That is what the Spirit is searching to communicate to us—that we are children of this Abba, whose Son takes our sin upon himself. The Father accepts the self-offering of the Son for us.[35]

We thus are invited to move directly from the spirit of bondage to the spirit of adoption by which we enter into a new family on the premise of a new spiritual birth, no longer servants or slaves to sin, but children entering into an inheritance.[36] That inheritance, eternal life with God, is offered to be unambiguously received. It is inwardly felt as a radical, assured gift, insofar as we listen to the testimony of the Spirit certified in the written word and in our hearts. We are confident of the divine-human reconciliation by this testimony of the Holy Spirit witnessing within our own spirits that we are children of God, attesting the truth of the cross, the

---

[32] #9 "The Spirit of Bondage and of Adoption," ii.9–10, 1:258–60; CH 7:201–10.
[33] B1:118, 404, 662f.; 2:167; 3:119; 4:26.
[34] #9 "The Spirit of Bondage and of Adoption," iii, 1:260–63.
[35] #9 "The Spirit of Bondage and of Adoption," iii, 1:260–63.
[36] #9 "The Spirit of Bondage and of Adoption," 1:423–24; 3:497–500.

mission of the Son made known through the power of the Spirit.[37]

Evangelical Freedom

In evangelical existence, one experiences oneself as free, not in a falsely fantasized liberty of moral sluggishness, but a true liberty to love the neighbor grounded in pardon. It is not only liberty from guilt but also for the life of faith active in love that the cross makes credible. By this the power of sin is broken. Sin may remain in fragmented forms amid the redeemed life, but its primal vitality is broken. It has no power over the faithful though its consequences and effects lie strewn all about.[38]

Now there is no condemnation. Light shines upon the reconciled soul. God who commanded light to shine, shines in the heart so as to attest the pardon of God. This is what Wesley designates evangelical life, life under grace, a new life of peace where one does not experience condemnation. This is the spirit of adoption into the family of God.

Note that there is a paradoxical parallelism between the beginning and mature stages—between the imagined liberty of the natural self, and the true liberty of the evangelical self. The freedom lost in moral despair and ambiguity is now regained in a more profound form. The peace that had been dissipated is regained in a more profound form—shalom, reconciliation with God, ending the tyranny of guilt and remorse, overcoming the spirit of bondage unto fear.[39] The false peace of the natural self is contrasted with the true peace of the reconciled self.[40]

This renewed person is enabled to say, Abba. Every step of life becomes receivable as the gift of this Father. God is welcomed not solely as righteous judge who places the radical claim of the law upon us, but as merciful, caring, disciplining, correcting, loving Abba. God still is the Holy One whose requirement has not diminished, but now we understand that God has taken our sin upon himself by his active obedience to the law and by his suffering obedience on the cross in which we participate by faith. Thereby we share in this new life of freedom, peace, light, truth, and pardon, clothed in the righteousness of Christ. All of these metaphors are taken captive to the truth made known on the cross.[41]

One is now wholly at rest, though no longer in a moral daze. One's eyes are realistically open to the history of sin, yet with the renewed serenity that comes from trusting God's pardon. The sequence moves from ignorance of self, to incriminating evidence of one's collusion with sin, and finally toward liberating grace.

This pivotal homily was preached on June 10, 1742, at Epworth, where Wesley's father had served for years as parish priest. More strikingly, it was preached in the graveyard adjacent to the church, from his father's tombstone! It is among the most theologically lucid of Wesley's homilies, showing how we move from deception to recognition and then to the glorious liberty of the sons and daughters of God, from false peace to no peace to true peace. Much of his revival preaching had to do precisely with clarifying these transitions.[42]

[37]#9 "The Spirit of Bondage and of Adoption," iii, 1:260–63.
[38]#9 "The Spirit of Bondage and of Adoption," iii, 1:260–63.
[39]SS 1:288.
[40]#9 "The Spirit of Bondage and of Adoption," iii.5, 1:262.
[41]#9 "The Spirit of Bondage and of Adoption," iv.1, 1:264.
[42]#9 "The Spirit of Bondage and of Adoption," iv.3, 4, 1:265–66.

The Almost Christian

Acts 26:28: "Almost thou persuadest me to be a Christian." [Homily #2 1741 B1:131–41; J#2 V:17–25]

The *almost* Christian has the form but not the power of godliness, as contrasted with the *altogether* Christian who walks daily in the way of evangelical existence by the steady, habitual reception of justifying and sanctifying grace.[43] This, one of the most preachable of all Wesley's sermons, is based upon the surprising comment of King Agrippa to Paul under arraignment: *"Almost thou persuadest me to be a Christian."*[44]

The Almost Christian

The almost Christian has the appearance of piety and religion, but without its power—pardon and holiness.[45] This person may keep the sabbath, not lie, do good, all with unflagging sincerity.[46] The almost Christian may be seeking a more just social order, not fornicating, not stealing, and this with all earnestness.[47] He may attend to public worship, receive the means of grace, do no harm to anyone.

What is missing? A desire to serve God? No, that desire may be fervent. A strong sense of religious commitment? No, the sense of duty may be felt so strongly as to appear oppressive.[48] Why then almost, and not altogether a Christian? What is lacking is that which is necessary and sufficient to the Christian life: full trust in God's merciful self-disclosure.

The almost Christian may come conceptually to the brink of evangelical existence and still never have felt the full import of what God has done for him. This person may appear to be a thoroughly decent person, even an intensely religious character, but with something crucial missing.

Implied in being almost a Christian is that humane honesty found wherever people are paying attention to truth and justice, seeking fairness to all, telling the truth, and seeking to be attentive to the less fortunate. These qualities even philistines expect of good persons.[49] "So true it is that the faith of a devil and the life of a heathen make up what most men call a good Christian!"[50]

For many years Wesley himself lived with utmost rigor as an almost Christian, lacking the joy of saving grace. He pointed candidly to his own earlier demeanor as prime example of the almost Christian.[51]

The Altogether Christian

The "altogether Christian" is infused with the love of God, which is always

---

[43]#2 "The Almost Christian," i, 1:131–33; cf. #4 "Scriptural Christianity," ii.5; cf. FA 11:176, 267–68, 536–37.

[44]JJW 2:478; 3:484.

[45]#2 "The Almost Christian," i.4, 1:132; cf. #150 "Hypocrisy in Oxford," ii.2; cf. B1:508; 2:465; 3:317.

[46]#9 "The Spirit of Bondage and of Adoption," iv.1.

[47]#2 "The Almost Christian," i.9, 1:135.

[48]#2 "The Almost Christian," i, 1:132.

[49]#2 "The Almost Christian," i, 1:132.

[50]#150 "Hypocrisy in Oxford," i.9, 4:399.

[51]#2 "The Almost Christian," i, 1:131–35; cf. *Journal*, Jan. 29, 1738: "I who went to America to convert others, was never myself converted to God," but a note was added later: "I am not sure of this." In his Jan. 4, 1739, *Journal*, he repeated that he was "not a Christian now" in the sense that he was conscious that he had not yet attained to perfect love. Five months after Aldersgate he wrote to his brother: "I was not a Christian till the 24th of May last past" (assuming the distinction between the faith of a servant and the faith of a son). Cf. letter to Charles, June 17, 1766; and #81, "In What Sense we are to Leave the World," sec. 23.

being made active and tangible in the love of the neighbor through faith. The Christian is one who altogether loves God, whose affections are wholly turned to the One who gives life. Enabled by the undistracted *love of God*, one is free to view all other goods in relation to the One giver of all creaturely goods, each one of which is capable of being (precisely because good) falsely worshiped. All loves are loved in relation to the love of God. The love of God "engrosses the whole heart . . . takes up all the affections . . . fills the entire capacity of the soul, and employs the utmost extent of all its faculties," when one is "crucified to the world."[52]

The pardoning love of God frees me to give full attention to *the love of the neighbor*, the person who meets me next. Having been loved in a costly way by God as sinner, I am made ready to become radically responsive to the next one that comes along my path, the one I now see before me. I do not choose the neighbor. He meets me unexpectedly, happens to me, comes instantly before my eyes as a surprising gift. Person-to-person meeting occurs in joyful awareness of the final I–Thou meeting.[53]

The altogether Christian lives by *faith*, by trusting in God's own righteousness made known on the cross. Faith is not merely intellectual assent to an idea of God or conceptual proposition, but far more the immediate entrusting of oneself to a person, God the Son, Jesus Christ, by the power of the Spirit.[54] Faith is *the sure trust and confidence in God that by the merits of Christ my sins are forgiven, and I reconciled in the favor with God.*[55] Out of this confidence there ensues a grateful spontaneous inclination to follow God's calling and obey God's claims, insofar as it lies within our power.[56]

Faith has as its consequence a comprehensive reordering of life in a new birth in which the self is no longer locked into guilt and fear, but altogether freed to love the neighbor.[57] Such is the life of the altogether Christian, who being regenerated, is daily receiving new life in Christ.

TERMS OF SALVATION

The Way to the Kingdom

Mark 1:15: "Repent and believe." [Homily #7 1746 B1:217–32; J#76–86]

The terms of salvation are: repent and believe. Early in the gospel narratives these terms are unambiguously stated: "*The kingdom of God is near, repent and believe the good news*" (Mark 1:15). To those who sincerely ask about the way to the kingdom, Scripture answers directly: repent and believe.[58]

The Kingdom of God as True Religion

To ask about the kingdom of God is to ask about the nature of true religion, which is a heart right toward God and humanity.[59] The kingdom is true religion in practice, not merely as outward

---

[52]#2 "The Almost Christian," ii.1, 1:137; Gal. 6:14.
[53]#2 "The Almost Christian," ii.2, 1:138.
[54]#2 "The Almost Christian," ii.3–6, 1:138–39.
[55]#2 "The Almost Christian," ii, 1:137–40. "The Doctrine of Salvation," "Faith and Good Works," sec. 14.
[56]B1:418–19, 634–35, 9:101–2.
[57]#2 "The Almost Christian," ii, 1:138–42; Gal. 5:6; #35, "The Law Established Through Faith, I," ii.3.
[58]Preached from his father's tombstone, the first of the series of "tombstone sermons" at Epworth, June 6, 1742.
[59]B1:217–25; 3:520.

act, tenet, or doctrine.[60] True religion is behaviorally defined, and is not adequately grasped in terms of outward ceremony, moral preachment, or conceptual argument about religion.[61] The kingdom of God is not meat or drink or any exterior good or outward thing, but righteousness, joy, and peace in the Holy Spirit (Rom. 14:17).[62]

The first great branch of true religion is that *active love of God* that finds all one's happiness in God, delighting in the Lord, desiring none beside God, giving the whole heart to God without a rival.[63]

The second is to *love the neighbor* as oneself, every soul God has made, even those unseen, "not excepting him whom thou knowest to be evil and unthankful, him that still despitefully uses and persecutes thee," all to be loved "with the same invariable thirst after his happiness" just as one thirsts for one's own happiness.[64] Such love fulfills the law by an inward righteousness that is not puffed up, and an outward righteousness that actively does good to all.[65]

The heart made right toward God and the neighbor empowers holiness, which welcomes and engenders happiness, for it begets peace and joy in the Holy Spirit (Rom. 14:17). This is a *peace* that only God can give and the world cannot take away, a peace that passes natural understanding because it is spiritually discerned, a peace that banishes fear. It is inwardly attested by the hushed witness of the Spirit that one is a child of God (Rom. 8:16).

This peace brings *joy* wrought in the heart by the Holy Spirit, enabling that calm, humble delight in God that is made possible by the divine-human reconciliation effected on the cross. One is made happy by the awareness that one's sins are entirely covered by grace.[66]

Such happiness and holiness conjoined is called the reign of God or kingdom of heaven in the sacred text. It is termed the kingdom of God because God is reigning in our hearts. Those who allow God to set up his throne in their hearts find themselves instantly filled with righteousness, peace, and joy.[67] It is called the kingdom of heaven because heaven is opening up our closed souls, coming to us in the Son who descends from heaven to bring us back with him to the presence of God the Father. This reign of God is at hand. With the Son's coming, its time is fulfilled. It is not far away from anyone this hour who responds to it in repentance and faith.[68]

The Kingdom of God as the Porch of Religion

"Our main doctrines, which include all the rest, are three—that of Repentance, of Faith, and of Holiness. The first of these we account, as it were, the porch of religion; the next, the door; the

---

[60]LJW 5:5.

[61]"The Character of a Methodist," sec. 1; #38 "A Caution Against Bigotry," ii.3. That this does not imply theological indifferentism is evident from "The Doctrine of Original Sin," iii.i; iv.iv; 1:220n.

[62]#7 "The Way to the Kingdom," i.7, 1:221; LJW 2:269–70; 8:218.

[63]#7 "The Way to the Kingdom," i.7, 8, 1:221; #6 "The Righteousness of Faith," ii.9.

[64]#7 "The Way to the Kingdom," i.8, 9, 1:222.

[65]FA 11:250f., 268, 273; CH 7:194–200.

[66]#7 "The Way to the Kingdom," i.11, 1:223–24.

[67]#7 "The Way to the Kingdom," i.12, 1:224.

[68]Letter to a Gentleman at Bristol, Jan. 6, 1758, LJW 3:246–48.

third, religion itself.''⁶⁹ The temple itself is the holy life of faith active in love.⁷⁰

"By *repentance* I mean conviction of sin, producing real desires and since4re resolutions of amendment; and by 'fruits meet for repentance,' forgiving our brother, ceasing from evil, doing good, using the ordinances of God, and in general obeying Him according to the measure of grace which we have received. But these I cannot as yet term good works, because they do not spring from faith and the love of God.''⁷¹

"Although both repentance, and the fruits thereof, are in some sense necessary before justification, neither the one nor the other is necessary in the same sense, or in the same degree, with faith. . . . For none of these has so direct, immediate a relation to justification as faith." Faith is proximately necessary to justification, while "repentance remotely, as it is necessary to faith. . . . And the fruits of repentance still more remotely, as they are necessary to the increase or continuance of repentance. And even in this ssense, they are only necessary on supposition,—if there be time and opportunity for them.''⁷²

The walk toward the kingdom begins with repentance and continues with

faith.⁷³ To repent, one must first recognize oneself as sinner.⁷⁴ *Metanoia* is a 180-degree turning: from sin to grace.⁷⁵ Repentance involves that moral seriousness about oneself that readies one to turn joyfully to the mercy of God.⁷⁶

Penitent Belief

Faith, the reception of that mercy, is not simply intellectual assent but trusting that the Word spoken on the cross and in the resurrection is for me, asddressed personally to me, and able to change me thoroughly. One who repents and believes has his feet already on the path to true religion, which is the love of God addressing us in the needs of the neighbor, where loving responsiveness is made possible through faith.⁷⁷

Peace with God means reconciliation with the holy One with whom one has been long estranged. This *shalom* is a key evidence of the kingdom of God and of true religion. Only God bestows this peace. Once bestowed itis not expended or delpeted except by our own decision to reject it. Grace enables this peace to be sustained as long as faith is receptive to it.⁷⁸ It is a taste of the world to come. It enables a life of righteousness, peace, and joy, a blessed

⁶⁹Letter to Thomas Church, June 17, 1746, LJW 2:268.
⁷⁰Letter to Thomas Church, June 17, 1746, LJW 2:268; cf. VII:396–97.
⁷¹Letter to Thomas Church, Feb. 2, 1756, 2:187, italics added; cf. IX:112.
⁷²"Principles of a Methodist Farther Explained," VIII:428; cf. #43 "The Scripture Way of Salvation," iii, 2:162–69; B1:349, 458, 477; 2:162; SS 2:394.
⁷³Letter to Thomas Church, Feb. 2, 1745, ii.1, LJW 224–25; 2:188; V:168.
⁷⁴#7 "The Way to the Kingdom," ii.1, 1:225; cf. "Of Repentance and Obedience," from discussion of Roman Catechism, X:94–102; B1:147, 245, 335–37, 403, 480f., 653; 2:230f.; 4:299f.
⁷⁵Since repentance means a true and deep knowing of oneself, the further one progresses in the reception of sanctifying grace, the more aware one is of one's sin. See #6 "The Righteousness of Faith," ii.6; and #14 "The Repentance of Believers."
⁷⁶#7 "The Way to the Kingdom," ii.1–2, 1:225–27; #6 "The Righteousness of Faith," ii.6; cf. B1:126f., 252f., 335f.; 3:113; 4:411f.
⁷⁷#7 "The Way to the Kingdom," ii.9–13, 1:230–31; cf. Hymns on Praying for Repentance, 7:188–201, and Hymns for Mourners convinced of Sin, *A Collection of Hymns for the Use of the People Called Methodists*, 7:210–234.
⁷⁸B1:349, 458, 477; 2:162; SS 2:394.

life that already anticipates the bliss that is to come eternally for those who love the Lord.[79]

FAITH

Three definitive homilies on faith were published in 1788: #106, 117, and 119. Their common theme: what the eye of faith can sense, the natural senses cannot. Faith is a vital spiritual sense that enables the believer to live spiritually, seeing beyond the visible to the invisible, eternal world.[80]

On Faith, Hebrews 11:6

Heb. 11:6: "Without faith it is impossible to please him." (Homily #106 1788 B3:491–501; J#106 VII:195–202)

Several providential dispensations of grace are seen in the gradual coming of faith into human history:[81]

● The general revelation of God's existence and justice to all people, commonly termed the *heathen* dispensation of grace to all who believe there is a God to be sought;

● The historical revelation to the people of Israel through the law, the *Mosaic* dispensation entrusted with the oracles of God;

● The *expectation of the coming* of the Christ as exemplified prototypically in John the Baptist, who was able to recognize the Lamb of God, and who preached repentance pointing to another yet to come; and finally

● *The coming of the fullness of faith in Jesus Christ*, the Christian dispensation of those who have received the spirit of adoption.[82]

Faith's Types and Stages

Within these dispensations, it is possible to enumerate a number of types of rudimentary faith that are distinguishable from the faith that saves.

1. While the empirical scientist is not usually thought of as a person of faith, there is a faith commitment in scientific inquiry. For it takes an immense axiomatic leap to enter into the realm of scientific inquiry by *assuming* the intelligibility of nature. *Scientific belief* often proceeds with the radical, unexamined faith assumption that the material world of causality can be meaningfully investigated.[83]

2. As to the *rationalistic faith* typical of academics, some lean toward the hedonic-sensual type, having "a downright appetite to mix with mud."[84] Others are more inclined toward an idealist-moral faith, who, though they may hold that God exists apart from matter, reject any knowledge of God through the history of biblical revelation. In either case both hedonic and moral rationalists, having voluntarily turned from hope in God, cling stubbornly to their own self-defined versions of rudimentary faith, distinguishable from the faith that saves.[85]

3. The primitive faith of the nations (or heathen faith) functions without divine revelation in the history of Israel, except as it is anticipatively grasped through reason and conscience. Lacking illumination rather than sincerity, the goodness of the heathen often shames those communities gathered by

---

[79]#7 "The Way to the Kingdom," ii.11–13, 1:231.

[80]B4:30–38, 53–56; EA 11:46–47, 54; JWO 275f., 293–95, 386–88, 395f.

[81]Relying upon John W. Fletcher, *The Doctrines of Grace and Justice*, 1777, sec. I, pp. 1–13.

[82]#106 "On Faith, Hebrews 11:6," proem.3 3:493.

[83]For some this takes the form of assuming that "there is nothing but matter in the universe," #106 "On Faith, Hebrews 11:6," i.i.

[84]#106 "On Faith, Hebrews 11:6," i.2.

[85]#106 "On Faith, Hebrews 11:6," i.1, 2, 3:493.

divine revelation in history.[86] "To believe the being and attributes of God is *the faith of an heathen.*"[87] It functions according to that light of conscience and reason that it has received.

4. The theistic and moral *faith of Islam* at times puts Christians to shame.[88] Wesley spoke of the writings of the medieval Muslim mystic, Abu Bakr Ibn Al-Tufail, as containing "all the principles of pure religion and undefiled," as one who had been "taught of God, by his inward voice, all the essentials of true religion."[89]

5. Wesley distinguished the faith of Judaism from that of Christianity in this way: "To believe the Old Testament and trust in Him that was to come was the faith of a Jew. To believe Christ gave himself for me is the faith of a Christian."[90] Wesley was disinclined to pass harsh judgment on modern Jews, leaving all judgment to God. Though "the veil is still upon their hearts" as to recognition of *Mashiach*, the anointed One, "it is not our part to pass sentence."[91] It is clear, however, that there is wonderful faith in the people of Israel who received the historical revelation of God through Moses and throughout the history of Israel and the prophets, leading to the messianic hope.

Of Jews Charles wrote: "Justly they claim the softest prayer from us."[92] Of their historical expectation of a renewed Israel, he wrote:

Rebuilt by his command,
Jerusalem shall rise,

Her temple on Moriah stand
Again, and touch the skies.

Send then thy servants forth,
To call the Hebrews home,
From east, and west, and south, and north,
Let all the wanderers come;
Where'er in lands unknown
The fugitives remain,
Bid every creature help them on,
Thy holy mount to gain.

. . . With Israel's myriads sealed
Let all the nations meet,
And show the mystery fulfilled,
Thy family complete.[93]

6. Pointing more definitely toward the coming Messiah so as to bridge Old and New Testaments, is the proto-Christian preaching of repentance seen in the unique and singular *faith of John the Forerunner*, the Baptist, a faith peculiar to himself, anticipatory of faith in the Son through the Spirit.[94]

7. The *formally orthodox faith of medieval scholasticism* conceptually contains all that is necessary for salvation, conceived as the faith of assent, even though it proceeds to add dogmas not revealed in Scripture. The formally orthodox faith of the *Protestant scholasticism* in general believes neither more nor less than what is found in Scripture as necessary to salvation. Yet in both Protestant and Catholic orthodoxy, insofar as faith is treated primarily as conceptual conviction of truths, it does not reach the depth of saving faith. Faith viewed as mere cerebral acknowl-

---

[86]B1:119; 3:494–95; SS 1:39.

[87]Letter to Theophilus Lessey, January 1787, LJW 7:362, italics added.

[88]#106 "On Faith, Hebrews 11:6," ii.3, 3:500; cf. LJW 6:118; CH 7:608; LJW 1:277; 5:250; 6:123, 371.

[89]#106 "On Faith, Hebrews 11:6," i.4, 3:494; Wesley knew him as Hai Ebn Yokton. He had read in 1734 *The Life of Ebenezer Yokton, An Exact Entire Mystic.* Cf. #44 "Original Sin," ii.4.

[90]Letter to Theophilus Lessey, January 1787, LJW 7:362; cf. LJW 7:307.

[91]#106 "On Faith, Hebrews 11:6," i.6, 3:495.

[92]CH 7:615.

[93]CH 7:617.

[94]#106 "On Faith, Hebrews 11:6," i.3–6, 3:494–95.

edgment of abstract propositional truth does not save, for even the devil may be aware of the truth of revelation, that God has come into our midst.[95] Wesley did not deny that many in the church of Rome and in the churches of Protestantism have received the saving faith that works through love, but he was also aware of a dismal neglect of the proclamation of saving faith in both traditions.[96]

Distinguishing the Faith of the Servant From the Faith of the Son or Daughter

To those with the *servile faith of a servant*, who fear God but have not learned to love God as Father, Wesley says: "You have already great reason to praise God that he has called you to his honourable service. Fear not. Continue crying unto him; 'and you shall see greater things than these.'"[97] The faith of the servant, or faith under the law, brings one closer to the fear of God and the working of righteousness.[98] The faith of the servant is preparatory to receiving adoption by the conviction that "the life that I now live, I live by *faith in the Son* of God, who loved me, and gave himself for me."[99]

The *filial faith embraced by sons and daughters* is rather "properly and directly a divine conviction whereby every child of God is enabled to testify, 'The life that I now live, I live by faith in the Son of God, who loved me, and gave himself for me.'" One is "living at that very moment in a state of accep-

tance," not as a servant but as a son or daughter freely adopted into the family of God. "They will receive the *faith* of the children of God by his *revealing* his only-begotten Son in their hearts." Because you are sons and daughters, "God hath sent forth the Spirit of his Son into your hearts, crying, 'Abba, Father;' that is, giving you a childlike confidence in him, together with a kind affection toward him." This inward witness of the Spirit "the servant hath not. Yet let no man discourage him; rather, lovingly exhort him to expect it every moment."[100]

In whatever proximate degree of faith one has thus far received or secured, one is called to press on fully to receive the Spirit of adoption as a child of God.[101] The history of religions as a history of varied modes of embryonic faith is thus viewed not negatively but positively as making ready for faith in God's own coming. "There is no reason why you should be satisfied with the faith of a materialist, a heathen, or a deist; nor indeed with that of a servant . . . press on till you receive the Spirit of adoption."[102]

On the Discoveries of Faith

Heb. 11:1: "Now faith is the evidence of things not seen." [Homily #117 1788 B4:28–38; J#110 VII:231–38]

Wesley argued for the incremental growth of faith through stages toward full maturity.

[95]On the faith of devils, see B1:119–20, 138–39; 9:52–53; SS 1:38, 63, 284.
[96]#106 "On Faith, Hebrews 11:6," i.7–10, 3:495–97.
[97]#106 "On Faith, Hebrews 11:6," i.11, 3:497; John 1:50.
[98]#9 "The Spirit of Bondage and of Adoption," iv.3, 4.
[99]Gal. 2:20; #106 "On Faith, Hebrews 11:6," i.12, 3:498.
[100]#106 "On Faith, Hebrews 11:6," sec. 10–12, 3:496–98. On the etymology and interpretation of *elenchos*, see B2:160–61, 167–68, 368–69; 4:187–88; 9:95, 177; FA 11:106–7, 444.
[101]On degrees of faith see B3:175–76; 3:491–98; 9:111, 164–65; LJW 2:214; 5:200; JJW 1:481–83; 2:328–29; JWO 68f., 356–62.
[102]#106 "On Faith, Hebrews 11:6," sec. 13, 3:498.

Sense Knowledge

Though some think that ideas are innate to persons, Wesley agreed with Locke that "there is nothing in the understanding which was not first perceived by some of the senses."[103] All the knowledge of nature that we have acquired is derived from the senses.[104]

The five senses have different degrees of extension, so that sight extends farther than hearing—one may see the moon but not hear the meteor that strikes it—and hearing much farther than smelling, tasting, or feeling.[105] But none of the empirical senses, however astute, can reach beyond the visible, temporal world.[106]

Faith's Knowing

Faith, beholding the evidences of what is not seen, unlike the physical senses, reaches beyond the visible world.[107] Faith is "the demonstrative evidence of things unseen, the supernatural evidence of things invisible, not perceivable by the eyes of flesh, or by any of our natural senses or faculties . . . whereby the spiritual man discerneth God."[108] The discerning appropriation of invisible evidences occurs by faith.

God has appointed faith to "supply the defects of sense." Faith's task begins where the natural senses end.[109] Being given an ability to see things not seen is of "the very essence of faith; love and obedience, the inseparable properties of it."[110]

What sort of knowing requires faith? Such matters as the origin and destiny of the soul, the spiritual creation, the Incarnation, the moral attributes of God, the Trinity, and the coming judgment are known by faith. *By faith one knows* that one has a soul, created in the image of God, and that having fallen from that image, one is "totally unable to quicken my own soul."[111] By faith one knows, grasps, and "sees" so to speak, that there are other orders of spiritual creation, some of whom blessedly dwell with God, and others who resist God in misery and unrighteousness.[112] By faith one knows that God, who transcends all creatures, was made flesh and died for our salvation. By faith one knows that God is infinite in power, wisdom, justice, mercy and holiness.

By faith the one God is known as Father, Son, and Spirit.[113] By faith we perceive that the righteous dwell with Christ. Faith looks toward the coming final judgment when the righteous will inherit the kingdom and the wicked will depart to the dissolution epitomized by fire.[114] The Spirit prepares us for this kingdom by convicting us of sin and teaching us to fear God's judgment and trust God's love.[115] Sense experience yields only minimal formal knowledge of these matters.

[103]Aristotle, *On the Soul* III.7 (430); 4:29n; EA sec. 32, 11:56.
[104]#117 "On the Discoveries of Faith," sec. 1, 4:29.
[105]#117 "On the Discoveries of Faith," sec. 1–2, 4:29–30; EA sec. 7, 11:46–7.
[106]#117 "On the Discoveries of Faith," sec. 2–3, 4:30.
[107]CH 7:194–95, 315–18, 489–90, 515–16.
[108]EA sec. 6, 11:46; B1:119–21, 138–39; LJW 4:174–76; 3:385.
[109]#117 "On the Discoveries of Faith," sec. 4, 4:30; B11:46–47.
[110]Minutes, 1744, June 25, Q8, JWO 138.
[111]#117 "On the Discoveries of Faith," sec. 5, 4:30–31.
[112]#117 "On the Discoveries of Faith," sec. 6, 4:31.
[113]#117 "On the Discoveries of Faith," sec. 7, 4:31–32.
[114]#117 "On the Discoveries of Faith," sec. 8, 4:32.
[115]#117 "On the Discoveries of Faith," sec. 11, 4:34.

The Growth of Faith
From Strength to Strength

Insofar as we have learned to obey God out of fear, we have the faith of a servant. We are called to press on until we learn to obey God out of grateful love, which is the great privilege of the children of God. The Spirit attests to our spirits our adoption as sons and daughters of the reconciling Father.[116] Beginning with new birth, the faith of the child of God grows toward spiritual maturity in "the faith of the fathers," being delivered from doubt and fear,[117] and from "all inward as well as outward sin, from evil desires and evil tempers, as well as from evil words and works."[118] Healthy faith grows steadily through gradual stages from being a babe in Christ still having anxieties and guilts, toward growing up as a maturing person gradually coming better to refract the holiness of God in one's behavioral life.[119]

As maturing persons in Christ they continue to grow from strength to strength, with the knowledge of God's Word abiding in them, toward "the consciousness of the divine favour without any intermission," leading toward full confidence that walks in the hope of dwelling and reigning with God eternally.[120] Praying without ceasing, and taking up their cross daily,[121] they are "able to comprehend, with all the saints, what is the length, and breadth, and height, and depth, and to know that love of Christ which passeth knowledge" (Eph. 3:18–19). "The more we exert our faith, the more 'tis increased."[122]

Walking by Sight and Walking by Faith

2 Cor. 5:7: "We walk by faith, not by sight." [Homily #119 1788 B4:48–59; J#113 VII:256–64]

Walking by Faith

Those who have been dead in trespasses have been quickened and given new senses to behold spiritual things. Adopted into the family of God as sons and daughters, they no longer walk by fear in a servile relationship with the Lawgiver.[123] No one can begin to walk by faith until first born of the Spirit. One is thereby given new senses evangelically to discern the requirement of faith.[124] " 'By this faith we are saved' from all uneasiness of mind, from the anguish of a wounded spirit, from discontent, from fear, and sorrow of heart."

Christians "walk by faith, not by sight" (2 Cor. 5:7), not by the five physical senses alone, but by the grace-enabled new sensibilities of faith. This homily offers a concise description of the life that proceeds step by step by faith insofar as it lives by grace.[125]

One cannot give this faith to oneself. One can only receive it from God. "The more you labour so to do, the more you will be convinced, 'it is the gift of God.' "[126]

---

[116]#117 "On the Discoveries of Faith," sec. 13–14, 4:35–36.

[117]#117 "On the Discoveries of Faith," sec. 15, 4:36.

[118]#117 "On the Discoveries of Faith," sec. 16, 4:37.

[119]LJW 2:215; 3:213–321; JWO 231–34.

[120]#117 "On the Discoveries of Faith," sec. 17, 4:37–38.

[121]SS 2:292.

[122]Minutes, 1744, June 25, Q13, JWO 138; cf. CH 7:690–94.

[123]#119 "Walking by Sight and Walking by Faith," sec. 1, 4:49; cf. #10 "The Witness of the Spirit, I," i.12; #106 "On Faith, Hebrews 11:6," i.10.

[124]#119 "Walking by Sight and Walking by Faith," sec. 2, 4:49.

[125]#119 "Walking by Sight and Walking by Faith," sec. 1–9, 4:49–52.

[126]EA sec. 8, 10, 11:47–48.

Lacking this new birth from above, we walk solely by sight, knowing only what the five senses reveal.[127] Nothing of the invisible world, full of God, is directly accessible to sight, sound, smell, touch or taste.[128] Our external senses serve us in our clay houses, but there is far more to life than body.[129] Physical senses "have nothing to do with the invisible world: they are not adapted to it."[130]

The Light That Enlightens This Walk

A succession of degrees of faith may be seen in the progression from the glimmering light of primitive crude faith of primitive cultures, from the faith of Noah through the faith of Socrates.[131]

Some inkling of God's presence remains in all generations of the history of religions. But all these "lights" together avail no further than faint twilight when compared to the light of revelation that can walk by faith in the Son. These forms of anticipatory faith are fulfilled by faith in God's own coming in Jesus Christ.[132]

Faith illumines where the senses fail. Walking by faith "opens eyes" to the life that is "hid with Christ in God."[133] The things that are seen are temporal, things not seen eternal. Those who live by faith walk each step by faith, judging each situation in relation to the invisible. They sojourn in the temporal world, but as citizens of an eternal city. They do not love the world or the things

of the world, but desire chiefly the glory that abides forever, seeking in the general tenor of their lives "the things that are above."[134]

True religion is not merely moral decency or harmlessness, however admirable, or the formal observance of divine ordinances. True religion is "no less than living in eternity, and walking in eternity; and hereby walking in the love of God and man—in lowliness, meekness, and resignation. This, and this alone, is that 'life which is hid with Christ in God.' He alone who experiences this 'dwells in God, and God in him.' "[135] True religion is to live and walk in the love of God and humanity by faith, so as to do God's will on earth as in heaven. Yet precisely this is regarded as madness by those who walk only by sight.[136]

Walking by faith is contrasted with dissipation, the art of forgetting God, studied inattention to the whole invisible world known by faith.[137] Those who walk by faith flee from dissipation, being completely and steadily attentive to God, having God in all their thoughts, eternity always before their eyes, having constant regard for that which remains unseen.[138]

REGENERATION

Regeneration is the birthing work of God the Spirit by which the pardoned sinner becomes a child of God, loving and serving God with the affections of

[127]B3:327; 4:30, 48–52, 288.
[128]#119 "Walking by Sight and Walking by Faith," sec. 4–7, 4:50–51.
[129]#119 "Walking by Sight and Walking by Faith," sec. 6, 4:50; cf. #28 "Sermon on the Mount, VIII," sec. 21.
[130]#119 "Walking by Sight and Walking by Faith," sec. 6, 4:50; cf. #10 "Witness of the Spirit, I, i.12; and #117 "On the Discoveries of Faith," sec. 8.
[131]#119 "Walking by Sight and Walking by Faith," sec. 8–10, 4:51–52.
[132]#119 "Walking by Sight and Walking by Faith," sec. 11–12, 4:53f.
[133]#119 "Walking by Sight and Walking by Faith," sec. 13, 4:54.
[134]#119 "Walking by Sight and Walking by Faith," sec. 16, 17, 4:56–57.
[135]#119 "Walking by Sight and Walking by Faith," sec. 18, 4:57.
[136]#119 "Walking by Sight and Walking by Faith," sec. 19, 4:57–58.
[137]#119 "Walking by Sight and Walking by Faith," sec. 20, 4:58.
[138]#119 "Walking by Sight and Walking by Faith," sec. 21, 4:59.

the heart, so as to receive the Spirit of adoption by whom we are enabled to say Abba, Father.[139]

The new birth brings into being not only a new life, but a new will, and a new beginning for the redeemed affections. A new spiritual nature is being offered by the mercy of God so that one is born again into a new capacity better to mirror the original image of God in humanity.[140] God's image in humanity, having become distorted by the intergenerational history of social and individual sin, original and actual, in this way is being renewed by the life-giving power of the Spirit.[141]

The regenerating work of the Spirit allows these our earthen vessels to yield so as to reflect anew the love, power, and goodness of God. This new life is quickened by faith made active in love. It is the renewal of the whole person in righteousness by the power of the Spirit.[142] The work of the Spirit is acting at each discrete phase to renew and energize the whole life of the baptized faithful. That we are made partakers of the divine nature means that we share in God's own life through this regenerating grace.

The Inseparability of Justification, Regeneration, and Adoption

If the cross embodies God's act for us, the new birth makes effective the outworking of God's act in us. Justification changes one's relation to God. New birth changes one's inmost motivation and disposition of soul. *Justification restores us by pardon to the favor of God. New birth restores us by faith to the image of God. Justification takes away the guilt of sin. New birth takes away the power of sin.*[143]

God's justifying act on the cross is conceptually distinct from our new birth of spirit, yet inseparable experientially—inseparable in point of time, yet distinct in nature. One does not first have a justification experience and subsequently a regeneration experience. It is amid, not chronologically following, the reception of justifying grace that one is reborn.[144]

In this rebirth the active agency is God's own Spirit imparting new life. The imputation of the gift of righteousness of the Son on the cross sets the context for an impartation—the actual subjective, motivational and behavioral giving of new life through the Spirit. The gift of atoning grace by the Son begins in us and is continued in us through the sanctifying grace empowered by the Spirit. In personal regeneration we experience the personal appropriation of the gift formally and juridically given on the cross.

Legal, Biological, and Filial Metaphors in Complementarity

By adoption we mean that the pardoned sinner becomes a child of God, welcomed and freely adopted into the family of God, sharing in that family fully, heir of the inheritance of that family, inheritor of eternal life, delivered from the power of the corruption that reigns in the history of sin.

In this way the born-again metaphor is intimately connected with both the teachings of justification and adoption. Justification is a *legal* metaphor showing that by our trust in Jesus Christ we

---

[139]Letter to Rev. Mr. Potter, Nov. 4, 1758, IX:89–90; and to Rev. Mr. Downes, Nov. 17, 1759, 12, IX:104.
[140]B1:279, 415f., 432–35; 2:186–201; 4:173; CH 7:234–83.
[141]CH 7:553–81.
[142]Letter to the Bishop of Gloucester, 11:459–539.
[143]LJW 1:327; 3:358; 4:38, 65; CH 7:234–83; B1:279, 415f., 432–35; 2:186–201; 4:173; 11:520–27.
[144]#107 "On God's Vineyard," i.6–10, 3:506–8.

are in fact accounted righteous, having been freed from the guilt and the penalty of our sin.

Regeneration is a *biological* metaphor, a word picture of a birth into a new life that has a new spiritual nature, a new motivational life engendered by the grace and love of God. The moral nature of the penitent believer is being quickened, enlivened spiritually into a life capable of faith, hope, and love.

Adoption is a *filial* metaphor pointing to inclusion within the family of God. The word picture is one of warmth, love, and belonging, showing that by our new relation and new life we have become his wanted children freed from the alien mastery of a creditor or oppressor, now having the witness of the Spirit that we are children of God. This adoption tells of a new relationship to God as Abba. It assumes a previous estrangement from the family that has now been overcome, so that the prodigal is again drawn back into the family, adopted into full rights of inheritance of that family.

We become sons and daughters in this family, born into this family, sustained daily by the preaching of the Word, sacramental life, and spiritual discipline. Even when we fall into sin, we are still supported by a community of faith that offers this Word, embodied in its sacrament, and accompanied by its admonition, that brings us back into a restored and renewed relationship to God.

The New Birth

John 3:7: "You must be born again." [Homily #45 1760 B2:186–201; J#45 VI:65–77]

Among issues decisively examined in this homily: Is new birth the equivalent of justification? What does it mean to be renewed in the image of God? To die to sin? If so prone to fall, how are we made able to stand? Why is rebirth necessary? In what sense is it even possible that one may be born again? How is new birth related to baptism?[145]

The Ordering of the Relation of Justification and New Birth

We are not first justified and then reborn, but by being justified are reborn. The two doctrines are intimately woven together. We are not talking about a chronological sequence in which justification first comes and then at some later date sanctification occurs. In the order of time neither is before the other. Chronologically you cannot say that justification precedes new birth. But in order of thinking, i.e., logically, there is a distinction between justification and new birth in that God's justifying activity of imputing righteousness is the logical precondition or presupposition of the Holy Spirit's impartation of the gift of new life to us. Justification is God's work *for us*, which calls forth the work of the Spirit *in us* to bring into birth our responsiveness to God's work for us.[146] These move together dynamically. Son and Spirit work together for our salvation.[147]

The justifying action of Christ for us is presupposed as logically prior to any talk of anything we can do in response to it. Justification is by grace alone through faith alone. New birth focuses special energy upon the new life that begins in response to justifying grace. The Protestant tradition has heard too little talk of the practical application of

[145]#45 "The New Birth," proem.2, 2:188.
[146]#45 "The New Birth," proem.1, 2:187; cf. #19 "The Great Privilege of those that are Born of God," proem.1; #5 "Justification by Faith," ii.1.
[147]#45 "The New Birth," iv.3, 2:198.

justification to the actual processes of behavioral change. That is what the bands and societies of Wesley were seeking to actualize and embody.[148]

Renewal in the Natural, Political, and Moral Image of God

We are not originally made to be sinners. We are made good and only then we choose to become sinners. But the fact that we are created good does not mean that we are created immutably good.[149]

There is a threefold working distinction in the Wesleyan evangelical tradition between the natural, political, and moral image of God in humanity. The original creation of humanity stood in the *natural* image of God by which human beings have free self-determining will and immortality. We are created in the image of God in the sense of having some measure of natural free will. When fallen, the will ceases being able to elicit moral goods on its own initiative.[150]

By the *political* image of God is meant that human beings are permitted and called to bring tranquil order and governance to the world, to have responsible dominion or stewardship over the earth. We are created in the image of God in the sense of having some measure of political competence to organize society toward relative justice and decent governance.[151]

Most importantly, we are made in the *moral* image of God, by being made for righteousness and holiness. What does it mean morally to refract the image of the holy God? Before the history of sin,

human nature was like a diamond, beautifully capable of gloriously refracting the holiness of God. With the Fall that capacity for refraction has been radically marred and reduced. With the history of sin, the natural, political, and moral image of God in us has not been altogether lost but has been grossly disfigured by that history.[152]

Able to Stand, Liable to Fall

Human beings are created in the image of God *able to stand but liable to fall*.[153] Those who understand this distinction will be very far along in grasping Wesley's basic anthropology. In the pre-fallen condition God gives the grace and power to human life to stand accountably before God so as to mirror this natural, political, and moral image; but this ability to stand was perpetually susceptible to mutation, forever alterable by freedom.[154]

No person is created immutable, for it is the very essence of personhood to be created with a self-determinative capacity to change. In this mutability human history did in fact change for the worse. That is the story of the Fall. Whatever good is given in creation is vulnerable to fallenness, to failure of the will to hear and respond adequately to the command of God.[155] If able to stand, the liability to falling is not necessitated. If liable to fall, the ability to stand is not immutable.

Death From Sin

In Adam's fall and Eve's fall, something in all of us has died, or is destined to die. The whole history of sin is a

---

[148]#45 "The New Birth," proem, 2:187–88.
[149]#45 "The New Birth," 1.2, 2:189.
[150]#45 "The New Birth," i.1, 2:188.
[151]#45 "The New Birth," i.1, 2:188.
[152]#45 "The New Birth," 1.1, 2:188.
[153]#45 "The New Birth," 1.2, 2:189.
[154]#45 "The New Birth," 1.3, 2:190.
[155]#45 "The New Birth," i.1, 2:189.

history of spiritual death that cannot awaken itself to new life.[156] This is the pervasive condition of the history of sin: spiritual death as exemplified prototypically by the case history of the first human beings. The death they died was not merely a death of the body, but a spiritual death in which life in God is lost and the image of God defaced.[157] The consequences of the first fall and each of our subsequent fallings of human freedom ripple on out to influence subsequent human sufferers.[158]

The answer to why we *must* be born again is best framed historically, not abstractly: we all actually share from the outset in this tangible history of sin and death. Every discrete act following from our freedom has become subject to corruption.[159]

This is the grounding assumption of all regeneration teaching. All who in Adam die must be born anew to mirror once again the divine goodness. We must be born anew because we have died, in the sense that the most vital spiritual root of our humanity has perished. This does not mean that the moral image of God is totally lost, but radically disfigured and shattered, remaining only in fragmented form.[160]

Whether One May Be Born Again

We get a refreshing glimpse of Wesley as a critical historical exegete in his homily "The New Birth." He was especially interested in the ways in which biblical metaphors were being refashioned in the intertestamental period. He was intrigued by the analogies between Jewish circumcision and Christian baptism. The expression "being born again" was not an expression first used by Jesus in his conversation with Nicodemus, but already available to the intertestamental Jewish tradition, referring to non-Jews who had converted to Judaism.[161] In that conversion, they went through a ritual cleansing process analogous to baptism, as a preparatory act to circumcision and actual entry into the covenant community. When ritually cleansed, the converts were said to be born again. Converts into Judaism were baptized as a type of dying to an old way and being born into a new way.[162]

This tradition illumines the radical nature of what John the Baptist was doing. For John was baptizing not non-Jews but Jews! That is precisely what made the Forerunner so controversial. Prior to the call of John, Gentiles could be converts to Judaism through this humbling ritual act of purification and cleansing that later became the pattern of Christian baptism. John's baptism was saying, the chosen people now must repent.[163]

The Mystery of Birth

How are we born again? Scripture does not offer an empirical description of the how of the new birth. Rather the opposite: We *do not know how* the Spirit works in this renewing process, but we *do know that* it happens.[164] While no one can disinterestedly describe the precise way the Spirit enables

---

[156]DOS IX:404–9.

[157]#45 "The New Birth," 1.3, 2:190.

[158]#45 "The New Birth," 1.4, 2:190.

[159]For further development of the effects of the Fall, see #44 "Original Sin," i.3; #57 "On the Fall of Man"; #130 "On Living without God," sec. 15.

[160]#45 "The New Birth," 1.4, 2:190.

[161]#45 "The New Birth," ii.1, 2, 2:190–91.

[162]#45 "The New Birth," ii.1–3, 2:190–91.

[163]#45 "The New Birth," ii.3, 2:191.

[164]#45 "The New Birth," ii.1, 2:191.

new birth, there can be little doubt that new life in Christ has come into being.

The basic scriptural analogy: The Spirit blows where it wills. Who can say where or how the Spirit moves or is going to move? Like wind, we know *that* the Spirit is there, but we cannot account for it precisely; no matter how much meteorological evidence we compile, there remain elements of chaotic absurdity in our conceptualities and vast holes in our data bases. God does not offer himself up neatly for our objective inquiry, for God being Spirit is not an object for our laboratory dissection. Objects are by definition visible. God is not reducible to anything visible.[165]

No one before being born knows what it means to be born. If I am a fetus in my mother's womb, I have some awareness that there is something outside my immediate environment, but no actual specific knowledge of what is ahead for me. It is a maturing, unfolding surprise.[166] That analogy is like the transition going on when the Spirit is awakening one to faithful sonship or daughterhood in the family of God.[167]

The Spirit is moving us from a lack of spiritual awareness to a birthing in which one becomes suddenly and dramatically aware of new life. New birth is "the change wrought in the whole soul by the almighty Spirit of God," when it is renewed after the image of God, "when the love of the world is changed into the love of God, pride into humility, passion into meekness," "whereby the 'earthly, sensual and devilish' mind is turned into 'the mind which is in Christ.' "[168] A new spiritual consciousness and life is given that elicits a healing *shalom*, a serenity that results from reconciliation with God.

Whether New Birth Is Requisite to Salvation

The text, "You must be born again" (John 3:7), provides the scriptural grounding of the teaching of the necessity of regeneration.[169] There is a precise requirement implied in the phrase: "you must," in order to live within and toward the coming reign of God (John 3:7). The sinner cannot be restored into the image of God until having once again received the renewed capacity to refract the holiness of God by which human happiness is restored.[170]

As long as ungodly passions and tempers "reign in any soul, happiness has no place there. But they must reign till the bent of our nature is changed, that is, till we are born again."[171] "Gospel holiness is no less than the image of God stamped upon the heart."[172]

Nothing necessitated the Fall. It was absurdly chosen.[173] There is no way to speak of the necessity of the new birth without recalling the fundamental predicament of human history (the enigma of sin) from its beginnings: Adam was given freedom, and the sufficient grace to sustain a day-by-day walk in a trusting relation with God.[174]

The Intended End of New Birth

The purposeful objective of this birth is a growing life of holiness, salvation,

---

[165]#45 "The New Birth," ii.2, 2:191.
[166]#45 "The New Birth," ii.4, 2:192–93.
[167]#45 "The New Birth," ii.4, 2:193.
[168]#45 "The New Birth," ii.5, 2:193–94; James 3:15; Phil. 2:5.
[169]DOS IX:307–14; cf. I:214.
[170]Letter to "John Smith," June 1746, LJW 2:71.
[171]#45 "The New Birth," iii.3, 2:195–96.
[172]#45 "The New Birth," iii.1, 2:194.
[173]#45 "The New Birth," i.1, 2:188.
[174]#45 "The New Birth," ii.3, 4, 2:189–90.

and happiness, where the image of God is being constantly renewed in the heart. No one lacking holiness will see the Lord (Heb. 12:14). Holiness is the necessary precondition of joy.[175] The text contends for "the necessity of holiness in order to glory—and consequently of the new birth, since none can be holy except he be born again."[176]

To be happy finally is to live an accountable life before God, fully enjoying the source and end of all good. This blessedness is not fully grasped as a hedonic, humanistic, individualistic, narcissistic happiness, for it is always set within the frame of eternity.[177]

Whether Baptism Constitutes the New Birth

The homily concludes with a delicate discussion of the relation of the sacrament of baptism and the new birth. Baptism, strictly speaking, is not the same as rebirth. Baptism is the sign of regeneration.[178] Regeneration is the thing signified and baptism is the sign.[179] Baptism sacramentally points to that reception of regenerating grace that is nascently present in baptism in the name of the Father, Son, and Spirit.[180] There is no baptism without water, the life-giving, cleansing physical element.[181]

Baptism is "the outward sign our one Lord has been pleased to appoint of all that inward and spiritual grace which he is continually bestowing upon his church. It is likewise a precious means

whereby this faith and hope are given to those that diligently seek him."[182]

Death and rebirth images are profoundly embedded in baptism.[183] That is what baptism bespeaks: a dying and a going down into death, and being raised anew with the risen Lord (Rom. 6). New birth of spirit may be embryonically anticipated in baptism, even while not maturely or experientially possessed. One cannot simply claim that because one is baptized, one is therefore reborn. "There may sometimes be the outward sign where there is not the inward grace."[184]

Although within the frame of reference of the established church, Wesley was assuming that with few exceptions most of his hearers were baptized, he was nonetheless insisting that even then they must be born again in the sense of receiving actively and joyfully the very regenerating grace of the Spirit that baptism offers and manifests and to which it points. The grace given with baptism is a participatory grace that looks toward further actualizing confirmation in our behavior, our choices. This is a standard article of Anglican teaching, that baptism is the sacramental seed of the grace of regeneration.[185]

Baptism is the charter of redemption, a constituting liturgical moment that then asks to be lived out. Though baptized only once on a particular day, we keep on living daily. The grace of baptism points beyond itself as a visible

---

[175]#45 "The New Birth," iii.1, 2:194.
[176]#45 "The New Birth," iii.2, 2:195.
[177]#45 "The New Birth," iii.2, 3, 2:195.
[178]B2:196–200; 1:428–30; FA 11:107, cf. 11:253; JWO 321–25.
[179]FA VIII:48–49; B1:143, 415, 428–30; 2:196–200.
[180]#74 "Of the Church," 3:49–50.
[181]#45 "The New Birth," iv.1, 2:196–97; cf. "Treatise on Baptism," 1756.
[182]#74 "Of the Church," 3:49.
[183]"On Baptism," JWO 317–32.
[184]#45 "The New Birth," iv.2, 2:197.
[185]Thirty-nine Articles, BCP; on the relation of baptism and subsequent decision see LJW 4:235; 5:330; JWO 318–31; CH 7:646–48.

event to this new birth and the beginnings of behavioral transformation.[186] So just showing your baptismal certificate is not enough. God wants to see a life lived out in response to the grace of baptism.[187]

"I tell a sinner, 'You must be born again.' 'No', say you, 'He was born again in baptism. Therefore he cannot be born again now.' Alas! What trifling is this? What if he was *then* a child of God? he is *now* manifestly a 'child of the devil'? . . . Therefore do not play upon words. He *must* go through an entire change of heart," without which "if either he or you die . . . your baptism will be so far from profiting you that it will greatly increase your damnation."[188]

"The being 'sealed by the Spirit' in the full sense of the word I take to imply two things: first, the receiving the whole image of God, the whole mind which was in Christ, as the wax receives the whole impression of the seal when it is strongly and properly applied; secondly the full assurance of hope, or a clear and permanent confidence of being with God in glory. Either of these may be given . . . separate from the other. When both are joined together, then I believe they constitute the seal of the Spirit. But even this admits of various degrees."[189]

Breathing Grace: Beginning and Continuing

Certainly a genuine gift is given to us in baptism, but grace has not thereby completed its work, but only begun it. The grace of baptism places one in this new community of response where this new circumcision of the heart is taking place. We ourselves must freely join in with God's Spirit working in us. Baptism enables and requires a renewal of our hearts, eliciting an inward change in us that seeks to become outwardly actualized in daily behavior.[190]

The analogies of birth and growth work complementarily but distinguishably. New birth is the beginning of the renewed spiritual life. One does not enjoy life or enter into this new family of God without spiritual birth. Birth in this sense simply means faith responding to the love of God on the cross. But one does not keep getting born and born and born. After one is born, one grows in the family, having been adopted into its inheritance.[191]

When you think of a fully matured intrauterine fetus, you have an unborn child that is completely potentiated and ready to come into full actualization as a human being, yet it is not until after birth that this one begins to breathe. The viable baby is not born and then breathes only one breath. Rather the baby is born, begins breathing, and then keeps on breathing, in a continuing process that is the basis of constant growth. It is this constant growth process, this constant reception of grace, that Wesley is concerned to interpret and enable. Breathing is a pivotal symbol of our constantly receiving grace upon grace, and ever anew responding to grace.

Before birth one's eyes are not yet opened. After birth one begins to breathe, to see with one's own eyes, which existed previously but did not see, and to hear with one's ears the

---

[186]B3:435–36.

[187]#45 "The New Birth," iv.1, 2, 2:196–98.

[188]FA Part I, i.5, 11:107.

[189]Letter to Hannah Ball, Oct. 4, 1771, LJW 5:280; cf. B9:64.

[190]#45 "The New Birth," iv.4, 2:199; on the distinction between inward and outward sin see B1:239–40, 245f., 336–44; 2:215f.

[191]#45 "The New Birth," ii.3, 2:191.

previously muffled sounds of providence.[192]

It is less accurate to say that life begins with birth than that breathing begins with birth, for before birth the fetus was alive. What new birth is all about is the birthing of these spiritual senses that have remained latent prior to birth. Breathing, hearing, seeing spiritually are all gifts of the new birth by which one may now receive the breath of life, behold the Way, and hear the divine address.[193]

Imagine what it would feel like to be born—suddenly entering an unfolding world of free action. Upon birth one sees the world one has not seen before. In spiritual birth one learns to hear in a new way, by listening to the word of Scripture and the address of the Spirit in one's daily walk.

The new birth involves attentive hearing and alert seeing. A new sensory apparatus comes with faith. One's spiritual senses begin gradually to be activated by this new spiritual birth. That does not mean that they immediately all work maximally as if in mature spiritual hearing and seeing, but they commence seeing and hearing. Birth is just a beginning, but nothing else can occur until it happens.

Keeping in mind this distinction, the new birth is not identical with sanctification. The new birth is the entrance to the life in which one begins to grow in holiness.[194] The former is accomplished in a moment, the latter is a progressive work. Countering William Law, who had equated regeneration with progressive sanctification, Wesley argued that the new birth was the beginning point of growth in sanc-

tification. "The same relation therefore which there is between our natural birth and our growth there is also between our new birth and our sanctification."[195]

The respiratory function that keeps us spiritually alive is a constant reception of grace, not a single momentary occurrence. Think of the sin of believers as returning voluntarily again into the stuffy atmosphere of an oxygen-deprived smoke-filled room. They may yet return to the freedom and open air of grace. Those who fall and stumble have the remedy of the Eucharist to complement the grace of baptism. If sin means voluntary transgression of a known law of God, then the life of grace means constantly being empowered by the Spirit to walk in the way of faith, trusting step by step in God's providing.[196]

Anyone who loves souls seeks a way of communicating with them candidly that they must be born again. Neither baptism, church attendance, nor a godly life can take the place of the new birth.[197]

Marks of the New Birth

John 3:8: "So is everyone that is born of the Spirit." [Homily #18 1748 B1:415–30; J#18 V:212–23]

The Spirit intends to work a thoroughgoing victory over our sins. Part of what makes classical Wesleyan teaching relatively aistinctive among Protestant options is that he held not to a perfunctory or minimal expectation of behavioral transformation, but a consummate and radical expectation.

While God's saving work finally remains a mystery of grace, nonetheless there are marks and visible fruits of the

---

[192]#45 "The New Birth," ii.4, 2:192; cf. #19 "The Great Privilege of those that are Born of God," i; FA, v.24–26.

[193]#45 "The New Birth," iv.4, 2:199–201.

[194]B2:194f., 198; 3:506f., 4:521f.

[195]#45 "The New Birth," iv.3, 2:198.

[196]#45 "The New Birth," iv.3–4, 2:198–201.

[197]#45 "The New Birth," iv.4, 2:200–201.

new birth. As God works for our renewal, we are not left without plausible evidences of this work.[198] The first mark of the new birth is:

Faith

Whoever from the heart *believes* that Jesus is the Christ is born of God. Regenerating, saving faith means not simply intellectual assent to propositions of revelation,[199] or speculative faith, but a disposition of the heart to trust in God that through the merits of Christ *my* sins are forgiven and I reconciled to favor with God.[200] This is not to disavow the intellectual component of faith, but the course of faith runs deeper than intellectual assent. What happened on the cross is meritorious for me, so that what is objectively done for humanity is applied and received by me through faith.

Whoever is born of the Spirit and abides in the Spirit and is nurtured by the Spirit, remains free from sin as long as he or she trustingly receives the empowerment of grace through the Spirit. The fruit of faith is precisely power over sin, inward and outward, and thus peace with God.

"No one who is born of God will continue to sin, because God's seed remains in him; he cannot go on sinning, because he has been born of God" (1 John 3:9).[201] The only way to understand that text is to test it out experientially, by finding out what it means to live practically by this regenerating grace. Only then will you see its fruit, which is freedom from sin. Some eisegetes may try to coerce the text to say

that what the writer of 1 John really meant was that whoever is born of God does not commit sin *habitually*. Wesley preferred to adhere closely to what the Greek text plainly says.[202] Seed points to the reimplanted divine nature and image given the one born of God by faith and baptism, who is "inwardly and universally changed." This renewal promises the complete cleansing of the maturing self, moment by moment, by this justifying and regenerating grace. It is from this that we receive a sense of serenity, consolation, and peace not only with ourselves and the neighbor toward whom we move in love, but peace with God, having been reconciled so as to reflect the love of God.[203]

Hope

The second mark of the new birth is a lively *hope* that testifies that we are children of God, along with the testimony of conscience that we are walking in simplicity and godly sincerity. It is not simply a biblically informed conscience testifying that we are so walking, but it is the direct witness of God's own Spirit with our spirit that we are children of God that gives this assurance, a firm sense that we are adopted into the family of God, and that this inheritance is eternal life. This dual testimony of my conscience with that of God's own Spirit in and with my own spirit is what yields hope, which finally reaches toward the end-time judgment and consummation of divine glory.[204] The hope is ultimately to receive the

---

[198] #18 "The Marks of the New Birth," proem, 1:417.

[199] FA 11:177.

[200] #18 "The Marks of the New Birth," i.3, 1:418.

[201] #18 "The Marks of the New Birth," i.5, 6, 1:420–21.

[202] "By living faith, whereby God is continually breathing spiritual life into his soul, and his soul is continually breathing out love and prayer to God, [the believer] does not commit sin," ENNT 911.

[203] #18 "The Marks of the New Birth," i.5, 1:420.

[204] B1:406f., 411f., 422–25; 2:223.

inheritance that is the final gift of faith's journey.[205]

There is intense joy in this hope. It is no dismal, depressing matter to share in this hope, as if focused despairingly upon what one does not have. Rather it is a serene, at times ecstatic, anticipatory reception of the gifts yet finally to be received—eternal bliss, the vision of God.[206]

Suffering is understood in relation to the providential purposes of God in history that are already in the process of being fulfilled. Meanwhile history is incomplete. The end of history is not yet. In this transient interim, faith elicits a living hope that sustains the believer through whatever drought or storm may come.[207]

Love

The third mark is *love*, which pours itself out caringly for the neighbor as having been cared for by God; loving our enemies as God has loved us while we were enemies of righteousness.[208] Love, which bears the fruit of faith in relation to the neighbor, is especially tested in relation to one perceived as foe. Even the antagonist can now be viewed in relation to the coming final divine reconciliation. In this way one is freed to love every person one meets in relation to the love of God, which is being poured out by the Holy Spirit in our hearts.[209]

Each one is called to earnest self-examination as to whether the marks of the new birth are being truly manifested: trusting in God, hoping amid suffering, and loving the neighbor in need. These are such visible evidences

of new birth that no one need feel deprived of assurance of salvation, or in the dark about one's reconciliation with God as Abba. By faith, hope, and love we are living out in practice a life of responsiveness to God in a joyful constant answerability of the whole heart and all of one's behavior to the love of God.[210]

By these evidences it is knowable that one, being born again, born of God, born of the Spirit, is a "child of God" by "the Spirit of adoption." These privileges "by the free mercy of God, are *ordinarily annexed to baptism* (which is thence termed by our Lord in a preceding verse, the being 'born of water and of the Spirit')."[211] Yet we are admonished not to say too cheaply: "I *was once* baptized, therefore I *am now* a child of God," or identify the new birth simply with the sacrament of baptism as such, as if to ignore behavioral responsiveness to the grace of baptism. For this forces any serious observer to ask whether "baptized whoremongers" are indeed living as children of God.[212]

The Great Privilege of Those That Are Born of God

1 John 3:9: "Whosoever is born of God, doth not commit sin." [Homily #19 1748 B1:431–43; J#19 V:223–33]

Relational and Real Change: Restoration of the Favor and Image of God

New birth begins the daily respiratory process of breathing in the grace and mercy of God, and breathing out the energies of new life. Justification is

---

[205]#18 "The Marks of the New Birth," ii.1–3, 1:422–23.
[206]#18 "The Marks of the New Birth," ii.4, 5, 1:423–25.
[207]#18 "The Marks of the New Birth," ii, 1:422–25.
[208]LJW 5:101, 203, 258, 323.
[209]#18 "The Marks of the New Birth," iii, 1:425–27.
[210]#18 "The Marks of the New Birth," iv, 1:427–30.
[211]#18 "The Marks of the New Birth," proem, 1:417, italics added.
[212]#18 "The Marks of the New Birth," iv.3, 1:429.

God's work on the cross for us, a completed work that implies an objective change in our relationship to God. As such it is not contingent upon our decision. It is simply a gift.[213] That new *relational*[214] gift intends and seeks a real change in us, imperatively requiring a new spiritual life responsive to that gift. Justification is therefore a relational (*"relative"*) change, while what follows after justification (new birth and growth in sanctifying grace) calls for *real*, substantive behavioral change.[215] God the Son on the cross is juridically establishing a new relationship between God and humanity. By new birth we are actually being born into that relationship so that we may continue to grow in it, in a real behavioral change that is answerable to the relational change offered on the cross.

God the Spirit seeks to transform fully and in consummate detail the fallen person so that the image of God is being actually reflected in human conduct. The offering and receiving of this new life is what is meant by being born of God. In this way the triune God is working economically and cooperatively to bring us this salvation by justification in the Son and sanctification through the Spirit.

Summing up: If by justification we are restored to the *favor* of God, by regeneration we are restored in the *image* of God. God's justifying action on the cross changes one's objective relation to God. New birth changes one's inmost motivation and disposition of soul. If justification is God's action *for us in the Son*, new birth is the inauguration of God's action *in us through the Spirit*. Justification takes away the *guilt* of sin. New birth takes away the *power* of sin. When the image of God is restored, the power of sin is made null.[216]

Exploring the Fetal Analogy

As the child in the womb has no knowledge of the world outside the womb, even though that world surrounds him, because the senses are not yet fully functional, so the fallen self has little or no knowledge of the spiritual world because its spiritual senses are not yet activated, awakened, ready to function. By analogy, the unregenerate self lives and "subsists by Him in whom all that have life 'live, and move, and have their being,' yet he is not *sensible* of God; he does not feel, he has no inward consciousness of His presence."[217]

One born of God is made sensible to God, and can employ never before used spiritual senses to come alive to grace. The newborn "by a kind of spiritual re-action returns the grace he receives in unceasing love, praise, and prayer."[218]

The Great Privilege of Those Reborn: The Grace Not to Sin

What is the unique privilege of those born of God? "Whoever is born of God *does not commit sin*" (1 John 3:9) as long as one shares in this responsiveness to grace, as long as one continues to breathe the invigorating air of grace.[219] The distinct gift of the Chris-

---

[213]#19 "The Great Privilege of those that are Born of God," proem.1, 2, 1:431.

[214]Wesley's term is *relative*, used archaically in the sense of *relational*.

[215]#19 "The Great Privilege of those that are Born of God," proem.2, 1:431.

[216]#19 "The Great Privilege of those that are Born of God," proem.2–4, 1:431–32.

[217]#19 "The Great Privilege of those that are Born of God," i.6, 1:433–34.

[218]#19 "The Great Privilege of those that are Born of God," ii.1, 1:435. Wesley was among the earliest known to use the term "re-action," cf. OED.

[219]#18 "Marks of the New Birth," i.3, 1:419.

tian life is to be delivered from the power of sin, and thus prepared for the holy and happy life.[220]

"By 'sin' I here understand outward sin, according to the plain, common acceptation of the word: an *actual voluntary 'transgression of the law'*; of the revealed, written law of God; of any commandment of God acknowledged to be such at the time that it is transgressed." It is just such offenses that those born of God are being enabled by grace to overcome.[221]

"Does not St. Paul say plainly that those who believe do not 'continue in sin'. . .? And does not St. John say most expressly: . . . 'For this purpose the Son of God was manifested, that he might destroy the works of the devil. Whosoever is born of God doth not commit sin' . . . it is not *we* that say this, but the Lord . . . This is the height and depth of what we (with St. Paul) call perfection—a state of soul devoutly to be wished for by all who have tasted of the love of God.'"[222]

The Duty Commensurable With the Privilege: Keeping Oneself From Temptation

The gift of the new birth is to be so steadily surrounded by sufficient grace that temptation can be continually turned aside. As long as this seed remains alive and nurtured in us, the adversary does not get close enough to us to do us mortal harm. So we are being guarded, hedged by grace from temptation and its consequent sin.[223]

Falling away begins with temptation, but keep in mind that temptation is by definition that which can be resisted. To be compelled is not the same as to be

tempted. Temptation is a seduction to which we are idolatrously inclined but not necessitated to collude.

The faithful are not unconditionally protected from falling into sin, as we see in the biblical accounts of David's lust and Peter's denial. When we neglect grace and incline our hearts to evil, we lose faith, failing to listen attentively to the steady witness of the Spirit. We decide we do not want to breathe clean air but polluted air. And so we fall away. It is not guaranteed that once having received justifying grace, one can then forever rest easily in Zion, regardless of one's subsequent behavior. Freedom remains always vulnerable to temptation.[224]

One born of God who keeps himself under the constraint of grace may fall temporarily, but no fall is irremediable. Wesley's formula: Though liable to fall, we remain able to stand.[225]

We are being given the possibility of not committing sin by ever-sufficient prevenient, justifying, and sanctifying grace. One may receive this grace in one moment, and succumb to temptation the next. There is no way to predict outcomes or to anticipate how freedom will react to the variable possibilities of grace meeting free agency in history. But the distinct privilege of the believer is to live the life of the new birth whereby sin has lost its absolute sway, though it continues to tempt freedom. Sin remains in the faithful, but does not reign.[226]

Regression From Grace to Sin

So long as one is living by faith, one is not committing sin. One may regress, however, from grace to sin, in the

---

[220]#19 "The Great Privilege of those that are Born of God," ii.1, 1:435–36.
[221]#19 "The Great Privilege of those that are Born of God," italics added, ii.2, 1:436.
[222]EA 53–56, 11:65–67.
[223]#19 "The Great Privilege of those that are Born of God," ii.2, 1:436.
[224]B2:142, 226.
[225]#19 "The Great Privilege of those that are Born of God," ii.4–10, 1:436–41.
[226]#19 "The Great Privilege of those that are Born of God," ii.4–10, 1:436–41.

following sequence: The seed remains in one born of God. The seed does not die. It may be reawakened by faith. Temptation arises within the conditions of finitude, amid the body/soul interface, escalated by demonic intensification.[227]

When that happens, we are admonished by the Spirit through conscience. By this admonition we know we are children of the Father, not parentless waifs. Growth in grace can be arrested at any point at which faith ceases to respond trustingly to grace.

Whenever we are tempted, the Spirit is always there to give counsel (*nouthesia*, admonition). Those attentive to the Spirit will hear early warning signals, and not fall into sin insofar as faith is sustained. Those who collude with the temptation may fall into sin and grieve the Spirit.

Tempted freedom may gradually "give way, in some degree, to the temptation, which now begins to grow pleasing."[228] The Spirit is grieved, faith weakened, and our love for God cools. The Spirit warns more sharply. We may try to turn off conscience, but seldom with undivided or enduring success.

We may turn away from the Spirit's address even more decisively so that evil tempters and wretched neurotic behavioral patterns begin to form themselves in us habitually.[229] When this happens it does not mean that we are ever completely out of the reach of the Spirit. Even then, the Spirit does not abandon the fallen, but continues to reprove, correct, and teach. But whenever we reinforce toxic behavioral patterns, it becomes psychologically harder to hear the address of the Spirit.

Finally we may spin into a syndrome in which evil desires[230] spread so cancerously that the living power of faith, hope, and love virtually vanish in a sea of despairing self-assertion, making one again prone to sin since the power of the Lord has left him, yet still the seed remains implanted and may be revitalized by faith.[231]

Daily Meeting Temptation

At each stage of falling we are choosing, not being necessitated, to fall. Those who freely collude are at first free to cease to collude, but with more collusion they grow ever less free. It is our personal responsibility when we collude with temptation. Those born of God do not commit sin insofar as they do not choose to fall step by step into this syndrome of collusion with temptation.[232]

Those born of God are charged to keep themselves so that the Adversary will not come within reach of touching them. Those born of God through justifying grace, grow through this constant respiratory process, continuing to breathe in the ever-new daily life of grace and breathe out the works of love.[233]

Christian care-giving focuses on helping pardoned sinners meet temptation, so as not to collude with the demonic at the moment when tempted to pride or gluttony. Amid all snares, as long as faith remains one has not turned away from saving grace. Even if faith remains in a weak form one has not lost access to saving grace.

---

[227]B1:438–41, 484, 693; 3:24f., 156–71; 4:194, 533.

[228]#19 "The Great Privilege of those that are Born of God," ii.9, 1:440.

[229]B1:416, 420f., 557f.

[230]It is not that desire as such is evil, but that evil desires may be transformed into desires made holy by faith active in love. SS 2:362n.

[231]#19 "The Great Privilege of those that are Born of God," ii.9, 10, 1:440–41; SS 2:275.

[232]#19 "The Great Privilege of those that are Born of God," ii.6–8, 1:438–39.

[233]#19 "The Great Privilege of those that are Born of God," ii.6–10, 1:438–41.

The faithful do well to examine carefully, in small accountable groups, specific ways in which they at early stages are beginning to be tempted. They are called to pray to be guarded against temptation, and to pray for the means of grace by which temptation can be resisted.[234]

It is therefore always an inward loss of faith that precedes outward, actual sin.[235] If we do not continue in love toward God and neighbor, the Spirit "will gradually withdraw, and leave us to the darkness of our own hearts."[236] Faith working by love leaves no room for inward or outward sin in a soul being made fully alive by grace.[237]

FURTHER READINGS

Soteriology

Collins, Kenneth. *John Wesley on Salvation.* Grand Rapids: FAP, Zondervan, 1989. Chap. 2 "Convincing Grace and Initial Repentance."

Mason, C. E. "John Wesley's Doctrine of Salvation." Master's Thesis, Union Theological Seminary, 1950.

Schilling, Paul. "John Wesley's Theology of Salvation." Chap. 2 in *Methodism and Society in Theological Perspective*, 44–64. Nashville: Abingdon, 1960.

---

[234]#19 "The Great Privilege of those that are Born of God," iii, 1:441–43.

[235]#19 "The Great Privilege of those that are Born of God," iii.2, 1:442; cf. B2:203, 206; SS 2:246.

[236]#19 "The Great Privilege of those that are Born of God," iii.3, 1:442.

[237]B1:559–60; 3:122–23, 303–4, 385–86, 612–13; JWO 68, 123–32, 231f., 279f., 376.

10

Sanctification

Since the teaching of entire sanctification is found abundantly in the ancient church tradition, it is viewed as a unique Wesleyan distinctive only by those inattentive to the patristic tradition. Yet it became a leading feature of the Wesleyan legacy in the Evangelical Revival. Many vectors of modern perplexities about Wesley focus here. One does an injustice to Wesley by viewing all his teaching in the light of this single point, yet those who disregard it miss something crucial in Wesley. In his *Plain Account of Christian Perfection*, Wesley reviewed four decades of his teaching on this subject.

ON ROOTING OUT SIN AFTER JUSTIFICATION

Plain Account of Christian Perfection
[XI:366–446]

Whether Consistently Taught

Wesley was convinced that he had not substantially changed his mind about sanctification teaching from his Oxford days until 1763 when he wrote the *Plain Account*. He thought he had consistently held to the expectation that

the Holy Spirit intends to transform our behavior, not partially but completely. The tenet went through modest changes of interpretation and defense, not of substance, but expression. It remained constant except for a few minor alterations that amount to little more than responses to challenges. Variable circumstances caused Wesley to argue the same case in different ways, and defend it against varied deconstructions.[1]

Wesley urged that all preachers in his connection of spiritual formation make a point of teaching the way of holiness to believers "constantly, strongly and explicitly," and that all class leaders should be attentive to this doctrine and "continually agonize" for its experiential appropriation.[2]

The Grand Depositum

Convinced that the traditions following Luther and Calvin had not grasped the full implications of the work the Holy Spirit intends to do in us, Methodists were called upon not merely to teach but to live the holy life, to bring it into being as an experienced reality. Wesley considered this "the grand de-

---

[1] *A Plain Account of Christian Perfection*, 1–5, XI:366–67.
[2] *A Plain Account of Christian Perfection*, 26, XI:443.

positum which God has lodged with the people called Methodists and for the sake of propagating this chiefly he appeared to have raised them up."[3]

Of the 1740 Preface to *Hymns and Sacred Poems*, Wesley later would write: "This is the strongest account we ever gave of Christian perfection; indeed too strong in more than one particular." Admitting that it had led to some misunderstandings, he nonetheless insisted that "there is nothing we have since advanced upon the subject, either in verse or prose, which is not either directly or indirectly contained in this preface. So that whether our present doctrine be right or wrong, it is howsoever the same which we taught from the beginning."[4]

The affirmations that invited misunderstanding, later to be refined, were that those walking in perfect love "are freed from evil thoughts, so that they cannot enter into them"; that "they are, in one sense, freed from temptation; for though numberless temptations fly about them, yet they wound them not."[5] They are not freed from the challenge of temptation, but rather, from any necessity to fall and are freed by sufficient grace to avert temptation. They situationally receive "unction from the Holy One which abideth in them, and teacheth them every hour, what they shall do."[6]

Kempis, Taylor, and Law

Three authors of the holy living tradition exercised a decisive influence on Wesley's early formation on this theme: Jeremy Taylor, Thomas à Kempis, and William Law. At age 23, 1725, Wesley read Anglican bishop Jeremy Taylor's *Rules and Exercises of Holy Living and Holy Dying*, which stressed the intentional resolution to lifelong purity of heart. Taylor called his readers to dedicate their entire lives wholly to God, every moment being seen in relation to eternity. "Instantly I resolved to dedicate all my life to God."[7]

In 1726 when Wesley read *The Imitation of Christ* by Thomas à Kempis,[8] he was further arrested by the notion of simplicity of intention, that purity of affection where one loves but one thing, has one design in all that is spoken or done, and a single desire ruling all tempers.[9] These gracious habits are "indeed 'the wings of the soul' without which she can never ascend to the mount of God."[10]

The same centeredness of intent he found in William Law's *Christian Perfection* and *A Serious Call to the Devout and Holy Life*. Wesley unequivocally decided that it was impossible to be a fractional Christian, but must yield all to God.[11] The rest of Wesley's long life expressed the embodiment of this teaching that he had deeply appropriat-

---

[3]#76 "On Perfection," iii.12, 3:86–87.

[4]*A Plain Account of Christian Perfection*, 13, XIV:381–82.

[5]The point here is not that temptation ceases objectively, but that it is being subjectively deprived by the grace-enabled, disciplined will of exercising unchecked power.

[6]HSP 1740 Pref. 7, XIV:324–25.

[7]*A Plain Account of Christian Perfection*, 2, XI:366; see also B3:123, 324, 580; 4:121 for reference to Bishop Taylor.

[8]On Thomas à Kempis see B2:375; 3:39, 580; 4:105, 182; 9:85; LJW 3:213; 4:239, 293.

[9]On purity of heart, or simplicity of intention see LJW 1:192; 2:190, 201; B1:306f., 510–14, 573–77, 608f., 672f., 698; 3:122f., 287–89; 4:120–23, 371–77.

[10]XI:367; Christian spirituality today is currently recovering this doctrine of simplicity of intention in writers like Thomas Merton, Henry Nouwen, and Richard Foster.

[11]*A Plain Account of Christian Perfection*, 4, XI:367; "And by my continued endeavor to keep his whole law, inward and outward to the uttermost of my power, I was persuaded that I should be accepted of Him, and that I was even then in a state of salvation." John Emory edition of Wesley, 1855, III.71.

ed so early, first at home under the instruction of his mother, Susanna, and in his early twenties at Oxford around the time of his ordination.

Christ Forming the Consecrated Person: From Above and Below

Mark well: The teaching of perfecting grace is not finally about the power of human freedom, but the power of grace totally to transform freedom.[12] This transformation is best understood as Christ's own forming in us, and secondarily as our yielding ourselves to be formed by Christ.

From the point of view of Christ forming himself in us, Christian perfection is the mind of Christ entering into us and taking us into himself in union with himself. Viewed from above, it is "all the mind which was in Christ enabling us to walk as Christ walked. It is the circumcision of the heart from all filthiness, from all inward as well as outward pollution."[13]

Viewed experientially, from a subjective, psychological, human point of view (from below), perfecting grace is seen as as an act of complete dedication, entire consecration, a radical and unreserved commitment of the self to the grace of the Spirit filling the soul. Grasped volitionally, "it is purity of intention, dedicating all the life to God. It is the giving God all our heart; it is one desire and design ruling all our tempers. It is the devoting, not a part, but all, our soul, body, and substance to God."[14]

Wesley's sanctification teaching is a complex constellation of ideas and exegetical explications. In most ways it is close to what some Reformed writers have called positional sanctification. There is a profound doctrine of sanctification in the Calvinist teaching of our sharing in the righteousness of Christ, assuming that our sanctification is already embedded in this juridical act.[15] This idea of sanctification Wesley strongly affirmed, yet with the recurring alarm that it might drift toward antinomian license. The only way he was refashioning it was by speaking steadily of the possibility and necessity of a full and unreserved consecration of the whole of one's redeemed powers for the remainder of one's life.[16]

Meanwhile Charles was writing hymns by which the societies were singing their way into celebrating the same teaching:

> In thee my wandering thoughts unite,
> Of all my works be thou the aim:
> Thy love attend me all my days,
> And my sole business be thy
> praise.[17]

Countering Objections to Sanctification Teaching

Some objected that Wesley was exalting the human possibility by wrongly, even Pelagianly, claiming that native humanity is of itself capable of achieving redemption. His reply made it clear that perfecting grace is a doctrine of grace, not anthropology or natural human competency. It is only by the power of grace that human willing is being reclaimed to its original purpose of righteousness, refracting the image of God.

---

[12]B2:97–121; 3:70–87; JWO 252f.; on crowning grace see CH 7:49.
[13]XI:444.
[14]PACP XI:366f.; cf. LJW 4:298. The holy living tradition from both Anglican and Puritan sources is crucial in this definition. Cf. B1:20–22, 37; 4:268.
[15]Calvin, *Institutes*, 3.11.10, 4:13; Commentaries, XVIII:561, XXII:334; John Owen, Works 3:468–538; Thomas Goodwin, Works, VI:85–95, 459–70; W. S. Chafer, *Systematic Theology*, VI:283–85.
[16]CH 7:589–93.
[17]HSP, 1739, 122.

Others objected that humanity is so far fallen into evil that talk of perfection is ludicrous and that we had better be speaking of the redeemed will as still tending inevitably toward evil. To the Manichean claim that it is self-evident that the self is so evil that there is no perfect responsiveness to God on the earth, Wesley answered that while created humanity is profoundly fallen into sin, grace perfectly reaches and addresses human follies with the intent of utterly transforming them. The faithful are not perfect in knowledge, not free from weakness, finitude, or temptation, but the Christian life aims toward unblemished love of God and neighbor that is not intrinsically unrealizable. There is, however, no perfection that does not admit of continual increase. It is not a static notion but rather dynamic, a *teleiōsis* and not a *perfectus*.

"We are justified by *faith alone*, and yet by such a faith as is *not alone*" in the sense of being fruitless.[18] "Faith alone is the condition of *present* salvation," on the assumption that when "faith is given, holiness commences in the soul; for that instant 'the love of God (which is the source of holiness) is shed abroad in the heart.' "[19] "This was the view of religion," which from the early age of thirty to the advanced age of seventy-four, "I scrupled not to term *perfection*. This is the view I have of it now."[20]

The Circumcision of The Heart

Rom. 2:29: "Circumcision is that of the heart, in the Spirit and not the letter." [Homily #17 1733 B1:398–414; J#17 V:202–12]

Before going to Georgia, on the first day of the year in 1733, Wesley preached at St. Mary's, Oxford, on what it means to be a Jew inwardly. The *leitmotif* is captured in the Pauline text: "A man is not a Jew if he is only one outwardly, nor is circumcision merely outward and physical. No, a man is a Jew if he is one inwardly; and circumcision is circumcision of the heart, by the Spirit, not by the written code" (Rom. 2:28, 29).

On Being a Jew Inwardly: Circumcision of the Heart Defined

Being a Jew inwardly, or "circumcision of the heart," is defined as that habitual disposition of soul to walk by faith in the way of holiness. It implies so trusting in the coming righteousness of Christ as to be renewed in the spirit of our minds that the body, as temple of the Spirit, manifests the holiness of God fully and without blemish. It implies being cleansed from sin, from corruption of both flesh and spirit, and in consequence being drawn toward those virtues that were in Christ Jesus. Only by complete trust in the atoning work is one enabled to fulfill the command to be perfect as our Father in heaven is perfect. It is accompanied by the confirmation of one's hope for reconciliation through the testimony of one's conscience, and through the testimony of the Holy Spirit to our spirit.

Circumcision of the heart is total commitment of the heart to God. Each circumcised individual is called to let every thought, word, action, and movement of the heart be ordered in relation to this source and end of our existence so that everything we do tends to the glory of God, loving all things in relation to the One most worthy of our love. All loves are loved in relation to the love of this One. The circumcised are called first to love God unreservedly, that all that we love may come into the orbit of this centering love. In this

---

[18]A Letter to the Rev. Mr. Horne, ii.3, B11:454.
[19]FA Part I, iii.10, 11:130.
[20]*A Plain Account of Christian Perfection*, 6, XI:369.

way the will is reordered so that all created things tend toward the glory of the Creator. Nothing thought to be good is pursued except in relation to the One eternally good.

Circumcision of the heart means complete consecration, entire sanctification. Those circumcised of heart are constantly being effectively renewed in the Spirit of Christ.[21] This is not the circumcision of the penis, but of the heart, for it is out of the heart that all words and deeds come.

Sharing in the Covenant Community

Circumcision has its origin in the hebraic rite by which infant males were brought into the covenant community, set apart as consecrated members of the people of God. Circumcision of the heart is a metaphor that reveals how God the Spirit places us in a new covenant community.[22] The New Testament debate about circumcision had to do with what is meant by one's entry into the covenant community. Baptism functions in analogy with circumcision, except that it is a rite not just for males, but all men and women who share Christ's death and resurrection.[23]

The Torah had promised that "The Lord your God will circumcise your hearts and the hearts of your descendants, so that you may love him with all your heart and with all your soul, and live" (Deut. 30:6). "A promise is implied in every commandment of God." What God commands, God offers sufficient grace to do.[24]

Jesus attested that the sum of the law is to love the Lord with all your heart, mind, and strength and the neighbor as yourself, so that whatever one fears, desires, seeks, or avoids is viewed in relation to the giver of life. Circumcision of the heart (as distinguished from "outward circumcision or baptism, or any other outward form") is a way of talking about the heart being set apart for the love of God and the neighbor.[25]

Being Sustained Daily in Humble Repentance, Faith, Hope, and Love

Those circumcised in heart are characterized by a daily mortification,[26] a dying to the world's idolatries, a profound meekness and "lowliness of mind" that makes way for faith, hope, and love. The penitent life that burns away pride and self-deception waters and nurtures saving faith, which allows and calls us to hope that the Spirit will provide us with the means of grace that leads to "Love divine, all loves excelling."[27]

Grace must first remove the pride that blocks us from hearing the word of God's mercy. Through *this humbling*, we become aware of how far our own natural capacities have fallen away from the goodness of God, and how we really cannot save or adequately help ourselves.[28] Repentance brings the realistic self-awareness that "in our best estate we are, of ourselves, all sin and vanity . . . that there is no whole part of our soul, that all the foundations of our nature are out of course."[29]

Sanctifying grace works to cleanse the person from multiple layers of inveterate ego-centricity. The tendency to see everything from one's own self-as-

---

[21]#17 "The Circumcision of the Heart," proem.1–3, 1:401–2.
[22]JWO 318–31.
[23]#17 "The Circumcision of the Heart," i, 1:402–9.
[24]#76, "On Perfection," ii.11, 3:80.
[25]#17 "The Circumcision of the Heart," i, 1:402.
[26]B2:245; SS 1:165; 2:289.
[27]LJW 1:248; 2:107, 110, 186.
[28]B1:403f., 409f., 479f.
[29]#17 "The Circumcision of the Heart," i.2, 1:403.

sertive point of view is being cut away. Circumcision is a cutting image, an incision that carries over metaphorically into the life of repentance. What happens in circumcision is a cutting away of a part of the male generative organ by which life is spawned, a sanctification metaphor, whereby this most crucial engendering function is being set aside for a holy purpose.

From the humility of repentance there may follow by grace *faith*, which is a sure trust in Christ who redeems us from our sin and reconciles us to God.[30] Faith leads to *hope* that quietly expects the Spirit to do his work in us. Hope is the expectation that the Spirit desires to provide us with sufficient means of grace by which our lives can be thoroughly reordered.[31] Unless we rejoice in hope that we are heirs of God's promise, we will not rise above our persistent weaknesses and impediments, and truly be led by the Spirit toward self-denial and taking up of the cross. Hope perseveres by "a lively expectation of receiving all good things at God's hand."[32] *Love* completes the circle, fulfills the law so that the love of God with all of one's heart, mind and strength and love of neighbor as oneself are not only envisioned but enabled.

Whether One Baptized Can be Half a Christian

It is an oxymoron to talk of being "half a Christian." One either believes the good news or one does not. What follows from that is either radically transforming of one's behavior or it falls short of unfeigned faith. One is either altogether a Christian, adopted into the family of God, or still trapped in the syndromes of being almost a Christian, with the servile, legalistic, wage-counting relation of a servant.[33]

Becoming a Christian at heart means not merely that one has received the grace of baptism, but that one having received it understands what the grace of baptism means. Christians are those who, having been baptized, take seriously the moral consequences of their baptism.

Those who have received the grace of baptism remain free to deny or disregard or forget or ignore the meaning of their baptism. Their mouths are not stopped. They are not forcibly prevented from falling from grace. The grace of baptism points quietly toward the new birth, toward concretely sharing in Christ's death and resurrection. Whether sanctifying grace is palpably experienced by those who have been once formally baptized depends not on whether God offers it but on whether they receive it.[34]

It appears as a hard saying to one dead to God and alive to the world to be called to "live wholly unto God," dying to the world. "Unless it be so qualified in the interpretation as to have neither use nor significance," the hearer will turn away, thinking such thoughts "foolishness."[35] To teach such things "runs the hazard of being esteemed" as "a setter forth of new doctrines," most having "so *lived away* the substance of that religion, the profession whereof they still retain, that no sooner are any of those truths proposed"[36] that distinguish true from false religion than they cry out: "You are bringing some strange ideas to our ears" (Acts 17:20).

---

[30] #17 "The Circumcision of the Heart," ii.2, 1:410.
[31] #17 "The Circumcision of the Heart," ii.5–8, 1:411–12.
[32] #17 "The Circumcision of the Heart," i.9, 1:406.
[33] #2 "The Almost Christian," i, 1:131–5; V:17–25.
[34] #17 "The Circumcision of the Heart," proem.3, i, 1:402–9.
[35] #17 "The Circumcision of the Heart," proem.2, 1:402.
[36] #17 "The Circumcision of the Heart," proem.1, 1:401; Acts 17:18–19.

Counting All Else Dross

It is useful here to recall the questions on sanctification embedded in the sermon "Catholic Spirit" (#39), where in the centerpiece of that homily, to avert latitudinarian distortions, there appeared a telling series of questions on the filling work of the Spirit that were to be assumed of anyone whose life is hid in Christ: "Is thy faith *energoumene di agapes*—filled with the energy of love? Dost thou love God? I do not say 'above all things,' for it is both an unscriptural and an ambiguous expression, but 'with all thy heart, and with all thy mind, and with all thy soul, and with all thy strength'? Dost thou seek all thy happiness in him alone? And dost thou find what thou seekest? Dost thy soul continually 'magnify the Lord, and thy spirit rejoice in God thy Saviour'?" "Is God the centre of thy soul? The sum of all thy desires? Art thou accordingly 'laying up' thy 'treasure in heaven' and 'counting all things else dung and dross'? Hath the love of God cast the love of the world out of thy soul? Then thou art 'crucified to the world.' 'Thou art dead' to all below, 'and thy life is hid with Christ in God.' If so then your heart is as my heart,"[37] so give me your hand. This is the catholic spirit that seeks companionship in Christ without succumbing to doctrinal diffusion.

The Character of a Methodist
[1739 VIII:339–47]

Whether Behavioral Descriptions of Sustained Responsiveness to Grace Are Disclosed in Scripture

In 1739 Wesley set forth distinguishing marks of the people labeled "Methodists," a term he did not like or choose, but knew had stuck, and with which he was willing to let providence do its work.[38] He hoped that with increased discernment, those who "hate what I am *called*, may love what I *am* by the grace of God."[39]

"The Character of a Methodist" stands as his best early descriptive statement of perfecting grace. What follows is Wesley's clearest delineation of the Christian life of complete steady responsiveness to saving grace.

He formed his thoughts around the ironic text: *"not as though I had already attained"* (Phil. 3:12, KJV). It must not be assumed that Wesley broadly claimed that he himself had attained what he was seeking to implement and enable in others. He never publicly asserted that he himself was living the life of complete responsiveness that he was convinced he was finding in many whose lives had been profoundly reshaped by the revival.[40] Later when William Dodd charged him with claiming that "A Methodist, according to Mr. Wesley, is one who is perfect, and sinneth not," Wesley retorted: "This is not 'according to Mr. Wesley.' I have told all the world I am not perfect; and yet you allow me to be a Methodist. *I tell you flat I have not attained the character I draw*. Will you pin it upon me in spite of my teeth?"[41]

Non-Starters in Defining the Altogether (Methodist) Christian

First a series of disclaimers as to what a Methodist (or altogether Christian) is *not*. One seeking to live the life of sustained accountability to God cannot be instantly differentiated by cloth-

---

[37]#39 "Catholic Spirit," i.14, 2:88.
[38]Cf. Letter to the Bishop of Gloucester 11:531–34; LJW 158, 152, 262; 2:375, 380; 8:47.
[39]"The Character of a Methodist," proem.4, VIII:339.
[40]"The Character of a Methodist," proem.1–4, VIII:339–40.
[41]Letter to the Editor of "Lloyd's Evening Post," March 5, 1767, LJW 3:43 (italics added).

ing, eating habits, quaint words, gestures, vocabulary, or anything external. There are indeed few outward indicators or body-language clues, as might be the case with many other more predictably uniformed pietists or countercultural demonstrators.[42]

What distinguishes a Methodist (in Wesley's sense) are not political or intellectual opinions or any sentiments that do not strike at the root of Christianity. Nor is a Methodist distinguished by the holding of a single special precious doctrinal interpretation or accent that defines all other doctrines. On such matters one is well-advised to think and let think in a tolerationist mood with honest respect for differing sincere opinions.[43] If such outward evidences do not distinguish a Methodist, what does?

So What Is a Methodist? Behavioral Marks Scripturally Identified

Look at it behaviorally. Do you happen upon anyone who wholeheartedly loves God? That, says Wesley, is what he means by a Methodist. What distinguishes the Methodist in Wesley's sense is praying without ceasing, loving the Lord with all one's heart, soul, mind, and strength, serving the neighbor in need, and not being enamored of the vices of the world. The love of God is shed abundantly abroad in such a heart.[44]

God's grace is the joy of his life, the source of life's meaning and value. He rejoices in God's gifts even amid disabilities, crying out with the Psalmist: "Whom have I in heaven but you? And earth has nothing I desire besides you. My flesh and my heart may fail, but God is the strength of my heart and my portion forever" (Ps. 73:25–26).[45] God's all-encompassing love has cast out his fear. In everything he gives thanks, saying the Lord gives, the Lord takes away, blessed be the name of the Lord. Whether in comfort or distress, sickness or health, life or death—from his heart he gives thanks to the One to whom he has committed all. Anxious about nothing, he does not despair or compulsively try to secure his future.[46]

The woman who is a Methodist—how does she appear behaviorally? She is happy in the divine love that has justified her, claimed her as a daughter for adoption into the family of God, and begotten her to a living hope. In whatever state she finds herself, she is content, and poised to follow God's will. In her the works of the flesh are being supplanted by the fruits of the Spirit. All her desires are toward God.[47]

What behavioral marks evidence a Methodist? Having cast his care upon One who infinitely cares for him, he continually presents himself upon the altar before God as a living sacrifice in response. All his talents are committed to the practical service of the neighbor, doing whatever is at hand to the glory of God whether in commerce, family, recreation, or religion, rejoicing in doing what God requires, not from fear but from gratitude.[48]

His heart set at liberty, he delights in God's commandments, loves the nearest one at hand as himself, regards the neighbor in relation to the love of God, loves even the supposed enemy without class distinction or social, racial, or gender partiality. He provides for the neighbor's good as earnestly as his

---

[42]"The Character of a Methodist," 1–3, VIII:340–41.
[43]"The Character of a Methodist," 1–4, VIII:340–41.
[44]"The Character of a Methodist," 4–8, VIII:341–43.
[45]"The Character of a Methodist," 5, VIII:341.
[46]"The Character of a Methodist," 6, 7, VIII:342–43.
[47]"The Character of a Methodist," 6, 7, VIII:342.
[48]"The Character of a Methodist," 9, VIII:343.

own. If it is not within his power to do good to those who hate him, he does not cease to pray for them. He prays without ceasing, with God as constant companion. Whatever things are good, wholesome, of good report, or just, he thinks on those things. He has fundamentally one desire: to serve his neighbor as God has loved and served him.[49]

He does not love the world. No matter how deteriorated the environing culture, this person is focused on valuing each one he meets in relation to the giver of diverse cultures and values. The ways of the world do not bring him to despair. He desires only God. The love of God is cleansing his heart from every unkind temper and malignant affection.[50]

It is love that has reclaimed his life, reaching into every crevice of his volition, driving out hatred, contentiousness, and pride, awakening kindness, longsuffering, and humility. He has a single eye, and because his eye is single, his whole body is full of light.[51] God's reign has begun in him. In all this he finds no grounds for self-congratulation.[52]

"Plain Old Christianity"

This is what a Methodist is, a Christian not in name only but in heart and life, renewed inwardly and outwardly in the image of God.[53] The marks of a Methodist are those found in anyone whose life is hid in Christ. What we have in these descriptions are the same characteristics manifested in one whose life is shaped by unfeigned responsiveness to God. It is not a different list. The Methodist is neither more or less than one who takes such promises with complete seriousness.[54]

This is "plain, old Christianity," and Methodists are not distinguished from other Christians in any other way.[55] They are merely seeking wholeheartedly to live the Christian life.[56]

Wesley derived this pattern of Christian perfection primarily from the Scriptures and secondarily from Ante-Nicene writers who spoke of it so cogently. In March of 1767 Wesley wrote: "Five- or six-and-thirty years ago [1729] I much admired the character of a perfect Christian drawn by Clemen Alexandrinus.[57] Five- or six-and-twenty years ago [1739] a thought came into my mind of drawing such a character myself, only in a more scriptural manner, and mostly in the very words of Scripture; this I entitled *The Character of a Methodist.*"[58]

Christian Perfection

Phil. 3:12: "Not as though I had already attained, either were already perfect."[59] [Homily #40 1741 (or earlier) B2:97–124; J#40 VI:1–22]

---

[49]"The Character of a Methodist," 8–10, VIII:343–44.
[50]"The Character of a Methodist'," 9, VIII:343; 3:110–11.
[51]On singularity of intent see B1:573–77, 608f., 672f.; 4:120–23, 371–77.
[52]"The Character of a Methodist," 10–11, VIII:343–44.
[53]LJW 2:71–75; 4:237; B3:202f.; 4:275, 398; 9:35.
[54]"The Character of a Methodist," 16–18, VIII:346–47.
[55]"The Character of a Methodist," 17, VIII:346. Methodism is described as "plain old Bible religion," B9:469; cf. LJW 4:131.
[56]"The Character of a Methodist," 18, VIII:347.
[57]*Christ the Educator* and *Stromateis*.
[58]Letter to the Editor of "Lloyd's Evening Post," March 5, 1767, LJW 5:43.
[59]Paul had just implied in verse 12 that he had not already laid hold of perfection and had not already arrived at this goal, when he then called upon his hearers in verse 15: "Let us therefore, as many as be perfect [*téleioi*, full grown, spiritually mature, ripe in understanding], be thus minded." To solve the seeming contradiction between verses 12 and 15 is the concern of this pastoral reflection.

Perfecting grace is admittedly a difficult doctrine to defend. By 1741 Wesley was receiving thoughtful challenges, and having to fend off serious objections. At times he must have been tempted to give up altogether on defending this tenet. Some in the connection were wondering why such a controversial and falsifiable doctrine should be taught at all.

The intractable answer for Wesley was that this teaching is found constantly in Scripture. Even if *teleiotēs* (perfecting grace) should cause offense among some, it could not as a recurrent scriptural term be sidestepped or parried by honest exegetes. It echos so frequently through the language of Scripture that it cannot be circumvented without abandoning a central theme of holy writ. Were it not so deeply embedded in so many beloved texts from Jesus, and from the Pauline, Petrine, and Johannine traditions, it might be more conveniently ignored or discarded. But its prevalence as a scriptural theme constrained his conscience.[60]

As a result of answering these arguments, Wesley began to shape the teaching more confidently. The Spirit is determined to renew the self totally, rejecting all halfway measures. Those who are receiving regenerating grace by the Spirit are being freed not only from all outward sin at the time of new birth but also from inward sin so as to grow toward the fullness of Christ.[61]

The Greek *teleiotēs* (Col. 3:14; Heb. 6:1) has been commonly translated as perfection, but also under metaphors of maturation and completeness. The Christian life is not a static *perfectus* in the sense of no further possible improvement, but a dynamic *teleiotēs* in the sense of the most excellent conceivable contextual functioning of the developing person. The Latin term *perfectus* tends to contort and reify the earlier Greek language tradition of *teleiotēs*. Since English is rooted far more in Latin than Greek, this becomes a fate-laden difference. Wesley himself was working constantly out of the Greek text, not the Latin Vulgate or the KJV in his daily meditations on Scripture. Therefore when we say *perfect*, our latinized English language yields to us a static notion of perfection. Wesley's references to "perfection" instead assumed the Greek notion of a perfecting (not perfected) grace, "a never ending aspiration for all of love's fullness," as found especially in the pre-Augustinian Eastern church writers.[62]

In What Ways It Is Improper to Say That Christians Are Perfect: What Teleiotēs Is Not

Wesley learned by rough experience to qualify his exegesis carefully. He patiently went through a detailed list of stipulations, indicating what Scripture does not mean by *teleiotēs*.

1. The Scripture promise of perfecting grace does not command or imply freedom from *ignorance*. The full reception of grace can occur in one who remains normally limited in knowing (since finite knowledge is intrinsic to the nature of human finitude). No finite human person is capable of infinite knowledge. Reason offers only proximate knowledge of "things relating to the present world."[63] The saints may know more than most about the ways of God, but still there is much more that they as ordinary human beings "know not."[64]

---

[60]Letter to William Dodd, March 12, 1756, LJW 3:167–72.
[61]B1:239/40, 245f., 336–44; 2:215f.
[62]Outler, Introduction, #40 "Christian Perfection," i.1, 2:98.
[63]#40 "Christian Perfection," i.1–4, 2:100–102.
[64]#40 "Christian Perfection," i.3, 2:101.

2. The perfecting grace of which Scripture speaks is not free from *mistakes*, which are an unavoidable consequence of our finitude and ignorance. Those walking with full maturity in love make mistakes of fact and circumstance.[65] Paul's admonition not to be deceived or mistaken in perception would be meaningless if this were not the case. When John said: "Ye know all things," (1 John 2:20, KJV) the implication is "all things needful for your souls' health."[66] "Every one may *mistake* as long as he lives . . . the most perfect have continual need of the merits of Christ, even for their actual transgressions, and may well say, for themselves as well as their brethren, "Forgive us our trespasses."[67]

3. The mature reception of perfecting grace does not imply freedom from *infirmities*,[68] which are not matters of moral decision, except as they have been habitually formed by collusions of freedom with temptation. By *infirmities* Wesley points to such things as slowness of understanding, poor memory, dull apprehension, or flawed speech.[69]

4. Nor does perfecting grace deliver the faithful from *temptation*. As Jesus was tempted, so are we. Trials and temptations continue to surround any who walk in this way, but each must be dealt with contextually by receiving grace upon grace.[70] Whatever the temptation, there is always a way open to deflect it. No necessity is laid upon us to sin. "The trials which a gracious Providence sends may be precious means of growing in grace, and particularly of increasing in faith, patience, and resignation."[71] No matter where one is in the sequence of stages of growth in grace, one never gets to the point where it is impossible to sin or inconceivable that one might again fall into unresponsiveness to grace.

Anyone whose feet are on the path of holiness will be guarding continually against the subtleties of spiritual pride and seeking to gain early victory over each temptation to sin as it arises. Only as one responds wholly to the will of God does sin lose its power. Those who are so responding to grace that grace is exercising increasing influence within the will, are prepared for whatever emerges. "The world, the flesh, and the devil are put under his feet; thus he rules over these enemies with watchfulness through the power of the Holy Spirit."[72]

What Teleiotēs *Is: In What Way Believers Are Being Perfected by Grace in This Life*

The unchallenged dominion of sin has been broken in those newly born from above. There is no ground upon which to legitimize continued sin in the life of the believer.[73]

The full and sustained maintenance of a way of life utterly dependent upon faith is not intrinsically impossible. If so the call to holiness in Scripture would be absurd.[74]

No believer is being asked to seek holiness apart from grace, but rather to reflect contextually insofar as possible

---

[65]JWO 254–58, 284–90.
[66]#40 "Christian Perfection," i.4, 5, 2:102.
[67]Minutes, 1758, Aug. 15, JWO 177.
[68]B1:241f.; 2:482f.; 4:166f.
[69]#40 "Christian Perfection," i.7, 2:103.
[70]#40 "Christian Perfection," i.8, 2:104.
[71]Letter to Hester Ann Roe, Oct. 6, 1776, LJW 6:234.
[72]Confession, Art. 11, *Book of Discipline*, 1988:72.
[73]#40 "Christian Perfection," ii.3, 2:106.
[74]#40 "Christian Perfection," ii.7, 2:107.

the holiness of God.[75] God is holy. It is possible for God's redeemed creatures proximately to image, as in a mirror, the goodness and holiness of God.[76]

Such a refraction normally occurs in stages that often move through a series of crises, as does life, not abruptly or nondevelopmentally. Those who look for a developmental doctrine of sanctification will find this homily the best place to examine it. Here Wesley shows how the Christian life may be viewed in terms of progressive stages of growth from newborn to adolescence to young adulthood to older adulthood. Each stage has a perfection applicable especially to that stage. It is not as if there is a maturity for neonates that is also applicable to young adults. No one expects an adolescent to express the kind of responsibility expected of a wise grandmother. Rather there is a peculiar maturity that pertains to being a child, and a different maturity that pertains to being an adolescent, and still a different one that pertains to being an adult. While the perfecting of love is often associated with mature age, Wesley specifically pointed out that there is a completeness that even newborn babes have, since the notion of maturity must be understood contextually within the frame of reference of what is possible at a given stage of development.[77]

"The generality of believers in *our* Church (yea, and in the Church of Corinth, Ephesus, and the rest, even in the Apostolic age), are certainly no more than babes in Christ; not young men, and much less fathers. But we have some, and we should certainly pray and expect that our Pentecost may fully come."[78]

All these points make it clear that we have here a doctrine of *teleiotēsis* (dynamic perfecting grace) rather than *perfectus* (static perfection).[79] The key idea is not that of getting to a fixed state of perfection in a motionless sense—a very un-Wesleyan notion, but rather being in a continuing process of growth in grace that has multiple moments of completion and fulfillment, where the refraction of inexhaustible love occurs at many points (in principle any point) along the way. The process of receiving sanctifying grace, since it is a process, is never capturable as a still photograph, but must be a history that can be conceived only narratively and lived out personally.

The first epistle of John does not misunderstand this dynamism in saying "If we claim to be without sin, we deceive ourselves" (1:8), for to say, "I have no sin," is to imply I have no need of the atoning work of God the Son to cleanse me from all sin. To stand in no need of Christ is to deceive oneself and make God a liar. But if we do confess that we have sinned, God will not only forgive but also cleanse us so that we may go and sin no more.

Having been made dead to sin, Christians are now alive to righteousness. Living without sin is the privilege of every Christian, who is being invited and enabled by grace to move gradually through this and that temptation seeking a consummate victory over each evil thought or temper.[80] Jesus experienced thoughts concerning evil, and anger of a grievous nature, yet did not sin, meeting each temptation as it came. Insofar as the risen Lord lives in the life of the believer, how could it be other-

[75]JJW 2:90, 275; 5:283f.
[76]#40 "Christian Perfection," ii.1–10, 2:105–9.
[77]#40 "Christian Perfection," ii.1–2, 2:105–6.
[78]LJW 6:221; cf. B11:503.
[79]#40 "Christian Perfection," ii.1, 2, 2:105–6.
[80]#40 "Christian Perfection," ii.21, 2:117; B3:313–15, 320f.

wise than that the believer is fully freed from sin?[81]

However far one travels on the way of holiness, there is always room the next moment to go further, to grow from grace to grace. There is no perfection that does not admit of continual increase, of further growth in grace. However matured, it is always further maturing, perpetually in process.[82]

The *teleiotēs* of which Scripture speaks does not imply that no further progression is possible, but that the faithful are going on from strength to strength. Paul says that they behold the love of God first as a faint image in an indistinct mirror, and only gradually are changed into this image from glory to glory by the Spirit of the same Lord.

On Perfection

Heb. 6:1: "Let us go on to perfection." [Homily #76 1784 B3:70–87; J#76 VI:411–24]

This homily remains in my view the most penetrating précis of Wesley's matured doctrine of perfection. In this late offering, dated 1784, the elderly Wesley gathered a lifetime of clarifications and disclaimers together in concentrated scope.

Christian Perfection Is Neither Angelic Nor Adamic Perfection

Christian perfection occurs within the theater of human history, not angelic creation. The life of perfect love within this world is neither angelic nor Adamic perfection, for we are corporeal creatures who have fallen from grace into a specific history of sin. Angels are not as liable to make perceptual mistakes as myopic humans.

Nor do we speak here of that perfection that is possible only for God, for we are not God. Thus, "the highest perfection which man can attain, while the soul dwells in the body, does not exclude ignorance, and error, and a thousand other infirmities." If so, all children of Adam and Eve need the work of God on the cross to atone for every transgression of the requirement of God.[83] Key scriptural descriptions of grace perfecting ordinary humanity are abundantly exhibited in the sacred text.

Its Center Is Love

"It is all comprised in that one word, love"—love toward God and the neighbor.[84] Christian perfection implies "loving God with all the heart, so that every evil temper is destroyed and every thought and word and work springs from and is conducted to that end by the pure love of God and our neighbour."[85] So to love is thereby to have the mind that is in Christ (Phil. 2:5), to bear the fruits of the Spirit of love (Gal. 5:22–23). One who loves puts on a new humanity renewed after the moral image of God that is "true righteousness and holiness" (Eph. 4:24), walking in the way of inward and outward righteousness with holiness of life issuing from holiness of heart (1 Peter 1:15).[86] It is the sacrificial offering of our very selves on the altar of grace, so as to participate in the Son's once-for-all sacrifice for sin, and share finally in salvation from all sin (Matt. 1:21).[87]

One who is crucified with Christ, in whom is the mind that was in Christ, "loveth his neighbour (every man) as himself; yea, as Christ loved us; them in particular that despitefully use him and

---

[81]#40 "Christian Perfection," ii.22–24, 2:116–18.
[82]#40 "Christian Perfection," ii.30, 2:121.
[83]#76 "On Perfection," i.1–2, 3:72–73.
[84]#76 "On Perfection," i.4, 3:74.
[85]Minutes, 1758, Aug. 15, JWO 177; cf. EA 11:66–67; FA 11:278.
[86]LJW 3:380; 5:56; B11:239, 416.
[87]#76 "On Perfection," i.4–12, 3:74–76.

persecute him . . . Indeed, his soul is all love, filled with the bowels of mercies, kindness, meekness, gentleness, long-suffering."[88] " 'Faith working by love' is the length and breadth and depth and height of Christian perfection."[89]

If Sin Is Conscious, Voluntary, Deliberate, and Intentional, Then Salvation From Sin Cannot Be Intrinsically Impossible

The question of the possibility of full salvation turns significantly on the definition of sin. Opponents of the New Testament teaching of perfection tend to redefine sin as involuntary. In Scripture, sin is characteristically deliberate, "a voluntary transgression of a known law."[90]

When Scripture says that all "sin is the transgression of the law" (1 John 3:4, KJV), the assumption is that each collusion with temptation could have been chosen otherwise. The text does not imply the reverse, that all "transgression of the law is sin." For some breaches of God's requirement are not strictly speaking sin because they are not willed, but due to inavoidable illnesses, spontaneous mistakes, and the limiting conditions of human finitude. With such a definition, miscalculations of judgment, infirmities, and ignorance can be reasonably distinguished from deliberate, voluntary sin. Wesley found it difficult to believe that any earnest reader of Scripture could "deny the possibility of being saved from sin in *my* sense of the word," with sin viewed as at some level chosen—willfully and without coercion.[91]

There is nothing in the teaching of perfecting grace that suggests that anyone is exempt from human weakness, ill health, events, and consequences of which one is unaware, or imprecisions common to human finitude. All these are sharply distinguished from intentional negations of a known requirement of God—Wesley's sense of the word *sin*. "There is no such perfection in this life, as implies . . . a freedom from ignorance, mistake, temptation, and a thousand infirmities necessarily connected with flesh and blood."[92]

Whether There Are Living Exemplars of the Life of Holiness

Does such a one exist? In answer to the objection that there are no living exemplars, Wesley conceded there are not many, that some are false, and others having received have lost it. Nevertheless, he thought some had experienced it over many years.[93] True, they may not measure up to the hyper-skeptic's uncritical idea of perfection, but they never could since the skeptic defines the standard of perfection as already intrinsically impossible.[94] Wesley indeed thought that there were persons in the range of his honest observation and experience who fully, consistently and in a sustained manner walked in the way of holiness, loving the neighbor in relation to God, loving God with their whole mind, strength and spirit.[95]

But can we empirically locate anybody who lives such a life? Have any such species ever been actually sighted or held up to rigorous scrutiny or exam-

---

[88]HSP 1745, Pref. 5, XIV:329.
[89]HSP 1739, Pref. 5, XIV:321; B1:559–60; 3:122–23, 303–4, 385–86, 612–13; JWO 68, 123–32, 231f., 279f., 376.
[90]On the volitional character of sin see B1:181, 124, 233, 315, 416; 3:71, 85.
[91]#76 "On Perfection," ii.9, 3:79–80.
[92]HSP 1745, Pref. 1, XIV:328.
[93]#76 "On Perfection," ii.12–15, 3:81–83.
[94]#76 "On Perfection," ii.16, 3:83.
[95]"Short Account of the Life and Death of the Rev. John Fletcher," XI:364.

ination? To Charles he conceded in 1767: "If there be *no living witnesses* of what we have preached for twenty years, I cannot, dare not preach it any longer."[96] If it turns out that there are no living saints and cannot be any, that would run contrary to repeated apostolic reference to living saints.

Assuming that he knew some who were living the life of complete responsiveness to divine love, Wesley answered that for good reason he would not pass around their addresses. Cynical detractors would mercilessly pounce upon their infirmities, weaknesses, mistakes, all of which those who are living responsively to sanctifying grace are admittedly still subject to. The piranha press would enjoy nothing more than to have a saint to try to devour.

There is another obvious reason why the best exemplars of the Christian life are never found advertising themselves as such. By this display they would evidence a pride precisely contrary to the life they would be seeking to embody. Nonetheless, Wesley was convinced that there were indeed persons who, unadvertised, embody the Christian life. Wesley could not believe that the life so clearly promised in the gospel was intrinsically impossible. That would make it a cruel joke. Yet this remains a potentially volatile teaching insofar as it tempts pride and is easily confused with pretending to erase the limits of finitude.

Herod's Search

Wesley was convinced that there were godly persons in his own connection of spiritual formation who were living a life hidden in Christ, fully accountable to sanctifying grace, but he was not willing to write out a list for others to vilify. Where there are saints, we do them no favor by issuing a press notice. "To some that make this inquiry one might answer, 'If I knew one here, I would not tell you. You are *like Herod, you only seek the young child to destroy it.*' But to the serious we answer, 'There are numberless reasons why there should be few, if any indisputable examples. What inconveniences would this bring on the person himself, set as a mark for all to shoot at! What a temptation would it be to others, not only to men who knew not God, but to believers themselves! How hardly would they refrain from idolizing such a person! And yet how unprofitable to gainsayers! For if they hear not Moses and the prophets . . . neither would they be persuaded though one rose from the dead.' "[97]

To Charles he wrote in July 9, 1766, warning against "setting perfection too high. That perfection which I believe, I can boldly preach; because I think I see five hundred witnesses of it. Of that [impossible, too lofty, supposed] perfection which you preach, you think you do not see any witnesses at all." Why then not "fall in plumb with Mr. Whitefield," who asks with imprecise criteria: "Where are the perfect ones?" If you accept skewed, insurmountable, impossible-to-fulfill criteria, "there are none upon earth; none dwelling in the body . . . no such perfection here as you describe . . . Therefore . . . to set perfection so high is effectually to renounce it."[98]

Why Be So Fond of Sin?

He mused that the opposers of this teaching were willing to concede most of its key points as long as the term *perfection* could be strictly avoided. They are willing to "allow all you say of

---

[96]Letter to Charles Wesley, Feb. 12, 1767, LJW 5:41.
[97]Minutes, 1747, June 17, Q12, JWO 170, italics added; Matt. 2:16–18; Luke 16:31.
[98]LJW 5:20.

the love of God and man; of the mind which was in Christ; of the fruit of the Spirit; of the image of God; of universal holiness; of entire self-dedication; of sanctification in spirit, soul, and body; yea, and of the offering up of all our thoughts, words and actions, as a sacrifice to God;—all this they will allow [if] we will allow sin, a little sin, to remain in us till death.''[99]

The homily culminates with a searching series of rhetorical questions: Why should detractors become so furious at those who are seeking complete responsiveness to grace? What rational objection can one have to people who love God with all their hearts? What explains our being so adverse to receiving the whole fruit of the Spirit? Why be so fond of sin?[100] Even if wrong in our exegesis, let us be left to live with our mistakes, lest we give up the contest against sin altogether.

Wesley continued to insist that this was why the Methodist people were called forth, to make plausible this teaching experientially. Meanwhile, it remains very much a question of conscience for modern preachers in Wesley's connection to decide whether or how to present these teachings. You can take meager comfort in the fact that no church official is likely to knock down your door and demand how long it has been since you preached on perfecting grace. It is not something that is going to be externally imposed on the preacher under modern church conditions. That leaves the matter to conscience for continued examination.

Whether Instantaneous or Gradual

How long does it take a farmer to plant a seed? Only a moment. But how long does it take the seed to grow? Only over time. Inward sanctification begins "in the moment we are justified, the seed of every virtue is then *instantaneously* sown in the soul. From that time the believer *gradually* dies to sin and grows in grace. Yet sin remains in him, yea, the seed of all sin, till he is sanctified through in spirit, soul, and body." To those who expect it not sooner, sanctification is "ordinarily not given till a little before death," but we ought to expect it sooner, aware that "the generality of believers [whom we have hitherto known] are not so sanctified till near death." "Yet this does not prove that we may not today" receive sanctifying grace before death.[101]

Wesley does not rule out an instantaneous work of the Spirit by which one fully receives the seed of the regenerated life, which then grows in time and bears ever-new fruit.[102] "I believe this perfection is always wrought in the soul by a simple act of faith; consequently, in an *instant*. But I believe *a gradual work, both preceding and following that instant.* As to the time: I believe this instant generally is the instant of death, the moment before the soul leaves the body. But I believe it may be ten, twenty, or forty years before."[103]

When critics accused Wesley of a view of sanctification that too abruptly "finishes the business of salvation once for all," Wesley replied: "I believe a gradual improvement in grace and

[99]#76 "On Perfection," iii.10, 3:85.
[100]#76 "On Perfection," iii.12, 3:86–87.
[101]Minutes, 1745, Aug. 2, Q1–4, JWO 152–53, italics added. For further reference to the distinction between instantaneous and gradual sanctification see B1:35, 350f.; 2:160, 168f., 220; 3:178; LJW 5:16, 333.
[102]LJW 5:16, 333; B2:168f.; 3:178.
[103]"Brief Thoughts on Christian Perfection," 1767, italics added; FA 11:70–71, 137–38; B3:204.

goodness" as a "testimony of our present sincerity toward God."[104]

"Neither, therefore, dare we affirm (as some have done) that this full salvation is at once given to true believers. There is, indeed, an instantaneous (as well as a gradual) work of God in the souls of his children; and there wants not, we know, a cloud of witnesses, who have received, in one moment, either a clear sense of the forgiveness of their sins, or the abiding witness of the Holy Spirit. But we do not know a single instance, in any place, of a person's receiving, in one and the same moment, remission of sins, the abiding witness of the Spirit, and a new, a clean heart."[105]

The Doctrinal Minutes

[JWO:134–76]

Refining the Definition
of Sanctification

The minutes of the earliest conferences from 1744–47 are foundational for what later would be called "Larger Minutes" or "Doctrinal Minutes."[106]

All basic Methodist doctrines were hammered out in dialogical form through conversation. The preachers came together under Wesley's leadership and made certain theological and disciplinary decisions.[107] These conversations established consensually agreed teachings at an early stage on key doctrinal themes: justification, salvation by faith, and especially sanctification.

Sanctification is the work of the Spirit by which God by grace seeks completely to mend the broken human condition, to bring our stunted lives to fulfillment, not partially, but wholly in a victory over all sin in this life, through a genuine renewal of all the redeemed powers of the believer.[108] It is that movement of faith that radically and continually commits the will by grace to trust in Christ's righteousness.

Sanctification, which begins at the moment of justification, is required of all and is given to all who earnestly desire it. Faith is its sole condition.[109] It is loving God with our whole being, all inward sin being removed.[110] Sanctification was defined in the 1747 Con-

---

[104]LLBL sec. 7, 11:338, against charge made by Edmund Gibson, Bishop of London; B1:201.

[105]HSP 1740, Pref. 9, XIV:326. Later this would cause some difference of opinion between John and Charles Wesley. To Charles he wrote on February 12, 1767: "Is there or is there not any instantaneous sanctification between justification and death? I say, Yes; you (often seem to) say, No." LJW 3:41.

[106]The conference records or minutes of early conferences are sometimes referred to as the "Doctrinal" or "Large" or "Larger Minutes." The minutes of the first six conferences were published in 1749 under the title "Doctrinal Minutes" (along with a separate tract called "Disciplinary Minutes," Dublin: S. Powell, 1749). In this edition Wesley had rearranged and systematically abstracted all the doctrinal decisions of the conferences from 1744 to 1747. Six editions of "Large Minutes" were published during Wesley's lifetime, an incremental compendium of the minutes from 1744 to 1753. Well into the twentieth century British Wesleyan candidates for ministry were required to read and subscribe the "Large Minutes," using the 1797 edition as a standard, JJW 3:302n.; B20:177. Wesley himself along with a committee of preachers edited the minutes of 1780. They "considered all the articles, one by one, to see whether any should be omitted or altered," JJW 6:289. After 1765 the minutes were published annually in order to "do all things openly," JJW 6:301. Cf. LJW 5:252, 259, 262, 5:52, 228; 6:215; 7:40, 210, 255, 296, 375; 8:68, 149.

[107]DSWT:21–29.

[108]*The Pentecost Hymns of John and Charles Wesley*, ed. Timothy L. Smith, Kansas City: Beacon Hill of Kansas City, 1982, 1–85.

[109]B11:130, 133.

[110]Minutes of June 16, 1747, JWO 167–72.

ference Minutes in this way: "to be renewed in the image of God, in righteousness and true holiness," faith being "both the condition and the instrument of it. When we begin to believe, then salvation begins. And as faith increases, holiness increases till we are created anew."[111] Faith has not abrogated the call to holiness,[112] nor has faith rescinded the requirement embedded in the text, "without holiness no one will see the Lord" (Heb. 12:14).[113]

It is not as if one is first justified by faith and then later or separately sanctified by something other than faith. One is justified and sanctified by the same faith alone, which from the beginning is becoming active in love.[114] In this way faith remains the operating premise of all subsequent acts of reception of sanctifying grace. If salvation begins with pardon, it continues with an ongoing life of holiness, which finds its full maturation only in the celestial city. The life of faith begins with justifying grace, and continues with a process of habitual growth in grace. Faith does not just occur at the beginning of this process but continues throughout the life that ensues.

Pardon is salvation begun; holiness is salvation by faith continued.[115] The justified are pardoned and received into God's favor so that insofar as they continue in faith they are promised eternal happiness with God.[116] This differs in tone from the early period of Oxford Holy Club theology, which tended to view sanctification as the

premise of justification. By 1738 Wesley had come to understand more profoundly the radical nature of the Protestant doctrine of justification by grace through faith, especially as manifesting itself in an emotive life of joy in the fruits of the Spirit.

"Being made perfect in love" means "loving the Lord our God with all our mind and soul and strength," so much so that one does not sin insofar as one is born of God.[117] While we cannot be certain of identifying those made perfect in love, short of martyrdom these are the "best proofs which the nature of the things admits . . . unblamable behaviour . . . [wherein] all their tempers, words, and actions were holy and unreprovable."[118]

How Sanctification Teaching Counters Antinomian Resistance to Using the Means of Grace

Antinomianism is "the doctrine which makes void the law through faith," holding that "Christ abolished the moral law," and that "Christian liberty is liberty from obeying the commandments of God; that it is bondage to do a thing because it is commanded; that a believer is not obliged to use the ordinances of God or to do good works."[119]

Countering antinomian tendencies, Paul taught that no one "can be justified or saved by the works of the law, either moral or ritual," including "all works that do not spring from faith in Christ." More precisely, the law that Christ has

---

[111]Minutes, 1744, June 26, Q1-2, JWO 140.

[112]#35 "The Law Established Through Faith, I," ii.1, 2:26.

[113]B11:115f.

[114]On the relation of justification and sanctification see B1:124, 187, 191, 431–34; 2:158, 418; 3:505–7; 4:519–21.

[115]SS 2:451–53; 2:163f.; 3:178.

[116]B3:266.

[117]Minutes, 1744, June 26, Q6–8, JWO 141.

[118]Minutes, 1744, June 26, Q9, JWO 141.

[119]Minutes, 1744, June 25, Q19–26, JWO 139–40; JJW 3:503–11.

abolished is "the ritual law of Moses."[120]

"Does not the truth of the gospel lie very near both to Calvinism and antinomianism? Indeed it does, as it were, within a hair's breadth. So that 'tis altogether foolish and sinful, because we do not quite agree either with one or the other, to run from them as far as ever we can." Wesleyans agree with Calvinists "in ascribing all good to the free grace of God, in denying all natural free-will and all power antecedent to grace. And, in excluding all merit." We come to "the very edge of antinomianism . . . in exalting the merits and love of Christ," and "in rejoicing evermore."[121]

The faithful await the gift of full salvation by attending "the general means which God hath ordained for our receiving his sanctifying grace. These in particular are prayer, searching the Scripture, communicating, and fasting."[122]

"There is no such perfection in this life, as implies . . . a dispensation from doing good, and attending all the ordinance of God."[123] They are to be repudiated who teach a supposed perfection that turns away from the privilege "as oft as they have opportunity, to eat bread and drink wine in remembrance of Him; to search the Scripture; by fasting, as well as temperance, to keep their bodies under, and bring them into subjection; and, above all, to pour out their souls in prayer, both secretly, and in the great congregation."[124]

The "Doctrinal Minutes" instruct the connection on how to seek this sanctifying grace so as to elicit an undivided and completely sound way of holy living, by searching the Scriptures, keeping the commandments, and using the means of grace. The Spirit intends to penetrate and dwell in every fissure of our broken human lives. The inhibitions to full salvation lie in ourselves, not in God's own Spirit.

"Good works follow this [justifying] faith, but cannot go before it. Much less can sanctification, which implies a continued course of good works, springing from holiness of heart. But entire sanctification goes before our justification at the last day."[125] The Spirit's mission is fully to refashion broken human life prior to, and not on the last day, and not merely passively awaiting final judgment.

A fair number of Charles Wesley's hymns were written specifically either to prove or guard "the doctrine of Christian perfection . . . against enthusiasts and Antinomians, who . . . cause the truth to be evil spoken of."[126] Wesley admonished Thomas Maxfield's antinomianism for "using faith rather as contradistinguished from holiness than as productive of it."[127]

Whether the Full Reception of Sanctifying Grace Is Possible in This Life Before the Article of Death

The consequential phrase, "entire sanctification" was definitively expli-

---

[120]Minutes, 1744, June 25, Q19–26, JWO 139–40.
[121]Minutes, 1745, August 2, Q22–25, JWO 151–52.
[122]Minutes, 1745, Aug. 2, Q6–11, JWO 153.
[123]HSP 1745, Pref. 1, XIV:328.
[124]HSP 1745, Pref. 2, XIV:328.
[125]Letter to Thomas Church, Feb. 2, 1745, LJW 2:187; cf. 1:318–19. This assumes a distinction between the full pardon that occurs with faith in justifying grace, and the final administering of that full pardon on the last day, in "final justification."
[126]HSP 1762, Preface, XIV:334; cf. CH 7:269n.
[127]Letter to Thomas Maxfield, Nov. 2, 1962, LJW 4:193.

cated in the Minutes of June 16, 1747.[128] It is more commonly realized by the faithful near death but it can be received earlier. Nothing tests living faith like dying. No experience brings us closer to a more radical penitence. Hence the fullest sanctification is often not realized until near death, for death is always the final challenge and trial of faith.[129] Nonetheless, grace is sufficient to allow it to be received before death. Otherwise one might be encumbered by the curious assertion that one must first die before one walks in the way of holiness.

On the basis of his experience in the revival, Wesley thought that many who were justified at one point in their life were never fully tested in faith until they neared death, where they were finally prepared to embody this life of holiness. But he never insinuates that one must wait until death before sanctifying grace is made available.[130] The controversy on sanctification hinged crucially around the question "whether we should expect to be saved from all sin before the article of death," which the "Doctrinal Minutes" assert as a scriptural promise.[131]

The Minutes concede "that many of those who have died in the faith, yea, the greater part of them we have known, were not sanctified throughout—not made perfect in love—till a little before death," and "that the term 'sanctified' is continually applied by St. Paul to all that were justified . . . consequently it behooves us to speak almost constantly of the state of justification, but rarely, at least in full and explicit terms, concerning entire sanctification."[132]

Wesley was convinced that some actually attain the perfect love promised in the Scripture. It is the Scripture that drew him toward these sanctification promises. He heard in the prayers of the church and the promises of Scripture the hope of a full manifestation of grace. He was convinced that he had met living saints in the revival, people walking fully in the way of holiness and living unreservedly the life of perfect love prior to death.[133]

Should Perfect Love in This Life Be Attested?

The Minutes show agreement that entire sanctification does not need to be preached all the time, yet must not be avoided or abandoned. Wesley did not require preachers in his connection to preach it, but they were required not to inveigh against it. Even today it remains a strong tradition in interpreting Methodist doctrinal standards that one should not preach against teleiotēs in a Methodist pulpit, though no one is forced to preach in favor of it.

Admittedly, when these terms are translated into modern moral categories, little of this seriousness pervades the contemporary ethos, except perhaps in the sphere of social transformation, and even there it is often poorly formed. But it is a deep stratum of evangelical history, which one will often hear echoing even in supposedly secularized places.

There are plausible grounds on which we are "apt to have a secret distaste to any who say they are saved from all sin," especially "if these are not what they profess," but this revulsion may come "partly from our slowness and

---

[128]See also B3:169, 174–79; 2:122–24; SS 1:151; 2:172, 191, 457.
[129]LJW 1:120, 6:213, 11:528.
[130]Minutes of June 16, 1747, JWO 169.
[131]Minutes, 1747, June 17, Q3–8, JWO 168–69, from Deut. 30:6; Ezek. 36:25, 29; Eph. 3:14–19, 5:25, 27; 2 Cor. 7:1; John 17:20, 23; 1 Thess. 5:23.
[132]Minutes, 1747, June 17, Q2, JWO 167–68.
[133]JJW 2:90, 275; 5:283f.; JJW 8:307.

unreadiness of heart to believe the works of God."[134]

The way of holiness must be attested with reserve: "Suppose one had attained to this, would you advise him to speak of it? Not to them who know not God; it would only provoke them to contradict and blaspheme."[135] Those who believe they are receiving perfecting grace do well to speak of their own experience with deep humility, modesty, meekness, and humble self-awareness. Young preachers if speaking publicly on Christian perfection are advised not to do so too minutely or circumstantially but rather in general and scriptural terms.[136]

The "Doctrinal Minutes" recommend that the preachers not preach on perfecting grace often or constantly, even though it is constantly to be expected. It should be treated chiefly in the presence of those who have readiness to hear it without engendering unnecessary distortions. Entire sanctification should be preached "scarce at all to those who are not pressing forward; to those who are, always by way of promise, always drawing rather than driving."[137] Since the judgmental or "harsh preaching" of perfection tends to "bring believers into a kind of bondage of slavish fear," "we should always place it in the most amiable light, so that it may excite only hope, joy and desire."[138]

Though promised to all, it remains difficult to communicate without misconstructions. The Methodist societies should seek to elicit a response to perfecting grace in all, but not to make it a contentious point of constant railing for those not rightly prepared to understand it. Union with Christ, purity of heart, and godliness cannot be neglected or diluted, but perfecting grace can be preached sparely and prudently depending on the context. Wesley asked all preachers in his connection the question still asked in Methodist ordinal services: "Do you expect to be made perfect in love in this life?"[139]

Scriptural Teaching on the Extent of Grace

A central teaching of Scripture concerns the radical extent of the promise of grace, so much so that perfecting grace is not doctrine merely permissible in Scripture, but integral to the gospel. God promised to "redeem Israel from *all* their sins" (Ps. 130:8). From all her impurities and idols she is promised cleansing (Ezek. 36:25). Christ loved the church and gave himself for her that he might "present her to himself as a radiant church, without stain or wrinkle or any other blemish, but holy and blameless" (Eph. 5:27). For this purpose the Son of God was manifested, that he might destroy all sin (1 John 3:8). Jesus prayed that his followers might all be one, and that they would be made perfect in love (John 17:22). Herein is our love made perfect, that we may have boldness in the day of judgment, because as he is, so are we in this world (1 John 4:17).

The call to "be perfect, therefore, as your heavenly Father is perfect" (Matt. 5:48) is a command given to living, not dead men. It would not have been commanded if impossible to fulfill. On the basis of these texts, there can be no doubt that the Scriptures are describing present Christian life, not merely an

---

[134]Minutes, 1747, June 17, Q15, JWO 171.
[135]Minutes, 1747, June 17, Q13, JWO 170.
[136]Minutes, Aug. 15, 1758, JWO 177.
[137]Minutes, 1745, Aug. 2, Q6–11, JWO 153.
[138]Minutes, 1747, June 17, Q16, JWO 171.
[139]*Book of Discipline,* UMC, 1988:232.

abstract description of a life that never happens. Yet we should be keenly aware of "the sinful nature which still remains in us," "but this should only incite us the more earnestly to turn unto Christ every moment."[140]

Are You Going on to Perfection?

Those who come up for full connection as preachers in the Wesleyan connection are asked a weighty series of questions not merely about Christian perfection as an idea, but more so about their own appropriation of it: "Have you faith in Christ?" "Are you going on to perfection?" "Do you expect to be made perfect in love in this life?" "Are you earnestly striving after it?" "Are you resolved to devote yourself wholly to God and His work?"[141]

By the time anyone in Wesley's connection is ordained, one must have thought carefully about these questions. They remain troubling to some. What follows seeks to answer, or more so to frame the context in which one's own answer might be made more meaningful, seeking not prematurely to ease conscience but inform it. Those who have not yet developed a defensible view of sanctification on which they are willing to stand and that they are willing to defend can do no better than directly study Wesley himself in answering these questions.

The disciplinary rubric softens modern ordinands and protects them from making a hard landing, for upon the examination the bishop is instructed to "explain to the conference the historic nature of the following questions, and seek to interpret their spirit and intent."[142] This language has embedded in

it a studied, intentional ambiguity. On the one hand, some, by explaining its historic nature, exalt it as normative; on the other hand, others, by showing its historic importance, by implication show that it belongs to the past, and perhaps does not need to be taken too seriously, since it is just a historical document. It deftly allows for either interpretation. The hearer is left to judge the questions as either archaic or perennially pertinent. In any event, these questions have been asked of Methodist preachers in full connection from the early days of the Methodist revival.

Defining Sanctification in the Confession, Article 11

For many in the Wesleyan tradition, including all United Methodists, the Confession stands as a constitutionally unrevisable summary of doctrine in the Wesleyan tradition. Three paragraphs of the Confession, Article 11, carefully define sanctification, perfection, and disclaimers about perfection, and deserve to be carefully studied by all who teach in the Wesleyan tradition.

Sanctification is the work of God's grace, not an expression of human ability. It assumes the work of the Spirit by which those who have been born again by justifying grace are cleansed from sin in their thoughts, words, and acts. God's work of grace does not intend partially but wholly to cleanse from sin. Two metaphors complement each other: cleansing and empowerment. We are being empowered, and enabled to live in accordance with God's will and to strive for holiness without which no one will see the Lord.

---

[140]Minutes, 1747, June 17, Q19–21, JWO 171.

[141]Book of Discipline, UMC 1992, para. 425. "These are the questions which every Methodist preacher from the beginning has been required to answer upon becoming a full member of an Annual Conference. These questions were formulated by John Wesley and have been little changed throughout the years," 227n.

[142]Book of Discipline, UMC 1992, para. 425.

"We believe sanctification is the work of God's grace through the Word and the Spirit by which those who have been born again are cleansed from sin in their thoughts words and acts, and are enabled to live in accordance with God's will, and to strive for holiness without which no one will see the Lord."[143]

Entire sanctification is complete responsiveness to perfecting grace. It is a right ordering of perfect love, righteousness, and true holiness, which every regenerate believer may obtain, by being delivered from the power of sin, loving God with all the heart, soul, mind, and strength, and the neighbor as oneself.

"Through faith in Jesus Christ this gracious gift may be received in this life." The way of holiness is not simply a road to be walked after death, but rather received in this life. The Spirit works in this receptive process "both gradually and instantaneously," by means of a gift and a giving process. This perfecting grace "should be sought earnestly by every child of God."[144]

It is doubtful that those who inveigh against the teaching of perfecting grace can in good conscience lead and preach in Methodist pulpits. The model deed of 1763 made clear that the doctrinal standards that apply to Methodist preaching should be judged in relation to the first four volumes of sermons, and Wesley's *Explanatory Notes Upon the New Testament*, which contain this teaching. Those offend against Methodist doctrine who inveigh against perfecting grace. It is not implied that one cannot have a contrary opinion about it—one may, provided that opinion is kept out of preaching.[145]

The Unique Doctrinal Status of the Unnumbered Methodist Protestant Disciplinary Article on Sanctification

Appended to the Twenty-five Articles in all United Methodist *Disciplines* is an unnumbered Article on Sanctification, adopted by the uniting conferences of 1939 and 1968. It has a special status, having been received from the Methodist Protestant Church tradition, which upon union was included in the discipline as an article of faith. Arguably, it is not expressly protected by the restrictive rules and is not strictly speaking one of the Twenty-five Articles of Religion, though constitutionally appended to them. Nonetheless it has appeared in every *Discipline* since unification (1939), and remains a concise and useful statement of that sanctification teaching generally accepted among Wesleyans.

In this Article sanctification is defined as the renewal of our fallen nature by the atoning work of the Son, and by the attesting work of the Spirit, received through faith, enabling the cleansing from *all* sins. We are not only delivered from the guilt of sin but washed from its pollution, saved from its power, and enabled through grace to love God with all our hearts and to walk in his holy commandments blamelessly.

FURTHER READING ON THE WORK OF THE SPIRIT IN SANCTIFICATION

Arnett, William M. "The Role of the Holy Spirit in Entire Sanctification in the Writings of John Wesley." WTJ 14 no. 2 (1979):15–30.

Cary, Clement. "Did Mr. Wesley Change His View on Sanctification?" In *Entire Sanctification*, edited by S. Coward. Louisville: Herald Press, 1900.

Collins, Kenneth. FW, 138-47.

[143]Confession, Art. 11; cf. LJW 8:256.
[144]Confession, Art. 11.
[145]DSWT:21–53.

Dorr, Donal. "Wesley's Teaching on the Nature of Holiness." LQHR 190 (1965): 234–39.

Harper, Steve. *John Wesley's Theology Today.* Grand Rapids: FAP, Zondervan, 1983. Chaps. 5 and 6, "Transformation (Effects of Salvation)" and "Growth in Grace."

Lindström, Harald G. A. *Wesley and Sanctification.* Nashville, Abingdon, op. cit.

Miley, John. *Systematic Theology.* Vol. 2. Chap. 8 on sanctification. New York: Hunt and Eaton, 1892–1894.

Monk, R. op. cit. "Sanctification." 107ff., 118ff.

Outler, Albert C. *The Wesleyan Theological Heritage, Essays,* edited by T. Oden and L. Longden. "A Focus on the Holy Spirit." Grand Rapids: FAP, Zondervan, 1991, pp. 159–75.

Page, Isaac E. and John Brash. *Scriptural Holiness: As Taught by John Wesley.* London: C. H. Kelly, 1891.

Runyan, Theodore, ed. *Sanctification and Liberation.* Nashville, Abingdon, 1981.

Weems, Lovett Hayes. *The Gospel According to Wesley: A Summary of John Wesley's Message.* Nashville: Discipleship Resources, 1982.

ON REMAINING SIN AFTER JUSTIFICATION

On Sin in Believers

2 Cor. 5:17: "If any man be in Christ, he is a new creature." [Homily #13 1763 B1:314–34; J#13 V:144–56]

No willful sin is consistent with life in Christ. "If a believer wilfully sins, he thereby forfeits his pardon. Neither is it possible he should have justifying faith again without previously repenting."[146] One may "forfeit the gift of God either by sins of omission or commission."[147]

Hence with Wesley as with Luther, the whole life of the believer is repentance.

Christ "cannot *reign* where sin *reigns*; neither will he *dwell* where any sin is *allowed.* But he *is* and *dwells* in the heart of every believer who is *fighting against all sin.*"[148] This then is a struggle. The believer is not being intimidated by the power of sin because the believer already knows that sin's power has been broken.

Whether Regenerate Believers Commit Sin

Wesley had repeatedly stressed the power bestowed by sufficient grace on justified and regenerate believers not to commit sin, a central feature of the holy living tradition.[149] The controversy that exploded around this idea came on one hand from those formed by the Lutheran tradition of *simul justus et peccator,*[150] and by the Calvinist tradition that stressed the perseverance of the saints and the eternal security of the saved, and on the other hand from Moravians who were teaching "sinless—even guiltless—perfection, as if the power not to sin meant the extirpation of all 'remains of sin.' "[151]

Wesley proposed a third alternative that hinged decisively on the distinction between voluntary and involuntary transgressions, "between 'sin properly so called' (i.e. the [deliberate] violation of a known law of God)—mortal if unrepented) and all 'involuntary transgressions' (culpable only if unrepented and not discarded when discerned or entertained)."[152] There remained an un-

---

[146]Minutes, 1744, June 25, Q9, JWO 138.

[147]Minutes, 1744, June 25, Q11, JWO 138.

[148]#13 "On Sin in Believers," iii.8, 1:323.

[149]As in #17 "The Circumcision of the Heart," and #19 "The Great Privilege of those that are Born of God."

[150]B1:233, 245n.

[151]#13 "On Sin in Believers," Outler's introduction, 1:314; on Wesley's rejection of sinless perfection see EA 11:65–66, 338–41; B1:318–32, 416–21; 9:53–55, 397f.

[152]#13 "On Sin in Believers," i.5, 1:315, in the tradition of the medieval and scholastic

stable tension, however, between Wesley's preaching of the great privilege (not to commit sin) and the realities of post-conversion life where sin remained even though it was not reigning.[153]

He insisted on juxtaposing the ancient ecumenical holy living tradition in the closest possible relation to the Reformation tradition of justification by grace through faith alone. When he shifted from one to another focus, he sometimes sounded as if the other were for a moment forgotten, but seen as a whole the corpus seeks to bring them into the closest homogeneity. By 1763 the need was evident to sort out the relationship with greater clarity, so he wrote Homily #13 "On Sin in Believers," "in order to remove a mistake which some were labouring to propagate: there is no sin in any that are justified"[154] (followed four years later by its sequel, Homily #14 "The Repentance of Believers").

Homily #13 corrected the inference that might be fairly drawn from some of Wesley's earlier sermons that after conversion the believer is *de facto* so entirely free from sin that there is no further possibility of sin (or even of finite error!), or that the presence of sinful desires proves one's lack of faith.[155] Keep in mind that the "great privilege of those born of God" is precisely that they are no longer bound to the reign of sin. This homily is a crucial addendum. Those who preach on Christian perfection should carefully read this and its companion homily as a corrective to the exaggerated edges of several sermons on entire freedom from sin.[156]

Hedging Against Despair

Much of the confusion had been spawned by "well-meaning men" under the direction of Nicholas von Zinzendorf, who imagined that "even the corruption of nature *is no more* in those who believe in Christ."[157] When pressed, they allowed that "sin did still remain *in the flesh*, but not *in the heart* of a believer. And after a time, when the absurdity of this was shown, they fairly gave up the point, allowing that sin did still *remain*, though not *reign*, in him that is born of God."[158]

Wesley was trying pastorally to protect believers against despair over deep-rooted sin. Some who having experienced justifying faith had then often experienced a backsliding despondency were disturbed over whether they still had saving faith. His purpose is to show that the struggle against sin continues after justification.

It would become a serious problem of pastoral care if each time one fell from faith one would then intensely despair over whether one had ever or ever would receive saving grace. Wesley was countering that forgiveness is constantly being offered and that one is never made absolutely immune to or incapable of falling.

The idea that the justified person is

---

distinction between mortal and venial sin, and between voluntary and involuntary transgression. On the distinction between deliberate and indeliberate see JWO 258f., 287.

[153]#13 "On Sin in Believers," i.6, 1:319. This was a theme that Wesley would repeatedly explore from one angle or another; see #8 "The First-fruits of the Spirit," iii.4–5; #40 "Christian Perfection," ii.3–5; #41 "Wandering Thoughts," iii.6; #82 "On Temptation," i.5.

[154]JJW, March 28, 1763.

[155]See also B1:65, 335–52; 2:164–67.

[156]See also B1:233, 245f., 314–34, 336–47, 435–41; 2:165f.; 4:157, 212.

[157]#13 "On Sin in Believers," i.5, 1:319.

[158]#13 "On Sin in Believers," i.5, 1:318–19; #19 "The Great Privilege of Those That are Born of God," ii, V:227–31.

JOHN WESLEY'S SCRIPTURAL CHRISTIANITY

free from all remnants of sin and temptation is a novel teaching (hence spurious, viewed apostolically) never found in the primitive church, patristic writers or in the central history of the Church of England.[159]

Quadrilateral Criteria Applied to Those Who Deny That Sin Remains in Believers

Wesley built his case on the basis of quadrilateral criteria. Only in a few places can the quadrilateral method be seen deliberately at work: here, and in the early part of *Original Sin*, and in the *Appeals*.[160] Accordingly, he offered four types of argument from *Scripture, reason, tradition*, and *experience*, against the position that there is no sin in those that are justified:

1. The position of absolute sinlessness after justification is contrary to *Scripture* (Gal. 5:17; 1 Cor. 1:2), especially all those passages in Paul's writings that insist that the flesh continually lusts against the spirit, and the spirit against the flesh.[161]

2. To say that there is no sin in believers is contrary to the *experience* of innumerable believers. Almost every believer has experienced some sort of ongoing struggle, having received saving faith, of contending with the consequences that follow from faith, and often with doubts as to whether one even had the faith or not. That is very common to the life of faith. One need not feel alienated or guilty or in despair when one goes through such a "wilderness state," a condition in which one having been delivered like Moses crossing the Red Sea, having gone through baptism, having gone through the waters and being born into a renewed life, one then finds oneself wandering in the wilderness still on the way to Canaan.[162]

3. Presumed absolute sinlessness after justification is a novel, hence untraditional doctrine, unheard of in the ancient church. It is a new doctrine and any doctrine that is new and unprecedented could not be a fully apostolic doctrine. The prayers of the whole Christian *tradition*, East and West, from the ancient Christian writers through the Reformation, confess that believers continue to struggle with sin.[163] Wesley applied the Vincentian rule of Christian antiquity, "whatever doctrine is *new* must be *wrong*," since unapostolic, "for the *old* religion is the only *true* one: and no doctrine can be right unless it is the same 'which was from the beginning.' "[164] "The perfection I hold is so far from being contrary to the doctrine of our Church, that it is exactly the same which every Clergyman prays for every Sunday: 'Cleanse the thoughts of our hearts by the inspiration of thy Holy Spirit, that we may perfectly love thee, and worthily magnify thy holy name.' I mean neither more nor less than this."[165]

4. Finally, it is by *reason* that a critique is applied to false premises. Wesley discussed the logical dilemma of the doctrine of complete freedom from sin after justification by showing that it has the logical effect of eliciting hopelessness. If this premise is true, then anyone who feels a sinful desire cannot be a believer. That merely leads

---

[159]#13 "On Sin in Believers," i, 1:317–19.

[160]Alternatively Wesley lists Scripture, reason, and experience as doctrinal norms, as in #14 "The Repentance of Believers," i.2, and on other occasions "Scripture, reason, and Christian antiquity," as in his Preface to his collected works, I, 1771.

[161]#13 "On Sin in Believers," iii, 1:321–25.

[162]#13 "On Sin in Believers," iii.7, 1:323.

[163]#13 "On Sin in Believers," i.2–4; iii.9.

[164]#13 "On Sin in Believers," iii.9, 1:324.

[165]"An Answer to Mr. Roland Hill's Tract, Entitled, 'Imposture Detected,' " X:450.

to despair, not faith. It elicits a double bind: If I think that any subsequent sin after justification negates my justification (disallowing penitent faith), and then if I feel mixed motives and sinful desires, I am likely to conclude that I have lost my faith. Thus reason concurs with Scripture, experience, and tradition that after faith one still may sin.[166]

The Struggle of Flesh and Spirit

The two contrary principles, flesh and spirit, continue to struggle and intermesh, latently or overtly, throughout every day of the life of faith.[167] In even the most mature believer there continues a dormant guerrilla war between flesh and spirit.[168] Anyone walking after the Spirit still feels inwardly these two contrary principles in quiescent tension. The Corinthian believers were described as carnal, even while their faith was growing.[169]

One may have weak faith. There are different degrees of faith.[170] One may have a tiny foothold on faith, yet even the foothold is the beginning of saving faith, which is being called to pray that faith might increase in strength.[171] The "almost Christian" is not even one with little faith. The "almost Christian" lacks the faith that trusts God's righteousness (that may be the only thing missing), although he or she may have many outward appearances of religiosity. One may be an "altogether Christian" and still continue to struggle with a weak or partially blinded faith. Faith may have been born without fully bearing the joyful fruits it could bear in due time.

Believers are "daily sensible of sin remaining in their heart, pride, self-will, unbelief; and of sin cleaving to all they speak and do, even their best actions and holiest duties. Yet at the same time they 'know that they are of God;' they cannot doubt of it for a moment. They feel his Spirit clearly 'witnessing with their spirit, that they are children of God.'"[172] They have not lost faith just because they experience an ongoing struggle with temptation, a continuing combat between flesh and spirit.[173]

In the Preface to the 1740 *Hymns and Sacred Poems*, Wesley poignantly described the ongoing struggle of those who having been "justified freely through faith" may "remain for days, or weeks, or months" in this peace, "and commonly suppose they shall not know war any more, till some of their old enemies, their bosom-sins, or the sin which did most easily beset them, (perhaps anger or desire,) assault them again, and thrust sore at them . . . Then arises fear, that they shall not endure to the end; and often doubt, whether God has not forgotten them, or whether they did not deceive themselves, in thinking their sins were forgiven . . . But it is seldom long before the Lord answers for himself, sending them the Holy Ghost, to comfort them, to bear witness continually with their spirit." "Now they see all the hidden abominations there; the depth of pride, and self, and hell: Yet" knowing they are heirs, "their spirit rejoiceth in God their Sav-

---

[166]#13 "On Sin in Believers," iii.10, 1:324.

[167]#13 "On Sin in Believers," iii.1–3, 1:321–22.

[168]CH 7:398–406, 460–63.

[169]#13 "On Sin in Believers," iii.2, 1:321.

[170]B3:175–76; 3:491–98; 9:111, 164–65; LJW 1:251; 2:214; 5:173, 200; JJW 1:481–83; 2:328–29; JWO 68f., 356–62; cf. B3:266.

[171]#13 "On Sin in Believers," iii, 1:321–25. In defense of degrees of faith, see #2 "The Almost Christian," JJW May 29, 1738; Minutes Aug. 2, 1745.

[172]#13 "On Sin in Believers," iii.7, 1:323.

[173]B1:235–36; 3:105–6; SS 1:164; 2:362; CH 7:398–406, 460–63.

iour, even in the midst of this fiery trial, which continually heightens both the strong sense they then have of their inability to help themselves, and the inexpressible hunger they feel after a full renewal in his image."[174]

Distinguishing Sin Reigning From Sin Remaining

Every faithful babe in Christ, having been baptized, and having received the new birth, and having begun to walk the way of holiness, remains subject to falling. The believer who shares by God's pardoning gift in God's holiness remains still on a long road leading toward mature responsiveness to grace.[175] The believer is "saved from sin; yet not entirely; It *remains*, though it does not *reign*."[176]

The Adversary "remains indeed where he once reigned but he remains in chains."[177] The demonic powers are chained up even though they rise up and howl. They pretend to have enduring power but in fact do not. Imagine an enemy in chains, and that you know the enemy is in chains, and yet the enemy is still capable of doing proximate harm, and creating a lot of penultimate noise and confusion.[178]

Sin no longer has any overwhelming power or hegemony over the life of the believer, although its consequences and residual effects continue.[179] When I by sinning harm my neighbor, the consequences of that sin may keep on rippling through the next year even though last year I sincerely repented. I cannot stop the world. It keeps on going. No one by being pardoned is suddenly exempt from having to struggle with the consequences of past sin. Faith teaches me that even though I may feel this ambiguity and conflict in my heart, nonetheless I am daily in the process of yielding myself up to the pardoning word, and therefore there is no condemnation. Sin no longer has radical power over the life of the believer, though its consequences echo.[180]

The False Premise of "Sinless Perfection"

Sin in believers remains a vexing daily challenge to be dealt with, but it does not have abiding power, for its power has been radically undermined by the grace of the Son on the cross. The demonic spirits have been bound up. Wesley disputed the fantasy of a sinless perfection that would imagine itself exempt from all future struggle with temptation, and all conflict between flesh and spirit.[181] Deploring the phrase "sinless perfection,"[182] Wesley preferred to speak of "perfect love."[183]

---

[174]HSP 1740 Pref. 11, XIV:327.

[175]#13 "On Sin in Believers," iii.8–10, 1:323–25. On the distinction between babes in Christ (who grasp pardon but not holiness) and those mature in Christ (who consecrate the full measure of their redeemed powers to steady responsiveness to grace) see #40 "Christian Perfection," ii.1; #83 "On Patience," sec. 10; *Notes* on Heb. 5:13–14; Letter to John Fletcher, Mar. 22, 1775.

[176]#13 "On Sin in Believers," iv.3, 1:327.

[177]#13 "On Sin in Believers," iv.11, 1:331.

[178]#13 "On Sin in Believers," iv, 1:325–32. For further reference to the distinction between remaining and reigning see also #1 "Salvation by Faith," ii.6; #19 "The Great Privilege of Those That are Born of God," ii.2; #128 "The Deceitfulness of the Human Heart," ii.5; JJW, Aug. 10, 1738.

[179]B1:233, 245f., 314–34, 336–47, 435–41; 2:165f.; 4:157, 212.

[180]#13 "On Sin in Believers," v, 1:332–34.

[181]"Principles of a Methodist," 11–13, VIII:363–65.

[182]EA 11:65–66, 338–41; B1:318–32, 416–21; 9:53–55, 397f.

So is the justified person free from all sin? In principle, "yes," because God's gift on the cross is the gift of freedom, and yet what is given sufficiently is received deficiently. Hence the gift does not exempt human freedom from its defining conditions of finitude and time, or from the daily struggle between flesh and spirit. As new creatures, we do not leave behind our creatureliness completely, but are restored to our original creation.

The further one walks in the way of holiness the more deeply one is aware of one's sin. It is a paradox of sin and grace, that those who turn out to be most keenly aware of their inadequacy are walking, breathing saints. Those least aware of their sin are the most distant from repentance. Repentance thus continues in the Christian life. It does not happen just once.

The Repentance of Believers

Mark 1:15: "Repent and believe the gospel." [Homily #14 1767 B1:355–53; J#14 V:156–70]

In What Manner Sin Cleaves to Believers' Words and Actions

Believers remain vulnerable to temptation to inordinate affections, and disordered loves not beheld in relation to the love of God.[184] However deeply rooted in faith, ordinary believers still struggle with continuing pride, self-will, and love of the world, shame, fear of rejection, evil surmisings, and impure intentions.[185]

Tempers that interfere with the love of neighbor, such as jealously, malice, covetousness, and envy, do not suddenly disappear when one has faith. One continues to be tempted to the idolatrous love of earthly things so as to neglect the love of the neighbor under the embrace of the love of God.[186] It is not uncommon for believers to continue to struggle with idolatry, since believers too continue to be tempted to imagine that temporal goods are absolute.

The whole of the spiritual life is a subtle equilibrium that is always susceptible to imbalance. When a child is at the point of learning to walk, it is difficult to maintain equilibrium. The problem of learning to walk in faith is likewise a problem of keeping equilibrium. The balance is subtle. Recipients of sanctifying grace are constantly tempted to imbalance, fallenness, and "backsliding."[187]

The backslider, having gotten a certain foothold in faith, slips and falls backward. Sin remains in the heart after conversion even when unrecognized,[188] in the subtle forms of pride, self-will, love of the world, the desire of the eyes, self-indulgence, the pride of life, the desire for glory.[189] Such temptations may recalcitrantly remain lodged within the context of the justified life.[190]

No self-aware believer could remain wholly oblivious that sin cleaves to his words and actions, as seen in sins of omission, inward defects without number, uncharitable interactions, actions not aiming at the glory of God, and in

---

[183]"Some Remarks on Mr. Hill's 'Review of All the Doctrines Taught by Mr. John Wesley,'" X:411; CH 7:183, 187, 506–7, 520–21.

[184]#14 "The Repentance of Believers," i.4, 5, 1:337–38.

[185]#14 "The Repentance of Believers," i.3–5, 1:337–38.

[186]#14 "The Repentance of Believers," i.7–9, 1:339–40.

[187]B3:210–26; 4:517–19; LJW 7:103, 351; 8:61, 111; JJW 5:40, 47, 54, 436; 8:31; CH 7:284–98, 628f.

[188]#14 "The Repentance of Believers," i.i, 1:336.

[189]#14 "The Repentance of Believers," i.3–7, 1:337–39.

[190]#14 "The Repentance of Believers," i.8–10, 1:339–42.

continuing post-conversion evidences of neurotic guilt and helplessness.[191] This struggle of flesh and spirit goes on in the heart, in one's affect and activity, both in sins committed and neglected.

But still in all of these things, believers, insofar as they have faith in God's atoning work, have no condemnation. They still have an advocate with the Father. That is what distinguishes the regenerate life.

The Continuing Congruence Between Repentance and Faith After Justification

Hence repentance remains equally necessary before and after the first repentance. Repentance and faith are needed first to enter the kingdom, and then recurrently to continue and grow in the kingdom.[192]

The call of the gospel to "repent and believe" does not subside after its first address. If one enters the Christian community initially by repenting and believing, so does one continue in it. Subsequently, repentance remains a daily integral concern of the Christian life, which is ever anew being offered the promise that God is not only willing but able "to save from all the sin that still remains in your heart."[193] In going " 'from faith to faith', when we have a faith to be cleansed from indwelling sin" we are "saved from all that *guilt*, that *desert* of punishment, which we felt before."[194]

The congruence between faith and repentance is rhythmic and dialectical: When repentance says, "Without him, I can do nothing," faith replies, "I can do all things through Christ strengthening me."[195] By repentance we recognize our need; by faith our need is met. In repentance we behold our limitations; in faith our grace-enabled capabilities.

The Cure for Sin After Justification

In receiving justifying grace, we are not immediately thereby made behaviorally whole. If we were it would be "absurd to expect a farther deliverance from sin" after justification.[196] Hence the paradox: those believers that are only slightly "convinced of the deep corruption in their hearts" tend to have "little concern about entire sanctification." A profound sense of our *demerit* is precisely needed before we can understand the full compass of the atoning work of Christ. It is not our native strength but our utter helplessness that best teaches us "truly to live upon Christ by faith, not only as our Priest, but as our King."[197]

"Immense harm" is done by imagining that the gradual reception of sanctifying grace is indistinguishable from the instantaneous reception of justifying grace, for this "entirely blocks up the way to any farther change."[198] After the reception of justifying grace, the believer hears God speaking with a word of power that not only cleanses but in time evicts sin, whereby the "evil root, the carnal mind, is destroyed; and inbred sin subsists no more." This uprooting occurs again by repentance and faith, but "in a peculiar sense different from that wherein we believed

[191]#14 "The Repentance of Believers," i.11–20, 1:341–46.
[192]#14 "The Repentance of Believers," proem.1–3, 1:335–36; B1:65, 225, 278, 335–52, 477; 2:164–67.
[193]#14 "The Repentance of Believers," ii.2, 1:347.
[194]#14 "The Repentance of Believers," ii.4, 1:348.
[195]#14 "The Repentance of Believers," ii.5, 1:350.
[196]#14 "The Repentance of Believers," iii.1, 1:350.
[197]#14 "The Repentance of Believers," iii.4, 1:352.
[198]#14 "The Repentance of Believers," iii.1, 1:350.

[for] justification," in a deepening faith that at length saves to the uttermost.[199]

A Call to Backsliders

Ps. 77:7–8: "Will the Lord absent himself for ever? And will he be no more entreated? Is his mercy clean gone for ever? And is his promise come utterly to an end for evermore?" [Homily #86 1778 B3:210–26; J#86 VI:514–27]

There is still hope for those who having "begun to run well" have "made shipwreck of the faith." But for the "uneasy" who earnestly desire change but think it impossible, the problem is different. They may be closer to salvation who think themselves furthest away.[200] More sinners are destroyed by despair than presumption. Many who once fought in spiritual combat now no longer strive, feeling victory impossible to attain.[201]

Wesley is here concerned with that form of despair among believers who, having experienced faith, enter into an extended period of the wilderness state, who tend to become disconsolate. They find themselves backsliding through a lengthy period of spiritual combat in which they are hardly producing the fruits of faith. Such are not beyond the grace of God.[202]

Why Backsliders May be Drawn to Despair

Backsliders may imagine there is no hope for them because they find it hard to conceive of being forgiven again having once been born anew in faith. Having received a full pardon once, they imagine that they cannot ever expect to receive it again. They reason wrongly by analogy from civil governance to eternal governance.[203] But God forgives many times, unlike civil justice.[204]

At first glance the origin of the backsliders' depression seems too deep to uproot. They may imagine they have so blasphemed the Spirit that there is no hope of further forgiveness (Matt. 12:31, 32).[205] The blasphemy against the Spirit of which Jesus spoke, however, is the specific act of explicitly abusing the divine name by attributing the Spirit's work to Satan or by directly declaring that Jesus worked by the power of Satan.[206]

Scrupulous backsliders may fantasize and mourn that they have committed that "sin that leads to death," as distinguished from sin that "does not lead to death" (1 John 5:16).[207] The death spoken of in that passage, however, is not eternal death, but the approach to death[208] of "notorious backsliders from high degrees of holiness" whose full redemption awaits the moment of death in order that they might be finally proved by faith meeting death to be ready for eternal life.[209]

They may become scrupulously disturbed by the text in Hebrews: "It is impossible for those who have once been enlightened, who have tasted the heavenly gift, who have shared in the

---

[199]#14 "The Repentance of Believers," ii.2, 1:347.
[200]#86 "A Call to Backsliders," proem.4, 5, 3:212.
[201]#86 "A Call to Backsliders," proem.1–3, 3:211.
[202]#86 "A Call to Backsliders," proem.4–5, 3:212.
[203]#86 "A Call to Backsliders," i.1, 3:213.
[204]#86 "A Call to Backsliders," ii.1, 3:217.
[205]#86 "A Call to Backsliders," i.2, 3:215; cf. 3:555–56; LJW 5:224.
[206]#86 "A Call to Backsliders," ii.2(6), 3:223.
[207]#86 "A Call to Backsliders," i.2.(1), 3:214.
[208]On the distinction between physical and spiritual (eternal, second) death see B2:287–88; 3:185–86; FA 11:64, 215, 230, 507–8; SS 1:117, 157; CH 7:68f., 86–7, 129–45, 379, 465.
[209]#86 "A Call to Backsliders," ii, 3:217–19.

Holy Spirit, who have tasted the goodness of the word of God, and the powers of the coming age, if they fall away, to be brought back to repentance'' (Heb. 6:4–5). And, "If we deliberately keep on sinning after we have received the knowledge of the truth, no sacrifice for sins is left'' (Heb. 10:26).[210] The sin involved in these passages, however, is the specific one of openly declaring "that Jesus is a deceiver of the people."[211] There is no scriptural reason for despair, unless one is making these specific denials.

Wesley countered these false imaginings with the plain evidences of the evangelical revival: Large numbers of "real apostates" were being restored to the way of holiness, in some cases to a higher level of grace than before. In some this change was occurring in an instant.[212]

Article 12 on Sin After Justification

Article 12 defined sin in believers. One may depart from whatever grace God has given, be it prevenient, justifying, or sanctifying grace, because grace does not suppress free choice. To receive justifying and sanctifying grace does not imply that one ceases to be free, but rather that one becomes free in a new way.

The believer remains subject to temptation and prone to fall though continuing inordinate desire. So at whatever stage one is in the curriculum of unfolding grace, there always remains the possibility of sin. Having walked in faith one may fall into sin. Any movement toward repentance is possible only by grace, not by one's natural power or initiative.

The Contrite Cannot Rightly Be Denied the Sacrament

Article 12 resists three distortions: that forgiveness is not offered a second time after having received justifying grace, that sin after justification is unpardonable, and that all sins are unpardonable sins against the Holy Spirit.[213] The Article stipulates: "Not every sin willingly committed after justification is sin against the Holy Ghost and unpardonable. Wherefore the grant of repentance is not to be denied to such as fall into sin after justification. After we have received the Holy Ghost we may depart from grace given and fall into sin and by the grace of God rise again and amend our lives. Therefore they are to be condemned who say they can no more sin as long as they live here, or deny the place of forgiveness to such as truly repent."

Sin against the Holy Spirit is that sin so hardened against the hearing of the Word and against one's own conscience that one has decided not to put oneself in a place where one can be pardoned.

Forgiveness is being offered on the condition of penitence. Those not truly penitent are not ready to receive this forgiveness. It is not that God's pardoning word on the cross remains unspoken unless we accept it. For it is in principle offered to all. Rather, contrition is the subjective condition of our readiness to receive what is already there, namely, the forgiveness of God.[214] For only "to such as truly repent this forgiveness is being offered." Amendment of life is required to authenticate repentance.

The offer of forgiveness is not to be denied penitents who fall into sin after justification. The church does an injustice when it denies to the contrite the

---

[210]#86 "A Call to Backsliders," i.2 (2–4), 3:214–15.
[211]#86 "A Call to Backsliders," ii.2, 3:219–22.
[212]#86 "A Call to Backsliders," ii, 3:222–26.
[213]Oden, DSWT 145–47, 199–200.
[214]B1:215, 229.

means of grace for their sins after justification, or the preaching of forgiveness to the penitent.

The prayer of absolution in the service of Holy Communion calls to mind among worshipers that forgiveness is addressed to all, yet there is a conditional premise that our pardon hinges on conscious readiness to receive it. We do not receive pardon from God without any reference to our repentance and faith. Once pardoned and delivered, the new beginning requires being strengthened and reconfirmed. One must ready oneself anew for each time of holy communion. Repentance recurs daily.

FURTHER READINGS ON SANCTIFICATION

Flew, R. Newton. *The Idea of Perfection in Christian Theology*. Oxford: OUP, 1934, 313–34.

Lindström, Harald G. A. *Wesley and Sanctification*. Nashville: Abingdon, n.d.

Peters, John L. *Christian Perfection and American Methodism*. New York: Abingdon, 1956.

Runyan, Theodore, ed. *Sanctification and Liberation*. Nashville: Abingdon, 1981.

Sangster, W. E. *The Path of Perfection*. London: Hodden and Sloughton, 1943.

Wood, J. A. *Christian Perfection as Taught by John Wesley*. Chicago: Christian Witness, 1885.

11

History and Eschatology

The dismal condition of the existing world must be seen in relation to the promise of the condition in which it will be when God's redemptive work is finished.

The General Spread of the Gospel

Isa. 11:9: "The earth shall be full of the knowledge of the Lord, as the waters that cover the sea." [Homily #63 1783 B2:485–99; J#63 VI:277–88]

Both Christian eschatology and ethics look toward the actual transformation of society as an implication of evangelical testimony, when "the earth will be full of the knowledge of the Lord as the waters cover the sea" (Isa. 11:9).[1]

The Present Dismal Condition of the World

It is evident from the present wretched condition of history that God's redemptive work is not yet complete. A pathetic pall of darkness, ignorance, and misery hovers over the face of the earth. Amid this unhappy condi-

tion, bluntly viewed, some are tempted to imagine that the Holy Spirit has withdrawn from it. They assume that as long as human sin is so recalcitrant, nothing is likely to change in any constitutional way. This invites a deadly cynicism and hopelessness about the possibility of human renewal.[2]

In his portrayal of the bleak picture of the present spiritual condition of the entire world, Wesley does not spare Western "Christendom." Special attention, however, is given to Islam and popular Near Eastern religions.[3]

In spite of this prevailing hollowness, and precisely through it, God's providential economy is gradually working itself out. God's purposes are in the process of being fulfilled despite all human resistances. There is still a long way to go. The Spirit still has much work to do with us.[4] Meanwhile time is on God's side.

Whether Transformation of the World Through the Power of the Gospel Is to Be Expected

However realistic Christian believers may be in examining the disheartening

---

[1]#63 "The General Spread of the Gospel," sec. 1, 2:485; cf. CH 7: 96, 606, 612, 687–89.
[2]#63 "The General Spread of the Gospel," sec. 7, 2:487.
[3]#63 "The General Spread of the Gospel," sec. 3–5, 2:486–87.
[4]#63 "The General Spread of the Gospel," sec. 2, 2:486.

proneness of humanity to sin, they may look with even temperament toward the renewing power of God the Spirit, who promises ultimately to transform this world and fulfill entirely the work God has begun. The hope for the future is not grounded in naturalistic optimism, but unmerited grace.[5] Faith takes it as an elementary premise of revelation that God's grace is working reliably to transform radically the whole human condition, even when this outworking is an enigma, seen from the sullied domain of empirical investigation.[6]

What we see happening in history is only the beginning, merely a fragment of a long process the end of which we do not yet see. But we can behold with the eyes of faith the promised end by trusting that the One who meets us on the cross will complete his work in and through the Spirit. A coming world is promised in which the loving knowledge of God is effectively producing uninterrupted holiness and happiness, covering the whole earth.[7]

Wesley viewed the evangelical revival as a concrete sign of hope and a model of the general spread of the gospel in world history. We need only reflect upon how grace is currently working in the revival, preveniently bringing persons toward repentance and justifying grace, and in due time sanctifying grace. In the same manner as God the Son has converted many by persuading them through atoning love, without demeaning or destroying their liberty, God the Spirit undoubtedly is able and willing to convert whole nations, and in due time, the whole world.[8]

As God raised up a few young, inconsiderable neophytes at Oxford to witness that "without holiness no one will see the Lord" (Heb. 12:14),[9] so God is doing in history on a vast scale. From Oxford the fire spread across England, Ireland, and to America, and even in the eighteenth century was looking toward Russia, Africa, China, and the Pacific rim.[10] As hearers were born again from above by the Spirit, so the leaven of renewal would spread from one to another.

Will the Spread of the Gospel Continue?

Assuming that such a work has begun, what reason do we have to think it will continue? Wesley's simple logical syllogism is gently pressed: If God can redeem cavalier, unprofitable, class-conscious Anglicans, God can work wonders with any sinner, and if so there is no intrinsic reason why the whole of the human condition cannot be changed.

More difficult to believe is the even more bleak assumption that God has wrought so glorious a work as the revival only to let it die away in a few years. Luther thought a particular revival of religion would likely last little more than thirty years. But as Wesley was writing, the Evangelical Revival had already been proceeding for fifty years, and was still going strong.[11] It is more reasonable to assume that "God will carry on his work in the same

---

[5]Concerning Wesley's mode of eschatological reasoning, see B1:169–72, 357–59, 494–95; see also hymns: CH 7:146–61, 716–17.

[6]#63 "The General Spread of the Gospel," sec. 9–16, 2:489–92.

[7]#63 "The General Spread of the Gospel," sec. 7–9, 2:487–89.

[8]#63 "The General Spread of the Gospel," sec. 10–13, 2:489–90.

[9]#63 "The General Spread of the Gospel," sec. 10–13, 2:490; B11:115f.

[10]#63 "The General Spread of the Gospel," sec. 11, 2:489.

[11]#63 "The General Spread of the Gospel," sec. 16, 2:492; cf. #107 "On God's Vineyard"; LJW, To William Black, Nov. 26, 1786.

manner as he has begun."[12] We are witnessing the spread of experiential knowledge and love of God reaching out to all the world. On this basis of scriptural and experiential Christianity, Wesley thought we have sufficient reason to look toward a time when all the inhabitants of the earth will be reestablished in universal holiness and happiness.[13]

The gospel is the good news of God's saving action within, and not merely beyond, history. That gospel is promised to spread and lengthen to its full extension. Now we see only a faint dawning of a vast historical process that in God's time will appear illumined in the full light of day.[14]

The Spirit patiently addresses us one by one, individually breaking down our resistances, nudging the ungodly toward faith. What happens quietly and inwardly in an individual's repentance and faith is precisely the window into the meaning of world history. Behold the patient ways of the Spirit. Those who look for a characteristically evangelical view of history will find its chief clue in the spread of the gospel one by one to all. Just notice what God is doing in your own heart, and you can then grasp something of what God is doing everywhere.[15]

This is not an argument for automatic humanistic progress in history or one based on optimism about human competency—ideas entirely foreign to Wesley. Hidden in the premise of this argument is an a priori judgment about

the Holy Spirit's sure determination to fulfill the mission of the Son.[16] By this grace, people are invited to experience scriptural Christianity, which intends to execute its commission to spread to all the inhabitants of the world.

Imperative Authorization
for World Mission

A world mission is envisioned in which knowledge of God is spreading to the unhearing nations of the world, even to the "remotest parts" of "Asia, Africa, and America."[17] Even in the mission to the Muslim world, ultimately even this "grand stumbling block" will be removed, but only when the sorry lives of professing Christians are replaced by faith active in love, when "their words will be clothed with divine energy, attended with the demonstration of the Spirit and of power."[18] "The holy lives of Christians will be an argument they [Muslims] will not know how to resist."[19]

God is able finally to gather Israel "out of all countries" and "cause them to dwell safely."[20] As this is occurring, "all those glorious promises made to the Christian Church" are being accomplished, where at length "violence shall no more be heard in thy land."[21]

It is not as if we are autonomously building the kingdom of God, but rather that God is working in us and through human willing and acting in order to bring about the larger purpose of redeeming the history of sin. God is carrying on the work of providence in

---

[12]#63 "The General Spread of the Gospel," sec. 14–16, 2:491–93.
[13]#63 "The General Spread of the Gospel," sec. 17–21, 2:493–95; cf. #4 "Scriptural Christianity."
[14]#63 "The General Spread of the Gospel," sec. 16, 2:492–93.
[15]#63 "The General Spread of the Gospel," sec. 13–18, 2:490–93.
[16]#63 "The General Spread of the Gospel," sec. 18–20, 2:493–95.
[17]#63 "The General Spread of the Gospel," sec. 18, 2:493.
[18]#63 "The General Spread of the Gospel," sec. 21, 2:495.
[19]#63 "The General Spread of the Gospel," sec. 22, 2:496.
[20]#63 "The General Spread of the Gospel," sec. 25, 2:498; Jer. 32:37–41.
[21]#63 "The General Spread of the Gospel," sec. 26, 2:498–99; Isa. 60:18–19, 61:11.

the same manner that it was begun and is moving steadily toward the dawn of the latter-day glory.[22]

Human Suffering in Eschatological View

Those who lack an overarching view of meaning in history are likely to remain especially vexed by the continuing problems of evil and suffering. Experiential Christianity's eschatological view of history is the only full and satisfactory answer to the salient objections against the wisdom and goodness of God that are so plausibly taken from the present state of the world, centering upon the objection that God is unjust because these present conditions of the world are unjust. Such an abstract, non-eschatological argument detaches present history from the future of history. Rather, the justice of God must be viewed eschatologically as a process very gradually working to restore the human condition.[23]

On Faith, Hebrews 11:1

Heb. 11:1: "Faith is the evidence of things not seen." [Homily #132 1791 B4:187–200; J#122 VII:326–35]

The Soul in Death

"What kind of existence shall I then enter upon, when my spirit has launched out of the body? How shall I feel myself . . .when the organs of hearing are mouldering into dust, in what manner shall I *hear*? When my brain is of no farther use, what means of *thinking* shall I have?"[24] What shall I be and do after my death? What will the intermediate state between death and the final resurrection be like, when my spirit is out of my body? Here Wesley engages in broad theological and exegetical conjectures concerning the immortal soul at the time of death.[25]

As a very old man he poignantly described himself already as "strangely connected with a little portion of earth, but this only for a while. In a short time I am to quit this tenement of clay, and remove into another state," which the living know not and the dead cannot tell.[26] "How strange, how incomprehensible, are the means whereby I shall then take knowledge even of the material world!"[27]

Admittedly, there is much of the invisible world of which we can "know nothing, and indeed we need to know nothing."[28] Most of our ideas and impressions remain conjectural, even with the most acute reasoning and widest data, lacking the promises of divine disclosure.

It is at least clear that we will go from one existence to another very different one.[29] From Scripture we learn that the spirits of the righteous are to be blessed by dwelling with God face to face, while those of the wicked remain infinitely distanced from the eternal blessedness of God.[30]

To those who ask: "Is heaven a state or a place?" the fitting response is:

---

[22] #63 "The General Spread of the Gospel," sec. 16, 2:492–93.
[23] #63 "The General Spread of the Gospel," sec. 27, 2:499.
[24] #132 "On Faith," Hebrews 11:1, sec. 2, 4:189.
[25] #132 "On Faith," Hebrews 11:1, sec. 1, 4:188; Letter to William Law, LJW 3:359. Letter to Sarah Wesley, April 12, 1788, LJW 8:54; cf. LJW 3:372; on knowledge of survival after death see B2:289f.; 4:288f.; 2:595–97; 4:52f., 299.
[26] #132 "On Faith," Hebrews 11:1, sec. 2, 4:188; cf. #119 4:49ff.; JJW, Dec. 15, 1788.
[27] #132 "On Faith," Hebrews 11:1, sec. 3, 4:189.
[28] #132 "On Faith," Hebrews 11:1, sec. 3, 4:189.
[29] #132 "On Faith," Hebrews 11:1, sec. 4, 4:180.
[30] #132 "On Faith," Hebrews 11:1, sec. 9, 4:194; B2:365–72; 3:41–43, 185–88, 196–97; 4:32–34.

"There is no opposition between these two ... It is the place wherein God more immediately dwells with those saints who are in a glorified state," the essential feature of which is "to see God, to know God, to love God. We shall then know both His nature, and His works of creation, of providence, and of redemption. Even in paradise, in the intermediate state between death and the resurrection, we shall learn more concerning these in an hour than we could in an age during our stay in the body."[31]

Faith's Grasp of the Invisible

What depths of understanding await us in the end. All that we can know of the future world by natural light is but "one degree better than utter darkness."

Only by divine revelation can we know of this coming world, and what we can know requires active faith.[32] "These things we have believed upon the testimony of God ... by this testimony we already know the things that now exist, though not yet seen."[33] All our speculations will pass away.

Meanwhile in order to know the spiritual world, we must be given a sensory competency of a quite different nature. Faith is that spiritual sense that lays hold of the invisible by trusting in God's revealed word. "By faith we understand" (Heb. 11:2), for faith is "being sure of what we hope for and certain of what we do not see" (Heb. 11:1).

Faith and the Intermediate State

The intermediate state is distinguished from heaven. In the intermediate state—whether Hades or Paradise—both the spirits of the righteous and unrighteous dwell separated by an impassable gulf, awaiting reunion with their bodies,[34] as portrayed in the parable of the Rich Man and Lazarus.[35] "In paradise the souls of good men rest from their labours and are with Christ from death to the resurrection."[36]

Those with God will experience eternal joy, abiding in "intimate communion" with the Lord, "continually ripening for heaven." "Inexpressibly happy," those "in Abraham's bosom"[37] "will be perpetually holier and happier, till they are received into 'the kingdom prepared for them.'"[38] The spirits of the righteous will "swiftly increase in knowledge, in holiness, and in happiness, conversing with the wise and holy souls that lived in all ages ... They will forget nothing. To forget is only incident to spirits that are clothed with flesh and blood."[39]

Whether Faith Sees

God employs incorporeal spirits to accomplish his purposes in the visible world. They converse with other spiritual beings. They advance in holiness and in the love of God and of humanity. They may be given "astonishing

---

[31]Letter to Mary Bishop, April 17, 1776, LJW 6:213; B2:289f.; 3:537–41; 4:190–92, 195–97, 211–13, 288f.; cf. LJW 6:26.
[32]#132 "On Faith," Hebrews 11:1, sec. 14, 15, 4:198.
[33]#132 "On Faith," Hebrews 11:1, sec. 16, 4:199.
[34]LJW 6:214.
[35]#132 "On Faith," Hebrews 11:1, sec. 4, 4:189; cf. #115 "Dives and Lazarus."
[36]Letter to George Blackall, Feb. 25, 1783, LJW 7:168; for his critique of medieval scholastic and Tridentine views of purgation see B2:292, 374f., 581.
[37]On the metaphor of Abraham's bosom, see B2:156; 3:35; 4:7, 33, 116, 190.
[38]#132 "On Faith," Hebrews 11:1, sec. 5, 4:191; cf. LJW 5:299, 306; 6:216, 224; JJW 5:195.
[39]#132 "On Faith," Hebrews 11:1, sec. 6, 4:192.

senses" to perceive the depths of the orders of beings, virtues, powers, and dominions that are imperceptible by physical senses.[40]

It is not improbable that righteous spirits may move about on the earth doing God's pleasure, ministering to persons on the earth by counteracting wicked spirits and protecting persons from harm.[41] Faith has eyes that enable the faithful to glimpse spirits of the just made perfect, in close relation with the living, ministering to their good, happy to be "permitted to minister to those whom they have left behind."[42]

Like angelic creatures, the saints in heaven will recognize each other, and enjoy communion with the patriarchs, prophets, apostles, and martyrs. They will be able to traverse "the whole universe in the twinkling of an eye, either to execute the divine commands or to contemplate the works of God."[43] Now we can thank God for the evidences of things unseen, and for the new senses of faith that are opened in our souls. We are called to give thanks "to God for enlightening us to these things which we would otherwise not know."[44]

The Signs of the Times

Matt. 16:3: "Ye can discern the face of the sky; but can ye not discern the signs of the times?" [Homily #66 1787 B2:521–33; J#66 VI:304–13]

The Times and Signs of Which Jesus Spoke

In the time of the coming of the anointed One, God took our nature to die for us. Expected by the prophets and announced by the Baptist, many signs and wonders attest his coming: the blind see, lame walk, lepers are cleansed, deaf hear, the dead are raised up, and the poor have the gospel preached to them.[45]

Many analogous signs are even now at hand. Yet how unprepared the gathered people are to see the signs of God's latter-day glory. It has long been promised that God would complete his mission to reconcile humanity through the ministry of the Holy Spirit. The kingdom is coming without observation, like a mustard seed growing silently, like a little leaven in the meal that gradually leavens the whole loaf.[46]

The Signs of These Times

During the six decades of evangelical awakenings in England and America in which Wesley taught,[47] such signs seemed to be abundantly appearing. The spiritually deaf were hearing the whispers of grace; the poor were hearing the gospel preached after decades of neglect. The spiritually blind were coming to see themselves through the eyes of faith in the light of Jesus Christ. They were being converted by the thousands. Profligates and merely formal religionists were turning to the active life of faith working through love, happy in life, triumphant in death.[48]

In this way God is revealing himself to the eyes of faith far more than to the wise and learned. There are many signs now at hand that point to the emergent completing, sanctifying work of the

---

[40] #132 "On Faith," Hebrews 11:1, sec. 7, 4:192.
[41] #132 "On Faith," Hebrews 11:1, sec. 11–12, 4:197.
[42] #132 "On Faith," Hebrews 11:1, sec. 12, 4:197.
[43] #132 "On Faith," Hebrews 11:1, sec. 11, 4:196.
[44] #132 "On Faith," Hebrews 11:1, sec. 17, 4:199.
[45] #66 "The Signs of the Times," i, 2:523–25.
[46] #66 "The Signs of the Times," ii, 2:525–27.
[47] 1729 to 1787 at this time of writing.
[48] #66 "The Signs of the Times," ii.8–9, 2:530.

Spirit.[49] The world mission of the church to the ends of the earth is reaching toward a new state of readiness.[50]

Why then is so much recalcitrant human consciousness still so unready to discern these signs? In a culture full of pride, ruled by disorderly passions, habitually loving the creature more than the Creator, it is not surprising that many hearts are hardened to God's gracious coming. This adulterous and sinful generation cannot see the signs of these times. The evidences are there for anyone to see, but our eyes are not open. No matter how radiant the emerging signs, even if they glare in our eyes, our jaded sensibilities remain closed to them. Lacking spiritual senses, which the new birth enables, we miss what is dramatically happening all about us in the history of revelation.[51] Our history is being lived out amid the gradual emergence of the advent of the latter-day glory, the completion of the redemptive purpose and beyond in fallen history.[52] Though incomplete, it shows trenchant signs of ever-fuller appearance. God is fulfilling his promises, and for those who have eyes to see, it is a mighty display of divine power and love throughout the whole earth. The evangelical revival offers a window into final eschatological fulfillment.[53]

Unlike some interpreters who were calculating a final reckoning on a particular date, Wesley did not speculate in detail on explicit predictions of final judgment.[54] He specifically rejected the amillennial interpretation that held that " 'the new Jerusalem came down from heaven' when Constantine the Great called himself a Christian . . . He would have come nearer to the mark if he had said, that was the time when a huge cloud of infernal brimstone and smoke came up from the bottomless pit.' "[55] But he did think that the revival was signaling that the triune God was at work in God's own time to bring his promises into final fulfillment.

The beast of Revelation 13, following much defensive Protestant exegesis, especially that of Johann Bengel, was interpreted by Wesley as a corrupted church, especially in the period following Gregory VII.[56] "When the 'beast' is destroyed, Satan is bound for a millennium, then loosed, to gather his great army with Gog and Magog for the final battle, where, with a great fire from heaven, his force is destroyed. He is finally cast into the lake of fire and brimstone to be tormented day and night."[57]

The Great Assize

Rom. 14:10: "Before the judgment seat of Christ." [Homily #15 1758 B1:354–75; J#15 V:171–85]

This is the only sermon Wesley is known to have preached in a civil court.[58] An assize was a periodic session of a superior court of law for trial of civil and criminal cases. It brought a demeanor of impressive solemnity wherever it was held.

The Great, or Last Assize was a

---

[49]#66 "The Signs of the Times," ii.1–4, 2:525–26.
[50]#66 "The Signs of the Times," ii.10, 2:531.
[51]#66 "The Signs of the Times," ii.1–7, 2:525–29.
[52]LJW 6:80; B1:215–16; 2:482; 4:33–34.
[53]LJW 1:284.
[54]LJW 8:63, 67.
[55]#66 "The Signs of the Times," ii.7, 2:529; cf. 3:449–50, 470.
[56]ENNT, Rev. 13.1–12.
[57]WC 124; ENNT on Rev. 13.
[58]Feb. 27, 1758 in Bedford; JJW 4:254.

euphemism for the Last Judgment.[59] However solemn any human court might seem, another is coming that will arouse far greater solemnity: the final day of judgment when all motives will come under divine investigative judgment.[60] Those who understand how inescapable will be this final judgment, will find their moral behavior transformed by the stark awareness of it.[61]

Circumstances Preceding the General Judgment

Scripture attests certain signs on earth—earthquakes,[62] floods, awesome events—by which the coming judgment will be signaled, accompanied by signs from the heavens: the sun will darken, the stars stop shining, the dead will rise at the last trump, and all will stand before the throne of the Lord who will gather the nations, and separate sheep from goats.[63]

The Judgment Itself

The Judgment itself is presided over by One who has empathically shared our frame, who knows what it means to be tempted yet without sin, who knows what it means to weep, face death, and die. *The Judge* is the incarnate Son who in his flesh has suffered the wounds of our transgressions, and because of his obedience unto death was exalted to the right hand of the Father.[64]

The duration of judgment: as long as it takes to deal fairly with each and every case. The present time (from creation to consummation) will end, and the day of the Lord will begin. We know that the day of the Lord will commence with the general resurrection, but how long it will continue is debatable, seeing that for the Lord one day is as a thousand years. So "day" need not be taken as a twenty-four-hour period of time, but an unspecified interval, perhaps extensive, seeing the task to be done. "Some of the ancient Fathers drew the inference that what is commonly called 'the day of judgment' would be indeed a thousand years. And it seems they did not go beyond the truth; nay probably they did not come up to it," for "it may not improbably comprise several thousand years. But God shall reveal this also in its season."[65] The venue of judgment is unspecified except as the great white throne, highly exalted above the earth.[66]

"It is then 'the dead, small and great,' will 'stand before God; and the books' will be 'opened'—the book of Scripture, to them who were entrusted therewith, the book of conscience to all mankind . . . thou wilt appear without any shelter or covering, without any possibility of disguise, to give a particular account of the manner wherein thou hast employed all thy Lord's goods."[67]

Those to be judged: all that ever have lived, to give account of their words and works. Everything done in darkness will be brought to light: actions, motives, every idle word, every

---

[59]Cf. LJW 4:345; 6:79; B1:147f., 359–66; 2:292–96; 3:187f., 400–402; 4:141–43, 319f.
[60]B11:316f., 404–6, 475f., 487–89; CH 7:132f., 146–61, 716f.
[61]#15 "The Great Assize," proem, 1:356; cf. 2:292–96.
[62]Remembering the Lisbon earthquake of Nov. 1, 1755, cf. "Serious Thoughts Occasioned by the Late Earthquake at Lisbon," 1755.
[63]#15 "The Great Assize," i.2–3, 1:358–59.
[64]#15 "The Great Assize," ii.1, 1:359; cf. 3:400–402.
[65]#15 "The Great Assize, ii.2, 1:360; CH 7:716–17.
[66]#15 "The Great Assize," ii.3, 1:361.
[67]#51 "The Good Steward," iii.2, 2:293; cf. Letters, To the Bishop of Gloucester, 11:487–8.

inward working of every human soul.[68] With consummate fairness their evil deeds will be remembered, and the faithful forgiven according to the gospel covenant.[69] The metaphor portrays each one standing before the Judge and in some way recollecting, witnessing, and beholding the entire history of their moral decision making before the cosmic audience.

The Investigative Judgment

The soul will then be examined:

The Judge of all will then inquire: "How didst thou employ thy *soul*? I entrusted thee with an immortal spirit, endowed with various powers and faculties, with understanding, imagination, memory, will, affections. I gave thee withal full and express directions how all these were to be employed. Didst thou employ thy *understanding*, as far as it was capable . . . ? Didst thou employ thy *memory* according to my will? In treasuring up whatever knowledge thou hadst acquired which might conduce to my glory . . . was thy *imagination* employed, not in painting vain images, much less such as nourish foolish and hurtful desires, but in representing to thee whatever would profit thy soul, and awaken thy pursuit of wisdom and holiness? . . . Were thy *affections* placed and regulated in such a manner as I appointed in my Word? Didst thou give me thy heart? . . . Was I the joy of thy heart, the delight of thy soul, the chief among ten thousand? . . Did the whole stream of thy affections flow back to the ocean from whence they came?"

The examination of lifelong trusteeship of the body will proceed:

The Lord will then inquire, "How didst thou employ thy *body* wherewith I entrusted thee. I gave thee a *tongue* to praise me therewith . . . Didst thou employ it, not in evil-speaking . . . but in such as was good, as was necessary or useful, either to thyself or others? Such as always tended, directly or indirectly, to 'minister grace to the hearers'? I gave thee, together with thy other senses those grand avenues of knowledge, *sight*, and *hearing*. Were these employed to those excellent purposes for which they were bestowed? . . . I gave thee hands and feet and various *members* wherewith to perform the works which were prepared for thee.'"[70]

The examination of the lifelong stewardship of goods and possessions will continue:

The Lord of all will next inquire, "How didst thou employ the *worldly goods* which I lodged in thy hands? Didst thou use thy *food* . . . to preserve thy body in health, in strength and vigour, a fit instrument for the soul? Didst thou use *apparel*, not to nourish pride or vanity, much less to tempt others to sin, but conveniently and decently. . . ? In what manner didst thou employ that comprehensive talent, *money*? . . . Not squandering . . . Not hoarding . . . But first supplying thy own reasonable wants, together with those of thy family; then restoring the remainder to me, through the poor, whom I had appointed to receive it; looking upon thyself as only one of that number of poor whose wants were to be supplied out of that part of my substance which I had placed in thy hands for this purpose; leaving thee the right of being supplied first, and the blessedness of giving rather than receiving?. . . Didst thou employ

---

[68]#15 "The Great Assize," ii.5, 1:362–63.

[69]#15 "The Great Assize," ii.2–6, 1:360–63. J. A. Bengel's commentary on Revelation, 1740, translated into English in 1757, had predicted the date for the millennium as 1836. Wesley was in many ways greatly indebted to Bengel, and had reproduced Bengel's chronological appendix in his own work. Though Wesley had sympathies with some aspects of Montanus, he did not sympathize with his specific chiliasm. Wesley hesitated to become entangled in a speculative attempt at apocalyptic chronology; cf. "The Real Character of Montanus," and #68 "The Wisdom of God's Councils," sec. 9; 1:350n; Jer. 31:34; Heb. 8:12.

[70]#51 "The Good Steward," iii.3, 4, 2:293–95.

whatever was pleasing in thy person or address, whatever *advantages* thou hadst by education . . . for the promoting of virtue?"[71]

The examination of the lifelong guardianship of time will inquire:[72]

"Didst thou employ that inestimable talent of time with wariness and circumspection, as duly weighing the value of every moment, and knowing that all were numbered in eternity? Above all, wast thou a good steward of my grace, preventing, accompanying, and following thee?. . . Then 'well done, good and faithful servant! . . . Enter thou into the joy of the Lord!' "[73]

The Vindication of Divine Mercy

In the investigative judgment, God will vindicate himself, his own justice and moral perfections, in the "amazing contexture of divine providence," by showing in such a plausible way why he permitted evil that the righteous will rejoice with joy unspeakable.

This vindication is necessary to display the wisdom, power, and mercy of God in their precise conjunction, where for each free agent "all the circumstances of their life should be placed in open view, together with all their tempers, and all the desires, thoughts, and intents of their hearts. Otherwise how would it appear out of what a depth of sin and misery the grace of God had delivered them?"[74]

On no other basis is a theodicy possible than that the justice of God is finally made clear through all transient ambiguities.[75] For the atoned-for faithful "It will be abundantly sufficient for them that 'all the transgressions which they had committed shall not be once mentioned unto them' to their disadvantage."[76]

The Separation

A great division will take place: Believers will mercifully receive a sentence of acquittal. "All their good desires, intentions, thoughts, all their holy dispositions, will also be then remembered" along with "their sufferings for the name of Christ."[77]

The wicked who have spurned the grace offered will be fairly judged according to their thoughts, words, deeds, tempers, affections, desires, motives, circumstances, and hear the dreadful sentence pronounced.[78] There is little fascination with damnation and minimal fixation upon specific conditions of reprobation.[79] The pronouncements on the last day remain fixed and irrevocable, since it is the last day.

Circumstances Following the General Judgment

After the execution of the sentence will come a great and holy conflagration, a consuming fire in the temporal heavens and earth, not as if rendering them nothing or to annihilation. Rather, they will undergo a change "like the formation of glass, after which the fire can have no further power over them."[80] The purpose of the fire is to purify and ready the cosmos for eternal

---

[71]#51 "The Good Steward," iii.5, 2:295.
[72]EA 11:60–62; cf. 2:286, 296–97; LJW 8:270.
[73]#51 "The Good Steward," iii.6, 2:296.
[74]#15 "The Great Assize," ii.10, 1:364–65.
[75]2:398–99.
[76]#15 "The Great Assize," ii.11, 1:365; Ezek. 18:22.
[77]#15 "The Great Assize," ii.12, 1:366; CH 7:146–61.
[78]#15 "The Great Assize," ii.12, 1:366.
[79]LJW 5:167, 270, 344.
[80]#15 "The Great Assize," iii.2, 1:367.

service in the celestial city.[81] Then will come the creation of new heavens and a new earth wherein the righteous shall dwell, and where the Lord will reign infinitely.[82]

The Contemporary Moral Relevance of the Consideration of Final Judgment

Earthly judges are given by God's providence the fearful requirement to be his ministers, to "execute justice, to defend the injured, and punish the wrong-doer."[83] Every earthly judgment rightly should be executed in humble faith, aware of one's accountability before the final Judge, and following in the way of the One who mixed justice and mercy with incomparable wisdom. All are called to bear in mind the coming judgment, its universality and inescapability, so as to form prudent present moral judgments.[84]

Of Hell

Mark 9:48: "The worm dieth not." [Homily #73 1782 B3:30–44; J#73 VI:381–91]

Even those who most love God do well to consider what has been revealed in Scripture concerning the final destiny of the unrighteous.[85] Jesus made repeated reference to the consequence of sin as final just punishment. The teaching of hell functions as a constraint upon the ungodly, and as a means of preserving the faithful from sin.[86] Hence this

teaching is as pertinent to believers as unbelievers.[87]

Hell is that final condition "where 'their worm does not die, and the fire is not quenched' " (Mark 9:48). The biblical teaching is "awful and solemn: suitable to His wisdom and justice," differing widely from the idle tales of pagan myths.[88]

What the Ungodly Lose

There is a distinction between what the ungodly *lose*, and what they *feel*. They lose God. Hell is fundamentally banishment from the presence of God, hence viewed as an absolute deprivation of the good.[89] The punishment of loss *(poena damni)* occurs when the soul separates from the body of the ungodly. At the moment of death the unrighteous experience the loss of all senses of pleasure, all sources of gratification. There is no beauty, no light, no music, no friendship. The only inward senses are feelings of shame and loss. The greatest loss is the loss of God. "Depart from me!" (Matt. 25:41).[90]

What the Ungodly Feel: Worm and Fire

But to the punishment of loss is added the punishment of sense, which is expressed in two metaphors that shape this exegesis: worm and fire. In death, whether buried or cremated, we face either worm or fire. In either case the worm dies or the fire goes out. But hell is posited as a place where this

---

[81]When his nephew Samuel became a Roman Catholic, Wesley may have been jesting when he wrote that if he has faith, "He may, indeed, roll a few years in purging fire; but he will surely go to heaven at last!" Letter to Charles Wesley, Jr., May 2, 1784, LJW 7:217.
[82]#15 "The Great Assize," iii.3, 1:368.
[83]#15 "The Great Assize," iv.1, 1:371.
[84]#15 "The Great Assize," iv.3–5, 1:372–75.
[85]SS 1:22; 2:412.
[86]Letter to William Law, IX:506–8.
[87]#73 "Of Hell," Pref. 1–3, 3:31–32.
[88]#73 "Of Hell," Pref. 4, 3:33; cf. 1:366–67.
[89]JJW 1:139n; 5:552; SS 1:22; 2:412.
[90]#73 "Of Hell," i.1–4, 3:34–35; 4:58–59.

desolation does not end, where the worm does not die and the fire is not quenched.

Anticipative intimations of this worming of conscience in present life are guilt, self-condemnation, shame, and remorse that wounds the spirit and unleashes unholy tempers, and hatred of God. These already give us some idea of hell's torment. The worm is the inner torment of a guilty conscience; the fire is the outward torment of material anguish.[91] This is what the unrighteous feel (*poena sensus*).

One does well to withstand the Adversary who can kill and cast into hell, for the condition is everlasting. The fire is not consumed, but continues. There is no company in hell, no respite from pain, no interval of relief, no sabbath rest, only uninterrupted night with uninterrupted misery. The term of the sentence is forever.[92] The fire is not to be viewed merely as symbolic but real, yet not necessarily according to our present finite, physical understanding of the reality of fire.[93]

But why does Scripture speak in such horrible terms? To rouse us to repent and believe, to abstain from evil in this life, and to receive the benefits of paradise: the society of angels, the spirits of just men made perfect, conversing face to face with God, drinking forever of the waters of life, and enjoying forever the glory of God. Such thoughts are meant to inspire hope in God, not despair over our misery.[94]

Countering William Law's Speculations Against Divine Judgment

[To William Law, Jan. 6, 1756, LJW 3:332–70; IV:466–509]

Whether God Lacks a Capacity for Anger Against Sin

In the later writings of William Law, after 1735, Wesley whiffed the stench of corruption of Enlightenment optimism, which deprived God of any capacity for negation or judgment. Wesley understood all too well why preachers might be tempted to preach such "smooth things" as Law's view that there is no punitive justice in God, no divine anger against sin. Here we have portrayed an ambivalent, irresolute divine Parent who refuses to punish his children, either in this world or the next.[95]

The rejoinder to such softheadedness is found in the constant testimony of Scripture that "whom the Lord loveth he chasteneth" (Heb. 12:6) and that "the Lord is . . . slow to anger, and plenteous in mercy. He will not always chide, neither will he keep his anger for ever" (Ps. 103:8,9, KJV).[96] "Had God never been angry, He could never have been reconciled," Wesley confessed personally. "I know He was angry with me till I believed in the Son of His love; and yet this is no impeachment to His mercy."[97]

A view that premises that God cannot be angry at sin cannot posit any final judgment other than "the various operations of self"— psychological, social, temporal, political—"No hell, no heaven, no revelation."[98] Against Law's contraction of hell to the general notion that "damnation is only that which springs up within you," Wesley argued for a real hell. He rehearsed the argument of Peter Browne's *Procedure, Extent and Limits of Human Under-*

---

[91]#73 "Of Hell," iii.1–2, 3:40–41.
[92]#73 "Of Hell," iii.3, 3:42.
[93]B4:12–23; cf. LJW 2:98; SS 2:412.
[94]#73 "Of Hell," iii.3, 3:42–44; VII:234–35, 247–55.
[95]On the divine anger against sin, see LJW 3:345–48; B1:359–66; 2:292–96; 3:187f., 400–402; 4:141–43, 319f.
[96]To William Law, ii.3, LJW 3:345–51; Prov. 13:24; Heb. 2:6–8.
[97]Letter to Mary Bishop, Feb. 7, 1778, LJW 6:298.
[98]To William Law, ii.7, LJW 3:370.

standing[99] to establish his case that the chief cause of eternal misery will be eternal exclusion from the beatific vision of God, that there will be future punishment of both body and soul, and that "the eternity of these punishments is revealed as plainly as word can express" in Scripture, which would not have been included in the sacred text if they had the purpose merely of frightening us.[100] "I have now, Sir, delivered my own soul," concluded Wesley, hoping that Mr. Law would come to his senses and renounce "all the high-flown bombast, all the unintelligible jargon of the Mystics, and come back to the plain religion of the Bible, 'We love him, because he first loved us.' "[101]

Wesley's tightest précis of eschatology appeared in his Letter to a Roman Catholic: "I believe God forgives all the sins of them that truly repent and unfeignedly believe his holy gospel; and that, at the last day, all men shall arise again, everyone with his own body. I believe that, as the unjust shall after their resurrection be tormented in hell for ever, so the just shall enjoy inconceivable happiness in the presence of God to all eternity."[102]

The New Creation

Rev. 21:5: "Behold, I make all things new." [Homily #64 1785 B2:500–10 J#64 VI:288–96]

The vision of the future in the Revelation of John presents a strange scene, remote from all our familiar sensibilities and natural apprehensions.[103] The text points to a mystery beyond finite knowing. Yet we must try to understand it as much as possible through our spiritual senses, "interpreting Scripture by Scripture, according to the analogy of faith."[104]

New Heavens, New Earth

The new heaven and earth are wrongly identified by some with a particular period of human history in which the riches of Constantine were poured upon Christendom ("a miserable way . . . of making void the whole counsel of God"). Rather, this refers to the end of this world and the beginning of the eternal age, to "things that will come to pass when this world is no more."[105]

Biblical cosmology envisioned not a single heaven, but heavens, not only the heaven of air, a higher heaven of stars (which we can to some degree see), but also a third heaven where God dwells, which will not be changed when the other heavens are renovated.[106]

*An Unmixed State
of Holiness and Happiness*

A universal restoration will follow a universal destruction, a new age to succeed this present age.[107] In the new

---

[99]350–51.

[100]To William Law, ii.7, LJW 3:368–70, quoting P. Browne, *Human Understanding*, 351; cf. Letter of Feb. 18, 1756, to Samuel Furly. On hell see LJW 2:133; 3:168, 263; B1:227f., 366f.; 3:37–40; 4:58f., 665–68; 3:30–44, 4:33.

[101]To William Law, ii.7, LJW 3:370.

[102]Letter to a Roman Catholic, sec. 10, JWO 495–96; cf. 1:227–28; cf. B2:365–72; 3:41–43, 185–88, 196–97; 4:32–34.

[103]#64 "The New Creation," sec. 1, 2:501.

[104]#64 "The New Creation," sec. 2, 2:501; see also #5 "Justification by Faith," sec. 2; #62 "The End of Christ's Coming," iii.5.

[105]#64 "The New Creation," sec. 4, 2:501–52.

[106]#64 "The New Creation," sec. 5–9, 2:502–3; CH 7:161–76; for further reference to heaven, see B2:289f, 392; 4:116, 288f.

[107]B2:455–50, 500–510; 9:108, 370, 407; CH 7:81, 85, 118–23, 251–55, 338f., 536f. On the destruction of death, see B2:482.

heaven will dwell righteousness, where all will be perfected in "exact order and harmony."[108]

The present physical elements are not brought to nothing but rather transformed, and divested of their power to destroy. The air will be refined, the water unpolluted, fire will no longer destroy or consume but purify so as to "retain its vivifying power,"[109] and the earth will be made perfect, with all the elements being "changed as to their qualities, although not as to their nature." This transmutation will elicit "a far nobler state of things, such as it has not yet entered into the heart of men to conceive—universal restoration, which is to succeed the universal destruction."[110]

The Paradise lost in the Fall will be restored. Envisioning a myriad of flowers, the wolf will indeed lie down with the lamb. All forms of animal creation, having been delivered from the "deplorable effects of Adam's apostasy" will abide together in peace.[111] Wesley further conjectured that the lower region of the air will no longer be agitated by hurricanes, tempests, and terrifying meteors,[112] and on earth no deserts, weeds, bogs, thorns, poisonous plants, or uncomfortable extremes of temperature.

Perfect love, the restoration of the divine image in humanity within history, is an anticipatory expression of the final restoration beyond history.[113]

The reign of Christ has already begun in the present dispensation. The believer tastes already the actual impartation of the glory to come. Present salvation is the earnest of final salvation.[114] Resurrected human life, refashioned in the divine image, will become equal with angels in swiftness and strength.[115]

There will be no more death, sorrow, pain or sin, but "an intimate, an uninterrupted union with God; a constant communion with the Father and his Son Jesus Christ, through the Spirit; a continual enjoyment of the Three-One God, and of all the creatures in him."[116] The redeemed will be restored to "an unmixed state of holiness and happiness far superior to that which Adam enjoyed in paradise."[117]

FURTHER READING ON ESCHATOLOGY:

Collins, Kenneth. FW, 189-204.

Downes, Cyril. "The Eschatological Doctrines of John and Charles Wesley." Ph.D. dissertation, Univ. of Edinburgh, 1974.

Harper, Steve. *John Wesley's Theology Today*. FAP, Zondervan, 1983. Chap. 8 on glorification. 107ff.

"John Wesley a Premillenarian," Christian Workers Magazine 17 (1916): 96–101.

Lindström, Harald. "Sanctification and Final Salvation." In *Eschatology*, Burtner and Chiles, 273ff.

Marino, Bruce. *Through a Glass Darkly: The Eschatological Vision of John Wesley*, Drew dissertation, 1994.

[108]#64 "The New Creation," sec. 10, 2:504; cf. 4:116.
[109]#64 "The New Creation," sec. 10, 2:504.
[110]#64 "The New Creation," sec. 7, 2:503; LJW 6:187; on cosmic redemption see B2:455–50, 500–510.
[111]#64 "The New Creation," sec. 17, 2:509.
[112]#64 "The New Creation," sec. 8, 2:503; see also #56 "God's Approbation of His Works," i.10.
[113]B1:57, 76; 3:175; 2:455–50, 500–510; CH 7:118–23, 251–55, 536f.
[114]#64 "The New Creation," sec. 1–4, 2:501.
[115]#64 "The New Creation," sec. 17, 2:509; #60 "The General Deliverance," i.5.
[116]#64 "The New Creation," sec. 18, 2:510; #55 "On the Trinity," sec. 17.
[117]#64 "The New Creation," sec. 18, 2:510; cf. 2:39f., 475–6; #5 "Justification by Faith," i.4; LJW 3:338; 4:98. On the golden chain of pardon, holiness, and heaven, see B3:149f.

Mercer, Jerry. "The Destiny of Man in John Wesley's Eschatology." WTJ 2 (1967): 56–65.

Monk, R. JWPH on Final Justification, 122ff.

Rall, Harris F. *Was John Wesley a Premillennialist?* Toronto: Methodist Book and Publ. House, 1921, 12f.

Strawson, William. "Wesley's Doctrine of the Last Things." LQHR 184 (1959): 240–49.

West, Nathaniel. *John Wesley and Premillennialism.* Louisville: Pentecostal Publ. Co., 1894.

Williams, Colin. JWTT, "Eschatology," 191ff.

Wilson, David D. "The Importance of Hell for John Wesley." PWHS 34 (1963): 12–16.

APPENDIX A

The references to the sermons are chiefly in the Bicentennial edition. For readers who have available only the oft-reprinted 14-volume Jackson edition, it will be useful to have available the following:

CORRELATION OF THE SERMONS IN THE BICENTENNIAL AND JACKSON EDITIONS

BICENTENNIAL OXFORD–ABINGDON EDITION	JACKSON 14-VOLUME REPRINT LOCATION	TOPIC AS TREATED IN THIS STUDY
SERMON NUMBER AND TITLE		
VOLUME 1 BICENTENNIAL EDITION		
#1, "Salvation by Faith"	V:7–16	Christology
#2, "The Almost Christian"	V:17–25	Christology
#3, "Awake, Thou That Sleepest" (Charles Wesley)	V:25–36	Soteriology
#4, "Scriptural Christianity"	V:37–52	Christology
#5, "Justification by Faith"	V:53–64	Christology
#6, "The Righteousness of Faith"	V:65–76	Christology
#7, "The Way to the Kingdom"	V:76–86	Soteriology
#8, "The First-fruits of the Spirit"	V:87–97	Pneumatology
#9, "The Spirit of Bondage and of Adoption"	V:98–111	Pneumatology
#10, "The Witness of the Spirit, Discourse I"	V:111–23	Pneumatology
#11, "The Witness of the Spirit, Discourse II"	V:123–34	Pneumatology
#12, "The Witness of Our Own Spirit"	V:134–44	Pneumatology
#13, "On Sin in Believers"	V:144–56	Repentance
#14, " The Repentance of Believers"	V:156–70	Repentance
#15 "The Great Assize"	V:171–85	Eschatology
#16, "The Means of Grace"	V:185–201	Pastoral Care
#17, "The Circumcision of the Heart"	V:202–12	Soteriology
#18, "The Marks of the New Birth	V:212–23	Soteriology
#19, "The Great Privilege of those that are Born of God"	V:223–33	Soteriology

VOLUME 3 BICENTENNIAL EDITION

#128, "The Deceitfulness of the Human Heart"	VII:335–43	Sin
#129, "Heavenly Treasure in Earthen Vessels"	VII:344–48	Anthropology
#130, "On Living Without God"	VII:349–54	Anthropology
#131, "The Danger of Increasing Riches"	VII:355–62	Ethics
#132, "On Faith, Heb. 11:1"	VII:326–35	Soteriology
#133, "Death and Deliverance"	[not present]	Eschatology
#134, "Seek First the Kingdom"	[not present]	Ethics
#135, "On Guardian Angels"	[not present]	Creation
#136, "On Mourning for the Dead"	VII:463–68	Pastoral Care
#137, "On Corrupting the Word of God"	VII:468–73	Method
#138A, "On Dissimulation"	[not present]	Pastoral Care
#138B–C, Two Fragments on Dissimulation	[not present]	Pastoral Care
#139, "On the Sabbath"	[not present]	Pastoral Care
#140, "The Promise of Understanding"	[not present]	Method
#141, "The Image of God"	[not present]	Anthropology
#142, "The Wisdom of Winning Souls"	[not present]	Pastoral Care
#143, "Public Diversions Denounced"	VII:500–508	Ethics
#144, "The Love of God"	[not present]	Theology
#145, "In Earth as in Heaven," a fragment	[not present]	Ethics
#146, "The One Thing Needful"	[not present]	Ethics
#147, "Wiser Than the Children of Light"	[not present]	Ethics
#148, "A Single Intention"	[not present]	Ethics
#149, "On Love"	VII:492–99	Ethics
#150, "Hypocrisy in Oxford," English text	VII:452–62	Ethics
#151, "Hypocrisy in Oxford," Latin text	[not present]	

SERMONS NOT BY JOHN WESLEY
BUT INCLUDED IN THE JACKSON
EDITION

"The Cause and Cure of Earthquakes" (Charles Wesley)	VII:386–99
"On the Resurrection of the Dead" (Benjamin Calamy)	VII:474–85
"On Grieving the Holy Spirit" (William Tully)	VII:485–92
"On the Holy Spirit" (John Gambold)	VII:508–20

APPENDIX B

BICENTENNIAL VOLUME TITLES

Volumes of the Bicentennial edition according to subject: [brackets indicate unpublished to date but scheduled:]

1–4 Sermons
[5, 6 *Explanatory Notes Upon the New Testament*]
7 *A Collection of Hymns for the Use of the People Called Methodists*
[8 Forms of Worship and Prayer]
9 *The Methodist Societies, History Nature and Design*
[10 The Methodist Societies, The Conference]
11 *The Appeals to Men of Reason and Religion and Certain Related Open Letters*
[12 Doctrinal Writings: Theological Treatises]
[13 Doctrinal Writings: The Defence of Christianity]
[14–15 Pastoral and Instructional Writings]
[16 Editorial Work]
[17 Natural Philosophy and Medicine]
18 *Journals and Diaries I 1735–38*
19 *Journals and Diaries II 1738–43*
20 *Journals and Diaries III 1743–54*
21 *Journals and Diaries IV 1753–65*
22 *Journals and Diaries V 1765–76*
[23–24 *Journals and Diaries VI–VII*]
25 *Letters I 1721–39*
26 *Letters II 1740–55*
[27–31 Letters]
[32–33 Bibliography of Publications of John and Charles Wesley]
[34 Miscellanea and General Index]

NAME INDEX

SCRIPTURE INDEX

SUBJECT INDEX